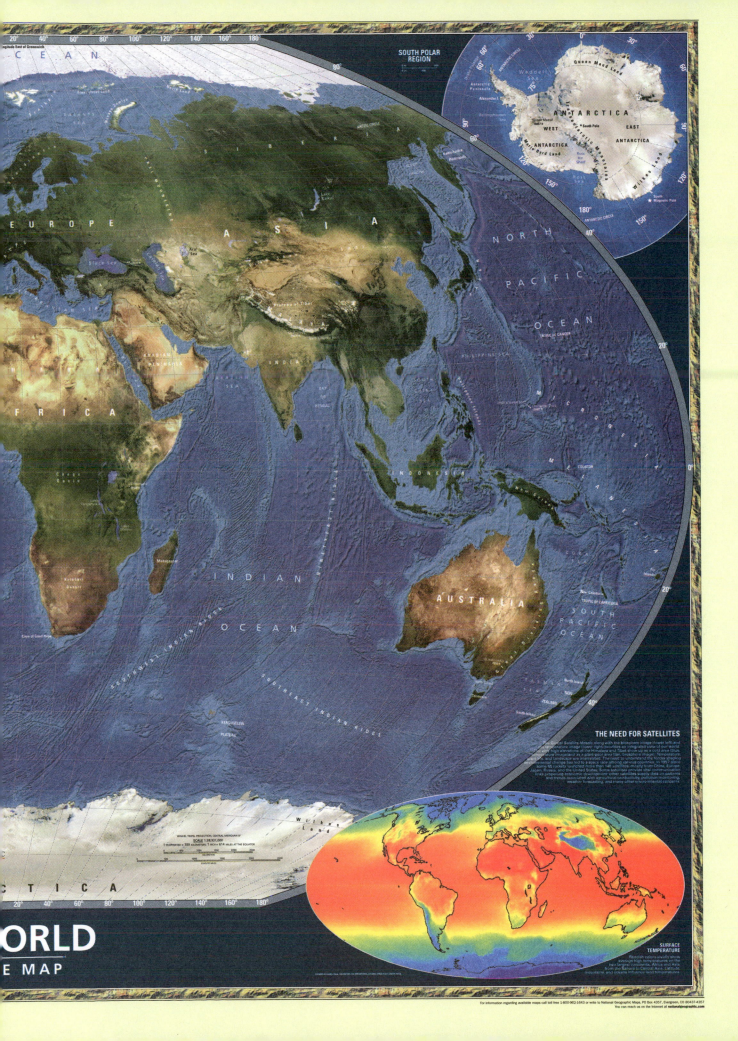

SOUTH POLAR
REGION

ANTARCTICA

THE NEED FOR SATELLITES

SURFACE
TEMPERATURE

ORLD
E MAP

This registration code provides access to documents

and other sources available at the

Worlds Together, Worlds Apart 3E StudySpace site:

wwnorton.com/studyspace

FMES-LKIC

THIRD EDITION
VOLUME B

Worlds Together, WORLDS APART

ROBERT TIGNOR

JEREMY ADELMAN

STEPHEN ARON

PETER BROWN

BENJAMIN ELMAN

STEPHEN KOTKIN

XINRU LIU

SUZANNE MARCHAND

HOLLY PITTMAN

GYAN PRAKASH

BRENT SHAW

MICHAEL TSIN

THIRD EDITION
VOLUME B
600 TO 1850

Worlds Together, WORLDS APART

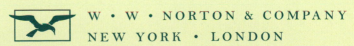

W · W · NORTON & COMPANY

NEW YORK · LONDON

W. W. Norton & Company has been independent since its founding in 1923, when William Warder Norton and Mary D. Herter Norton first published lectures delivered at the People's Institute, the adult education division of New York City's Cooper Union. The firm soon expanded its program beyond the Institute, publishing books by celebrated academics from America and abroad. By mid-century, the two major pillars of Norton's publishing program—trade books and college texts— were firmly established. In the 1950s, the Norton family transferred control of the company to its employees, and today—with a staff of four hundred and a comparable number of trade, college, and professional titles published each year—W. W. Norton & Company stands as the largest and oldest publishing house owned wholly by its employees.

Editor: Jon Durbin
Developmental Editor: Alice Vigliani
Copy Editor: Ellen Lohman
Project Editor: Rebecca Homiski
Photo Editor: Stephanie Romeo
Production Manager: Benjamin Reynolds
Managing Editor, College: Marian Johnson
Marketing Manager: Tamara McNeill
Emedia Editor: Steve Hoge
Design Director: Rubina Yeh
Ancillary Editor: Lorraine Klimowich
Editorial Assistant: Jason Spears
Layout Artist: Brad Walrod
Composition: TexTech, Inc.
Cartographer: Carto-Graphics/Alice Thiede

The Library of Congress has cataloged the one-volume edition as follows:

Worlds together, worlds apart : a history of the world from the beginnings of humankind to the present / Robert Tignor ... [et al.]. — 3rd ed.
       p. cm.
    Includes bibliographical references and index.
    ISBN 978-0-393-93492-2 (hardcover)
 1. World history.   I. Tignor, Robert L.
    D21.W94 2011
    909—dc22

                                                                2010036837

This edition:
ISBN: 978-0-393-93496-0 (pbk.)

W. W. Norton & Company, Inc., 500 Fifth Avenue, New York, NY 10110
wwnorton.com

W. W. Norton & Company Ltd., Castle House, 75/76 Wells Street, London W1T 3QT

4 5 6 7 8 9

Contents in Brief

Contents

Chapter 10   Becoming "The World," 1000–1300 CE   363

CHAPTER 12 CONTACT, COMMERCE, AND COLONIZATION, 1450–1600 447

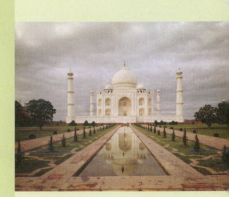

Global Connections & Disconnections Features

Primary Sources

Maps

Preface

The New Edition

Worlds Together, Worlds Apart has set the standard for two editions for those instructors who want to teach a globally integrated world history survey course. Just as the dynamic field of world history evolves, so has Worlds Together, Worlds Apart with each edition. With the Third Edition, Worlds Together, Worlds Apart continues to offer a highly coherent, cutting-edge survey of the field, while becoming more streamlined and accessible for a wider range of students. The Third Edition offers a number of improvements over the first two. First, the chapters are shorter. We cut the narrative by 50,000 words, reducing its length by nearly 20 percent. We shrank the text to highlight even more clearly the distinctive world history stories and themes that each chapter is built around. Readers should be in little doubt now about what truly counted globally in each of the time periods that the chapters cover. The new edition should also be a good page turner for students for while we reduced the length of the book to just over 840 pages, we did not dramatically cut back on the map, illustration, and primary-source programs. By shortening the text, we also wanted to allow instructors to make greater use of outside reading materials, especially primary sources, which are so vital to understanding the life and thought of people living in different time periods and locations. Second, pedagogically, we have re-written the chapter introductions to emphasize the themes even more strongly. We have also added a new pedagogy feature called "Storylines," which is designed to provide the reader with a snapshot of the main chapter themes and show how they relate to each major region of the world. We also went through all the pedagogical features with great care to make sure that the prose and questions were pitched at a good level for a wide range of students. Third, we are pleased to announce the publication of Worlds Together, Worlds Apart: A Companion Reader. Long-time users of the book have been asking for a primary-source reader designed to accompany Worlds Together, Worlds Apart since its First Edition. The companion reader has been carefully assembled by Ken Pomeranz, Laura Mitchell, and James Given, all of whom teach the world history survey course at the University of California, Irvine, and all of whom have been teaching with Worlds Together, Worlds Apart for many years. The companion reader contains nearly 150 primary sources (both visual and textual) and will greatly enhance an instructor's ability to teach students how to analyze primary sources, while building off the key themes and topics of Worlds Together, Worlds Apart. Finally, Norton StudySpace offers an exciting new feature called World History Tours powered by Google Maps. These digitally based tours trace global developments over time, touching down on locations to launch documents and images for analysis. For example, the Silk Road tour follows the bubonic plague from its eastern origins to Europe, chronicling this movement through journals and images from the Muslim world, Italy, and England.

Since work began on *Worlds Together, Worlds Apart*, world history has gained even more prominence in college classrooms and historical studies. Courses in the history of the world now abound, often replacing the standard surveys of European history and western civilization overviews. Graduate history students receive training in world history, and journals routinely publish studies in this field. A new generation of textbooks was needed to help students and instructors make sense of this vast, complex, and rapidly evolving field.

We believe that *Worlds Together, Worlds Apart* remains the most cutting-edge, engaging, readable, and useful text available for all students of world history. We also believe that this text, one that has advanced the teaching of this field, could have only grown out of the highly collaborative effort of a team of scholars and teachers rather than the more typical single- or two-author efforts. Indeed, the idea to build each chapter around stories of world history significance and the execution of this model grew out of our monthly team meetings and our joint writing efforts during the development stage. As a team-driven text, *Worlds Together, Worlds Apart* also has the advantage of area experts to make sure the material is presented accurately, which is always a challenge for the single- or two-author texts, especially in world history. Finally, our book also reads with a single voice due to the extraordinary efforts of our general editor, and leader, Robert Tignor, who with every edition makes the final major sweep through the text to make sure that the voice, style, and level of detail are consistent throughout. Building on these distinctive strengths, we have worked hard and thoughtfully to make the Third Edition of *Worlds Together, Worlds Apart* the best one so far. While there are many exciting additions to the main text and support package, we have made every effort to remain true to our original vision.

OUR GUIDING PRINCIPLES

Five principles inform this book, guiding its framework and the organization of its individual chapters. The first is that **world history is global history**. There are many fine histories of the individual regions of the world, which we have endeavored to make good use of. But unlike the authors of many other so-called world histories, we have chosen not to deal with the great regions and cultures of the world as separate units, reserving individual chapters to East Asia, South Asia, Southwest Asia, Europe, Africa, and the Americas. Our goal is to place each of these regions in its largest geographical context. Accordingly, we have written chapters that are truly global in that most major regions of the world are discussed in each one. We achieved these globally integrated chapters by building each around a significant world history story or theme. There are a number of wonderful examples throughout the book, including the peopling of the earth (Chapter 1), the building of the Silk Road (Chapter 6), the rise of universal religions (Chapters 8 and 9), the Black Death (Chapter 11), the effects of New World silver on the economies of the world (Chapter 13), alternative visions to nineteenth-century capitalism (Chapter 15), the rise of nation states and empires (Chapter 16), and so on. It would be misleading, of course, to say that the context is the world, because none of these regions, even the most highly developed commercially, enjoyed commercial or cultural contact with peoples all over the globe before Columbus's voyage to the Americas and the sixteenth century. But the peoples living in the Afro-Eurasian landmass, probably the single most important building block for our study, were deeply influenced by one another, as were the more scattered peoples living in the Americas and in Africa below the Sahara. Products, ideas, and persons traveled widely across the large land units of Eurasia, Africa, and the Americas. Indeed, Afro-Eurasia was not divided or thought of as divided into separate landmasses until recent times. It is in this sense that our world history is global.

The second principle informing this work is **the importance of chronology in framing world history**. Rather than telling the story of world history by analyzing separate geographical areas, we have elected to frame the chapters around significant world history themes and periods that transcended regional and cultural boundaries—moments or periods of meaningful change in the way that human beings organized their lives. Some of these changes were dramatic and affected many people. Environments changed; the earth became drier and warmer; humans learned to domesticate plants and animals; technological innovations in warfare, political organization, and commercial activities occurred; and new religious and cultural beliefs spread far and wide. These changes swept across large landmasses, paying scant heed to preexisting cultural and geographical unity. They affected peoples living in widely dispersed societies. In other cases, changes occurred in only one locality while other places retained their traditions or took alternative routes. Chronology helps us understand the ways in which the world has, and has not, shared a common history.

The third principle is **historical and geographical balance**. Ours is not a history focused on the rise of the West. We seek to pay attention to the global histories of all peoples and not to privilege those developments that led directly into European history as if the rest of the history of the world was but a prelude to the rise of western civilization. We deal with peoples living outside Europe on their own terms and try to see world history from their perspective. Even more significantly, while we describe societies that obviously influenced Europe's historical development, we do so in a context very different from that which western historians have stressed. Rather than simply viewing these cultures in terms of their role in western development, we seek to understand them in their own terms and to illuminate the ways they influenced other parts of the world. From our perspective, it is historically inaccurate to annex Mesopotamia and Egypt to western civilization, because these territories lay well outside Europe and had a large influence on Africa, South Asia, and East Asia as well as on Europe. Indeed, our presentation of Europe in the period leading up to and including the founding of the Roman Empire is different from many of the standard treatments. The Europeans we describe are rather rough, wild-living, warring peoples living on the fringes of the settled parts of the world and looked down on by more politically stable communities. They hardly seem to be made of the stuff that will catapult Europeans to world leadership a millennium later—indeed, they were very different people from those who, as the result of myriad intervening and contingent events, founded the nineteenth- and twentieth-century empires whose ruins are still all around us.

Our fourth principle is **an emphasis on connections and what we call disconnections across societal and cultural boundaries**. World history is not the history of separate regions of the world at different periods of time. It is the history of the connections among peoples living often at great distances from one another, and it is also the history of the resistances of peoples living within and outside societies to connections that threatened to put them in subordinate positions or to rob them of their independence.

A stress on connections inevitably foregrounds those elements within societies that promoted long-distance ties. Merchants are important, as are military men and political potentates seeking to expand their polities. So are scholars and religious leaders, particularly those who believed that they had universalistic messages with which to convert others to their visions. Perhaps most important of all in pre-modern world history, certainly the most understudied, are the nomadic pastoral peoples, who were often the agents for the transmission of products, peoples, and ideas across long and harsh distances. They exploded onto the scene of settled societies at critical junctures, erasing old cultural and geographical barriers and producing new unities, as the Arabs did in the seventh century CE and the Mongols in the thirteenth century. *Worlds Together, Worlds Apart* is not intended to convey the message that the history of the world is a story of increasing integration. What for one ruling group brought benefits in the form of increased workforces, material prosperity, and political stability often meant enslavement, political subordination, and loss of territory for other groups. The historian's task, then, is not only to represent the different experiences of increased connectedness, describing worlds that came together, but also to be attentive to the opposite trends, describing peoples and communities that remained apart.

The fifth and final principle is that **world history is a narrative of big themes and high-level comparisons**. *Worlds*

Together, Worlds Apart is not a book of record. Indeed, in a work that covers the whole of the historical record of humankind from the beginnings of history to the present, the notion that no event or individual worthy of attention would be excluded is the height of folly. We have sought to offer clear themes and interpretations in order to synthesize the vast body of data that often overwhelms histories of the world. Our aspiration is to identify the main historical forces that have moved history, to highlight those monumental innovations that have changed the way humans lived, and to describe the creation and evolution of those bedrock institutions, many of which, of course, endure. In this regard, self-conscious cross-cultural comparisons of developments, institutions, and even founding figures receive attention to make students aware that some common institutions, such as slavery, did not have the same features in every society. Or, in the opposite fashion, the seemingly diverse terms that were used, say, to describe learned and religious men in different parts of the world—monks in Europe, ulama in Islam, Brahmans in India, and scholar-gentries in China—often meant much the same thing in very different settings. We have constructed *Worlds Together, Worlds Apart* around big ideas, stories, and themes rather than filling the book with names and dates that encourage students only to memorize rather than understand world history concepts.

OUR MAJOR THEMES

The primary organizing framework of *Worlds Together, Worlds Apart*—one that runs through the chapters and connects the different parts of the volume—is the theme of **interconnection and divergence**. While describing movements that facilitated global connectedness, this book also shows how different regions developed their own ways of handling or resisting connections and change. Throughout history, different regions and different population groups often stood apart from the rest of the world until touched by traders or explorers or missionaries or soldiers. Some of these regions welcomed global connections. Others sought to change the nature of their connections with the outside world, and yet others resisted efforts to bring them into the larger world. All, however, were somehow affected by their experience of connection. Yet, the history of the world is not simply one of increasing globalization, in which all societies eventually join a common path to the present. Rather, it is a history of the ways in which, as people became linked, their experience of these global connections diverged.

Besides the central theme of interconnection and divergence, other themes also stand out in *Worlds Together, Worlds Apart*. First, the book discusses **how the recurring efforts of people to cross religious, political, and cultural borders brought the world together**. Merchants and educated men and women traded goods and ideas. Whole communities, in addition to select groups, moved to safer or more promising environments. **The transregional crossings of ideas, goods, and peoples produced transformations and conflicts**—a second important theme. Finally, the movement of ideas, peoples, products, and germs over long distances upset the balance of power across the world and within individual societies. Such movements changed the relationship of different population groups with other peoples and areas of the world and led over time to dramatic shifts in the ascendancy of regions. **Changes in power arrangements within and between regions explain which parts of the world and regional groups benefited from integration and which resisted it.** These three themes (exchange and migration, conflict and resistance, and alterations in the balance of power) weave themselves through every chapter of this work. While we highlight major themes throughout, we tell the stories of the people caught in these currents of exchange, conflict, and changing power relations, paying particular attention to the role that gender and the environment play in shaping the evolution of societies.

The history of the world is not a single, sweeping narrative. On the contrary, the last 5,000 years have produced multiple histories, moving along many paths and trajectories. Sometimes these histories merge, intertwining themselves in substantial ways. Sometimes they disentangle themselves and simply stand apart. Much of the time, however, they are simultaneously together and apart. In place of a single narrative, the usual one being the rise of the West, this book maps the many forks in the road that confronted the world's societies at different times and the surprising turns and unintended consequences that marked the choices that peoples and societies made, including the unanticipated and dramatic rise of the West in the nineteenth century. Formulated in this way, world history is the unfolding of many possible histories, and readers of this book should come away with a reinforced sense of the unpredictability of the past, the instability of the present, and the uncertainty of the future.

OVERVIEW OF VOLUME ONE

Volume One of *Worlds Together, Worlds Apart* deals with the period from the beginnings of human history through the Mongol invasions of the thirteenth century and the spread of the Black Death across Afro-Eurasia. It is divided into eleven chapters, each of which marks a distinct historical period. Hence, each chapter has an overarching theme or small set of themes that hold otherwise highly diverse material together.

Chapter 1, "Becoming Human," presents biological and cultural perspectives on the way that early hominoids became truly human. We believe that this chapter is important in establishing the global context of world history. We believe too that our chapter is unique in its focus on how humans became humans, so we discuss how early humans became bipedal and how they developed complex cognitive processes such as language and artistic abilities. Recent research indicates that *Homo sapiens* originated in Africa, probably no more than 200,000 years ago. These early men and women walked out of the African landmass sometime between 120,000 and 50,000 years ago, gradually populating all regions of the world. What is significant in this story is that the different population groups around the world, the so-called races of humankind, have only recently broken off from one another. Also in this chapter, we describe the domestication of plants and animals and the founding of the first village settlements around the globe.

NEW: Discussions of the role that dogs played in human evolution and the latest findings on the origins of humans.

Chapter 2, "Rivers, Cities, and First States, 4000–2000 BCE," covers the period during which five of the great river basins experienced extraordinary breakthroughs in human activity. On the flood plains of the Tigris and Euphrates in Mesopotamia, the Nile in Egypt, the Indus valley in modern-day northern India and Pakistan, and the Yellow and Yangzi rivers in China, men and women mastered annual floods and became expert in seeding and cultivating foodstuffs. In these areas, populations became dense. Riverine cultures had much in common. They had highly developed hierarchical political, social, and cultural systems, priestly and bureaucratic classes, and organized religious and cultural systems. But they also differed greatly, and these differences were passed from generation to generation. The development of these major complex societies certainly is a turning point in world history.

Extensive climatic and technological changes serve as major turning points for **Chapter 3, "Nomads, Territorial States, and Microsocieties, 2000–1200 BCE."** Drought, environmental degradation, and political instability brought the first riverine societies to a crashing end around 2000 BCE. When aridity forced tribal and nomadic peoples living on the fringes of the settled populations to move closer to settled areas, they brought with them an insurmountable military advantage. They had become adept at yoking horses to war chariots, and hence they were in a position to subjugate or intermarry with the peoples in the settled polities in the river basins. Around 2000 BCE these peoples established new territorial kingdoms in Mesopotamia, Egypt, the Indus valley, and China, which gave way a millennium later (1000 BCE) to even larger, militarily and politically more powerful states. In the Americas, the Mediterranean, sub-Saharan Africa, and the

Pacific worlds, microsocieties arose as an alternative form of polity in which peoples lived in much smaller-scale societies that showcased their own unique and compelling features.

NEW: Expanded discussions of how the Egyptian pyramids were built and their role in Egyptian cosmology and fuller integration of material on the environmental catastrophe that shaped the third millennium BCE.

Chapter 4, "First Empires and Common Cultures in Afro-Eurasia, 1200–350 BCE," describes the different ways in which larger-scale societies grew and became unified. In the case of the world's first empires, the neo-Assyrian and Persian, political power was the main unifying element. Both states established different models that future empires would emulate. The Assyrians used brutal force to intimidate and subjugate different groups within their societies and neighboring states. The Persians followed a pattern that relied less on coercion and more on tributary relationships, while reveling in cultural diversity. The Zhou state in China offered yet a third way of political unity, basing its rule on the doctrine of the mandate of heaven, which legitimated its rulers' succession as long as they were able to maintain stability and order. Vedic society in South Asia offers a dramatically different model in which religion and culture were the main unifying forces. Religion moves to the forefront of the narrative in other ways in this chapter. The birth of monotheism occurred in the Zoroastrian and Hebrew faiths and the beginnings of Buddhism. All three religions endure today.

NEW: Revised and expanded discussion of the origins of Judaism.

The last millennium before the common era witnessed some of the most monumental developments in human history. In the six and half centuries discussed in **Chapter 5, "Worlds Turned Inside Out, 1000–350 BCE,"** teachers and thinkers, rather than kings, priests, and warriors, came to the fore. Men like Confucius, the Buddha, Plato, and Aristotle, to name only the best known of this brilliant group, offered new insights into the natural world and provided new guidelines for how to govern justly and live ethically. In this era, small-scale societies, benefiting from more intimate relationships, took the place of the first great empires, now in decline. These highly individualistic cultures developed new strategies for political organization, even including experimenting with a democratic polity. In Africa, the Bantu peoples spread across sub-Saharan Africa, and the Sudanic peoples of Meroe created a society that blended Egyptian and sub-Saharan influences. These were all dynamic hybrid societies building on existing knowledge. Equally dramatic transformations occurred in the Americas, where the Olmec and Chavín peoples were creating hierarchical societies of the like never before seen in their part of the world.

NEW: Increased discussion of the first millennium as an "axial age."

Chapter 6, "Shrinking the Afro-Eurasian World, 350 BCE–250 CE," describes three major forces that simultaneously integrated large segments of the Afro-Eurasian landmass culturally and economically. First, Alexander and his armies changed the political and cultural landscape of North Africa and Southwest and South Asia. Culturally, Alexander spread Hellenism through North Africa and Southwest and central Asia, making it the first cultural system to achieve a transregional scope. Second, it was in the post-Alexander world that these commercial roads were stabilized and intensified. For the first time, a trading network, known as the Silk Road, stretching from Palmyra in the West to central Asia in the East, came into being. Buddhism was the first religion to seize on the Silk Road's more formal existence as its followers moved quickly with the support of the Mauryan Empire to spread their ideas into central Asia. Finally, we witness the growth of a "silk road of the seas" as new technologies and bigger ships allowed for a dramatic expansion in maritime trade from South Asia all the way to Egypt and East Africa.

Chapter 7, "Han Dynasty China and Imperial Rome, 300 BCE–300 CE," compares Han China and the Roman Empire, the two political, economic, and cultural systems that dominated much of the Afro-Eurasian landmass from 200 BCE to 200 CE. Both the Han Dynasty and the Roman Empire ruled effectively in their own way, providing an instructive comparative case study. Both left their imprint on Afro-Eurasia, and rulers for centuries afterward tried to revive these glorious polities and use them as models of greatness. This chapter also discusses the effect of state sponsorship on religion, as Christianity came into existence in the context of the late Roman Empire and Buddhism was introduced to China during the decline of the Han.

Out of the crumbling Roman Empire new polities and a new religion emerged, the major topic of **Chapter 8, "The Rise of Universal Religions, 300–600 CE."** The Byzantine Empire, claiming to be the successor state to the Roman Empire, embraced Christianity as its state religion. The Tang rulers patronized Buddhism to such a degree that Confucian statesmen feared it had become the state religion. Both Buddhism and Christianity enjoyed spectacular success in the politically fragmented post-Han era in China and in the feudal world of western Europe. These dynamic religions represent a decisive transformation in world history. Christianity enjoyed its eventual successes through state sponsorship via the Roman and Byzantine empires and by providing spiritual comfort and hope during the chaotic years of Rome's decline. Buddhism grew through imperial sponsorship and significant changes to its fundamental beliefs, when adherents to the faith deified Buddha and created notions of an afterlife. In Africa a wide range of significant developments and a myriad of cultural practices existed; yet large common cultures also arose. The Bantu peoples spread throughout the southern half of the landmass, spoke closely related languages, and developed similar political institutions based on the prestige of individuals of high achievement. In the Americas the Olmecs established their own form of the city-state, while the Mayans owed their success to a decentralized common culture built around a strong religious belief system and a series of spiritual centers.

NEW: Revised discussions of what enables a religion to become "universal."

In **Chapter 9, "New Empires and Common Cultures, 600–1000 CE,"** in a relatively remote corner of the Arabian Peninsula another world religion, Islam, exploded with world-changing consequences. The rise of Islam provides a contrast to the way in which universalizing religions and political empires interacted. Islam and empire arose in a fashion quite different from Christianity and the Roman Empire. Christianity took over an already existing empire—the Roman—after suffering persecution at its hands for several centuries. In contrast, Islam created an empire almost at the moment of its emergence. By the time the Abbasid Empire came into being in the middle of the eighth century, Islamic armies, political leaders, and clerics exercised power over much of the Afro-Eurasian landmass from southern Spain, across North Africa, all the way to Central Asia. The Tang Empire in China, however, served as a counterweight to Islam's power both politically and intellectually. Confucianism enjoyed a spectacular recovery in this period. With the Tang rulers, Confucianism slowed the spread of Buddhism and further reinforced China's development along different, more secular pathways. Japan and Korea also enter world history at this time, as tributary states to Tang China and as hybrid cultures that mixed Chinese customs and practices with their own. The Christian world split in this period between the western Latin church and the eastern Byzantine church. Both branches of Christianity played a role in unifying societies, especially in western Europe, which lacked strong political rule.

NEW: Reorganized to integrate material on the agricultural revolutions that spread across Afro-Eurasia as a result of the rise of Islam between 600 and 1000 BCE.

In the three centuries from 1000 to 1300 (**Chapter 10, "Becoming 'the World,' 1000–1300 CE"**) Afro-Eurasia experienced an unprecedented rise in prosperity and population that even spread into West and East Africa. Just as importantly, the world in this period divided into regional zones that are recognizable today. And trade grew rapidly.

A view of the major trading cities of this time demonstrates how commerce transformed cultures. Sub-Saharan Africa also underwent intense regional integration via the spread of the Mande-speaking peoples and the Mali Empire.

The Americas witnessed their first empire in the form of the Chimu peoples in the Andes. This chapter ends with the Mongol conquests of the twelfth and thirteenth centuries, which brought massive destruction. The Mongol Empire, however, once in place, promoted long-distance commerce, scholarly exchange, and travel on an unprecedented scale. The Mongols brought Eurasia, North Africa, and many parts of sub-Saharan Africa into a new connectedness. The Mongol story also underscores the important role that nomads played throughout the history of the early world.

NEW: Expanded discussion of the Crusades.

The Black Death brought Afro-Eurasia's prosperity and population growth to a catastrophic end as discussed in **Chapter 11, "Crises and Recovery in Afro-Eurasia, 1300s–1500s."** The dying and destruction of the fourteenth century saw traditional institutions give way and forced peoples to rebuild their cultures. The polities that came into being at this time and the intense religious experimentation that took place effected a sharp break with the past. The bubonic plague wiped out as much as two-thirds of the population in many of the densely settled locations of Afro-Eurasia. Societies were brought to their knees by the Mongols' depredations as well as by biological pathogens. In the face of one of humanity's grimmest periods, peoples and societies demonstrated tremendous resilience as they looked for new ways to rebuild their communities, some turning inward and others seeking inspiration, conquests, and riches elsewhere. Volume One concludes on the eve of the "Columbian Exchange," the moment when "old" worlds discovered "new" ones and a vast series of global interconnections and divergences commenced.

NEW: Expanded discussion of the Renaissance.

OVERVIEW OF VOLUME TWO

The organizational structure for Volume Two reaffirms the commitment to write a decentered, global history of the world. Christopher Columbus is not the starting point, as he is in so many modern world histories. Rather, we begin in the eleventh and twelfth centuries with two major developments in world history: the Mongols and the Black Death. The first, set forth in **Chapter 10, "Becoming 'the World,' 1000–1300 CE,"** describes a world that was divided for the first time into regions that are recognizable today. This world experienced rapid population growth, as is shown by a simple look at the major trading cities from Asia in the East to the Mediterranean in the West. Yet nomadic peoples remain a force as revealed in the Mongol invasions of Afro-Eurasia.

NEW: Expanded discussion of the Crusades.

Chapter 11, "Crises and Recovery in Afro-Eurasia, 1300s–1500s," describes how the Mongol warriors, through their conquests and the integration of the Afro-Eurasian world, spread the bubonic plague, which brought death and depopulation to much of Afro-Eurasia. Both these stories set the stage for the modern world and are clear-cut turning points in world history. The primary agents of world connection described in this chapter were dynasts, soldiers, clerics, merchants, and adventurers who rebuilt the societies that disease and political collapse had destroyed.

NEW: Expanded discussion of the Renaissance.

The Mongols joined the two hemispheres, as we describe in **Chapter 12, "Contact, Commerce, and Colonization, 1450s–1600,"** bringing the peoples and products of the Western Hemisphere into contact and conflict with Eurasia and Africa. It is the collision between the Eastern and Western Hemispheres that sets in motion modern world history and marks a distinct divide or turning point between the pre-modern and the modern. Here, too, disease and increasing trade linkages were vital. Unprepared for the advanced military technology and the disease pool of European and African peoples, the Amerindian population experienced a population decline even more devastating than that caused by the Black Death.

NEW: Expanded discussion of the Protestant Reformation.

Europeans sailed across the Atlantic Ocean to find a more direct, less encumbered route to Asia and came upon lands, peoples, and products that they had not expected. One item, however, that they had sought in every part of the world and that they found in abundance in the Americas was precious metal. In **Chapter 13, "Worlds Entangled, 1600–1750,"** we discuss how New World silver from Mexico and Peru became the major currency of global commerce, oiling the long-distance trading networks that had been revived after the Black Death. The effect of New World silver on the world economy was so great that it, even more than the Iberian explorations of the New World, brought the hemispheres together and marks the true genesis of modern world history. Sugar also linked the economies and polities of western Europe, Africa, and the Americas and was a powerful force in a triangular trade centered on the Atlantic Ocean. This trade involved the shipment of vast numbers of African captives to the Americas, where they toiled on sugar, tobacco, cotton, and rice slave plantations.

Chapter 14, "Cultures of Splendor and Power, 1500–1780," discusses the Ottoman scientists, Safavid and Mughal artists, and Chinese literati, as well as European thinkers, whose notable achievements were rooted in their own cultures but tempered by awareness of the intellectual activities of others. In this chapter, we look closely at how culture is created as a historical process and describe how the massive increase in wealth during this period, growing out of global trade, led to one of the great periods of cultural flourishing in world history.

NEW: Discussions of the Seven Years' War as the first global war.

Around 1800, transformations reverberated outward from the Atlantic world and altered economic and political relationships in the rest of the world. In **Chapter 15, "Reordering the World, 1750–1850,"** we discuss how political revolutions in the Americas and Europe, new ideas about how to trade and organize labor, and a powerful rhetoric of freedom and universal rights underlay the beginning of "a great divide" between peoples of European descent and those who were not. These forces of laissez-faire capitalism, industrialization, the nation-state, and republicanism not only attracted diverse groups around the world; they also threatened groups that put forth alternative visions. Ideas of freedom, as manifested in trading relations, labor, and political activities, clashed with a traditional world based on inherited rights and statuses and further challenged the way men and women had lived in earlier times. These political, intellectual, and economic reorderings changed the way people around the world saw themselves and thus represent something quite novel in world history.

NEW: Discussions of "industriousness" and how the work habits of westerners were changing in the period before the Industrial Revolution.

These new ways of envisioning the world did not go unchallenged, as **Chapter 16, "Alternative Visions of the Nineteenth Century,"** makes clear. Here, intense resistance to evolving modernity reflected the diversity of peoples and their hopes for the future. Wahabbism in Islam, the strongman movement in Africa, Indian resistance in America and Mexico, socialism and communism in Europe, the Taiping Rebellion in China, and the Indian Mutiny in South Asia catapulted to historical prominence prophets and leaders whose visions often drew on earlier traditions and led these individuals to resist rapid change.

NEW: Streamlined discussions comparing the alternative visions of the nineteenth century.

Chapter 17, "Nations and Empires, 1850–1914," discusses the political, economic, military, and ideological power that thrust Europe and North America to the fore of global events and led to an era of nationalism and modern imperialism, new forces in world history. Yet this period of seeming European supremacy was to prove short-lived.

As **Chapter 18, "An Unsettled World, 1890–1914,"** demonstrates, even before World War I shattered Europe's moral certitude, many groups at home (feminists, Marxists, and unfulfilled nationalists) and abroad (anti-colonial nationalists) had raised a chorus of complaints about European and North American dominance. As in Chapter 14, we look at the processes by which specific cultural movements rose and reflected the concerns of individual societies. Yet here, too, syncretistic movements emerged in many cultures and reflected the sway of global imperialism, which by then had become a dominant force.

NEW: Revised discussions of cultural modernism.

Chapter 19, "Of Masses and Visions of the Modern, 1910–1939," briefly covers World War I and then discusses how, from the end of World War I until World War II, different visions of being modern competed around the world. It is the development of modernism and its effects on multiple cultures that integrate the diverse developments discussed in this chapter. In the decades between the world wars, proponents of liberal democracy struggled to defend their views and often to impose their will on authoritarian rulers and anticolonial nationalists.

NEW: Discussions of the Spanish Civil War as a global phenomenon.

Chapter 20, "The Three-World Order, 1940–1975," presents World War II and describes how new adversaries arose after the war. A three-world order came into being—the First World, led by the United States and extolling capitalism, the nation-state, and democratic government; the Second World, led by the Soviet Union and favoring authoritarian polities and economies; and the Third World, made up of former colonies seeking an independent status for themselves in world affairs. The rise of this three-world order dominates the second half of the twentieth century and constitutes another major theme of world history.

NEW: Expanded discussions of the Holocaust.

In **Chapter 21, "Globalization, 1970–2000,"** we explain that, at the end of the cold war, the modern world, while clearly more unified than before, still had profound cultural differences and political divisions. At the beginning of the twenty-first century, capital, commodities, peoples, and ideas move rapidly over long distances. But cultural tensions and political impasses continue to exist. It is the rise of this form of globalism that represents a vital new element as humankind heads into a new century and millennium.

We close with an **Epilogue**, which tracks developments since the turn of the millennium. These last few years have brought profound changes to the world order, yet we hope readers of *Worlds Together, Worlds Apart* will see more clearly how this most recent history is, in fact, entwined with trends of much longer duration that are the chief focus of this book.

NEW: Fully up-to-date on the global financial collapse, wars in the Middle East, and the Obama presidency.

INNOVATIVE PEDAGOGICAL PROGRAM, MADE BETTER

Worlds Together, Worlds Apart is designed for maximum readability. The crisp, clear, and succinct narrative, built around memorable world history stories and themes, is reinforced through a highly innovative pedagogical program designed to help students think critically and master the core content. All the pedagogical elements have been carefully revised for the Third Edition to ensure that students will find them highly useful. Highlights of this innovative program are described below.

NEW "STORYLINES" FEATURE

New "Storylines" features provide a thematic snapshot of the chapter and appear right after the chapter introduction. Each "Storylines" feature highlights the chapter themes and shows how they apply to each region of the world.

STELLAR MAP PROGRAM WITH NEW GUIDING QUESTIONS

The book's more than 120 beautiful maps are designed to reinforce the main stories and themes in each chapter. Most chapters open with a beautiful two-page map of the world to highlight the main storyline of the chapter. Within the chapter are four to five more maps that focus on the regions covered. Enhanced captions with new guiding questions help students learn how to read historical maps and to understand the relationship between geography and history.

REVISED FOCUS-QUESTION SYSTEM

The focus-question system has been fully revised and now contains more manageable questions in order to help the reader remain alert to key concepts and questions on every page of the text. Focus questions guide students' reading in three ways: (1) a focus question box at the beginning of the chapter previews the chapter's contents, (2) relevant questions reappear at the start of the section where they are discussed, and (3) running heads on right-hand pages keep these questions in view throughout the chapter.

PRIMARY-SOURCE DOCUMENTS WITH NEW QUESTIONS FOR ANALYSIS

The authors have selected three to five primary-source documents for each chapter that reinforce the chapter's main themes and help students learn how to analyze primary sources. Many of them challenge students to see world history through the eyes of others and from different perspectives. The questions for analysis after each document have been carefully revised to draw students into the document, moving from simpler to more complex. Additional primary sources are available in *Worlds Together, Worlds Apart: A Companion Reader* and in the Digital History Reader, which is part of the Norton StudySpace website.

GLOBAL CONNECTIONS & DISCONNECTIONS

Each chapter contains one thematic feature built around key individuals or phenomena that exemplify the main emphasis of the text. Among the many topics are how historians use technology to date bones and objects from early history, the use of ritual funeral objects in the contexts of religion and trade, the role of libraries in early world history, the travels of Marco Polo and Ibn Battuta, coffee drinking and coffeehouses in different parts of the world, cartography and maps as expressions of different worldviews, the growth of universities around the world, and Che Guevera as a radical visionary who tried to export revolution throughout the Third World.

STREAMLINED CHAPTER CHRONOLOGIES

Chapter chronologies appear at the end of each chapter, and they are organized regionally rather than temporally. The chapter chronologies have been streamlined for the Third Edition to make it easier for students to identify the most important events, to track unifying concepts, and to see influences across cultures and societies within a given time period.

REVISED STUDY QUESTIONS

New Study Questions appear at the end of each chapter. Each question has been carefully crafted to ensure that students can identify chapter themes, master core content, and identify the most important comparisons and connections from the reading.

FURTHER READINGS

A section at the back of the book includes an ample list of up-to-date suggestions for further reading, broken down by chapter and annotated so that students can see what each work covers.

RESOURCES FOR INSTRUCTORS

INSTRUCTOR'S MANUAL

Amy Hudnall and Neva Specht
Appalachian State University
Includes chapter outlines, lecture ideas, classroom activities, recommended books, recommended film lists with annotations, and recommended websites.

TEST BANK/COMPUTERIZED TEST BANK

Sara Jorgensen and Andrea Becksvoort
University of Tennessee, Chattanooga
The Test Bank has been revised in accordance with the Norton Assessment Guidelines. Questions are organized around a Concept Map and are ranked by knowledge type, difficulty, and section reference.

All Norton test banks are available with Exam View Test Generator software, allowing instructors to effortlessly create, administer, and manage assessments. The convenient and intuitive testmaking wizard makes it easy to create customized exams with no software learning curve. Other key features include the ability to create paper exams with algorithmically generated variables and to export files directly to Blackboard, WebCT, and Angel.

INSTRUCTOR'S RESOURCE DISC

This helpful classroom presentation tool features:
- Lecture PowerPoint slides that include a suggested classroom-lecture script in the notes field. These are particularly helpful to first-time teachers of the course.
- A separate set of art PowerPoints featuring photographs and maps, retouched for in-class projection.

DOWNLOADABLE INSTRUCTOR'S RESOURCES

wwnorton.com/instructors
Instructional content for use in lecture and distance education, including coursepacks, test banks, PowerPoint lecture slides, images, figures, and more.

COURSEPACKS

Available at no cost to professors or students, Norton coursepacks for online or hybrid courses are available in a variety of formats, including all versions of Blackboard and WebCT. With just a simple download from our instructor's website, an instructor can bring high-quality Norton digital media into a new or existing online course (no extra student passwords required), and it's theirs to keep forever. Content includes chapter-based assignments, test banks and quizzes, interactive learning tools, and selected content from the StudySpace website.

NORTON GRADEBOOK

With the free, easy-to-use Norton Gradebook, instructors can easily access StudySpace student quiz results and avoid email inbox clutter. No course setup required. For more information and an audio tour of the Gradebook, visit wwnorton.com/college/nrl/gradebook.

NORTON ONLINE

Norton Online provides a seamless and flexible online learning environment featuring proven resources that help students succeed. By integrating Norton's market-leading textbooks with interactive tools in an easy-to-use learning-management system, Norton Online provides a high-quality online course that can be used right away or customized to suit an instructor's specific needs.

RESOURCES FOR STUDENTS

STUDYSPACE: YOUR PLACE FOR A BETTER GRADE

StudySpace tells students what they know, shows them what they need to review, and then gives them an organized study plan to master the material.

Students rely on effective and well-designed online resources to help them succeed in their courses—StudySpace is unmatched in providing a one-stop solution that's closely aligned with their textbook. This free and easy-to-navigate website offers students an impressive range of exercises, interactive-learning tools, assessment, and review materials, including:

Quiz+ Quiz+ doesn't just tell students how they did; it shows them how they can do better. With Quiz+, students are presented with a targeted study plan that offers specific page references and links to the ebook and other online learning tools.

NEW: World History Tours powered by Google Maps. These tours trace global developments over time, touching down on locations to launch documents and images for analysis.

NEW: Nearly 100 new documents increase the collection of readings to 350 sources. Each source is accompanied by a media analysis worksheet that offers students a simple guided method to *Observe* a document's primary themes, *Express* an opinion or respond to the author's objective, and *Connect* the document to broader historical relevance.

Engaging Review Materials include chapter summaries and outlines, focus questions, flashcards with audio pronunciations, and diagnostic quizzes.

More Help with Geography: iMaps offer students tools to view maps one layer of information at a time, focusing on specific geographic sections.

Map Review Worksheets provide each map in the textbook as a label-less image; students are given a list of labels to connect to the map. These worksheets can be printed out so that the exercises can be completed off line.

Chrono-Sequencers: These interactive chapter chronologies challenge students to reassemble sequences of events and reinforce their understanding of the flow of history.

Research Topics and Documents: Each chapter clusters primary sources around a topic, complete with an opening question and introduction to help students focus on the connections between the documents.

EBOOK AND CUSTOM VERSIONS

Ebook: Same great book, *one-third* the price!

An affordable and convenient alternative, Norton ebooks retain the content and design of the print book and allow students to highlight and take notes with ease, print chapters as needed, and search the text. Norton ebooks are available online and as downloadable PDFs. They can be purchased directly from our website or with a registration folder that can be sold in the bookstore.

Chapter Select

With Chapter Select instructors can create a custom ebook that contains only the chapters they want to assign. For more information, go to norton**ebooks**.com: includes pricing and purchasing details as well as instructions about how to create a custom ebook using Chapter Select.

ACKNOWLEDGMENTS

*World*s *Together*, *World*s *Apart* would never have happened without the full support of Princeton University. In a highly unusual move, and one for which we are truly grateful, the university helped underwrite this project with financial support from its 250th Anniversary Fund for undergraduate teaching and by allowing release time for the authors from campus commitments.

The history department's support of the effort over many years has been exceptional. Four chairs made funds and departmental support available, including the department's incomparable administrative talents. We would be remiss if we did not single out the department manager, Judith Hanson, who provided us with assistance whenever we needed it. We also thank Eileen Kane, who provided help in tracking down references and illustrations and in integrating changes into the manuscript. We also would like to thank Pamela Long, who made all of the complicated arrangements for ensuring that we were able to discuss matters in a leisurely and attractive setting. Sometimes that meant arranging for long-distance conference calls. She went even further and proofread the entire manuscript, finding many errors that we had all overlooked.

We drew shamelessly on the expertise of the departmental faculty, and although it might be wise simply to include a roster of the Princeton history department, that would do an injustice to those of whom we took most advantage. So here they are: Mariana Candido, Robert Darnton, Sheldon Garon, Anthony Grafton, Molly Greene, David Howell, Harold James, William Jordan, Emmanuel Kreike, Michael Mahoney, Arno Mayer, Kenneth Mills, John Murrin, Susan Naquin,

Willard Peterson, Theodore Rabb, Bhavani Raman, Stanley Stein, and Richard Turits. When necessary, we went outside the history department, getting help from L. Carl Brown, Michael Cook, Norman Itzkowitz, Martin Kern, Thomas Leisten, Heath Lowry, and Peter Schaefer. Two departmental colleagues—Natalie Z. Davis and Elizabeth Lunbeck—were part of the original team but had to withdraw because of other commitments. Their contributions were vital, and we want to express our thanks to them. David Gordon, now at Bowdoin College, used portions of the text while teaching an undergraduate course at the University of Durban in South Africa and shared comments with us. Shamil Jeppie, like David Gordon a graduate of the Princeton history department, now teaching at the University of Cape Town in South Africa, read and commented on various chapters.

Beyond Princeton, we have also benefited from exceptionally gifted and giving colleagues who have assisted this book in many ways. Colleagues at Louisiana State University, the University of Florida, the University of North Carolina, the University of Pennsylvania, and the University of California at Los Angeles, where Suzanne Marchand, Michael Tsin, Holly Pittman, and Stephen Aron, respectively, are now teaching, pitched in whenever we turned to them. Especially helpful have been the contributions of James Gelvin, Naomi Lamoreaux, Gary Nash, and Joyce Appleby at UCLA; Michael Bernstein at Tulane University; and Maribel Dietz, John Henderson, Christine Kooi, David Lindenfeld, Reza Pirbhai, and Victor Stater at Louisiana State University. It goes without saying that none of these individuals bears any responsibility for factual or interpretive errors that the text may contain. Xinru Liu would like to thank her Indian mentor, Romila Thapar, who changed the way we think about Indian history.

The quality and range of reviews on this project were truly exceptional. The final version of the manuscript was greatly influenced by the thoughts and ideas of numerous instructors. We wish to particularly thank our consulting reviewers, who read multiple versions of the manuscript from start to finish.

First Edition Consultants
Hugh Clark, Ursinus College
Jonathan Lee, San Antonio College
Pamela McVay, Ursuline College
Tom Sanders, United States Naval Academy

Second Edition Consultants
Jonathan Lee, San Antonio College
Pamela McVay, Ursuline College
Steve Rapp, Georgia State University
Cliff Rosenberg, City University of New York

First Edition Reviewers
Lauren Benton, New Jersey Institute of Technology
Ida Blom, University of Bergen, Norway

Ricardo Duchesne, University of New Brunswick
Major Bradley T. Gericke, United States Military Academy
John Gillis, Rutgers University
David Kenley, Marshall University
John Kicza, Washington State University
Matthew Levinger, Lewis and Clark College
James Long, Colorado State University
Adam McKeown, Columbia University
Mark McLeod, University of Delaware
John Mears, Southern Methodist University
Michael Murdock, Brigham Young University
David Newberry, University of North Carolina, Chapel Hill
Tom Pearcy, Slippery Rock State University
Oliver B. Pollak, University of Nebraska, Omaha
Ken Pomeranz, University of California, Irvine
Major David L. Ruffley, United States Air Force Academy
William Schell, Murray State University
Major Deborah Schmitt, United States Air Force Academy
Sarah Shields, University of North Carolina, Chapel Hill
Mary Watrous-Schlesinger, Washington State University

Second Edition Reviewers
William Atwell, Hobart and William Smith Colleges
Susan Besse, City University of New York
Tithi Bhattacharya, Purdue University
Mauricio Borrerero, St. John's University
Charlie Briggs, Georgia Southern University
Antoinne Burton, University of Illinois, Urbana-Champaign
Jim Cameron, St. Francis Xavier University
Kathleen Comerford, Georgia Southern University
Duane Corpis, Georgia State University
Denise Davidson, Georgia State University
Ross Doughty, Ursinus College
Alison Fletcher, Kent State University
Phillip Gavitt, Saint Louis University
Brent Geary, Ohio University
Henda Gilli-Elewy, California State Polytechnic University, Pomona
Fritz Gumbach, John Jay College
William Hagen, University of California, Davis
Laura Hilton, Muskingum College
Jeff Johnson, Villanova University
David Kammerling-Smith, Eastern Illinois University
Jonathan Lee, San Antonio College
Dorothea Martin, Appalachian State University
Don McGuire, State University of New York, Buffalo
Pamela McVay, Ursuline College
Joel Migdal, University of Washington
Anthony Parent, Wake Forest University
Sandra Peacock, Georgia Southern University
David Pietz, Washington State University
Jared Poley, Georgia State University

John Quist, Shippensburg State University
Steve Rapp, Georgia State University
Paul Rodell, Georgia Southern University
Ariel Salzman, Queen's University
Bill Schell, Murray State University
Claire Schen, State University of New York, Buffalo
Jonathan Skaff, Shippensburg State University
David Smith, California State Polytechnic University, Pomona
Neva Specht, Appalachian State University
Ramya Sreeniva, State University of New York, Buffalo
Charles Stewart, University of Illinois, Urbana-Champaign
Rachel Stocking, Southern Illinois University, Carbondale
Heather Streets, Washington State University
Tim Teeter, Georgia Southern University
Charlie Wheeler, University of California, Irvine
Owen White, University of Delaware
James Wilson, Wake Forest University

Third Edition Reviewers

Henry Antkiewicz, Eastern Tennessee State University
Anthony Barbieri-Low, University of California, Santa Barbara
Andrea Becksvoort, University of Tennessee, Chattanooga
Hayden Bellonoit, United States Naval Academy
John Bloom, Shippensburg University
Kathryn Braund, Auburn University
Catherine Candy, University of New Orleans
Karen Carter, Brigham Young University
Stephen Chappell, James Madison University
Jessey Choo, University of Missouri, Kansas City
Timothy Coates, College of Charleston
Gregory Crider, Wingate University
Denise Davidson, Georgia State University
Jessica Davidson, James Madison University
Sal Diaz, Santa Rosa Junior College
Todd Dozier, Baton Rouge Community College
Richard Eaton, University of Arizona
Lee Farrow, Auburn University, Montgomery
Bei Gao, College of Charleston
Behrooz Ghamari-Tabrizi, University of Illinois, Urbana-Champaign
Steven Gish, Auburn University, Montgomery
Jeffrey Hamilton, Baylor University
Barry Hankins, Baylor University
Brian Harding, Mott Community College
Tim Henderson, Auburn University, Montgomery
Marjorie Hilton, University of Redlands
Richard Hines, Washington State University
Lisa Holliday, Appalachian State University
Jonathan Lee, San Antonio College
David Kalivas, University of Massachusetts, Lowell

Christopher Kelley, Miami University, Ohio
Kenneth Koons, Virginia Military Institute
Michael Kulikowski, Pennsylvania State University
Benjamin Lawrence, University of California, Davis
Lu Liu, University of Tennessee, Knoxville
David Longfellow, Baylor University
Harold Marcuse, University of California, Santa Barbara
Dorothea Martin, Appalachian State University
David Mayes, Sam Houston State University
James Mokhiber, University of New Orleans
Mark Munzinger, Radford College
David Murphree, Virginia Tech University
Joshua Nadel, North Carolina Central University
Wing Chung Nq, University of Texas, San Antonio
Robert Norrell, University of Tennessee, Knoxville
Chandrika Paul, Shippensburg University
Beth Pollard, San Diego State University
Timothy Pytell, California State University, San Bernardino
Stephen Rapp, Professional Historian
Alice Roberti, Santa Rosa Junior College
Aviel Roshwald, Georgetown University
James Sanders, Utah State University
Lynn Sargeant, California State University, Fullerton
William Schell, Murray State University
Michael Seth, James Madison University
Barry Stentiford, Grambling State University
Gabrielle Sutherland, Baylor University
Lisa Tran, California State University, Fullerton
Michael Vann, California State University, Sacramento
Peter Von Sivers, University of Utah
Andrew Wackerfuss, Georgetown University
Ted Weeks, Southern Illinois University, Carbondale
Angela White, Indiana University of Pennsylvania
Jennifer Williams, Nichols State University
Andrew Wise, State University of New York, Buffalo
Eloy Zarate, Pasadena City College
William Zogby, Mohawk Valley Community College

We also want to thank Nancy Khalek (Ph.D. Princeton University), who now teaches at Brown University. Nancy was our jack-of-all-trades who helped in any way she could. She attended all the monthly meetings during the development of the early volume. She provided critiques of the manuscript, helped with primary research, worked on the photo program and the Global Connections & Disconnections features, and contributed content to the student website. She was invaluable. For the Third Edition, Nancy has authored a number of the new digital World History Tours powered by Google Maps. We would also like to thank Neva Specht and Amy Hudnall (both from Appalachian State University), who have authored the Instructor's Manual for the last two editions. They have filled the manual with many wonderful classroom exercises and a highly useful annotated suggested films list. Finally, we'd like to thank our two newcomers, Sara Jorgensen and Andrea Becksvoort (both from the University of Tennessee, Chattanooga) for thoroughly revising the test bank.

Our association with the publisher of this volume, W. W. Norton & Company, has been everything we could have asked for. Jon Durbin took us under the wing of the Norton firm. He attended all of our monthly meetings for the first two editions spanning the better part of four years across the creation of both volumes. How he put up with some of our interminable discussions will always be a mystery, but his enthusiasm for the endeavor never flagged, even when we seemed to grow weary. He has brought the same energy and determination to the Third Edition. Sandy Lifland was the ever-watchful and ever-careful development editor for each volume for the First Edition and a good portion of the Second Edition. She let us know when we were making sense and when we needed to explain ourselves more fully. Alice Falk was our talented and insightful co-developmental editor for the Second Edition. Between the efforts of Sandy and Alice, our vision became a reality. For the Third Edition, Alice Vigliani was an unimaginably superb development editor. She took a book that we were all very proud of, and she has helped bring it closest to our original vision. She responded immediately to all queries, kept everyone on an even keel, shrank the text where it was too wordy, and demanded that we add color and vitality where the writing flagged. If the Third Edition showcases the big world history stories better than ever, and it is easier to read and more accessible than the first two (and we believe that this is the case), we owe these improvements to her. Rebecca

Homiski did a fabulous job as our project editor on the Second and Third editions, coordinating the responses of up to twelve authors on both volumes combined and locking down all the details on the project. We also want to thank Ellen Lohman for copyediting the manuscript ably and with just the right touch for the Second and Third Editions. Stephanie Romeo led the charge again, finding all the new photos we requested, and Rubina Yeh integrated the new "Storylines" features and the new chapter chronologies into her already gorgeous design. Debra Morton-Hoyt has provided us again with what have to be the most distinctive and appealing world history book covers in the field. Ben Reynolds guided the manuscript through the production process, and Jason Spears capably pulled together all the important loose ends to get the manuscript ready for copyediting, working on the photo captions, glossary, and art manuscript, among other tasks. On the media front, we want to thank Steve Hoge for creating the Norton StudySpace website, which includes the impressive Norton Digital History Reader and the exciting new Norton World History Tours powered by Google Maps. On the print ancillary front, we'd like to thank Lorraine Klimowich and Rachel Comerford for finding an excellent group of authors to create the instructor's manual and test bank. Carla Zimowsk, the information officer for the history department at Princeton University, simplified the multiple transmission of revised chapters among all twelve of the authors, no easy task. She made what is a very complicated set of procedures easy to understand and workable.

Finally, we must recognize that while this project often kept us apart from family members, their support held our personal worlds together.

About the Authors

ROBERT TIGNOR (Ph.D. Yale University) is Professor Emeritus and the Rosengarten Professor of Modern and Contemporary History at Princeton University and the three-time chair of the history department. With Gyan Prakash, he introduced Princeton's first course in world history nearly twenty years ago. Professor Tignor has taught graduate and undergraduate courses in African history and world history and written extensively on the history of twentieth-century Egypt, Nigeria, and Kenya. Besides his many research trips to Africa, Professor Tignor has taught at the University of Ibadan in Nigeria and the University of Nairobi in Kenya.

JEREMY ADELMAN (D.Phil. Oxford University) is currently the Director of the Council for International Teaching and Research at Princeton University and the Walter S. Carpenter III Professor of Spanish Civilization and Culture. He has written and edited five books, including *Republic of Capital: Buenos Aires and the Legal Transformation of the Atlantic World*, which won the best book prize in Atlantic history from the American Historical Association, and most recently *Sovereignty and Revolution in the Iberian Atlantic*. Professor Adelman is the recent recipient of a Guggenheim Memorial Foundation Fellowship and the Frederick Burkhardt Award from the American Council of Learned Societies.

STEPHEN ARON (Ph.D. University of California, Berkeley) is professor of history at the University of California, Los Angeles, and executive director of the Institute for the Study of the American West, Autry National Center. A specialist in frontier and Western American history, Aron is the author of *How the West Was Lost: The Transformation of Kentucky from Daniel Boone to Henry Clay* and *American Confluence: The Missouri Frontier from Borderland to Border State*. He is currently editing the multi-volume *Autry History of the American West* and writing a book with the tentative title *Can We All Just Get Along: An Alternative History of the American West*.

PETER BROWN (Ph.D. Oxford University) is the Rollins Professor of History at Princeton University. He previously taught at London University and the University of California, Berkeley. He has written on the rise of Christianity and the end of the Roman Empire. His works include *Augustine of Hippo, The World of Late Antiquity, The Cult of the Saints, Body and Society, The Rise of Western Christendom*, and *Poverty and Leadership in the Later Roman Empire*. He is presently working on issues of wealth and poverty in the late Roman and early medieval Christian worlds.

BENJAMIN ELMAN (Ph.D. University of Pennsylvania) is professor of East Asian studies and history at Princeton University. He is currently serving as the chair of the Princeton East Asian Studies Department. He taught at the University of California, Los Angeles, for over fifteen years. His teaching and research fields include Chinese intellectual and cultural history, 1000–1900; the history of science in China, 1600–1930; the history of education in late imperial China; and Sino-Japanese cultural history, 1600–1850. He is the author of five books: *From Philosophy to Philology: Intellectual and Social Aspects of Change in Late Imperial China; Classicism, Politics, and Kinship: The Ch'ang-chou School of New Text Confucianism in Late Imperial China; A Cultural History of Civil Examinations in Late Imperial China; On Their Own Terms: Science in China, 1550–1900*; and *A Cultural History of Modern Science in China*. He is the creator of Classical Historiography for Chinese History at www.princeton.edu/~classbib/, a bibliography and teaching website published since 1996.

STEPHEN KOTKIN (Ph.D. University of California, Berkeley) is professor of European and Asian history as well as international affairs at Princeton University. He formerly directed Princeton's program in Russian and Eurasian studies (1996–2009). He is the author of *Magnetic Mountain: Stalinism as a Civilization, Uncivil Society: 1989 and the Implosion of the Communist Establishment*, and *Armageddon Averted: The Soviet Collapse, 1970–2000*. He is a coeditor of *Mongolia in the Twentieth Century: Landlocked Cosmopolitan*. Professor Kotkin has twice been a visiting professor in Japan.

XINRU LIU (Ph.D. University of Pennsylvania) is associate professor of early Indian history and world history at the College of New Jersey. She is associated with the Institute of World History and the Chinese Academy of Social Sciences. She is the author of *Ancient India and Ancient China, Trade and Religious Exchanges, AD 1–600; Silk and Religion, an Exploration of Material Life and the Thought of People, AD 600–1200; Connections across Eurasia, Transportation, Communication, and Cultural Exchange on the Silk Roads*, co-authored with Lynda Norene Shaffer; and *A Social History of Ancient India* (in Chinese). Professor Liu promotes South Asian studies and world history studies in both the United States and the People's Republic of China.

SUZANNE MARCHAND (Ph.D. University of Chicago) is professor of European and intellectual history at Louisiana State University, Baton Rouge. Professor Marchand also spent a number of years teaching at Princeton University. She is the author of *Down from Olympus: Archaeology and Philhellenism in Germany, 1750–1970* and *German Orientalism in the Age of Empire: Religion, Race and Scholarship*.

HOLLY PITTMAN (Ph.D. Columbia University) is professor of art history at the University of Pennsylvania, where she teaches art and archaeology of Mesopotamia and the Iranian Plateau. She also serves as curator in the Near East Section of the University of Pennsylvania Museum of Archaeology and Anthropology. Previously she served as a curator in the Ancient Near Eastern Art Department of the Metropolitan Museum of Art. She has written extensively on the art and culture of the Bronze Age in the Middle East and has participated in excavations in Cyprus, Turkey, Syria, Iraq, and Iran, where she currently works. Her research investigates works of art as media through which patterns of thought, cultural development, and historical interactions of ancient cultures of the Near East are reconstructed.

GYAN PRAKASH (Ph.D. University of Pennsylvania) is professor of modern Indian history at Princeton University and a member of the Subaltern Studies Editorial Collective. He is the author of *Bonded Histories: Genealogies of Labor Servitude in Colonial India, Another Reason: Science and the Imagination of Modern India*, and *Mumbai Fables*. Professor Prakash edited *After Colonialism: Imperial Histories and Postcolonial Displacements* and *Noir Urbanisms*, coedited *The Space of the Modern City* and *Utopia/Dystopia*, and has written a number of articles on colonialism and history writing. He is currently working on a history of the city of Bombay. With Robert Tignor, he introduced the modern world history course at Princeton University.

BRENT SHAW (Ph.D. Cambridge University) is the Andrew Fleming West Professor of Classics at Princeton University, where he is director of the Program in the Ancient World. He was previously at the University of Pennsylvania, where he chaired the Graduate Group in Ancient History. His principal areas of specialization as a Roman historian are Roman family history and demography, sectarian violence and conflict in Late Antiquity, and the regional history of Africa as part of the Roman Empire. He has published *Spartacus and the Slaves Wars*; edited the papers of Sir Moses Finley, *Economy and Society in Ancient Greece*; and published in a variety of books and journals, including the *Journal of Roman Studies*, the *American Historical Review*, the *Journal of Early Christian Studies*, and *Past & Present*.

MICHAEL TSIN (Ph.D. Princeton) is associate professor of history and international studies at the University of North Carolina at Chapel Hill. He previously taught at the University of Illinois at Chicago, Princeton University, Columbia University, and the University of Florida. Professor Tsin's primary interests include the histories of modern China and colonialism. He is the author of *Nation, Governance, and Modernity in China: Canton, 1900–1927*. He is currently writing a social history of the reconfiguration of Chinese identity in the twentieth century.

NORTH

AMERICA

ATLANTIC
OCEAN

PACIFIC
OCEAN

SOUTH

AMERICA

SAHARA

Niger R.

0   1000   2000 Miles

0   1000   2000 Kilometers

THE GEOGRAPHY OF THE ANCIENT AND MODERN WORLDS

Today, we believe the world to be divided into continents, and most of us think that it was always so. Geographers usually identify six inhabited continents: Africa, North America, South America, Europe, Asia, and Australia. Inside these continents they locate a vast number of subcontinental units, such as East Asia, South Asia, Southeast Asia, the Middle East, North Africa, and sub-Saharan Africa. Yet this geographical understanding would have been completely alien to premodern men and women, who did not think that they inhabited continents bounded by large bodies of water. Lacking a firm command of the seas,

they saw themselves living on contiguous landmasses, and they thought these territorial bodies were the main geographical units of their lives. Hence, in this volume we have chosen to use a set of geographical terms, the main one being *Afro-Eurasia*, that more accurately reflect the world that the premoderns believed that they inhabited.

The most interconnected and populous landmass of premodern times was Afro-Eurasia. The term *Eurasia* is widely used in general histories, but we think it is in its own ways inadequate. The preferred term from our perspective must be *Afro-Eurasia*, for the interconnected

landmass of premodern and indeed much of modern times included large parts of Europe and Asia and significant regions in Africa. The major African territories that were regularly joined to Europe and Asia were Egypt, North Africa, and even parts of sub-Saharan Africa.

Only gradually and fitfully did the divisions of the world that we take for granted today take shape. The peoples inhabiting the northwestern part of the Afro-Eurasian landmass did not see themselves as European Christians, and hence as a distinctive cultural entity, until the Middle Ages drew to a close in the twelfth and thirteenth centuries. Islam did not arise and extend its influence throughout the middle zone of the Afro-Eurasian landmass until the eighth and ninth centuries. And, finally, the peoples living in what we today term the *Indian subcontinent* did not feel a strong sense of their own cultural and political unity until the Delhi Sultanate of the thirteenth and fourteenth centuries and the Mughal Empire, which emerged at the beginning of the sixteenth century, brought political unity to that vast region. As a result, we use the terms *South Asia, Vedic society,* and *India* in place of *Indian subcontinent* for the premodern part of our narrative, and we use *Southwest Asia* and *North Africa* to refer to what today is designated as the *Middle East*. In fact, it is only in the period from 1000 to 1300 that some of the major cultural areas that are familiar to us today truly crystallized.

9

NEW EMPIRES AND COMMON CULTURES, 600–1000 CE

I n 754 CE, the Muslim caliph (ruler) al-Mansur decided to relocate his capital city. Islam was barely a century old, yet flourishing under its second dynasty, the Abbasids. Al-Mansur wanted to relocate power away from Damascus (the capital of Islam's first dynasty) to the Abbasids' home region on the Iranian plateau to signal its new dawn. After traveling the length of the Tigris and Euphrates rivers in search of a perfect site, the caliph decided to build his capital near an unimposing village called Baghdad.

He had good reasons for this selection. The site lay between Mesopotamia's two great rivers at the juncture of the canals that linked them. It was also a powerful symbolic location: close to the ancient capital of the Sasanian Empire, Ctesiphon, where the Arch of Khusro was still standing. It was also the site of earlier Sumerian and Babylonian power. By building at Baghdad, al-Mansur could reaffirm Mesopotamia's centrality in the world and exalt the universalizing ambitions of Islam. Within five years of laying the first brick, towering walls surrounded what soon became known as the "round city," so named because of the way in which the different segments radiated out from the administrative and religious center."

Al-Mansur's choice had enduring effects. As the new capital of Islam, Baghdad also became a vital crossroads for commerce. Overnight, the city exploded into a bustling world entrepôt. Chinese goods arrived by land and sea; commodities from Inner Eurasia flowed in over the Silk Road; and cargo-laden camel caravans wound across Baghdad's western desert, linking the capital with Syria, Egypt, North Africa, and southern Spain. In effect, the unity that the Abbasids imposed from Baghdad intensified the movement of peoples, ideas, innovations, and commodities.

Baghdad's eminence and prosperity reflected its role as the center of the Islamic world. Yet, while Islam was gaining ground in central Afro-Eurasia, Chinese might was surging in East Asia—powerfully under the Tang—and Christianity was striving to extend its domains and add to its converts. Unquestionably, however, the two imperial powerhouses of this period were Islam and Tang China, and they are the focus of this chapter.

Islam and Tang China were manifestly different worlds. The Islamic state had a universalizing religious mission: to bring humankind under the authority of the religion espoused by the Prophet Muhammad. In contrast, the Tang had no such grandiose religious aspirations, and while the ruling elite supported religious pluralism within China, they did not use Buddhism to expand their control into areas outside China. Instead, the Tang rulers expected that their neighbors would emulate Chinese institutions and pay tribute as symbols of respect to the greatness of the Tang Empire. As Islam's warriors and scholars crossed into Europe and as Chinese influences took deeper root in East Asia, religion and empire once again intertwined to serve as the social foundation across much of Afro-Eurasia.

RELIGIONS AND EMPIRES

> → *Why did the new religion of Islam arise in the Arabian Peninsula, and what outside factors influenced Muhammad's religious messages?*

How religion and empire connect can vary in important ways. In the cases of Christianity and Buddhism, empire was the main vehicle for their growth. In the case of Islam, though, it was religion that created empire. Having swept aside their predecessors in Southwest Asia, Muslim leaders had to form their own institutional system; and as their spiritual aspirations spread, the political imagination evolved into an imperial one. Although they borrowed from the Byzantines and Persians, their reason for establishing an empire was new: to secure, defend, and spread their religion. Whereas Christianity, Buddhism, and Zoroastrianism converted already-existing empires to their own views, Islam created its empire from scratch.

Given the recent surge of religious energy across Afro-Eurasia, it was perhaps only a matter of time before a prophetic figure would arise among the Arabs. Christianity and Buddhism were laying claim to universal truths, spreading their faiths across wide geographic areas outside their places of origin, and competing groups now had to speak the language of universal religion. Only the Tang dynasty resisted the universalizing faiths, as Confucianism and Daoism withstood the upsurge of Chinese Buddhism—revealing that China would follow a different path by maintaining past traditions. In the seventh century, Arab peoples would become

Focus Questions

→ *Why did the new religion of Islam arise in the Arabian Peninsula, and what outside factors influenced Muhammad's religious messages?*

→ *What factors created a common cultural outlook among Muslim communities in Afro-Eurasia during this era?*

→ *How did the Tang state balance its restoration of Confucian principles with the growth of new universal religions?*

→ *To what extent did Japanese and Korean polities imitate Tang China?*

→ *How did two Christianities come to exist in western Afro-Eurasia?*

MAIN THEMES

→ *The universalizing religion of Islam, based on the message of the prophet Muhammad, originates on the Arabian Peninsula and spreads rapidly across Afro-Eurasia.*

→ *Two distinctly different imperial powerhouses—Islam and Tang China—dominate much of Afro-Eurasia.*

→ *Christianity splits over doctrinal and political differences, leading to a western church based on the papacy in Rome and Eastern Orthodoxy based in Constantinople.*

FOCUS ON *Faith and Empire*

The Islamic Empire

✦ Warriors from the Arabian Peninsula defeat Byzantine and Sasanian armies and establish an Islamic empire stretching from Morocco to South Asia.

✦ The Abbasid state takes over from the Umayyads, crystallizes the main Islamic institutions of the caliphate and Islamic law, and promotes cultural achievements in religion, philosophy, and science.

✦ Disputes over Muhammad's succession lead to a deep and enduring split between Sunnis and Shiites.

Tang China

✦ The Tang dynasty dominates East Asia, including Japan and Korea.

✦ Tang dynasts balance Confucian ideals with Buddhist thought and practice.

✦ A common written language and shared philosophy, rather than a universalizing religion, integrate the Chinese state.

Christian Europe

✦ Monks, nuns, and Rome-based popes spread Christianity throughout western Europe.

✦ Constantinople-based Eastern Orthodoxy survives the spread of Islam.

---

the makers of their own universal faith, which would join and jostle with predecessors in Afro-Eurasia.

THE ORIGINS AND SPREAD OF ISLAM

→ *What factors created a common cultural outlook among Muslim communities in Afro-Eurasia during this era?*

Islam began inside Arabia. Despite its remoteness and sparse population, by the sixth century CE Arabia was brushing up against exciting outside currents: long-distance trade, religious debate, and imperial politics. Byzantine and Sasanian imperial pressures already had intruded deeply into Arabia (see Chapter 8); commodities from Egypt, Syria, and Iraq cir-

culated in local markets; and learned men debated the doctrines of Christianity and Judaism. The Hijaz—the western region bordering the Red Sea—knew the outside world through trading routes reaching up the coast to the Mediterranean. While one of the world's major universalizing faiths would be born in a remote region of Southwest Asia, Islam would quickly take advantage of the dynamic trade routes stretching across Southwest Asia and North Africa to spread its faith and political empire.

Mecca, in the Hijaz, was not an imposing place. A pre-Islamic poet wrote that its "winter and summer are equally intolerable. No waters flow . . . [and there is] not a blade of grass on which to rest the eye; no, nor hunting. [Here there are] only merchants, the most despicable of professions" (Peters, p. 23). Hardly more than a village of simple mud huts, Mecca's inhabitants sustained themselves less as traders than as caretakers of a revered sanctuary called the kaaba. They regarded this collection of unmortared rocks piled on top of one another as the dwelling place of deities, whom the polytheistic Meccans worshipped. Here a great prophet was born.

Mecca. At the great mosque at Mecca, which many consider the most sacred site in Islam, hundreds of thousands of worshippers gather for Friday prayers. Many are performing their religious duty to go on a pilgrimage to the holy places in the Arabian Peninsula.

A VISION, A TEXT

Born in Mecca around 570 CE into a well-respected tribal family, **Muhammad** enjoyed only moderate success as a trader. Little in his early life suggested that momentous events would soon occur. Then came a revelation, which would convert this broker of commodities into a proselytizer of a new faith. In 610 CE, while Muhammad was on a month-long spiritual retreat in a cave near Mecca, he believed that God came to him in a vision and commanded him to recite these words:

> Recite in the Name of the Lord who createth,
> Createth man from a clot
> Recite: And thy Lord is the most Bounteous who
>   teacheth by the pen
> Teacheth man that which he knew not.

Further revelations followed. The early ones were like the first: short, powerful, emphasizing a single, all-powerful God (Allah), and full of instructions for Muhammad's fellow Meccans to carry this message to nonbelievers. The words were eminently memorable, an important feature in an oral culture where poetry recitation was the highest art form. Muhammad's early preaching had a clear message. He urged his small band of followers to act righteously, to set aside false deities, to submit themselves to the one and only true God, and to care for the less fortunate—for the Day of Judgment was imminent. Muhammad's most insistent message was the oneness of God, a belief that has remained central to the Islamic faith ever since.

These teachings, compiled into an authoritative version after the Prophet's death, constituted the foundational text of Islam: the **Quran.** Its 114 chapters, known as suras, occur in descending order of length; the longest has three hundred verses and the shortest, a mere three. Accepted as the very word of God, they flowed without flaw through God's perfect instrument, the Prophet Muhammad. (See Primary Source: The Quran: Two Suras in Praise of God.) Like the Jewish Torah, the Christian Bible, and other foundational texts, this one proclaimed the tenets of a new faith to unite a people and to expand its spiritual frontiers. Its message already had universalist elements, though how far it was to be extended, whether to the tribesmen living in the Arabian Peninsula or well beyond, was not at all clear at first.

Muhammad believed that he was a prophet in the tradition of Moses, other Hebrew prophets, and Jesus, and that he communicated with the same God that they did. As we have seen, Christian and Jewish communities existed in the Arabian Peninsula at this time. The city of Yathrib (later called Medina) held a substantial Jewish community. Just how deeply Muhammad understood the tenets of Judaism and Christianity is difficult to determine, but his professed indebtedness to their tradition is a part of Islamic belief.

THE MOVE TO MEDINA

Muslims date the beginning of the Muslim era from the year 622 CE. At this time Muhammad and a small group of followers, opposed by Mecca's leaders because of their radical

Primary Source

THE QURAN: TWO SURAS IN PRAISE OF GOD

These two suras from the Quran are relatively short, but they convey some of the essence of Muhammad's message. The Quran opens with a sura known as the fatiha ("of the opening"), which in its powerfully prayerlike quality lends itself to frequent recitation. Sura 87, "The Most High," provides a deeper insight into the nature of humanity's relationship with God.

The Fatiha

In the Name of God the Compassionate the merciful
Praise be to God, Lord of the Universe,
The Compassionate, the Merciful,
Sovereign of the Day of Judgement!
You alone we worship, and to You alone we turn for help.
Guide us to the straight path,
The path of those whom You have favoured,
Not of those who have incurred Your wrath,
Nor of those who have gone astray.   (1.1–1.7)

The Most High

In the Name of God, the Compassionate, the merciful
Praise the name of your Lord, the Most High, who has
    created all things and proportioned
them; who has ordained their destinies and guided them;
    who brings forth the green pasture, then turns it to
    withered grass.
We shall make you recite our revelations, so that you
    shall forget none of them except as God pleases. He

has knowledge of all that is manifest, and all that is
hidden.
We shall guide you to the smoothest path. Therefore give
    warning, if warning will avail. He that fears God will
    heed it, but the wicked sinner will flout it. He shall
    burn in the gigantic Fire, where he shall neither die
    nor live. Happy shall be the man who purifies himself,
    who remembers the name of his Lord and prays,
Yet you prefer this life, although the life to come is
    better and more lasting.
All this is written in earlier scriptures; the scriptures of
    Abraham and Moses.   (87.1–87.19)

→ *What themes do these passages reveal about Islam's view of the relationship between God and mortals?*

→ *Do you find any similarities to the tenets of Judaism and Christianity as you have encountered them in this volume?*

SOURCE: From *The Koran*, translated and with notes by N. J. Dawood (Penguin Classics 1956, Fifth revised edition 1990). Copyright © N. J. Dawood, 1956, 1959, 1966, 1968, 1974, 1990, 1993, 1997, 1999, 2003. Reproduced by permission of Penguin Books Ltd.

religious tenets and their challenge to the ruling elite's authority, escaped to Medina. Known as *the hijra* ("breaking off of relations" or "departure"), the perilous 200-mile journey yielded a new form of communal unity: the *umma* ("band of the faithful").

The city of Medina had been facing tribal and religious tensions, and by inviting Muhammad and his followers to take up residence there, its elders hoped that his leadership and charisma would bring peace and unity to their city. Early in his stay Muhammad promulgated a document, the Constitution of Medina, requiring the community's people to refer all disputes to God and him. Medina thus became the birthplace of a new faith called **Islam** ("submission"—in this case, to the will of God) and a new community called Muslims ("those who submit"). Now the residents were expected to replace traditional family, clan, and tribal affiliations with loyalty to Muhammad as the one and true Prophet of God. From Medina the faithful broadcast their faith and their mission, at first mainly by military means, to the recalcitrants of Mecca and then to all of Arabia and then later to the entire world. In this way, Islam joined Christianity in seeking to bring the whole known world under its authority.

CONQUESTS

In 632, in his early sixties, the Prophet passed away. Islam might have withered without its leader, but the movement remained vibrant thanks to the energy of the early followers—especially Muhammad's first four successors, the "rightly

بشدلرسب ول ولنیکم السب تجدوغی وقت قریسلکو کلنے
قوز قیدی ایکتجی سبب اولدلیکم کاولرکشه هیت اولدوز ذیے

The Battle of Badr. This image depicts the battle of Badr, which took place in 624 and marked the beginning of Muhammad's reconquest of Mecca from his new base in the city of Medina.

(the world of warfare), seeking nothing less than world dominion. Within fifteen years Muslim soldiers had grasped Syria, Egypt, and Iraq—centerpieces of the former Byzantine and Sasanian empires that now became pillars undergirding an even larger Islamic empire. Mastery of desert warfare and inspired military leadership yielded these astonishing exploits, as did the exhaustion of the Byzantine and Sasanian empires after generations of warfare.

The Byzantines saved the core of their empire by pulling back to the highlands of Anatolia, where they had readily defensible frontiers. In contrast, the Sasanians gambled all on a final effort: they hurled their remaining military resources against the Muslim armies, only to be crushed. Having lost Iraq and unable to defend the Iranian plateau, the Sasanian Empire passed out of existence, its remnants absorbed into a new imperial regime. The result: Islam acquired political foundations within a generation of its birth.

AN EMPIRE OF ARABS

Creating an empire and stabilizing it were two different things. We have seen some come and go, like Alexander's. Others had more stamina. How would Islam fare? For a while, it was unclear. After the assassination of the last of the "rightly guided caliphs," Ali, a political vacuum opened. At this point a branch of one of the Meccan clans, the Umayyads, laid claim to Ali's legacy. Having been governors of the province of Syria under Ali, this first dynasty moved the core of Islam out of Arabia to the Syrian city of Damascus. They also introduced a hereditary monarchy to resolve leadership disputes. These adaptable, cosmopolitan traders ruled from Damascus until the Abbasids overthrew them in 750 CE.

By then, the core practices and beliefs of every Muslim had crystallized as the five "pillars" of Islam, which found clear expression in the Quran. Building on long-standing Arabian customs and certain familiar Jewish practices, these pillars undergirded Islamic practice early in Muhammad's career as a prophet and gave the imperial system a doctrinal and legal structure and a broad appeal to diverse populations.

The five pillars of Islam established clear-cut demands on believers. Converts were expected to adhere to and repeat the phrase that there is no God but God and that Muhammad was His Prophet. They were required to pray five times daily facing Mecca, to fast from sunup until sundown during the month of Ramadan, to make a pilgrimage to Mecca at least once in a lifetime if their personal resources permitted, and to pay alms in the form of taxation that would alleviate the hardships of the poor. These core doctrines, especially the crucial pillar affirming belief in one God and the prophecy of Muhammad, likely attracted early converts.

There was, however, a political limit to Islam's welcoming embrace. Although tolerant of conquered populations, Umayyad dynasts did not permit non-Arabic-speaking con-

guided caliphs." The Arabic word *khalīfa* means "successor," and in this context it referred to Muhammad's successors as political rulers over Muslim peoples and the expanding state. Their breakthrough was to institutionalize the new faith. They set the new religion on the pathway to imperial greatness and linked religious uprightness with territorial expansion, empire-building, and an appeal to all peoples.

Now Islam's expansive spiritual force galvanized its political authority. But what kind of polity would this be? Driven by religious fervor and a desire to acquire the wealth of conquered territories, Muslim soldiers embarked on military conquests and sought to found a far-reaching territorial empire. This expansion of the Islamic state was one aspect of the struggle that they called *jihad.* From the outset Muslim religious and political leaders divided the world into two units: the *dar al-Islam* (or the world of Islam) and the *dar al-harb*

verts to hold high political offices. Not until the overthrow of Umayyad rule did the "Arabs only" empire come to an end and non-Arab populations become incorporated into the Islamic core. This changed the nature of the emerging empire. For as the political center of Islam moved out of Arabia to Syria (at Damascus), and then with the Abbasids to Mesopotamia, ethnic and geographical diversity replaced what had been ethnic purity. Thus even as the universalizing religion strove to create a common spiritual world, it became more diverse within its political dimensions.

THE ABBASID REVOLUTION

As the Umayyad dynasts spread Islam beyond Arabia, some peoples resented the rulers' high-handed ways. For example, the central Asian province of Khurasan was home to many converts who chafed at their subordination to Arab peoples. Here, religious reformers and political dissidents stressed doctrines of religious purity and depicted the Umayyads as irreligious and politically repressive.

A coalition emerged under the Abbasi family, which claimed descent from the Prophet. Soon disgruntled provincial authorities and their military allies, as well as non-Arab converts, joined the movement. These individuals had embraced Islam and learned Arabic, only to discover that they were still second-class citizens. After amassing a sizable military force, the Abbasid coalition trounced the Umayyad ruler in 750 CE. Thereafter the center of the caliphate shifted to Iraq (at Baghdad; recall the opening anecdote about al-Mansur), signifying the eastward sprawl of the faith and its empire. It also represented a success for non-Arab groups within Islam without eliminating Arab influence at the dynasty's center—the capital, Baghdad, in Arabic-speaking Iraq.

Ultimately, conversion to Islam rested on the zeal of evangelizers and the faith's appeal to converts. Some turned to it for practical reasons, seeking reduced taxes or enhanced power. Others, particularly those living in ethnically and religiously diverse regions, welcomed the message of a single all-powerful God and a single community united by a clear code of laws; they saw it as offering superior answers to thorny secular and spiritual questions. Not only did the Abbasids open Islam to Persian peoples, but they also embraced Greek and Hellenistic learning, Indian science, and Chinese innovations. In this fashion, Islam, drawing its original impetus from the teachings and actions of a prophetic figure, followed the trajectory of Christianity and Buddhism and became a faith with a universalist message and appeal. It owed much of its success to its ability to merge the contributions of vastly different geographic and intellectual territories into a rich yet unified culture (see Map 9-1).

THE CALIPHATE   An early challenge for the Abbasid rulers was to determine how traditional, or "Arab," they could

be and still rule so vast an empire. They chose to keep the bedrock political institution of the early Islamic state—the **caliphate**. Signifying both the political and spiritual head of the Islamic community, this institution had arisen as the successor to Muhammad's shining leadership. Although the caliphs exercised political and spiritual authority over the Muslim community, they did not inherit his prophetic powers. Nor were they authorities in religious doctrine. That power was reserved for religious scholars, called **ulama**; some of these men were schooled in Islamic law, others were experts in Quranic interpretation, and still others were religious thinkers.

Imperial rule reflected borrowed practices from successful predecessors. The caliphates' leadership style was a mixture of Persian absolute authority and the royal seclusion of the Byzantine emperors who lived in palaces far removed from their subjects. Imperial Islam mingled absolute authority with decentralized power through its envoys in the provinces. This involved a delicate and ultimately unsustainable balancing act. As the empire expanded it became increasingly decentralized, enabling wily regional governors and competing caliphates in Spain and Egypt to grab power. The political result was an Islamic world shot through with multiple centers of power, nominally led by a weakened Abbasid caliphate. Even as Islam's political center diffused, though, its spiritual center remained fixed in Mecca, where many of the faithful gathered to circle the kaaba and to reaffirm their devotion to Islam as part of their pilgrimage obligation.

THE ARMY   The Abbasids, like all rulers, relied on force to integrate their empire. For imperial Islam (as for the Romans), exercising military power required marshalling warriors and soldiers from across Afro-Eurasia.

How "Arab" should the Muslim armies be? In the early stages, leaders had conscripted military forces from local Arab populations, creating citizen armies. But as Arab populations settled down in garrison cities, the Abbasid rulers turned to professional soldiers from the empire's peripheries. Now they recruited from Turkish-speaking communities in central Asia, and from the non-Arab, Berber-speaking peoples of North Africa and West Africans. Their reliance on foreign—that is, non-Arab—military personnel represented a major shift in the Islamic world. Not only did the change infuse the empire with dynamic new populations, but soon these groups gained political authority (just as the "barbarians" had done in the last centuries of the Roman Empire; see Chapters 6 and 8). Having begun as an Arab state and then incorporated strong Persian influence, the Islamic empire now especially embraced Turkish elements from the pastoral belts of central Asia.

ISLAMIC LAW (THE *SHARIA*) AND THEOLOGY   In the Abbasid period, not just the caliphate but also Islamic law took shape. The **sharia** stands as the crucial foundation of

Islam. It covers all aspects of practical and spiritual life, providing legal principles for marriage contracts, trade regulations, and religious prescriptions such as prayer, pilgrimage rites, and ritual fasting. It reflects the work of generations of religious scholars, rather than soldiers, courtiers, and bureaucrats. And it has remained vital throughout the Muslim world, independent of empires, to the present day.

Early Muslim communities prepared the ground for the *sharia,* endeavoring (guided by the Quran) to handle legal matters in ways that they thought Muhammad would have wanted. However, because the Quran mainly addressed family concerns, religious beliefs, and social relations (such as marriage, divorce, inheritance, dietary restrictions, and treatment of women) but not other legal questions, local judges exercised their own judgment where the Quran was silent. The most influential early legal scholar was an eighth-century Palestinian-born Arab, al-Shafi'i, who wanted to make the empire's laws entirely Islamic. He insisted that Muhammad's laws as laid out in the Quran, in addition to his sayings and actions as written in later reports (*hadith*), provided all the legal guidance that Islamic judges needed.

The triumph of scholars such as Shafi'i was deeply significant: it placed the *ulama,* the Muslim scholars, at the heart of Islam. *Ulama,* not princes and kings, became the lawmakers, insisting that the caliphs could not define religious law. Only the scholarly class could interpret the Quran and determine which *hadith* were authentic. The *ulama*'s ascendance opened a sharp division within Islam: between the secular realm, where caliphs and their representatives exercised power, and the religious sphere, where religious officials and scholars (judges, experts on Islamic jurisprudence, teachers, and holy men) exercised their authority.

GENDER IN EARLY ISLAM Pre-Islamic Arabia was one of the last regions in Southwest Asia where patriarchy had not triumphed. Instead, men still married into women's families and moved to those families' locations, as was common in tribal communities. Some women engaged in a variety of occupations and even, if they became wealthy, married more than one husband. But contact with the rest of Southwest Asia, where men's power over women prevailed, was already altering women's status in the Arabian Peninsula before the birth of Muhammad.

Muhammad's relations with women reflected these changes. As a young man, he married a woman fifteen years his senior—Khadija, an independent trader—and took no other wives before she died. It was Khadija to whom he went in fear following his first revelations. She wrapped him in a blanket and assured him of his sanity. She was also his first convert. Later in life, however, he took younger wives and insisted on their veiling. He

→ *What factors created a common cultural outlook among Muslim communities in Afro-Eurasia during this era?*

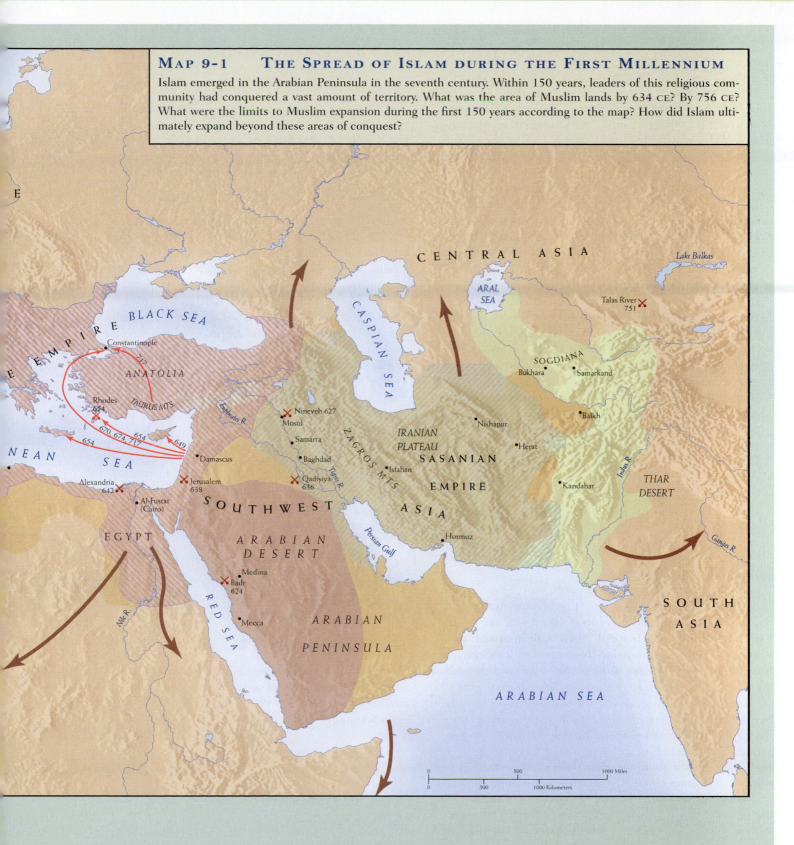

MAP 9-1 THE SPREAD OF ISLAM DURING THE FIRST MILLENNIUM

Islam emerged in the Arabian Peninsula in the seventh century. Within 150 years, leaders of this religious community had conquered a vast amount of territory. What was the area of Muslim lands by 634 CE? By 756 CE? What were the limits to Muslim expansion during the first 150 years according to the map? How did Islam ultimately expand beyond these areas of conquest?

PREMODERN LIBRARIES: FROM ROYAL ARCHIVES TO REPOSITORIES OF UNIVERSAL KNOWLEDGE

Libraries invariably accompanied urbanization, centralized governments, and writing. In the ninth and tenth centuries the biggest, most carefully organized, and most actively used libraries were in the Islamic and Chinese empires. These were great centers of learning and government; their cultures extolled the written word.

The Islamic world had special respect for books and libraries, for in the Quran Muhammad had brought the very words of God to his followers. Later generations added to Islam's traditions by collecting sayings attributed to the Prophet, his companions, and the early caliphs (*hadith*); writing treatises on religious law (*sharia*); and assimilating the knowledge of Greeks, Persians, Indians, and Chinese. Moreover, since Egypt and Southwest Asia had seen the world's earliest writing, these areas—the heartland of Islam—already had strong literary and library traditions.

The world's first libraries arose in Mesopotamia, where writing itself originated. These facilities were quite different from modern repositories of learning. They did house literary masterpieces (such as the Sumerian *Epic of Gilgamesh*), but they mainly served as government archives, holding important records that future rulers and bureaucrats might need to consult. Most likely the first storehouse of written materials was that of King Ashurbanipal of Assyria in the seventh century BCE. Like other monarchs aspiring to universal sway, he collected all significant literary works. His library at Nineveh contained as many as 25,000 tablets preserving omens, incantations, and hymns;

it also held the literatures of the many Mesopotamian languages, including Assyrian, Sumerian, Ugaritic, and Aramaic.

Because the "books" of Ashurbanipal II's library were clay tablets etched in cuneiform, hardened through baking in kilns, they were safe from fire—the destroyer of many later libraries. Those in its famous successor in Alexandria were not so fortunate. Housed in several buildings, that magnificent library was the pride of Ptolemy I and Ptolemy II (r. 323–285, 285–246 BCE), two enlightened kings who believed that Greek arts, sciences, and literature were an unmatched legacy for future generations. They set their administrators the task of collecting anything written in Greek. Though the size of Alexandria's holdings is unknown (as few as 40,000 scrolls or as many as half a million works), it was almost unimaginably large for the period. But beginning in the first century BCE, these collections were repeatedly subject to burning and looting. By the fourth century CE the immense body of literature was almost entirely lost.

The Muslims led the way, as impressive libraries arose in the heartland of Islam. They appeared first in the early mosques, including those in Cairo, Damascus, and Baghdad. But book and manuscript collecting spread rapidly to the outskirts of the Islamic world, where libraries in Timbuktu in West Africa, Samarkand in central Asia, and Jakarta in Southeast Asia earned high reputations for their extraordinary collections of religious and scientific treatises.

---

married his favorite wife, Aisha, when she was only nine or ten years old.

Hence, by the time Islam reached Southwest Asia and North Africa, where strict gender rules and women's subordinate status were entrenched, the new faith was adopting a patriarchal outlook. Muslim men could divorce freely; women could not. A man could take four wives and numerous concubines; a woman could have only one husband. Well-to-do women, always veiled, lived secluded from male society. Still, the Quran did offer women some protections. Men had to treat each wife with respect if they took more than one. Women could inherit property (although only half of what a man inherited). Infanticide was taboo. Marriage dowries went

directly to the bride rather than to her guardian, indicating women's independent legal standing; and while a woman's adultery drew harsh punishment, its proof required eyewitness testimony. The result was a legal system that reinforced men's dominance over women but empowered magistrates to oversee the definition of male honor and proper behavior.

THE BLOSSOMING OF ABBASID CULTURE

The arts flourished during the Abbasid period, a blossoming that left its imprint throughout society. Within a century, Ara-

Compared with those in Christian Europe, the Muslim libraries were immense. The library at Cordova (in Muslim Spain) reportedly held 600,000 books, or more than two books for every household in the city. Ibn Sina, the great Muslim scholar of the eleventh century, marveled at the library holdings of the Saminid court in Persia. There he found Greek books that he had not seen anywhere else and that were barely known to even the best Muslim scholars. Probably the largest collection was Cairo's vast House of Learning, assembled by the Fatimid caliphs. At its height it may have held 1.5 million books. By contrast, Germany's Reichenau, one of the largest monastic libraries in Christian Europe, had only 450 volumes in parchment—almost one-third of them prayer books. It did, however, have a catalog and a system of interlibrary loans that served monasteries across Germany, northern Italy, and France.

China was very much the equal of the Islamic world in its wealth of libraries. The Chinese had invented paper during the Western Han dynasty and printing during the Tang era. As a result, scholarship, book production, and libraries became vital to the region's cultural fabric. Accompanying the classical works printed for literati were works of popular literature and primers that circulated among a common audience.

The Chinese infatuation with the printed word bred an elite class of bibliophiles (book collectors). These individuals located source materials and created the reference works necessary to found coherent scholarly disciplines. Although Chinese libraries housed printed books, unpublished manuscripts formed a more substantial portion of many collections.

Under the Han, private libraries did not exceed 10,000 "rolls" (each holding about a chapter) of books or manuscripts. But under the Tang, many Buddhist monasteries accumulated thousands of books and religious sutras. Some 30,000 rolls, for example, survived in the precious Buddhist grottoes of Dunhuang along the Silk Road. The largest collection graced the imperial library in the capital. Here in this library scholars toiled as collators and editors to recompile the Confucian classics and dynastic histories for the civil service examination system—and for posterity. The Tang imperial catalog indicates that by the early eighth century this library contained some 54,000 unique titles and, including duplicates, about 200,000 rolls. Then as now, libraries were crucial repositories of knowledge and culture.

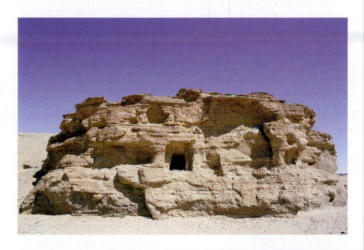

Dunhuang Cave Temple. Buddhist temples such as this one served as repositories for tens of thousands of manuscript rolls.

bic had superseded Greek as the Muslim world's preferred language for poetry, literature, medicine, science, and philosophy. Like Greek, it spread beyond native speakers to become the language of the educated classes.

Arabic scholarship now made significant contributions, including the preservation and extension of Greek and Roman thought and the transmission of Greek and Latin treatises to Europe. Scholars at Baghdad translated the principal works of Aristotle; essays by Plato's followers; works by Hippocrates, Ptolemy, and Archimedes; and the medical treatises of Galen. To house such manuscripts, patrons of the arts and sciences—including the caliphs—opened magnificent libraries. (See Global Connections & Disconnections:

Premodern Libraries: From Royal Archives to Repositories of Universal Knowledge.)

The intense borrowing, translating, storing, and diffusing of written works brought worlds together. The Muslim world absorbed scientific breakthroughs from China and other areas, incorporated the use of paper from China, adopted siege warfare from China and Byzantium, and applied knowledge of plants from the ancient Greeks. From Indian sources, scholars borrowed a numbering system based on the concept of zero and units of ten—what we today call Arabic numerals. Arab mathematicians were pioneers in arithmetic, geometry, and algebra, and they expanded the frontiers of plane and spherical trigonometry.

ISLAM IN A WIDER WORLD

As Islam spread and became decentralized, it generated dazzling and often competitive dynasties in Spain, North Africa, and points farther east. Each dynastic state revealed the Muslim talent for achieving high levels of artistry far from its heartland. As more peoples came under the roof provided by the Quran, they invigorated a broad world of Islamic learning and science. But growing diversity led to a problem: Islam's political structures could not hold its widely dispersed believers under a single regime. Although its polities shared many legal elements (especially those controlled by Islamic texts and its enforcers), in terms of secular power Islam was deeply divided—and remains so to this day (see Map 9-2).

DAZZLING CITIES IN SPAIN One extraordinary Muslim state arose in Spain under Abd al-Rahman III, al-

Nasir (the Victorious; r. 912–961 CE), the successor ruler of a Muslim kingdom founded there over a century earlier. Abd al-Rahman brought peace and stability to a violent frontier region where civil conflict had disrupted commerce and intellectual exchange. His evenhanded governance promoted amicable relations among Muslims, Christians, and Jews, and his diplomatic relations with Christian potentates as far away as France, Germany, and Scandinavia generated prosperity across western Europe and North Africa. He expanded and beautified the capital city of Cordoba, and his successor made the Great Mosque of Cordoba one of Spain's most stunning sites.

The Great Mosque of Cordoba, known in Spanish as la Mezquita, is the oldest standing Muslim building on the Iberian Peninsula. It is a stirring tribute to the architectural brilliance and religious zeal of Iberia's Muslims. Conceived of in 785 CE by the Umayyad ruler Abd al-Rahman I, it was

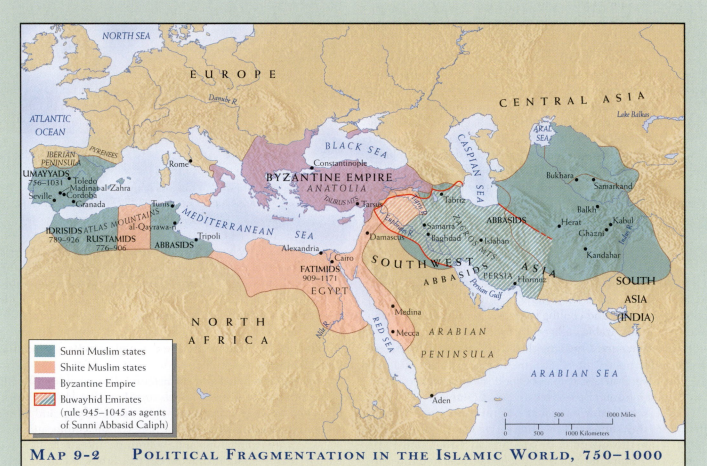

MAP 9-2   POLITICAL FRAGMENTATION IN THE ISLAMIC WORLD, 750–1000

By 1000, the Islamic world was politically fractured and decentralized. The Abbasid caliphs still reigned in Baghdad, but they wielded very limited political authority. Looking at the map, first point to Baghdad and then point out all the areas under Abbasid control. What are the regions where major Islamic powers emerged? What areas were Sunni versus Shiite? Why were the Abbasids unable to sustain political unity in the Islamic world?

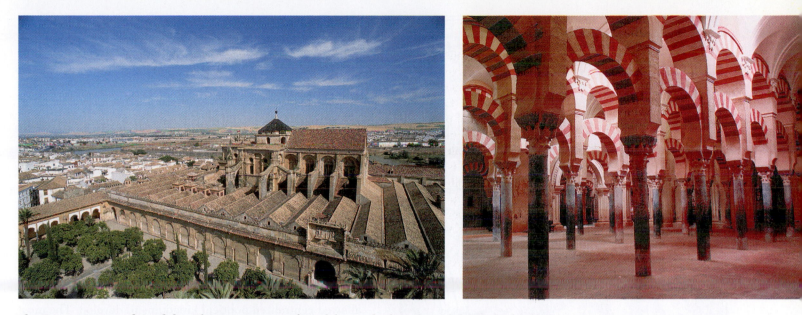

The Great Mosque of Cordoba. The great mosque of Cordoba was built in the eighth century by the Umayyad ruler Abd al-Rahman I and added to by other Muslim rulers, including al-Hakim II, who succeeded Abd al-Rahman III, considered by many historians to have been the most powerful and effective of the Spanish Umayyad caliphs.

finished within a year of the laying of the foundations. It arose on a site with a rich cultural and political history. Here had existed a Roman temple and later a Gothic church, which after the Arab Muslim conquest housed both Muslim and Christian believers (the latter permitted by the Muslim conquerors to worship under the same roof). Convinced that this building could no longer accommodate the area's increasing Muslim population, Abd al-Rahman I sketched out the plan of the mosque. He commanded that it be built in the form of a perfect square. Its most striking features were alternating red and white arches, made of jasper, onyx, marble, and granite and fashioned from materials from the Roman temple and other buildings in the vicinity. These huge double arches hoisted the ceiling to forty feet and filled the interior with light and cooling breezes. Around the doors and across the walls Arabic calligraphy proclaimed Muhammad's message and asserted the superiority of Arabic as God's chosen language.

At this time, competition among rival rulers spurred artistic creativity. Soon the Islamic world resembled a series of dazzling lanterns, each vying to outdo the others in brilliance. When Abd al-Rahman III built an extravagant city, Madinat al-Zahra, next to Cordoba, his goal was to overshadow the splendor of Islam's most fabled cities, including Baghdad and al-Qayrawān (in northeast Tunisia). He surrounded the city's administrative offices and mosque with verdant gardens of lush tropical and semitropical plants, tranquil pools, fountains that spouted cooling waters, and sturdy aqueducts that carried potable water to the city's inhabitants. Madinat al-Zahra was meant to be paradise on earth.

A CENTRAL ASIAN GALAXY OF TALENT The other end of the Islamic empire, 8,000 miles east of Spain, enjoyed an equally spectacular cultural flowering. In a territory where Greek culture had once sparkled and where Sogdians had become leading intellectuals, Islam was now the dominant faith and the source of intellectual ferment.

The Abbasid rulers in Baghdad delighted in surrounding themselves with learned men from this region. The Barmaki family, who for several generations held high administrative offices under the Abbasids, came from the central Asian city of Balkh. They had been Buddhists living under the serene gaze of the great carved Buddhas of Bamiyan (see Chapter 8). This family prospered under Islam and enjoyed remarkable influence in Baghdad. Loyal servants of the caliph, they made sure that all wealth and talent from the crossroads of Asia found their way to Baghdad, as they themselves had done.

In turn, the Barmakis were devoted patrons of the arts. They promoted and collected Arabic translations of Persian, Greek, and Sanskrit manuscripts, and they encouraged central Asian scholars to enhance their learning by moving to Baghdad. One of their protégés, the Islamic cleric al-Bukhari (d. 870 CE), was Islam's most dedicated collector of *hadith*, which provided vital knowledge about the Prophet's life.

Others made notable contributions to science and mathematics. Al-Khwarizmi (c. 780–850 CE) modified Indian digits into Arabic numerals and wrote the first book on algebra. The renowned Abbasid philosopher al-Farabi (d. 950 CE), from a Turkish military family, also made his way to Baghdad, where he studied Hellenistic Christian teachings. Although he considered himself a Muslim, he thought good societies

Ibn Sina. Ibn Sina was a versatile scholar, most famous for his *Canon of Medicine*.

Yet the region's intellectual vitality remained strong, for young men of learning found patrons among local rulers. Consider Ibn Sina, known in the west as Avicenna (980–1037 CE). He grew to adulthood in Bukhara, practiced medicine in the courts of various Islamic rulers, and spent his later life in central Persia. Schooled in the Quran, Arabic secular literature, philosophy, geometry, and Indian and Euclidean mathematics, Ibn Sina was a master of many disciplines. His *Canon of Medicine* stood as the standard medical text in both Southwest Asia and Europe for centuries.

ISLAM IN SUB-SAHARAN AFRICA   Islam also crossed the Sahara Desert and penetrated well into Africa, carried by traders and scholars (see Map 9-3). By the seventh and eighth centuries, Islamic adventurers were pouring into sub-Saharan West Africa, where they exchanged weapons and textiles for gold, salt, and slaves. Trade did more than join West Africa to North Africa. It also generated prodigious wealth, which allowed centralized political kingdoms to develop. The most celebrated was Ghana, which lay at the terminus of North Africa's major trading routes.

Of Ghana, scholars know little. The first to mention it was a Baghdadi scholar, who in the eighth century described it as "the land of gold." A century later, an Arab geographer wrote of "the kingdom of Ghana, the king of which is very powerful. In his country there are gold mines. Under his authority are other kingdoms . . . and gold is found in all of these regions" (Fage, p. 15). Although Muslim traders frequented the state, its rulers were not Muslims. Still, Ghana's pomp and power impressed visitors; in 1067–1068, a geographer from the Muslim province of Andalusia in Spain, wrote of a resplendent king who heard "grievances against officials in a domed pavilion around which stand ten horses covered with gold-embroidered materials. Behind the king stand ten pages holding shields and swords decorated with gold and on his right are the sons of the (vassal) kings of his country wearing splendid garments and their hair plaited with gold" (Levtzion and Spaulding, p. 16). (See also Primary Source: Ghana as Seen by a Muslim Observer in the Eleventh Century.)

Seafaring Muslim traders carried Islam into East Africa via the Indian Ocean. There is evidence of a small eighth-century Islamic trading community at Lamu, along the northern coast of present-day Kenya; and by the mid-ninth century other coastal trading communities had sprung up. They all exported ivory and, possibly, slaves. On the island of Pate, off the coast of Kenya, the inhabitants of Shanga constructed the region's first mosque. This simple structure was replaced 200 years later by a mosque capable of holding all adult members of the community when they gathered for their Friday prayers. By the tenth century, the East African coast featured a mixed African-Arab culture. The region's evolving Bantu language absorbed Arabic words and before long gained a new name, Swahili (derived from the Arabic plural of the word meaning "coast").

would succeed only if their rulers implemented political tenets espoused in Plato's *Republic*. He championed a virtuous "first chief" to rule over an Islamic commonwealth in the same way that Plato had favored a philosopher-king.

In the eleventh century the Abbasid caliphate began to decline, weakening under overextension and the influx of outsider groups (the same problems the Roman Empire had faced). Scholars no longer trekked to the court at Baghdad.

→ *What factors created a common cultural outlook among Muslim communities in Afro-Eurasia during this era?*

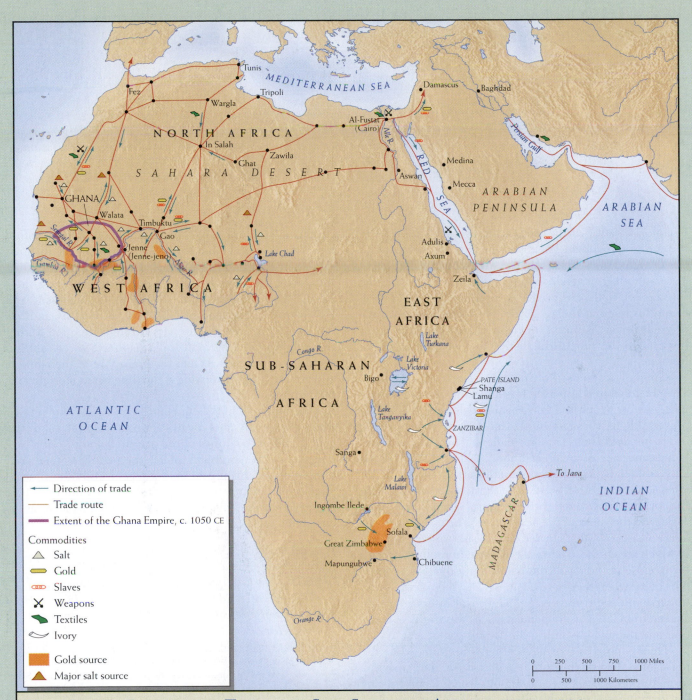

MAP 9-3   ISLAM AND TRADE IN SUB-SAHARAN AFRICA, 700–1000

Islamic merchants and scholars, not Islamic armies, carried Islam into sub-Saharan Africa. Trace the trade routes in Africa, being sure to follow the correct direction of trade. According to the map key and icons, what commodities were Islamic merchants seeking below the Sahara? What were the major trade routes and the direction of trade in Africa? How did trade and commerce lead to the geographic expansion of the Islamic faith?

Primary Source

GHANA AS SEEN BY A MUSLIM OBSERVER IN THE ELEVENTH CENTURY

The following excerpt is from an eleventh-century manuscript written by a Muslim serving under the Umayyads in Spain. Its author, Abdullah Abu Ubayd al-Bakri, produced a massive general geography and history of the known world, as did many Muslim scholars of the period. This manuscript has special value because it provides information about West Africa, a region in which the Spanish rulers had great interest and into which Islam had been spreading for several centuries.

Ghana is the title of the king of the people. The name of the country is Aoukar. The ruler who governs the people at the present time—the year 460 AH (after the Hijra and 1067–68 CE)—is called Tenkamein. He came to the throne in 455 AH. His predecessor, who was named Beci, began his reign at the age of 85. He was a prince worthy of great praise as much for his personal conduct as for his zeal in the pursuit of justice and his friendship to Muslims. . . .

Ghana is composed of two towns situated in a plain. The one inhabited by Muslims is large and contains twelve mosques, in which the congregants celebrate the Friday prayer. All of these mosques have their imams, their muezzins, and their salaried readers. The city possesses judges and men of great erudition. . . . The city where the king resides is six miles away and carries the name el-Ghaba, meaning "the forest." The territory separating these two locations is covered with dwellings, constructed out of rocks and the wood of the acacia tree. The dwelling of the king consists of a chateau and several surrounding huts, all of which are enclosed by a wall-like structure. In the ruler's town, close to the royal tribunal, is a mosque where Muslims come when they have business with the ruler in order to carry out their prayers. . . . The royal interpreters are chosen from the Muslim population, as was the state treasurer and the majority of the state ministers. . . .

The opening of a royal meeting is announced by the noise of a drum, which they call a *deba*, and which is formed from a long piece of dug-out wood. Upon hearing the drumming, the inhabitants assemble. When the king's coreligionists [people of the same religion] appear before him, they genuflect and throw dust on their heads. Such is the way in which they salute their sovereign. The Muslims show their respect for the king by clapping their hands. The religion of the Negroes is paganism and fetishism. . . . The land of Ghana is not healthy and has few people. Travelers who pass through the area during the height of the agricultural season are rarely able to avoid becoming sick. When the grains are at their fullest and are ready for harvesting is the time when mortality affects visitors.

The best gold in the land comes from Ghiarou, a town located eighteen days journey from the capital. All of the gold found in the mines of the empire belongs to the sovereign, but the sovereign allows the people to take gold dust. Without this precaution, the gold would become so abundant that it would lose much of its value. . . . It is claimed that the king owns a piece of gold as large as an enormous rock.

→ *From this excerpt, how much can you learn about the kingdom of Ghana? Try drawing a sketch of the region based on the description in the second paragraph.*
→ *What influence did Islam have in the empire? What aspects of the excerpt reveal the extent of Islam's acceptance?*
→ *What elements of Ghana most interested the author?*

SOURCE: Abou-Obeïd-el-Bekri, *Description de l'Afrique septentrionale*, revised and corrected edition, translated by [William] Mac Guckin de Slane (Paris: A. Maisonneuve, 1965), pp. 327–31; translated from the French by Robert Tignor.

Jenne Mosque. This fabulous mosque arose in the kingdom of Mali when that kingdom was at the height of its power. The mosque speaks to the depth and importance of Islam's roots in the Malian kingdom.

OPPOSITION WITHIN ISLAM, SHIISM, AND THE RISE OF THE FATIMIDS

Islam's whirlwind rise generated internal tensions from the start. It is hardly surprising that a religion that extolled territorial conquests and created a large empire in its first decades would also spawn dissident religious movements that challenged the existing imperial structures. Muslims shared a reverence for a basic text and a single God, but little else. Religious and political divisions grew deeper as Islam spread into new corners of Afro-Eurasia. Once the charismatic prophet died, believers disagreed over who should take his place and how to preserve authority. Strains associated with selecting the first four caliphs after Muhammad's death left a legacy of protest; to this day, they represent the greatest challenge facing Islam's efforts to create a unified culture.

SUNNIS AND SHIITES The most powerful opposition movement arose in North Africa, lower Iraq, and the Iranian plateau. The questions that fueled disagreements were who should succeed the Prophet, how the succession should take place, and who should lead Islam's expansion into the wider world. The vast majority of Muslims today are **Sunnis** (from the Arabic word meaning "tradition"). They accept the political succession to the Prophet through the four rightly guided caliphs and then to the Umayyad and Abbasid dynasties was the correct one. Dissidents, like the Shiites,

contest this version. Over time the Sunnis and Shiites diverged even more than these political disputes would have indicated. Both groups had their own versions of the *sharia*, their own collections of *hadith*, and their own theological tenets.

Shiites ("members of the party of Ali"), among the earliest dissidents, felt that the proper successors should have been Ali, who had married the Prophet's daughter Fatima, and his descendants. Ali was one of the early converts to Islam and one of the band of Meccans who had migrated with the Prophet to Medina. The fourth of the rightly guided caliphs, he ruled over the Muslim community from 656 to 661 CE, dying at the hands of an assassin who struck him down as he was praying in a mosque in Kufa, Iraq. Shiites believe that Ali's descendants, whom they call *imams,* have religious and prophetic power as well as political authority—and thus should enjoy spiritual primacy. Shiism appealed to groups whom the Umayyads and Abbasids had excluded from power; it became Islam's most potent dissident force and created a permanent divide within Islam. Shiism was well established in the first century of Islam's existence.

FATIMIDS After 300 years of struggling, the Shiites finally seized power. Repressed in Iraq and Iran, Shiite activists made their way to North Africa, where they joined with dissident Berber groups to topple several rulers. In 909 CE, a Shiite religious and military leader, Abu Abdallah, overthrew the Sunni ruler there. Thus began the Fatimid regime.

After conquering Egypt in 969 CE, the Fatimids set themselves against the Abbasid caliphs of Baghdad, refusing to acknowledge their legitimacy and claiming to speak for the whole Islamic world. The Fatimid rulers established their capital in a new city that arose alongside al-Fustat, the old Umayyad capital. They called this place al-Qahira (or Cairo), "the Victorious," and promoted its beauty. Early on they founded a place of worship and learning, the al-Azhar mosque, which attracted scholars from all over Afro-Eurasia and spread Islamic learning outward; they also built other elegant mosques and centers of learning. The Fatimid regime lasted until the late twelfth century, though its rulers made little headway in persuading the Egyptian population to embrace their Shiite beliefs. Most of the population remained Sunnis.

AGRICULTURE IN THE MUSLIM WORLD

At the time Islam was spreading, the Muslim world was also experiencing significant developments in agriculture; indeed, rural bounty gave the new belief system resources to plow into its expansion.

By now, India had replaced Mesopotamia as the source of a dazzling array of new crops. Most of them originated in Southeast Asia, made their way to India, and dispersed from there throughout the Muslim world. These crops included rice, taro, sour oranges, lemons, limes, and most likely coconut palm trees, sugarcane, bananas, plantains, and mangoes. Sorghum and possibly cotton and watermelons arrived from Africa. Only the eggplant was indigenous to India. Although these staple crops spread quickly to East Asia, their westward movement was slower. Not until the Muslim conquest of Sindh in northern India in 711 CE did territories to the west fully discover the crop innovations pioneered in Southeast Asia.

India fascinated the Arabs, and they exploited its agricultural offerings to the hilt. Soon a revolution in crops and diet swept through the Muslim world. Sorghum supplanted millet and the other grains of antiquity because it was hardier, had higher yields, and required a shorter growing season. Citrus trees added flavor to the diet and provided refreshing drinks during the summer heat. Increased cotton cultivation led to a greater demand for textiles.

For over three hundred years, farmers from northwest India to Spain, Morocco, and West Africa made impressive use of the new crops. They increased agricultural output, slashed fallow periods, and grew as many as three crops on lands that formerly yielded one. (See Map 9-4.) As a result, farmers could feed larger urban communities; as cities grew, the countryside became more densely populated and even more productive.

Al-Azhar Mosque. The mosque of al-Azhar is Cairo's most important ancient mosque. Built in the tenth century by the Fatimid conquerors and rulers of Egypt, it quickly became a leading center for worship and learning, frequented by Muslim clerics and admired in Europe.

→ *What factors created a common cultural outlook among Muslim communities in Afro-Eurasia during this era?*

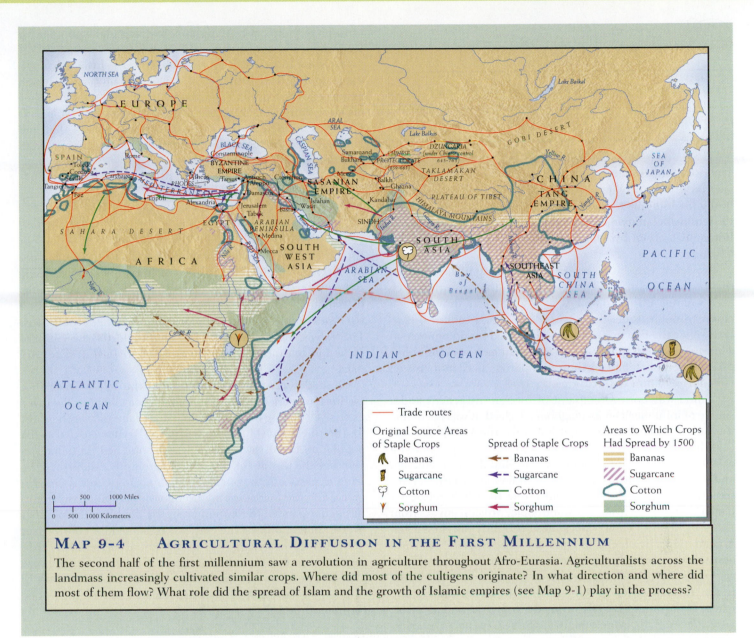

MAP 9-4   AGRICULTURAL DIFFUSION IN THE FIRST MILLENNIUM
The second half of the first millennium saw a revolution in agriculture throughout Afro-Eurasia. Agriculturalists across the landmass increasingly cultivated similar crops. Where did most of the cultigens originate? In what direction and where did most of them flow? What role did the spread of Islam and the growth of Islamic empires (see Map 9-1) play in the process?

By 1000 CE Islam, which had originated as a radical religious revolt in a small corner of the Arabian Peninsula, had grown into a vast political and religious empire. It had become the dominant political and cultural force in the middle regions of Afro-Eurasia. Like its rival in this part of the world, Christianity, it aspired to universality. But unlike Christianity, it was linked from its outset to political power. Muhammad and his early followers created an empire to facilitate the expansion of their faith while their Christian counterparts inherited an empire when Constantine embraced the new faith. A vision of a world under the jurisdiction of Muslim caliphs, adhering to the dictates of the *sharia*, drove Muslim armies, merchants, and scholars to territories thousands of miles away from Mecca and Medina. Yet the impulse to expand ran out of energy at the fringes of Islam's reach, creating political fragmentation within the Muslim world and leaving much of western Europe and China untouched. But it also had important internal consequences: Muslims were no longer the minority within their own lands, owing to the conversion of Christians, Jews, and other populations under Muslim emperors.

THE TANG STATE

> → *How did the Tang state balance its restoration of Confucian principles with the growth of new universal religions?*

The rise of the Sui and Tang empires in China, and their impact on Korea and Japan, paralleled Islam's explosion out of Arabia and its impact throughout Afro-Eurasia. Once again the landmass had two centers of power, as Islam replaced the Roman Empire in counterbalancing the power and wealth of China.

However, this bipolar world differed significantly from that of the Roman and Han empires: in the centuries since their waning, Eurasian and African worlds had drawn much closer through trade, conversion, and regular political contacts. Now the two powerhouses competed for dominance in central Asia, sharing influences and even mobile populations that weaved back and forth across porous borders between Islamic and Chinese territories.

China was both a recipient of foreign influences and a source of influences on its neighbors. Indeed, it was becoming the hub of East Asian integration. Like the Umayyads and the Abbasids, the **Tang dynasty** (608–907 CE) promoted a cosmopolitan culture. Under its rule Buddhism, medicine, and mathematics from India gave China's chief cities an international flavor. Buddhist monks from Bactria; Greeks, Armenians, and Jews from Constantinople; Muslim envoys from Samarkand and Persia; Vietnamese tributary missions from Annam; nomadic chieftains from the Siberian plains; officials and students from Korea; and monkish visitors from Japan all rubbed elbows in the streets of Chang'an and Luoyang. Ideas traveled east as well—notably to Korea and Japan, where Daoism and Buddhism made inroads. Similarly, Chinese statecraft, as expressed through the Confucian classics, struck the early Koreans and Japanese as the best model for their own state building.

AGRICULTURE IN CHINA

The agrarian transformation that swept through South Asia and the Muslim world also took East Asia by storm (see above). Indeed, China received the same crops that Islamic cultivators were carrying westward. Rice was critical. New varieties entered from the south, and groups migrating from the north (after the collapse of the Han Empire) eagerly took them up. Soon Chinese farmers became the world's most intensive wet-field rice cultivators. Early- and late-ripening seeds supported two or three plantings a year. Champa rice, introduced from central Vietnam, was especially popular for its drought resistance and rapid ripening.

Because rice needs ample water, Chinese hydraulic engineers went into the field to design water-lifting devices, which peasant farmers used to construct hillside rice paddies. They also dug more canals linking rivers and lakes (see Map 9-5) and even drained swamps, alleviating the malaria that had long troubled the region. Their efforts yielded a booming and constantly moving rice frontier.

TERRITORIAL EXPANSION UNDER THE TANG DYNASTY

After the fall of the Han, China had faced a long period of political instability (see Chapter 8). Ultimately, though, Tang rulers restored Han models of empire building. Their claims that an imperial system could outperform small states found a receptive audience in a populace fatigued by internal chaos. The Tang dynasty expanded the boundaries of the Chinese state and reestablished its dominance in East and central Asia.

A sudden change in the course of the Yellow River (not the first such environmental calamity; see Chapter 7) caused extensive flooding on the North China plain and set the stage for the emergence of the Tang dynasty. Revolts ensued as the population faced starvation. Li Yuan marched on Chang'an and took the throne for himself. He promptly established the Tang dynasty and began building a strong central government. First he increased the number of provinces and counties and expanded the bureaucracy. By doubling the number of government offices, the emperor tightened his control over individual governors. By 624 CE the initial steps of establishing the Tang dynasty were complete. But the fruits of these gains slipped into the hands of Li Yuan's ambitious son Li Shimin, who forced his father to abdicate and took the throne for himself in 627 CE.

THE ARMY AND IMPERIAL CAMPAIGNING

The Chinese empire created armies, and big armies reinforced the empire on a massive scale. An expanding Tang state required a large and professionally trained army, capable of defending far-flung frontiers and squelching rebellious populations. Toward these efforts the Tang built a military organization of aristocratic cavalry and peasant soldiers. The cavalry regularly clashed on the northern steppes with encroaching nomadic peoples, who also fought on horseback; at its height the Tang military had some 700,000 horses. At the same time, between 1 and 2 million peasant soldiers garrisoned the south and toiled on public works projects.

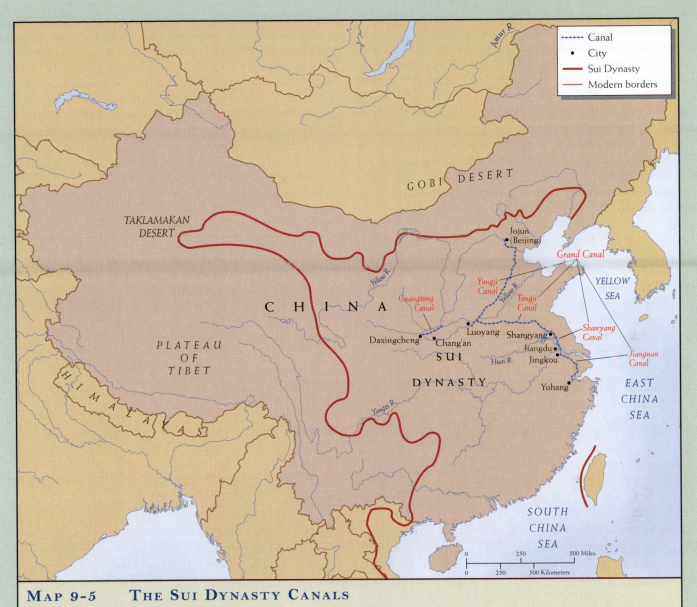

MAP 9-5   THE SUI DYNASTY CANALS

China, like the Islamic world, experienced a population explosion during this period. Where are the Sui dynasty canals on the map and the two areas showing population concentration? Why do you think the population concentrations are located along the canals? What other roles might the canals have played in addition to fostering population growth in this period within China?

Much like the Islamic forces, the Tang's frontier armies increasingly relied on pastoral nomadic soldiers from the Inner Eurasian steppe. Notable were the Uighurs, Turkish-speaking peoples who had moved into western China and by 750 CE constituted the empire's most potent military force. These hard-riding and hard-drinking warriors galvanized fearsome cavalries, fired longbows at distant range, and wielded steel swords and knives in hand-to-hand combat. The Tang military also pushed the state into Tibet, the Red River valley in northern Vietnam, Manchuria, and Bohai (near Korea).

By 650 CE, as Islamic armies were moving toward central Asia, the Tang were already the region's new colossus. At the empire's height, Tang armies controlled more than 4 million square miles of territory—an area as large as the entire

Islamic world in the ninth and tenth centuries. Once the Tang administrators brought South China's rich farmlands under cultivation (by draining swamps, building an intricate network of canals and channels, and connecting lakes and rivers to the rice lands), the state was able to collect taxes from roughly 10 million families, representing 57 million individuals. Most of these taxes took the form of agricultural labor, which propelled the expansion of cultivated frontiers throughout the south.

In spite of the Abbasid Empire's precocious spread, China in 750 CE was the most powerful, most advanced, and best administered empire in the world (see Map 9-6). Korea and Japan recognized its superiority in every material aspect of life. Mus-

lims were among the people who arrived at Chang'an to pay homage. Persians, Armenians, and Turks brought tribute and merchandise via the busy Silk Road or by sea, and other travelers and traders came from Southeast Asia, Korea, and Japan.

The peak of Chinese power occurred just as the Abbasids were expanding into Tang portions of central Asia. Rivalry brought these worlds together, but not peaceably. Muslim forces drove the Tang from Turkistan in 751 CE at the battle of Talas River, and their success emboldened groups such as the Sogdians and Tibetans to challenge the Tang in the west. As a result, the Tang retreated into the old heartlands along the Yellow and Yangzi rivers. They even saw their capital fall to invading Tibetans and Sogdians. Thereafter misrule, court

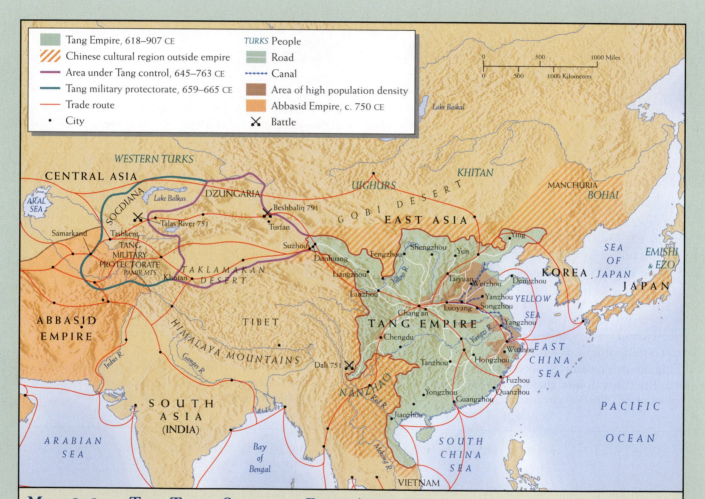

MAP 9-6   THE TANG STATE IN EAST ASIA, 750 CE

The Tang dynasty, at its territorial peak in 750, controlled a state that extended from central Asia to the East China Sea. What foreign areas are under Tang control? What areas were heavily influenced by Tang government and culture? How can we tell from the map that China was undergoing an economic revolution during the Tang period? How did the Tang maintain order and stability in such a large, dynamic realm?

China Trade. In this seventh-century silk painting, we see envoys from the busy Silk Road bearing tribute to gain access to the lucrative China trade.

intrigues, economic exploitation, and popular rebellions weakened the empire, but the dynasty held on for over a century more until northern invaders toppled it in 907 CE.

ORGANIZING AN EMPIRE

The Tang Empire, a worthy successor to the Han, ranks as one of China's great dynastic polities. Although its rulers emulated the Han in many ways (for example, by compiling a legal code based on the Han's), they also introduced new institutions.

CONFUCIAN ADMINISTRATORS Despite the Tang's reliance on military force, the day-to-day control of the empire required an efficient and loyal civil service. Whereas a shared spiritual commitment to Islam held together the multilingual, multiethnic, and even multireligious Islamic empire, the Tang found other ways to integrate remote territories and diverse groups. Their ingenious efforts produced an empire-wide political culture based on Confucian teachings composed in the written language of Mandarin-speaking officials and classically educated elites.

Chinese integration began at the top. Entry into the ruling group required knowledge of Confucian ideas and all of the commentaries on the Confucian classics. It also required skill in the intricate classical Chinese language, in which this literature was written. These skills were as crucial in forging a Chinese cultural and political solidarity as Islam was for the Abbasid state or Christianity was for Europe and the Byzantine Empire.

Most important in reinforcing the Tang state were the world's first fully written **civil service examinations.** These examinations, which tested sophisticated literary skills and the Confucian classics, were the only route to the top echelons of power and the ultimate means of uniting the Chinese state. Candidates for office, whom local elites recommended, gathered in the capital triennially to take qualifying exams. They had been trained since the age of three in the Classics and Histories, either by their families or in Buddhist temple schools. Most failed the grueling competition, however. Those who were successful underwent further trials to evaluate their character and determine the level of their appointments. New officials were selected from the pool of graduates on the basis of social conduct, eloquence, skill in calligraphy and mathematics, and legal knowledge. (See Primary Source: The Pressures of Maintaining Empire by Examination.) When Emperor Li Shimin observed the new officials obediently parading out of the

Tang Official. Tang officials were selected through competitive civil examinations in order to limit the power of Buddhist and Daoist clerics. This painted clay figure of a Tang official c. 717 was excavated in 1972.

THE PRESSURES OF MAINTAINING EMPIRE BY EXAMINATION

Young and old competed equally in the Tang examination halls. The rituals of success were alluring to youths, while the tortures of failure weighed heavily on older competitors still seeking an elusive degree. For all, the tensions of seeing the posted list of successful candidates—following years of preparation for young boys, and even more years of defeat for old men—were intensely personal responses to success or failure. The few who passed would look back on that day with relief and pride.

In the Southern Court they posted the list. (The Southern Court was where the Board of Rites ran the administration and accepted documents. All prescribed forms together with the stipulations for each [degree] category were usually publicized here.) The wall for hanging the list was by the eastern wall of the Southern Court. In a separate building a screen was erected which stood over ten feet tall, and it was surrounded with a fence. Before dawn they took the list from the Northern Court to the Southern Court where it was hung for display.

In the sixth year of Yuanhe [AD 811] a student at the University, Guo Dongli, broke through the thorn hedge. (The thorn hedge was below the fence. There was another outside the main gate of the Southern Court.) He then ripped up the ornamental list [*wenbang*]. It was because of this that afterwards they often came out of the gateway of the Department [of State Affairs] with a mock list. The real list was displayed a little later.

> → *Why were the stakes so high in the civil examinations? What happened to those who failed?*
> → *Was the Tang civil examination system an open system that tested talent—that is, a meritocracy?*
> → *Can you relate to the candidates' anxiety in terms of your own experiences—for example, waiting for college acceptance letters or your year-end grade point average?*

SOURCE: Wang Dingbao (870–940), quoted in Oliver J. Moore, *Rituals of Recruitment in Tang China* (Leiden: Brill, 2004), p. 175.

examination hall, he slyly noted, "The heroes of the empire are all in my pocket!" (Miyazaki, *China's Examination Hell*, 13). Overall, the civil service system gave rise in China to the perennial belief in the value of a classically trained **meritocracy** (rule by persons of talent), which lasted into modern times.

Having assumed the mandate of heaven (see Chapter 4), the Tang rulers and their supporters sought to establish a code of moral values for the whole empire. Building on Han models, they expanded the state school in the capital into an empire-wide series of select schools that accepted only fully literate candidates for the civil examinations. They also allowed the use of Daoist classics as texts for the exams, believing that the early Daoists represented an important stream of ancient wisdom. Ultimately the Tang amalgamated this range of texts, codes, and tests into a common intellectual and moral credo for the governing classes.

Although official careers were in theory open to anyone of proven talent, in practice they were closed to certain groups. Despite Empress Wu's prominence (see below), women were not permitted to serve, nor were sons of merchants, nor those who could not afford a classical education. Over time, Tang civil examinations forced aristocrats to compete with commoner southern families, whose growing wealth (from trade) and access to educational resources made them the equals of the old elites. Through examinations, this new elite eventually outdistanced the sons of the northern aristocracy in the Tang government by out-studying them.

The system also brought a few benefits to the poor by underscoring education as the primary avenue for success. Even impoverished families sought the best classical education they could afford for their sons. Although few succeeded in the civil examinations, many boys and even some girls learned the fundamentals of reading and writing. In fact, the Buddhists played a crucial role in extending education across society: as part of their charitable mission, their temple schools introduced many children to primers based on classical texts. Buddhist monks would never admit that many in their own ranks had initially hoped to become Confucian officials, but in reality quite a few entered the clergy only after not qualifying for or failing the civil examinations.

CHINA'S FEMALE EMPEROR Not all Tang power brokers were men. Women also wielded influence in the court—usually behind the scenes, but sometimes publicly. Consider Empress Wu, who dominated the court in the late seventh and early eighth centuries. She deftly exploited the examination system to check the power of aristocratic families and consolidated courtly authority by creating groups of loyal bureaucrats, who in turn preserved loyalty to the dynasty at the local level.

Born into a noble family, Wu Zhao played music and mastered the Chinese classics as a young girl. By age thirteen, because she was witty, intelligent, and beautiful, Wu was recruited to Li Shimin's court, where she became his favorite concubine. She also fell in love with his son. When Li Shimin died, his son assumed power and became the Emperor Gaozong. Wu became the new emperor's favorite concubine and gave birth to the sons he required to succeed him. As the mother of the future emperor, Wu enjoyed heightened political power. Subsequently, she took the place of Gaozong's Empress Wang by accusing her (falsely) of killing Wu's newborn daughter. Gaozong believed Wu and married her.

After Gaozong suffered a stroke, Wu became administrator of the court, a position equal to the emperor's. She created a secret police force to spy on her opposition, and she jailed or killed those who stood in her way, including Empress Wang. Upon the emperor's death Wu outmaneuvered her eldest sons, placed her youngest son in power, and named herself as his regent. Shortly thereafter she seized power in her own right as Empress Wu (r. 684–705 CE), becoming the only female ruler in Chinese history. She expanded the military and recruited her administrators from the civil examination candidates to oppose her enemies at court.

Challenging Confucian beliefs that subordinated women, Wu elevated their position. She ordered scholars to write biographies of famous women, and she empowered her mother's clan by assigning high political posts to her relatives. Later, she moved her court from Chang'an to Luoyang, where she tried to establish a new "Zhou dynasty" in imitation of the Confucian period.

Empress Wu. When she seized power in her own right as Empress Wu, Wu Zhao became the first and only female ruler in Chinese history.

Despite Wu's ruthless climb to power, her rule was relatively benign and competent. She elevated Buddhism over Daoism as the favored state religion, invited the most gifted Buddhist scholars to her capital at Luoyang, built Buddhist temples, and subsidized spectacular cave sculptures. In fact, Chinese Buddhism achieved its highest officially sponsored development in this period.

EUNUCHS Tang rulers protected themselves and their possessions, including their women, with loyal and well-compensated men. So did the Abbasids. The caliphs in Baghdad chose young male slaves as their personal guards, although males known as **eunuchs** (who were surgically castrated as youths and thus sexually impotent) also protected the harem. Similarly, Tang emperors relied on castrated males from the lower classes to protect the royal family. By the late eighth century, more than 4,500 eunuchs were fully entrenched in the Tang Empire's institutions, wielding significantly more court power than the male slaves in Baghdad.

The Chief Eunuch controlled the military. Through him, the military power of court eunuchs extended to every province and garrison station in the empire, forming an all-encompassing network. In effect, the eunuch bureaucracy mediated between the emperor and the provincial governments.

Under Emperor Xianzong (r. 806–820 CE), eunuchs acted as a third pillar of the government, working alongside the official bureaucracy and the imperial court. By establishing clear career patterns for eunuchs that paralleled those in the civil service, Xianzong sparked a striking rise in their levels of literacy and their cultural attainments. Yet by 838 CE, the delicate balance of power among throne, eunuchs, and civil officials had evaporated. Eunuchs became an unruly political force in late Tang politics, and their scheming plots equaled those of the slaves guarding the Abbasid caliph and his harem.

AN ECONOMIC REVOLUTION

In both the Abbasid caliphate and Tang China, political stability fueled remarkable economic achievements. Highlighting China's success were rising agricultural production based on an egalitarian land allotment system, an increasingly fine handicrafts industry, a diverse commodity market, and a dynamic urban life.

An earlier dynasty, the Sui, had started this economic progress by reunifying China and building canals, especially the Grand Canal linking the north and south (see again Map 9-5). The Tang continued by centering their efforts on the Grand Canal and the Yangzi River, which flows from west to east. These waterways aided communication and transport

The Tang Court. This tenth-century painting of elegant ladies of the Tang imperial court enjoying a feast and music (*left*) tells us a great deal about the aesthetic tastes of elite women in this era. It also shows the secluded "inner quarters," where court ladies passed their daily lives far from the hurly-burly of imperial politics. Castrated males, known as eunuchs (*right*), guarded the harem and protected the royal family of Tang emperors. By the late eighth century, eunuchs were fully integrated into the government and wielded a great deal of military and political power.

throughout the empire and helped raise living standards. The south grew richer, largely through the backbreaking labor of immigrants from the north. Fertile land along the Yangzi became China's new granary, and areas south of the Yangzi became its demographic center.

Chinese merchants took full advantage of the Silk Road to trade with India and the Islamic world; but when rebellions in northwest China and the rise of Islam in central Asia jeopardized the land route, the "silk road by sea" became the avenue of choice. From all over Asia and Africa, merchant ships arrived in South China ports bearing intoxicating cargoes of spices, medicines, and jewelry in exchange for Chinese silks and porcelain (see again Map 9-6). Chang'an became the richest city in the world, with its million or so residents including foreigners of every description.

In the large cities of the Yangzi delta—in some ways a nascent industrial heartland—workshops proliferated. Their reputations spread far and wide for the elegance of their wares, which included rich brocades (silk fabrics), fine paper, intricately printed woodblocks, unique iron casts, and exquisite porcelains. Art collectors especially valued Tang "tricolor pottery," fired up to 900 degrees Celsius in the Sui (1200–1300°C in Song) and decorated with brilliant hues of yellow, green, white, brown, and blue. Meanwhile, Chi-

nese artisans transformed locally grown cotton into highest-quality clothing. The textile industry prospered as painting and dyeing technology improved and superb silk products generated significant tax revenue. Such Chinese luxuries dominated the trading networks that reached Southwest Asia, Europe, and Africa via the Silk Road and the Indian Ocean.

ACCOMMODATING WORLD RELIGIONS

The early Tang emperors tolerated remarkable religious diversity, for the Confucian ideology at heart was secular. Although it posited a heaven from which the ruling dynasty claimed the authority to govern, it did not promise an afterlife or threaten nonbelievers with eternal damnation. Thus Nestorian Christianity, Zoroastrianism, and Manichaeanism (a radical Christian sect) had entered China from Persia during the time of the Sasanian Empire. Islam came later. These spiritual impulses—together with Buddhism and the indigenous teachings of Daoism and Confucianism—spread throughout the Tang Empire and at first did not conflict with state power.

THE GROWTH OF BUDDHISM Buddhism, in particular, thrived under Tang rule. In fact, many students from Korea and Japan journeyed to China in the Tang's early years to study it. Initially, Emperor Li Shimin distrusted Buddhist monks because they avoided serving the government and paying taxes. Yet after Buddhism gained acceptance as one of the "three ways" of learning—joining Daoism and Confucianism—Li endowed huge monasteries, sent emissaries to India to collect texts and relics, and commissioned Buddhist paintings and statuary. Caves along the Silk Road, such as those at Dunhuang, provided ideal venues for monks to paint the inside walls of caves where religious rites and meditation took place. Soon the caves boasted "bright" color paintings and massive statues of the Buddha and the bodhisattvas. Before long, giant carvings of the Buddha in northwestern temple sanctuaries dotted the trading routes to central Asia, and temples filled with ornate statuary offered religious refuge throughout South China.

ANTI-BUDDHIST CAMPAIGNS By the mid-ninth century, the Tang Empire contained nearly 50,000 monasteries and hundreds of thousands of Buddhist monks and nuns. (In contrast, Charlemagne's empire in France had only 700 major monasteries.) Such success by a foreign religion, in conjunction with the initial decline of the Tang dynasty, threatened China's Confucian and Daoist leaders. So they attacked Buddhism, arguing that its values conflicted with Confucian and Daoist traditions.

One of the first to attack was the scholar-official Han Yu, who represented the rising literati from the south. His Memorial of 819 protested the emperor's plan to bring a relic of the Buddha to the capital for exhibition. Striking a note that would have been inconceivable under the early Tang's cosmopolitanism, Han Yu attacked Buddhism as a foreign doctrine of barbarian peoples who were different in language, culture, and knowledge. These objections earned him exile to the southern province of Guangdong.

Yet, two decades later the state began suppressing Buddhist monasteries and confiscating their wealth, fearing that religious loyalties would undermine political ones. Increasingly intolerant Confucian scholar-administrators argued that the Buddhist monastic establishment threatened the imperial order. They accused Buddhists of undermining kinship values and traditional family relations. They claimed that members of the clergy were conspiring to destroy the state, the family, and the body.

Gradually the Tang government began challenging the power of monastic communities. Piecemeal measures against the monastic orders gave way in the 840s CE to open persecution. Emperor Wuzong, for instance, closed more than 4,600 monasteries and destroyed 40,000 temples and shrines. More than 260,000 Buddhist monks and nuns endured a forced return to secular life, after which the state parceled out monastery lands to taxpaying landlords and peasant farmers. To expunge the cultural impact of Buddhism, classically trained literati revived ancient prose styles and the teachings of Confucius and his followers. Linking classical scholarship, ancient literature, and Confucian morality, they constructed a cultural fortress that reversed the early Buddhist successes in China.

The persecution of Buddhism in this period raises two important points. First, in China, it was government (the Tang) that brought religion (the Buddhist monastic communities) under its control; in Latin Europe, in contrast, it was religion (the Christian church) that dominated government (the

One of the Four Sacred Mountains. This monastery on Mount Song is famous because in 527 an Indian priest, Bodhidharma, arrived there to initiate the Zen school of Buddhism in China.

feudal states). Second, because the Chinese bureaucracy was steeped in the traditions of Confucianism and Daoism, it had a power base that Buddhism lacked. China's most prominent universalizing religion was thus vulnerable once Emperor Wuzong began to persecute it.

Ultimately, the Tang era represented the triumph of homegrown ideologies (Confucianism and Daoism) over universalizing religion (Buddhism). The result was persistent religious pluralism within China.

THE FALL OF TANG CHINA

China's deteriorating economic conditions in the ninth century led to peasant uprisings, some led by unsuccessful examination candidates. These revolts eventually brought down the dynasty. In the tenth century, China fragmented into regional states and entered a new era of decentralization. Even the Song dynasty that emerged in 960 CE could not overcome the disunity. Only the Mongols, invading steppe peoples, were later able to restore the glory of the Han and Tang empires.

EARLY KOREA AND JAPAN

> → *To what extent did Japanese and Korean polities imitate Tang China?*

While China was opening up to the cultures of its western regions, its own culture was reaching out to the east—to Korea and, eventually, to Japan (see Map 9-7). Being colored by Buddhism, these influences were somewhat flexible and less distinctly Chinese, although Confucianism in Japan, Korea, and Vietnam was tailored to each country's scale and needs. To comprehend Korean and Japanese history of this era, we need to explore developments that predated the Koryo kingdom of Korea and the Japanese experience of the ninth and tenth centuries.

EARLY KOREA

Scholars have documented Chinese cultural influences in Korea as early as the third century BCE. By the fourth century CE, three independent states had emerged on the peninsula. This division into the "Three Kingdoms" of Korea lasted until 668 CE, when one of these states, Silla, gained control over the entire peninsula and unified it.

UNIFICATION UNDER THE SILLA Unification enabled the Koreans to establish a government modeled on the Tang imperial state. Now Silla dispatched annual embassies to the Chinese capital and regularly sent students and monks. As a result, literary Chinese became the written language of Korean elites—not their vernacular (as Latin did among diverse populations in medieval Europe). Koreans much later in the fifteenth century devised a phonetic system for writing their own language based on simplified Chinese characters, but most official writing continued in the literary Chinese form.

In spite of Chinese influences the loyalty of most non-Chinese Koreans was to their kinship groups. These early Koreans believed that birth, not displays of learned achievement, should be the source of influence in religious and political life. Korean holy men and women (known today as shamans), who interceded with gods, demons, and ancestral spirits, remained prominent in local village life. The culture stressed small-scale agriculture for harvesting grains, fishing along the coasts, and hunting in the vast northern forests.

Silla's fortunes became entwined with the Tang's to such an extent that once the Tang declined, Silla also began to fragment. Moreover, it had never established a full-blown Tang-style government.

THE KORYO DYNASTY In 936 CE, Wang Kon, a rebel leader, absorbed Silla into the northern-based Koryo kingdom, an act that tenuously reunified the country. The Koryo dynasty (from which the country's modern name derives) began to construct a new cultural identity by enacting a bureaucratic system, which replaced the archaic tribal system that the Silla had maintained. The Koryo went beyond earlier Silla reforms and fully established Tang-style civil service examinations to select officials who would govern at court and in the provinces. Wang Kon's heirs consolidated control over the peninsula and strengthened its political and economic foundations by following the Tang's bureaucratic and land allotment systems.

During this period Korea, like Tang China itself, suffered continual harassment from northern tribes such as the Khitan. This particular group exploited the fall of the Tang dynasty to control northern Chinese lands after 907 CE, establishing themselves in what is modern-day Manchuria. Reflecting the repercussions of this troubled period, Korean artisans anxiously carved wooden printing blocks for 81,258 scriptures from the Buddhist canon as an offering to the Buddha to protect them from invading enemies—but in vain. The Korean royal family at the time was under siege, and they hoped that the woodblocks would elicit a change in fortune. The scriptures were hidden away in a single temple, and when rediscovered they represented the most comprehensive and intact version of the Buddhist canon written in the Chinese script. After being overwhelmed by the Khitan in 1010, the Koryo dynasty revived, only to be invaded by the Mongols in 1231 (see Chapter 10). Nevertheless, the dynasty managed to last until 1392.

→ *To what extent did Japanese and Korean polities imitate Tang China?*

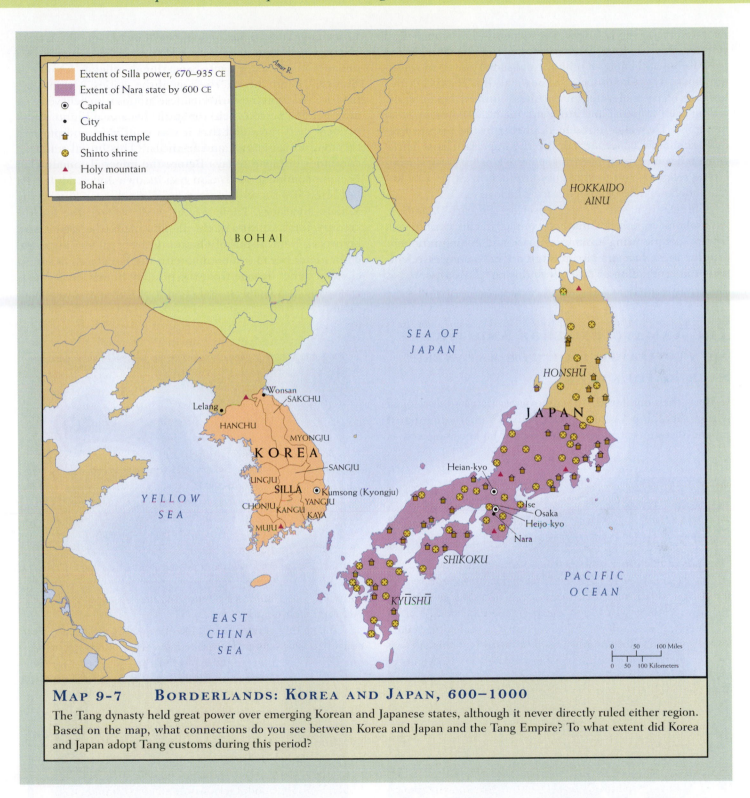

Extent of Silla power, 670–935 CE
Extent of Nara state by 600 CE
⊙ Capital
• City
Buddhist temple
⊛ Shinto shrine
▲ Holy mountain
Bohai

MAP 9-7 BORDERLANDS: KOREA AND JAPAN, 600–1000

The Tang dynasty held great power over emerging Korean and Japanese states, although it never directly ruled either region. Based on the map, what connections do you see between Korea and Japan and the Tang Empire? To what extent did Korea and Japan adopt Tang customs during this period?

EARLY JAPAN

Like Korea, Japan also felt influences emanating from China, and it responded by thwarting and accommodating them at the same time. But Japan enjoyed added autonomy: it was an archipelago of islands, more easily separated from the main-land although also internally more fragmented. Beginning in the Ice Age, tribal groups known as the Jomon (from 10,000 years ago to 400 BCE) and the Yayoi (400 BCE–250 CE) dom-inated prehistoric Japan. The early Jomon wandered into "Japan" when it was still part of the Asian mainland (see Chapter 1). Thereafter, several nomadic groups from Asia migrated to Japan via Korea. Subsequently, in the mid-third century, a warlike group also originating in Asia arrived by sea from Korea and imposed military and social power on southern Japan. These conquerors—known as the "Tomb Culture" because of their elevated burial sites—unified Japan by extolling their imperial ancestors and maintaining their social hierarchy. They also introduced a belief in the power of female shamans, who married into the imperial clans. These women became rulers of early Japanese kinship groups, combining religious and political power much like the early Korean holy men and women described above.

Chinese dynastic records describe the early Japanese, with whom imperial China had contact in this period, as a "dwarf" people who maintained a rice and fishing economy. The Japanese farmers also mastered Chinese-style sericulture: the production of raw silk by raising silkworms.

THE YAMATO EMPEROR AND THE SHINTO ORIGINS OF THE JAPANESE SACRED IDENTITY

In time, the complex aristocratic society that had developed within the Tomb Culture gave rise to a Yamato-dominated Japanese state that incorporated native Japanese as well as

Korean migrants. In becoming the ruling faction, the Yamato clan elevated themselves along with their belief system, based on ancestor worship, into a national religion known as **Shinto.** (Shinto means "the way of the deities.") Shinto beliefs derived from the early Japanese groups who believed that after death a person's soul (or spirit) became a Shinto *kami*, or local deity, provided that it was nourished and purified through proper rituals and festivals. (This burial tradition continues in Japan today.) Before the imperial Yamato clan became dominant, each clan had its own ancestral deities; but after 500 CE all Japanese increasingly worshipped the Yamato ancestors. Their origins went back to the fourth-century Tomb Culture of the Yamato plain (the region now known as Nara, south of Osaka). Other regional ancestral deities later became subordinate to the Yamato deities, who claimed direct lineage from the primary Shinto deity Amaterasu, the Sun Goddess and creator of the sacred islands of Japan.

Tomb Culture. Daisenryo Kofun, in Osaka, is allegedly the tomb of Emperor Nintoku, dating from the fifth century.

Creation Myth. Tsukioka Yoshitoshi (1839–1892) depicted Japan's creation myth in "Amaterasu Appearing from the Cave." To lure Amaterasu, the goddess of the sun, out so that light would return to the world, the other gods performed a ribald dance.

PRINCE SHOTOKU AND THE TAIKA POLITICAL RE-FORMS After 587 CE the Soga kinship group—originally from Korea but by 500 CE a minor branch of the Yamato imperial family—became Japan's leading family and controlled the Japanese court through intermarriage. Soon, they were attributing everything that was innovative in their culture to their own Prince Shotoku (574–622 CE), a direct descendant of the Soga and thus of the Yamato imperial family as well.

Contemporary Japanese scribes claimed that Prince Shotoku, rather than Korean immigrants, introduced Buddhism to Japan and that his illustrious reign sparked Japan's rise as an exceptional island kingdom. Shotoku promoted both Buddhism and Confucianism, thus enabling Japan, like its neighbor China, to be accommodating to numerous religions. Although earlier Korean immigrants had laid the groundwork for the growth of these views, Shotoku was credited with introducing these faiths into the native religious culture, Shinto. The prince also had ties with several Buddhist temples modeled on Tang pagodas and halls; one of these, in Nara (Japan's first imperial capital), is Horyuji Temple, the oldest surviving wooden structure in the world. Its frescoes include figures derived from the art of Iran and central Asia. They are a reminder that within two centuries Buddhism had dispersed its visual culture along the full length of the Silk Road—from Afghanistan to China, and then on to Korea and the island kingdom of Japan.

Political integration under Prince Shotoku did not mean political stability, however. In 645 CE, the Nakatomi kinship group seized the throne and eliminated the Soga and their allies. Via intermarriage with the imperial clan, the Nakatomi became the new spokesmen for the Yamato tradition. Thereafter Nakatomi no Kamatari (614–669 CE) enacted a series of reforms, known as the Taika Reform, which reflected Confucian principles of government allegedly enunciated by Shotoku. These reforms enhanced the power of the ruler, no longer portrayed simply as an ancestral kinship group leader but now depicted as an exalted "emperor" (*tenno*) who ruled by the mandate of heaven, as in China, and exercised absolute authority.

MAHAYANA BUDDHISM AND THE SANCTITY OF THE JAPANESE STATE Religious influences continued to flow into Japan, contributing to spiritual pluralism while bolstering the Yamato rulers. Although Prince Shotoku and later Japanese emperors turned to Confucian models for government, they also dabbled in occult arts and Daoist purification rituals. In addition, the Taika edicts promoted Buddhism as the state religion of Japan. Although the imperial family continued to support native Shinto traditions, association with Buddhism gave the Japanese state extra status by lending it the prestige of a universal religion whose appeal stretched to Korea, China, and India.

State-sponsored spiritual diversity led native Shinto cults to formalize a creed of their own. Indeed, the introduction of Confucianism and Buddhism motivated Shinto adherents to assemble their diverse religious practices into a well-organized belief system. Shinto priests now collected ancient liturgies, and Shinto rituals (such as purification rites to ward off demons and impurities) gained recognition in the official Department of Religion.

Prince Shotoku Taishi. Shotoku was instrumental in the establishment of Buddhism in Japan, although his actual historical role was overstated. In this hanging scroll painting from the early fourteenth century (*left*), he is idealized as a sixteen-year-old son, holding an incense censer and praying for the recovery of his sick father, the Emperor Yomei (r. 585–587 CE). The main hall of the Horyuji Temple in Nara, Japan (*right*).

Although the Japanese welcomed elements of the Buddhist faith, they did not fully accept the traditional Buddhist view that the state was merely a vehicle to propagate moral and social justice for the ruler and his subjects. Instead, the Japanese saw their emperor (the embodiment of the state) as an object of worship, a sacred ruler, one in a line of luminous Shinto gods, a supreme *kami*—a divine force in his own right. Thus, Buddhism as imported from China and Korea changed in Japan to serve the interests of the state (much as Christianity served the interests of European monarchs, and Islam served the Islamic dynasties).

THE CHRISTIAN WEST

> → *How did two Christianities come to exist in western Afro-Eurasia?*

Seen from the Mediterranean and the Islamic worlds, Europe by now seemed little more than a warrior-dominated realm. In the fifth century, the mighty Roman military machine gave way to a multitude of warrior leaders whose principal allegiances were local affiliations. Yet major innovations were under way. The leading force was Christianity, and its universalizing agents were missionaries and monks. The political ideal of the Roman Empire cast a vast shadow over the western Europeans, but the inheritor of the mantle of Rome was a spiritual institution—the Roman Catholic Church—whose powerful head, the pope, was based in Rome (see Map 9-8.)

CHARLEMAGNE'S FLEDGLING EMPIRE

In 802 CE, Harun al-Rashid, the ruler of Baghdad, sent the gift of an elephant to Charlemagne, the king of the Franks, in northern Europe. The elephant caused a sensation among the Franks, who saw the gift as an acknowledgment of Charlemagne's power. In fact, Harun often sent rare beasts to distant rulers as a gracious reminder of his own formidable power. In his eyes, Charlemagne's "empire" was a minor principality.

This was an empire that Charlemagne ruled for over forty years, often traveling 2,000 miles a year on campaigns of plunder and conquest. He ultimately controlled much of western Europe, which was a significant accomplishment; yet compared with the Islamic world's rulers, he was a political lightweight. His empire had a population of less than 15 million; he rarely commanded armies larger than 5,000; and he had a rudimentary tax system. At a time when the palace quarters of the caliph at Baghdad covered nearly 250 acres,

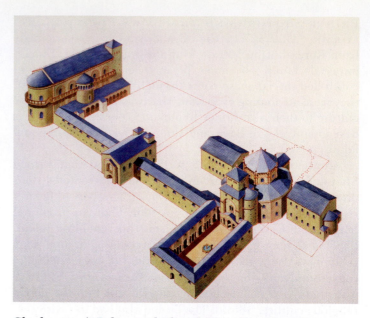

Charlemagne's Palace and Chapel. Though not large by Byzantine or Islamic standards, Charlemagne's palace and chapel were heavy with symbolic meaning. A royal hall for banqueting in Frankish, "barbarian" style was linked by a covered walkway to the imperial domed chapel, which was meant to look like a miniature version of the Hagia Sophia of Constantinople. Outside the chapel was a courtyard, like that outside the shrine of Saint Peter at Rome.

Charlemagne's palace at Aachen was merely 330 by 655 feet. Baghdad itself was almost 40 square miles in area, whereas there was no "town" outside the palace at Aachen. It was little more than a large country house set in open countryside, close to the Ardennes woods where Charlemagne and his Franks loved to hunt wild boar on horseback.

He and his men were representatives of the warrior class that dominated post-Roman western Europe. For a time, Roman rule had imposed an alien way of life in this rough world. After that empire faded, however, war became once again the duty and joy of the aristocrat. Buoyed up by their chieftains' mead—a heavy beer made with honey, "yellow, sweet and ensnaring"—young men eagerly followed their lords into battle "among the war horses and the blood-stained armor" (Aneirin, *Y Gododdin,* ll. 102, 840).

And although the Franks vigorously engaged in trade, that trade was based on war. In fact, Europe's principal export at this time was Europeans, and the massive sale of prisoners of war financed the Frankish empire. From Venice, which grew rich from its role as middleman, captives were sent as slaves across the sea to Alexandria, Tunis, and southern Spain. The main victims of this trade were Slavic-speaking peoples, tribal hunters and cultivators from eastern Europe. Their long oppression is preserved in the English language, for the medieval Latin *sclavus* ("Slavic") replaced the classical Latin *servus* to denote "slave"; *servus,* by contrast, applied to those

→ *How did two Christianities come to exist in western Afro-Eurasia?*

MAP 9-8   CHRISTENDOM, 600–1000 CE

The end of the first millennium saw much of Europe divided between two versions of Christianity, each with different traditions. Locate Rome and Constantinople on the map, the two seats of power in Christianity. According to the map, what were the two major regions where Christianity held sway? In what directions did Latin Christianity and Orthodox Christianity spread? Why do you suppose the Catholic Church based in Rome was successful in expanding to the west, but not to the east? Why do you suppose Orthodox Christianity based in Constantinople expanded into eastern Europe, but not into the west?

who stayed at home and became "serfs"—peasants tied for life to the estates of the aristocracy.

Yet this seemingly uncivilized and inhospitable zone offered fertile ground for Christianity to sink down roots. Although its worldwide expansion did not occur for centuries, its spiritual conquest of European peoples established institutions and fired enthusiasms that would later drive believers to carry its message to faraway lands.

A CHRISTIANITY FOR THE NORTH

Charlemagne's empire was unquestionably primitive when compared with the Islamic empire or the Tang Empire of China. What made it significant was its location. Far removed from the old centers of high culture, it was a polity of the borderlands. It also featured an expansionist Christianity that drew energy from its rough frontier mentality. Indeed, Christianity now entered a world profoundly different from the Mediterranean cities in which it had taken form.

AUGUSTINE AND THE UNIVERSAL CATHOLIC CHURCH Christians of the west felt that theirs was the one truly universal religion. (See Primary Source: Christendom on the Edge: A View of Empire in Ireland.) Their goal was to bring rival groups into a single "catholic" church that was replacing a political unity lost in western Europe when the Roman Empire fell.

As far back as 410 CE, reacting to the Goths' sack of Rome, the Christian bishop Augustine of Hippo (a seaport in modern Algeria) had laid down the outlines of this belief. His book *The City of God* assured contemporary Christians that the barbarian takeover happening around them was not the end of the world. The "city of God" would take earthly shape in the form of the Catholic Church, and the Catholic Church was not just for Romans—it was for all times and for all peoples, "in a wide world which has always been inhabited by many differing peoples, that have so many different customs and languages, so many different forms of organization and so many languages, and who have had so many different religions" (Augustine, *City of God,* 14.1). Only one organization would bring them all to paradise: the Catholic Church.

Several developments gave rise to this attitude. First, the arrival of Christianity in northern Europe had provoked a cultural revolution. Preliterate societies now encountered a sacred text—the Bible—in a language that seemed utterly strange. Latin had become a sacred language, and books themselves were vehicles of the holy. The bound codex (see Chapter 8), which had replaced the clumsy scroll, was still a messy object. It had no divisions between words, no punctuation, no paragraphs, no chapter headings. Readers who knew Latin as a spoken language could understand the script. But Irishmen, Saxons, and Franks could not, for they had never spoken Latin. Hence the care lavished in the newly Christian north on the Latin scriptures. The few parchment texts that circulated there were carefully prepared with words separated, sentences correctly punctuated and introduced by uppercase letters, and chapter headings provided. They were far more like this textbook than anything available to Romans at the height of the empire.

Second, those who produced the Bibles were starkly different from ordinary men and women. They were monks and nuns. **Monasticism** had originated in Egypt, but it suited the missionary tendencies of Christianity in northern Europe particularly well. (The root of "monastic" and "monk" is the Greek *monos,* "alone": a man or a woman who chose to live alone, without the support of marriage or family.) Monasticism placed small groups of men and women in the middle of societies with which they had nothing in common. It appealed to a deep sense that the very men and women who had little in common with "normal" people were best suited to mediate between believers and God. Laypersons (common believers, not clergy) gave gifts to the monasteries and offered them protection. In return, they gained the prayers of monks and nuns and the reassurance that although they themselves were warriors and men of blood, the monks' and nuns' intercessions would keep them from going to hell.

Celtic Bible. Unlike the simple codex of early Christian times, the Bible came to be presented in Ireland and elsewhere in the northern world as a magical book. Its pages were filled with mysterious, intricate patterns, which imitated on parchment the jewelry and treasure for which early medieval warlords yearned.

CHRISTENDOM ON THE EDGE: A VIEW OF EMPIRE IN IRELAND

A young Christian Briton of Roman citizenship who lived near Hadrian's Wall experienced the pull of Christianity around 400. Captured by Irish slave raiders as a teenager, Patricius spent six years herding pigs on the Atlantic coast of Mayo. He escaped but years later returned in order to convert his former captors to Christianity. He believed that in making the fierce Irish Christians, he also made them "Romans." He thus brought Christianity to the Atlantic edge of the known world. Patricius is remembered today as Saint Patrick.

16 But after I reached Ireland, well, I pastured the flocks every day. . . . I would even stay in the forests and on the mountain and would wake to pray before dawn in all weathers, snow, frost, rain. . . .

17 And it was in fact there that one night while asleep I heard a voice saying to me: 'You do well to fast, since you will soon be going to your home country;' and again, very shortly after, I heard this prophecy: 'See, your ship is ready.' And it was not near at hand but was perhaps two hundred miles away, and I had never been there and did not know a living soul there. And then I soon ran away and abandoned the man with whom I had been for six years . . . till I reached the ship.

23 And again a few years later I was in Britain with my kinsfolk. . . . And it was there that I saw one night in a vision a man coming as it were from Ireland . . . with countless letters, and he gave me one of them, and I read the heading of the letter, 'The Voice of the Irish,' and as I read these opening words aloud, I imagined at that very instant that I heard the voice of those who were beside the forest of Foclut which is near the western sea; and thus they cried, as though with one voice: 'We beg you, holy boy, to come and walk again among us.'

→ *What does this passage reveal about life in the Celtic worlds?*

→ *How many voices or visions does Patricius experience in this passage? What other religious figure have you read about in this chapter who had a vision or a revelation?*

→ *Based on your reading, how do St. Patrick's spiritual experiences compare to those of rulers and priests in the older Christian communities of Rome and Constantinople?*

SOURCE: *St. Patrick: His Writings and Muirchu's Life*, edited and translated by A. B. E. Hood (London: Phillimore, 1978), pp. 41, 44–46, 50.

MONKS, NUNS, AND POPES With the spread of monasticism, the Christianity of the north took a decisive turn. In Muslim (as in Jewish) societies, religious leaders emphasized what they had in common with those around them: many Islamic scholars, theologians, and mystics were married men just like the public, even merchants and courtiers. In the Christian West, the opposite was true: warrior societies honored small groups of men and women (the monks and nuns) who were utterly unlike themselves: unmarried, unfit for warfare, and intensely literate in an incomprehensible tongue. Even their hair looked different. Unlike warriors, these men were close-shaven; by contrast, the Orthodox clergy of the eastern Roman empire grew long, silvery beards (signifying wisdom and maturity; not, as in the west, the warrior's masculine strength). Catholic monks and priests shaved their heads as well.

The Catholic Church of northern Europe owed its missionary zeal to the same principles that explained the spread of Buddhism: it was a religion of monks, whose communities represented an otherworldly alternative to the warrior societies of the time. By 800 CE, most regions of northern Europe held great monasteries, many of which were far larger than the local villages. Supported by thousands of serfs donated by kings and local warlords, the monasteries became powerhouses of prayer that kept the regions safe.

Northern Christianity also gained new ties to an old center: the city of Rome. The Christian bishop of Rome had always enjoyed much prestige. But being only one bishop among many, he often took second place to his peers in Carthage, Alexandria, Antioch, and Constantinople. Though people spoke of him with respect as *papa* ("the grand old man"), many others shared that title.

Monasticism. The great monasteries of the age of Charlemagne, such as the St. Gallen Monastery (*left*), were like Roman legionary settlements. Placed on the frontiers of Germany, they were vast, stone buildings, around which entire towns would gather. Their libraries, the largest in Europe, were filled with parchment volumes, carefully written out and often lavishly decorated in a "northern," Celtic style. Monasticism was also about the lonely search for God at the very end of the world, which took place in these Irish monasteries (*right*) on the Atlantic coast. The cells, made of loose stones piled in round domes, are called "beehives."

By 800 CE, this picture had changed. As believers looked down from the distant north, they saw only one *papa* left in western Europe: Rome's pope. The papacy as we know it arose because of the fervor with which the Catholic Church of western Europe united behind one symbolic center, represented by the popes at Rome and the desire of new Christians in northern borderlands to find a religious leader for their hopes.

Charlemagne recognized this desire very well. In 800 CE, he went out of his way to celebrate Christmas Day by visiting the shrine of Saint Peter at Rome. There, Pope Leo III acclaimed him as the new "emperor" of the west. The ceremony ratified the aspirations of an age. A "modern" Rome—inhabited by popes, famous for shrines of the martyrs, and protected by a "modern" Christian monarch from the north—was what his subjects wanted.

THE AGE OF THE VIKINGS

Harun's elephant died in 813 CE, one year before Charlemagne himself. The elephant's death was noteworthy because the Franks viewed it as an omen of coming disasters. The great beast keeled over when his handlers marched him out to confront a Viking army from Denmark. In the next half-century, the Vikings from Scandinavia exposed the weakness of Charlemagne's self-confident regime. His empire of bor-

derland peoples met its match on the widest border of all: that between the European landmass and the mighty Atlantic (see Map 9-9).

The Vikings' motives were announced in their name, which derives from the Old Norse *vik*, "to be on the warpath." The **Vikings** sought to loot the now-wealthy Franks and replace them as the dominant warrior class of northern Europe. It was their turn to extract plunder and to sell droves of slaves across the water. They succeeded because of a deadly technological advantage: ships of unparalleled sophistication, developed by Scandinavian sailors in the Baltic Sea and the long fjords of Norway. Light and agile, with a shallow draft, they could penetrate far up the rivers of northern Europe and even be carried overland from one river system to another. Under sail, the same boats could tackle open water and cross the unexplored wastes of the North Atlantic.

In the ninth century, the Vikings set their ships on both courses. They emptied northern Europe of its treasure, sacking the great monasteries along the coasts of Ireland and Britain and overlooking the Rhine and the Seine—rivers that led into the heart of Charlemagne's empire. At the same time, Norwegian adventurers colonized the uninhabited island of Iceland, and then Greenland. By 982 CE, they had even reached the New World and established a settlement at L'Anse aux Meadows on the Labrador coast. Viking goods have been found as far west as the Inuit settlements of Baffin Island to

The Coronation of Charlemagne. This is how the coronation of Charlemagne at Rome in 800 CE was remembered in medieval western Europe. This painting stresses the fact that it was the pope who placed the crown on Charlemagne's head, thereby claiming him as a ruler set up by the Catholic Church for the Catholic Church. But in 800 contemporaries saw the pope as recognizing the fact that Charlemagne had already deserved to be emperor. The rise of the papacy to greater prominence and power in later medieval Europe caused this significant "re-remembering" of the event.

the north of Hudson Bay, carried there along trading routes by Native Americans.

The consequences of this spectacular reach across the ocean to America were short-lived, but the penetration of eastern Europe had lasting effects. Supremely well equipped to traverse long river systems, the Vikings sailed east along the Baltic and then turned south, edging up the rivers that crossed the watershed of central Russia. Here the Dnieper, the Don, and the Volga begin to flow south into the Black Sea and the Caspian. By opening this link between the Baltic and what is now Kiev in modern Ukraine, the Vikings created an avenue of commerce that linked Scandinavia and the Baltic directly to Constantinople and Baghdad. And they added yet more slaves: Muslim geographers bluntly called this route "The Highway of the Slaves."

THE SURVIVAL OF THE CHRISTIAN EMPIRE OF THE EAST

On reaching the Black Sea, the Vikings made straight for Constantinople. In 860 CE, more than 200 Viking long ships gathered ominously in the straits of the Bosporus, beneath the walls of Constantinople. What they found was not Charlemagne's rustic Aachen, but a proud city with a population exceeding 100,000 surrounded by well-engineered late Roman walls.

The Vikings had come up against a state hardened by battle. For two centuries the empire of "East Rome," centered on Constantinople, had held Islamic armies at bay. From 640 to 840 CE they faced almost yearly campaigns launched by the Islamic empire of Damascus and Baghdad, powerhouses that grew to be ten times greater than their own. For years on end, Muslim armies and navies came within striking distance of Constantinople. Each time they failed, outmaneuvered by highly professional generals and blocked by a skillfully

Oseberg Ship. The Viking ship was a triumph of design. It could be rowed up the great rivers of Europe, and, at the same time, its sail could take it across the Atlantic.

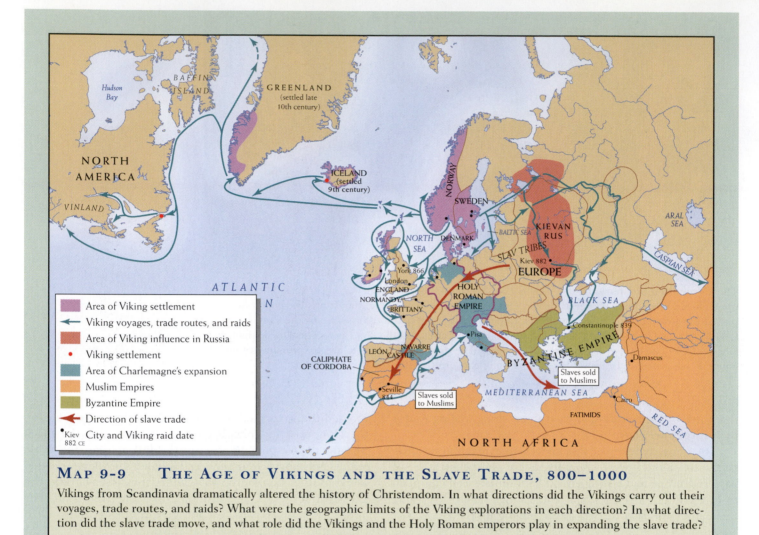

MAP 9-9   THE AGE OF VIKINGS AND THE SLAVE TRADE, 800–1000

Vikings from Scandinavia dramatically altered the history of Christendom. In what directions did the Vikings carry out their voyages, trade routes, and raids? What were the geographic limits of the Viking explorations in each direction? In what direction did the slave trade move, and what role did the Vikings and the Holy Roman emperors play in expanding the slave trade?

constructed line of fortresses that controlled the roads across Anatolia. The Christian empire of East Rome fought the caliphs of Baghdad to a draw. The Viking fleet was even less well suited to assault Constantinople, as the empire of "East Rome" had a deadly technological advantage in naval warfare: Greek fire, a combination of petroleum and potassium that, when sprayed from siphons, would explode in a great sheet of flame on the water. A previous emperor had used it to destroy the Muslim fleet as it lay at anchor within sight of Constantinople. Now, a century and a half later, the experience and weaponry of East Rome were too much for the Vikings, and their raid was a spectacular failure.

GREEK ORTHODOX CHRISTIANITY In the long run, the sense of having outlasted so many military emergencies bolstered the morale of East Roman Christianity and led to its unexpected flowering. Not just Constantinople but Justinian's glorious church, the Hagia Sophia—its heart—had survived. That great building and the solemn Greek liturgy that reverberated within its domed spaces might not impress Catholic Franks, but upon seeing it the Scandinavian adventurers were awestruck. Here was the central church of a Christian empire that for half a millennium had represented all that was most venerable in the Christian tradition. In the tenth century, as Charlemagne's empire collapsed in western Europe, large areas of eastern Europe became Greek Orthodox, not Catholic. As a result, Greek Christianity gained a spiritual empire in Southwest Asia.

The conversion of Russian peoples and Balkan Slavs to Greek Orthodox Christianity was a complex process. It reflected a deep admiration for Constantinople on the part of Russians, Bulgarians, and other Slav princes. It was an admiration as intense as that of any Western Catholic for the Roman popes. This admiration amounted to awe, as shown by the famous story of the conversion to Greek Christianity of the rulers of Kiev (descendants of Vikings):

> The envoys reported[,] . . . "We went among the Germans [the Catholic Franks] and we saw them performing many ceremonies in their churches; but we beheld no glory there. Then we went to Greece [in fact, to Constantinople and Hagia Sophia], and the Greeks led us to the edifices where they worship their God, and we knew not whether we were in heaven or on earth. For on earth there is no such splendor or such beauty, and we are at a loss to describe it. . . . [W]e can not forget that beauty. (Cross and Sherbowitz-Westor, *The Russian Primary Chronicle*, 111)

By the year 1000, there were two Christianities: the new and confident "borderland" **Roman Catholicism** of western Europe, and an ancient **Greek Orthodoxy,** protected against extinction by the iron framework of a "Roman" state inherited from Constantine and Justinian. Together both strands of the faith constituted the realm of **Christendom:** the entire portion of the world in which Christianity prevailed. Western Catholics believed that their church was destined to expand everywhere. East Romans were less euphoric but more tenacious. They believed that their church would forever survive the regular ravages of invasion. It was a significant difference in attitude and neither side liked the other. East Romans considered the Franks barbarous and grasping; Western Catholics contemptuously called the East Romans "Greeks" and condemned them for their "Byzantine" cunning.

Thus, like Islam, the Christian world was divided. But its differences were not about the basic tenets of the faith, like those of Shiite and Sunni Islam. They were differences in heritage, customs, and levels of civilization. At that time, the orthodox world was considerably more ancient and more cultured than the world of the Catholic west. And it dealt with Islam differently. At Constantinople, eastern Christianity held off Muslim forces that constantly threatened the integrity of the great city and its Christian hinterlands. In the west, by contrast, Muslim expansionism reached all the way to the Iberian Peninsula. Western Christendom, led by the Roman papacy, did not feel the same intimidation from Islam. It set about spreading Christianity to pagan tribes in the north, and it began to contemplate retaking lands from the Muslims.

The period 600–1000 CE saw heightened movement across cultural boundaries as well as an insistence on the distinctiveness of individual societies. Commodities, technological innovations, ideas, merchants, adventurers, and scholars traveled from one end of Afro-Eurasia to the other, and up and down coastal Africa. Spreading religion into new frontiers accompanied this mercantile activity. The proximity of the period's two powerhouses—Abbasid Islam and Tang China—facilitated the dynamic movement.

Jelling Stone. Carved on the side of this great stone, Christ appears to be almost swallowed up in an intricate pattern of lines. For the Vikings, complicated interweaving like serpents or twisted gold jewelry was a sign of majesty: hence, in this, the first Christian monument in Denmark, Christ is part of an ancient pattern of carving, which brought good luck and victory to the king.

CONCLUSION

Despite the intermixing, new political and cultural boundaries were developing that would split this landmass in ways it could never have imagined. The most important dividing force was Islam, which challenged and slowed the spread of Christianity. As a consequence, Afro-Eurasia's major cultural zones began to compete in terms of religious and cultural doctrines. The Islamic Abbasid Empire pushed back the borders of the Tang Empire. But the conflict grew particularly intense between the Islamic and Christian worlds, where the clash involved faith as well as frontiers.

The Tang Empire revived Confucianism, insisting on its political and moral primacy as the foundation of a new imperial order, and it embraced the classical written language as another unifying element. By doing so the Tang counteracted universalizing foreign religions—notably Buddhism but also Islam—spreading into the Chinese state. The same adaptive strategies influenced new systems on the Korean peninsula and in Japan.

In some circumstances, faith followed empire and relied on rulers' support or tolerance to spread the word. This was the case especially in East Asia. At the opposite extreme, empire followed faith—as in the case of Islam, whose believers endeavored to spread their empire in every conceivable direction. The Islamic empire and its successors represented a new force: expanding political power backed by one God whose instructions were to spread his message. In the worlds of Christianity, a common faith absorbed elements of a common culture (shared books, a language for learned classes). But in the west, political rulers never overcame inhabitants' intense allegiance to local authority.

While universalizing religions expanded and common cultures grew, debate raged within each religion over foundational principles. In spite of the diffusion of basic texts in "official" languages, variations of Christianity, Islam, and Buddhism proliferated as each belief system spread. The period demonstrated that religion, reinforced by prosperity and imperial resources, could bring peoples together in unprecedented ways. But it could also, as the next chapter will illustrate, drive them apart in bloodcurdling confrontations.

Review and research materials are available at StudySpace: ⊚ WWNORTON.COM/STUDYSPACE

KEY TERMS

caliphate (p. 327)

Christendom (p. 359)

civil service examinations (p. 343)

eunuchs (p. 345)

Greek Orthodoxy (p. 359)

Islam (p. 325)

jihad (p. 326)

meritocracy (p. 344)

monasticism (p. 354)

Muhammad (p. 324)

Quran (p. 324)

Roman Catholicism (p. 359)

sharia (p. 327)

Shiites (p. 337)

Shinto (p. 350)

Sunnis (p. 337)

Tang dynasty (p. 340)

ulama (p. 327)

Vikings (p. 356)

Chronology

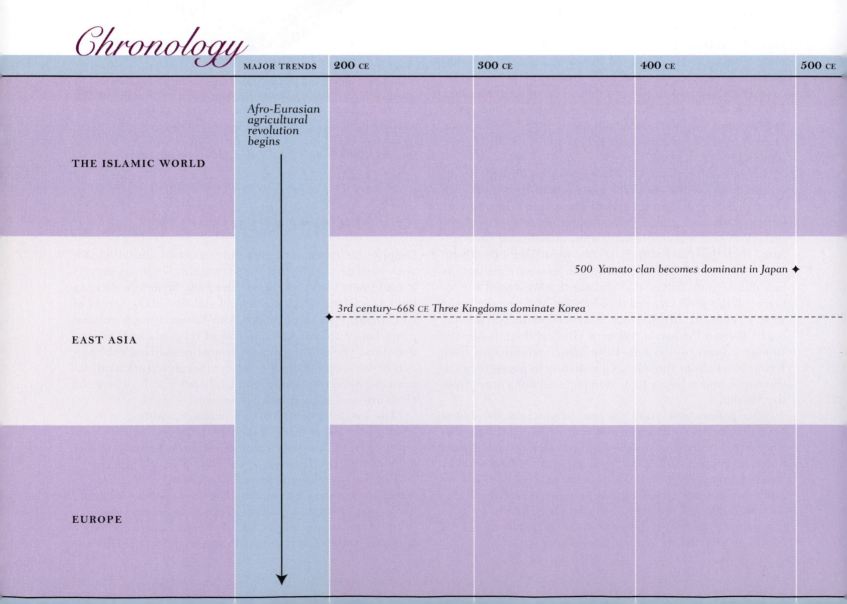

	MAJOR TRENDS	200 CE	300 CE	400 CE	500 CE
THE ISLAMIC WORLD	Afro-Eurasian agricultural revolution begins				
EAST ASIA			3rd century–668 CE *Three Kingdoms dominate Korea*		500 *Yamato clan becomes dominant in Japan* ◆
EUROPE					

STUDY QUESTIONS

1. Analyze the impact of the spread of Islam on Afro-Asian societies. How did the large Islamic empire shape the movement of peoples, ideas, innovations, and commodities across the vast landmass?

2. Describe the process through which an expanding Islam fostered an agricultural revolution. What crops and cultivation techniques were involved?

3. Compare and contrast the spread of Islam, Christianity, and Buddhism between 600 and 1000. What was the geographic range of each religious community? Through which methods did each religion gain new converts?

4. Explain the origins and basic concepts of Islam. How similar to and different from other religions that began in Southwest Asia—such as Judaism, Christianity, and Zoroastrianism—was this new religious outlook?

5. Analyze the successes and failures of Islamic leaders in creating one large empire to govern Islamic communities. What opponents challenged this goal?

6. Describe the Tang dynasty's attempts to restore political unity to East Asia. How did Tang leaders react to the growth of universal religions within their realm?

7. Describe the state structure that emerged in Korea and Japan during this era. How did other developments in Afro-Eurasia, such as the spread of universal religions, shape these new states?

8. Compare and contrast Christian communities in western Europe to those in eastern Europe and the Byzantine Empire. What factors contributed to each region's distinctiveness?

9. Analyze the Vikings' impact on world history during this era. How did they shape developments in the Christian world especially?

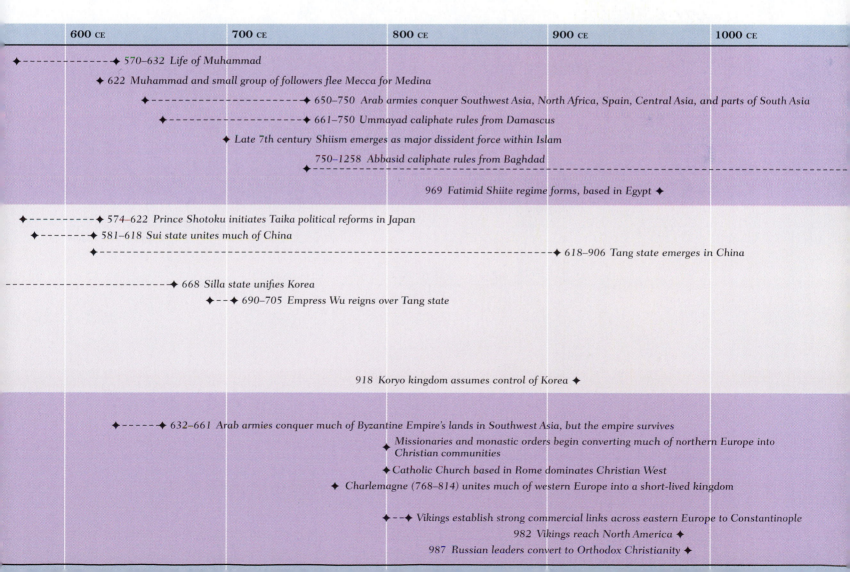

	600 CE	700 CE	800 CE	900 CE	1000 CE

570–632 Life of Muhammad

622 Muhammad and small group of followers flee Mecca for Medina

650–750 Arab armies conquer Southwest Asia, North Africa, Spain, Central Asia, and parts of South Asia

661–750 Ummayad caliphate rules from Damascus

Late 7th century Shiism emerges as major dissident force within Islam

750–1258 Abbasid caliphate rules from Baghdad

969 Fatimid Shiite regime forms, based in Egypt

574–622 Prince Shotoku initiates Taika political reforms in Japan

581–618 Sui state unites much of China

618–906 Tang state emerges in China

668 Silla state unifies Korea

690–705 Empress Wu reigns over Tang state

918 Koryo kingdom assumes control of Korea

632–661 Arab armies conquer much of Byzantine Empire's lands in Southwest Asia, but the empire survives

Missionaries and monastic orders begin converting much of northern Europe into Christian communities

Catholic Church based in Rome dominates Christian West

Charlemagne (768–814) unites much of western Europe into a short-lived kingdom

Vikings establish strong commercial links across eastern Europe to Constantinople

982 Vikings reach North America

987 Russian leaders convert to Orthodox Christianity

10

BECOMING "THE WORLD," 1000–1300 CE

I n the late 1270s two Christian monks, Bar Sāwmā and Markōs, voyaged into the heart of Islam. They were not Europeans. They were Uighurs, a Turkish people of central Asia, many of whom had converted to Christianity centuries earlier. Sent by the mighty Mongol ruler Kubilai Khan as he prepared to become the first emperor of China's Yuan dynasty, the monks were supposed to worship at the temple in Jerusalem. But the Great Khan also had political ambitions. He was eager to conquer Jerusalem, held by the Muslims. Accordingly, he dispatched the monks as agents to make alliances with Christian kings in the area and to gather intelligence about his potential enemy in Palestine.

By 1280, conflict and conquest had transformed many parts of the world. But friction was simply one manifestation of cultures brushing up against one another. More important was trade. Indeed, Bar Sāwmā and Markōs lingered at the magnificent trading hub of Kashgar in far western China, where caravan routes converged in a market for jade, exotic spices, and precious silks. Later, at Baghdad, the monks parted ways. Bar Sāwmā visited

Constantinople (where the king gave him gold and silver), Rome (where he met with the pope at the shrine of Saint Peter), and Paris (where he saw that city's vibrant university) before deciding to return to China, where the Christians of the east awaited his reports. In the end, neither monk ever returned. Yet their voyages exemplified the crisscrossing of people, money, and goods along the trade routes and sea-lanes that connected the world's regions. For just as religious conflict was a hallmark of this age, so was a surge in trade, migration, and global exchange.

The period brought to a climax many centuries of human development, and it ushered in a new, very long cycle of cultural interaction from which emerge three interrelated themes. First, trade was shifting from land-based routes to sea-based routes. Coastal trading cities began to dramatically expand. Second, intensified trade and linguistic and religious integration generated the world's four major cultural "spheres," whose inhabitants were linked by shared institutions and beliefs: China, India, Islam, and Europe. Not all cultures turned into "spheres," though. In the Americas and sub-Saharan Africa there was not the same impulse to integrate regions, which remained more fragmented but thrived nonetheless. Third, the rise of the Mongol Empire represented the peak in the long history of ties and tensions between settled and mobile peoples. From China to Persia and as far as eastern Europe, the Mongols ruled over much land in the world's major cultural spheres.

COMMERCIAL CONNECTIONS

> → *What factors led to the explosion of global trading between 1000 and 1300?*

REVOLUTIONS AT SEA

By the tenth century, sea routes were eclipsing land networks for long-distance trade. Improved navigational aids, refinements in shipbuilding, better mapmaking, and new legal arrangements and accounting practices made shipping easier and slashed the costs of seaborne trade. The numbers testify to the power of the maritime revolution: while a porter could carry about 10 pounds over long distances, and animal-drawn wagons could move 100 pounds of goods, the Arab dhows plying the Indian Ocean were capable of transporting up to 5 tons of cargo. (**Dhows** are ships with triangle-shaped sails, called lateens, that maximize the monsoon trade winds on the Arabian Sea and the Indian Ocean.) As a result some coastal ports, like Mogadishu in eastern Africa, became vast transshipment centers for a thriving trade across the Indian Ocean.

A new navigational instrument spurred this boom: the needle compass. This Chinese invention initially identified prom-

Focus Questions

Ⓢ WWNORTON.COM/STUDYSPACE

→ *What factors led to the explosion of global trading between 1000 and 1300?*

→ *How did trade and migration affect sub-Saharan Africa between 1000 and 1300?*

→ *How did trade, conversion, and migration affect the Islamic world between 1000 and 1300?*

→ *In what ways did India remain a cultural mosaic?*

→ *What transformations in communication, education, and commerce promoted a distinct Chinese identity during this era?*

→ *How were Southeast Asia, Japan, and Korea influenced by sustained contact with other regions?*

→ *How did Christianity produce a distinct identity among the diverse peoples of Europe?*

→ *Where did societies in the Americas demonstrate strong commercial expansionist impulses?*

→ *How did Mongol conquests affect cross-cultural contacts and regional development in Afro-Eurasia?*

ising locations for houses and tombs, but eleventh-century sailors from Canton used it to find their way on the high seas. The device spread rapidly. Not only did it allow sailing under cloudy skies, but it also improved mapmaking. And it made all the oceans, including the Atlantic, easier to navigate.

Now shipping became less dangerous. Navigators relied on lateen-rigged dhows between the Indian Ocean and the Red Sea, heavy junks in the South China seas, and Atlantic "cogs," which linked Genoa to locations as distant as the Azores and Iceland. They also enjoyed the protection of political authorities, such as the Song dynasts in China, in guiding the trading fleets in and out of harbors. The Fatimid caliphate in Egypt, for instance, profited from maritime trade and defended merchant fleets from pirates. Armed convoys of ships escorted commercial fleets in a system called *karim* (a loose confederation of shippers banding together to protect convoys) that regularized the ocean traffic. The system soon spread to North Africa and southern Spain. Most *karimi* firms were family-based, and they sent young men of the family, sometimes servants or slaves, to work in India. Housewives in Cairo could expect gifts from their husbands to arrive with the *karimi* fleet.

Changes in navigation ushered in the demise of overland routes. Silk Road merchants eventually gave up using camel trains, caravansaries (inns for travelers), and oasis hubs as they switched to the sea-lanes. The shift took centuries, but overland routes and camels were no match for multiple-masted cargo ships.

Dhow. This modern dhow in the harbor of Zanzibar displays the characteristic triangle sail. The triangle sail can make good use of the trade monsoon and thus has guided dhows on the Arabian Sea since ancient times.

COMMERCIAL CONTACTS

The opening of the sea-lanes also tapped into changes occurring in world agriculture (see Map 10-1). By 1000 CE, major innovations in irrigation techniques, carried out over many centuries and in numerous locations, had yielded enormous returns. New strains of cereals—and in the Americas, the refinement of maize—led to grain cultivation in vast areas that had been too cold and arid to sustain them previously. Clover, alfalfa, and other newly domesticated grasses became fodder for healthier, stronger, and fatter animals. Agriculture pushed into new regions, buoying population growth and surpluses that now could be shipped over great distances.

GLOBAL COMMERCIAL HUBS

Long-distance trade spawned the growth of commercial cities. These entrepôts became cosmopolitan nerve centers of an increasingly integrated world. (**Entrepôts** are transshipment centers, located between borders or in ports, where traders exchange commodities and replenish supplies.) Beginning in the late tenth century, four places became major anchorages of the maritime trade: in the west, the Egyptian port cities of Alexandria and Cairo; in the east, the Chinese city of Quanzhou; in the Malaysian Archipelago, the city of Melaka; and near the tip of the Indian peninsula, the port of Quilon. These hubs thrived under the political stability of powerful dynasts who recognized that the free-for-all of trade and market life would generate wealth for their regimes. Yemeni rulers, for instance, offered shelter to *karimi* fleets in return for taxes collected on cargoes; so did Egyptian governments for fleets moving through the Red Sea.

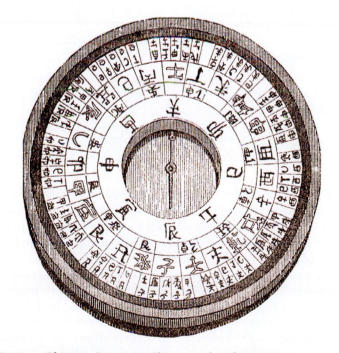

Antique Chinese Compass. Chinese sailors from Canton started to use needle compasses in the eleventh century. By the thirteenth century, needle compasses were widely used on ships in the Indian Ocean and were starting to appear in the Mediterranean.

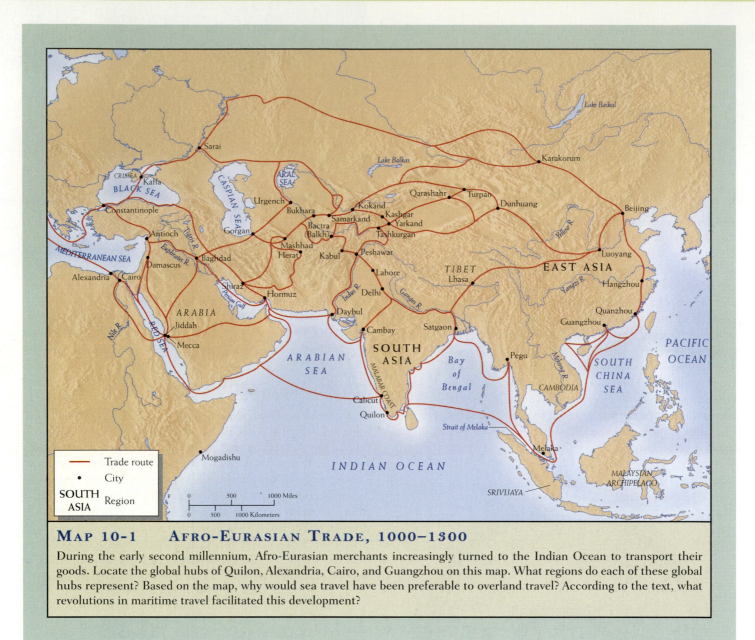

MAP 10-1 AFRO-EURASIAN TRADE, 1000–1300

During the early second millennium, Afro-Eurasian merchants increasingly turned to the Indian Ocean to transport their goods. Locate the global hubs of Quilon, Alexandria, Cairo, and Guangzhou on this map. What regions do each of these global hubs represent? Based on the map, why would sea travel have been preferable to overland travel? According to the text, what revolutions in maritime travel facilitated this development?

THE EGYPTIAN ANCHORAGE Cairo and Alexandria were the Mediterranean's main maritime commercial centers. Cairo was home to numerous Muslim and Jewish trading firms, and Alexandria was their lookout post on the Mediterranean.

Silk yarn and textiles were the most popular commodities in the global trade involving Egypt. It was through Alexandria that Europeans acquired silks from China, especially the coveted *zaytuni* (satin) fabric from Quanzhou. Spanish silks also passed through Alexandria, heading to eastern Mediterranean markets. But the entrepôts handled much more. Goods from the Mediterranean included olive oil, glassware, flax, corals, and metals. Gemstones and aromatic perfumes poured in from India. Also changing hands were minerals and

chemicals for dyeing or tanning, and raw materials such as timber and bamboo. The real novelties were paper and books. Hand-copied Bibles, Talmuds, legal and moral works, grammars in various languages, and Arabic books became the first best sellers of the Mediterranean.

Cairo and Alexandria prospered under Islamic leaders' commercial institutions. Success required states to protect merchants from predators. Armed convoys sent by Fatimid caliphs to escort commercial fleets in the Mediterranean and the Red Sea were so effective that fleets arrived on schedule and were relied on for postal service. Thus, when an Egyptian trader in Quilon (India) around 1100 was delayed on his journey home, he could send a consoling message to his wife in Cairo. He apologized for his absence but promised gifts

Mazu. Many Quanzhou sailors sought protection at the shrine of the goddess Mazu. According to legend, before assuming godhood Mazu had performed many miracles. Her temple became prominent after 1123, when Quanzhou's governor survived a storm at sea while returning from Korea. After that, sailors and their families burned incense for the goddess and prayed for her aid in keeping them safe at sea.

including pearl bracelets, red silk garments, a bronze basin, a ewer, and a slave girl: "I shall send them, if God wills it, with somebody who is traveling home in the *Karim*" (Goitein, "New Light," 179).

The Islamic legal system also promoted a favorable business environment. Consider how legal specialists got around the rule that might have brought commerce to a halt—the *sharia*'s (see Chapter 9) prohibition against earning interest on loans. With the clerics' blessing, Muslim traders formed partnerships between those who had capital to lend and those who needed money to expand their businesses. These partnerships enabled owners of capital to entrust their money or commodities to agents who, after completing their work, returned the investment and a share of the profits to the owners—and kept the rest as their reward. The English word "risk" derives from the Arabic *rizq*, the extra allowance paid to merchants in lieu of interest.

THE ANCHORAGE OF QUANZHOU   In China, Quanzhou was as busy as Cairo and Alexandria. The Song government set up offices of Seafaring Affairs in its three major ports: Canton, Quanzhou, and an area near present-day Shanghai in the Yangzi delta. In return for a portion of the taxes, these offices registered cargoes, sailors, and traders, while guards kept a keen eye on the traffic.

All foreign traders were guests of the governor, who doubled as the Chief of Seafaring Affairs. Part of his mandate was to summon favorable winds for shipping. Every year, the governor took his place on a high perch facing the harbor, in front of a rock cliff filled with inscriptions that recorded the wind-calling rituals. Traders of every origin witnessed the rite, then joined the dignitaries for a sumptuous banquet.

Ships departing from Quanzhou and other Chinese ports were junks—large, flat-bottomed ships with internal sealed bulkheads and stern-mounted rudders. Their multiple watertight compartments increased stability; the largest ones boasted four decks, six masts, and a dozen sails and could carry 500 men. Those departing Quanzhou headed for Srivijaya (Java) in the Malay Archipelago, navigating through the Strait of Melaka, a choke point between the South China Sea and the Indian Ocean. The final destination was Quilon on the coast of southwest India. Traders heading farther west in Arab-dominated seas unloaded their cargo and boarded small Arabian dhows.

Arabs, Persians, Jews, and Indians (as well as Chinese) traded at Quanzhou, and some stayed on to manage their businesses. Perhaps as many as 100,000 Muslims lived there during the Song dynasty. And traders could become power brokers in their own right. Consider the Pu family, which owned several hundred ships ferrying goods between India and Islamic countries. For generations the family made donations for public projects such as bridges, and the contributions garnered them official positions.

Although most foreign merchants did not reside apart from the rest of the city, they had their own buildings for

MAIN THEMES

→ *Trade routes shift from land to sea, transforming coastal cities into global trading hubs and elevating Afro-Eurasian trade to unprecedented levels.*

→ *Intensified trade, linguistic, and religious integration generate the foundational cultural spheres that we recognize today: China, India, Islam, and Europe.*

→ *The rise of the Mongol Empire integrates the world's foundational cultural spheres.*

FOCUS ON *Foundational Cultural Spheres*

The Islamic World

◆ Islam undergoes a burst of expansion, prosperity, and cultural diversification but remains politically fractured.

◆ Arab merchants and sufi mystics spread Islam over great distances and make it more appealing to other cultures, helping to transform Islam into a foundational world.

◆ Islam travels across the Sahara Desert; the powerful gold- and slave-supplying empire of Mali arises in West Africa.

China

◆ The Song dynasty reunites China after three centuries of fragmented rulership, reaching into the past to re-establish a sense of a "true" Chinese identity as the Han, through a widespread print culture and denigration of outsiders.

◆ Breakthroughs in iron metallurgy allow agricultural expansion to support 120 million people and undergird Han commercial success.

◆ China undergoes the world's first manufacturing revolution: gunpowder, porcelain, and handicrafts are produced on a large scale for widespread consumption.

India

◆ India remains a mosaic under the canopy of Hinduism despite cultural interconnections and increasing prosperity.

◆ The invasion of Turkish Muslims leads to the Dehli Sultanate, which rules over India for three centuries, strengthening cultural diversity and tolerance.

Christian Europe

◆ Catholicism becomes a "mass" faith and helps to create a common European cultural identity.

◆ An emphasis on religious education spawns numerous universities and a new intellectual elite.

◆ Feudalism causes a fundamental reordering of the elite–peasant relationship, leading to agricultural and commercial expansion.

◆ Europe's growing confidence is manifest in the Crusades and Reconquista, an effort to drive Islam out of Christian lands.

---

religious worship. A mosque from this period is still standing on a busy street. Hindu traders living in Quanzhou worshipped in a Buddhist shrine where statues of Hindu deities stood alongside those of Buddhist gods.

THE CROSSROADS OF AFRO-EURASIA: MELAKA Because of its strategic location and proximity to Malayan tropical produce, Melaka became a key cosmopolitan city. Indian, Javanese, and Chinese merchants and sailors spent months at a time in such ports selling their goods, purchasing return cargo, and waiting for the winds to change so they could reach their next destination. During peak season, Southeast Asian ports teemed with colorfully dressed foreign sailors,

local Javanese artisans who produced finely textured batik handicrafts (using melted wax applied to cloth before dipping it into blue and brown dyes), and money-grubbing traders. The latter converged from all over Asia to flood the markets with their merchandise and to search for pungent herbs, aromatic spices, and agrarian staples such as quick-ripening strains of rice to ship out. In a sense, each bustling port represented the cosmopolitan mosaic that Southeast Asia had become.

THE TIP OF INDIA In the tenth century, the Chola dynasty in south India supported a nerve center of maritime trade between China and the Red Sea and the Mediterranean. Although the Chola golden age lasted only about two generations, trade continued to flourish. Many Muslim traders settled in Malabar, on the southwest coast of the Indian peninsula, and Quilon became a major cosmopolitan hub. Dhows arrived, laden not only with goods from the Red Sea and Africa but also with traders, sojourners, and fugitives. Chinese junks unloaded silks and porcelain, and picked up passengers and commodities for East Asian markets. Sailors and traders strictly observed the customs of this entrepôt, for it was good business to respect others' norms and values while doing business with them.

Muslims, the largest foreign community, lived in their own neighborhoods. They shipped horses from Arab countries to India and the southeast islands, where kings viewed them as symbols of royalty. Because the animals could not survive in those climates, the demand was constant. There was even trade in elephants and cattle from tropical countries, though most goods were spices, perfumes, and textiles. Traders knew each other well, and personal relationships were key. When striking a deal with a local merchant, a Chinese trader would mention his Indian neighbor in Quanzhou and that family's residence in Quilon. Global commercial hubs relied on friendship and family to keep their businesses thriving across religious and regional divides.

SUB-SAHARAN AFRICA COMES TOGETHER

> → *How did trade and migration affect sub-Saharan Africa between 1000 and 1300?*

During this period sub-Saharan Africa's relationship to the rest of the world changed dramatically. Before 1000 CE sub-Saharan Africa had never been a world entirely apart, but now its integration became firmer. Africans and outsiders were determined to overcome the sea, river, and desert barriers that had blocked sub-Saharan peoples from participating in long-distance trade and intellectual exchanges (see Map 10-2). Increasingly, interior hinterlands found themselves touched by the commercial and migratory impulses emanating from the Indian Ocean and Arabian Sea transformations.

WEST AFRICA AND THE MANDE-SPEAKING PEOPLES

Once the camel bridged the Sahara Desert (see Chapter 9), the flow of commodities and ideas linked sub-Saharan Africa to the Muslim world of North Africa and Southwest Asia. As the savanna region became increasingly connected to developments in Afro-Eurasia, Mande-speaking peoples emerged as the primary agents for integration within and beyond West Africa. Exploiting their expertise in commerce and political organization, the Mande edged out rivals.

The Mande, or Mandinka, homeland was a vast area between the bend in the Senegal River to the west and the bend of the Niger River to the east (1,000 miles wide), stretching from the Senegal River in the north to the Bandama River in the south (more than 2,000 miles). This was where the kingdom of Ghana had arisen (see Chapter 9) and where Ghana's successor state—the Mandinka state of Mali, discussed below—emerged around 1100.

The Mande-speaking peoples were constantly on the go and marvelously adaptable. By the eleventh century they were spreading their cultural, commercial, and political hegemony from the high savanna grasslands southward into the woodlands and tropical rainforests stretching to the Atlantic Ocean. Those dwelling in the rainforests organized small-scale societies led by local councils, while those in the savanna lands developed centralized forms of government under sacred kingships. These peoples believed that their kings had descended from the gods and that they enjoyed the gods' blessing.

As the Mande broadened their territory to the Atlantic coast, they gained access to tradable items that residents of the interior were eager to have—notably kola nuts and malaguetta peppers, for which the Mande exchanged iron products and textile manufactures. By 1300 the Mandinka merchants had followed the Senegal River to its outlet on the coast and then pushed their commercial frontiers farther inland and down the coast. Thus, even before European explorers and traders arrived in the mid-fifteenth century, West African peoples had created dynamic networks linking the hinterlands with coastal trading hubs.

From the eleventh century to the late fifteenth century, the most vigorous businesses were those that spanned the Sahara Desert. The Mande-speaking peoples, with their far-flung commercial networks and highly dispersed populations, dominated this trade as well. Here one of the most prized commodities was salt, mined in the northern Sahel around the city of Taghaza; it was in demand on both sides of the Sahara. Another valuable commodity was gold, mined within the Mande homeland and borne by camel caravans to the far northern side of the Sahara, where traders exchanged it for various manufactures. Equally important in West African commerce were slaves, who were shipped to the settled Muslim communities of North Africa and Egypt.

THE EMPIRE OF MALI

As booming trade spawned new political organizations, the empire of Mali became the Mande successor state to the kingdom of Ghana. Founded in the twelfth century, it exercised political sway over a vast area for three centuries.

The Mali Empire represented the triumph of horse warriors, and its origins are enshrined in an epic involving the dynasty's founder, the legendary Sundiata, *The Epic of Sundiata*. Many

MAP 10-2   SUB-SAHARAN AFRICA, 1300

Increased commercial contacts influenced the religious and political dimensions of sub-Saharan Africa at this time. Compare this map to Map 9-3 (p. 335). Where had strong Islamic communities emerged by 1300? According to this map, what types of activity were affecting the Mande homeland? To what extent had sub-Saharan Africa "come together"?

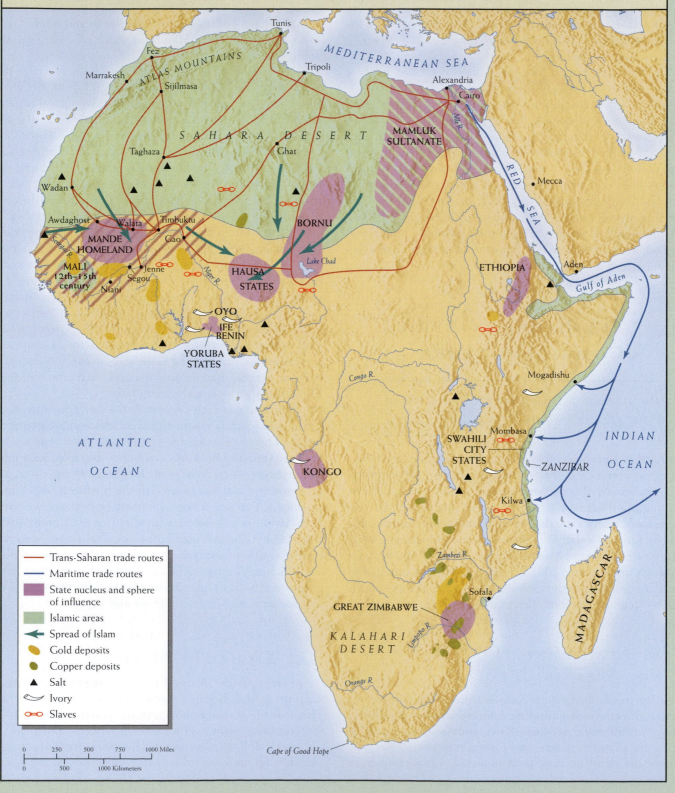

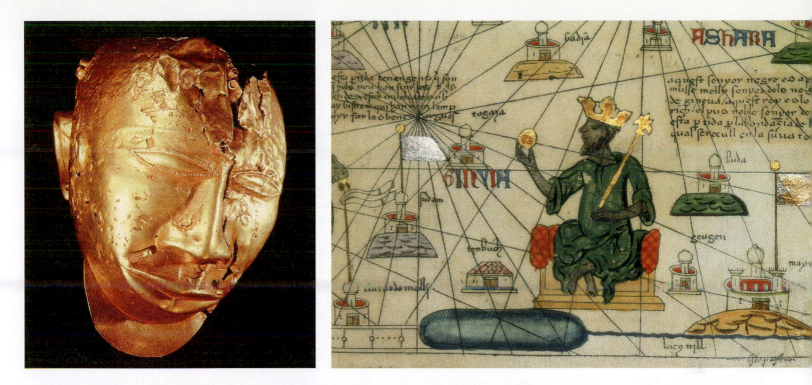

West African Asante Gold. Although this gold head from the kingdom of Asante (*left*) was made in the eighteenth century, it shows the artistic abilities of the West African peoples. The head probably belonged to the Asante ruler, known as the Asantehene, and symbolized his power and wealth. This 1375 picture (*right*) shows the king of Mali on his throne, surrounded by images of gold.

historians believe that Sundiata actually existed, noting that the Arab historian Ibn Khaldun referred to him by name and reported that he was "their [Mali's] greatest king" (Levtzion and Pouwels, p. 64). His triumph, which occurred in the fourteenth century, marked the victory of new cavalry forces over traditional footsoldiers. Henceforth, horses—which had always existed in some parts of Africa—became prestige objects of the savanna peoples, symbols of state power. (See Primary Source: An African Epic.)

Under the Mali Empire, commerce was in full swing. With Mande trade routes extending to the Atlantic Ocean and spanning the Sahara Desert, West Africa was no longer an isolated periphery of the central Muslim lands. Mali's most famous sovereign, Mansa Musa (r. 1312–1332), made a celebrated hajj, or pilgrimage to Mecca, in 1325–1326, traveling through Cairo and impressing crowds with the size of his retinue and his displays of wealth, especially many dazzling items made of gold.

Mansa Musa's visit to Cairo was a sensation in its time. The stopover in one of Islam's primary cities astonished the Egyptian elite and awakened much of the world to the fact that Islam had spread far below the Sahara and that a sub-Saharan state could mount such an ostentatious display. Mansa Musa spared no expense to impress his hosts. He sent ahead an enormous gift of 50,000 dinars (a unit of money widely used in the Islamic world at this time), and his entourage included soldiers, wives, consorts, and as many as 12,000 slaves, many wearing rich brocades woven of Persian silks. And there was gold—a lot of it. He brought immense quantities and distributed it lavishly during his three-month stay. Preceding his retinue as it crossed the desert were 500 slaves, each carrying a golden staff. The caravan also included around 100 camels, each bearing two 300-pound sacks of gold.

The Mali Empire boasted two of West Africa's largest cities. Jenne, an ancient entrepôt, was a vital assembly point for caravans laden with salt, gold, and slaves preparing for journeys west to the Atlantic coast and north over the Sahara. The city had originated as an urban settlement around 200 BCE; by 1000 CE most substantial structures were made of brick. Around the city ran an impressive wall over eleven feet thick at its base and extending over a mile in length. More spectacular was the city of Timbuktu; founded around 1100 as a seasonal camp for nomads, it grew in size and importance under the patronage of various Malian kings. By the fourteenth century it was a thriving commercial and religious center famed for its two large mosques, which are still standing. Timbuktu was also renowned for its intellectual vitality. Here, West African Muslim scholars congregated to debate the tenets of Islam and to ensure that the faithful, even when distant from the Muslim heartland, practiced their religion with no taint of pagan observances. These clerics acquired treatises on Islam from all over the world for their personal libraries, remnants of which remain to this day.

Primary Source

AN AFRICAN EPIC

The traditional story of the founding of the kingdom of Mali was passed down orally from generation to generation by griots, counselors and other official historians to the royal family. Only in 1960 was it finally written down in French. The narrative recounts the life of Sundiata, the heroic founder of the Mali state. The following passage provides insight into the role of the narrator (the griot) in the Malian kingdom, as well as some of the qualities of good and bad rulers.

Griots know the history of kings and kingdoms and that is why they are the best counsellors of kings. Every king wants to have a singer to perpetuate his memory, for it is the griot who rescues the memories of kings from oblivion, as men have short memories.

Kings have prescribed destinies just like men, and seers who probe the future know it. They have knowledge of the future, whereas we griots are depositories of the knowledge of the past. But whoever knows the history of a country can read its future.

Other peoples use writing to record the past, but this invention has killed the faculty of memory among them. They do not feel the past any more, for writing lacks the warmth of the human voice. . . .

I, Djeli Mamoudou Kouyaté, am the result of a long tradition. For generations we have passed on the history of kings from father to son. The narrative was passed on to me without alteration and I deliver it without alteration, for I received it free from all untruth.

Listen now to the story of Sundiata, the Na'Kamma, the man who had a mission to accomplish.

At the time when Sundiata was preparing to assert his claim over the kingdom of his fathers, Soumaoro was the king of kings, the most powerful king in all the lands of the setting sun. The fortified town of Sosso was the bulwark of fetishism against the word of Allah. For a long time Soumaoro defied the whole world. Since his accession to the throne of Sosso he had defeated nine kings whose heads served him as fetishes in his macabre chamber. Their skins served as seats and he cut his footwear from human skin. Soumaoro was not like other men, for the jinn had revealed themselves to him and his power was beyond measure. So his countless sofas [soldiers] were very brave since they believed their king to be invincible. But Soumaoro was an evil demon and his reign had produced nothing but bloodshed. Nothing was taboo for him. His greatest pleasure was publicly to flog venerable old men. He had defiled every family and everywhere in his vast empire there were villages populated by girls whom he had forcibly abducted from their families without marrying them.

→ *Are you able to understand the function of the griot after reading this passage?*

→ *How reliable do you think this kind of oral history is?*

→ *Soumaoro, the adversary of Sundiata, exemplified the characteristics of a bad ruler. What were they? Can you tell, indirectly, what the characteristics of a good ruler (like Sundiata) were?*

SOURCE: *Sundiata: An Epic of Old Mali*, translated by D. T. Niane (Harlow: Longman Group, 1965), pp. 40–41.

EAST AFRICA AND THE INDIAN OCEAN

Africa's eastern and southern regions were also integrated into long-distance trading systems. Because of monsoon winds, East Africa was a logical end point for much of the Indian Ocean trade. Thus Swahili peoples living along that coast became brokers for the trade coming and going from the Arabian Peninsula, the Persian Gulf territories, and the western coast of India. Merchants in the city of Kilwa along the coast of present-day Tanzania brought ivory, slaves, gold, and other items from the interior and shipped them to destinations around the Indian Ocean.

The most valued commodity in the trade was gold. Shona-speaking peoples grew rich by mining the ore in the highlands between the Limpopo and Zambezi rivers. By the year 1000, the Shona had founded up to fifty small religious and political centers, each one erected from stone to display

Great Zimbabwe. These walls surrounded the city of Great Zimbabwe, which was a center of the gold trade between the East African coastal peoples and traders sailing on the Indian Ocean. Great Zimbabwe flourished during the thirteenth, fourteenth, and fifteenth centuries.

THE TRANS-SAHARAN AND INDIAN OCEAN SLAVE TRADE

African slaves were as valuable as African gold in shipments to the Mediterranean and Indian Ocean markets. There had been a lively trade in African slaves (mainly from Nubia) into pharaonic Egypt well before the Common Era. After Islam spread into Africa and sailing techniques improved, the slave trade across the Sahara Desert and Indian Ocean boomed.

Although the Quran attempted to mitigate the severity of slavery, requiring Muslim slave owners to treat their slaves kindly and praising manumission as an act of **piety** (a strong sense of religious duty and devoutness, often inspiring extraordinary actions), nonetheless the African slave trade flourished under Islam.

Slave Market. Slaves were a common commodity in the marketplaces of the Islamic world. Turkish conquests during the years from 1000 to 1300 put many prisoners into the slave market.

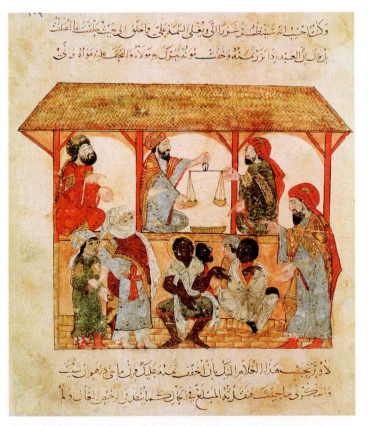

its power over the peasant villages surrounding it. Around 1100 one of these centers, Great Zimbabwe, stood supreme among the Shona. Built on the fortunes made from gold, its most impressive landmark was a massive elliptical building—32 feet high, 17 feet thick in parts, and extending more than 800 feet—made of stone so expertly that its fittings needed no grouting. The buildings of Great Zimbabwe probably housed the king and may also have contained smelters for melting down gold.

One of the key meeting grounds of the Indian Ocean trading system was the island of Madagascar. So intense was the interchange of peoples, plants, and animals from mainland Africa and around the rest of the Indian Ocean that Madagascar became one of the most multicultural places in the world at this time. Among the early inhabitants of the island were seafarers from Indonesia who plied the oceans with seaworthy outrigger canoes, likely picking up Bantu-speaking mainlanders from East Africa. The first evidence of human settlement there dates to the eighth century CE. Subsequently the island became a regular stopover point, as well as an import-export market, for traders crossing the Indian Ocean.

Africans became slaves during this period much as they had before: some were prisoners of war; others were considered criminals and sold into slavery as punishment. Their duties were varied. Some slaves were pressed into military service, rising in a few instances to positions of high authority. Others with seafaring skills worked as crewmen on dhows or as dockworkers. Still others, mainly women, were domestic servants, and many became concubines of Muslim political figures and businessmen. Slaves also did forced labor on plantations, the most oppressive being the agricultural estates of lower Iraq. There, slaves endured fearsome discipline and revolted in the ninth century. Yet in this era plantation-slave labor like that which later became prominent in the Americas was the exception, not the rule. Slaves were more prized as additions to family labor or as status symbols for their owners.

ISLAM IN A TIME OF POLITICAL FRAGMENTATION

> → *How did trade, conversion, and migration affect the Islamic world between 1000 and 1300?*

Islam underwent the same burst of expansion, prosperity, and cultural diversification that swept through the rest of Afro-Eurasia (see Map 10-3 and Map 10-4). However, whereas prosperity fostered greater integration in other regions, the peoples of Islam remained politically fractured. As in China, efforts to unite under a common rulership failed, giving way to defeats by marauding outsiders. The attempt to uphold centralized rule ended cataclysmically in 1258 with the Mongol sacking of Baghdad. But unlike China, Muslim leaders were unable to reunite after their collapse.

BECOMING THE "MIDDLE EAST"

Islam responded to political fragmentation by undergoing major changes, many prompted by contacts (and conflicts) with neighbors. Commercial networks, sustained by Muslim merchants, carried the word of the Quran far and wide. As Islam spread, it attracted more converts.

Decisive in the spread of Islam was a popular form of the religion, highly mystical and communal, called **Sufism.** The term *Sufi* comes from the Arabic word for wool (*suf*), which many of the early mystics wrapped themselves in to mark their penitence. Seeking closer union with God, they also performed ecstatic rituals such as repeating over and over again the name of God. In time, groups of devotees gathered to read aloud the Quran and other religious tracts. Although

Dervishes. Today, the whirling dance of dervishes is almost a tourist attraction, as shown in this picture from the Jerash Cultural Festival in Jordan. Though Sufis in the early second millennium CE were not this neatly dressed, the whirling dance was an important means of reaching union with God.

many clerics despised the Sufis and loathed their seeming lack of theological rigor, the movement spread with astonishing speed. Sufism's emotional content and strong social bonds, sustained in Sufi brotherhoods or lodges, made its appeal to common folk irresistible. Sufi missionaries carried the universalizing faith to India, across the Sahara Desert, and to many other distant locations. It was from within these brotherhoods that Islam became truly a religion for the people.

Sufism had an intellectual and artistic dynamism that complemented its missionizing zeal. This was especially true of poetry, where the mystics' desire to experience God's love found ready expression. Most admired of Islam's mystical love poets was Jalal al-Din Rumi, spiritual founder of the Medlevi Sufi order that became famous for the ceremonial dancing of its whirling devotees, known as dervishes. Rumi, who wrote in Persian, celebrated all forms of love, spiritual and sexual, and preached a universalistic religious message:

What is to be done of Muslims? For I do not recognize myself.
I am neither Christian, nor Jew, nor Gabr (Zoroastrian), nor Muslim.

Another Sufi mystic and advocate of the universality of religions, the Spanish Muslim poet Ibn Arabi, wrote in Arabic:

My heart has been of every form; it is a pasture for gazelles and a convent for Christian monks.
And a temple for idols and the pilgrim's kaaba, and the tables of the Torah and the book of the Quran.

As trade increased and more converts appeared in the Islamic lands, urban and peasant populations came to understand the faith practiced by the political, commercial, and scholarly upper classes even while they remained attached to their

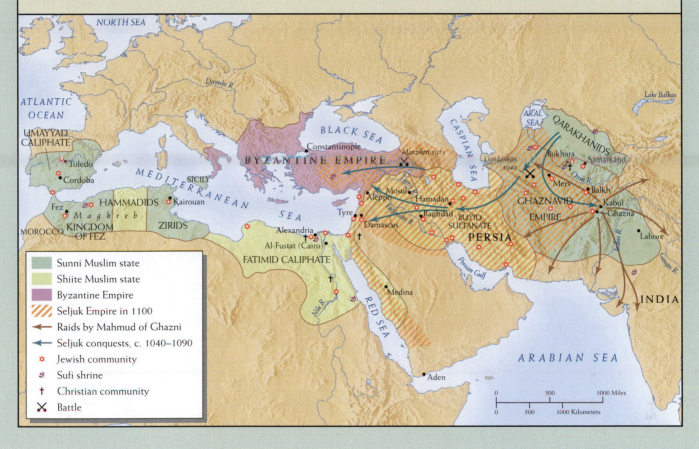

MAP 10-3   ISLAM BETWEEN 900 AND 1200

The Muslim world experienced political disintegration in the first centuries of the second millennium. According to the map key, what were the two major types of Muslim states in this period and what were the two major empires? What were the sources of instability in this period according to the map? As Islam continued to expand in this period, what challenges did it face?

Legend:
- Sunni Muslim state
- Shiite Muslim state
- Byzantine Empire
- Seljuk Empire in 1100
- Raids by Mahmud of Ghazni
- Seljuk conquests, c. 1040–1090
- Jewish community
- Sufi shrine
- Christian community
- Battle

Sufi brotherhood ways. Islam became even more accommodating, embracing Persian literature, Turkish ruling skills, and Arabic-language contributions in law, religion, literature, and science. In this way the world acquired a "core" region centered in what we now call the Middle East (the lands west of the "Far East" of China and Japan, and including the "Near East" of the eastern Mediterranean), united by a shared faith and pulsating with religious and commercial energies.

AFRO-EURASIAN MERCHANTS

By the thirteenth century, as the old Islamic heartland became the crossroads for commercial networks, Muslim merchants were the world's premier traders. As diverse as their businesses, these merchants were proof that a universal religion, an imagined political unity (projected by the Abbasid caliphate), the spread of the Arabic language, and Islamic law allowed entrepreneurs of varied backgrounds to flourish. The traders were not only Muslims but also Armenians, Indians, and Jews; working out of Islam's major cities; and they all had connections with families in North Africa and central Asia. (See Primary Source: The Merchants of Egypt.)

Long-distance trade surged under the protection of a sophisticated legal framework. The traders drew up elaborate contracts knowing that if breaches of contract occurred, they could take their cases to the courts. Many Jewish, Armenian, and Christian merchants went before Islamic judges, whose expertise in commercial matters they admired. Yet legal recourse was rarely necessary because the merchant community was self-policing—its members severely punished those who violated trust, sometimes ending their careers. Relying on partnerships, letters of credit, and a thorough knowledge of local trading customs and currencies, traders and their customers were confident that agreements made in India would be honored in Southeast Asia, Egypt, and North Africa.

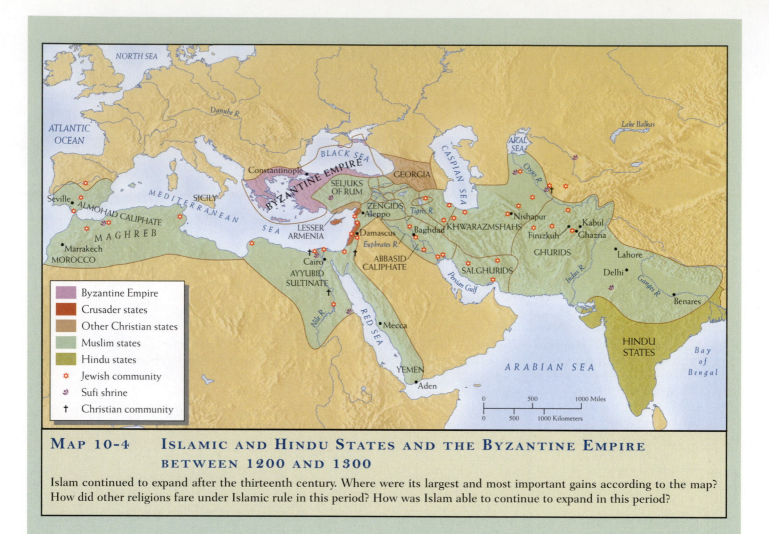

MAP 10-4   ISLAMIC AND HINDU STATES AND THE BYZANTINE EMPIRE BETWEEN 1200 AND 1300

Islam continued to expand after the thirteenth century. Where were its largest and most important gains according to the map? How did other religions fare under Islamic rule in this period? How was Islam able to continue to expand in this period?

DIVERSITY AND UNIFORMITY IN ISLAM

Not until the ninth and tenth centuries did Muslims become a majority within their own Abbasid Empire (see Chapter 9). From the outset, Muslim rulers and clerics had to deal with large non-Muslim populations, even as these groups were converting to Islam. Rulers through the dhimma system accorded non-Muslims religious toleration as long as the non-Muslims accepted Islam's political dominion. Thus Jewish, Christian, and Zoroastrian communities were free to choose their own religious leaders and to settle internal disputes in their own religious courts. They did, however, have to pay a special tax, the *jizya,* and be deferential to their rulers. The dhimma system spared the Islamic world some of the religious conflict that afflicted other areas, and it made Islamic cities hospitable environments for traders from around the world.

While tolerant, Islam was an expansionist, universalizing faith. Intense proselytizing carried the sacred word to new frontiers and, in the process, reinforced the spread of Islamic institutions that supported commercial exchange. There were also moments of intense religious passion within Islam's frontiers, especially when Muslim rulers feared that Christian minorities would align with the Europeans pressing on their borders. Ugly incidents left some Christian churches in flames. Pressures to convert to Islam were unremitting at this time. After a surge of conversions to Islam from the ninth century onward, for example, the Christian Copts of Egypt shrank to a small community and never recovered their numbers.

POLITICAL INTEGRATION AND DISINTEGRATION

Just as the Islamic faith was increasing its reach from Africa to India and ultimately to Southeast Asia, its political institutions began to fragment. From 950 to 1050, it appeared that Shiism would be the vehicle for uniting the Islamic

Primary Source

THE MERCHANTS OF EGYPT

The most comprehensive collection of eleventh- and twelfth-century commercial materials from the Islamic world comes from a repository connected to the Jewish synagogue in Cairo. (It was the custom of the Jewish community to preserve, in a special storeroom, all texts that mention God.) These papers, a rich source of information about the Jewish community in Egypt at that time, touch on all manner of activities: cultural, religious, judicial, political, and commercial. The following letter is addressed to Joseph ibn 'Awkal, one of Egypt's leading merchants in the eleventh century.

Dear and beloved elder and leader, may God prolong your life, never take away your rank, and increase his favors and benefactions to you.

I inform you, my elder, that I have arrived safely. I have written you a letter before, but have seen no answer. Happy preoccupations—I hope. In that letter I provided you with all the necessary information.

I loaded nine pieces of antimony (kohl), five in baskets and four in complete pieces, on the boat of Ibn Jubār—may God keep it; these are for you personally, sent by Mūsā Ibn al-Majjānī. On this boat, I have in partnership with you—may God keep you—a load of cast copper, a basket with (copper) fragments, and two pieces of antimony. I hope God will grant their safe arrival. Kindly take delivery of everything, my lord.

I have also sent with Banāna a camel load for you from Ibn al-Majjānī and a camel load for me in partnership with you—may God keep you. He also carries another partnership of mine, namely, with 'Ammā r Ibn Yijū, four small jugs (of oil).

With Abū Zayd I have a shipload of tin in partnership with Salāma al-Mahdawī. Your share in this partnership with him is fifty pounds. I also have seventeen small jugs of s[oap]. I hope they arrive safely. They belong to a man [called . . .]r b. Salmūn, who entrusted them to me at his own risk. Also a bundle of hammered copper, belonging to [a Muslim] man from the Maghreb, called Abū Bakr Ibn

Rizq Allah. Two other bundles, on one is written Abraham, on the other M[. . .]. I agreed with the shipowner that he would transport the goods to their destination. I wish my brother Abū Nasr—may God preserve him—to take care of all the goods and carry them to his place until I shall arrive, if God wills.

Please sell the tin for me at whatever price God may grant and leave its "purse" (the money received for it) until my arrival. I am ready to travel, but must stay until I can unload the tar and oil from the ships.

Please take care of this matter and take from him the price of five skins (filled with oil). The account is with Salāma.

Al-Sabbāgh of Tripoli has bribed Bu 'l-'Alā the agent, and I shall unload my goods soon.

Kindest regards to your noble self and to my master [. . . and] Abu 'l-Fadl, may God keep them.

> ➔ List all the different kinds of commodities that the letter talks about.
> ➔ How many different people are named as owners, partners, dealers, and agents?
> ➔ What does the letter reveal about the ties among merchants and about how they conducted their business?

SOURCE: *Letters of Medieval Jewish Traders*, translated with introductions and notes by S. D. Goitein (Princeton, NJ: Princeton University Press, 1973), pp. 85–87.

---

world. While the Fatimid Shiites established their authority over Egypt and much of North Africa (see Chapter 9), the Abbasid state in Baghdad fell under the sway of a Shiite family. Each group created universities (in Cairo and Baghdad, respectively), ensuring that leading centers of higher learning were Shiite. But divisions also sapped Shiism, as Sunni Muslims began to challenge Shiite power and establish their own strongholds. The last of the Shiite Fatimid rulers gave way to

a new Sunni regime in Egypt. In Baghdad, the Shiite Buyid family surrendered to a group of unrelated Sunni strongmen.

The new strongmen were mainly Turks. Their people had been migrating into the Islamic heartland from the Asian steppes since the eighth century, bringing superior military skills and an intense devotion to Sunni Islam. Once established in Baghdad, they founded outposts in Syria and Palestine, and then moved into Anatolia after defeating

Byzantine forces in 1071. But this Turkish state also crumbled, as tribesmen quarreled for preeminence. Thus by the thirteenth century the Islamic heartland had fractured into three regions. In the east (central Asia, Iran, and eastern Iraq), the remnants of the old Abbasid state persevered. Caliphs succeeded one another, still claiming to speak for all of Islam yet deferring to their Turkish military commanders. Even in the core of the Islamic world (Egypt, Syria, and the Arabian Peninsula), where Arabic was the primary tongue, military men of non-Arab origin held the reins of power. Farther west (in the Maghreb), Arab rulers prevailed—but there the influence of Berbers, some from the northern Sahara, was extensive. Islam was a vibrant faith, but its polities were splintered.

WHAT WAS ISLAM?

Buoyed by Arab dhows on the high seas and carried on the backs of camels, following commercial networks, Islam had been transformed from Muhammad's original goal of creating a religion for Arab peoples. By 1300, its influence spanned Afro-Eurasia. It attracted urbanites and rural peasants alike, as well as its original audience of desert nomads. Its extraordinary universal appeal generated an intense Islamic cultural flowering in 1000 CE.

Some people worried about the preservation of Islam's true nature as, for example, Arabic ceased to be the language of many Islamic believers when it spread beyond the Arab peoples. True, the devout read and recited the Quran in its original tongue, as the religion mandated. But Persian was now the language of Muslim philosophy and art, and Turkish was the language of law and administration. Moreover, Jerusalem and Baghdad no longer stood alone as Islamic cultural capitals. Other cities, housing universities and other centers of learning, promoted alternative, vernacular versions of Islam. In fact, some of the most dynamic thought came from Islam's fringes.

At the same time, heterogeneity fostered cultural blossoming in all fields of high learning. Arabic remained a preeminent language of science, literature, and religion in 1300. Indicative of Islam's and Arabic's prominence in thought was the legendary Ibn Rushd (1126–1198). Known as Averroës in the western world, where scholars pored over his writings, he wrestled with the same theological issues that troubled western scholars. Steeped in the writings of Aristotle, Ibn Rushd became Islam's most thoroughgoing advocate for the use of reason in understanding the universe. His knowledge of Aristotle was so great that it influenced the thinking of the Christian world's leading philosopher and theologian, Thomas of Aquino (Thomas Aquinas, 1225–1274). Above all, Ibn Rushd believed that faith and reason could be compatible. He also argued for a social hierarchy in which learned

men would command influence akin to Confucian scholars in China or Greek philosophers in Athens. Ibn Rushd believed that the proper forms of reasoning had to be entrusted to the educated class—in the case of Islam, the *ulama*—which would serve the common folk.

Equally powerful works appeared in Persian, which by now was expressing the most sophisticated ideas of culture and religion. Best representing the new Persian ethnic pride was Abu al-Qasim Firdawsi (920–1020), a devout Muslim who also believed in the importance of pre-Islamic Sasanian traditions. In the epic poem *Shah Namah,* or *Book of Kings,* he celebrated the origins of Persian culture and narrated the history of the Iranian highland peoples from the dawn of time to the Muslim conquest. As part of his effort to extol a pure Persian culture, Firdawsi attempted to compose his entire poem in Persian unblemished by other languages, even avoiding Arabic words.

By the fourteenth century, Islam had achieved what early converts would have considered unthinkable. No longer a religion of a minority of peoples living amid Christian, Zoroastrian, and Jewish communities, it had become the people's faith. The agents of conversion were mainly Sufi saints and Sufi brotherhoods—not the *ulama,* whose exhortations had little impact on common people. The Sufis had carried their faith far and wide to North African Berbers, to Anatolian villagers, and to West African animists (who believed that things in nature have souls). Indeed, Ibn Rushd worried about the growing appeal of what he considered an "irrational" piety. But his message failed, because he did not appreciate that Islam's expansionist powers rested on its appeal to common folk. While the *sharia* was the core of Islam for the educated and scholarly classes, Sufism spoke to ordinary men and women.

INDIA AS A CULTURAL MOSAIC

> → *In what ways did India remain a cultural mosaic?*

Trade and migration affected India, just as it did the rest of Asia and Africa. As in the case of Islam, India's growing cultural interconnections and increasing prosperity produced little political integration. Under the canopy of Hinduism it remained a cultural mosaic; in fact, the Islamic faith now joined others to make the region even more diverse (see Map 10-5). India, in this sense, illustrates how cross-cultural integration can just as easily preserve diversity as promote internal unity.

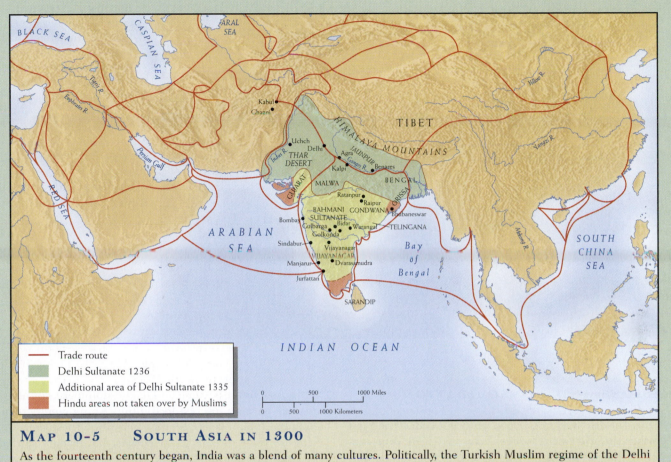

MAP 10-5   SOUTH ASIA IN 1300

As the fourteenth century began, India was a blend of many cultures. Politically, the Turkish Muslim regime of the Delhi Sultanate dominated the region. Use the map key to identify the areas dominated by the Delhi Sultanate. How do you suppose the trade routes helped to spread the Muslims' influence in India? Now use the key to find the Hindu areas. Based on your reading, what factors accounted for Hinduism's continued appeal despite the Muslims' political power?

RAJAS AND SULTANS

Turks spilled into India as they had the Islamic heartlands, bringing their newfound Islamic beliefs. But the newcomers encountered an ethnic and religious mix that they would add to without upsetting the balance. India became an intersection for the trade, migration, and culture of Afro-Eurasian peoples. Moreover, with 80 million inhabitants in 1000 CE, it had the second-largest population in the region, not far behind China's 120 million.

Before the Turks arrived, India was splintered among rival chiefs called *rajas*. (**Rajas** considered themselves kings; the term also denotes the head of a family or the person who controlled land and resources.) These leaders solicited support from high-caste Brahmans by giving them land. Much of it was uncultivated, so the Brahmans set out to make it arable: they built temples, converted the indigenous hunter-gatherer peoples to the Hindu faith, and then taught the converts how to cultivate the land. In this way the Brahmans simultaneously spread their faith and expanded the agrarian tax base for themselves and the rajas. The Brahmans reciprocated the rajas' support by compiling elaborate genealogies for them and endowing them with a lengthy (and legitimizing) ancestry. For their part, the rajas demonstrated that they were well versed in Sanskrit culture, including equestrian skills and courtly etiquette, and became the patrons of artists and poets. Ultimately, many of the warriors and their heirs became Indian rajas. However, the Turkish invaders were armed with Islam, so the conquerors remained sultans instead of becoming rajas. (Unlike rajas, **sultans** were political leaders who combined a warrior ethos with a devotion to Islam.)

Hindu Temple. When Buddhism started to decline in India, Hinduism was on the rise. Numerous Hindu temples were built, many of them adorned with ornate carvings like this small tenth-century temple in Bhubaneshwar, east India.

INVASIONS AND CONSOLIDATIONS

When the Turkish warlords began entering India, the rajas had neither the will nor resources to resist them after centuries of fighting off invaders. The Turks introduced their own customs while accepting local social structures, such as the caste system. Concerned to promote Islamic culture, the Turks constructed grandiose mosques and built impressive libraries where scholars could toil and share their wisdom with the court. Previous invaders from central Asia had reinforced the rajas' power base through intermarriage. But the Turks upset the balance of the raja kingdoms. For example, Mahmud of Ghazna (971–1030) launched many expeditions from the Afghan heartland into northern India and wanted to make his capital, Ghazni, a center of Islamic learning in order to win status within Islam. Subsequently, Muhammad Ghuri in the 1180s led another wave of Islamic Turkish invasions from Afghanistan and dispersed across the Delhi region in northern India. Wars raged between the Indus and Ganges rivers until one by one, all the way to the lower Ganges valley, the fractured kingdoms of the rajas toppled.

The most powerful and enduring of the Turkish Muslim regimes of northern India was the **Delhi Sultanate** (1206–1526), whose rulers strengthened the cultural diversity and tolerance that were already a hallmark of the Indian social order. Sultans recruited local artisans for numerous building projects, and palaces and mosques became displays of Indian architectural tastes adopted by Turkish newcomers. But the sultans did not force their subjects to convert, so that South Asia never became an Islamic-dominant country. Nor did they have an interest in the flourishing commercial life along the Indian coast. So they permitted these areas to develop on their own. Persian Zoroastrian traders settled on the coast around modern-day Mumbai (Bombay). The Malabar coast to the south became the preserve of Arab traders. The Delhi Sultanate was a rich and powerful regime that brought political integration but did not enforce cultural homogeneity.

WHAT WAS INDIA?

During the eleventh, twelfth, and thirteenth centuries India became the most diverse and, in some respects, most tolerant region in Afro-Eurasia. It is from this era that India as an impressive but fragile mosaic of cultures, religions, and ethnicities truly arises. Not even Islam's entry into the region undermined this intense cultural mixing.

When the Turks arrived, the local Hindu population, having had much experience with foreign invaders and immigrants, assimilated these intruders as they had done earlier peoples. And the Turks cooperated. Before long, they thought of themselves as Indians who, however, retained their Islamic beliefs and steppe ways. They continued to wear their distinctive trousers and robes and flaunted their horse-riding skills. At the same time, the local population embraced some of their conquerors' ways, donning the tunics and trousers that characterized Central Asian peoples.

Lodi Gardens. The Lodi Dynasty was the last Delhi sultan dynasty. Lodi Gardens, the cemetery of Lodi sultans, places central Asian Islamic architecture in the Indian landscape, thereby creating a scene of "heaven on the earth."

Diversity and cultural mixing became most visible in the multiple languages that flourished in India. Although the sultans spoke Turkish languages, they regarded Persian literature as a high cultural achievement and made Persian their courtly and administrative language. Meanwhile, most of their Hindu subjects spoke local languages (which had evolved out of Sanskrit) and followed their caste regulations. Despite living under Muslim rulers, the subject populations adhered to their local adaptations of the Hindu faith. Here the rulers did what Muslim rulers did with Christian and Jewish communities living in their midst: they collected the *jizya* tax and permitted communities to worship as they saw fit and to administer their own communal law. Ultimately, Islam proved in India that it did not have to be a conquering religion to prosper. As rulers, sultans granted lands to ulama (Islamic scholars) and Sufi saints, much as Hindu rajas had earlier granted lands to Brahmans (see Chapter 8). These scholars and saints in turn attracted followers to their large estates and forests to enjoy the benefits of membership in a community of believers.

Although newcomers and locals cleaved to separate religious traditions, nonetheless their customs began to merge.

Sultans maintained their steppe lifestyle and equestrian culture and took delight in the fact that their subjects adopted Central Asian–style clothing. Within only a few decades, once the subject peoples realized that sultans and Islam were there to stay, they embraced the fashions of the court. In turn, their Muslim rulers understood that ruling effectively meant mastering the local language. Before long, court scholars and Sufi holy men were writing and teaching proficiently in local dialects. Hindustani was the result, an Indian language incorporating Persian and Arabic words; in time, it became the root language of Hindi and Urdu.

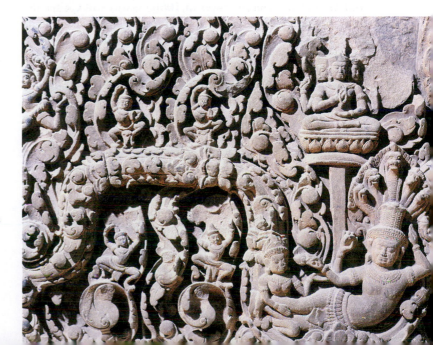

Vishnu. With Buddhism disappearing from India, Buddha was absorbed by the cult of Vishnu and became one of the incarnations of the Hindu god. This late-twelfth-century Angkor Wat–style sculpture from Cambodia shows Vishnu asleep; from his nostril sprouts the lotus that will give birth to Buddha.

This exchange of skills among diverse communities was not confined to governance and religion. It spilled over into the economic arena as well. The foreign artisans who had arrived with their rulers brought silk textiles, rugs, and appliances to irrigate gardens that the leading families of Delhi cherished. Soon the artisans' talents were influencing local manufacturing techniques. Native-born Indians learned from Muslims how to extract long filaments from silk cocoons and were themselves weaving fine silk textiles.

Although Buddhism had been in decline in India for centuries, it, too, became part of the cultural intermixing of these centuries. As Vedic Brahmanism evolved into Hinduism (see Chapter 8), it absorbed many Buddhist doctrines and practices, such as *ahimsa* (non-killing) and vegetarianism. The two religions became so similar that Hindus simply considered the Buddha to be one of their deities—an incarnation of the great god Vishnu. Many Buddhist moral teachings mixed with and became Hindu stories. Artistic motifs reflect a similar process of adoption and adaptation. Goddesses, some beautiful and others fierce, appeared alongside Buddhas, Vishnus, and Sivas as their consorts. The Turkish invaders' destruction of major monasteries in the thirteenth century deprived Buddhism of local spiritual leaders. Lacking dynastic support, Buddhists in India were thus more easily assimilated into the Hindu population or converted to Islam.

SONG CHINA: INSIDERS VERSUS OUTSIDERS

> → *What transformations in communication, education, and commerce promoted a distinct Chinese identity during this era?*

The preeminent world power in 1000 CE was still China, despite its recent turmoil. Once dampened, that turbulence yielded to a long era of stability and splendor—a combination that made China a regional engine of Afro-Eurasian prosperity.

After the end of the Tang dynasty (907 CE), North and South China splintered into regional kingdoms, mostly led by military generals. In 960 CE one of those generals, Zhao Kuangyin, ended the fragmentation. Overthrowing the boy emperor of his own kingdom, Zhao reunified China by conquering regional kingdoms. After his death, his younger brother annexed the remaining kingdoms. Thus, the Song dynasty took over the mandate of heaven.

The following three centuries witnessed many economic and political successes, but northern nomadic tribes kept the Song from completely securing their reign (see Map 10-6 and Map 10-7). Their efforts to deter these warriors were ulti-mately unsuccessful, and in 1127 the Song lost control of northern China to the Jurchen (ancestors of the Manchu, who would rule China from the seventeenth until the twentieth century). After reconstituting their dynasty in southern China, their empire's most economically robust region, the Song enjoyed another century and a half of rule before falling to the Mongols.

CHINA'S ECONOMIC PROGRESS

China, like India and the Islamic world, participated in Afro-Eurasia's powerful long-distance trade. Indeed, Chinese merchants were as energetic as their Muslim and Indian counterparts. Yet China's commercial successes could not have occurred without the country's strong agrarian base—especially its vast rice fields, which sustained a population that reached 120 million. Agriculture benefited from breakthroughs in metalworking that yielded stronger iron plows, which the Song harnessed to sturdy water buffalo to extend the farming frontier. In 1078, for example, total Song iron production reached between 75,000 and 150,000 tons, roughly the equivalent of European iron production in the early eighteenth century. The Chinese piston bellows were a marvel, and of a size unsurpassed until the nineteenth century.

Manufacturing also flourished. In the early tenth century, Chinese alchemists mixed saltpeter with sulfur and charcoal to produce a product that would burn and could be deployed on the battlefield: gunpowder. Soon, Song entrepreneurs were inventing a remarkable array of incendiary devices that flowed from their mastery of techniques for controlling explosions. Moreover, artisans produced increasingly light, durable, and exquisitely beautiful porcelains. Before long, their porcelain (now called "china") was the envy of all Afro-Eurasia. Also flowing from the artisans' skillful hands were vast amounts of clothing and handicrafts, made from the fibers grown by Song farmers. In effect, the Song Chinese oversaw the world's first manufacturing revolution, producing finished goods on a large scale for consumption far and wide.

MONEY AND INFLATION

Expanding commerce transformed the role of money and its wide circulation. By now the Song government was annually minting nearly two million strings of currency, each containing 1,000 copper coins. In fact, the supply of metal currency could not match the demand. (The result: East Asia's thirst for gold from East Africa.) At the same time, merchant guilds in northwestern Shanxi developed the first letters of exchange, called "flying cash." These letters linked northern traders with their colleagues in the south. Before long,

→ *What transformations in communication, education, and commerce promoted a distinct Chinese identity during this era?*

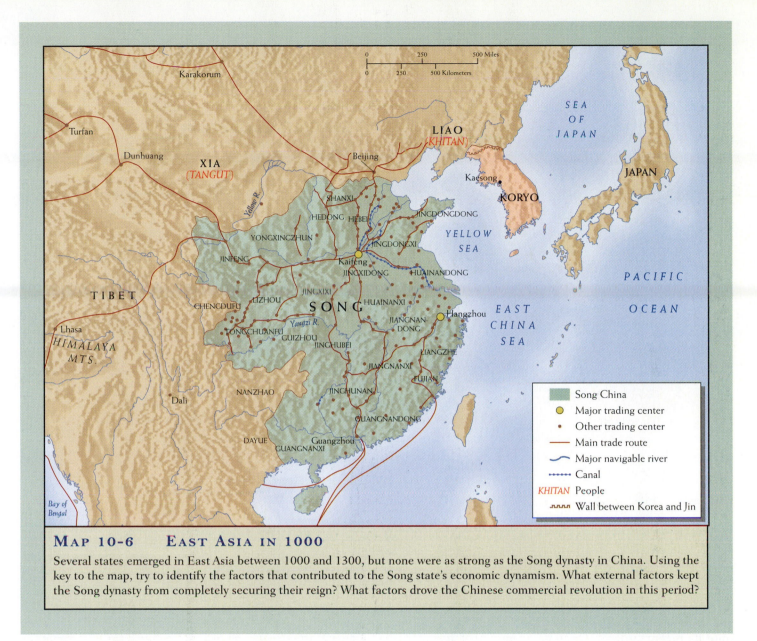

MAP 10-6   EAST ASIA IN 1000

Several states emerged in East Asia between 1000 and 1300, but none were as strong as the Song dynasty in China. Using the key to the map, try to identify the factors that contributed to the Song state's economic dynamism. What external factors kept the Song dynasty from completely securing their reign? What factors drove the Chinese commercial revolution in this period?

printed money had eclipsed coins. Even the government collected more than half its tax revenues in cash rather than grain and cloth. The government also issued more notes to pay its bills—a practice that ultimately contributed to the world's first case of runaway inflation.

NEW ELITES

Song emperors ushered in a period of social and cultural vitality. They established a central bureaucracy of scholar-officials chosen through competitive civil service examinations. Zhao Kuangyin, or Emperor Taizu (r. 960–976 CE), himself administered the final test for all who had passed the highest-level palace examination. In subsequent dynasties, the emperor was the nation's premier examiner, symbolically demanding oaths of allegiance from successful candidates. By 1100 these ranks of learned men had accumulated sufficient power to become China's new ruling elite.

The introduction of the civil service examination system was crucial to a dramatic shift in power from a hereditary aristocracy to a less wealthy but more highly schooled class of scholar officials. Consider the career of the infamous Northern Song reformer Wang Anshi (1021–1086), who ascended to power from a commoner family outside of Hangzhou in the south. He owed his rise to power to success

MAP 10-7   EAST ASIA IN 1200

The Song dynasty regularly dealt with "barbarian" neighbors. What were the major "barbarian" tribes during this period? Approximately what percentage of Song China was lost to the Jin in 1126? How did the "barbarian" tribes affect the Han Chinese identity in this period?

in Song state examinations—a not insignificant achievement, for in nearby Fujian province alone, of the roughly 18,000 candidates who gathered triennially to take the provincial examination, over 90 percent failed! After gaining the emperor's ear, Wang eventually challenged the political and cultural influence of the old Tang dynasty elites from the northwest.

NEGOTIATING WITH NEIGHBORS

As the Song flourished, nomads on the outskirts eyed the Chinese successes closely. To the north, Khitan, Tungusic, Tangut, and Jurchen nomadic societies formed their own dynasties and adopted Chinese techniques. Located within the "greater China" established by the Han and Tang dynasties,

Wang Anshi. He owed his rise from a commoner family to a powerful position as a reformer to the Song state examinations.

these non-Chinese nomads saw China proper as an object of conquest.

In military power the Song dynasts were relatively weak: despite their sophisticated weapons, they could not match their steppe foes when the latter united against them. Yes, steel tips improved the arrows that their soldiers shot from their crossbows, and flame throwers and "crouching tiger catapults" sent incendiary bombs streaking into their enemies' ranks; none of these breakthroughs was secret. Warrior neighbors on the steppe mastered the new arts of war more fully than did the Song dynasts themselves.

China's strength as a manufacturing powerhouse made economic diplomacy an option, so the Song relied on "gifts" and generous trade agreements with the borderlanders. For example, after losing militarily to the Khitan Liao dynasty, the Song agreed to make annual payments of 100,000 ounces of silver and 200,000 bolts of silk. The treaty allowed them to live in relative peace for more than a century. Securing peace meant emptying the state coffers and then printing more paper money. The resulting inflation added economic instability to military weakness, making the Song an easy target when Jurchen invaders made their final assault.

WHAT WAS CHINA?

Paradoxically, the increasing exchange between outsiders and insiders within China hardened the lines that divided them and gave residents of China's interior a highly developed sense of themselves as a distinctive people possessing a superior culture. Exchanges with outsiders nurtured a "Chinese" identity among those who considered themselves true insiders and referred to themselves as Han. Improvements in communications and education further intensified this Han sense that they were the authentic Chinese, and that outsiders were radically different. Driven from their ancient homeland in the eleventh century, they grew increasingly suspicious and resentful toward the outsiders living in their midst. They called these outsiders "barbarians" and treated them accordingly.

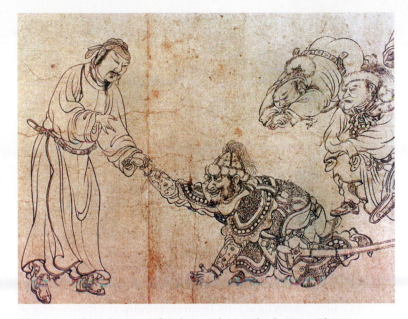

Chinese and Barbarian. After losing the north, the Han Chinese grew resentful of outsiders. They drew a dividing line between their own agrarian society and the nomadic warriors, calling them "barbarians." Such identities were not fixed, however. Chinese and so-called barbarians were mutually dependent.

Vital in crystallizing this sense of a distinct Chinese identity was print culture. In fact, of all Afro-Eurasian societies in 1300, the Chinese were the most advanced in their use of printing and book publishing and circulation. The Song government used its plentiful supply of paper to print books, especially medical texts, and to distribute calendars. The private publishing industry also expanded. Printing houses throughout the country produced Confucian classics, works on history, philosophical treatises, and literature—all of which figured in the civil examinations. Buddhist publications, too, were available everywhere. The dramatic expansion of the print culture was further emblematic of this great period of stability and splendor in China.

CHINA'S NEIGHBORS ADAPT TO CHANGE

→ *How were Southeast Asia, Japan, and Korea influenced by sustained contact with other regions?*

Feeling the pull of Chinese economic and political gravity, cultures around China's rim consolidated internal political authority to resist being swallowed up, while increasing their commercial transactions.

THE RISE OF WARRIORS IN JAPAN

In Japan, rulers sought to create a stable regime out of feuding warrior factions, so they combined the Heian court's imperial authority with the military power of provincial warriors. At first, entrenched court nobles in the new capital of Heian (today's Kyoto) dominated Japan (see Map 10-7); later, rough-and-ready warriors won possession of the throne to "protect" its sanctity as an object of popular veneration.

The most influential of these ruling groups was the Fujiwara family, ancestors of the Nakatomi kinship group (see Chapter 9). During the tenth and eleventh centuries the Fujiwara presided over Japanese society in what is known as the Heian period (794–1185). They exchanged poetry written in classical Chinese and their native language, and dressed in the elegant costumes that have influenced Japanese taste up to this day.

In time, however, power shifted to elites in the provinces. In a new hierarchy of land tenures, peasant cultivators were at the bottom, managers and estate officials in the middle, and absentee patrons at the top. Soon these large estates controlled more than half of Japan's rice land, and the state's revenue and power plummeted. In the midst of such privatization, Heian aristocrats became politically weak but culturally influential—while the hinterlands provided their economic wealth.

Heian aristocrats disdained the military and even abolished the conscription system used to raise imperial armies. In the provinces, however, trained warriors affiliated with kinship groups gathered strength. Protected by lightweight leather armor, these expert horsemen defended their private estates with remarkable long-range bowmanship and superbly crafted, single-edged long steel swords for close combat. Formidable in warfare, they formed local warrior organizations in the outlying regions and prepared the way for the rise of a warrior or samurai society.

Japan now smoldered with multiple sources of political and cultural power: an endangered aristocracy, an imperial family, and local samurai warriors. It was a combustible mix of refined high culture in the capital versus uncouth warriors in the provinces. Such a mix generated social intrigue in marriage politics and political double-dealing in the capital. Lady Murasaki Shikibu (c. 976–c. 1031), writing in native Japanese script, captured this world of elegant lives and sordid affairs of courtiers and their women in *The Tale of Genji*, Japan's—and possibly the world's—first novel. (See Primary Source: *The Tale of Genji*.)

SOUTHEAST ASIA: A MARITIME MOSAIC

Southeast Asia, like India, now became a crossroads of Afro-Eurasian influences. Its sparse population (probably around 10 million in 1000 CE—tiny compared with that of China and India) was not immune, however, to the foreign influences riding the sea-lanes into the archipelago. Indeed, the Malay Peninsula became home to many trading ports and stopovers for traders shuttling between India and China, because it connected the Bay of Bengal and the Indian Ocean with the South China Sea (see Map 10-8).

"INDO-CHINESE" INFLUENCES   Indian influence had been prominent both on the Asian mainland and in island portions of Southeast Asia since 800 CE, but Islamic expansion into the islands after 1200 gradually superseded these influences. Only Bali and a few other islands far to the east of Malaya preserved their Vedic religious origins. Elsewhere in Java and Sumatra, Islam became the dominant religion. In Vietnam and northern portions of mainland Southeast Asia, Chinese cultural influences and northern schools of Mahayana Buddhism were especially prominent.

Heiji Rebellion. This illustration from the Kamakura period depicts a battle during the Heiji Rebellion, which was fought between rival subjects of the cloistered emperor Go-Shirakawa in 1159. Riding in full armor on horseback, the fighters on both sides are armed with devastating long bows.

Primary Source

THE TALE OF GENJI

Lacking a written language of their own, Heian aristocrats adopted classical Chinese as the official written language while continuing to speak Japanese. Men at the court took great pains to master the Chinese literary forms, but Japanese court ladies were not expected to do so. Lady Murasaki Shikibu, the author of The Tale of Genji, *hid her knowledge of Chinese, fearing that she would be criticized. In the meantime, the Japanese developed a native syllabary (a table of syllables) based on Chinese written graphs. Using this syllabary, Murasaki kept a diary in Japanese that gave vivid accounts of Heian court life. Her story—possibly the world's first novel—relates the adventures of a dashing young courtier named Genji. In the passage below, Genji evidently speaks for Murasaki in explaining why fiction can be as truthful as a work of history in capturing human life and its historical significance.*

Genji . . . smiled, and went on: "But I have a theory of my own about what this art of the novel is, and how it came into being. To begin with, it does not simply consist in the author's telling a story about the adventures of some other person. On the contrary, it happens because the storyteller's own experience of men and things, whether for good or ill— not only what he has passed through himself, but even events which he has only witnessed or been told of—has moved him to an emotion so passionate that he can no longer keep it shut up in his heart. Again and again something in his own life or in that around him will seem to the writer so important that he cannot bear to let it pass into oblivion. There must never come a time, he feels, when men do not know about it. That is my view of how this art arose.

"Clearly then, it is no part of the storyteller's craft to describe only what is good or beautiful. Sometimes, of course, virtue will be his theme, and he may then make such play with it as he will. But he is just as likely to have been struck by numerous examples of vice and folly in the world around him, and about them he has exactly the same feelings as about the pre-eminently good deeds which he encounters: they are more important and must all be garnered in. Thus anything whatsoever may become the subject of a novel, provided only that it happens in this mundane life and not in some fairyland beyond our human ken.

"The outward forms of this art will not of course be everywhere the same. At the court of China and in other foreign lands both the genius of the writers and their actual methods of composition are necessarily very different from ours; and even here in Japan the art of storytelling has in course of time undergone great changes. There will, too, always be a distinction between the lighter and the more serious forms of fiction. . . . So too, I think, may it be said that the art of fiction must not lose our allegiance because, in the pursuit of the main purpose to which I have alluded above, it sets virtue by the side of vice, or mingles wisdom with folly. Viewed in this light the novel is seen to be not, as is usually supposed, a mixture of useful truth with idle invention, but something which at every stage and in every part has a definite and serious purpose."

→ *According to this passage, what motivates an author to write a story (i.e., fiction)?*

→ *Genji feels it is appropriate for a writer to address not only "what is good or beautiful" but also "vice and folly." What explanation does he give? Do you agree?*

SOURCE: *Sources of Japanese Tradition,* compiled by Ryūsaku Tsunoda, Wm. Theodore de Bary, and Donald Keene (New York: Columbia University Press, 1964), vol. 1, pp. 177–79.

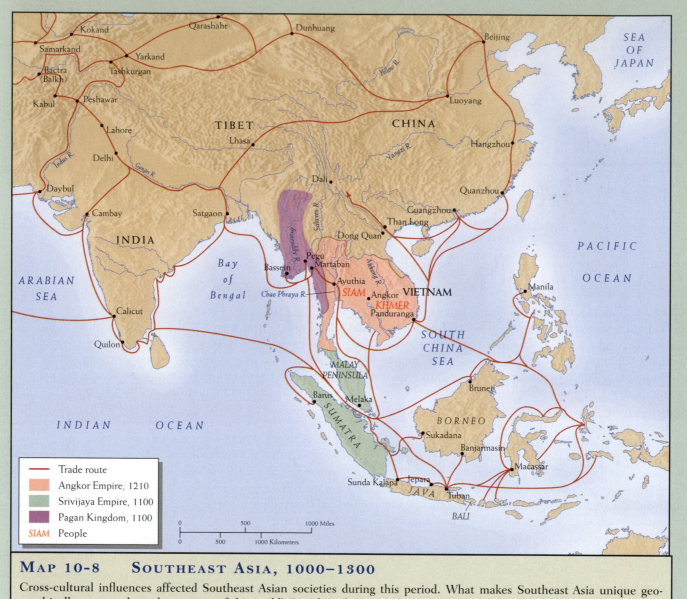

MAP 10-8   SOUTHEAST ASIA, 1000–1300

Cross-cultural influences affected Southeast Asian societies during this period. What makes Southeast Asia unique geographically compared to other regions of the world? Based on the map, why were the kingdoms of Southeast Asia exposed to so many cross-cultural influences? In this chapter, the term "mosaic" describes both South and Southeast Asia. Compare Map 10-5 with this map, and explain how the mosaic of Southeast Asia differed from the mosaic of India.

MAINLAND BUFFER KINGDOMS During this period Cambodian, Burmese, and Thai peoples founded powerful mixed polities along the Mekong, Salween, Chao Phraya, and Irriwaddy river basins of the Asian mainland. Important Vedic and Buddhist kingdoms emerged here as political buffers between the strong states in China and India and brought stability and further commercial prosperity to the region.

Consider the kingdom that ruled Angkor in present-day Cambodia. With their capital in Angkor, the Khmers (889–

1431) created the most powerful and wealthy empire in Southeast Asia. Countless water reservoirs enabled them to flourish on the great plain to the west of the Mekong River after the loss of eastern territories. Public works and magnificent temples dedicated to the revived Vedic gods from India went hand in hand with the earlier influence of Indian Buddhism. Eventually the Khmer kings united adjacent kingdoms and extended Khmer influence to the Thai and Burmese states along the Chaophraya and Irriwaddy rivers.

Angkor Wat. Mistaken by later European explorers as a remnant of Alexander the Great's conquests, the enormous temple complexes built by the Khmer people in Angkor borrowed their intricate layout and stupa (a moundlike structure containing religious relics) architecture from the Brahmanist Indian temples of the time. As the capital, Angkor was a microcosm of the world for the Khmer, who aspired to represent the macrocosm of the universe in the magnificence of Angkor's buildings and their geometric layout.

One of the greatest temple complexes in Angkor exemplified the Khmers' heavy borrowing from Vedic Indian architecture. Angkor aspired to represent the universe in the magnificence of its buildings. As signs of the ruler's power, the pagodas, pyramids, and terra-cotta friezes (ornamented walls) presented the life of the gods on earth. The crowning structure of the royal palace was the magnificent temple of **Angkor Wat,** possibly the largest religious structure ever built. In ornate detail and with great artistry, its buildings and statues represented the revival of the Hindu pantheon within the Khmer royal state. Far less Buddhist influence is visible.

CHRISTIAN EUROPE

> → *How did Christianity produce a distinct identity among the diverse peoples of Europe?*

In the far western corner of Afro-Eurasia, people were building a culture revealingly different. Although their numbers were small compared with the rest of Afro-Eurasia in 1000 CE (36 million in Europe, compared to 80 million in India and 120 million in China), their population would soar to 80 million before the arrival of the Black Death in the fourteenth century.

This was a region of contrasts. On the one hand, the period 1000–1300 witnessed an intense localization of politics because there was no successor to the Roman Empire or Charlemagne's (see Chapter 9). On the other hand, the territory united under a shared sense of its place in the world. Indeed, some inhabitants even began to believe in the existence of something called "Europe" and increasingly referred to themselves as "Europeans" (see Map 10-9).

WESTERN AND NORTHERN EUROPE

The collapse of Charlemagne's empire had exposed much of northern Europe to invasion, principally from the Vikings, and left the peasantry with no central authority to protect them from local warlords. Armed with deadly weapons, these strongmen collected taxes, imposed forced labor, and became the unchallenged rulers of society. Within this growing warrior aristocracy, northern France led the way. The Franks (later called Frenchmen) were the trendsetters of eleventh- and twelfth-century western Europe.

The most important change was the peasantry's subjugation to the knightly class. Previously, well-to-do peasants had carried arms as "free" men. The moment the farmers lost the right to carry arms, they were no longer free. They slipped back to being mere agricultural laborers. Each peasant toiled under the authority of a lord, who controlled every detail of his or her life. This was the basis of a system known as **feudalism.**

Assured of control of the peasantry, feudal lords watched over an agrarian breakthrough—which fueled a commercial transformation that drew Europe into the rest of the global trading networks. Lordly protection and more advanced metal tools like axes and plows, combined with heavier livestock to pull plows through the root-infested sods of northern

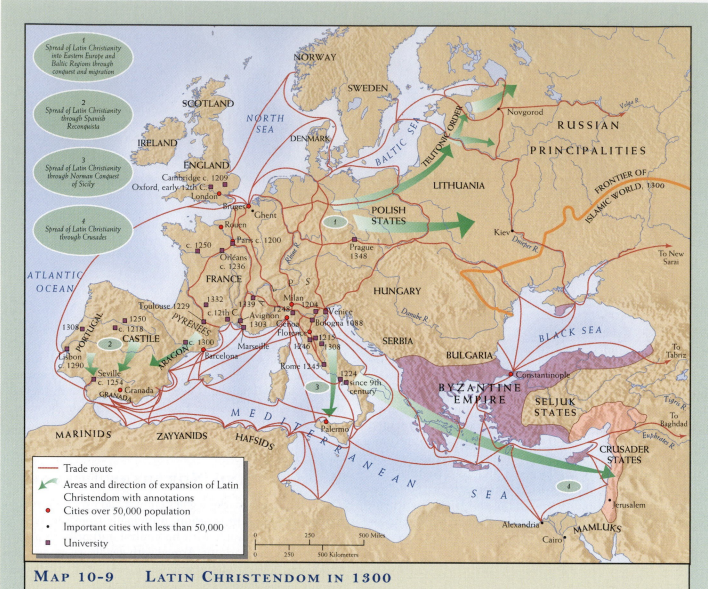

MAP 10-9   LATIN CHRISTENDOM IN 1300

Catholic Europe expanded geographically and integrated culturally during this era. According to this map, into what areas did western Christendom successfully expand? What factors contributed to the growth of a widespread common culture and shared ideas? How did long-distance trade shape the history of the region during this time?

Europe, led to massive deforestation. Above this clearing activity stood the castle. Its threatening presence ensured that the peasantry stayed within range of the collector of rents for the lords and of tithes (shares of crops, earmarked as "donations") for the church. In this blunt way, "feudalism" harnessed agrarian energy to its own needs. The population of western Europe as a whole leaped forward, most spectacularly in the north. As a result, northern Europe (from England to Poland) ceased to be an underdeveloped "barbarian" appendage of the Mediterranean.

EASTERN EUROPE

Nowhere did pioneering peasants develop more land than in the wide-open spaces of eastern Europe, the region's land of opportunity. Between 1100 and 1200, some 200,000 farmers emigrated from Flanders (modern Belgium), Holland, and northern Germany into eastern frontiers. Well-watered landscapes, covered with vast forests, filled up what are now Poland, the Czech Republic, Hungary, and the Baltic states. "Little Europes," whose castles, churches, and towns echoed

The Bayeux Tapestry. This tapestry was prepared by a queen and her ladies to celebrate the victories of William, known as the Conqueror because of his successful invasion of England in 1066. It shows the fascination of the entire "feudal" class, even women, with war on which they depended—great horses, tightly meshed chain mail, long shields, and the stirrups that made such cavalry warfare possible.

the landscape of France, now replaced economies that had been based on gathering honey, hunting, and the slave trade. For a thousand miles along the Baltic Sea, forest clearings dotted with new farmsteads and small towns edged inward from the coast up the river valleys.

The social structure here was a marriage of convenience between migrating peasants and local elites. The area offered the promise of freedom from the feudal lords' arbitrary justice and imposition of forced labor. Even the harsh landscape of the eastern Baltic (where the sea froze every year and impenetrable forests blocked settlers from the coast) was preferable to life in the feudal west. For their part, the elites of eastern Europe—the nobility of Poland, Bohemia, and Hungary and the princes of the Baltic—wished to live well, in the "French"

Olavinilinna Castle. This castle in Finland was the easternmost extension of a "western," feudal style of rule through great castles. It was built at the very end of the Baltic, to keep away the Russians of Novgorod.

style. But they could do so only if they attracted manpower to their lands by offering newcomers a liberty that they had no hope of enjoying in the west.

THE RUSSIAN LANDS

In Russian lands, western settlers and knights met an eastern brand of Christian devotion. This world looked toward Byzantium, not Rome. Russia was a giant borderland between the steppes of Eurasia and the booming feudalisms of Europe. Its cities lay at the crossroads of overland trade and migration, and Kiev became one of the region's greatest cities. Standing on a bluff above the Dnieper River, it straddled newly opened trade routes. With a population exceeding 20,000, including merchants from eastern and western Europe and the Middle East, Kiev was larger than Paris—larger even than the much-diminished city of Rome.

Kiev looked south to the Black Sea and to Constantinople. Under Iaroslav the Wise (1016–1054), it became a small-scale Constantinople on the Dnieper. A stone church called St. Sophia stood (as in Constantinople) beside the imperial palace. Indeed, with its distinctive "Byzantine" domes, it was a miniature Hagia Sophia (see Chapter 8). Its highest dome towered a hundred feet above the floor, and its splendid mosaics depicting Byzantine saints echoed the religious art of Constantinople. But the message was political as well, for the ruler of Kiev was cast in the mold of the emperor of Constantinople. He now took the title *tsar* from the ancient Roman name given to the emperor, Caesar. From this time onward, *tsar* was the title of rulers in Russia.

The Russian form of Christianity replicated the Byzantine style of churches all along the great rivers leading to the trading cities of the north and northeast. These were not agrarian centers, but hubs of expanding long-distance trade.

Hagia Sophia, Novgorod.
The cathedral of Novgorod (as that of Kiev) was called Hagia Sophia. It was a deliberate imitation of the Hagia Sophia of Constantinople, showing Russia's roots in a glorious Roman/Byzantine past that had nothing to do with western Europe.

(See Primary Source: The Birch Bark Letters of Novgorod.) Each city became a small-scale Kiev, and thus a smaller-scale echo of Constantinople. The Orthodox religion looked to Byzantium's Hagia Sophia rather than the Catholic faith associated with the popes in Rome. Russian Christianity remained the Christianity of a borderland—vivid oases of high culture set against the backdrop of vast forests and widely scattered settlements.

WHAT WAS CHRISTIAN EUROPE?

In this era Catholicism became a universalizing faith that transformed the region becoming known as "Europe." The Christianity of post-Roman Europe had been a religion of monks, and its most dynamic centers were great monasteries. Members of the laity were expected to revere and support their monks, nuns, and clergy, but not to imitate them. By 1200, all this had changed. The internal colonization of western Europe—the clearing of woods and founding of villages—ensured that parish churches arose in all but the wildest landscapes. Their spires were visible and their bells were audible from one valley to the next. Church graveyards were the only places where good Christians could be buried; criminals' and outlaws' bodies piled up in "heathen" graves outside the cemetery walls. Even the bones of the believers helped make Europe Christian.

Now the clergy reached more deeply into the private lives of the laity. Marriage and divorce, previously considered family matters, became a full-time preoccupation of the church. And sin was no longer an offense that just "happened"; it was a matter that every person could do something about. Soon, regular confession to a priest became obligatory for all Catholic, western Christians. The followers of Francis of Assisi (1182–1226) emerged as an order of preachers who brought a message of repentance. They did not tell their audiences to enter the monastery (as would have been the case in the early Middle Ages). Instead, their listeners were to weep, confess their sins to local priests, and strive to be better Christians. Franciscans instilled in the hearts of all believers a Europe-wide Catholicism based on daily remorse and daily contemplation of the sufferings of Christ and his mother, Mary. From Ireland to Riga and Budapest, Catholic Christians came to share a common piety.

UNIVERSITIES AND INTELLECTUALS Vital to the creation of Europe's Christian identity was the emergence of universities, for it was during this era that Europe acquired its first class of intellectuals. Since the late twelfth century, scholars had gathered in Paris, where they formed a *universitas*—a term borrowed from merchant communities, where it denoted a type of union. Those who belonged to the *universitas* enjoyed protection by their fellows and freedom to continue their trade. Similarly protected by their own "union," the scholars of Paris began wrestling with the new learning from Arab lands. When the bishop of Paris forbade this undertaking, they simply moved to the Left Bank of the Seine, so as to place the river between themselves and the bishop's officials, who lived around the cathedral of Notre Dame.

The scholars' ability to organize themselves gave them an advantage that their Arab contemporaries lacked. For all his

Primary Source

THE BIRCH BARK LETTERS OF NOVGOROD

The city of Novgorod was a vibrant trading center with a diverse population. From 1951 onward, Russian archaeologists in Novgorod have excavated almost a thousand letters and accounts scratched on birch bark and preserved in the sodden, frequently frozen ground. Reading them, we realize how timeless people's basic concerns can be.

First, we meet the merchants. Many letters are notes by creditors of the debts owed to them by trading partners. The sums are often expressed in precious animal furs. They contain advice to relatives or to partners in other cities:

> Giorgii sends his respects to his father and mother: Sell the house and come here to Smolensk or to Kiev: for the bread is cheap there.

Then we meet neighborhood disputes:

> From Anna to Klemiata: Help me, my lord brother, in my matter with Konstantin. . . . [For I asked him,] "Why have you been so angry with my sister and her daughter. You called her a cow and her daughter a whore. And now Fedor has thrown them both out of the house."

There are even glimpses of real love. A secret marriage is planned:

> Mikiti to Ulianitza: Come to me. I love you, and you me. Ignato will act as witness.

And a poignant note from a woman was discovered in 1993:

> I have written to you three times. What is it that you hold against me, that you did not come to see me this Sunday? I regarded you as I would my own brother. Did I really offend you by that which I sent to you? If you had been pleased you would have torn yourself away from company and come to me. Write to me. If in my clumsiness I have offended you and you should spurn me, then let God be my judge. I love you.

→ *What does the range of people writing on birch bark tell us about these people?*

→ *Think of the messages you send to friends and relatives today. Even if texting and e-mailing seem centuries distant from writing on birch bark, can you relate in any way to these ancient letter-writers?*

SOURCE: A. V. Artsikhovskii and V. I. Borkovski, *Novgorodskie Gramoty na Bereste*, 11 vols. (Moscow: Izd-vo Akademii nauk SSSR, 1951–2004), document nos. 424, 531, 377, and 752.

---

genius, Ibn Rushd had to spend his life courting the favor of individual monarchs to protect him from conservative fellow Muslims, who frequently burned his books. Ironically, European scholars congregating in Paris could quietly absorb the most persuasive elements of Arabic thought, like Ibn Rushd's. Yet they endeavored to prove that Christianity was the only religion that fully met the aspirations of all rational human beings. Such was the message of the great intellectual Thomas Aquinas, who wrote *Summa contra Gentiles* (Summary of Christian Belief against Non-Christians) in 1264.

The Europe of 1300 was more culturally unified than in previous centuries. It was permeated by Catholicism, and its leading intellectuals extolled the virtues of Christian learning. Such a confident region was not, however, a tolerant place for heretics, Jews, or Muslims.

CHRISTIAN EUROPE ON THE MOVE: THE CRUSADES AND IBERIA

By the tenth and eleventh centuries, western Christianity was on the move, spreading into Scandinavia, southern Italy, the Baltic, and eastern Europe. Its ambitions to reconquer Spain and Portugal (which had been under Islamic control since the eighth century CE) demonstrated one of the effects of feudal power: the lords' self-confidence, their belief in their military capability, and their pious sense of destiny were all inflated. Besides, the wealth of the east was irresistible to those whose piety entwined with an appetite for plunder. Yet the two Christendoms formed an uneasy alliance to roll back the expanding frontiers of Islam. The result: Europeans zealously took war outside their own borders.

Global Connections & Disconnections

THE CRUSADES FROM DUAL PERSPECTIVES

In 1095, Pope Urban II called for the First Crusade in the following words:

> Oh, race of Franks, race from across the mountains, race chosen and beloved by God, as shines forth in very many of your works, set apart from all nations by the situation of your country, as well as by your Catholic faith and the honor of the Holy Church! To you our discourse is addressed, and for you our exhortation is intended. We wish you to know what a grievous cause has led us to your country, what peril, threatening you and all the faithful, has brought us.

The "grievous cause" was the occupation of the Holy City of Jerusalem by the Islamic empire. Formed within the complex relationship between the Byzantine Empire and the western Christian papacy and kingdoms of Europe, the religious motivation behind the Crusades became the subject of many literary renditions of the tumultuous events. It also generated emotionally stirring and polemical (argumentative) writing, depicting either a Muslim or Christian enemy (depending on the work's author).

Polemics are often passionate, harsh, and emotional. They also inspire and reinforce the conviction of fellow believers, with little concern for accuracy. Thus authors of polemic in the time of the Crusades were usually too biased or too misinformed to present accurate portraits of their enemies. But occasionally, firsthand accounts in the form of chronicles and histories offer us unique glimpses into Christian-Muslim relations in the age of the Crusades.

Consider Usāmah ibn Munqidh (1095–1188), the learned ruler of the city of Shaizar in western Syria. Skirmishes, truces, and the ransoming of prisoners were part of his daily life, and Usāmah socialized with his Frankish neighbors as much as he fought with them. He offers a dismissive opinion of his enemies. Basically, they struck him as "animals possessing the virtues of courage and fighting, but nothing else." In particular, their medical practice appalled him. More strange, the Franks allowed their wives to walk about freely and to talk to strangers unaccompanied by male guardians. How could men be at once so brave and yet so lacking in a proper, Arab sense of honor, which would lead a man to protect his women? Unlike other Muslim authors of his time, however, Usāmah does not refer to the Franks in derogatory terms such as "infidels" or "devils." In fact, he occasionally refers to some of them as his companions and writes of a Frank who called him "my brother" (*An Arab-Syrian Gentleman and Warrior in the Time of the Crusades,* 16).

CRUSADES In the late eleventh century, western Europeans launched a wave of attacks known as the **Crusades.** The First Crusade began in 1095, when Pope Urban II appealed to the warrior nobility of France to put their violence to good use: they should combine their role as pilgrims to Jerusalem with that of soldiers, and free Jerusalem from Muslim rule. What the clergy proposed was a novel kind of war. Whereas previously war had been a dirty business and a source of sin, now the clergy told the knights that good and just wars were possible. Such wars could cancel out the sins of those who waged them.

Starting in 1097, an armed host of around 60,000, men moved all the way from northwestern Europe to Jerusalem. This was a huge crowd. But it was divided. Knights in heavy armor led, as they did in Europe. But in the eastern Mediterranean they depended on poor masses who joined the movement to help besiege cities and construct a network of castles as the Christian knights drove their frontier forward. Later Crusaders brought their wives, especially those from the upper class. As in many colonial societies away from the homeland, these women felt freer. Eleanor of Aquitaine, for example, led her own army. Also, queens were crucial in opening up to the local populations. Consider the Armenian queen, Melisende (r. 1131–1152): regarded as wise and experienced in affairs of the state, she was popular with local Christians. As a result, the society of the Crusader states remained more open to women and the lower classes than in Europe. Above all, the Crusades could not have happened without the sailors and merchants of Italy. It was the fleets of Venice, Genoa, and Pisa that transported the later Crusaders and supplied their kingdom.

Christian authors had similar interests in documenting the customs of their enemies in battle. Jean de Joinville (1224/1225–1317) was a chronicler of medieval France. During one crusade, while in the service of the king, Joinville had occasion to note the Muslims' social behavior:

> Whenever the Sultan was in the camp, the men of the personal Guard were quartered all round his lodging, and appointed to guard his person. At the door of the Sultan's lodging there was a little tent for the Sultan's door-keepers, and for his musicians, who had Arabian horns and drums and kettledrums; and they used to make such a din at daybreak and at nightfall that people near them could not hear one another speak, and that they could be heard plainly all through the camp. The musicians never dared sound their instruments in the daytime unless by the order of the Chief of the Guard. Thus it was, that whenever the Sultan had a proclamation to make he used to send for the Chief of the Guard, and give him the order; and then the Chief would cause all the Sultan's instruments to be sounded; and thereupon all the host would come to hear the Sultan's commands.

Although scholars regard such literary renditions with caution, they are useful for gleaning personal details that other types of works omit. The colorful accounts by authors such as Usāmah ibn Munqidh and Joinville are invaluable resources for the social history of the Crusaders.

Jeane de Joinville. Joinville dictating his Memoir of St. Louis, in which he described the Seventh Crusade.

There were five Crusades in all, spread out over two centuries. None of the coalitions, in the end, created permanent Christian kingdoms in the lands they "reconquered." Only a small proportion of Crusaders remained in southwest Asia, and those who did met their match in Muslim armies. (See Global Connections & Disconnections: The Crusades from Dual Perspectives.) Part of the problem was that few Crusaders had any intention of becoming colonists. Only a small proportion remained to defend the Kingdom of Jerusalem after the First Crusade. Most knights returned home, their epic pilgrimage completed. The remaining fragile network of Crusader lordships could barely threaten the Islamic heartlands.

Muslim leaders, however, did not see the Frankish knights as a threat. For them, the Crusades were irrelevant. And as far as the average Muslim of the region was concerned, the Cru-saders hardly mattered at all. Jerusalem and Palestine had always been fringe areas in the Middle East. Real prosperity and the capital cities of Muslim kingdoms lay inland, away from the coast—at Cairo, Damascus, and Baghdad. The assaults' long-term effect was to harden Muslim feelings against the Franks and the millions of non-Western Christians who had previously lived peacefully in Egypt and Syria. Muslims viewed the Crusaders as brave but uncivilized warriors. A neighboring Muslim wrote: "The Franks possess none of the virtues of men except courage. . . . Nobody counts for them except knights." Their lack of medical knowledge shocked this observer. He noted that they would rather chop off a man's leg than administer ointments, as Muslim doctors would have advised.

Other campaigns of Christian expansion were more successful. Consider the Spanish driving the Muslims out of the

Crusader. Kneeling, this Crusader promises to serve God (as he would serve a feudal lord) by going to fight on a Crusade (as he would fight for any lord to whom he had sworn loyalty). The two kinds of loyalty—to God and to one's lord—were deliberately confused in Crusader ideology. Both were about war. But fighting for God was unambiguously good, while fighting for a lord was not always so clear-cut.

Iberian Peninsula. Beginning with the capture of Toledo in 1061, the Christian kings of northern Spain (who could count on support from Christian neighbors across the Pyrenees) slowly pushed back the Muslims. Eventually they reached the heart of Andalusia and conquered Seville, adding more than 100,000 square miles of territory to Christian Europe. Another force from northern France crossed Italy to conquer Muslim-held Sicily, ensuring Christian rule in the strategically located mid-Mediterranean island. These two conquests—not the Crusaders' fragile foothold at the edge of the Middle East—turned the tide in relations between Christian and Muslim power.

THE AMERICAS

> → *Where did societies in the Americas demonstrate strong commercial expansionist impulses?*

During this period, the Americas were untouched by the connections reverberating across Afro-Eurasia. After all, navigators still could not cross the large oceans that separated the Americas from other lands. Yet, here, too, commercial and expansionist impulses fostered closer contact among peoples who lived there.

ANDEAN STATES

Growth and prosperity in the Andean region gave rise to South America's first empire. Known as the Chimú Empire, it developed early in the second millennium in the fertile Moche Valley bordering the Pacific Ocean (see Map 10-10). Ultimately the Moche people expanded their influence across numerous valleys and ecological zones, from pastoral highlands to rich valley floodplains to the fecund fishing grounds of the Pacific Coast. As their geographical reach grew, so did their wealth. The Chimú regime lasted until Incan armies invaded in the 1460s and incorporated the Pacific state into their own immense empire.

A THRIVING LOWLAND ECONOMY The Chimú economy was successful because it was highly commercialized. Agriculture was its base, and complex irrigation systems turned the arid coast into a string of fertile oases capable of feeding an increasingly dispersed population. Cotton became a lucrative export to distant markets along the Andes. Parades of llamas and porters lugged these commodities up and down the steep mountain chains that are the spine of South America. As in China, a well-trained bureaucracy oversaw the construction and maintenance of canals, with a hierarchy of provincial administrators watching over commercial hinterlands.

Between 850 and 900 CE, the Moche peoples founded their biggest city, Chan Chan, with a core population of 30,000 inhabitants. A sprawling walled metropolis, covering nearly ten square miles with extensive roads circulating through neighborhoods, it boasted ten huge palaces at its center. Protected by thick walls thirty feet high, these opulent residence halls bespoke the rulers' power. Within the compound, emperors erected mortuary monuments for storing their accumulated riches: fine cloth, gold and silver objects, splendid *Spondylus* shells, and other luxury goods. Around the compound spread neighborhoods for nobles and artisans; farther out stood rows of commoners' houses.

AN INVENTIVE HIGH-LAND STATE The Andes also saw its first highland empires during this period. On the shores of the plateau lake Titicaca, the people of Tiahuanaco forged a high-altitude state. Though neither as large nor as wealthy as the Chimú Empire, its residents converted the inhospitable highlands into an environment where farmers and herders thrived. There is evidence of long-distance trade with neighbors in semitropical valleys, and even signs of highlanders migrating to the lowlands to produce agrarian staples for their kin in the mountains. Dried fish and cotton came from the coast; fruits and vegetables came from lowland valleys. Trade sustained an enormous urban population of up to 115,000 people. Looming over the skyline of Tiahuanaco was an imposing pyramid of massive sandstone blocks. Its advanced engineering system conveyed water to the summit, from which an imitation rainfall coursed down the carefully carved sides—an awesome spectacle of engineering prowess in such an arid region.

CONNECTIONS TO THE NORTH

Additional hubs of regional trade developed farther north, showing once again that even in areas of relative geographic isolation, cultures could flourish and interact within expanding regional spheres. The Toltecs and the Cahokians are superb examples.

MAP 10-10 ANDEAN STATES

Although the Andes region of South America was isolated from Afro-Eurasian developments before 1500, it was not stagnant. Indeed, political and cultural integration brought the peoples of this region closer together. Where are the areas of the Chimú Empire and Tiahuanaco influence on the map? What kinds of ecological niches did they govern? According to your reading, how did each polity encourage greater cultural and economic integration?

Andean States. The image to the left shows what remains of Chan Chan. The city covered fifteen square miles and was divided into neighborhoods for nobles, artisans, and commoners, with the elites living closest to the hub of governmental and spiritual power. The buildings of Tiahuanaco (below) were made of giant, hand-hewn stones assembled without mortar. Engineers had not discovered the principle of curved arches and keystones and instead relied on massive slabs atop gateways. Gateways were important symbolic features, for they were places where people acknowledged the importance of sun and moon gods.

THE TOLTECS IN MESOAMERICA By 1000 CE, Mesoamerica had seen the rise and fall of several complex societies. Caravans of porters worked the intricate roads that connected the coast of the Gulf of Mexico to the Pacific, and the southern lowlands of Central America to the arid regions of modern Texas (see Map 10-11). The region's heartland was the rich valley of central Mexico. Here the Toltecs filled the political vacuum left by the decline of Teotihuacán (see Chapter 8) and tapped into the commercial network radiating from the valley.

The Toltecs were a combination of migrant groups, refugees from the south, and farmers from the north. They settled northwest of Teotihuacán as the city waned, making their capital at Tula. They relied on a maize-based economy supplemented by beans, squash, and dog, deer, and rabbit meat. Their rulers, however, made sure that enterprising merchants provided them with status goods such as ornamental pottery, rare shells and stones, and precious skins and feathers.

Tula was a commercial hub, a political capital, and a ceremonial center. While its layout differed from Teotihuacán's, many features revealed borrowings from other Mesoamerican peoples. Temples consisted of giant pyramids topped by colossal stone soldiers, and ball courts where subjects and conquered peoples alike played their ritual sport were ubiquitous. The architecture and monumental art bespoke the mixed and migratory origins of the Toltecs: a combination of Mayan and Teotihuacáno influences. At its height, the Toltec capital teemed with 60,000 people—a huge metropolis by contemporary European standards.

THE CAHOKIANS IN NORTH AMERICA Cities took shape at the hubs of trading networks all across North America. The largest was **Cahokia,** along the Mississippi River near modern-day East St. Louis. A city of about 15,000, it approximated the size of London at the time. Farmers and hunters settled in the region around 600 CE, attracted by its rich soil, its woodlands for fuel and game, and its access to the trading artery of the Mississippi. Eventually, fields of maize and other crops fanned out toward the horizon. The hoe replaced the trusty digging stick, and satellite towns erected granaries to hold the increased yields.

Now Cahokia became a commercial center for regional and long-distance trade. The hinterlands produced staples for Cahokia's urban consumers, and in return its crafts rode inland on the backs of porters and to distant markets in canoes. The city's woven fabrics and ceramics were especially desirable. In exchange, traders brought mica from the Appalachian Mountains, seashells and sharks' teeth from the Gulf of Mexico, and copper from the upper Great Lakes. Indeed, Cahokia became more than an importer and exporter:

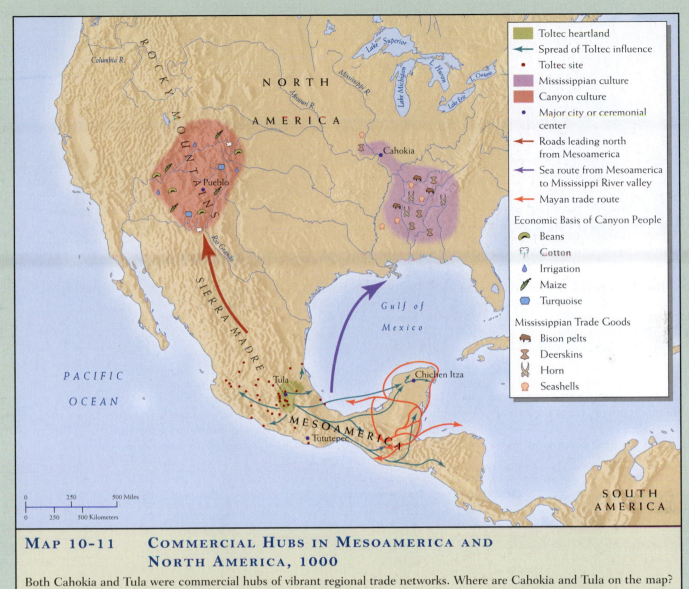

MAP 10-11   COMMERCIAL HUBS IN MESOAMERICA AND NORTH AMERICA, 1000

Both Cahokia and Tula were commercial hubs of vibrant regional trade networks. Where are Cahokia and Tula on the map? According to the map, what kinds of goods circulated through these cities? How much political influence on the surrounding region do you think each city had?

it was the entrepôt for an entire regional network trafficking in salt, tools, pottery, woven stuffs, jewelry, and ceremonial goods.

Dominating Cahokia's urban landscape were enormous mounds (thus the nickname "mound people"). These earthen monuments reveal a sophisticated design and careful maintenance: for example, their builders applied layers of sand and clay to prevent the foundations from drying and cracking. It was from these artificial hills that the people paid homage to spiritual forces. Of course, building this kind of infra-

structure without draft animals, hydraulic tools, or even wheels was labor-intensive, so the Cahokians recruited neighboring people to help. A palisade around the city protected the metropolis from marauders.

Ultimately the city outgrew its environment, and its success bred its downfall. As woodlands fell to the axe and arable soil lost nutrients, timber and food became scarce. Because the city lacked a means of transportation to ship bulky items over long distances (in contrast to the sturdy dhows of the Arabian Sea and the bulky junks of the China Sea), its river

Toltec Temple. Tula, the capital of the Toltec Empire, carried on the Mesoamerican tradition of locating ceremonial architecture at the center of the city. The Pyramid of the Morning Star cast its shadow over all other buildings. And above them stood columns of the Atlantes, carved Toltec god-warriors, the figurative pillars of the empire itself. The walls of this pyramid were likely embellished with images of snakes and skulls. The north face of the pyramid has the image of a snake devouring a human.

canoes could carry only limited cargoes. Thus Cahokia's commercial networks met their limits. When the creeks that fed its water system could not keep up with demand, engineers changed their course, but to no avail. By 1350 the city was practically empty. Nevertheless, Cahokia was a remarkable entrepôt while it lasted. It represented the growing networks of trade and migration, and the ability of North Americans to organize vibrant commercial societies.

Cahokia Mounds. This is all that is left of what was once a large city organized around temple mounds in what today is Illinois. The largest of the temples, known as Monks' Mound, was likely a burial site, with four separate terraces for crowds to gather. Centuries of neglect and erosion have taken their toll on what was once the largest human-made earthen mound in North America.

THE MONGOL TRANSFORMATION OF AFRO-EURASIA

> → *How did Mongol conquests affect cross-cultural contacts and regional development in Afro-Eurasia?*

The world's sea-lanes grew crowded with ships; ports buzzed with activity. Commercial networks were clearly one way to integrate the world. But just as long-distance trade connected people, so could conquerors—as we have seen throughout the history of the world. Now, transformative conquerors came from the Inner Eurasian steppes, the same place that centuries earlier had unleashed horse-riding warriors such as the Xiongnu (see Chapters 6 and 7).

Like the Xiongnu and the Kushans before them, the Mongols not only conquered but intensified trade and cultural exchange. By consolidating a latticework of states across northern and central Asia, they created an empire that straddled east and west (see Map 10-12). It was unstable and not as durable as other dynasties. It did not even have a shared faith; the mother of the conquering emperors, Hulagu and Kubilai Khan, was a devout Christian, reflecting Nestorian missionaries' centuries-long efforts to convert the animistic nomads. Many Europeans prayed that the entire empire would convert. But it did not; the Mongols were a religious patchwork of Afro-Eurasian belief systems. Yet they brought far-flung parts of the world together as they conquered territories much larger than their own.

WHO WERE THE MONGOLS?

The **Mongols** were a combination of forest and prairie peoples. Residing in circular, felt-covered tents, which they shared with some of their animals, they lived by hunting and livestock herding. They changed campgrounds with the seasons. Life on the steppes was such a constant struggle that only the strong survived. Their food, primarily animal products, provided high levels of protein, which built up their muscle mass and their strength. Always on the march, their society resembled a perpetual standing army with bands of well-disciplined military units led by commanders chosen for their skill.

MILITARY SKILLS Mongol archers were uniquely skilled. Wielding heavy compound bows made of sinew, wood, and horns, they were deadly accurate at over 200 yards—even at full gallop. Their small but sturdy horses, capable of withstanding extreme cold, bore saddles with high supports in front and back, enabling the warriors to maneuver at high speeds. With their feet secure in iron stirrups, the archers could rise in their saddles to aim their arrows without stopping. These expert horsemen often remained in the saddle all day and night, even sleeping while their horses continued on. Each warrior kept many horses, replacing tired mounts with fresh ones so that the armies could cover up to seventy miles per day.

Mongol Warriors. This miniature painting is one of the illustrations for *History* by Rashid al Din, the most outstanding scholar under the Mongol regimes. Note the relatively small horses and strong bows used by the Mongol soldiers.

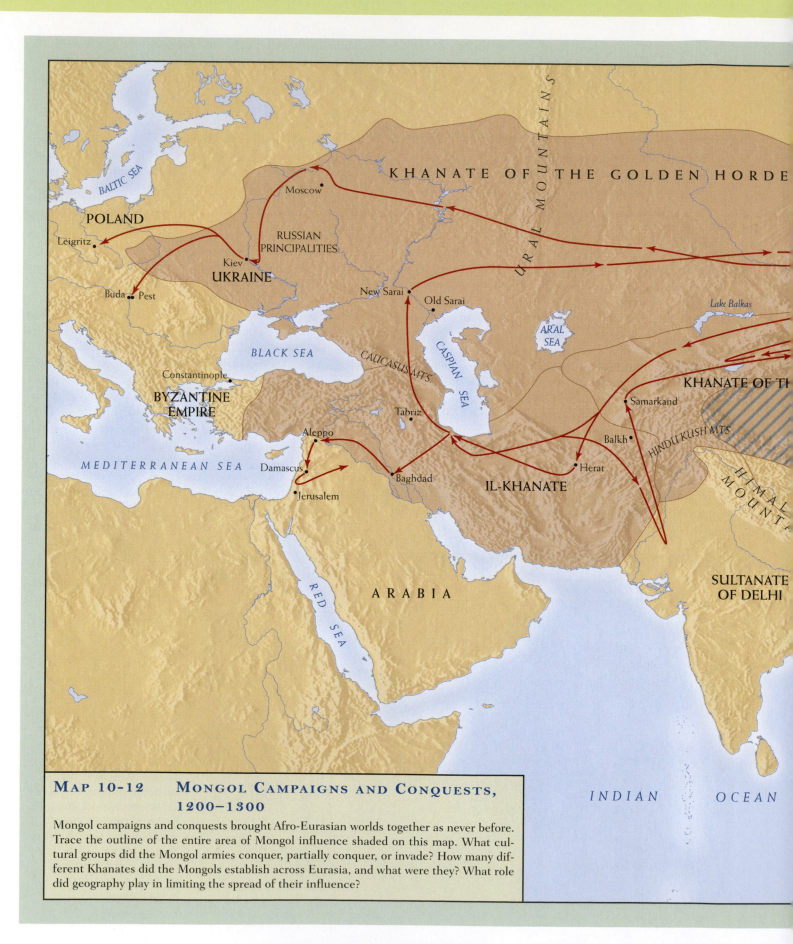

MAP 10-12   MONGOL CAMPAIGNS AND CONQUESTS, 1200–1300

Mongol campaigns and conquests brought Afro-Eurasian worlds together as never before. Trace the outline of the entire area of Mongol influence shaded on this map. What cultural groups did the Mongol armies conquer, partially conquer, or invade? How many different Khanates did the Mongols establish across Eurasia, and what were they? What role did geography play in limiting the spread of their influence?

Global Connections & Disconnections

THE TRAVELS OF MARCO POLO AND IBN BATTUTA

The most famous of the thirteenth- and fourteenth-century travelers were Marco Polo and Ibn Battuta. They encountered a world linked by trade routes that often had as their ultimate destination the imperial court of the Great Khan in China. These two men, and less celebrated travelers, observed worlds that were highly localized and yet culturally unified.

In 1271, Marco Polo (1254–1324), the son of an enterprising Venetian merchant, set out with his father and uncle on a journey to East Asia. Making their way along the fabled Silk Road across central Asia, the Polos arrived in Xanadu, the summer capital of the Mongol Empire, after a three-and-a-half-year journey. There they remained for more than two decades. When they returned

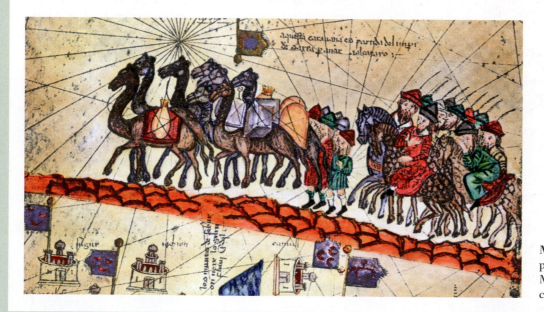

Marco Polo. This medieval painting shows the caravan of Marco Polo's father and uncle crossing Asia.

KINSHIP NETWORKS AND SOCIAL ROLES Mongol tribes solidified their conquests by extending kinship networks, thus building an empire out of an expanding confederation of familial tribes. The tents (households) were interrelated mostly by marriage: they were alliances sealed by the exchange of daughters. Conquering men married conquered women, and conquered men were selected to marry the conquerors' women. Chinggis Khan may have had more than 500 wives, most of them daughters of tribes that he conquered or that allied with him.

Women in Mongol society were responsible for child-rearing, shearing and milking livestock, and processing pelts for clothing. But they also took part in battles. Kubilai Khan's niece Khutulun became famous for besting men in wrestling matches and claiming their horses as spoils. Although women were often bought and sold, Mongol wives had the right to

own property and to divorce. Elite women even played important political roles. Consider Sorghaghtani Beki, Kubilai Khan's mother, who helped to engineer her sons' rule. Illiterate herself, she made sure that each son acquired a second language to aid in administering conquered lands. She gathered Confucian scholars to prepare Kubilai Khan to rule China. Chabi, Kubilai's senior wife, followed a similar pattern, offering patronage to Tibetan monks who set about converting the Mongol elite in China to Tibetan Buddhism.

CONQUEST AND EMPIRE

The nomads' need for grazing lands contributed to their desire to conquer the splendors of distant fertile belts and rich cities. Then, as they acquired new lands, they increasingly craved

Ibn Battuta. During his journey, Ibn Battuta traveled throughout Africa. In this woodcut, he is depicted in Morocco.

A half-century after Polo began his travels, the Moroccan-born scholar Muhammad ibn Abdullah ibn Battuta (1304–1369) embarked on a journey of his own. Then just twenty-one, he vowed to visit the whole of the Islamic world without traveling the same road twice. It was an ambitious goal, for Islam's domain extended from one end of the Eurasian landmass to the other and far into Africa as well. On his journey, Ibn Battuta eventually covered some 75,000 miles. Along his way, he claimed to have met at least sixty rulers, and in his book he recorded the names of more than 2,000 persons whom he knew personally.

The writings of Marco Polo and Ibn Battuta provide a wealth of information on the well-traversed lands of Africa, Europe, and Asia. What they and other travelers observed was the extreme diversity of Afro-Eurasian peoples, reflecting numerous ethnicities, political formations, and religious faiths. In addition, they observed that the vast majority of people lived deeply localized lives, primarily seeking to obtain the basic necessities of everyday life. Yet, they were also aware the same societies welcomed trade and cultural exchange. In fact, they wrote most eloquently about how each of the four major cultural systems of the landmass—Christian, Muslim, Indian, and Chinese—struggled to define itself. Interestingly, if Ibn Battuta and Marco Polo had been able to travel in the "unknown" worlds—the African hinterlands, the Americas, and Oceania—they would have witnessed to varying degrees similar phenomena and challenges.

to Venice in 1295, fellow townsmen greeted them with astonishment, believing that the Polos had perished years before. So, too, Marco Polo's published account of his travels generated an incredulous reaction. Some of his European readers considered his tales of eastern wonders to be mere fantasy, yet others found their appetites for Asian splendor whetted by his descriptions.

control of richer agricultural and urban areas nearby to increase their wealth and power through tribute. Trade disputes also likely spurred their expeditions. The Mongols depended on settled peoples for grain and manufactured goods (including iron for tools, wagons, weapons, bridles, and stirrups), and their first expansionist forays followed caravan routes.

The expansionist thrust began in 1206 under a united cluster of tribes. A gathering of clan heads acclaimed one of those present as Chinggis (Genghis) Khan, or Supreme Ruler. Chinggis (c. 1155–1227) subsequently launched a series of conquests southward across the Great Wall of China, and westward to Afghanistan and Persia. The Mongols also invaded Korea in 1231. The armies of Chinggis's son reached both the Pacific Ocean and the Adriatic Sea. His grandsons founded dynasties in China, in Persia, and on the southern Eurasian steppes. One of them, Kubilai Khan, enlisted thousands of Koryo men and ships for (ill-fated) invasions of Japan. Thus, a realm took shape that touched all four of Afro-Eurasia's main worlds.

Mongol raiders ultimately built a permanent empire by incorporating conquered peoples and some of their ways. Their feat of unification was far more surprising and sudden than the ties developed incrementally by traders and travelers on ships. Now, Afro-Eurasian regions were connected by land and by sea, in historically unparalleled ways.

MONGOLS IN CHINA

Mongol forces under Chinggis Khan entered northern China at the beginning of the thirteenth century, defeating the Jin army that was no match for the Mongols' superior cavalry on the North China plain. But below the Yangzi River, where the climate and weather changed, the Mongol horsemen fell ill from diseases such as malaria, and their horses perished from the heat. To conquer the semitropical south, the Mongols took to boats and fought along rivers and canals. **Kubilai Khan** (1215–1294) seized the grandest prize of all—southern China—after 1260. His cavalries penetrated the higher plateaus of southwest China and then attacked South China's economic heartland from the west. The Southern Song army fell before his warriors brandishing the latest gunpowder-based weapons (which the Mongols had borrowed from Chinese inventors only to be used against them).

THE FALL OF HANGZHOU Hangzhou, the last Song capital, succumbed in 1276. Rather than see the invaders pillage the city and their emperors' tombs, the Southern Song bowed to the inevitable. Kubilai Khan's most able commander, Bayan, led his crack Mongol forces in seizing town after town, ever closer to the capital. The Empress Dowager tried to buy them off, proposing substantial tribute payments, but Bayan had his eye on the prize: Hangzhou, which fell under Mongol control but survived reasonably intact. Bayan escorted the emperor and the Empress Dowager to Beijing, where Kubilai treated them with honor. Within three years, Song China's defeat was complete. With all of South China in their grip, the Mongols established the Yuan dynasty with a new capital at Dadu ("Great Capital," present-day Beijing).

Although it fell to Mongol control, Hangzhou survived reasonably intact. It was still one of the greatest cities in the world when the Venetian traveler Marco Polo visited in the 1280s and the Muslim traveler Ibn Battuta in the 1340s. Both men agreed that neither Europe nor the Islamic world had anything like it. (See Global Connections & Disconnections: The Travels of Marco Polo and Ibn Battuta.)

OUTSIDERS TAKE CONTROL The Mongol conquest both north and south changed the political and social landscape. However, Mongol rule did not impose rough steppeland ways on the "civilized" urbanite Chinese. Outsiders, non-Chinese, took political control. They themselves were a heterogeneous group of Mongols, Tanguts, Khitan, Jurchen, Muslims, Tibetans, Persians, Turks, Nestorians, Jews, Armenians—a conquering elite that ruled over a vast Han majority. The result was a segmented ruling system in which incumbent Chinese elites governed locally, while newcomers managed the central dynastic polity and collected taxes for the Mongols.

MONGOL REVERBERATIONS IN SOUTHEAST ASIA

Southeast Asia also felt the whiplash of conquest. Circling Song defenses in southern China, the Mongols galloped southwest and conquered states in Yunnan and in Burma. From there, in the 1270s, the armies headed directly back east into

Mongols on Horseback. Even after the Mongols became the rulers of China, the emperors remembered their steppe origin and maintained the skills of horse-riding nomads. This detail from a thirteenth/fourteenth-century silk painting shows Kubilai Khan hunting.

the soft underbelly of the Song state. In this sweep, portions of mainland Southeast Asia became annexed to China for the first time. Even the distant Khmer regime felt repercussions when the Mongol fleet (which grew out of the conquered Song navy) passed by on its way to attack Java—unsuccessfully—in 1293. Kubilai Khan used the conquered Chinese fleets to push his expansionism onto the high seas—with little success during the unsuccessful 1274 and 1281 invasions of Japan from Korea. The ill-fated Javanese expedition was his last.

THE FALL OF BAGHDAD

In the thirteenth century, Mongol tribesmen streamed out of the steppes, crossing the whole of Asia and entering the eastern parts of Europe. Mongke Khan, a grandson of Chinggis, made clear the Mongol aspiration for world domination: he appointed his brother Kubilai to rule over China, Tibet, and the northern parts of India; and he commanded another brother, Hulagu, to conquer Iran, Syria, Egypt, Byzantium, and Armenia.

When Hulagu reached Baghdad in 1258, he encountered a feeble foe and a city that was a shadow of its former glorious self. Merely 10,000 horsemen faced his army of 200,000 soldiers, who were eager to acquire the booty of a wealthy city. Even before the battle had taken place, Baghdadi poets were composing elegies for their dead and mourning the defeat of Islam.

The slaughter was vast. Hulagu himself boasted of taking the lives of at least 200,000 people. The Mongols pursued their adversaries everywhere. They hunted them in wells, latrines, and sewers and followed them into the upper floors of buildings, killing them on rooftops until, as an Iraqi Arab historian observed, "blood poured from the gutters into the streets. . . . The same happened in the mosques" (Lewis, pp. 82–83). In a few weeks of sheer terror, the venerable Abbasid caliphate was demolished. Hulagu's forces showed no mercy to the caliph himself, who was rolled up in a carpet and trampled to death by horses, his blood soaked up by the rug so it would leave no mark on the ground. With Baghdad crushed, the Mongol armies pushed on to Syria, slaughtering Muslims along the way.

In the end, the Egyptian Mamluks stemmed the advancing Mongol armies and prevented Egypt from falling into their hands. The Mongol Empire had reached its outer limits. Better at conquering than governing, the Mongols struggled to rule their vast possessions in makeshift states. Bit by bit, they ceded control to local administrators and dynasts who governed as their surrogates. There was also chronic feuding among the Mongol dynasts themselves. In China and in Persia, Mongol rule collapsed in the fourteenth century.

Mongol conquest reshaped Afro-Eurasia's social landscape. Islam would never again have a unifying authority like the caliphate or a powerful center like Baghdad. China, too, was divided and changed, but in other ways. The Mongols introduced Persian, Islamic, and Byzantine influences on China's architecture, art, science, and medicine. The Yuan policy of benign tolerance also brought elements from Christianity, Judaism, Zoroastrianism, and Islam into the Chinese mix. The Mongol thrust thus led to a great opening, as fine goods, traders, and technology flowed from China to the rest of the world in ensuing centuries. Finally, the Mongol state promoted an Afro-Eurasian interconnectedness that this huge landmass had not known before and would not experience again for hundreds of years. Out of conquest and warfare would come centuries of trade, migration, and increasing contacts among Africa, Europe, and Asia.

 CONCLUSION

Between 1000 and 1300, Afro-Eurasia was forming large cultural spheres. As trade and migration spanned longer distances, these spheres prospered and became more integrated. In central Afro-Eurasia, Islam was firmly established, its merchants, scholars, and travelers acting as commercial and cultural intermediaries joining the landmass together, as they spread their universalizing faith. As seaborne trade expanded, India, too, became a commercial crossroads. Merchants in its port cities welcomed traders arriving from Arab lands to the west, from China, and from Southeast Asia. China also boomed, pouring its manufactures into trading networks that reached throughout Afro-Eurasia and even into Africa. Christian Europe had two centers, both of which were at war with Islam. In the east, Byzantium was a formidable empire with a resplendent and unconquerable capital city, Constantinople, in many ways the pride of Christianity. In the west, the Catholic papacy had risen from the ashes of the Roman Empire and sought to extend its ecclesiastical authority over Rome's territories in western Europe.

Trade helped outline the parts of the world. The prosperity it brought also supported new classes of people—thinkers, writers, and naturalists—who clarified what it meant to belong to the regions of Afro-Eurasia. By 1300, learned priests and writers had begun to reimagine these regions as more than just territories: they were maturing into cultures with definable—and defensible—geographic boundaries. Increasingly these intellectuals delivered their messages to commoners as well as to rulers.

Neither the Americas nor sub-Saharan Africa saw the same degree of integration, but trade and migration in these areas did have profound effects. Certain African cultures flourished as they encountered the commercial energy of trade on the Indian Ocean. Indeed, Africans' trade with one another linked coastal and interior regions in an ever more integrated world. American peoples also built cities that dominated cultural areas and thrived through trade. American cultures shared significant features: reliance on trade, maize, and the exchange of goods such as shells and precious feathers. And larger areas honored the same spiritual centers.

By 1300, trade, migration, and conflict were connecting Afro-Eurasian worlds in unprecedented ways. When Mongol armies swept into China, into Southeast Asia, and into the heart of Islam, they applied a thin, surface-like coating of political integration to these widespread regions and built on existing trade links. At the same time, most people's lives remained quite local, driven by the need for subsistence and governed by spiritual and governmental representatives acting at the behest of distant authorities. Still, locals noticed the evidence of cross-cultural exchanges everywhere—in the clothing styles of provincial elites, such as Chinese silks in Paris or Quetzal plumes in northern Mexico; in enticements to move (and forced removals) to new frontiers; in the news of faraway conquests or advancing armies. Worlds were coming together within themselves and across territorial boundaries, while remaining apart as they sought to maintain their own identity and traditions. In Afro-Eurasia especially, as the movement of goods and peoples shifted from ancient land routes to sea-lanes, these contacts were more frequent and far-reaching. Never before had the world seen so much activity connecting its parts. Nor within them had there been so much shared cultural similarity—linguistic, religious, legal, and military. Indeed, by the time the Mongol Empire arose, the regions composing the globe were those that we now recognize as the cultural spheres of today's world. These were truly worlds together and worlds apart.

Review and research materials are available at StudySpace: ⓢ WWNORTON.COM/STUDYSPACE

KEY TERMS

Angkor Wat (p. 389)	*karim* (p. 365)
Cahokia (p. 398)	Kubilai Khan (p. 405)
Crusades (p. 394)	Mongols (p. 401)
Delhi Sultanate (p. 380)	piety (p. 373)
dhows (p. 364)	rajas (p. 379)
entrepôts (p. 365)	Sufism (p. 374)
feudalism (p. 389)	sultans (p. 379)

Chronology

	700 CE	800 CE	900 CE	1000 CE
SUB-SAHARAN AFRICA			Mandinka merchants establish vast commercial networks linking West Africa ✦	
THE AMERICAS			c. 1000 Cahokia flourishes as a commercial hub in Mississippi River valley ✦	
			c. 900 Moche people found Chan Chan ✦	
			c. 900–1100 Toltec Empire in Mexico Valley ✦ - - - - - - - - - - - - - - - - - - -	
				1000–1460 Chimú Empire ✦ - - -
THE ISLAMIC WORLD				
SOUTH ASIA			Turkish invasions from Central Asia begin ✦	
EAST ASIA	794–1185 Heian period in Japan ✦ -			
			Song dynasty founded 960 ✦	
			918–1392 Koryo dynasty rules ✦ - - - - - - - - - - -	
			Gunpowder invented ✦	
SOUTHEAST ASIA				
		899–1431 Khmer kingdom ✦ -		
CHRISTIAN EUROPE				

STUDY QUESTIONS

1. List the four major cultural regions in Afro-Eurasia, and briefly explain the defining characteristics of each. What did the various people and groups in these geographic areas all have in common that distinguished them from others?

2. Explain the role of global commercial hubs in India, China, and Egypt in fostering commercial contacts across Afro-Eurasia. How did they reflect revolutions in maritime transportation?

3. Which areas of sub-Saharan Africa were parts of the larger Afro-Eurasian world by 1300? How did contact with other regions shape political and cultural developments in sub-Saharan Africa?

4. Describe the cultural diversity within the Islamic world during this era. How did diverse Islamic communities achieve a uniform regional identity?

5. Analyze the impact of Muslim Turkish invaders on India. To what extent did India remain distinct from the Islamic world in this era?

6. Describe how the Song dynasty reacted to the military strength of its nomadic pastoral neighbors. How did these relationships foster a distinct Chinese identity?

7. Compare and contrast cultural and political developments in Korea, Japan, and Southeast Asia during this era. How did other regional cultures influence these societies?

8. Describe how Christianity expanded its geographic reach during this era. How did this expansion affect Latin Christianity in western Europe and Orthodox Christianity in eastern Europe?

9. Analyze the extent to which peoples in the Americas established closer contact with each other. How extensive were these contacts compared with those in the Afro-Eurasian world?

10. Describe the empire that the Mongols created in the thirteenth century. How did their policies promote greater contact among the various regions of Afro-Eurasia?

	1100 CE	1200 CE	1300 CE	1400 CE

◆ *Kingdom of Mali emerges*   ◆ *Swahili emerges as a distinct language linking the coast of East Africa*

◆ *Great Zimbabwe*

1325–1326 King Mansa Musa of Mali (ruled 1312–1332) completes the hajj ◆

◆ *1071 Turkish forces defeat Byzantine armies at Manzikert*

◆ *1258 Mongol forces sack Baghdad, end Abassid caliphate*

1206–1526 Turkish warriors found Delhi Sultanate in northern India

◆ *Buddhism loses almost all influence in India*

◆ *1274–1281 Japan fends off Mongol invasions*

◆ *1279 Mongols conquer Southern Song dynasty*

◆ *1127 Song dynasty loses North China to Jurchen Jin dynasty*

1192–1333 Kamakura shogunate ◆

1280–1368 Yuan dynasty ◆

◆ *Islamic influence increases in city-states*

◆ *Mongols invade southwestern China and Burma*

1061–1492 Spanish Reconquista

1095–1272 Crusades

CRISES AND RECOVERY IN AFRO-EURASIA, 1300–1500

When Mongol armies besieged the Genoese trading outpost of Caffa on the Black Sea in 1346, they not only damaged trading links between East Asia and the Mediterranean but also unleashed a devastating disease: the bubonic plague. Defeated Genoese merchants and soldiers withdrew, inadvertently taking the germs with them aboard their ships. By the time they arrived in Messina, Sicily, half the passengers were dead. The rest were dying. People waiting on shore for the ships' trade goods were horrified at the sight and turned the ships away. Desperately, the captains went to the next port, only to face the same fate. Despite these efforts at isolation, Europeans could not keep the plague (called the Black Death) from reaching their shores. As it spread from port to port it eventually contaminated all of Europe, killing about one-third of the population.

This story illustrates the disruptive effects of the Mongol invasions on Afro-Eurasian societies. Although the invasions ushered in an age of intensified cultural and political contact, the channels of exchange—the land trails and sea-lanes of human

411

voyagers—became accidental conduits for deadly microbes. These germs devastated societies far more decisively than did Mongol warfare. They were the real "murderous hordes" of world history, infecting people from every community, class, and culture they encountered. So staggering was the Black Death's toll that population densities did not recover for 200 years. Most severely affected were regions that the Mongols had brought together: settlements and commercial hubs along the old Silk Road and around the Mediterranean Sea and the South China Sea. While segments of the Indian Ocean trading world experienced death and disruption, South Asian societies, which had escaped the Mongol conquest, also escaped the dying and political disruptions associated with the Black Death.

During the fourteenth and fifteenth centuries—following population loss, political crises, and social disorders—peoples struggled to remake their societies. This chapter explores the ways in which Afro-Eurasian peoples restored what they thought was valuable from the old while discarding what they felt had failed them, in favor of radically new institutions and ideas. Considering how grievously people suffered and how many had died, it is surprising that so much of the old (particularly religious beliefs and institutions) survived, though in modified forms. What was truly new and would prove enduring was a group of imperial dynasties that emerged all across Afro-Eurasia: national monarchies in Europe, Ottoman sultans in Anatolia, Safavids in Persia, Mughals in India, and Ming dynasts in China. The aftermath of Mongol rule and of the Black Death witnessed the transformation of the political setting in Afro-Eurasia. Focusing on the formation of new states with highly centralized forms of rulership, this chapter explores how societies coped with the long-term impact of the Mongol invasions and the Black Death.

COLLAPSE AND INTEGRATION

> → *Why was the plague so devastating, and what were the key factors in rebuilding societies after it subsided?*

Although the Mongol invasions overturned political systems, the plague devastated society itself. Rulers could explain to their people the assaults of "barbarians," but it was much harder to make sense of an invisible enemy. Many concluded that mass death was God's wish. However, the upheaval gave ruling groups the opportunity to consolidate power by making dynastic matches through marriage, establishing new armies and taxes, and creating new systems to administer their states.

THE BLACK DEATH

The spread of the Black Death out of inner Asia was the fourteenth century's most significant historical development (see Map 11-1). The disease stemmed from a combination of bubonic, pneumonic, and septicaemic plague strains, and it caused a staggering loss of life. Among infected populations, death rates ranged from 25 to 50 percent.

How did the **Black Death** spread so far? One explanation may lie in climatic changes. A drying up of the central Asian steppe borderlands, where bubonic plague had existed for centuries, may have forced rodents out of their usual dwelling places and pressed pastoral peoples, who carried the strains,

Focus Questions

→ *Why was the plague so devastating, and what were the key factors in rebuilding societies after it subsided?*

→ *What were the major differences among the three Islamic dynasties?*

→ *How did the disasters of the fourteenth century change Western Christendom?*

→ *How did the Ming centralize their authority?*

to move closer to settled agricultural communities. So, it is thought, began the migration of microbes. But what spread the germs across Afro-Eurasia was the Mongols' trading network. The first outbreak in a heavily populated region occurred in the 1320s in southwestern China. From there, the disease spread through China and then took its death march along the major trade routes. The main avenue of transmission was across central Asia to the Crimea and the Black Sea, and from there by ship to the Mediterranean Sea and the Italian city-states. Secondary routes were by sea: one from China to the Red Sea, and another across the Indian Ocean, through the Persian Gulf, and into the Fertile Crescent and Iraq. All routes terminated at the Italian port cities, where ships with dead and dying men aboard arrived in 1347. From

there, what Europeans called the Pestilence or the Great Mortality engulfed the western end of the landmass.

The Black Death struck an expanding Afro-Eurasian population, made vulnerable because its members had no immunities to the disease and because its major realms were thoroughly connected through trading networks. Rodents, mainly rats, carried the plague bacilli that caused the disease. Fleas transmitted the bacilli from rodent to rodent, as well as to humans. The epidemic was terrifying, for its causes were unknown at the time. Infected victims died quickly—sometimes overnight—and in great agony, coughing up blood and oozing pus and blood from ugly black sores the size of eggs. Some European sages attributed the ravaging of their societies to an unusual alignment of Saturn, Jupiter, and Mars. Many believed that God was angry with mankind. One Florentine historian compared the plague to the biblical Flood and believed that the end of mankind was imminent.

The Black Death wrought devastation throughout much of the landmass. The Chinese population plunged from around 120 million to 80 million over the course of a century. Europe saw its numbers shrink by one-third. When farmers were afflicted, food production collapsed. Famine then followed and killed off the weak survivors. Worst afflicted were the crowded cities, especially coastal ports. Some cities lost up to two-thirds of their population. Refugees from the cities fled their homes, seeking security and food in the countryside. The shortage of food and other necessities led to rapidly rising prices, work stoppages, and unrest. Political leaders added to their unpopularity by repressing the unrest. The great Arab historian Ibn Khaldun (1332–1406), who lost his mother and father and a number of his teachers to the Black Death in Tunis, underscored the sense of desolation: "Cities and buildings were laid waste, roads and way signs were obliterated, settlements and mansions became empty, dynasties and tribes grew weak," he wrote. "The entire world changed."

Plague Victim. The plague was highly contagious and quickly led to death. Here the physician and his helper cover their noses to avoid the unbearable stench emanating from the patient; they can do little to help the victim as they do not understand what causes the boils, internal bleeding, or violent coughing that afflict him.

REBUILDING STATES

Starting in the late fourteenth century, Afro-Eurasians began the task of reconstructing both their political order and their trading networks. (By then the plague had died down, though it continued to afflict peoples for centuries.) However, the rebuilding of military and civil administrations—no easy task—also required political legitimacy. Rulers needed to revive confidence in themselves and their polities, which they did by fostering beliefs and rituals that confirmed their legitimacy and by increasing their control over subjects.

The basis for power was the **dynasty**—the hereditary ruling family that passed control from one generation to the next. Dynasties sought to establish their legitimacy in three ways. First, ruling families insisted that their power derived from a divine calling: Ming emperors in China claimed for

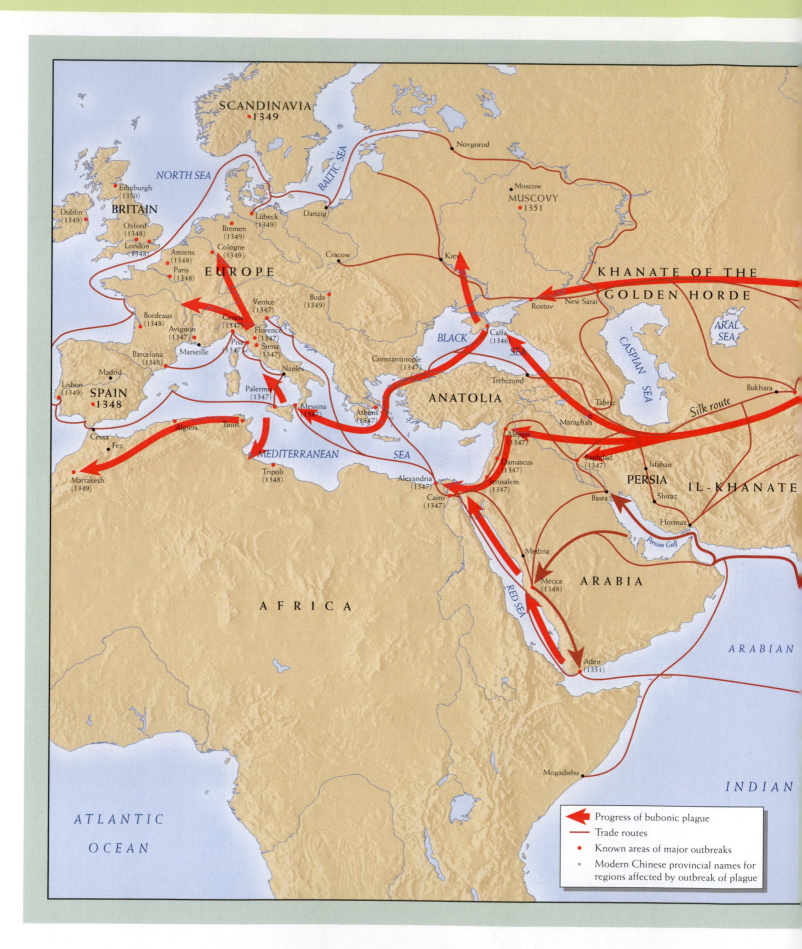

SCANDINAVIA
• 1349

NORTH SEA

BALTIC SEA

Novgorod

Edinburgh
(1350)

BRITAIN

Moscow
MUSCOVY
• 1351

Dublin
(1349)

Oxford
(1348)

London
(1348)

Lübeck
(1349)

Danzig

Bremen
(1349)

Cologne
(1349)

Amiens
(1348)

Paris
(1348)

EUROPE

Buda
(1349)

Cracow

Kiev

KHANATE OF THE
GOLDEN HORDE

Rostov

New Sarai

ARAL
SEA

Bordeaux
(1348)

Venice
(1347)

Genoa
(1347)

Florence
(1347)

Caffa
(1346)

BLACK

CASPIAN
SEA

Avignon
(1347)

Pisa
(1347)

Siena
(1347)

Constantinople
(1347)

SEA

Trebizond

Silk route

Bukhara

Barcelona
(1348)

Marseille

Naples

Tabriz

Madrid

Palermo
(1347)

ANATOLIA

Maraghah

PERSIA

IL-KHANATE

Lisbon
(1349)

SPAIN
• 1348

Messina
(1347)

Athens
(1347)

Aleppo
(1347)

Isfahan

Ceuta

Algiers

Tunis

MEDITERRANEAN

SEA

Damascus
(1347)

Baghdad
(1347)

Shiraz

Fez

Jerusalem
(1347)

Basra

Alexandria
(1347)

Hormuz

Marrakesh
(1349)

Tripoli
(1348)

Cairo
(1347)

Persian Gulf

Medina

Mecca
(1348)

ARABIA

AFRICA

RED SEA

Aden
(1351)

ARABIAN

Mogadishu

INDIAN

ATLANTIC

OCEAN

→ Progress of bubonic plague
— Trade routes
• Known areas of major outbreaks
✳ Modern Chinese provincial names for
regions affected by outbreak of plague

MAP 11-1   THE SPREAD OF THE BLACK DEATH

The Black Death was an Afro-Eurasian pandemic of the fourteenth century. What was the origin point of the Black Death? What were the main trade routes that allowed the Black Death to spread across Afro-Eurasia? Can you explain why certain parts of Afro-Eurasia were more severely affected than others?

MAIN THEMES

→ *The Black Death spreading out of Inner Asia brings a staggering loss of life, claiming one-third of the population.*
→ *Afro-Eurasians remake their societies in the wake of the plague's devastation.*
→ *Something old remains: religious beliefs and institutions. And something new appears: radically different imperial dynasties in Europe, Anatolia, Persia (Iran), India, and China.*

FOCUS ON *Rebuilding States*

Islamic Dynasties

+ Ottoman, Safavid, and Mughal empires replace the Mongols.
+ Ottomans overrun Constantinople and become the primary Sunni regime in the Islamic world.
+ Safavids come to power in Iran as a Shiite state less tolerant of diversity than the Ottomans.
+ Mughals replace the Delhi Sultanate in South Asia and continue to accommodate diverse religious beliefs.

China

+ The Ming dynasty replaces the Mongol Yuan dynasty and rebuilds a strong state from the ground up.
+ An elaborate, centralized bureaucracy oversees the revival of infrastructure and long-distance trade.

Western Christendom

+ Devastation from the Black Death provokes revolt and extremist religious movements.
+ New national monarchies appear in Portugal, Spain, France, and England.
+ A rebirth of classical learning (the Renaissance) originates in Italian city-states and spreads throughout western Europe.

themselves what previous dynasts had asserted—the "mandate of heaven"—while European monarchs claimed to rule by "divine right." Either way, ruling households asserted that they were closer to the gods than to commoners. Second, leaders squelched squabbling among potential heirs by establishing clear rules about succession to the throne. Many European nations tried to standardize succession by passing titles to the eldest male heir, but in practice there were countless complications and quarrels. In the Islamic world, successors could be designated by the incumbent or elected by the community; here, too, struggles over succession were frequent. Third, ruling families elevated their power through conquest or alliance—by ordering armies to forcibly extend their domains, or by marrying their royal offspring to rulers of other states or members of other elite households. Once it established legitimacy, the typical royal family would consolidate power by enacting coercive laws and punishments and sending emissaries to govern far-flung territories. It would also establish standing armies and new administrative structures to collect taxes and to oversee building projects that proclaimed royal power.

The innovative state-building that occurred in the wake of the plague's devastation would not have been as successful had it not drawn on older traditions. In China, the Ming renounced the Mongol legacy by emphasizing their role in restoring Han rulership and by rejecting the Mongol eagerness to expand. In Europe, a cultural flourishing based largely on ancient Greek and Roman models gave rise to thinkers who proposed novel views of governance. The peoples of the Islamic world held fiercely to their religion as two successor states—the Ottoman Empire and the Safavid state—absorbed numerous Turkish-speaking groups. A third Islamic state—the Mughal Empire—drew on local traditions of religious and cultural tolerance as it built a new regime on the foundations of the weakened Delhi Sultanate (see Chapter 10). Many of these regimes lasted for centuries, promoting political institutions and cultural values that became deeply embedded in the fabric of their societies.

ISLAMIC DYNASTIES

> → *What were the major differences among the three Islamic dynasties?*

The devastation of the Black Death following hard on the heels of the Mongol destruction of Islam's most important city and capital of the Abbasid Empire, Baghdad (see Chapter 10), eliminated Islam's old political order. Nonetheless, these two catastrophes prepared the way for new Islamic states to emerge. Of these, the Ottoman, the Safavid, and the Mughal dynasties ultimately grew powerful enough to become empires themselves.

THE MONGOL LEGACY AND THE RISE OF NEW ISLAMIC DYNASTIES

Rather than assimilate the peoples they defeated, the Mongols, whose numbers were always small, often assimilated themselves into the cultures they had conquered. For example, they adopted the Turkish language, and they converted to Islam. In addition, the Mongols fared better when they were closer to the steppe grasses, where their horses could graze. They had a harder time in urban centers. The Mongol Il-khans in Persia made Maraghah in Azerbaijan their capital, even though it was little more than an enlarged military encampment, in preference to the great administrative center of Baghdad. Still, Mongol armies in Persia as well as China suffered a decline in prowess (Mongol rule in the southern Russian steppes lasted longer). Mongol rule had always had two components. One was an ability to terrorize opponents into voluntarily submitting by such tactics as parading the heads of resisters on pikes. But this strategy began to lose effectiveness and sometimes even backfired. The other Mongol tactic had involved borrowing skills from across the empire and promoting the exchange of technologies and knowledge. But new groups aspiring to rule could do this, too.

Muslim peoples had no respite following the Mongol conquests. The Black Death reached Baghdad by 1347, perhaps carried there by an Azerbaijani army that besieged the city. By the next year, the plague had overtaken Egypt, Syria, and Cyprus; one report from Tunis records the deaths of more than 1,000 people a day in that North African city. Animals, too, were afflicted. One Egyptian writer commented: "The country was not far from being ruined. . . . One found in the desert the bodies of savage animals with the bubos under their arms. It was the same with horses, camels, asses, and all the beasts in general, including birds, even the ostriches." In the eastern Mediterranean, the plague left much of the Islamic world in a state of near political and economic collapse.

As new polities emerged from this economic and demographic crisis, they had to build from the ground floor. Warrior chiefs and religious leaders vied to fill the political vacuum. After Mongol power waned, the new rulers—notably the Ottomans in Anatolia and the Safavids in western Persia—operated out of strategic locations in the Islamic heartland and gradually rebuilt state institutions.

Through migration, warfare, and the eventual consolidation of post-Mongol states, Islam's domain expanded. Prior to the Mongol invasions, the political, economic, and cultural centers of the Islamic world were in Egypt, Syria, and Iraq. Most of these territories' inhabitants spoke Arabic, the language of the Prophet Muhammad—hence the language of Islamic devotion and theology. These areas, along with the Arabian Peninsula, contained Islam's most holy cities: Mecca, Medina, Jerusalem, Damascus, Cairo, Baghdad, and various other cities in Iraq. Even before the Mongol invasions, Turks had migrated into these regions and Persian had become a rival language of Islamic poetry and philosophy. Yet it was the Mongol invasions, which brought devastation to Persia and Iraq and an influx of nomadic peoples, that enabled a new Islamic world to appear. (See Primary Source: Qalandar Dervishes in the Islamic World.)

THREE ISLAMIC EMPIRES This new Islamic world, now including large numbers of Turkish- and Persian-speaking populations, occupied a vast geographical triangle. It stretched from Anatolia in the west to Khurasan in the east and to the southern apex at Baghdad. Of course, the old Arabic-speaking Islamic world remained vital, still at the heart of Islam geographically, but it now had to cede authority to the new rulers and religious men.

The Ottomans, the Safavids, and the Mughals emerged as the dominant states in the old Islamic world in the early sixteenth century. They exploited the rich agrarian resources of the Indian Ocean regions and the Mediterranean Sea basin, and they benefited from a brisk seaborne and overland trade. By the mid-sixteenth century the Mughals controlled the northern Indus River valley; the Safavids occupied Persia; and the Ottomans ruled Anatolia, the Arab world, and much of southern and eastern Europe.

Despite sharing core Islamic beliefs, each empire had unique political features. The most powerful, the **Ottoman Empire,** occupied the pivotal area between Europe and Asia. The Ottomans embraced a Sunni view of Islam, while adopting traditional Byzantine ways of governance and trying new ways of integrating the diverse peoples of their expanding territories. The Safavids, though adherents of the Shiite vision of Islam, were at the same time ardently devoted to the pre-Islamic traditions of Persia (present-day Iran). An internally cohesive people, their rulers were not so effective at expanding

QALANDAR DERVISHES IN THE ISLAMIC WORLD

The Qalandar dervish order sprang up in Damascus, Syria, and Egypt in the thirteenth century and spread rapidly throughout the Islamic world. In reaction to the period's widespread unrest, its members renounced the world and engaged in highly individualistic practices as they moved from place to place. The educated elite, however, criticized them as ignorant hypocrites living on alms obtained from gullible common folk. One of their practices was chiromancy, or palm-reading. In this excerpt Giovan Antonio Manavino, a European observer of Ottoman society, gives an obviously biased account of the Qalandars, whom he called the torlaks.

Dressed in sheepskins, the *torlaks* [Qalandars] are otherwise naked, with no headgear. Their scalps are always clean-shaven and well rubbed with oil as a precaution against the cold. They burn their temples with an old rag so that their faces will not be damaged by sweat. Illiterate and unable to do anything manly, they live like beasts, surviving on alms only. For this reason, they are to be found around taverns and public kitchens in cities. If, while roaming the countryside, they come across a well-dressed person, they try to make him one of their own, stripping him naked. Like Gypsies in Europe, they practice chiromancy, especially for women who then provide them with bread, eggs, cheese, and other foods in return for their services.

Amongst them there is usually an old man whom they revere and worship like God. When they enter a town, they gather around the best house of the town and listen in great humility to the words of this old man, who, after a spell of ecstasy, foretells the descent of a great evil upon the town. His disciples then implore him to fend off the disaster through his good services. The old man accepts the plea of his followers, though not without an initial show of reluctance, and prays to God, asking him to spare the town the imminent danger awaiting it. This time-honored trick earns them considerable sums of alms from ignorant and credulous people.

→ *Describe the way the Qalandar dervishes dressed, where they congregated, and how they obtained food. How did their lifestyle reflect the turmoil of the times?*

→ *Why do you think the Qalandars chose individualistic practices rather than communal living?*

→ *Why do you think Manavino is so critical of the Qalandars?*

SOURCE: Ahmet T. Karamustafa, "Dervish Groups in the Ottoman Empire, 1450–1550" from *God's Unruly Friends: Dervish Groups in the Islamic Later Middle Period, 1200–1550*, pp. 6–7. Oneworld Publications, Oxford, 2006. Reprinted with the permission of Oneworld Publications.

---

beyond their Persian base. The Mughals ruled over the wealthy but divided realm that is much of today's India, Pakistan, and Bangladesh; here they carried even further the region's religious and political traditions of assimilating Islamic and pre-Islamic Indian ways. Their wealth and the decentralization of their domain made the Mughals constant targets for internal dissent and eventually for external aggression.

THE RISE OF THE OTTOMAN EMPIRE

Although the Mongols considered Anatolia to be a borderland region of little economic importance, their military forays against the Anatolian Seljuk Turkish state in the late thirteenth century opened up the region to new political forces. The ultimate victors here were the Ottoman Turks. They transformed themselves from warrior bands roaming the borderlands between Islamic and Christian worlds into rulers of a settled state and, finally, into sovereigns of a far-flung, highly bureaucratic empire (see Map 11-2).

Under their chief, Osman (r. 1299–1326), the Turkish Ottomans formalized a stern and disciplined warrior ethos, and they triumphed over their rivals by assimilating the techniques of settled administration from their neighbors. Other warrior bands, which lived off the land and fought for booty under charismatic military leaders, had little regard for artisans, merchants, bureaucrats, and clerics. By contrast, the

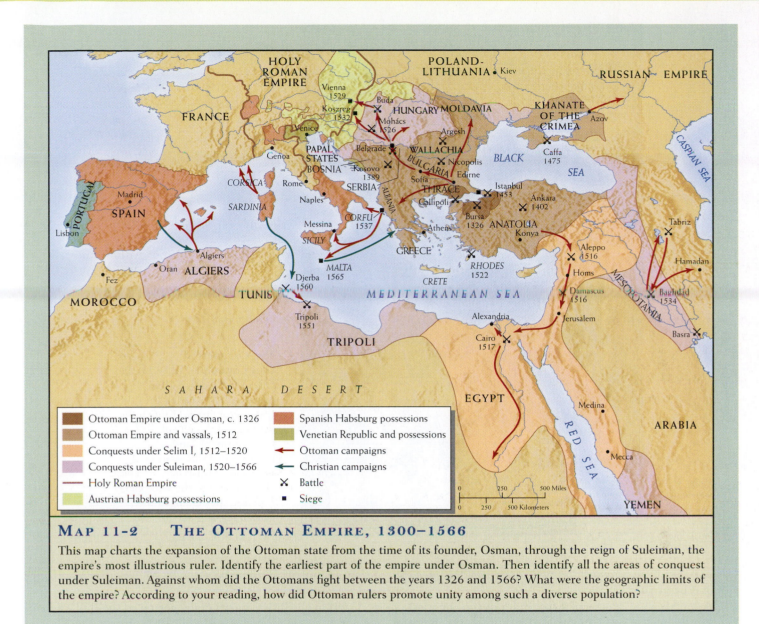

MAP 11-2   THE OTTOMAN EMPIRE, 1300–1566

This map charts the expansion of the Ottoman state from the time of its founder, Osman, through the reign of Suleiman, the empire's most illustrious ruler. Identify the earliest part of the empire under Osman. Then identify all the areas of conquest under Suleiman. Against whom did the Ottomans fight between the years 1326 and 1566? What were the geographic limits of the empire? According to your reading, how did Ottoman rulers promote unity among such a diverse population?

Ottomans realized that the consolidation of power depended on attracting just these groups. In time, not only did the Ottoman state (based in Bursa in western Anatolia) win the favor of Islamic clerics, but it also became the champion of Sunni Islam throughout the Islamic world.

By the mid-fourteenth century, the Ottomans had expanded into the Balkans, becoming the most powerful force in the eastern Mediterranean and western Asia. The state controlled a vast territory, stretching in the west to the Moroccan border, in the north to Hungary and Moldavia, in the south through the Arabian Peninsula, and in the east to the Iraqi-Persian border. At the top of the Ottomans' elaborate hierarchy stood the sultan. Below him was a military and civilian bureaucracy, whose task was to demand obedience and revenue from subjects. The bureaucracy's vigilance enabled the sultan to expand his realm, which in turn forced him to invest in an even larger bureaucracy.

THE CONQUEST OF CONSTANTINOPLE   The empire's spectacular expansion was primarily a military affair. To recruit followers, the Ottomans promised wealth and glory to new subjects. This was an expensive undertaking, but territorial expansion generated vast financial and administrative rewards. Moreover, by spreading the spoils of conquest and lucrative administrative positions, rulers bought off potentially discontented subordinates. Still, without military might, the Ottomans would not have enjoyed the successes associated with the brilliant reigns of Murad II

The Conquest of Constantinople. In 1453, the Ottomans, led by Sultan Mehmed, later called the Conqueror, broke through the defenses of the city of Constantinople and incorporated this bastion of Byzantine Christian civilization into the Ottoman Empire. They changed the city's name to Istanbul and made it their own capital.

(r. 1421–1451) and his aptly named successor, Mehmed the Conqueror (r. 1451–1481).

Mehmed's most spectacular triumph was the conquest of Constantinople, an ambition for Muslim rulers ever since the birth of Islam. Mehmed left no doubt that this was his primary goal: shortly after his coronation he vowed to capture the capital of the Byzantine Empire, a city of immense strategic and commercial importance. He knew this feat would require a large and well-armed fighting force, for the heavily fortified city had kept Muslims at bay for almost a century. First he built a fortress of his own, on the European bank of the Bosporus strait, to prevent European vessels from reaching the capital. Then, by promising his soldiers free access to booty and portraying the city's conquest as a holy cause, he amassed a huge army that outnumbered the defending force of 7,000 by more than tenfold. For forty days his troops bombarded Constantinople's massive walls with artillery that included enormous cannons built by Hungarian and Italian engineers. On May 29, 1453, Ottoman troops overwhelmed the surviving soldiers and took the ancient Roman and Chris-

tian capital of Byzantium—which Mehmed promptly renamed Istanbul.

Although Christians generally portrayed the "fall" of Constantinople as an insult and a disaster, in fact the Muslim conquest had cultural benefits for western Europe. Many Christian survivors fled to ports in the west, bringing with them classical and Arabic manuscripts previously unknown in Europe. The well-educated, Greek-speaking émigrés generally became teachers and translators, thereby helping to revive Europeans' interest in classical antiquity and spreading knowledge of ancient Greek (which had virtually died out in medieval times). These manuscripts and teachers would play a vital role in Europe's Renaissance.

The Ottomans followed their capture of Constantinople with other military successes that put many of Christian Europe's great cities in peril. Their forces sacked Athens in 1458, then took Bosnia in 1463. In 1480 the Ottomans launched an invasion of Italy. They captured one port city; but Mehmed II's death, and fights between his sons for control of the empire, prevented further conquests in Italy. The

Ottomans then turned to the Balkans and central Europe, invading Hungary in 1492 and Croatia in 1493. Their inroads so frightened the French king that he decided to invade Italy himself in order to lead his own crusade against the Ottomans.

Meanwhile, Mehmed made Istanbul the Ottoman capital, adopting Byzantine administrative practices to unify his enlarged state and incorporating many of Byzantium's powerful families into it. From Istanbul, Mehmed and his successors would continue their expansion, eventually seizing all of Greece and the Balkan region. As a result, Ottoman navies increasingly controlled sea-lanes in the eastern Mediterranean, curtailing European access to the rich ports that handled the lucrative caravan trade. By the late fifteenth century, Ottoman forces menaced another of Christendom's great capitals, Vienna, and European merchants feared that never again would they obtain the riches of Asia via the traditional overland route.

THE TOOLS OF EMPIRE BUILDING Having penetrated the heartland of Christian Byzantium, under Selim (r. 1512–1520) and Suleiman (r. 1520–1566), the Ottomans turned their expansionist designs to the Arab world. During the latter's reign the Ottomans reached the height of their territorial expansion, with Suleiman himself leading thirteen major military campaigns and many minor engagements. An exceptional military leader, Suleiman was an equally gifted administrator. His subjects called him "the Lawgiver" and "the Magnificent" in recognition of his attention to civil bureaucratic efficiency and justice for his people. His fame spread to Europe, where he was known as "the Great Turk." Under Suleiman's administration, the Ottoman state ruled over 20 to 30 million people. By the time Suleiman died, the Ottoman Empire bridged Europe and the Arab world. Istanbul by then was a dynamic imperial hub, dispatching bureaucrats and military men to oversee a vast domain.

The Suleymaniye Mosque. Built by Sultan Suleiman to crown his achievements, the Suleymaniye Mosque was designed by the architect Sinan to dominate the city and to have four tall minarets from which the faithful were called to prayer.

Ottoman dynastic power was, however, not only military; it also rested on a firm religious foundation. At the center of this empire were the sultans, who combined a warrior ethos with an unwavering devotion to Islam. Describing themselves as the "shadow of God" on earth, they claimed to be caretakers for the welfare of the Islamic faith. Throughout the empire, the sultans devoted substantial resources to the construction of elaborate mosques and to the support of Islamic schools. As self-appointed defenders of the faithful, the sultans assumed the role of protectors of the holy cities on the Arabian Peninsula and of Jerusalem, defending the realm's internal cohesion and constantly striving to extend the borders of Islam. Thus the Islamic faith helped to unite a diverse and sprawling imperial populace, with the sultan's power fusing the sacred and the secular.

ISTANBUL AND THE TOPKAPI PALACE   Istanbul reflected the splendor of this awesome empire. After the Ottoman conquest, the sultans' engineers rebuilt the city's crumbling walls, while their architects redesigned homes, public buildings, baths, inns, and marketplaces to display the majesty of Islam's new imperial center. To crown his achievements, Suleiman ordered the construction of the Suleymaniye Mosque, which sat opposite the Hagia Sophia. That domed Byzantine cathedral was formerly the most sacred of Christian cathedrals, the largest house of worship in all of Christendom, but Suleiman had it turned into a mosque. Moreover, the Ottoman dynasts welcomed (indeed, forcibly transported) thousands of Muslims and non-Muslims to the city and revived Istanbul as a major trading center. Within twenty-five years of its conquest, its population more than tripled; by the end of the sixteenth century, 400,000 people regularly swarmed through its streets and knelt in its mosques, making it the world's largest city outside China.

Istanbul's **Topkapi Palace** reflected the Ottomans' view of governance, the sultans' emphasis on religion, and the continuing influence of Ottoman familial traditions—even in the administration of a far-flung empire. Laid out by Mehmed II, the palace complex reflected a vision of Istanbul as the center of the world. As a way to exalt the sultan's magnificent power, architects designed the complex so that the buildings containing the imperial household nestled behind layers of outer courtyards, in a mosaic of mosques, courts, and special dwellings for the sultan's harem.

The growing importance of Topkapi Palace as the command post of empire represented a crucial transition in the history of Ottoman rulers. Not only was the palace the place where future bureaucrats received their training; it was also the place where the chief bureaucrat, the grand vizier, carried out the day-to-day running of the empire. Whereas the early sultans had led their soldiers into battle personally and had met face-to-face with their kinsmen, the later rulers withdrew into the sanctity of the palace, venturing out only occasionally for grand ceremonies. Still, every Friday, subjects queued up outside the palace to introduce their petitions, ask for favors, and seek justice. If they were lucky, the sultans would be there to greet them—but they did so behind grated glass, issuing their decisions by tapping on the window. The palace thus projected a sense of majestic, distant wonder, a home fit for semidivine rulers.

And Topkapi was indeed a home—for the increasingly sedentary sultan and his harem. Among his most cherished quarters were those set aside for women. At first, women's influence in the Ottoman polity was slight. But as the realm consolidated, women became a powerful political force. The harem, like the rest of Ottoman society, had its own hierarchy of rank and prestige. At the bottom were slave women; at the top were the sultan's mother and his favorite consorts. As many as 10,000 to 12,000 women inhabited the palace, often

The Topkapi Palace. A view of the inner courtyard of the seraglio, where the sultan and his harem lived.

in cramped quarters. Those who had the ruler's ear conspired to have him favor their own children, which made for widespread intrigue. When a sultan died, the entire retinue of women would be sent to a distant palace poignantly called the Palace of Tears, because the women who occupied it wept at the loss of the sultan and their own banishment from power.

DIVERSITY AND CONTROL The fact that the Ottoman Empire endured into the twentieth century owed much to the ruling elite's ability to win the favor of exceedingly diverse populations. After all, neither conquest nor conversion eliminated cultural differences in the empire's distant provinces. Thus, for example, the Ottomans' language policy was one of flexibility and tolerance. Although Ottoman Turkish was the official language of administration, Arabic was the primary language of the Arab provinces, the common tongue of street life. Within the empire's European corner, the sounds and cadences of various languages continued to prevail. From the fifteenth century onward, the Ottoman Empire was more multilingual than any of its rivals.

In politics, as in language, the Ottomans showed flexibility and tolerance. The imperial bureaucracy permitted extensive regional autonomy. In fact, Ottoman military cadres perfected a technique for absorbing newly conquered territories into the empire by parceling them out as revenue-producing units among loyal followers and kin. Regional appointees could collect local taxes, part of which they earmarked for Istanbul and part of which they pocketed for themselves. (This was a common administrative device for many world dynasties ruling extensive domains.)

Like other empires, the Ottoman state was always in danger of losing control over its provincial rulers. Local rulers—the group that the imperial center allowed to rule locally—found that great distances enabled them to operate independently from central authority. These local authorities kept larger amounts of tax revenues than Istanbul deemed proper. So, to clip local autonomy, the Ottomans established a corps of infantry soldiers and bureaucrats (called janissaries) who owed direct allegiance to the sultan. The system at its high point involved a conscription of Christian youths from the empire's European lands. This conscription, called the *devshirme,* required each village to hand over a certain number of males between the ages of eight and eighteen. Uprooted from their families and villages, selected for their fine physiques and good looks, these young men were converted to Islam and sent to farms to build up their bodies and learn Turkish. A select few were moved on to Topkapi Palace to learn Ottoman military, religious, and administrative techniques. Some of these men later enjoyed exceptional careers in the arts and sciences—such as the architect Sinan, who designed the Suleymaniye Mosque. Recipients of the best education available in the Islamic world, trained in Ottoman ways, instructed in the use of modern weaponry, and shorn of all family connections, the *devshirme* recruits were prepared to serve the sultan (and the empire as a whole) rather than the interests of any particular locality or ethnic group.

The *Devshirme.* A miniature painting from 1558 depicts the *devshirme* system of taking non-Muslim children from their families in the Balkan Peninsula as a human tribute in place of cash taxes, which the poor region could not pay. The children were educated in Ottoman Muslim ways and prepared for service in the sultan's civil and military bureaucracy.

The Ottomans thus artfully balanced the decentralizing tendencies of the outlying regions with the centralizing forces of the imperial capital. Relying on a careful mixture of faith, patronage, and tolerance, the sultans curried loyalty and secured political stability. Indeed, so strong and stable was the polity that the Ottoman Empire dominated the coveted and highly contested crossroads between Europe and Asia for many centuries.

THE SAFAVID EMPIRE IN IRAN

The Ottoman dynasts were not the only rulers to extend Islam's political domain. In Persia, too, a new empire arose in the aftermath of the Mongols. The legitimacy of the Safavid Empire, like that of the Ottoman, rested on an Islamic foundation. But the Shiism espoused by Safavid rulers was quite different from the Sunni faith of the Ottomans, and these contrasting religious visions shaped distinct political systems.

More so than in Anatolia, the Mongol conquest and decline brought terrible destruction and political instability to Persia. Initially, Mongol conquerors refused to embrace the majority population's Islamic faith. Instead, for over seven decades the Mongol rulers practiced a form of religious toleration. Various Mongol autocrats permitted Jews to serve the state as viziers (administrators) and employed Christians as auxiliary soldiers. But in 1295, the khan of the Persian state adopted Islam as the state religion. (A **khan** is a ruler who was acclaimed at an assembly of elites and supposedly descended from Chinngis Khan [see Chapter 10] on the male line; those not descended from Chinggis continually faced challenges to their legitimacy.) When the Mongol order slipped into decline soon after, no power arose to dominate the area. The region between Konya in eastern Anatolia and Tabriz in Persia and including Iraq fell into disorder, with warrior chieftains squabbling for preeminence. Adding to the

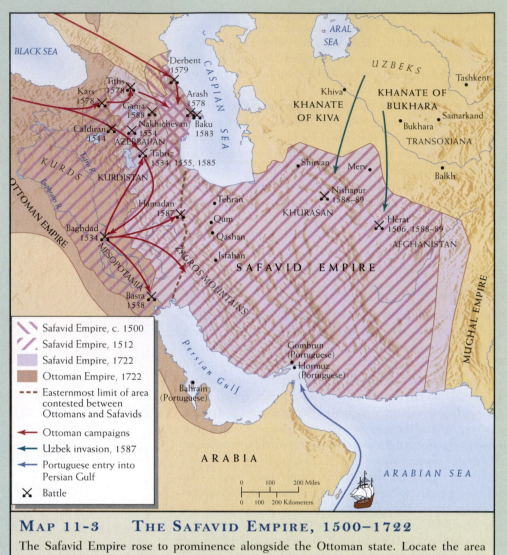

MAP 11-3 THE SAFAVID EMPIRE, 1500–1722

The Safavid Empire rose to prominence alongside the Ottoman state. Locate the area where it originated. With which empire did the Safavids fight the most battles? Why were most of the battles limited to the regions of Azerbaijan, Kurdistan, and Mesopotamia? What were the geographical and political limits on the growth of the Safavid Empire?

volatility were various populist Islamic movements, some of which urged followers to withdraw from society or to parade around without clothing. Among the more prominent movements was a Sufi brotherhood led by Safi al-Din (1252–1334), which gained the backing of religious adherents and Turkish-speaking warrior bands. However, his successors, known as Safaviyeh or Safavids, embraced Shiism.

The Safavid aspirants to power rallied support from tribal groups in badly devastated parts of Persia by promising to restore good governance. They also steeped themselves in the separatist sacred tradition of Shiism. As a result, of the three great Islamic empires, the Safavid state became the most single-mindedly religious, persecuting those who did not follow its Shiite form of Islam. When the most dynamic of Safi al-

Din's successors, Ismail (r. 1501–1524), took power in Tabriz, he required that the call to prayer announce that "there is no God but Allah, that Muhammad is His prophet, and that Ali is the successor of Muhammad." Rejecting his advisers' counsel to tolerate the Sunni creed of the vast majority of the city's population, Ismail made Shiism the official state religion. He offered the people a choice between conversion to Shiism or death, exclaiming at the moment of conquest that "with God's help, if the people utter one word of protest, I will draw the sword and leave not one of them alive." In 1502, Ismail proclaimed himself the first shah of the Safavid Empire. (**Shah** is the Persian word for king or leader, a title that many other cultures adopted as well.) Under Ismail and his successors, the Safavid shahs restored Persian sovereignty over the entire region traditionally regarded as the homeland of Persian speakers (see Map 11-3).

In the hands of the Safavids, Islam assumed an extreme and often militant form. The Safavids revived the traditional Persian idea that rulers were ordained by God, believing the shahs to be divinely chosen. Some Shiites even went so far as to affirm that there was no God but the shah. Moreover, Persian Shiism fostered an activist clergy who (in contrast to Sunni clerics) saw themselves as political and religious enforcers against any heretical authority. They compelled Safavid leaders to rule with a sacred purpose. Because the Safavids did not tolerate diversity, unlike the Ottomans, they never had as expansive an empire. Whatever territories they conquered, the Safavids ruled much more directly, based on central—and theocratic—authority.

THE DELHI SULTANATE AND THE EARLY MUGHAL EMPIRE

A quarter century after the Safavids seized power in Persia, another Islamic dynasty, the Mughals, emerged in South Asia. Like the Ottomans and Safavids, the Mughals created a regime destined to last for many centuries. But unlike those other empires, the Mughals did not replace a Mongol regime. Instead, they erected their state on the foundations of the old Delhi Sultanate, which had come into existence in 1206. Although spared the devastating effects of the Mongols and the Black Death, nonetheless the peoples of India had to deal with an invading nomadic force every bit as destructive as the Mongols: the warriors of Tamerlane. His military forays crushed the Delhi Sultanate and opened the way for a new, even more powerful regime.

THE DECLINING DELHI SULTANATE In 1303, when Mongol forces had moved toward South Asia, the Delhi Sultanate was at its height. Its formidable military force extended imperial authority to most of the northern Indus River valley and cast a shadow over the political map of the south. The reigning sultan raised a sufficiently powerful army to drive the Mongols back toward Afghanistan. They never again disturbed the tranquility of the sultanate.

Although military strength was the foundation of the sultanate's power, it was also, ironically, a vulnerable institution. Toward the late fourteenth century, a decline in government revenues and a rise in expenditures combined to reduce resources for the military. Quarreling among nobles further weakened the sultanate and left it vulnerable to a Turkish, rather than Mongol, invader. This was a force led by Timur (Tamerlane), a Turkish warrior from central Asia. Sweeping down from the northwest, Timur's army sacked Delhi and pillaged and annexed the Punjab, an area around the headwaters of the Indus River. Thereafter death and destruction engulfed the city and much of the northern Indus River valley. Thousands were taken prisoner and carried off as slaves. Artisans

and stonemasons who had constructed Delhi's beautiful buildings were carted away to work similar magic on the conqueror's city of Samarkand (in present-day Uzbekistan). Yet, as summer approached, a time when semiarid Delhi chokes with dust and the temperature hovers between 100 and 110 degrees Fahrenheit, Timur abandoned the scorching plains of northern India and returned home. Still, his conquest accelerated the fragmentation of the Delhi Sultanate.

RIVALRIES, RELIGIOUS REVIVAL, AND THE FIRST MUGHAL EMPEROR A wave of religious revival followed in the wake Timur's conquests. Bengal broke away from Delhi and soon embraced a Sufi form of mystical Islam, emphasizing personal union with God. Here, too, a special form of Hinduism, called Bhakti Hinduism, put down deep roots. Its

Raid on Delhi. Timur's swift raid on Delhi in 1398 was notable for the death and destruction it caused. This sixteenth-century miniature captures the plunder and violence.

devotees preached the doctrine of divine love. In the Punjab, previously a core area of the Delhi Sultanate, a new religion known as Sikhism came into being. **Sikhism** largely followed the teachings of Nanak (1469–1539). Although born a Hindu, he was inspired by Islamic ideals and called on his followers to renounce the caste system and to treat all believers as equal before God. (See Primary Source: Nanak's Teachings in India.)

Following Timur's attack, rival kingdoms and sultanates asserted their independence, leaving the Delhi Sultanate a mere shadow of its former self. It became just one of several competing powers in northern India, ruled first by the Sayyids and then by the Afghan dynasty of the Lodis. Surrounded by resurgent Hindu and Islamic polities, the weakened sultanate experienced something of a revival in the Lodi era. But the attempt by the last Lodi sultan to consolidate power by clipping the wings of the Afghan nobility provoked the governor of the Punjab to invite the Turkish prince Babur (the "Tiger") to India in 1526. A great-grandson of Timur, Babur traced his lineage to both the Turks and the Mongols (he was said to be a descendant of Chinggis Khan). For years, Babur had longed to conquer India. Massing an army of Turks and Afghans armed with matchlock cannons, he easily breached the wall of elephants put together by defenders of the sultan. Delhi fell, and the sultanate came to an end. Babur proclaimed himself emperor and spent

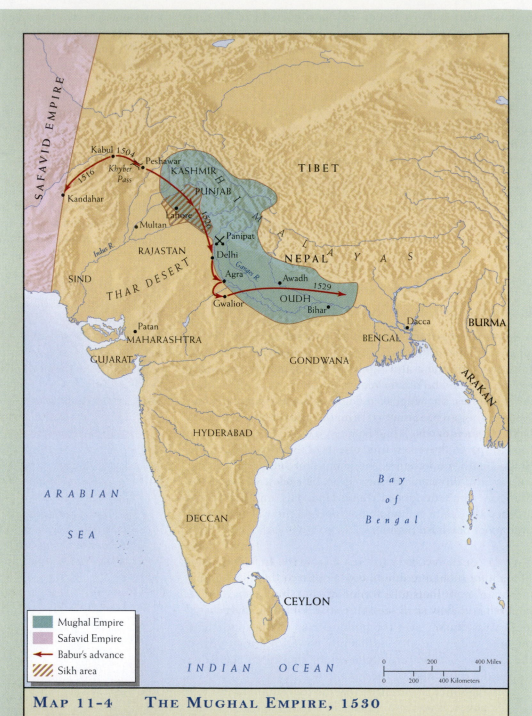

MAP 11-4   THE MUGHAL EMPIRE, 1530

Compare the Mughal state with the other major Asian empires of this period, notably the Ottoman, Safavid, and Ming states (see Maps 11-2, 11-3, 11-6). What geographic characteristic distinguished the Mughal state at this time from the others? Where in the landmass did the new state arise, and what effect do you think its place of origin had on the nature of Mughal rule? Based on their geographic location, to what religious traditions did the Mughals need to be sensitive?

NANAK'S TEACHINGS IN INDIA

Nanak (1469–1539), generally recognized as the founder of Sikhism, lived in northern India and participated in the religious discussions that were prominent at the time. As in western Europe and Islamic Southwest Asia, this was a period of political turmoil and intense personal introspection. The following excerpts demonstrate Nanak's views on the failings of the age and his use of Islamic and Hindu ideas to elaborate a unique spiritual perspective. Nanak stressed the unity of God, an emphasis that reflected Islamic influences. Nonetheless, his insistence on the comparative unimportance of prophets ran counter to Islam, and his belief in rebirth was strictly Hindu.

There is but one God, whose name is true, the Creator, devoid of fear and enmity, immortal, unborn, self-existent; God the great and bountiful. Repeat His Name.

Numberless are the fools appallingly blind;
Numberless are the thieves and devourers of others' property;
Numberless are those who establish their sovereignty by force;
Numberless the cutthroats and murderers; Numberless the liars who roam about lying;
Numberless the filthy who enjoy filthy gain;
Numberless the slandered who carry loads of calumny on their heads;
Nanak thus described the degraded.
So lowly am I, I cannot even once be a sacrifice unto Thee. Whatever pleaseth Thee is good.
O Formless One, Thou art ever secure.

The Hindus have forgotten God, and are going the wrong way.
They worship according to the instruction of Narad.
They are blind and dumb, the blindest of the blind.
The ignorant fools take stones and worship them.
O Hindus, how shall the stone which itself sinketh carry you across?

What power hath caste? It is the reality that is tested.
Poison may be held in the hand, but man dieth if he eat it.
The sovereignty of the True One is known in every age.
He who obeyeth God's order shall become a noble in His court.

Those who have meditated on God as the truest of the true have done real worship and are contented;
They have refrained from evil, done good deeds, and practiced honesty;
They have lived on a little corn and water, and burst the entanglements of the world.
Thou art the great Bestower; ever Thou givest gifts which increase a quarterfold.
Those who have magnified the great God have found Him.

→ *Identify all the "numberless" groups that Nanak lists. What range of social classes do they represent? How does this enumeration reflect the tumultuous times?*
→ *What criticisms of Hindu worship does Nanak raise?*
→ *What lines reveal his belief in rebirth?*
→ *How does Nanak expect true believers to behave?*

SOURCE: "Nanak's Teachings in India" from *Sources of Indian Tradition*, ed. William Theodore de Bary, © 1958 Columbia University Press. Reprinted with permission of the publisher.

the next few years snuffing out the remaining resistance to his rule (see Map 11-4). Thus he laid the foundation of the Mughal Empire, the third great Islamic dynasty (discussed in detail in Chapter 12).

By the sixteenth century, then, the Islamic heartland had seen the emergence of three new empires. Their differences were obvious, especially in the religious sphere. The Ottomans were Sunni Islam's most fervent champions, determined to eradicate the Shiite heresy on their border where an equally determined Persian Safavid dynasty sought to expand the realm of Shiism. In contrast to these dynasties' sectarian religious commitments, the Mughals of India, drawing on well-established Indian traditions of religious and cultural tolerance, were open-minded toward non-Muslim believers and sectarian groups within the Muslim community. Yet, the political similarities of these imperial dynasties were equally clear-cut. Although these states did not hesitate to go to war against each other, they shared similar styles of rule. All established their legitimacy via military prowess, religious backing, and a loyal bureaucracy. This combination of spiritual and military weaponry enabled emperors, espousing Muhammad's preachings, to claim vast domains. Islam also bound together rulers and those whom they ruled. Moreover, their religious differences did not prevent the movement of goods, ideas, merchants, and scholars across political and religious boundaries—even across the most divisive boundary of all, that between Sunni Iraq and Shiite Persia.

WESTERN CHRISTENDOM

> → *How did the disasters of the fourteenth century change Western Christendom?*

In western Afro-Eurasia, the period 1100–1300 was one of prosperity, population growth, and cultural flowering. Known as the High Middle Ages, this era saw spectacular advances in the arts, technology, learning, architecture, and banking. Expanding populations freed up laborers to move from the countryside to the cities. London, with a population of some 60,000 within its walls and 10,000 or more outside them, was only one city to experience a housing crunch; in some of its poorer sections, up to twelve people slept in a single room. Though excluded from many crafts and professions, women made gains in retail trades, weaving, and food production. Wives often supervised shops or took goods to local fairs, where producers met to exchange their wares.

During the High Middle Ages, Europe's 80 million inhabitants remained largely rooted to their local communities, but growing wealth allowed some to widen their horizons. Bologna, Paris, Oxford, and Cambridge had universities (with medical, law, and theology faculties), and a few scholars had begun to appreciate the learning of Arabs and earlier Greeks and Romans. Thomas Aquinas (1225–1274), a leading philosopher and theologian, had laid out the main tenets of western Christianity and resolved questions of faith and reason to the satisfaction of clerical and secular intellectuals. Florentine bankers opened establishments in commercial port cities, and Greek shipbuilders expanded their trade. New devices like mechanical clocks and the compass improved the accuracy of measurements on sea and on land, while spinning wheels increased the pace of cloth production. But all of this prosperity, population growth, and innovation would be halted by the tragedies of the fourteenth century.

REACTIONS, REVOLTS, AND RELIGION

Disastrous climatic changes struck first. Beginning around 1310, extremely harsh winters and rainy summers shortened the growing seasons and played havoc with harvests. Exhausted soils no longer supplied the resources to feed and clothe growing urban and rural populations. Nobles squeezed the peasantry hard in an effort to maintain their luxurious lifestyle. States raised taxes to balance their growing expenditures. In this context, Europe endured the first of several disasters: famine. It appeared in 1315 and did not let up for seven cruel years, by which time millions had died of starvation or of diseases against which the malnourished population had little resistance. But this was merely the prelude to a century and more of warfare, epidemic disease, famine, and social unrest.

THE PLAGUE IN EUROPE   In the wake of famine came the Black Death, starting around 1347 and ravaging the Italian Peninsula; then it seized France, the Low Countries, (present-day Netherlands, Belgium, and Luxembourg), Germany, and England in its deathly grip. The overcrowded and unsanitary cities were particularly vulnerable. Bremen lost at least 8,000 souls, perhaps two-thirds of its population; Hamburg, another port city, at least as many. The poor, sleeping in crowded quarters, were especially at risk. But master bakers, bankers, and aristocrats died too, unless they were able to flee to the relatively safer countryside in time to escape infection. No one had seen dying on such a scale. Some 25 to 50 percent of Europe's total population perished between 1347 and 1351.

After 1352, the epidemic died down, having killed all those with no natural immunities and most of the original carriers of the disease, the European black rat. But the plague would return every seven years or so for the rest of the century, as well as sporadically through the entire fifteenth century, killing the young and those who had managed to escape exposure in the first epidemic. The European population continued to decline, until by 1450 many areas had only one-quarter the number of a century earlier. Indeed, it took three centuries to return to population levels that existed prior to the Black Death.

Disaster on this scale had enduring psychological, social, economic, and political effects. Many individuals turned to pleasure, even debauchery, determined to enjoy themselves before it came their turn to die. Others retreated into a personal spirituality, convinced that they needed to put their lives in order before passing on to the next life. Occasionally, eccentric groups took shape. The Beghards, or Brethren of the Free Speech, claimed to be in a state of grace that allowed them to do as they pleased—including adultery, free love, nudity, and murder. By contrast, the Flagellants were so sure that man had incurred God's wrath that they whipped them-

Primary Source

FLAGELLANTS IN ENGLAND

Like the Qalandar dervishes in the Islamic realm (see p. 000), European Flagellants renounced the world and engaged in public self-punishment in reaction to the warfare, famines, and plagues of the fourteenth century. The Flagellants carried whips (flagella) with metal pieces run through knotted thongs, which they used to beat and whip themselves until they were bruised, swollen, and bloody. Robert of Avesbury here describes the actions of Flagellants in England during the reign of King Edward III.

In that same year of 1349, about Michaelmas [29 September], more than 120 men, for the most part from Zeeland or Holland, arrived in London from Flanders. These went barefoot in procession twice a day in the sight of the people, sometimes in St Paul's church and sometimes elsewhere in the city, their bodies naked except for a linen cloth from loins to ankle. Each wore a hood painted with a red cross at front and back and carried in his right hand a whip with three thongs. Each thong had a knot in it, with something sharp, like a needle, stuck through the middle of the knot so that it stuck out on each side, and as they walked one after the other they struck themselves with these whips on their naked, bloody bodies; four of them singing in their own tongue and the rest answering in the manner of the Christian litany. Three times in each procession they would all prostrate themselves on the ground, with their arms outstretched in the shape of a cross. Still singing, and beginning with the man at the end, each in turn would step over the others, lashing the man beneath him once with his whip, until all of those lying down had gone through the same ritual. Then each one put on his usual clothes and, always with their hoods on their heads and carrying their whips, they departed to their lodgings. It was said that they performed a similar penance every night.

→ *Describe how the Flagellants dressed, and identify the languages they spoke. What elements of Christianity did these characteristics display?*
→ *Why do you think the Flagellants whipped themselves?*
→ *How did the Flagellants differ from the Qalanders?*

SOURCE: Robertus de Avesbury, "Flagellants in England" from *The Black Death*, Rosemary Horrox, trans./ed., pp. 153–54. Copyright © Rosemary Horrox 1994. Reprinted with permission of Manchester University Press.

selves to atone for human sin. They also bullied communities that they visited, demanding to be housed, clothed, and fed. (See Primary Source: Flagellants in England.)

For many who survived the plague, Thomas Aquinas's rational Christianity no longer appealed, and disappointment with the clergy smoldered. Famished peasants resented priests and monks for living lives of luxury in violation of church tenets. In addition, they despaired at the absence of clergy when they were so greatly needed. In fact, many clerics had perished while attending to their parishioners. Others had fled to rural retreats far from the ravages of the Black Death, leaving their followers to fend for themselves.

THE CHURCH'S RESPONSE In the aftermath of famine and plague, religious authorities struggled to reclaim their power. The late medieval western church found itself divided at the top (at one point there were three popes) and challenged from below, both by individuals pursuing alternative kinds of spirituality and by increasing demands on the clergy and church administration. Facing challenges to its right to define religious doctrine and practices, the church identified all that was suspect and demanded strict obedience to the true faith. This entailed the persecution of heretics, Jews, Muslims, homosexuals, prostitutes, and "witches." But during this period the church also expanded its charitable and bureaucratic

Peasant Revolts. Long before the French Revolution, European peasants vented their anger against their noble masters. Lacking armaments and supplies, they usually lost—as this image of the brutal suppression of the French Jacquerie of 1358 depicts.

functions, providing alms to the urban poor and registering births, deaths, and economic transactions.

Persecution and administration cost money. Indeed, the needs as well as the extravagances of the clergy spurred certain questionable money-making tactics. One was the selling of indulgences (certificates that reduced one's time in purgatory, where souls continued the repentance that would eventually make them fit for heaven). This sort of unconventional fund raising, and the growing gap between the church's promises and its ability to bring Christianity into people's everyday lives, more than the persecutions, eventually sparked the Protestant Reformation (see Chapter 12).

A WEAKENING FEUDAL ORDER Just as the mayhem of the fourteenth and fifteenth centuries unleashed hostility toward the church, it also undermined the feudal order. Since the Roman era, peasant uprisings had occasionally erupted. But now they escalated into large-scale insurrections. In France and England, massive revolts signaled the peasants' resentment against lords who failed to protect them from marauding military bands, as well as their exasperation with feudal restrictions that now seemed—for the few survivors of plague and famine—too much to bear. In 1358 the French revolt, or **Jacquerie**, broke out (the term derived from "Jacques Bonhomme," a name that contemptuous masters used for all peasants). Armed with only knives and staves, the peasantry went on a rampage, killing hated nobles and clergy and burning and looting all the property they could get their hands on. At issue was the peasants' insistence that they

should no longer be tied to their land or have to pay for the tools they used in farming.

A better-organized uprising took place in England in 1381. Although the **English Peasants' Revolt** began as a protest against a tax levied to raise money for a war on France, it was also fueled by post-plague labor shortages: serfs demanded the freedom to move about, and free farm workers called for higher wages and lower rents. When landlords balked at these demands, aggrieved peasants assembled at the gates of London. The protesters demanded abolition of the feudal order, but the king ruthlessly suppressed them. Nonetheless, in both France and England a free peasantry gradually emerged as labor shortages made it impossible to keep peasants bound to the soil.

STATE BUILDING AND ECONOMIC RECOVERY

In the wake of famine, plague, and peasant uprisings, Europe's rulers tried to rebuild their polities and consolidate their power. Although their efforts at state building pale in comparison with those of the empires rising in Asia, one family, the Habsburgs, established a powerful and long-lasting dynasty. They provided emperors for the Holy Roman Empire from 1440 to 1806. Yet the Habsburg monarchs never succeeded in restoring an integrated empire to western Europe (as Chinese dynasts had done by claiming the mandate of heaven).

Moreover, language did not unite Europeans. While the written literary Chinese script remained a key administrative tool for China's dynasts, and in the Islamic world Arabic was the common language of faith, Persian the language of poetry, and Turkish the language of administration, in Europe Latin lost ground as rulers chose various regional dialects to be their official state language. In 1450 Europe had no central government, no official tongue, and only a few successful commercial centers, mostly in the Mediterranean basin (see Map 11-5). Feudalism had left a legacy of political fragmentation and enshrined privileges, which made the consolidation of a unified Christian Europe even more difficult to achieve.

Those who sought to rule the emerging states faced numerous obstacles. For example, rival claimants to the throne financed threatening private armies. Also, the clergy demanded and received privileges and often meddled in politics themselves. The church's huge landholdings and exemptions from taxation made it, too, a formidable economic powerhouse. And once the printing press became available in the 1460s, printers circulated anonymous pamphlets criticizing the court and the clergy. Some states had consultative bodies—such as the Estates General in France, the Cortes in Spain, or Parliament in England—in which princes formally asked representatives of their people for advice and, in the case of the English

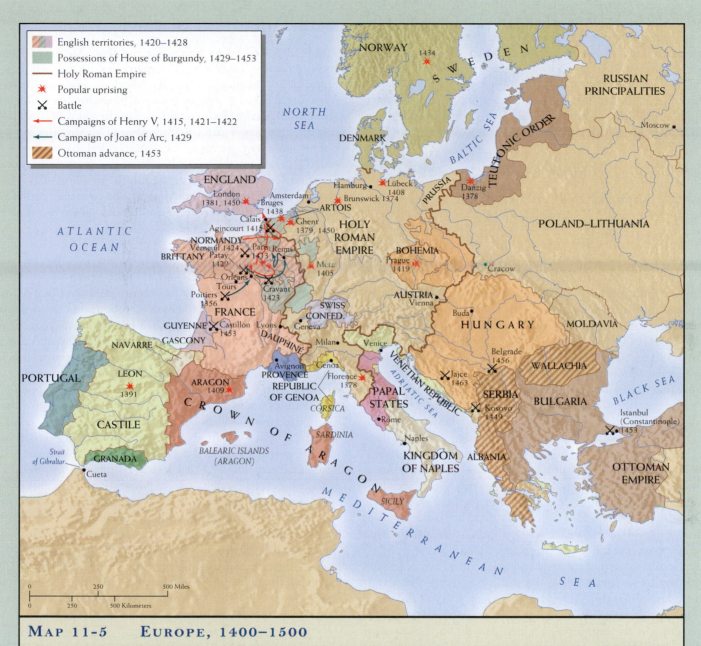

MAP 11-5   EUROPE, 1400–1500

Europe was a region divided by dynastic rivalries during the fifteenth century. Locate the most powerful regional dynasties on the map: Portugal, Castile, Aragon, France, England, and the Holy Roman Empire. In what country did the heaviest fighting occur? Why do you think one state was the scene for so many battles? On the basis of this map, predict which European territories and polities would become powerful in subsequent centuries, and which would not.

Parliament, for consent to new forms of taxation. Such bodies gave no voice to most nonaristocratic men and no representation to women. But they did allow the collective expression of grievances against high-handed policies.

Out of the chaos of famine, disease, and warfare, the diverse peoples of Europe found a political way forward. This path involved the formation of centralized national monarchies, much as the Ottomans, Safavids, Mughals, and Ming were accomplishing in Asia. (A **monarchy** is a political system in which one individual holds supreme power and passes that power on to his or her next of kin.) Often in competition with the new monarchies a sprinkling of city-states survived, in which a handful of wealthy and influential voters selected their leaders. Consolidation of these polities occurred sometimes through strategic marriages but more often through warfare, both between local princely families and with outsiders. Political stabilization was swiftest in southern Europe, where economies rebounded through trade with Southwest Asia. The stabilization of Italian city-states such as Venice and Florence, and of monarchical rule in Portugal and Spain, led to an economic and cultural flowering known as the Renaissance (see below).

POLITICAL CONSOLIDATION AND TRADE IN PORTUGAL

Portugal's fortunes demonstrate how political stabilization and the revival of trade entwined. After the chaos of the fourteenth century, Spain, England, and France followed the Portuguese example and established national monarchies. In Spain and Portugal, warfare against Muslims would help unite Christian territories, and Mediterranean trade would add valuable income to state coffers. In northern Europe, by contrast, lack of access to lucrative trade routes, in addition to internal feuding, regional warfare, and (after 1517) religious fragmentation, would delay recovery for decades.

Through the fourteenth century, Portuguese Christians devoted themselves to fighting the **Moors**, who were Muslim occupants of North Africa, the western Sahara, and the Iberian Peninsula. Decisive in this struggle was the Portuguese decision to cross the Strait of Gibraltar and seize the Moorish Moroccan fortresses at Ceuta, in North Africa: their ships could now sail between the Mediterranean and the Atlantic without Muslim interference. With that threat diminished, the Portuguese perceived their neighbor, Castile (part of what is now Spain), as their chief foe. Under João I (r. 1385–1433) the Castilians were defeated, and the monarchy could seek new territories and trading opportunities in the North Atlantic and along the West African coasts. João's son Prince Henrique, "Henry the Navigator," further expanded the family's domain by supporting expeditions down the coast of Africa and offshore to the Atlantic islands of the Madeiras and the Azores. The west and central coasts of Africa and the islands of the North and South Atlantic, including the Cape Verde Islands, São Tomé, Principe, and Fernando Po, soon became Portuguese ports of call.

The Portuguese monarchs granted the Atlantic islands to nobles as hereditary possessions on condition that the grantees colonize them, and soon the colonizers were establishing lucrative sugar plantations. In gratitude, noble families and merchants threw their political weight behind the king. Subsequent monarchs continued to reduce local elites' authority and to ensure smooth succession for members of the royal family. This political consolidation enabled Portugal to thrive in the wake of the Black Death.

DYNASTY BUILDING AND RECONQUEST IN SPAIN

The road to dynasty in Spain was arduous. Medieval Spain comprised rival kingdoms that quarreled ceaselessly. Also, Spain lacked religious uniformity: Muslims, Jews, and Christians lived side by side in relative harmony, and Muslim armies still occupied strategic posts in the south. Over time, however, marriages and the formation of kinship ties among nobles and between royal lineages yielded a new political order. One by one, the major houses of the Spanish kingdoms intermarried, culminating in the fateful wedding of Isabella of Castile and Ferdinand of Aragon. Thus, Spain's two most important provinces were joined, and Spain became a state to be reckoned with.

THE UNION OF CASTILE AND ARAGON   By the time Isabella and Ferdinand married in 1469, Spain was recovering from the miseries of the fourteenth century. (Castile and Aragon's population, for instance, rebounded from about 6 million in 1450 to 8.5 million in 1482.) This was more than a marriage of convenience. Castile was wealthy and populous; Aragon enjoyed an extended trading network in the Mediterranean. Together, the monarchs brought unruly nobles and distant towns under their domain. They topped off their achievements by marrying their children into other European royal families—especially the Habsburgs, central Europe's most powerful dynasty.

The new rulers also sent Christian armies south to push Muslim forces out of the Iberian Peninsula. By the mid-fifteenth century only Granada, a strategic lynchpin overlooking the straits between the Mediterranean and the Atlantic, remained in Muslim hands. After a long and costly siege, Christian forces captured the fortress there. This was a victory of enormous symbolic importance, as joyous as the fall of Constantinople was depressing. Many people in Spain thumped their chests in pride, unaware or unconcerned that at the same time Ottoman armies were conquering large sections of southeastern Europe.

THE INQUISITION AND WESTWARD EXPLORATION Just as the Safavid rulers had tried to stamp out all non-Shiite forms of Islam within their domains, so Isabella and Ferdinand sought to drive all non-Catholics out of Spain. Terrified by Ottoman incursions into Europe, in 1481 they launched the **Inquisition**, taking aim especially against *conversos*—converted Jews and Muslims, whom they suspected were Christians only in name. When Granada fell, the crown ordered the expulsion of all Jews from Spain; after 1499, a more tolerant attempt to convert the Moors by persuasion gave way to forced conversion—or emigration. All told, almost half a million people were forced to flee the Spanish kingdoms.

So strong was the tide of Spanish fervor by late 1491 that the monarchs listened now to a Genoese navigator whose pleas for patronage they had previously rejected. Christopher Columbus promised them unimaginable riches that could finance their military campaigns and bankroll a crusade to liberate Jerusalem from Muslim hands. Off he sailed with a royal patent that guaranteed the monarchs a share of all he discovered. Soon the Spanish economy was reorienting itself toward the Atlantic, and Spain's merchants, missionaries, and soldiers were preparing for conquest and profiteering in what had been, just a few years before, a blank space on the map.

THE STRUGGLES OF FRANCE AND ENGLAND, AND THE SUCCESS OF SMALL STATES

Warfare and strategic marriages allowed the Portuguese and Spanish monarchies to consolidate state power and to lay the foundations for revived commerce. But by no means were all states immediately successful. In France and England, the great age of European monarchy had yet to dawn.

When French forces finally pushed the English back across the English Channel in the Hundred Years' War (1337–1453), the French House of Valois began a slow process of consolidating royal power. Although diplomatic marriages helped the French crown expand its domain, two more centuries of royal initiatives and civil war were required to tame the powerful nobility. In England, even thirty years of civil war between the houses of Lancaster and York did not settle which one would take the throne. Both families in this War of the Roses ultimately lost out to the Tudors, who seized the throne in 1485. (See Global Connections & Disconnections: Joan of Arc: A Charismatic Leader in a Time of Social Turmoil.)

Even where stable states did arise, they were fairly small compared to the Ottoman and Ming empires. In the mid-sixteenth century, Portugal and Spain, Europe's two most expansionist states, had populations of 1 million and 9 million, respectively. England, excluding Wales, was a mere 3 million in 1550. Only France with 17 million had a population close to the Ottoman Empire's 25 million. And these numbers paled in comparison with Ming China's population of nearly 200 million in 1550 and Mughal India's 110 million in 1600.

But in Europe, small was advantageous. Portugal's relatively small population meant that the crown had fewer groups to instill with loyalty. Also, in the world of finance, the most successful merchants were those inhabiting the smaller Italian city-states and, a bit later, the cities of the northern Netherlands. The Florentines developed sophisticated banking techniques, created extensive networks of agents throughout Europe and the Mediterranean, and served as bankers to the popes. Venetian merchants enjoyed a unique role in the exchange of silks and spices from the eastern Mediterranean. It was in these prosperous city-states that the Renaissance began.

EUROPEAN IDENTITY AND THE RENAISSANCE

Europe's political and economic revival included a powerful outpouring of cultural achievements, led by Italian scholars and artists and financed by bankers, churchmen, and nobles. Much later, scholars coined the word **Renaissance** ("rebirth") to characterize the expanded cultural production of the Italian city-states, France, the Low Countries, England, and the Holy Roman Empire in the period 1430–1550. What was being "reborn" were ancient Greek and Roman art and learning—knowledge that could illuminate a world of expanding horizons and support the rights of secular individuals to exert power in it. Although the Renaissance was largely funded by popes and Christian kings, it broke the medieval church's monopoly on answers to the big questions and opened the way for secular forms of learning and a more human-centered understanding of the cosmos.

THE ITALIAN RENAISSANCE The Renaissance, ironically, was all about the new: new exposure, that is, to the old—to classical texts and ancient art and architectural forms. Although some Greek and Roman texts were known in Europe and the Islamic world, the fall of Constantinople and the invention of the printing press made others accessible to western scholars for the first time. Scholars now realized that the pre-Christian Greeks and Romans had known more: about how to represent and care for the human body; about geography, astronomy, and architecture; about how to properly govern states and armies. It was no longer enough to understand Christian doctrine and to trust medieval authorities; one had to accurately retranslate the original sources, which required the learning of languages and of history. This dive backward into ancient Greece and Rome became known as **humanism**, which sums up the aspiration to know more about the human experience beyond what the Christian scriptures offered.

Wealthy families, powerful rulers, and the Catholic Church were the sponsors of Renaissance achievement. For example, by the 1480s the di Medici family had been patronizing art based on ancient models for three generations. The Medici were bankers, but also influential political players in Florence and Rome. The family contributed greatly to making Florence one of the showplaces of Renaissance art and architecture, as well as the center stage for early Renaissance philosophy. Cosimo di Medici (1389–1464) funded the completion of the sumptuous Duomo, or cathedral of Florence, topped by the architect Brunelleschi's masterful dome, the largest built since antiquity. Cosimo's grandson, Lorenzo the Magnificent, supported many of the great Renaissance artists, including Leonardo da Vinci, Sandro Botticelli, and Michelangelo Buonarotti.

The artists who flourished in Florence, Rome, and Venice embraced their own form of humanism. In their case, the

JOAN OF ARC: A CHARISMATIC LEADER IN A TIME OF SOCIAL TURMOIL

The immense historical impact of a French peasant girl, Joan of Arc, demonstrates the importance of charismatic individuals—even women in male-dominated societies—during periods of social turmoil. As Europe endured plagues, famines, and war, its people sought help through the special talents of women, even in areas like warfare. Indeed, if not for Joan of Arc, the country we know today as France might not exist.

Appearing on the scene in 1429, as the English seemed to be winning the Hundred Years' War, she rallied the French against the English occupiers and turned the tide of the war. By giving religious sanction, as well as military succor, to the Valois monarch Charles VII, she made possible the consolidation of France and left Europe an inspiring image of the female warrior-saint.

The world of Joan's childhood was a chaotic one, in which English lords were laying claim to various French-speaking principalities. By 1420, Valois authority had been greatly eroded, and English armies were conquering more and more French towns. In 1428, the English laid siege to Orléans, a large town in north-central France. To contemporaries, it seemed a symbolic battle: as Orléans went, they thought, so the war would go—and so would God wish it to go.

This is the point at which the paths of a seventeen-year-old peasant girl and the monarch of France crossed. Beginning at about age thirteen, the shy girl had received visions of saints who instructed her to rescue Orléans and bring France's ruler to be crowned king at Reims Cathedral. (He had not been crowned there, in the tradition of all French kings, because the English armies controlled Reims, Paris, and northern France.) For five years Joan resisted, but at last she obeyed her celestial advisers. Granted an audience with Charles VII in 1429, Joan impressed him with her piety and her passionate devotion to the Valois crown. He concluded that God really had sent her to serve France's cause—and his own. Joan won command of 7,000 to 8,000 men; then, wearing a suit of armor and brandishing a sword, she marched to relieve Orléans. Joan directed the assault with brilliance and inspired the French forces; her charisma came not only from a tradition of female Christian "seers," but also from the peculiarity of her appearance (a young woman in male attire) and her appeal to French speakers who resented rule by English "outsiders." After driving the English from Orléans, she then pressed on to Reims; here, thanks to her military victories, Charles VII was crowned, fulfilling her visions. He was now king of France—and

though the war continued, the tide now turned in favor of the French.

The tide for Joan, however, turned for the worse. Although she continued to direct the troops with remarkable savvy, she failed to force open the gates of Paris, and jealous courtiers around Charles began to question her divine authority. She was wounded, then taken prisoner. After a year in English captivity she faced the Inquisition and was found guilty of heresy, on the grounds that her visions were false and misleading. On May 30, 1431, she was burned at the stake in the marketplace in the town of Rouen. Since that time she has stood as a heroic and charismatic martyr, and the French have often invoked her name to awaken patriotism against foreign threats.

The fact that this young, illiterate woman played such an important role in the history of European warfare and state formation testifies to the fact that male aristocrats, intellectuals, and clerics were not the only important actors. At the right place, at the right time, a woman could use courage, faith, and intelligence to make her visions prevail.

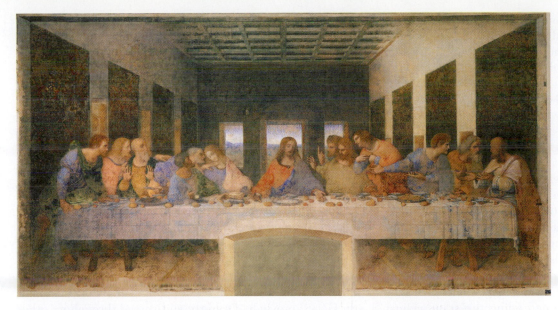

Renaissance Masterpieces. Leonardo da Vinci's *The Last Supper* (*above*) depicts Christ's disciples reacting to his announcement that one of them will betray him. Michelangelo's *David* (*right*) stands over thirteen feet high and was conceived as an expression of Florentine civic ideals.

return to ancient sources meant reviving the principles of the Greek architect Vitruvius and the imitation of nude classical sculpture. Their masterpieces, like Leonardo's *Last Supper* or Michelangelo's *David*, used the technique of perspective and classical treatments of the body to give vivacity and three-dimensionality to paintings and sculptures—even religious ones. Raphael's madonnas portrayed the Virgin Mary as a beautiful individual and not just as a symbol of chastity; similarly, Michelangelo's Sistine Chapel ceiling gave Adam the beautiful body of a Greek god so that viewers could appreciate the glory of the Creation. Of course, these artists also hoped to draw attention to their own achievements, and they were not disappointed. For soon northern European princes, too, sought out artists and humanists who could bring this inspiring new style to their courts.

THE RENAISSANCE SPREADS   By the sixteenth century, increasing economic prosperity, the circulation of books and images, and interstate competition were spreading Renaissance culture throughout Europe. Philip II of Spain, for example, purchased more than 1,000 paintings during his reign; Henry IV of France and his queen, Marie de Medici, invested a fortune in renovating the Louvre, building a new royal residence at Fontainebleau, and hiring Peter Paul Rubens to paint grand canvases. Courtiers built up-to-date palaces and invited scholars to live on their estates; Dutch, German, and French merchants also patronized the arts. All wanted their sons to be educated in the humanistic manner. Some families and religious institutions offered women access to the new learning, and some men encouraged their sisters, daughters, and wives

to expand their horizons. The well-educated nun Caritas Pirckheimer (1467–1532), for example, exchanged learned letters and books with male humanists in the German states. Studying Greek, Latin, and ancient rhetoric did not make the commercial elite equal to the aristocrats, or women equal to men, but this sort of education did enable some non-nobles to obtain social influence and to criticize the ruling elites.

THE REPUBLIC OF LETTERS   Since political and religious powers were not united in Europe (as they were in China and the Islamic world), scholars and artists could play one side against the other, or, alternatively, could suffer both clerical and political persecution. Michelangelo completed commissions for the Medici, for the Florentine Wool Guild, and for Pope Julius II. Peter Paul Rubens painted for the courts of France, Spain, England, and the Netherlands, as well as selling paintings on the open market. These two painters, renowned for showing a great deal of flesh, frequently offended conservative church officials, but their secular patrons kept them in oils. The Dutch scholar Desiderius Erasmus was able to ridicule the church because he had the patronage of English, Dutch, and French supporters. Fleeing persecution in Rome, the philosopher Giordano Bruno found a warm welcome in England—but made the mistake of thinking he was forgiven, and returned to Rome only to be burned at the stake.

The search for patrons and the flight from persecution, especially after the Reformation, made Europe's educated elite increasingly cosmopolitan (as it had in China and the Islamic empires). Scholars met one another in royal palaces and cultural centers such as Florence, Antwerp, and Amsterdam.

Seeking specialized information or rare books, they formed what was known as "the republic of letters"—a network of correspondents who were more interested in individual knowledge or talent than in noble titles or clerical rank.

COMPETING IDEAS OF GOVERNANCE Gradually, a network of educated men and women took shape that was not wholly dependent on either the church or the state. Thus these individuals acquired the means to challenge political, clerical, and aesthetic authority. Of course, they could also use their learning to defend the older elites: for example, numerous lawyers and scholars continued to work for the popes in defending the papacy. At the same time, in contrast, men like Erasmus and Martin Luther (the leading figure of the Reformation) looked to secular princes to support their critical scholarship.

Neither in Florence nor elsewhere did the Renaissance produce a consensus about who should rule. The Florentines pioneered a form of civic humanism under which all citizens were to devote themselves to defending the state against tyrants and foreign invaders; according to this view, the state would reward their civic virtue by ensuring their liberty. Yet it was also a Florentine, Niccolò Machiavelli, who wrote the most famous treatise on authoritarian power, *The Prince* (1513). Machiavelli argued that political leadership was not about obeying God's rules but about mastering the amoral means of modern statecraft. Holding and exercising power were ends in themselves, he claimed; civic virtue was merely a pretense on the part of those (like the Medici family he knew so well) who simply wanted to keep the upper hand.

The Renaissance produced a culture of critics who went back to classical ideas in order to go forward, to address the challenges and opportunities of an expanding world. This was not a movement that trickled down much to the common people, although they, too, surely were moved by the sight of the Duomo in Florence, or indirectly touched by the spread of printed books. The Renaissance transformed the European elite, however, making it more cosmopolitan and knitting together the artists and scholars who constituted "the republic of letters." By orienting the elite toward ancient models (for poetry, rhetoric, statecraft, geography, medicine, and architecture) instead of medieval ones, the Renaissance revolutionized European culture—even if it could not unify the states and peoples who cultivated it.

MING CHINA

> → *How did the Ming centralize their authority?*

Like the Europeans, the Chinese saw their stable worldview and political order crumble under the cataclysms of human and bacterial invasions. Moreover, like the Europeans, people in China had long regarded outsiders as "barbarians." Together, the Mongols and the Black Death upended the political and intellectual foundations of what had appeared to be the world's most integrated society. The Mongols brought the Yuan dynasty to power; then the plague devastated China and prepared the way for the emergence of the Ming dynasty.

CHAOS AND RECOVERY

China had been ripe for the plague's pandemic. Its population had increased significantly under the Song dynasty (960–1279) and subsequent Mongol rule. But by 1300, hunger and scarcity began to spread as resources stretched thin. A weakened population was especially vulnerable to plague. For seventy years, the Black Death ravaged China and shattered the Mongols' claim to a mandate from heaven. In 1331, plague may have killed 90 percent of the population in Bei Zhili (modern Hebei) province. From there it spread throughout other provinces, reaching Fujian and the coast at Shandong. By the 1350s, most of China's large cities suffered severe outbreaks.

The reign of the last Yuan Mongol rulers was a time of utter chaos. Even as the Black Death was engulfing large parts of China, bandit groups and dissident religious sects were undercutting the state's power. As in other realms devastated by the plague, popular religious movements foretold impending doom. Most prominent was the **Red Turban Movement**, which took its name from its soldiers' red headbands. This movement blended China's diverse cultural and religious traditions, including Buddhism, Daoism, and other faiths. Its leaders emphasized strict dietary restrictions, penance and ceremonial rituals in which the sexes freely mixed, and made proclamations that the world was drawing to an end.

In these chaotic times, only a strong military movement capable of overpowering other groups could restore order. That intervention began at the hands of a poor young man who had trained in the Red Turban Movement: Zhu Yuanzhang. He was an orphan from a peasant household in an area devastated by disease and famine, and a former novice at a Buddhist monastery. At age twenty-four Zhu joined the Red Turbans, after which he rose quickly to become a distinguished commander. Eventually, his forces defeated the Yuan and drove the Mongols from China.

It soon became clear that Zhu had a much grander design for all of China than the ambitions of most warlords. When he took the important city of Nanjing in 1356, he renamed it Yingtian ("In response to Heaven"). Buoyed by subsequent successful military campaigns, twelve years later Zhu (r. 1368–1398) proclaimed the founding of the Ming ("brilliant") dynasty. Soon thereafter, his troops met little resistance when they seized the Yuan capital of Beijing, causing the Mongol emperor to flee to his homeland in the steppe. It would, however, take Zhu almost another twenty years to reunify the entire country.

CENTRALIZATION UNDER THE MING

Zhu and successive Ming emperors had to rebuild a devastated society from the ground up. Although in the past China had experienced natural catastrophes, wars, and social dislocation, the plague's legacy was devastation on an unprecedented scale. It left the new rulers with the formidable challenge of rebuilding the great cities, restoring respect for ruling elites, and reconstructing the bureaucracy.

IMPERIAL GRANDEUR AND KINSHIP   The rebuilding began under Zhu, the Hongwu ("expansive and martial") Emperor, whose extravagant capital at Nanjing reflected imperial grandeur. When the dynasty's third emperor, the Yongle ("perpetual happiness") Emperor, relocated the capital to Beijing, he flaunted an even more grandiose style. Construction here mobilized around 100,000 artisans and 1 million laborers. The city had three separate walled enclosures. Inside the outer city walls sprawled the imperial city; within its walls lay the palace city, the Forbidden City. Traffic within the walled sections navigated through boulevards leading to the different gates, above which imposing towers soared. The palace compound, where the imperial family resided, had more than 9,000 rooms. Anyone standing in the front courts, which measured more than 400 yards on a side and boasted marble terraces and carved railings, would gasp at the sense of awesome power. That was precisely the effect the Ming emperors wanted (just as the Ottoman sultans did in building Topkapi Palace).

Marriage and kinship buttressed the power of the Ming imperial household. The dynasty's founder married the adopted daughter of a leading Red Turban rebel (her father, according to legend, was a convicted murderer), thereby consolidating his power and eliminating a threat. Empress Ma, as she was known, became Hongwu's principal wife and was praised for her compassion. Emerging as the kinder face of the regime, she tempered the harsh and sometimes cruel disposition of her spouse. He had numerous other consorts as well, including Korean and Mongol women, who bore him twenty-six sons and sixteen daughters.

BUILDING A BUREAUCRACY   Faced with the challenge of reestablishing order out of turmoil, Hongwu initially sought to rule through his many kinsmen—by giving imperial princes generous stipends, command of large garrisons, and significant autonomy in running their domains. However, when the princes' power began to threaten the court, Hongwu slashed their stipends, reduced their privileges, and took control of their garrisons. No longer dependent on these men, he established an imperial bureaucracy beholden only to him and to his successors. These officials won appointments through their outstanding performance on a reinstated civil service examination.

In addition, Hongwu took other steps to install a centralized system of rule. He assigned bureaucrats to oversee the manufacture of porcelain, cotton, and silk products, as well as tax collection. He reestablished the Confucian school system as a means of selecting a cadre of loyal officials (not unlike the Ottoman janissaries and administrators). He also set up local networks of villages to rebuild irrigation systems and to supervise reforestation projects to prevent flooding—with the astonishing result that the amount of land reclaimed nearly

The Forbidden City. The Yongle Emperor relocated the capital to Beijing, where he began the construction of the Forbidden City, or imperial palace. The palace was designed to inspire awe in all who saw it.

Chinese Irrigation. Farmers in imperial China used sophisticated devices to extract water for irrigation, as depicted in this illustration from the Yuan Mongol period.

tripled within eight years. Historians estimate that Hongwu's reign oversaw the planting of about 1 billion trees, including 50 million sterculia, palm, and varnish trees around Nanjing. Their products served in building a maritime expedition fleet in the early fifteenth century. For water control, 40,987 reservoirs underwent repairs or new construction.

Now the imperial palace not only projected the image of a power center, it *was* the center of power. Every official received his appointment by the emperor through the Ministry of Personnel. Hongwu also eliminated the post of prime minister (he executed the man who held the post) and henceforth ruled directly. Ming bureaucrats literally lost their seats and had to kneel before the emperor. In one eight-day period, Hongwu reputedly reviewed over 1,600 petitions dealing with 3,392 separate matters. The drawback, of course, was that he had to keep tabs on this immense system, and his bureaucrats were not always up to the task. Indeed, Hongwu constantly juggled personal and impersonal forms of authority, sometimes fortifying the administration, sometimes undermining it lest it become too autonomous. In due course, he nurtured a bureaucracy far more extensive than those of the Islamic empires. The Ming thus established the most highly centralized system of government of all the monarchies of this period. (See Primary Source: The Hongwu Emperor's Proclamation.)

RELIGION UNDER THE MING

The Ming's zeal extended to the religious pantheon as well. Citing the mandate of heaven, the emperor revised and strengthened the elaborate protocol of rites and ceremonies that had undergirded dynastic power for centuries. As well as underscoring the emperor's centrality, official rituals (such as those related to the gods of soil and grain) reinforced political and social hierarchies.

Under the guise of "community" gatherings, rites and sacrifices solidified the Ming order by portraying the rulers as the moral and spiritual benefactors of their subjects. On at least ninety occasions each year, the emperor engaged in sacrificial rites, providing symbolic communion between the human and the spiritual worlds. These lavish festivities reinforced the ruler's image as mediator between otherworldly affairs of the gods and worldly concerns of the empire's subjects. The message was clear: the gods were on the side of the Ming household.

As an example of religious rituals reinforcing hierarchies, the emperor sanctioned official cults that were either civil or military—and further distinguished as great, middle, or minor, as well as celestial, terrestrial, or human categories. Official cults, however, often conflicted with local faiths. In

Primary Source

THE HONGWU EMPEROR'S PROCLAMATION

This proclamation by the founder of the Ming dynasty, the Hongwu Emperor (r. 1368–1398), reveals how he envisioned reconstructing the devastated country as his own personal project. He sought a return to austerity by denouncing the morally corrosive effect of money and material possessions, and he especially distrusted his officials. Although frustrated in his efforts, Hongwu nonetheless set the tone for the centralization of power in the person of the emperor.

To all civil and military officials:

I have told you to refrain from evil. Doing so would enable you to bring glory to your ancestors, your wives and children, and yourselves. With your virtue, you then could assist me in my endeavors to bring good fortune and prosperity to the people. You would establish names for yourselves in Heaven and on earth, and for thousands and thousands of years, you would be praised as worthy men.

However, after assuming your posts, how many of you really followed my instructions? Those of you in charge of money and grain have stolen them yourselves; those of you in charge of criminal laws and punishments have neglected the regulations. In this way grievances are not redressed and false charges are ignored. Those with genuine grievances have nowhere to turn; even when they merely wish to state their complaints, their words never reach the higher officials. Occasionally these unjust matters come to my attention. After I discover the truth, I capture and imprison the corrupt, villainous, and oppressive officials involved. I punish them with the death penalty or forced labor or have them flogged with bamboo sticks in order to make manifest the consequences of good or evil actions. . . .

Alas, how easily money and profit can bewitch a person! With the exception of the righteous person, the true gentleman, and the sage, no one is able to avoid the temptation of money. But is it really so difficult to reject the temptation of profit? The truth is people have not really tried.

Previously, during the final years of the Yuan dynasty, there were many ambitious men competing for power who did not treasure their sons and daughters but prized jade and silk, coveted fine horses and beautiful clothes, relished drunken singing and unrestrained pleasure, and enjoyed separating people from their parents, wives, and children. I also lived in that chaotic period. How did I avoid such snares? I was able to do so because I valued my reputation and wanted to preserve my life. Therefore I did not dare to do these evil things. . . .

In order to protect my reputation and to preserve my life, I have done away with music, beautiful girls, and valuable objects. Those who love such things are usually "a success in the morning, a failure in the evening." Being aware of the fallacy of such behavior, I will not indulge such foolish fancies. It is not really that hard to do away with these tempting things.

→ *What criticisms does Hongwu level against the Mongol Yuan, whose rule he overthrew?*

→ *What crimes does he accuse his own officials of committing, and what punishments does he carry out?*

→ *Why would this Chinese emperor issue a decree that focuses on defining moral behavior?*

SOURCE: Lily Hwa, "Proclamations of the Hongwu Emperor." Reprinted with the permission of The Free Press, a division of Simon & Schuster, Inc., from *Chinese Civilization: A Sourcebook,* Second Edition, Revised and Expanded by Patricia Buckley Ebrey. Copyright © 1993 by Patricia Buckley Ebrey. All rights reserved.

---

this regard, they revealed the limits of Ming centralism. Consider Dongyang, a hilly interior region. As was common in Ming China, the people of Dongyang supported Buddhist institutions. Guan Yu, a legendary martial hero killed centuries earlier, was enshrined in a local Buddhist monastery there. But he was also worshipped as part of a state cult. Herein lay the problem: the state cult and the Buddhist monastery were

separate entities, and imperial law held that the demands of the state cult prevailed over those of the local monastery. So the state-appointed magistrates in Dongyang kept a watchful eye on local religious leaders, although the magistrates refrained from tampering directly in the monastery's affairs. Although the imperial government insisted that people honor their contributions to the state, Dongyang's residents delivered

Ming Deities. A pantheon of deities worshipped during the Ming, demonstrating the rich religious culture of the period.

most of their funds to the Buddhist monks. So strong were local sentiments and contributions that even the officials siphoned revenues to the monastery.

MING RULERSHIP

Religious sources of political power were less essential for the Ming dynasty than for the Islamic dynasties. Conquest and defense helped establish the realm, and bureaucracy kept it functioning. The empire's remarkable scale (see Map 11-6) required a remarkably complex administration. To many outsiders (especially Europeans, whose region was in a state of constant war), Ming stability and centralization appeared to be political wizardry.

In terms of the structures underlying Ming power, the usual dynastic dilemmas were present. The emperor wished to be seen as the special guardian of his subjects. He wanted their allegiance as well as their taxes and labor. But during hard times, poor farmers were reluctant to provide resources—taxes or services—to distant officials. For these reasons alone, Hongwu preferred to entrust management of the rural world to local leaders, whom he appointed as village chiefs, village elders, or tax captains. (In fact, a popular Chinese proverb was: "The mountain is high and the emperor is far away.") Within these communities, the dynasty created a social hierarchy based on age, sex, and kinship. While women's labor remained critical for the village economy, the government reinforced a gender hierarchy by promoting women's chastity and constructing commemorative arches for widows who refrained from remarrying. The Ming thus produced a more elaborate system for classifying and controlling its subjects than did the other Afro-Eurasian dynasties.

The Ming Empire, like the European and Islamic states, also faced periodic unrest and rebellion. Rebels often proclaimed their own brand of religious beliefs, just as local elites resented central authority. Outright terror helped stymie threats to central authority. In a massive wave of carnage, Hongwu slaughtered anyone who posed a threat to his authority, from the highest of ministers to the lowliest of scribes. From 1376 to 1393, four of his purges condemned close to 100,000 subjects to execution.

Yet, despite the emperor's immense power, the Ming Empire remained under-governed. Indeed, as the population multiplied, there were too few loyal officials to handle local affairs. By the sixteenth and early seventeenth centuries, for example, some 10,000 to 15,000 officials shouldered the responsibility of managing a population exceeding 200 million people. Nonetheless, Hongwu bequeathed to his descendants a set of tools for ruling that drew on subjects' direct loyalty to the emperor and on the intricate workings of an extensive bureaucracy. His legacy enabled his successors to balance local sources of power with centralizing ambitions.

TRADE UNDER THE MING

In the fourteenth century, China began its economic recovery from the devastation of disease and political turmoil. Gradually, political stability allowed trade to revive. Now the new dynasty's merchants reestablished China's preeminence in long-distance commercial exchange. Chinese silk and cotton textiles, as well as fine porcelains, ranked among the world's most coveted luxuries. Wealthy families from Lisbon to Kalabar loved to wash their hands in delicate Chinese bowls and to flaunt fine wardrobes made from bolts of Chinese dyed linens and smoothly spun silk. When a Chinese

MAP 11-6   MING CHINA, 1500S

The Ming state was one of the largest empires at this time—and the most populous. It had a long seacoast and even longer internal borders. What were of the two Ming capitals, and what were the three main seaport trading cities? According to the map, where did the Ming rulers expect the greatest threat to their security? How did the Ming rulers view foreign contact and exchange during this period?

merchant ship sailed into port, trading partners and onlookers crowded the docks to watch the unloading of precious cargoes.

OVERSEAS TRADE: SUCCESS AND SUSPICION   During the Ming period, Chinese traders based in ports such as Hangzhou, Quanzhou, and Guangzhou (Canton) were as energetic as their Muslim counterparts in the Indian Ocean.

These ports were home to prosperous merchants and the point of convergence for vast sea-lanes. Leaving the mainland ports, Chinese vessels carried precious wares to offshore islands, the Pescadores, and Taiwan. From there, they sailed on to the ports of Kyūshū, the Ryūkyūs, Luzon, and maritime Southeast Asia. As entrepôts for global goods, East Asian ports flourished. Former fishing villages developed into major urban centers.

The Ming dynasty viewed overseas expansion with suspicion, however. Hongwu feared that too much contact with the outside world would cause instability and undermine his rule. In fact, he banned private maritime commerce in 1371. But enforcement was lax, and by the late fifteenth century maritime trade once again surged. Because much of the thriving business took place in defiance of official edicts, it led to constant friction between government officials and maritime traders. Although the Ming government ultimately agreed to issue licenses for overseas trade in the mid-sixteenth century, its policies continued to vacillate. To Ming officials, the sea represented problems of order and control rather than opportunities.

MARITIME EXPLORATION AND AFTERMATH One spectacular exception to the Ming's attitude toward maritime trade was a series of officially sponsored expeditions in the early fifteenth century. It was the ambitious Yongle Emperor who took the initiative. One of his loyal followers was a Muslim whom the Ming army had captured as a boy. The youth was castrated and sent to serve at the court (as a eunuch, he could not continue his family line and so theoretically owed sole allegiance to the emperor). Given the name **Zheng He** (1371–1433), he grew up to be an important military leader. The emperor entrusted him with venturing out to trade, collect tribute, and display China's power to the world.

From 1405 to 1433, Zheng He commanded the world's greatest armada and led seven naval expeditions. His larger ships stretched 400 feet in length (Columbus's *Santa Maria*

was 85 feet), carried hundreds of sailors on four tiers of decks, and maneuvered with sophisticated rudders, nine masts, and watertight compartments. The first expedition set sail with a flotilla of 62 large ships and over 200 lesser ones. All 28,000 men aboard pledged to promote Ming glory.

Zheng He and his entourage aimed to establish tributary relations with far-flung territories—from Southeast Asia to the Indian Ocean ports, to the Persian Gulf, and to the east coast of Africa (see Map 11-7). These expeditions did not seek territorial expansion, but rather control of trade and tribute. Zheng traded for ivory, spices, ointments, exotic woods, and even some wildlife, including giraffes, zebras, and ostriches. He also used his considerable force to intervene in local affairs, exhibiting China's might in the process. If a community refused to pay tribute, Zheng's fleet would attack it. He encouraged rulers or envoys from Southeast Asia, India, Southwest Asia, and Africa to visit his homeland. When local rulers were uncooperative, Zheng might seize them and drag them all the way to China to face the emperor, as he did the rulers of Sumatra and Ceylon.

As spectacular as they were, Zheng's accomplishments could not survive the changing tides of events at home. Although many items gathered on his voyages delighted the court, most were not the stuff of everyday commerce. The expeditions were glamorous but expensive, and they came to an abrupt halt in 1433. Never again did the Ming undertake such large-scale maritime ventures. In fact, as early as 1424, when the Yongle Emperor died, the expeditions had already lost their most enthusiastic patron. Moreover, by the mid-

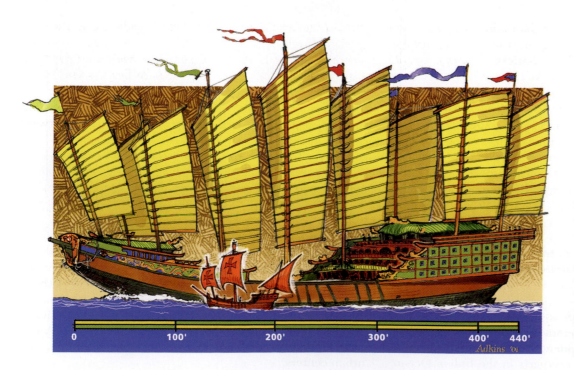

Zheng He's Ship. A testament to centuries of experience in shipbuilding and maritime activities, the largest ship in Zheng He's armada in the early fifteenth century was about five times the length of Columbus's *Santa Maria* (pictured next to Zheng's ship) and had nine times the capacity in terms of tonnage. It had nine staggered masts and twelve silk sails, all designed to demonstrate the grandeur of the Ming Empire.

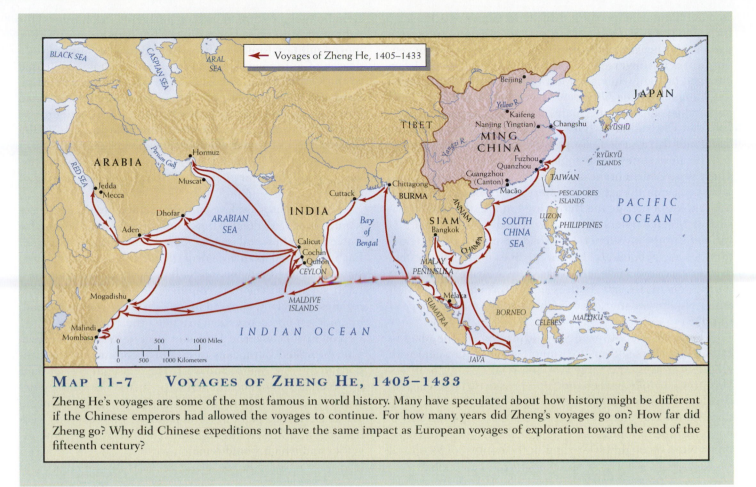

MAP 11-7   VOYAGES OF ZHENG HE, 1405–1433

Zheng He's voyages are some of the most famous in world history. Many have speculated about how history might be different if the Chinese emperors had allowed the voyages to continue. For how many years did Zheng's voyages go on? How far did Zheng go? Why did Chinese expeditions not have the same impact as European voyages of exploration toward the end of the fifteenth century?

fifteenth century, there was a revival of military threats from the north. At that time the Ming court was shocked to discover that during a tour of the frontiers, the emperor had been captured and held hostage by the Mongols. Recalling how the maritime-oriented Song dynasty had been overrun by invaders from the north (see Chapter 10), Ming officials withdrew imperial support for seagoing ventures and instead devoted their energies to overland ventures and defense.

Even though maritime commerce continued without official patronage, the abrupt withdrawal of imperial support led to the decline of Chinese naval power and opened the way for newcomers and rivals. Southeast Asians took advantage by constructing large oceangoing vessels, known as *jong*, which plied the regional trade routes from the fifteenth century to the early sixteenth century. These ships weighed an average of 350 to 500 tons (the largest weighed 1,000 tons) and carried 1,000 men on board. They transported cargoes and passengers not only to southern China, but also to the Indian Ocean as far west as Calicut and the Red Sea. Muslims also occupied the vacuum left by the Chinese, sailing west from ports such as Calicut across the

Indian Ocean to Mombassa and Mogadishu, and east to Melaka (Malacca). In addition, Japanese pirates commandeered some of the trade. The Chinese decision to focus on internal trade and defending northern borders just at the time others began to look outward and overseas was, in a way, as monumental as that of Mehmed to take Constantinople, or that of Columbus to attempt a perilous westward voyage across "the Ocean Sea."

 ## CONCLUSION

How could all the dying and devastation that came with the Black Death not have transformed the peoples of Afro-Eurasia? Much did change, but certain underlying ideals and institutions endured. What changed were mainly the political regimes, which took the blame for the catastrophes. The Delhi Sultanate, the Abbasid Empire, and the Yuan dynasty collapsed. In contrast, universal religions and wide-ranging cultural systems persisted even though they underwent vast transformations. The Ming dynasts in China set the stage for a long tenure by claiming as had previous rulers the mandate of heaven and stressing China's place at the center of their universe. A strict Shiite version of Islam emerged in Iran, while a fervent form of Sunni Islam found its champion in the Ottoman Empire. In Europe, national monarchies appeared in Spain, Portugal, France, and England. Yet Christianity, whose clerics had so often failed the dying and the disabled, swept back with renewed vigor.

The new states and empires had notable differences. These were evident in the ambition of a Ming warlord who established a new dynasty, the military expansionism of Turkish households bordering the Byzantine Empire, the unifying vision of Mughal rulers in northern India, and the desire of various European rulers to consolidate power. But interactions among peoples also mattered: an eagerness to reestablish and expand trade networks, and a desire to convert unbelievers to "the true faith"—be it a form of Islam, a variant of Hinduism, an exclusive Christianity, or a local type of Buddhism.

The dynasties all faced similar problems. They had to establish legitimacy, ensure smooth succession, deal with religious groups, and forge working relationships with nobles, townspeople, merchants, and peasants. Yet each state developed distinctive traits as a result of political innovation, traditional ways of ruling, and borrowing from neighbors. European monarchies achieved significant internal unity, often through warfare and in the context of a cultural Renaissance. Ottoman rulers perfected techniques for ruling an ethnically and religiously diverse empire: they moved military forces swiftly, allowed local communities a degree of autonomy, and trained a bureaucracy dedicated to the Ottoman and Sunni Islamic way of life. The Ming fashioned an imperial system based on a Confucian-trained bureaucracy and intense subordination to the emperor so that it could manage a mammoth population. The rising monarchies of Europe, the Shiite regime of the Safavids in Persia, and the Ottoman state all blazed with religious fervor and sought to eradicate or subordinate the beliefs of other groups.

The new states displayed unprecedented political and economic powers. All demonstrated military prowess, a desire for stable hierarchies and secure borders, and a drive to expand. Each legitimized its rule via dynastic marriage and succession, state-sanctioned religion, and administrative bureaucracies. Each supported vigorous commercial activity. The Islamic regimes, especially, engaged in long-distance commerce and, by conquest and conversion, extended their holdings.

For Europeans, the Ottoman conquests were decisive. They provoked Europeans to establish commercial connections to the east, south, and west. The consequences of their new toeholds would be momentous—just as the Chinese decision to turn *away* from overseas exploration and commerce marked a turning point in world history. Both decisions were instrumental in determining which worlds would come together and which would remain apart.

Chronology

	1300	1400
EUROPE	◆---◆ *1315–1322 Famine in Europe* *1337–1453 Hundred Years' War in France* ◆------------- ◆ *1347 Black Death reaches Italian port cities* ◆ *1358 Jacquerie Revolt in France*	 ◆ *1381 English Peasants' Revolt*
SOUTH ASIA	◆ *1303 Delhi Sultanate army repulses Mongols*	◆ *1398 Timur sacks Delhi*
EAST ASIA	◆ *1320 Black Death begins in China* ◆-----------------◆ *1368–1398 Reign of Hongwu Empe* *1403–1424 Reign of Yongle Emperor in China* ◆------------◆ *1405–1433 Zheng He's voyages from China* ◆----------------◆	
THE ISLAMIC WORLD	◆---------------◆ *1299–1326 Osman begins to build Ottoman Empire* *1421–1451 Murad II expands the Ottoman Empire* ◆---------	

Review and research materials are available
at StudySpace: 🄪 WWNORTON.COM/STUDYSPACE

KEY TERMS

Black Death (p. 412)
dynasty (p. 413)
English Peasants' Revolt (p. 430)
humanism (p. 433)
Inquisition (p. 432)
Jacquerie (p. 430)
khan (p. 424)
monarchy (p. 431)

Moors (p. 432)
Ottoman Empire (p. 417)
Red Turban Movement (p. 436)
Renaissance (p. 433)
shah (p. 424)
Sikhism (p. 426)
Topkapi Palace (p. 422)
Zheng He (p. 442)

STUDY QUESTIONS

1. Explain how the Black Death, or bubonic plague, spread throughout Afro-Eurasia. What human activity facilitated its diffusion?
2. Describe the long-term consequences of bubonic plague for the Afro-Eurasian world. What were the plague's social, political, and economic ramifications in various parts of the landmass?
3. Identify the three main Islamic dynasties that emerged after the bubonic plague. How were they similar, and how were they different?
4. Describe how the Ming dynasty centralized its power in China in the fourteenth and fifteenth centuries. What political innovations did it pursue, and what traditions did it sustain?
5. Describe the goals of the Ming dynasty's maritime exhibitions. Why did the government later abandon them?
6. Explain why the bubonic plague undermined the feudal order of the Catholic Church. How did regional monarchs in Europe capitalize on this development?
7. What were the key features of the Renaissance in Europe? How did it spread and change?

	1500	1600

◆ ◆------------------◆ *1455–1485 War of the Roses in England*

◆ *1469 Castile and Aragon united*

◆ *1492 Spaniards take Granada from Muslims*

◆ *1526 Babur founds Mughal Empire in India*

a (Ming dynasty)

◆

◆------------------◆ *1451–1481 Mehmed II expands the Ottoman Empire*

◆ *1453 Ottoman armies conquer Constantinople*

◆ *1501 Shiism becomes Safavid state religion*

◆------------◆ *1501–1524 Shah Ismail reigns over Safavid Empire*

◆----------------------------◆ *1520–1566 Suleiman consolidates Ottoman Empire*

12

CONTACT, COMMERCE, AND COLONIZATION, 1450–1600

In 1519, five ships under the command of Ferdinand Magellan set out from the Spanish mainland. Nearly three years later a single vessel returned, having successfully circumnavigated the globe. This achievement came at a high cost: four ships had been lost, and only 18 men out of 265 had staved off scurvy, starvation, and stormy seas to complete the journey. Magellan himself had died. But the survivors had become the first true world travelers. Unlike earlier adventurers who penetrated Eurasia and Africa, Magellan's transoceanic passage connected these worlds with others that, from an Afro-Eurasian viewpoint, had been apart—the Americas.

The voyages of Magellan and other European mariners intensified westerners' contact with Asia's vibrant commercial networks and gave Europeans access to a region they called the New World. Although Christopher Columbus did not intend to "discover" America when he went looking for Asia, his voyages convinced Europeans that there were still new territories to exploit and people to convert to Christianity. Moreover, in colonizing the Americas, Europeans drew on connections with West Africa.

Indeed, African laborers became vital to agriculture and mining in the American colonies. Soon the New World's riches were prominent participants in the commercial circuits of Afro-Eurasia.

This chapter introduces the initial European conquest and colonization of the Americas. In the narrative of world history, few events surpass Columbus's voyages of discovery, which opened up worlds about which Afro-Eurasians had no previous knowledge. For the first time since the Ice Age migrations, peoples again moved from Afro-Eurasian landmasses to the Americas. So did animals, plants, commercial products, and—most momentous—deadly germs.

It was enormously significant that Europeans, rather than Asians or Africans, first stumbled upon the Americas and then exploited their resources. For Europeans, too, now became empire builders—but of a different nature. Their empires were overseas, far from the homeland. While the new colonies generated vast riches, they also brought unsettling changes to those who sought to make and maintain empires.

Despite the significance of Europeans' activity in the Americas, most Africans and Asians were barely aware of its importance to them. As the chapter demonstrates, Asian empires in Ottoman-controlled lands and in India and China continued to flourish after recovering from the Black Death. Nor was Europe's attention exclusively on the Americas, for its national monarchies competed for sway at home. Religious revolt in the form of the Protestant Reformation intensified these rivalries. In the wake of Columbus, the drive to build and protect empires across oceans—as well as religious conflicts abroad and at home—scattered peoples, splattered blood, and shattered worlds.

THE OLD TRADE AND THE NEW

> → *What was old and what was new in sixteenth-century world trade?*

Well before the products of the Americas entered the circuits of Afro-Eurasian trade, commerce had recovered from the destruction wrought by the Black Death. Just as political leaders had rebuilt states by mixing traditional and innovative ideas, merchant elites revived old trade patterns while establishing new networks. Increasingly, traffic across seas supplemented, if not supplanted, the overland transportation of goods. The Indian Ocean and China Seas emerged as the focal points of Afro-Eurasia's maritime commerce. Across these waters moved an assortment of goods, coordinated by Arab, Persian, Indian, and Chinese merchants who often settled in foreign lands. There they facilitated trade and mixed with locals.

European mariners and traders, searching for new routes to South and East Asia, began exploring the Atlantic coast of Africa. Lured by spices, silks, and slaves, and aided by new maritime technology, Portuguese expeditions made their way around Africa and onward to India. Meanwhile, Spanish monarchs sponsored Columbus's bid to reach Asia by sailing west across the Atlantic. Portuguese and Spanish ventures alike sought to convert "heathen" peoples to Christianity and to reap the riches abounding in Asian ports. Although Euro-

Focus Questions

Ⓖ WWNORTON.COM/STUDYSPACE

→ *What was old and what was new in sixteenth-century world trade?*

→ *How did the Portuguese attitude toward trade enable the Portuguese to exploit and dominate their trading partners?*

→ *What did European conquerors adopt and change from the New World traditions they encountered?*

→ *What military and maritime technologies advanced Portuguese exploration?*

→ *What caused the political rivalries and religious rifts that divided Europe in the fifteenth and sixteenth centuries?*

→ *Why did trade expand and wealth increase in sixteenth-century Asia?*

peans still had little to offer would-be trading partners in Asia, their developing capability in overseas trade would lay the foundations for a new kind of global commerce.

THE REVIVAL OF THE CHINESE ECONOMY

China's economic dynamism was the crucial ingredient to Afro-Eurasia's global economic revival following the devastation wrought by the Black Death. Under the Ming dynasty, commerce rebounded and the Chinese achieved impressive economic expansion.

China's vast internal economy, not external trade, was the mainspring of the country's progress. After the Ming dynasty relocated its capital from Nanjing in the prosperous south to the northern city of Beijing, Chinese merchants, artisans, and farmers exploited the surging domestic market. Reconstruction of the Grand Canal now opened a major artery that allowed food and riches from the economically vibrant lower Yangzi area to reach the capital region of Beijing. Urban centers, such as Nanjing with a population approaching a million and Beijing at half a million, became massive and lucrative markets.

Along China's elaborate internal trading networks flowed silk and cotton textiles, rice, porcelain ceramics, paper, and many other products. The Ming's concern about the potentially disruptive effects of trade did not dampen this activity, and efforts to curb overseas commerce (following Zheng He's voyages; see Chapter 11) were largely unsuccessful. Merchants not only were tolerated but often thrived. And despite

Chinese Porcelain Box. The shape, coloring, and texture of this Chinese porcelain writing box are a tribute to the exquisite craftsmanship that went into its production. This box was also a symbol of flourishing world trade and a typical example of what the French called "chinoiserie," the possession of which was a hallmark of taste and cultivation among the rich and the status-conscious in Europe.

strictures on overseas trade, coastal cities remained active harbors (see Map 12-1).

Although the Chinese kept the best products for themselves, their silks and porcelain were esteemed across Afro-Eurasia. But what did foreign buyers have to trade with the Chinese? The answer was silver, which became essential to the Ming monetary system. Whereas their predecessors had used paper money, Ming consumers and traders mistrusted anything other than silver or gold for commercial dealings. Once the rulers adopted silver as a means of tax payment in the 1430s, it became the predominant medium for larger transactions.

However, China did not produce sufficient silver for its growing needs—a situation that foreigners learned to exploit. Indeed, silver and other precious metals were about the only commodities for which the Chinese would trade their precious manufactures. Through most of the sixteenth century, China's main source of silver was Japan, which one Florentine merchant called the "silver islands." Chinese and European merchants alike plied the routes from Japanese ports to the Chinese mainland.

After the 1570s, however, the Philippines, now under the control of the Spanish, became a gateway for silver coming from the New World. The Ming had developed a commercial fleet, which enabled their merchants to ship goods to Manila in exchange for silver (as well as firearms, sugar, potatoes, and tobacco). Despite official attempts to control trade, China became the final repository for much of the world's silver for roughly two hundred years. According to one estimate, one-third of all silver mined in the Americas wound up in Chinese hands. This influx fueled China's phenomenal economic expansion. New World silver also bought Europeans greater access to China's coveted goods.

THE REVIVAL OF INDIAN OCEAN TRADE

China's economic expansion occurred within the revival of Indian Ocean trade. In fact, many of the same merchants seeking trade with China developed a brisk commerce that tied the whole of the Indian Ocean together. As a result, ports in East Africa and the Red Sea again enjoyed links with coastal cities of India, South Asia, and the Malay Peninsula. Muslims dominated this trade.

India was the geographic and economic center of these trade routes. With a population expanding as rapidly as China's, its large cities (such as Agra, Delhi, and Lahore) each boasted nearly half a million residents. India's manufacturing center, Bengal, exported silk and cotton textiles and rice throughout South and Southeast Asia. Like China, India had a favorable trade balance (meaning they were exporting more than they were importing) with Europe and West Asia, exporting textiles and pepper (a spice that Europeans prized) in exchange for silver.

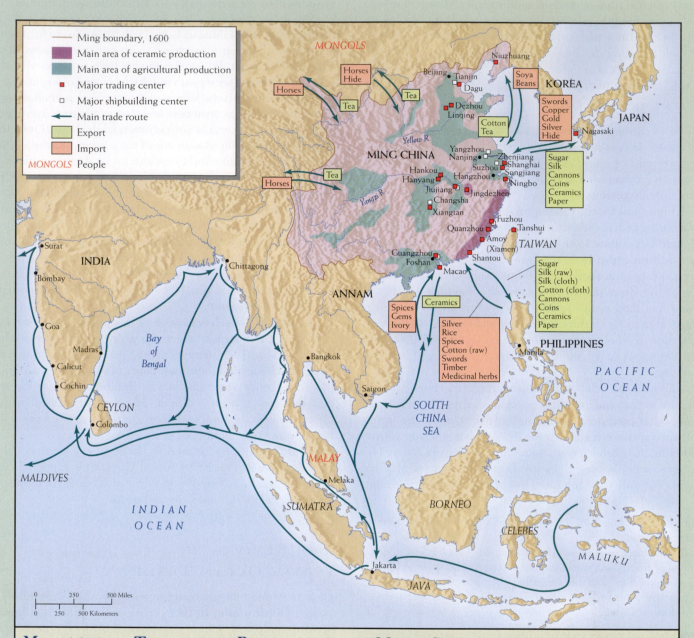

MAP 12-1 TRADE AND PRODUCTION IN MING CHINA

The Ming Empire in the early seventeenth century was the world's most populous state and arguably its wealthiest. According to this map, what were the main items involved in China's export-import trade, and what were some of the regions that purchased its exports? In what way does the activity represented on this map indicate why China was the world's leading importer of silver at this time? Locate the major trading and shipbuilding centers, and then explain how important the export trade was to the Ming Empire's prosperity.

In dealing with China, Indian merchants faced the same problem as Europeans and West Asians: they had to pay with silver. So they became as dependent on gaining access to silver as others who were courting Chinese commerce. But unlike Chinese merchants, Indian and Islamic traders in the region's commercial hubs did not obey one overarching political authority. This gave them considerable autonomy from political affairs and allowed them to occupy strategic positions in long-distance trade. Meanwhile, rulers all along the Indian Ocean enriched themselves with customs duties while flaunting their status with exotic goods. For glorifying sovereigns and worshipping deities, luxuries such as silks, porcelains, ivory, gold, silver, diamonds, spices, frankincense, myrrh, and incense were in high demand. Thus the Indian Ocean trade connected a vast array of consumers and producers long before Europeans arrived on the scene.

Of the many port cities supporting Indian Ocean commerce, none was more important than Melaka, located at a choke point between the Indian Ocean and the South China Sea. Melaka had no hinterland of farmers to support it, so it thrived exclusively as an entrepôt (a commercial hub for long-distance trade) for world traders, thousands of whom resided in the city or passed through it. Indeed, Melaka's merchants were a microcosm of the region's diverse commercial community. Arabs, Indians, Armenians, Jews, East Africans, Persians, and eventually western Europeans established themselves there to profit from the commerce that flowed in and out of the port.

OVERLAND COMMERCE AND OTTOMAN EXPANSION

In the fifteenth and sixteenth centuries, seaborne commerce eclipsed but did not eliminate overland caravan trading. In fact, along some routes, overland commerce thrived anew.

One well-trafficked route linked the Baltic Sea, Muscovy, the Caspian Sea, the central Asian oases, and China. Other land routes carried goods to the ports of China and the Indian Ocean; from there, they crossed to the Ottoman Empire's heartland and went by land farther into Europe.

Of the many entrepôts that sprang up along caravan routes, none enjoyed more spectacular success than Aleppo in Syria. Thanks to its prime location at the end of caravan routes from India and Baghdad, Aleppo came to overshadow its Syrian rivals, Damascus and Homs. A vital supply point for Anatolia and the Mediterranean cities, Aleppo by the late sixteenth century was the most important commercial center in southwest Asia.

The Aleppans, like others within the Ottoman Empire, revered successful merchants. In popular stories such as *The Thousand and One Nights*, they celebrated these wealthy traders as shrewd men who amassed enormous wealth by mastering the intricacies of the caravan trade. Those close to the trade recognized how difficult the merchant's task was. The caravans gathered on the city's edge, where animals were hired, tents sewn, and saddles and packs arranged. Large caravans involved 600 to 1,000 camels and up to 400 men; smaller parties required no more than a dozen animals. Whatever the size, a good leader was essential. Only someone who knew the difficult desert routes and enjoyed the confidence of nomadic Bedouin tribes (which provided safe passage for a fee) could hope to make the journey profitable.

Overland Caravans and Caravanserais. Muslim governments and merchants' associations constructed inns, or caravanserais, along the major trading routes. These areas were capable of accommodating a large number of traders and their animals in great comfort.

MAIN THEMES

→ *European voyagers and colonizers "discover" the Americas (the so-called New World) and connect Afro-Eurasia with the Americas for the first time since the Ice Age.*

→ *Not only do peoples move back and forth between Afro-Eurasia and the Americas; so do plants, animals, cultural products, and diseases—the Columbian exchange.*

→ *Europeans create empires at great distances from their homelands, fail to enslave Native Americans, and bring in African captives as slave laborers, creating the Atlantic System.*

FOCUS ON *Regional Impacts of European Colonization and Trade*

Europe

+ Portugal creates a trading empire in the Indian Ocean and the South China Sea.
+ Spain and Portugal establish colonies in the Americas, discover silver, and establish export-oriented plantation economies.
+ As the balance of power in Europe shifts, the Protestant Reformation breaks out in northern and western Europe, splitting the Catholic Church.

The Americas

+ Native Americans, lacking immunity to European diseases, perish everywhere.
+ Spanish conquest and disease destroy the two great Native American empires in Mexico (the Aztecs) and Peru (the Incas).

Africa

+ Trade in African captives fuels the Atlantic slave trade, which furnishes labor for European plantations in the Americas.

Asia

+ Asian empires—the Mughals in India, the Ming in China, the Safavids in Iran, and the Ottomans in western Asia and the eastern Mediterranean—barely notice the Americas but profit economically from enhanced global trade.

Ottoman authorities took a keen interest in the caravan trade, since the state gained considerable tax revenue from it. To facilitate the caravans' movement, the government maintained refreshment and military stations along the route. The largest had individual rooms to accommodate the chief merchants and could provide lodging for up to 800 travelers, as well as care for all their animals. But gathering so many traders, animals, and cargoes could also attract marauders, especially desert tribesmen. To stop the raids, authorities and merchants offered cash payments to tribal chieftains as "protection money." This was a small price to pay in order to protect the caravan trade, whose revenues ultimately supported imperial expansion.

EUROPEAN EXPLORATION AND EXPANSION

→ *How did the Portuguese attitude toward trade enable the Portuguese to exploit and dominate their trading partners?*

The Muslim conquest of Constantinople, Europe's gateway to the east (see Chapter 11), sent shock waves through Christendom and prompted Europeans to probe unexplored links to the east. That entailed looking south and west—and venturing across the seas. (See Map 12-2.) Taking the lead were the Portuguese, whose search for new routes to Asia led them first to Africa.

THE PORTUGUESE IN AFRICA AND ASIA

Europeans had long believed that Africa was a storehouse of precious metals. In fact, a fourteenth-century map, the Catalan Atlas, depicted a single black ruler controlling a vast quantity of gold in the interior of Africa. Thus, as the price of gold skyrocketed during and after the Black Death, ambitious men decided to venture southward in search of this commodity and its twin, silver. These intrepid adventurers did not allow their fears of the world they anticipated encountering to overcome their ambitions. The first Portuguese sailors expected to find giants and Amazons, seas of darkness, and distant lands of savages and cannibals. After all, stories and myths had shaped their views of the places and peoples they would encounter.

The Catalan Atlas. This 1375 map shows the world as it was then known. Not only does it depict the location of continents and islands, but it also includes information on ancient and medieval tales, regional politics, astronomy, and astrology.

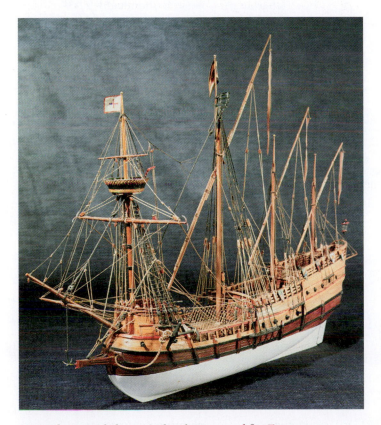

Caravel. Caravels became the classic vessel for European exploration. They had many decks and plenty of portholes for cannons, could house a large crew, and had lots of storage for provisions, cargo, and booty.

NAVIGATION AND MILITARY ADVANCES Innovations in maritime technology and information from other mariners helped Portuguese sailors navigate the treacherous waters along the African coast. In the former category were new vessels. The carrack worked well on bodies of water like the Mediterranean; the caravel could nose in and out of estuaries and navigate unpredictable currents and winds. By using highly maneuverable caravels and perfecting the technique of tacking (sailing into the wind rather than before it), the Portuguese advanced far along the West African coast. In addition, newfound expertise with the compass and the astrolabe helped them determine latitude. The Portuguese also applied knowledge absorbed from ancient Greeks and Arabs and had assistance from Muslim mariners who shared their wide experience of Africa and the Indian Ocean.

The Portuguese success in the Indian Ocean was also partly the result of a revolution in military technology that owed much to borrowings from Asia. It began with the adaptation of a Chinese technology: gunpowder. The Ottomans used it to conquer Constantinople in 1453 with enormous cannons and 800-pound cannonballs. In 1492, Christians used cannons to breach the walls of Granada. Europeans also used smaller cannons, which were more mobile and propelled iron balls in relatively flat trajectories, to destroy old fortifications. When mounted against warships' gunwales, such cannons could bombard ports and rival navies—or merchant

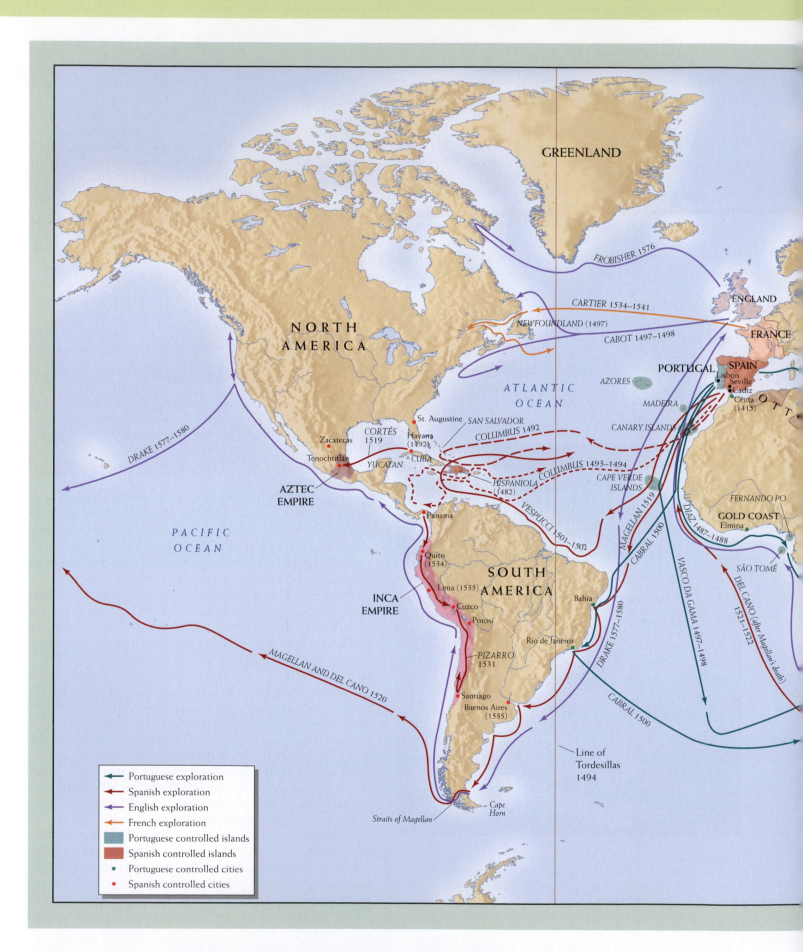

GREENLAND

NORTH AMERICA

FROBISHER 1576

CARTIER 1534–1541

ENGLAND

NEWFOUNDLAND (1497)

CABOT 1497–1498

FRANCE

PORTUGAL SPAIN

Lisbon
Seville
Cadiz
Ceuta
(1415)

AZORES

ATLANTIC OCEAN

MADEIRA

St. Augustine *SAN SALVADOR*

CANARY ISLANDS

Zacatecas

CORTÉS 1519

Havana
(1492)

COLUMBUS 1492

CUBA

COLUMBUS 1493–1494

CAPE VERDE ISLANDS

YUCATAN

HISPANIOLA (1482)

FERNANDO PO

Tenochtitlán

AZTEC EMPIRE

GOLD COAST

Elmina

DRAKE 1577–1580

Panama

VESPUCCI 1501–1502

MAGELLAN 1519

CABRAL 1500

DÍAZ 1487–1488

PACIFIC OCEAN

Quito (1534)

SOUTH AMERICA

Bahia

VASCO DA GAMA 1497–1498

SÃO TOMÉ

DEL CANO 1521–1522

INCA EMPIRE

Lima (1535)

Cuzco

Potosí

Rio de Janeiro

PIZARRO 1531

MAGELLAN AND DEL CANO 1520

Santiago

Buenos Aires (1535)

DRAKE 1577–1580

CABRAL 1500

DEL CANO (after Magellan's death) 1521–1522

Line of Tordesillas 1494

Cape Horn

Straits of Magellan

Portuguese exploration
Spanish exploration
English exploration
French exploration
Portuguese controlled islands
Spanish controlled islands
Portuguese controlled cities
Spanish controlled cities

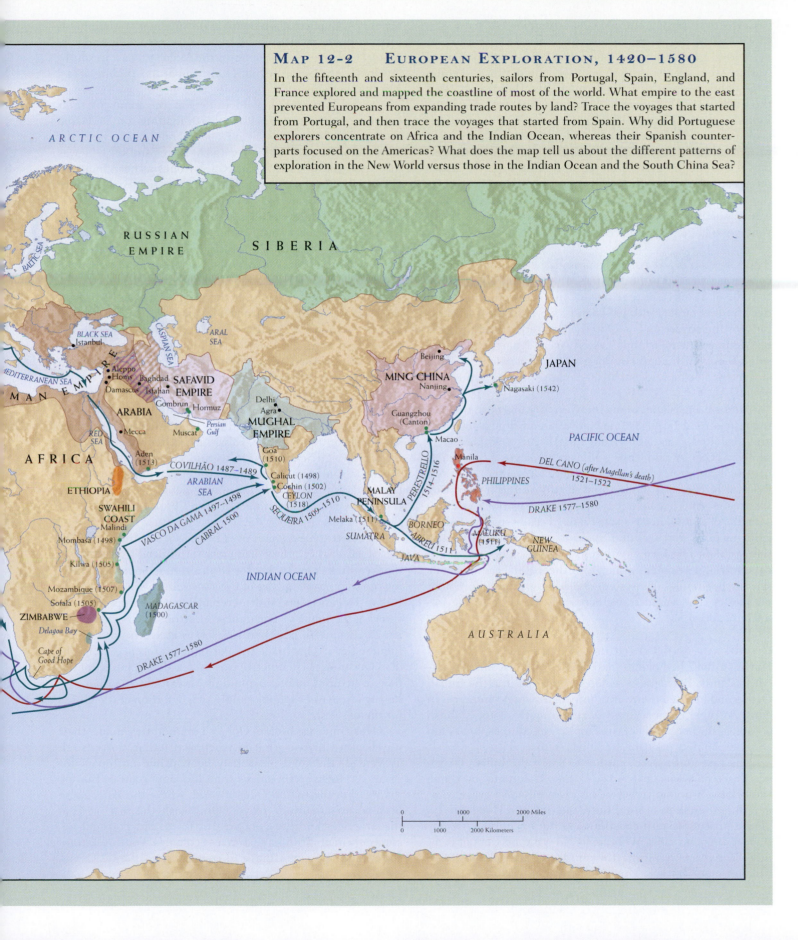

MAP 12-2   EUROPEAN EXPLORATION, 1420–1580

In the fifteenth and sixteenth centuries, sailors from Portugal, Spain, England, and France explored and mapped the coastline of most of the world. What empire to the east prevented Europeans from expanding trade routes by land? Trace the voyages that started from Portugal, and then trace the voyages that started from Spain. Why did Portuguese explorers concentrate on Africa and the Indian Ocean, whereas their Spanish counterparts focused on the Americas? What does the map tell us about the different patterns of exploration in the New World versus those in the Indian Ocean and the South China Sea?

vessels—to shift the nature of ocean commerce toward military ends.

Within Europe the main beneficiaries of this revolution in warfare were the dynastic rulers, who could afford to equip large fighting forces with new armaments. Whereas in 1415 the English king had won the Battle of Agincourt against the French with fewer than 10,000 men, by 1492 the Spanish crown amassed a huge force of 60,000 Christian soldiers to drive the Moors out of Granada. Tactics shifted, too. In medieval Europe, a day of combat or a short siege of castles often settled matters. But by the mid-sixteenth century, battles often involved lengthy and inconclusive struggles. This way of war, more costly in money and manpower, gave an advantage to larger, centralized states.

SUGAR AND SLAVES Africa and the islands along its coast soon proved to be far more than a stop-off en route to India or a source of precious metals. Africa became a valued trading area, and its islands were prime locations for growing sugarcane—a crop that had exhausted the soils of Mediterranean islands, where it had been cultivated since the twelfth century. Along what they called the Gold Coast, the Portuguese established many fortresses and ports of call.

After seizing islands along the West African coast, the Portuguese introduced sugarcane cultivation on large plantations and exploited slave labor from the African mainland. The Madeira, Canary, and Cape Verde archipelagos in particular became laboratories for plantation agriculture, for their rainfall and fertile soils made them ideally suited for growing sugarcane. And because it took droves of workers to cultivate, harvest, and process sugarcane, a ready supply of slave labor enabled Portugal and Spain to build sizeable plantations in their first formal **colonies** (regions under the political control of another country). In the 1400s, these islands saw the beginnings of a system of plantation agriculture built on slavery that would travel across the Atlantic in the following century.

COMMERCE AND CONQUEST IN THE INDIAN OCEAN Having established plantation colonies on West Africa's outlying islands, Portuguese seafarers ventured into the Indian Ocean and inserted themselves into its thriving commerce. In Asia, Portugal never wanted to rule directly or to establish colonies. Rather, its seaborne empire aimed to exploit Asian commercial networks and trading systems.

The first Portuguese mariner to reach the Indian Ocean was Vasco da Gama (1469–1524). Like Columbus, da Gama was relatively unknown before his extraordinary voyage commanding four ships around the Cape of Good Hope. He explored Africa's eastern coast but did not encounter friendly traders or great riches. What he found was a network of commercial ties spanning the Indian Ocean, as well as skilled Muslim mariners who knew the currents, winds, and ports

of call. Da Gama took on board a Muslim pilot at Malindi for instruction in navigating the Indian Ocean's winds and currents. He then sailed straight for the Malabar coast in southern India, one of the region's most important trading areas, arriving there in 1498.

To the Portuguese, who traded in the name of their crown, commercial access was worth fighting for. Da Gama was briefly taken hostage near Calicut, and though eventually allowed to take on a valuable cargo of spices and silks, he was incensed at the insult. While exiting from southern India, da Gama roughed up everyone he encountered, making sure local fishermen watched and spread the news.

On the difficult voyage back to Lisbon, da Gama lost more than half of his crew, but he had proved the feasibility—and profitability—of trade via the Indian Ocean. When he returned to Calicut in 1502 with a beefed-up contingent, he asserted Portuguese supremacy by boarding all twenty ships in the harbor and cutting off the noses, ears, and hands of their sailors. Then he burned the ships with the mutilated sailors on board. The Portuguese repeated their shows of force in strategic locations, especially the three naval choke points: Aden at the base of the Red Sea, Hormuz in the Persian Gulf, and Melaka at the tip of the Malay Peninsula. Once established in the key ports, the Portuguese attempted to take over the trade or, failing this, to tax local merchants. Although they did not hold Aden for long, they solidified control in Sofala, Kilwa, and other important ports on the East African coast, Goa and Calicut in India, and Macao in southern China. From these strongholds, the Portuguese soon commanded the most active sea-lanes of the Indian Ocean. (See Primary Source: Portuguese Views of the Chinese.)

To assert their domain over Indian Ocean trade (west of the Melaka Strait), the Portuguese introduced a pass system that required ships to pay for *cartazes*—documents identifying the ship's captain, size of the ship and crew, and its cargo. Indian Ocean rulers and merchants got cartazes for free, showing the limits of Portuguese control. Others calculated it was cheaper to pay than risk losses at sea from the Portuguese fleet. What made the Portuguese presence in the Indian Ocean world distinctive was that it did not interrupt the flow of luxuries among Asian and African elites; rather, the Portuguese naval captains simply kept a portion of the profits for themselves.

Over time, as Indian Ocean commodities made their way back to Lisbon, that city eclipsed Italian ports (such as Venice) that had previously been prime entrepôts for Asian goods. Even so, spices were less important in Europe than *within* the Indian Ocean world, where the Portuguese became an important player. Only with the discovery of the Americas and the conquest of Brazil did Portugal become an empire with large overseas colonies. For this to transpire, mariners would have to traverse the Atlantic Ocean itself.

PORTUGUESE VIEWS OF THE CHINESE

When the Portuguese arrived in China, they encountered an empire whose organizational structure and ideological orientation were quite different from their own. Written in 1517, this Portuguese report reflects misrepresentations that characterized many Europeans' views of China for centuries to come. It also signaled an aggressive European expansionism that celebrated brute force as a legitimate means to destroy and conquer those who stood in the way.

God grant that these Chinese may be fools enough to lose the country; because up to the present they have had no dominion, but little by little they have gone on taking the land from their neighbors; and for this reason the kingdom is great, because the Chinese are full of much cowardice, and hence they come to be presumptuous, arrogant, cruel; and because up to the present, being a cowardly people, they have managed without arms and without any practice of war, and have always gone on getting the land from their neighbors, and not by force but by stratagems and deceptions; and they imagine that no one can do them harm. They call every foreigner a savage; and their country they call the kingdom of God.

Whoever shall come now, let it be a captain with a fleet of ten or fifteen sail. The first thing will be to destroy the fleet if they should have one, which I believe they have not; let it be by fire and blood and cruel fear for this day, without sparing the life of a single person, every junk being burnt, and no one being taken prisoner, in order not to waste the provisions, because at all times a hundred Chinese will be found for one Portuguese.

→ *What do you think was the main purpose of this report?*
→ *How could this observer's views be so inaccurate?*
→ *What is the irony in the comment "They call every foreigner a savage" followed by instructions to destroy, burn, and not spare "the life of a single person"?*

SOURCE: Letters from Canton, translated and edited by D. Ferguson, *The Indian Antiquary* 31 (January 1902), in J. H. Parry, *European Reconnaissance: Selected Documents* (New York: Walker, 1968), p. 140.

THE ATLANTIC WORLD

> → *What did European conquerors adopt and change from the New World traditions they encountered?*

Western European Christendom, in opening new sea-lanes in the Atlantic, set the stage for an epochal transformation in world history. New technologies aided European expansion, but diseases made the difference. In their encounters with the peoples of the Americas, Europeans introduced more than new cultures to this isolated world; they also brought devastating pathogens that caused a catastrophic decline of Amerindian populations. This decimation enabled Europeans to conquer and colonize the Americas, but it resulted in severe labor shortages. Thus began the large-scale introduction of slave laborers imported from Africa. After 1500, most of the people who made the Atlantic voyage were not Europeans but Africans. As a supplier of slave labor, Africa became the third corner in a triangular world order. Born of the links among the peoples and resources of Europe, Africa, and the Americas, this emerging "Atlantic Ocean system" enriched the Europeans. Through their access to the precious metals of the Americas, they now had something to offer their trading partners in Asia.

Crossing the Atlantic was a feat of monumental importance in world history. It did not occur, however, with an aim to discover new lands. Columbus had wanted to voyage into the "Ocean Sea" so as to open a more direct—and more lucrative—route to Japan and China. Fired by their victory at Granada, Ferdinand and Isabella had agreed to finance his trip, hoping for riches to bankroll a crusade to liberate Jerusalem from Muslim hands. Just as Columbus had no idea he would find a "New World," Spain's monarchs (not to mention its merchants, missionaries, and soldiers) never dreamed that soon they would be preparing for conquest and profiteering in what had been, just a few years before, a blank space on the map. (Thus the term **New World**, as applied to the Americas, reflects the Europeans' view that anything previously unknown to them was "new," even if it had existed and supported societies long before European explorers arrived on its shores.)

Although discovering the Americas was not Columbus's goal, it took scarcely a generation for Europeans to realize the significance of their accidental find. As news of Columbus's voyage spread through Europe, ambitious mariners prepared to sail west. By 1550, all of Europe's powers were scrambling, not just for a share of Indian Ocean action but also for spoils from the Atlantic. In the process, they began destroying the societies and dynasties of the New World. The devastation of its peoples coincided with a sharpening of European rivalries.

WESTWARD VOYAGES OF COLUMBUS

Few figures in history embody their age more than Christopher Columbus. His three ships set sail from Spain in early 1492, stopped in the Canary Islands for supplies and repairs, and cast off into the unknown. When he stepped onto the beach of San Salvador (in the Bahamas) on October 12, 1492, Columbus ushered in a new era in world history. He did not, however, return with the precious Asian commodities he had sought. Columbus would search in vain over three subsequent voyages for the valuable products of the South China Sea and the Indian Ocean.

It is important to see Columbus as a man of his time. Like other expansion-minded Europeans, he aimed to Christianize

Columbus. As Columbus made landfall and encountered Indians, he planted a cross to indicate the spiritual purpose of the voyage and read aloud a document proclaiming the sovereign authority of the king and queen of Spain. Quickly, he learned there was barter for precious stones and metals.

the world while enriching himself and his backers. These goals—to save souls and to make money—drove the European colonization of the Americas and the formation of an Atlantic system. Still, it is noteworthy that Columbus's voyages aimed not to create something new but to generate revenues to cover the conquest of Granada and the reconquest of the Holy Land.

FIRST ENCOUNTERS

When Columbus made landfall in the Caribbean Sea, he unfurled the royal standard of Ferdinand and Isabella and claimed the "many islands filled with people innumerable" for Spain. It is fitting that the first encounter with Caribbean inhabitants, in this case the Tainos, drew blood. Columbus noted, "I showed them swords and they took them by the edge and through ignorance cut themselves." The Tainos had their own weapons but did not forge steel—and thus had no knowledge of such sharp edges.

For Columbus, the Tainos' naiveté in grabbing his sword symbolized the child-like primitivism of these people, whom he would mislabel "Indians" because he thought he had arrived off the coast of Asia. In Columbus's view the Tainos had no religion, but they did have at least some gold (found initially hanging as pendants from their noses). Likewise, Pedro Alvares Cabral, a Portuguese mariner whose trip down the coast of Africa in 1500 was blown off course across the Atlantic, wrote that the people of Brazil had all "the innocence of Adam." He also noted that they were ripe for conversion and that the soils "if rightly cultivated would yield everything." But, as with Africans and Asians, Europeans also developed a contradictory view of the peoples of the Americas. From the Tainos, Columbus learned of another people, the Caribs, who (according to his informants) were savage, warlike cannibals. For centuries, these contrasting images—innocents and savages—structured European (mis)understandings of the native peoples of the Americas.

We know less about what the Indians thought of Columbus or other Europeans on their first encounters. Certainly the Europeans' appearance and technologies inspired awe. The Tainos fled into the forest at the approach of European ships, which they thought were giant monsters; others thought they were floating islands. European metal goods, in particular weaponry, struck them as otherworldly. The strangely dressed white men seemed godlike to some, although many Indians soon abandoned this view. The natives found the newcomers different not for their skin color (only Europeans drew the distinction based on skin pigmentation), but for their hairiness. Indeed, the Europeans' beards, breath, and bad manners repulsed their Indian hosts. The newcomers' inability to live off the land also stood out.

In due course, the Indians realized not just that the strange, hairy people bearing metal weapons were odd trading partners, but that they meant to stay and to force the native population to labor for them. However, by the time the Indians were aware of the upheaval that the Spaniards wrought, it was too late. The explorers had become **conquistadors** (conquerors).

FIRST CONQUESTS

First contacts between peoples gave way to dramatic conquests; then conquests paved the way to mass predation. Explorers became exploiters. After the first voyage, Columbus claimed that on Hispaniola (present-day Haiti and the Dominican Republic) "he had found what he was looking for"—gold. That was sufficient to persuade the Spanish crown to invest in larger expeditions. Whereas Columbus first sailed with three small ships and 87 men, ten years later the Spanish outfitted an expedition with 2,500 men.

Between 1492 and 1519, the Spanish experimented with institutions of colonial rule over local populations on the Caribbean island that they renamed Hispaniola. Ultimately they created a model that the rest of the New World colonies would adapt. But the Spaniards faced problems that would recur. The first was Indian resistance. As early as 1494, starving Spaniards raided and pillaged Indian villages. When the Indians revolted, Spanish soldiers replied with punitive expeditions and began enslaving them to work in mines extracting gold. As the crown systematized grants (*encomiendas*) to the conquistadors for control over Indian labor, a rich class of *encomenderos* arose who enjoyed the fruits of the system. Although the placer gold mines soon ran dry, the model of granting favored settlers the right to coerce Indian labor endured. In return, those who received the labor rights paid special taxes on the precious metals that were extracted. Thus, both the crown and the *encomenderos* benefited from the extractive economy. The same cannot be said of the Indians, who perished in great numbers from disease, dislocation, malnutrition, and overwork.

It is no surprise that quarrels over spoils followed the conquests. The family of Columbus, in particular, had been granted a commercial monopoly on his discoveries, but some of the settlers challenged Columbus's authority. To prevent insurrection, the crown granted more *encomiendas* to other Spanish claimants. As special grants became a common feature of Spanish colonialism, less favored settlers grew disenchanted. When the Indians and the gold supplies began to disappear, many settlers pulled up their stakes and returned to Spain. Others looked for untapped territories that might yield precious metals.

Not all joined the rush for riches or celebrated the conquistadors and *encomenderos*. Dominican friars protested the abuse of the Indians, seeing them as potential converts who were equal to the Spaniards in the eyes of God. In 1511, Father Antonio Montesinos accused the settlers of barbarity:

"By what right do you wage such detestable wars on these people who lived idly and peacefully in their own lands, where you have consumed infinite numbers of them with unheard-of murders and desolations?" Dissent and debate would be a permanent feature of Spanish colonialism in the New World.

THE AZTEC EMPIRE AND THE SPANISH CONQUEST

As Spanish colonists saw the bounty of Hispaniola dry up, they set out to discover and conquer new territories. Finding their way to the mainlands of the American landmasses, they encountered larger, more complex, and more militarized societies than those they had overrun in the Caribbean.

On the mainland, great civilizations had arisen centuries before, boasting large cities, monumental buildings, and riches based on wealthy agrarian societies. In both Mesoamerica, starting with the Olmecs (see Chapter 5), and the Andes, with the Chimú (see Chapter 10), large polities had laid the foundations for subsequent Aztec and Incan empires. The latter states were powerful. But they also represented the evolution of states and commercial systems untouched by Afro-Eurasian developments; as worlds apart, they were unprepared for the kind of assaults that European invaders had honed. In pre-Columbian Mesoamerica and then the Andes, warfare was more ceremonial, less inclined to wipe out enemies than to make them tributary subjects. As a result, the wealth of these empires made them irresistible to outside conquerors they never knew, and their habits of war made them vulnerable to conquests they could never foresee.

AZTEC SOCIETY In Mesoamerica, the ascendant Mexicas had created an empire known to us as "Aztec." Around Lake Texcoco, Mexica cities grew and formed a three-city league in 1430, which then expanded through the Central Valley of Mexico to incorporate neighboring peoples. Gradually the **Aztec Empire** united numerous small, independent states under a single monarch who ruled with the help of counselors, military leaders, and priests. By the late fifteenth century, the Aztec realm may have embraced 25 million people. Tenochtitlán, the primary city situated on an immense island in Lake Texcoco, ranked among the world's largest.

Tenochtitlán spread in concentric circles, with the main religious and political buildings in the center and residences radiating outward. The city's outskirts connected a mosaic of floating gardens producing food for urban markets. Canals irrigated the land, waste served as fertilizer, and high-yielding produce found easy transport to markets. Entire households worked: men, women, and children all had roles in Aztec agriculture.

Extended kinship provided the scaffolding for Aztec statehood. Marriage of men and women from different villages solidified alliances and created clan-like networks. In

Tenochtitlán. At its height, the Aztec capital Tenochtitlán was as populous as Europe's largest city. As can be seen from this map, it spread in concentric circles, with the main religious and political buildings in the center and residences radiating outward.

Tenochtitlán, powerful families married their children to each other or found nuptial partners among the prominent families of other important cities. (Certain ruling houses in Europe were solidifying alliances in much the same way at this time; see Chapter 11.) Not only did this practice concentrate power in the great city, but it also ensured a pool of potential successors to the throne. Soon a lineage emerged to create a corps of "natural" rulers. Priests legitimized the new emperor in rituals to convey the image of a ruler close to the gods and to distinguish the elite from the lower orders.

A hierarchy at the village level provided the bedrock for layers of increasingly centralized political authority. Local elders developed representative councils, which selected delegates to a committee that elected the dominant civil authority, the chief speaker. As Aztec power spread, the chief speaker became a full-blown emperor. He was, however, not supreme; instead, he jockeyed with rival religious and military power-wielders. Thus at the top of the Aztec social pyramid stood a small but antagonistic nobility. This hierarchically organized society held itself together through a shared understanding of the cosmos. The Aztecs believed that the universe was prone to unceasing cycles of disaster that would eventually end in apocalypse. Such an unstable cosmos exposed mortals to repeated creations and destructions of their world. The priesthood governed relationships between people and their deities. Their challenge: balancing (1) a belief that history was destined to run in cycles with (2) a faith that mortals could influence the gods, and their own fate, through religious rituals.

Ultimately Aztec power spread though much of Meso-america, but the empire's constant wars and conquests deprived it of stability. In successive military campaigns, the Aztecs subjugated their neighbors, feeding off plunder and then forcing subject peoples to pay tribute of crops, gold, silver, textiles, and other goods that financed Aztec grandeur. Such conquests also provided a constant supply of humans for sacrifice, because the Aztecs believed that the great god of the sun required human hearts to keep on burning and blood to replace that given by the gods to moisten the earth through rain. Priests escorted captured warriors up the temple steps and tore out their hearts, offering their lives and blood as a sacrifice to the sun god. Allegedly, between 20,000 and 80,000 men, women, and children were slaughtered in a single ceremony in 1487, with the four-person-wide line of victims stretching for over two miles. In this marathon of bloodletting, knife-wielding priests collapsed from exhaustion and surrendered their places to fresh executioners.

Those whom the Aztecs sought to dominate did not submit peacefully. From 1440, the empire faced constant turmoil as subject peoples rebelled against their oppressive overlords. Tlaxcalans and Tarascans along the Gulf of Mexico waged a relentless war for freedom, pinning down entire divisions of Aztec armies. To pacify the realm, the empire diverted more and more men and money into a mushrooming military. By the time the electoral committee chose Moctezuma II as emperor in 1502, divisions among elites and pressures from the periphery placed the Aztec Empire under extreme stress.

CORTÉS AND CONQUEST Not long after Moctezuma became emperor, news arrived from the coast of strange sightings of floating mountains (ships) bearing pale, bearded men and monsters (horses and dogs). Moctezuma consulted with his ministers and soothsayers, wondering if these men were the god Quetzalcóatl and his entourage. The people of Tenochtitlán saw omens of impending disaster. Moctezuma sank into despair, hesitating over what to do. He sent emissaries bearing jewels and prized feathers; later he sent sorcerers to confuse and bewitch the newcomers. But he did not prepare for any military engagement. After all, Mesoamericans had

Cortés Meets Mesoamerican Rulers. (*Left*) This colonial image depicts the meeting of Cortés (second from right) and Moctezuma (seated on the left), with Doña Marina serving as an interpreter and informer for the Spanish conquistador. Notice at the bottom what are likely Aztec offerings for the newcomer. (*Right*) This detail from a twentieth-century Mexican mural depicts the meeting of Cortés and the king of Tlaxcala (enemy of the Aztecs). As Mexicans began to celebrate their mixed-blood heritage, Doña Marina (in the middle) became the symbolic mother of the first mestizos.

no idea of the interlopers' destructive potential in weaponry and germs.

Aboard one of the ships was Hernán Cortés (1485–1547), a former law student from one of the Spanish provinces. He would become the model conquistador, just as Columbus was the model explorer. For a brief time, Cortés was an *encomendero* in Hispaniola; but when news arrived of a potentially wealthier land to the west, he set sail with over 500 men, eleven ships, sixteen horses, and artillery.

When the expedition arrived near present-day Veracruz, Cortés acquired two translators, including the daughter of a local Indian noble family. The daughter, who became known as Doña Marina, was a "gift" to the triumphant Spaniards from the ruler of the Tabasco region (a rival to the Aztecs). Fluent in several languages, Doña Marina displayed such linguistic skills and personal charms that she soon came to Cortés's attention. She became his lover and ultimately revealed several Aztec plots against the tiny Spanish force. Doña Marina subsequently bore Cortés a son, who is considered one of the first mixed-blooded Mexicans (**mestizos**).

With the assistance of Doña Marina and other native allies, Cortés marched his troops to Tenochtitlán. Upon entering, he gasped in wonder that "this city is so big and so

remarkable" that it was "almost unbelievable." One of his soldiers wrote, "It was all so wonderful that I do not know how to describe this first glimpse of things never heard of, seen or dreamed of before."

How was this tiny force to overcome an empire of many millions with an elaborate warring tradition? Crucial to Spanish conquest was their alliance, negotiated through translators, with Moctezuma's enemies—especially the Tlaxcalans. After decades of yearning for release from the Aztec yoke, the Tlaxcalans and other Mesoamerican peoples embraced Cortés's promise of help. The Spaniards' second advantage was their method of warfare. The Aztecs were seasoned fighters, but they fought to capture, not to kill. Nor were they familiar with gunpowder or sharp steel swords. Although outnumbered, the Spaniards killed their foe with abandon, using superior weaponry, horses, and war dogs. The Aztecs, still unsure who these strange men were, allowed Cortés to enter their city. With the aid of the Tlaxcalans and a handful of his own men, in 1519 Cortés captured Moctezuma, who became a puppet of the Spanish conqueror. (See Primary Source: Cortés Approaches Tenochtitlán.)

Within two years, the Aztecs realized that the newcomers were not gods and that Aztec warriors, too, could fight to kill. When Spanish troops massacred an unarmed crowd in

The Conquest of the Aztecs. (*Left*) Diego Rivera's idealized account of the Spanish defeat of the Aztec warriors portrays Spanish soldiers with muskets and horses mowing down brave but technologically outgunned Indians. Of course, Rivera's efforts to accentuate Spanish brutality led him to exclude important factors in the fall of Tenochtitlán: Aztec rivals who joined with Spaniards, and diseases. In fact, guns and horses were important but not decisive in the Spanish conquest. (*Right*) This image of the conquest was drawn by a converted Indian later in the sixteenth century and relied on indigenous oral histories and familiar artistic forms. Observe the importance of Indians fighting Indians, and the conventional frontal images of bodies with profiles of heads.

Tenochtitlán's central square while Cortés was away, they provoked a massive uprising. The Spaniards led Moctezuma to one of the palace walls to plead with his people for a truce, but the Aztecs kept up their barrage of stones, spears, and arrows—striking and killing Moctezuma. Cortés returned to reassert control; but realizing this was impossible, he gathered his loot and escaped. Left behind were hundreds of Spaniards, many of whom were dragged up the temple steps and sacrificed by Aztec priests.

With the Tlaxcalans' help, Cortés regrouped. This time he chose to defeat the Aztecs completely. He ordered the building of boats to sail across Lake Texcoco to bombard the capital with artillery. Even more devastating was the spread of smallpox, brought by the Spanish, which ran through the soldiers and commoners like wildfire. Still, led by a new ruler, Cuauhtémoc, the Aztecs rallied and nearly drove the Spaniards from Tenochtitlán. In the end starvation, disease, and lack of artillery vanquished the Aztec forces. More died from disease than from fighting—the total number of Aztec casualties may have reached 240,000. As Spanish troops retook the capital, they found it in ruins, with a population too weak to resist. Cuauhtémoc himself faced execution, thereby ending the royal Mexica lineage. The Aztecs lamented their defeat in verse: "We have pounded our hands in despair against the adobe walls, for our inheritance, our city, is lost and dead." Cortés became governor of the new Spanish colony, renamed "New Spain." He promptly allocated *en-* *comiendas* to his loyal followers and dispatched expeditions to conquer the more distant Mesoamerican provinces.

The Mexica experience taught the Spanish an important lesson: an effective conquest had to be swift—and it had to remove completely the symbols of legitimate authority. Their winning advantage, however, was disease. The Spaniards unintentionally introduced germs that made their subsequent efforts at military conquest much easier.

THE INCAS

The other great Spanish conquest occurred in the Andes, where Quechua-speaking rulers, called Incas, had established an impressive polity. From its base in the valley of Cuzco, the **Inca Empire** encompassed a population of 4 to 6 million. But the Incas were internally split. Lacking a clear inheritance system, the empire suffered repeated convulsions.

In the early sixteenth century, the struggle over who would succeed Huayna Capac, the Inca ruler, was especially fierce. Huascar, his "official" son, took Cuzco (the capital), while Atahualpa, his favored son, governed the province of present-day Ecuador. Open conflict might have been averted were it not for Huayna's premature death. His killer was probably smallpox, which swept down the trade routes from Mesoamerica into the Andes (much as the bubonic plague had earlier spread through Afro-Eurasian trade routes; see Chapter 11).

CORTÉS APPROACHES TENOCHTITLÁN

When the Spanish conquered the Aztec Empire, they defeated a mighty power. The capital, Tenochtitlán, was probably the same size as Europe's biggest city. Glimpsing Tenochtitlán in 1521, Hernán Cortés marveled at its magnificence. But to justify his acts, he claimed to be bringing civilization and Christianity to the Aztecs. Note the contrast between Cortés's admiration for Tenochtitlán and his condemnation of Indian beliefs and practices—as well as his claim that he abolished cannibalism, something the Aztecs did not practice (although they did sacrifice humans).

This great city of Tenochtitlán is built on the salt lake. . . . It has four approaches by means of artificial causeways. . . . The city is as large as Seville or Cordoba. Its streets . . . are very broad and straight, some of these, and all the others, are one half land, and the other half water on which they go about in canoes. . . . There are bridges, very large, strong, and well constructed, so that, over many, ten horsemen can ride abreast. . . . The city has many squares where markets are held. . . . There is one square, twice as large as that of Salamanca, all surrounded by arcades, where there are daily more than sixty thousand souls, buying and selling. . . . [I]n the service and manners of its people, their fashion of living was almost the same as in Spain, with just as much harmony and order; and considering that these people were barbarous, so cut off from the knowledge of God and other civilized peoples, it is admirable to see to what they attained in every respect. . . .

It happened . . . that a Spaniard saw an Indian . . . eating a piece of flesh taken from the body of an Indian who had been killed. . . . I had the culprit burned, explaining that the cause was his having killed that Indian and eaten him, which was prohibited by Your Majesty, and by me in Your Royal name. I further made the chief understand that all the people . . . must abstain from this custom. . . . I came . . . to protect their lives as well as their property, and to teach them that they were to adore but one God . . . that they must turn from their idols, and the rites they had practised until then, for these were lies and deceptions which the devil . . . had invented. . . . I, likewise, had come to teach them that Your Majesty, by the will of Divine Providence, rules the universe, and that they also must submit themselves to the imperial yoke, and do all that we who are Your Majesty's ministers here might order them. . . .

→ *What does Cortés's report tell us about the city of Tenochtitlán?*

→ *Why does Cortés justify his actions to the degree he does?*

→ *Cortés writes, "I came . . . to protect their lives as well as their property." Based on your reading of the chapter text, would you say he accomplished these objectives?*

SOURCE: *Letters of Cortés*, translated by Francis A. MacNutt (New York: G. P. Putnam, 1908), pp. 244, 256–57.

With the father gone, Atahualpa declared war on his brother, crushed him, forced him to witness the execution of all his supporters, and then killed him and used his skull as a vessel for maize-beer.

When the Spaniards arrived in 1532 they found an internally divided empire, a situation they quickly learned to exploit. Francisco Pizarro, who led the Spanish campaign, had been inspired by Cortés's victory and yearned for his own glory. Commanding a force of about 600 men, he invited Atahualpa to confer at the town of Cajamarca. There he laid a trap. As columns of Inca warriors and servants covered with colorful plumage and plates of silver and gold entered the main square, the Spanish soldiers were awed. One recalled, "many of us urinated without noticing it, out of sheer terror." But Pizarro's plan worked. His guns and horses shocked the Inca forces. Atahualpa himself fell into Spanish hands, later to be decapitated. Pizarro's conquistadors overran Cuzco in 1533 and then vanquished the rest of the Inca forces, a process that took decades in some areas. (See Global Connections & Disconnections: The Voice of the Conquered: Guaman Poma de Ayala.)

Meanwhile, Spaniards began arriving in droves at the new capital of Lima. They staked their own claims for *encomiendas*, outdoing each other with greed, and soon were at war

THE VOICE OF THE CONQUERED: GUAMAN POMA DE AYALA

After defeating the Inca armies, Spanish conquerors tightened their hold over the central Andes. They created new political authorities, invited victors to set up silver mines and trading networks using forced native laborers, and licensed missionaries to go out into Andean communities to consolidate a more difficult "spiritual conquest." In reaction, Andean peoples resisted. They fled the mines, plundered trade routes, and kept fighting, now with the use of Spanish weaponry. The conquered Andeans also used techniques of the conquerors themselves, like the Spanish language and Spanish books, to resist Spanish control.

One of the strongest voices of the conquered was a native Andean, Felipe Guaman Poma de Ayala (c. 1535–c. 1615). His illustrated history of the Inca kingdoms, *Primer nueva crónica y bien gobierno,* fiercely criticized colonial rule while urging the Spanish king to adopt a new model of "good government."

The author's native tongue was Quechua, but he was schooled (possibly by missionaries) in Spanish language and culture. With his bilingual skills, he was drafted as an interpreter in Christian campaigns to wipe out heresy and idol worship in the Andes. In this capacity, he read books belonging to missionaries and learned of the Spaniards' religious, political, and historical traditions. He also served as an interpreter for Andeans who challenged the conquistadors' land claims.

Guaman Poma narrated the history of the Inca Empire, recounted the arrival and victory of the Spanish, and then described the misery of everyday life under colonial authority. Relying on his own experiences and centuries of oral culture, he told an epic tale—very much in a Spanish mode—of the tragic fate of a non-Spanish people. Indeed, the book accepted in many ways the Andean destiny, while denouncing colonialism. He was pro-Andean, but he celebrated Catholicism and Spanish monarchical rule.

As a chronicler of the Andean peoples before the Spanish conquest, Guaman Poma argued that his people were innocents—in this sense, already a Christian people—well before the conquest. They lived, according to the author, by Christian principles and knew but one God, "though they were barbarous, knowing nothing." Indeed, his history of the Incas begins with biblical creation, includes the arrival in South America of one of Noah's sons, and ends with the rule of Inca Huayna Capac. While much of his historical account was fabrication, claiming Christian roots enabled the Andean author to denounce the conquistadors as treasonous usurpers. They had killed the natural and legitimate Inca rulers and were thus eternally doomed.

Primer nueva crónica culminated in a detailed account of everyday life in the colony. It charted the system of forced labor in the mines, the burdens of Spanish taxes,

---

with one another. In 1541, one faction assassinated Pizarro himself. Rival factions kept up a brutal war until the Spanish king issued new laws to prevent *encomiendas* from being heritable. This act sought to block the establishment of a powerful aristocracy, to deter uncontrollable civil war, and to reinforce loyalty to Madrid (since once an *encomendero* died, his title would revert to the crown).

The defeat of the New World's two great empires had enormous repercussions for world history. First, it meant that Europeans had their way with the human and material wealth of the Americas. Second, it gave Europeans a market for their own products—goods that found little favor in Afro-Eurasia. Finally, it opened a new frontier that the Europeans could colonize as staple-producing provinces. Now, following the Portuguese push into Africa and Asia (as well as a Russian push into northern Asia; see Chapter 13), the New World

conquest introduced Europeans to a new scale of imperial expansion. The outcome, however, would destabilize Europe itself.

THE COLUMBIAN EXCHANGE

The Spanish came to the Americas for gold and silver, but the Indians taught them about unknown crops, especially potatoes and corn. Europeans also took away tomatoes, beans, cacao, peanuts, tobacco, and squash. These staples transformed European diets and fueled a population explosion across Afro-Eurasia. In China, for example, corn could grow in areas too dry for rice and too wet for wheat.

What did the Indians get from this hemispheric transfer, which historians call the **Columbian exchange**? The term

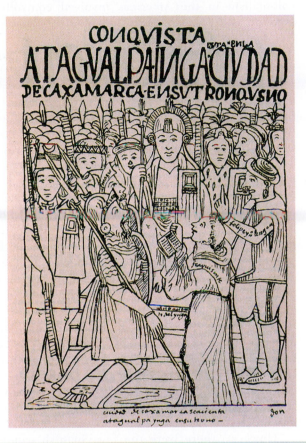

and the hypocrisy of missionaries who seized Indian property and failed to defend Indian lives. Guaman Poma wrote that the colonists violated Christian precepts of justice and their own laws. He added that, given the origins of the Andean peoples and their colonial fates, the king of Spain had a moral as well as a political duty to protect his Christian subjects in the Andes: he should free them from sinful authorities and create a sovereign Andean state as a universal Christian kingdom ruled from Madrid. Guaman Poma simultaneously denounced colonialism while affirming his loyalty to the king.

For all his skills at bridging the cultural and political divide between Andeans and Spaniards, Guaman Poma was not optimistic. His images, especially, portrayed irreconcilable differences between the conquered and their conquerors. Isolation, not understanding, characterized the colonial experience for Guaman Poma.

Pizarro and the Incas. This illustration is by the Andean native Guaman Poma, whose c. 1587 epic of the conquest of Peru depicted many of the barbarities of the Spanish. Here we see the conquistador Pizarro and a Catholic priest appealing to Atahualpa—before betraying and then killing him.

refers to the movements between Afro-Eurasia and the Americas of previously unknown plants, animals, people, and products that followed in the wake of Columbus's voyages. To the Indians, the Spanish brought wheat, grapevines, and sugarcane. But the most profound and destructive effect was not immediately visible. For millennia, the isolated populations of the Americas had been cut off from Afro-Eurasian microbe migrations. Africans, Europeans, and Asians had long interacted, sharing disease pools and gaining immunities; in this sense, in contrast, the Amerindians were indeed "worlds apart." Sickness spread from almost the moment the Spaniards arrived. One Spanish soldier noted, upon entering the conquered Aztec capital, "the streets were so filled with dead and sick people that our men walked over nothing but bodies." Native American accounts of the fall of Tenochtitlán recalled the smallpox epidemic more vividly than the fighting.

Even worse, no sooner had smallpox done its work than Indians faced a second pandemic: measles. Then came pneumonic plague and influenza. As each wave retreated, it left a population more emaciated than before, even less prepared for the next wave. The scale of death remains unprecedented: imported pathogens wiped out up to 90 percent of the Indian population. A century after smallpox arrived on Hispaniola in 1519, no more than 5 to 10 percent of the island's population was left alive. Diminished and weakened by disease, Amerindians could not resist European settlement and colonization of the Americas. Thus were Europeans the unintended beneficiaries of a horrifying catastrophe.

Environmental effects were manifold. In addition to crops, Europeans transported livestock such as cattle, swine, and horses to the New World. In the highland regions north of the valley of central Mexico (where Native Americans

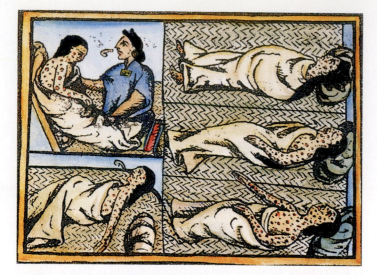

Disease and Decimation of Indians. The real conqueror of Native Americans was not so much guns as germs. Even before Spanish soldiers seized the Aztec capital, germs had begun decimating the population. The first big killer was smallpox, recorded here by an Indian artist, covering the bodies of victims.

had once maintained irrigated, highly productive agricultural estates), Spanish settlers opened up large herding ranches. An area that had once produced maize and squash now supported herds of sheep and cattle. Without natural predators, these animals reproduced with lightning speed, destroying entire landscapes with their hooves and their foraging. On the islands of the West Indies, described by Columbus as "roses of the sea," the Spanish found lush tropical and semi-tropical forests. As the Europeans cleared trees and other vegetation for sugar plantations, they undermined the habitat of many large mammals and birds. Before long, nearly all of the islands' tall trees as well as many shrubs and ground plants were gone, and residents lamented the absence of bird song. Over ensuing centuries, the flora and fauna of the Americas took on an increasingly European appearance—a process that the historian Alfred Crosby has called ecological imperialism.

SPAIN'S TRIBUTARY EMPIRE

Like the Europeans who sailed into the Indian Ocean to join existing commercial systems, the Spaniards sought to exploit the wealth of indigenous empires without fully dismantling them. Those Native Americans who survived the original encounters could be harnessed as a means to siphon tribute payments to the new masters. Spain could thereby extract wealth without extensive settlement. In Mexico and Peru, where the Inca Empire suffered the same fate as the Aztecs, conquistadors decapitated native communities but left much of their social and economic structure intact—including net-

works of tribute. But unlike the European penetration of the Indian Ocean, the occupation of the New World went beyond the control of commercial outposts. Instead, European colonialism in the Americas involved controlling large amounts of territory—and ultimately the entire landmass (see Map 12-3).

By fusing traditional tribute-taking with their own innovations, Spanish masters made villagers across their new American empire deliver goods and services. But because the Spanish authorities also bestowed *encomiendas*, those favored individuals could demand labor from their lands' Indian inhabitants—for mines, estates, and public works. Whereas Aztec and Inca rulers had used conscripted labor to build up their public wealth, the Spaniards did so for private gain.

Most Spanish migrants were men; only a few were women. One, Inés Suárez, reached the Indies only to find her husband, who had arrived earlier, dead. She then became mistress of the conquistador Pedro de Valdivia, and the pair worked as a conquering team. Initially, she joined an expedition to conquer Chile as Valdivia's domestic servant, but she soon became much more—nurse, caretaker, advisor, and guard, having uncovered several plots to assassinate her lover. Suárez even served as a diplomat between warring Indians and Spaniards in an effort to secure the conquest. Later, she helped to rule Chile as the wife of Rodrigo de Quiroga, governor of the province. Admittedly, hers was an exceptional story. More typical were women who foraged for food, tended wounded soldiers, and set up European-style settlements.

However, there were too few Spanish women to go around, so Spanish men consorted with local women. Although the crown did not approve the taking of concubines, the practice was widespread. From the onset of colonization, Spaniards also married into Indian families. After conquering the Incas, Pizarro himself wedded an Inca princess, thereby (or so he hoped) inheriting the mantle of local dynastic rule. As a result of intermarriages, mestizos became the fastest-growing segment of the population of Spanish America.

Spanish migrants and their progeny preferred towns to the countryside. Ports excepted, the major cities of Spanish America were the former centers of Indian empires. Mexico City took shape on the ruins of Tenochtitlán; Cuzco arose from the razed Inca capital. In their architecture, economy, and most intimate aspects, the Spanish colonies adopted as much as they transformed the worlds they encountered.

SILVER

For the first Europeans in the Americas, the foremost measure of success was the gold and silver that they could hoard for themselves and their monarchs. But in plundering massive

→ *What did European conquerors adopt and change from the New World traditions they encountered?*

MAP 12-3   THE SPANISH AND PORTUGUESE EMPIRES IN THE AMERICAS, 1492–1750

This map examines the growth of the Spanish and Portuguese empires in the Americas over two and a half centuries. Identify the natural resources that led the Spaniards and Portuguese to focus their empire-building where they did. What were the major export commodities from these colonized areas? Looking back to Map 12.2, why do you think Spanish settlement covered so much more area than Portuguese settlement? According to your reading, how did the production and export of silver and sugar shape the labor systems that evolved in both empires?

Silver. Silver was an important discovery for Spanish conquerors in Mesoamerica and the Andes. Conquerors expanded the customs of Inca and Aztec labor drafts to force the natives to work in mines, often in brutal conditions.

amounts of silver, the conquistadors introduced it to the world's commercial systems, which electrified them. In the twenty years after the fall of Tenochtitlán, conquistadors took more precious metals from Mexico and the Andes than all the gold accumulated by Europeans over the previous centuries.

Having looted Indian coffers, the Spanish entered the business of mining directly, opening the Andean Potosí mines in 1545. Between 1560 and 1685, Spanish America sent 25,000 to 35,000 tons of silver annually to Spain. From 1685 to 1810, this sum doubled. The two mother lodes were Potosí in present-day Bolivia and Zacatecas in northern Mexico. Silver brought bounty not only to the crown but also to a privileged group of families based in Spain's colonial capitals; thus private wealth funded the formation of local aristocracies.

Colonial mines epitomized the Atlantic world's new economy. They relied on an extensive network of Indian labor, at first enslaved, subsequently drafted. Here again, the Spanish adopted Inca and Aztec practices of requiring labor from subjugated villages. Each year, under the traditional system, village elders selected a stipulated number of men to toil in the shafts, refineries, and smelters. Under the Spanish, the digging, hauling, and smelting taxed human limits to their capacity—and beyond. Mortality rates were appalling. (See Primary Source: Silver, the Devil, and Coca Leaf in the Andes.) The system pumped so much silver into European commercial networks that it transformed Europe's relationship to all its trading partners, especially those in China and India. It also shook up trade and politics within Europe itself.

PORTUGAL'S NEW WORLD COLONY

> → *What military and maritime technologies advanced Portuguese exploration?*

No sooner did Europeans—starting with the Portuguese and Spanish—venture into the seas than they carved them up to prevent a free-for-all. The Treaty of Tordesillas of 1494, drawn up by the pope, had foreseen that the non-European world—the Americas, Africa, and Asia—would be divided into spheres of interest between Spain and Portugal. Yet the treaty was unenforceable. No less interested in immediate riches than the Spanish, the Portuguese were disappointed by the absence of tributary populations and precious metals in the areas set aside for them. What they did find in Brazil, however, was abundant, fertile land on which favored persons received massive royal grants. These estate owners governed their plantations like feudal lords (see Chapter 10).

COASTAL ENCLAVES

Hemmed in along the coast, the Portuguese created enclaves. Unlike the Spanish, they rarely intermarried with Indians, most of whom had fled or had died from imported diseases. Failing to find established cities, the colonists remained in more dispersed settlements. By the late seventeenth century, Brazil's white population was 300,000.

The problem was where to find labor to work the rich lands. Because there was no centralized government to deal with the labor shortage, initially the Portuguese settlers tried to enlist the dispersed native population; but when recruitment became increasingly coercive, Indians turned on the settlers, whom they perceived to be interlopers. Some fought. Others fled to the vast interior. Reluctant to pursue the Indians inland, the Portuguese hugged their beachheads, extracting brazilwood (the source of a beautiful red dye) and sugar from their coastal enclaves.

African slaves became the solution to this labor problem. What had worked for the Portuguese on sugarcane plantations in the Azores and other Atlantic islands now found application on their Brazilian plantations. Especially in the northeast, in the Bay of All Saints, the Atlantic world's first vast sugar-producing commercial center appeared.

SUGAR PLANTATIONS

Along with silver, sugar emerged as the most valuable export from the Americas. It also was decisive in rearranging relations between peoples around the Atlantic. Cultivation of sugarcane

Primary Source

SILVER, THE DEVIL, AND COCA LEAF IN THE ANDES

When Spanish colonists forced thousands of Andean Indians to work in the silver mines of Potosí, they permitted the chewing of coca leaves (which are now used to extract cocaine). Chewing the leaves gave Indians a mild "high," alleviated their hunger, and blunted the pain of hard work and deteriorating lungs. The habit also spread to some Spaniards. In this document, Bartolomé Arzáns de Orsúa y Vela, a Spaniard born in Potosí in 1676, expresses how important coca was to Indian miners and how harmful it was for Spaniards who fell under its spell. By the time the author wrote his observations in the late seventeenth century, the use of the coca leaf had become widespread.

I wish to declare the unhappiness and great evil that, among so many felicities, this kingdom of Peru experiences in possessing the coca herb. . . . No Indian will go into the mines or to any other labor, be it building houses or working in the fields, without taking it in his mouth, even if his life depends on it. . . .

Among the Indians (and even the Spaniards by now) the custom of not entering the mines without placing this herb in the mouth is so well established that there is a superstition that the richness of the metal will be lost if they do not do so. . . .

The Indians being accustomed to taking this herb into their mouths, there is no doubt that as long as they have it there they lose all desire to sleep, and since it is extremely warming, they say that when the weather is cold they do not feel it if they have the herb in their mouths. In addition, they also say that it increases their strength and that they feel neither hunger nor thirst; hence these Indians cannot work without it.

When the herb is ground and placed in boiling water and if a person then takes a few swallows, it opens the pores, warms the body, and shortens labor in women; and this coca herb has many other virtues besides. But human perversity has caused it to become a vice, so that the devil (that inventor of vices) has made a notable harvest of souls with it, for there are many women who have taken it—and still take it—for the sin of witchcraft, invoking the devil and using it to summon him for their evil deeds. . . .

With such ferocity has the devil seized on this coca herb that—there is no doubt about it—when it becomes an addiction it impairs or destroys the judgment of its users just as if they had drunk wine to excess and makes them see terrible visions; demons appear before their eyes in frightful forms. In this city of Potosí it is sold publicly by the Indians who work in the mines, and so the harm arising from its continued abundance cannot be corrected; but neither is that harm remediable in other large cities of this realm, where the use and sale of coca have been banned under penalties as severe as that of excommunication and yet it is secretly bought and sold and used for casting spells and other like evils.

Would that our lord the king had ordered this noxious herb pulled up by the roots wherever it is found. . . . Great good would follow were it to be extirpated from this realm: the devil would be bereft of the great harvest of souls he reaps, God would be done a great service, and vast numbers of men and women would not perish (I refer to Spaniards, for no harm comes to the Indians from it).

→ *Why would the Spaniards ban the sale of the coca herb everywhere except Potosí?*

→ *Why would Bartolomé believe that no harm would come to the Indians for taking the coca herb?*

→ *How does this document reveal the central role of the Catholic Church in Spanish colonial thinking? Find several words and phrases that express this outlook.*

SOURCE: R. C. Padden, ed., "Claudia the Witch," pp. 117–21, from *Tales of Potosí*. Copyright © 1975 by Brown University Press. Reprinted by permission of University Press of New England, Lebanon, NH, and the author.

Mission São Miguel. The Jesuits were avid missionaries in the Spanish and Portuguese empires and often tried to shelter native peoples from conquistadors and labor recruiters. Missions, like this one, in the borderlands between Brazil and Spanish colonies were targets of attack from both sides.

had originated in India, spread to the Mediterranean region, and then reached the coastal islands of West Africa. The Portuguese transported the West African model to Brazil, and other Europeans took it to the Caribbean. By the early seventeenth century, sugar had become a major export from the New World. By the eighteenth century, its production required continuous and enormous transfers of labor from Africa, and its value surpassed that of silver as an export from the Americas to Europe.

Most Brazilian sugar plantations were fairly small, employing between 60 and 100 slaves. But they were efficient enough to create an alternative model of empire, one that resulted in full-scale colonization and dislocation of the existing population. The slaves lived in wretched conditions: their barracks were miserable, and their diets were insufficient to keep them alive under backbreaking work routines. Moreover, these slaves were disproportionately men. As they rapidly died off, the only way to ensure replenishment was to import more Africans. This model of settlement relied on the transatlantic flow of slaves.

BEGINNINGS OF THE TRANSATLANTIC SLAVE TRADE

Although African slaves were imported into the Americas starting in the fifteenth century, the first direct voyage carrying them from Africa to the Americas occurred in 1525. The transatlantic slave trade began modestly in support of one commodity, sugar. As European demand for sugar increased, the slave trade expanded. From the time of Columbus until 1820, five times as many Africans as Europeans moved to the Americas: approximately 2 million Europeans (voluntarily) and 10 million Africans (involuntarily) crossed the Atlantic.

First to master long-distance seafaring, the Portuguese also led the way in human cargo. Trade in slaves grew steadily throughout the sixteenth century, then surged in the seventeenth and eighteenth centuries (see Chapter 13). Initially, all European powers participated—Portuguese, Spanish, Dutch, English, and French. Eventually, New World merchants in both North and South America also established direct trade links with Africa.

Well before European merchants arrived off its western coast, Africa had known long-distance slave trading. In fact, the overall number of Africans sold into captivity in the Muslim world exceeded that of the Atlantic slave trade. Moreover, Africans maintained slaves themselves. African slavery, like its American counterpart, was a response to labor scarcities. In many parts of Africa, however, slaves did not face permanent servitude. Instead, they were assimilated into families, gradually losing their servile status and swelling the size and power of their adopted lineage-based groups.

With the additional European demand for slaves to work New World plantations alongside the ongoing Muslim slave trade, pressure on the supply of African slaves intensified. Only a narrow band stretching down the spine of the African landmass, from present-day Uganda and the highlands of Kenya to Zambia and Zimbabwe, escaped the impact of Asian and European slave traders.

Within Africa, the social and political consequences were not fully evident until the great age of the slave trade in the eighteenth century, but already some economic consequences were clear. The overwhelming trend was to further limit Africa's population. Indeed, African laborers fetched high enough prices to more than cover the costs of their capture and transportation across the Atlantic.

By the late sixteenth century, important pieces had fallen into place to create a new Atlantic world, one that could not have been imagined a century earlier. This was the three-cornered **Atlantic system**, with Africa supplying labor, the Americas land and minerals, and Europeans the technology and military power to hold the system together. In time, the wealth flows to Europe and the slave-based development of the Americas would alter the world balance of power.

THE TRANSFORMATION OF EUROPE

> → *What caused the political rivalries and religious rifts that divided Europe in the fifteenth and sixteenth centuries?*

Instead of uniting Europeans, the Atlantic system deepened the region's internal divides. In particular, the growing wealth of the Spanish Empire added to the Habsburg dynasty's power and attracted the attention of jealous competitors. On top of the transformations wrought by transatlantic opportu-

THE TRANSFORMATION OF EUROPE | **471**

→ *What caused the political rivalries and religious rifts that divided Europe in the fifteenth and sixteenth centuries?*

nities and rivalries, a split within the Roman Catholic Church (the Reformation, discussed below) led to profound religious rifts among states and brought additional divisions to the continent.

THE HABSBURGS AND THE QUEST FOR UNIVERSAL EMPIRE IN EUROPE

The European dream of a continent-wide empire, which had persisted since the fall of ancient Rome, found expression under the Habsburg dynasts. They were heirs to the eastern half of Charlemagne's empire. Here a loose confederation of principalities, the **Holy Roman Empire,** continued to obey an emperor elected by elite lower-level sovereigns (dukes, archbishops, and kings of individual states like Bavaria). After 1273, the emperor usually came from the Austrian house of Habsburg. The Holy Roman Empire included territory incorporated into the Netherlands, Germany, Austria, Belgium, Croatia, and parts of Italy, Poland, and Switzerland. Although the realm was enormous, it never enjoyed effectively centralized power.

In 1519, the Habsburg prince Charles V was elected Holy Roman Emperor, and for a few decades he controlled a transatlantic empire larger than any before or since. As grandson of Spanish monarchs Isabella and Ferdinand and of Holy Roman Emperor Maximilian I, Charles inherited both Spain and its territories in the Americas, as well as the Habsburgs' traditional central European holdings. Overstretched by trying to keep such an ambitious empire intact, and unable to prevent some central European princes from embracing the new Protestant faith, Charles abdicated in 1556 and divided the realm between his younger brother Ferdinand and his son Philip. Ferdinand (r. 1556–1564) took the Austrian, German, and central European territories that straddled the Danube and became Holy Roman Emperor in 1556, enabling the Austrian Habsburgs to maintain dominance over central Europe.

Philip II (r. Spain 1556–1598) received Spain, Belgium, the Netherlands, southern Italy, and the New World possessions. Moreover, he inherited the Portuguese throne (from his mother), adding Portugal and its colonial possessions to his empire. This gave him a monopoly on Atlantic commerce. Yet the Spanish Habsburgs had to defend their empire against Dutch revolts, as well as confront Ottoman harassment on land and at sea. The size and wealth of Habsburg Spain continued to provoke enormous tension within Europe.

CONFLICT IN EUROPE AND THE DEMISE OF UNIVERSAL EMPIRE

As the situation on the European mainland grew tense, French, English, and Dutch elites envied the riches of Portuguese and Spanish colonial possessions. These rivals yearned for their own profitable colonies. But in their New World explorations, the French, English, and Dutch had not yet found gold and silver, nor had they discovered an easier route to Asia. Still, they managed to claim a share of the wealth of the Americas by stealing it on the high seas. Some of the plunderers were pirates who raided for their own benefit; others were privateers who stole with official sanction and shared the profits with their monarchs. Often the distinction between pirate and privateer was blurred.

The most famous raider was Sir Francis Drake, whom the English crown commissioned to plunder Spanish possessions. Circling the globe between 1577 and 1580, Drake plundered one Spanish port after another. His favorite hunting ground was the Caribbean, where Mesoamerican and Andean silver, loaded onto Spanish galleons (heavy, square-rigged ships used for war or commerce), made lucrative targets. Besides, the many islands provided natural shelter. Although Drake undertook his exploits for personal gain, Queen Elizabeth approved of his assaults on the Spanish Empire and rewarded him with a knighthood.

To retaliate against English plundering and to prevent Elizabeth from supporting the Dutch revolt, the Spanish sailed a mighty armada of 130 ships and almost 20,000 men into the English Channel. But England amassed even more vessels from its Royal Navy and private merchant fleet. The subsequent defeat of the Spanish fleet saw the burning and destruction of many prized battleships. Thereafter the conflict between a rising England and Spain continued in other seas, and Drake returned to privateering. When news of Drake's death in the Caribbean (from yellow fever) arrived in Madrid, the Spanish court erupted in jubilation. However, two months later an English fleet sailed into Spain's premier port of Cádiz, occupied the city for two weeks, burned 200 Spanish ships, and seized massive treasure from the Indies. Spain, the powerhouse of the Atlantic world, had been severely humbled. Two years later a despondent King Philip died. The dream of universal empire within Europe had failed, largely because Christendom continued to be at war with itself.

THE REFORMATION

Like the Renaissance, the **Protestant Reformation** in Europe began as a movement devoted to returning to ancient sources—in this case, to biblical scriptures. Long before Martin Luther came on the scene, some scholars and believers had despaired of the Catholic Church's ability to satisfy their longings for deeper, more individualized religious experience. But interpreting Christian doctrine for oneself was still very dangerous in the fourteenth and fifteenth centuries, for the church feared that heresies and challenges to its authority would arise if laypersons were allowed to read the scriptures as they pleased. The church was right: for when Luther and his followers seized the right to read and interpret the Bible in a new way, they paved the way for a "Protestant" Reformation that split Christendom for good.

MARTIN LUTHER CHALLENGES THE CHURCH   The opening challenge to the authority of the pope and the Catholic Church originated in Germany. Here a monk and a professor of theology, Martin Luther (1483–1546), used his knowledge of the Bible to criticize the church's ideas and practices. He sought no revolution but hoped to persuade church leaders to make reforms.

Beginning his career as a pious Catholic believer, Luther nonetheless believed that mortals were so given to sin that none would ever be worthy of salvation. In 1516, Luther found an answer to his quest for salvation in reading Paul's Letters to the Romans: since no human acts could be sufficient to earn admittance to heaven, individuals could only be saved by their faith in God's grace. God's free gift of forgiveness, Luther believed, did not depend on taking sacraments or performing good deeds. This faith, moreover, was something Christians could obtain just from reading the Bible—rather than by having a priest tell them what to believe. Finally, Luther concluded that Christians did not need specially appointed mediators to speak to God for them; all were,

in his eyes, priests, equally bound by God's laws and obliged to minister to one another's spiritual needs.

These became the three main principles that launched Luther's reforming efforts: (1) belief that faith alone saves, (2) belief that the scriptures alone hold the key to Christian truth, and (3) belief in the priesthood of all believers. But other things motivated Luther as well: corrupt practices in the church, such as the keeping of mistresses by monks, priests, and even popes; and the selling of indulgences, certificates that would supposedly shorten the buyer's time in Purgatory. In the 1510s, clerics were hawking indulgences across Europe in an effort to raise money for the sumptuous new Saint Peter's basilica in Rome.

In 1517, Luther formulated ninety-five statements, or theses, and posted them on the doors to the Wittenberg cathedral, hoping to stir up his colleagues in debate. Before long his theses made him famous—and bolder in his criticisms. In a widely circulated pamphlet called *On the Freedom of the Christian Man* (1520), he upbraided "the Roman Church, which in past ages was the holiest of all" for having "become

The Reformation. Reformation images played an important role in the often violent polemics of the period. In this rather tame image, Luther preaches to Christ and the godly (*left*), while the pope (*right*) doles out indulgences to wealthy sinners.

THE TRANSFORMATION OF EUROPE | **473**

→ *What caused the political rivalries and religious rifts that divided Europe in the fifteenth and sixteenth centuries?*

a den of murderers beyond all other dens of murderers, a thieves' castle beyond all other thieves' castles, the head and empire of every sin, as well as of death and damnation." As Luther's ideas spread, a highly important "colleague" entered the debate: Pope Leo X.

The church and the Habsburg emperor, Charles V, demanded that Luther take back his criticisms and theological claims. When he refused, he was declared a heretic and narrowly avoided being burned at the stake. Luther wrote many more pamphlets attacking the church and the pope, whom he now described as the anti-Christ. In 1525, he attacked another aspect of Catholic doctrine by marrying a former nun, Katharina von Bora. In Luther's view, God approved of human sexuality within the bonds of marriage, and encouraging marriage for both the clergy and the laity was the only way to prevent illicit forms of sexual behavior. Luther also translated the New Testament from Latin into German so that laypersons could have direct access, without the clergy, to the word of God. This act spurred many other daring scholars across Europe to undertake translations of their own, and it encouraged the Protestant clergy to teach children (and adults) to read their national languages.

OTHER "PROTESTANT" REFORMERS Spread by printed books and ardent preachers in all the common languages of Europe, Luther's doctrines won widespread support. In fact, many German princes embraced the reformed faith to assert their independence from the Holy Roman Emperor. Those who followed the new faith identified themselves as "Protestants," and they promised that their reformed version of Christianity provided both an answer to individual spiritual needs and a new moral foundation for community life. The renewed Christian creed appealed to commoners as well as elites, especially in communities that resented rule by Catholic "outsiders" (like the Dutch, who resented being ruled by Philip II, an Austrian prince who lived in Spain). Thus the reformed ideas took particularly firm hold in the German states, France, Switzerland, Scandinavia, the Low Countries, and England.

Some zealous reformers, like Jean Calvin (1509–1564) in France, modified Luther's ideas. To Luther's emphasis on the individual's relationship to God, Calvin added a focus on moral regeneration through church discipline and the autonomy of religious communities. He laid out the doctrine of predestination—the notion that each person is "predestined" for damnation or salvation even before birth. The "elect," he thought, should also be free to govern themselves, a doctrine that upheld radical political dissent (as in the case of Puritans in England) and the rule of the clergy (as in the Swiss city-state of Geneva). Calvinism proved especially popular in Switzerland, the Netherlands, northeastern France, and Scotland (where it was called Presbyterianism). In contrast, those who remained loyal to the original Protestant cause now described themselves as Lutherans.

In England, Henry VIII (r. 1509–1547) and his daughter Elizabeth (r. 1558–1603) crafted a moderate reformed religion—a "middle way"—called Anglicanism, which retained many Catholic practices and a hierarchy topped by bishops. (American followers would later call themselves Episcopalians, from the Latin word for bishop, *episcopus*). Although Anglican rule was imposed on Ireland, most nonelite Irishmen remained Catholic. The Scots maintained a fierce devotion to their Presbyterian Church, ensuring a measure of religious diversity within the British Isles. In England, as with the rest of Europe, more radical Protestant sects like Anabaptists and Quakers also developed. While all Protestants were opposed to Catholicism and distrustful of the papal hierarchy, these different communities sometimes developed animosities toward one another as well (see Map 12-4).

COUNTER-REFORMATION AND PERSECUTION The Catholic Church responded to Luther and Calvin by embarking on its own renovation, which became known as the **Counter-Reformation**. At the Council of Trent, whose twenty-five sessions stretched from 1545 to 1563, Catholic leaders reaffirmed numerous things: the church's doctrines, sacraments, acts of charity, papal supremacy, the clergy's distinctive role, and the insistence that priests, monks, and nuns remain celibate. But the council also enacted reforms to answer the Protestants' assaults on clerical corruption. In contrast to many of their predecessors, the popes who headed the Catholic Church late in the sixteenth century became renowned for their piety and asceticism. They also installed bishops and abbots who generally steered clear of unscrupulous practices. Taking on the Protestant theological challenge, Catholicism gave greater emphasis to individual spirituality. Like the Protestants, the reformed Catholics carried their message overseas—especially through an order established by Ignatius Loyola (1491–1556). Loyola founded a brotherhood of priests, the Society of Jesus, or **Jesuits**, dedicated to the revival of the Catholic Church. From bases in Lisbon, Rome, Paris, and elsewhere in Europe, the Jesuits opened missions as far as South and North America, India, Japan, and China.

Yet the Vatican continued to use repression and persecution to combat what it regarded as heretical beliefs. Priests in Augsburg performed public exorcisms, seeking to free Protestant parishioners from possession by "demons." The Index of Prohibited Books (a list of books and theological treatises banned by the Catholic Church) and the medieval Inquisition (from 1184) were weapons against those deemed to be the church's enemies. But the proliferation of printing presses and the spread of Protestantism made it impossible for the Catholic Counter-Reformation to turn back the tide leading toward increased autonomy from the papacy.

Both Catholics and Protestants persecuted witches. Between about 1500 and 1700, up to 100,000 people, mostly women, were accused of being witches. Many were tried,

MAP 12-4 **RELIGIOUS DIVISIONS IN EUROPE AFTER THE REFORMATION, 1590**

The Protestant Reformation divided Europe religiously and politically. Within the formerly all-Catholic Holy Roman Empire, what Protestant groups took hold? Looking at the map, can you identify any geographic patterns in the distribution of Protestant communities? In what regions would you expect Protestant-Catholic tensions to be the most intense?

tortured, burned at the stake, or hanged. Older women, widows, and nurses were especially vulnerable to charges of cursing or poisoning babies. Other charges included killing livestock, causing hailstorms, and scotching marriage arrangements. People also believed that weak and susceptible women might have sex with the devil or be tempted to do his bidding. Clearly, by no means did the Reformation—or the Catholic response to it—make Europe a more tolerant society.

RELIGIOUS WARFARE IN EUROPE

The religious revival led Europe into another round of ferocious wars. Their ultimate effect was to weaken the Holy Roman Empire and strengthen the English, French, and Dutch. Already in the 1520s, the circulation of books presenting Luther's ideas sparked peasant revolts across central Europe. Some peasants, hoping that Luther's assault on the church's authority would help liberate them, rose up against repressive feudal landlords. In contrast to earlier wars in which one noble's retinue fought a rival's, the defense of the Catholic mass and the Protestant Bible brought crowds of simple folk to arms. Now wars between and within central European states raged for nearly forty years. In 1555, the exhausted Holy Roman Emperor Charles V was compelled to allow the German princes the right to choose Lutheranism or Catholicism as the official religion within their domains (Calvinism was still outlawed). However, this concession did not end Europe's religious wars.

Religious conflicts both weakened European dynasties and whetted their appetite for conquest abroad. Spain, with its massive empire and its silver mines in the New World, spent much of its new fortune waging war in Europe. Most debilitating was its costly effort to subdue recently acquired Dutch territories. After a series of wars spanning nearly a hundred years, Catholic Spain finally conceded the Protestant Netherlands its independence.

Wars took their toll on the Spanish Empire, which was soon wallowing in debts; not even the riches of its American silver mines could bail out the court. In the late 1550s, Philip II could not meet his obligations to creditors. Within two decades, Spain was declared bankrupt three times. Its decline opened the way for the Dutch and the English to extend their trading networks into Asia and the New World. Competition between the latter two bred trade wars, indicating that religious differences were not the only sources of inter-European strife.

Religious conflicts also sparked civil wars. In France, the divide between Catholics and Protestants exploded in the St. Bartholomew's Day Massacre of 1572. Catholic crowds rampaged through the streets of Paris murdering Huguenot (Protestant) men, women, and children and dumping their bodies into the Seine River; parades of rioters displayed Protestants' severed heads on pikes. The number of dead reached 3,000 in Paris and 10,000 in provincial towns. Slaughter on this scale did not break the Huguenots' spirit, but it did bring more disrepute to the monarchy for failing to ensure peace. This was the beginning of the end of the Valois dynasty. Another round of warfare exhausted the French and brought Henry of Navarre, a Protestant prince, to the throne. To become king, Henry IV converted to Catholicism. Shortly thereafter he issued the Edict of Nantes, a proclamation that declared France a Catholic country but also tolerated some Protestant worship.

St. Bartholomew's Day Massacre. An important wedding between French Catholic and Huguenot families in Paris was scheduled for August 24, 1572, St. Bartholomew's Day, but instead of reconciliation, that day saw a massacre, as Catholics tried to stamp out Protestantism in France's capital city.

As princes sought to resolve religious questions within their domains, states increasingly became identified with one or another form of Christian faith—and, for Protestants, with a national language. In this way, religious strife propelled forward the process of state building and the forming of national identities. At the same time, religious conflict fueled rivalries for wealth and territory overseas. Thus, Europe entered its age of overseas exploration as a collection of increasingly powerful yet irreconcilably competitive rival states, whose differences stemmed not just from language but from the ways they worshipped the Christian God.

PROSPERITY IN ASIA

↠ *Why did trade expand and wealth increase in sixteenth-century Asia?*

While Europe was experiencing religious warfare, Asian empires were expanding and consolidating their power, and trade was flourishing. If anything, the arrival of European sailors and traders in the Indian Ocean strengthened trading ties across the region and enhanced the political power and expansionist interests of Asia's imperial regimes. These regimes have left their mark on world history. The Ming dynasty's elegant manufactures enjoyed worldwide renown, and its ability to govern vast numbers of highly diverse peoples led outsiders to consider China the model imperial state. The Mughal ruler, Akbar, and the Ottoman sultan, Suleiman the Magnificent (see Chapter 11), were equally effective and esteemed rulers.

MUGHAL INDIA AND COMMERCE

The **Mughal Empire** became one of the world's wealthiest just when Europeans were establishing sustained connections with India. These connections, however, only touched the outer layer of Mughal India, one of Islam's greatest regimes. Established in 1526, it was a vigorous, centralized state whose political authority encompassed most of modern-day India. During the sixteenth century, it had a population of between 100 and 150 million.

The Mughals' strength rested on their military power (see Chapter 11). The dynasty's founder, Babur, had introduced horsemanship, artillery, and field cannons from central Asia, and gunpowder had secured his swift military victories over northern India. Under his grandson, Akbar (r. 1556–1605), the empire enjoyed expansion and consolidation that continued (under his own grandson, Aurangzeb) until it covered almost all of India (see Map 12-5). Known as the "Great Mughal," Akbar was skilled not only in military tactics but also in the art of alliance making. Deals with Hindu chieftains through favors and intermarriage also undergirded his empire.

Mughal rulers were flexible toward their realm's diverse peoples, especially in spiritual affairs. Though its primary commitment to Islam stood firm, the imperial court also patronized other beliefs, displaying a tolerance that earned it widespread legitimacy. The contrast with Europe, where religious differences drove deep fractures within and between states, was stark. Unlike European monarchs, who tried to enforce religious uniformity, Akbar studied comparative religion and hosted regular debates among Hindu, Muslim, Jain, Parsi, and Christian theologians. Ultimately he introduced at his court a "Divine Faith" (*Dīn-i Ilāhī*) that was a mix of Quranic, Catholic, and other influences; it emphasized virtues such as piety, prudence, gentleness, liberality, and a yearning for God. In part, *Dīn-i Ilāhī* reflected Akbar's desire to strengthen his position against the *ulama* and his interest in philosophical skepticism. Akbar had both a Hindu and a Christian wife (besides a Muslim wife, as well as concubines of many nationalities and religions), and his palace boasted temples to each faith. His tolerance kept a multifaceted spiritual kingdom under one political roof.

Akbar's court benefited from commercial expansion in the Indian Ocean. Although the Mughals possessed no ocean navy, merchants from Mughal lands used overland routes and rivers to exchange Indian cottons, tobacco, saffron, betel leaf, sugar, and indigo for Iranian melons, dried fruits, nuts, silks, carpets, and precious metals, or for Russian pelts, leathers, walrus tusks, saddles, and chain-mail armor. Every year, Akbar ordered 1,000 new suits stitched of the most exquisite material. His harem preened in fine silks dripping with gold, brocades, and pearls. Carpets, mirrors, and precious metals adorned nobles' households and camps, while perfume and wine flowed freely. Soldiers, servants, and even horses and elephants sported elaborate attire.

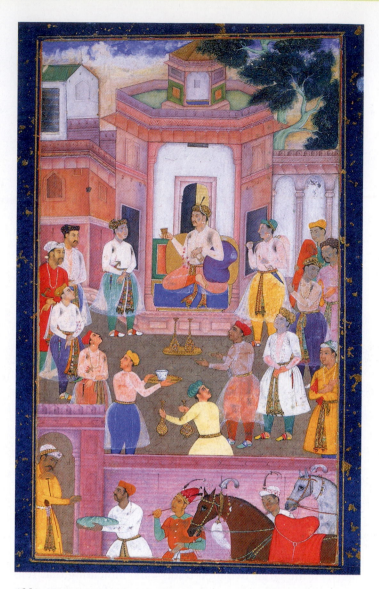

Akbar Hears a Petition. In keeping with the multiethnic and multireligious character of Akbar's empire, the image reflects the diversity of peoples seeking to have their petitions heard by the Mughal emperor.

During the sixteenth century, expanded trade with Europe brought more wealth to the Mughal polity, while the empire's strength limited European incursions. Although the Portuguese occupied Goa and Bombay on the Indian coast, they had little presence elsewhere and dared not antagonize the Mughal emperor. In 1578, Akbar recognized the credentials of a Portuguese ambassador and allowed a Jesuit missionary to enter his court. Thereafter, commercial ties between Mughals and Portuguese intensified, but the merchants were still restricted to a handful of ports. In the 1580s and 1590s, the Mughals ended the Portuguese monopoly on trade with Europe by allowing Dutch and English merchantmen to dock in Indian ports.

→ *Why did trade expand and wealth increase in sixteenth-century Asia?*

MAP 12-5   EXPANSION OF THE MUGHAL EMPIRE, 1556–1707

Under Akbar and Aurangzeb, the Mughal Empire expanded and dominated much of South Asia. Yet, by looking at the trading ports along the Indian coast, one can see the growing influence of Portuguese, Dutch, French, and English interests. Look at the dates for each port, and identify which traders came first and which came last. Compare this map with Map 12-2 (showing the earlier period 1420–1580): to what extent do the trading posts shown here reflect increased European influence in the region? How would these European outposts have affected Mughal policies?

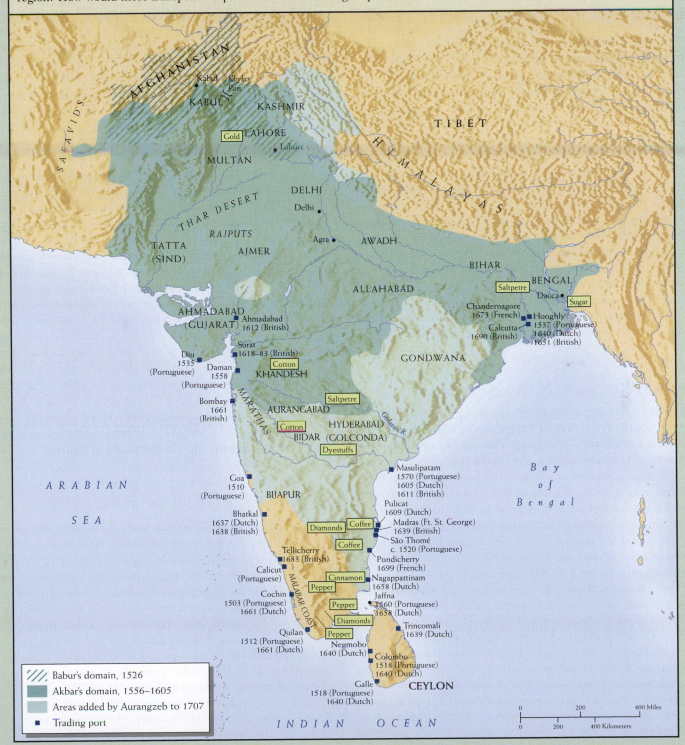

Akbar used the commercial boom to overhaul his revenue system. Until the 1560s, the Mughal state relied on a network of decentralized tribute collectors called *zamindars*. These collectors possessed rights to claim a share of the harvest while earmarking part of their earnings for the emperor. But the Mughals did not always receive their agreed share and the peasants resented the high levies, so local populations resisted. As flourishing trade bolstered the money supply, Akbar's officials monetized the tax assessment system and curbed the *zamindars'* power. After other centralizing reforms, increased imperial revenues helped finance military expeditions and the extravagant beautification of Akbar's court.

Such fiscal policies reinforced the empire's growing commercialization. To generate cash to pay taxes, peasants had to sell their produce in the market—so market towns and ports flourished. Meanwhile, in the countryside, dealers in grain and money helped peasants get their produce to market. Up to one-third the value of burgeoning rural produce filled state coffers. Now the *zamindars* evolved from private tribute lords into servants of the state, though they continued to pocket a share of the peasants' income.

Centered in northern India, the Mughal Empire used surrounding regions' wealth and resources—military, architectural, and artistic—to glorify the court. Over time, the enhanced wealth caused friction among Indian regions, and even between merchants and rulers. Yet as long as merchants relied on rulers for their commercial gains, and as long as rulers balanced local and imperial interests, the realm remained unified and kept Europeans on the outskirts of society.

PROSPERITY IN MING CHINA

In the late sixteenth century, China also prospered from increased commerce. Like the Mughals, the Ming seemed unconcerned with the increasing appearance of foreigners, including Europeans bearing silver. As in India, the Ming confined European traders to port cities. Silver from the Americas did, however, circulate widely in China. It allowed employers to pay their workers with money rather than with produce or goods. It also contributed to soaring production in agriculture and handicrafts. Through the sixteenth century, rural industries in China flourished. A cotton boom, for example, made spinning and weaving China's largest industry.

One measure of greater prosperity under the Ming was its population surge. By the mid-seventeenth century, China's population probably accounted for more than one-third of the total world population. Although 90 percent of Chinese people lived in the countryside, large numbers filled the cities. Beijing, the Ming capital, grew to over 1 million; Nanjing, the secondary capital, nearly matched that number. Cities offered diversions ranging from literary and theatrical societies to schools of learning, religious societies, urban associations, and manufactures from all over the empire. The elegance and material prosperity of Chinese cities dazzled European visitors. One Jesuit missionary described Nanjing as surpassing all other cities "in beauty and grandeur. . . . It is literally filled with palaces and temples and towers and bridges. . . . There is a gaiety of spirit among the people who are well mannered and nicely spoken." (In contrast, see Primary Source: Commentary on Foreigners from a Ming Official.)

Urban prosperity fostered entertainment districts where people could indulge themselves anonymously and in relative freedom. Some Ming women found a place here as refined entertainers and courtesans, others as midwives, poets, sorcerers, and matchmakers. Female painters, mostly from scholar-official families, emulated males who used the home and garden for creative pursuits. The expanding book trade also accommodated women, who were writers as well as readers, not to mention literary characters and archetypes (especially of Confucian virtues). But Chinese women made their greatest fortunes inside the emperor's Forbidden City as healers, consorts, and power brokers.

To be sure, by the mid-sixteenth century Ming rule faced a variety of problems, from piracy along the coasts to ineptness in the state. Corruption and perceptions of social decay elicited even more criticism. Consider Wang Yangming, a government official and scholar of neo-Confucian thought who urged commitment to social action. Arguing for the unity of knowledge and action, he claimed that one's own thoughts and intuition, rather than observations and external principles (as earlier neo-Confucian thinkers had emphasized), could provide the answers to problems. His more radical followers suggested, against traditional belief, that women were equal to men intellectually and should receive full educations—a position that earned these radicals banishment from the elite establishment. But even as such new ideas and the state's weaknesses created discord, Ming society remained commercially vibrant. This vitality survived the dynasty's fall in 1644, laying the foundation for increased population growth and territorial expansion in subsequent centuries.

ASIAN RELATIONS WITH EUROPE

Europeans' overseas expansion had originally looked toward Asia, and now the products from their New World colonies enabled them to realize some of those dreams. The Portuguese led the way, being the first Europeans to join the overseas trading networks bridging East Africa and China. Before long, they became either important commercial intermediaries or collectors of customs duties from Asian traders. In 1557, the Portuguese arrival at Macao, a port along the southern coast of China, enabled them to penetrate China's expanding import-export trade. Within five years the number of Portuguese in Macao neared 1,000 (see again Map 12-1).

True, Macao hosted many more Melakans, Indians, and Africans, who all enlivened the port. Moreover, although Ming authorities permitted a Portuguese presence there, the court refused to establish an official relationship with European

Primary Source

COMMENTARY ON FOREIGNERS FROM A MING OFFICIAL

Although China had a long history of trade with the outside world, Ming officials were often hostile toward contact with foreigners. The bureaucrat He Ao (Ho Ao) wrote this commentary around 1520, portraying the Europeans (whom he called Feringis) as unruly, untrustworthy, and a threat to the country's security. Such sentiments were also common among officials in subsequent centuries, even as China thrived in the commercial exchanges of an increasingly connected world.

The Feringis are most cruel and crafty. Their arms are superior to those of other foreigners. Some years ago they came suddenly to the city of Canton, and the noise of their cannon shook the earth [these were cannon shots fired as a salute by the fleet of Fernão Peres]. Those who remained at the post-station [places where foreigners were lodged] disobeyed the law and had intercourse with others. Those who came to the Capital were proud and struggled [among themselves?] to become head. Now if we allow them to come and go and to carry on their trade, it will inevitably lead to fighting and bloodshed, and the misfortune of our South may be boundless.

In the time of our ancestors, foreigners came to bring tribute only at fixed periods, and the law provided for precautionary measures, therefore the foreigners who could come were not many. But some time ago the Provincial Treasurer, Wu T'ing-chü, saying that he needed spice to be sent to the Court, took some of their goods no matter when they came. It was due to what he did that foreigner ships have never ceased visiting our shores and that barbarians have lived scattered in our departmental cities. Prohibition and precaution having been neglected, the Feringis became more and more familiar with our fair ways. And thus availing themselves of the situation the Feringis came into our port.

I pray that all the foreign junks in our bay and the foreigners who secretly live (in our territory) be driven away, that private intercourse be prohibited and that our strategical defence be close, so that that part of our country will have peace.

→ *According to this document, what was the Chinese view of foreigners?*

→ *How does this document compare to the earlier report from the European trader? (See Primary Source reading on p. 457.)*

→ *In this translation,* intercourse *means "commerce" or "business." Find the two places where this term occurs. Does the context indicate a difference of opinion between officials and merchants in Ming China?*

SOURCE: T'ien-Tse Chang, *Sino-Portuguese Trade from 1514 to 1644: A Synthesis of Portuguese and Chinese Sources* (Leyden: E. J. Brill, 1934), pp. 51–52. Reprinted by permission of Koninklijke Brill NV.

traders. Like the Mughals, the Ming confined the merchants to a coastal enclave. In fact, in 1574 the Chinese built a wall at the isthmus connecting Macao with the mainland; this barrier, and the soldiers who guarded it, restricted Portuguese access to inland trade. Nonetheless the Portuguese became important shippers of China's prized porcelains and silks throughout Asia and beyond to Europe. They also dominated the silver trade from Japan.

Seeing how much the Portuguese were earning on Asian trade, the Spanish, English, and Dutch also ventured into Asian waters. With its monopoly on American silver, Spain enjoyed a competitive advantage. In 1565, the first Spanish trading galleon reached the Philippines; in 1571, after capturing Manila and making it a colonial capital, the Spanish established a brisk trade with China. Each year, ships from Spain's colonies in the Americas crossed the Pacific to Manila, bearing cargoes of silver. They returned carrying porcelain and silks for well-to-do European consumers. Merchants in Manila also procured silks, tapestries, and feathers from the China Seas for shipment to the Americas, where the mining elite eagerly awaited these imports.

The year 1571 was decisive in the history of the modern world, for in that year Spain inaugurated a trade circuit that made good on Magellan's earlier achievement. As Spanish ships circled the globe from the New World to China and from China back to Europe, the world became commercially interconnected. Silver solidified the linkage, being the only foreign commodity for which the Chinese had an insatiable demand. From the mother lodes of the Andes and Mesoamerica, silver made the commerce of the world go round.

Other Europeans, too, wanted their share of Asia's wealth. The English and the Dutch reached the South China Sea late

Macao. This Chinese painting depicts the Portuguese enclave of Macao on the southern border of China around 1800.

in the sixteenth century. Captain James Lancaster made the first English voyage to the East Indies between 1591 and 1594. Five years later, 101 English subscribers pooled their funds and formed a joint-stock company (an association in which each member owned shares of capital). This English East India Company soon won a royal charter granting it exclusive rights to import East Indian goods. Soon the company displaced the Portuguese in the Arabian Sea and the Persian Gulf. Doing a brisk trade in indigo, saltpeter, pepper, and cotton textiles, the English East India Company eventually acquired control of ports on both coasts of India—Fort St. George (Madras; 1639), Bombay (1661), and Calcutta (1690).

It is tempting to see the Europeans' arrival in the South China Sea and the Indian Ocean as the beginning of the end of Asian autonomy. This was hardly the case, however. Through the sixteenth century, Europeans forged very weak connections to Asian societies. For the moment, the Europeans' increased presence enhanced the wealth and might of Asian dynasties.

CONCLUSION

In this multicentered world of the fifteenth century, Europe was a poor cousin. However, a new spirit of adventure and achievement animated its peoples, stirred up by the rediscovery of antiquity (the Renaissance), an ambitious mercantile elite, and the spiritual fervor of the Reformation and Counter-Reformation. Learning from Arab seamen, European sailors perfected techniques for sailing into dangerous waters. Desiring Asian luxury goods, European merchants and mariners were eager to exploit trade routes leading eastward. More important, Europe's location promoted expansion across the largely unknown Atlantic Ocean. With the Ottomans controlling Constantinople and the eastern Mediterranean, Atlantic sea-lanes offered an alternative route to Asia. As Europeans searched for routes around Islamic territory, they first sailed down the coast of Africa and then across the Atlantic.

Encountering the "New World" was an accident of monumental significance. In the Americas, Europeans found riches. Mountains of silver and rivers of gold gave them the currency they needed for dealing with Asian traders. Europeans also found opportunities for exchange, conquest, and colonization. Yet, establishing these transatlantic empires heightened tensions within Europe, as rivals fought over the spoils and a religious schism turned into a divisive political and spiritual struggle.

Thus two conquests characterize this age of increasing world interconnections. The Islamic conquest of Constantinople drove Europeans to find new links to Asia, thereby demonstrating Islam's pivotal role in shaping modern world history. In turn, the Spanish conquest of the Aztecs and the Incas gave Europeans access to silver, which bought them an increased presence in Asian trading networks.

American Indians also played an important role, as Europeans sought to conquer their lands, exploit their labor, and

Chronology

	1500	1510	1520	1530	1540
EUROPE	◆ 1492 Christians complete reconquest of Granada		◆ 1517 Luther posts 95 theses		
			1519–1522 Magellan's ship circumnavigates the globe ◆----◆		
AMERICAS	◆ 1492 Columbus discovers the New World		1519–1522 Magellan's ship circumnavigates the globe ◆----◆		
			◆----◆ 1519–1522 Cortés conquers the Aztecs		
			1533 Pizarro conquers the Incas ◆		
SOUTH ASIA	◆ 1498 Da Gama sails to the Indian Ocean				
		◆----◆ 1508–1511 Portuguese establish Indian Ocean bases			
			1519–1522 Magellan's ship circumnavigates the globe ◆----◆		
EAST ASIA			1519–1522 Magellan's ship circumnavigates the globe ◆----◆		

confiscate their gold and silver. Sometimes Indians worked with Europeans, sometimes under Europeans, sometimes against Europeans—and sometimes none were left to work at all. Then Europeans brought in African laborers, compounding the calamity of the encounter with the tragedy of slavery. Out of the catastrophe of contact, a new oceanic system arose to link Africa, America, and Europe. This was the Atlantic system. Unlike the tributary and trading orders of the Indian Ocean and China Seas, the Atlantic Ocean supported a system of formal imperial control and settlement of distant colonies. These would become more important to how worlds connected and collided in the following centuries.

Review and research materials are available at StudySpace: Ⓖ WWNORTON.COM/STUDYSPACE

KEY TERMS

Atlantic system (p. 470)
Aztec Empire (p. 459)
colonies (p. 456)
Columbian exchange (p. 464)
conquistadors (p. 459)
Counter-Reformation (p. 473)
Holy Roman Empire (p. 471)
Inca Empire (p. 462)
Jesuits (p. 473)
mestizos (p. 461)
Mughal Empire (p. 476)
New World (p. 457)
Protestant Reformation (p. 471)

STUDY QUESTIONS

1. Describe the new trade patterns in the Afro-Eurasian world during the fifteenth century. How similar and different were they from trade patterns during the Mongol period?
2. Describe how Spain created a vast empire in the Americas. How did the spread of lethal disease influence this outcome?
3. Explain the Columbian exchange. What consequences did it have on regions both beyond the Atlantic world and within it?
4. Compare and contrast Spain's "tributary empire" in the Americas with Portugal's "seaborne empire" in the Indian Ocean. Why did these empires pursue such different strategies?
5. Explain what conditions promoted the strengthening of regional dynasties in Europe in the sixteenth century as opposed to the growth of one large European empire.
6. Explain the transformation of the African slave trade during this period. What role did the growth of sugar plantations play?
7. How did the emergence of the Atlantic system transform Europe, the Americas, and Africa. To what extent was each region transformed?
8. Compare and contrast political and commercial developments in the Mughal and Ming dynasties during the sixteenth century. How did the expansion of global commerce affect each region?
9. Evaluate to what extent an increased European presence altered the political balance of power in Asia at this time. How did Asian dynasties react to increased European contacts?
10. Explain the role of silver in transforming global trade patterns during the sixteenth century. Which regions and dynasties benefited from the increased use of silver for monetary transactions?

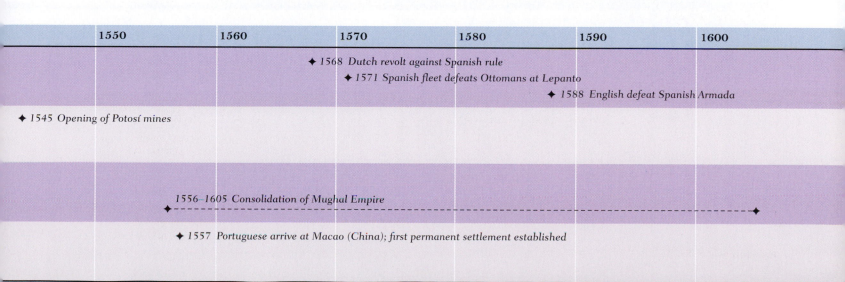

	1550	1560	1570	1580	1590	1600

◆ 1568 Dutch revolt against Spanish rule
◆ 1571 Spanish fleet defeats Ottomans at Lepanto
◆ 1588 English defeat Spanish Armada
◆ 1545 Opening of Potosí mines
1556–1605 Consolidation of Mughal Empire
◆ 1557 Portuguese arrive at Macao (China); first permanent settlement established

WORLDS ENTANGLED,
1600–1750

In 1720, a financial panic engulfed Europe, making rich men into paupers and ruining many political careers. The panic arose from a speculative mania over anticipated profits from trade with the Americas. A group of British merchants established the South Sea Trading Company to compete with French firms and obtained privileged trading rights with all of Spanish America. Most coveted was the exclusive right to sell African slaves to Spanish colonies. As enthusiasm for such companies soared, eager investors sent share prices skyrocketing. But rumors of fantastic spoils gave way to word that the original investors were dumping their shares and that the companies were worthless. Then the speculative bubble burst. Share prices plummeted, nearly all the new companies went bankrupt, and many older firms collapsed. The so-called South Sea Bubble reflected the euphoria—and the perils—of global trade and investment.

From 1600 to 1750, global trading networks propelled commerce across the world's oceans. Sugar flowed from Brazil and the Caribbean, spices from Southeast Asia, cotton textiles from India, silks from China, and, increasingly, silver from Mesoamerica and the Andes. New World silver was especially crucial to these networks: it gave Europeans a commodity to exchange with

Asians, and it tilted the balance of wealth and power in a westerly direction across Afro-Eurasia.

Imperial expansion and transoceanic trade now brought the world together as never before. Europeans conquered and colonized more of the Americas, the demand for African slaves to work New World plantations leaped upward, and global trade intensified. Conquest, colonization, and commerce created riches for some but also provoked bitter rivalries. In the Americas, Spain and Portugal faced new competitors—primarily England and France. With religious tensions added to the mix, the stage was set for decades of bloody warfare in Europe and the Americas. At the same time, rulers in India, China, and Japan enlarged their empires, while Russia's tsars incorporated Siberian territories into their domain. Meanwhile, the Ottoman, Safavid, and Mughal dynasties, though resisting most European intrusions, found their stability profoundly shaken by the forces that entangled the world.

ECONOMIC AND POLITICAL EFFECTS OF GLOBAL COMMERCE

> → *How did global economic integration affect economic and political systems?*

Global trade affected not only merchant groups and their sponsoring nations but also individual rulers and common people. Increasing economic ties brought new places and products into world markets: furs from French North America, sugar from the Caribbean, tobacco from British colonies on the American mainland, and coffee from Southeast Asia

and the Middle East. (See Global Connections & Disconnections: Stimulants, Sociability, and Coffeehouses.) Such products became so important that interruptions in availability sometimes destabilized economic and political systems. For example, gold and silver from the Americas were vital to the global networks (see Map 13-1). The supply of precious metals might fall when political disturbances caused work stoppages, or surge when new mines opened. Commodity prices could soar or drop, bringing prosperity to some and bankruptcy to others.

Closer economic contact enhanced the power of certain states and destabilized others. It bolstered the legitimacy of England and France, and it prompted strong local support of new rulers in Japan and parts of sub-Saharan Africa. But also in England, France, Japan, Russia, and Africa, linkages led to civil wars and social unrest. In the Ottoman state, outlying provinces slipped from central control; the Safavid regime foundered and then ended; the Ming dynasty gave way to the Qing. In India, rivalries among princes and merchants eroded the Mughals' authority, compounding the instability caused by peasant uprisings.

EXTRACTING WEALTH: MERCANTILISM

Transformations in global relations began in the Atlantic, where the extraction and shipment of gold and silver siphoned wealth from the New World (the Americas) to the Old World (Afro-Eurasia). Mined by Indian and African workers and delivered into the hands of merchants and monarchs, silver from the Andes and Mesoamerica boosted the world's supply. In addition, a boom in gold production made Brazil the world's largest producer of that metal at this time.

American mining was so lucrative for Spain and Portugal that other European powers wanted a share in the bounty, so they, too, launched colonizing ventures in the New World. Although these latecomers found few precious minerals,

Focus Questions

STIMULANTS, SOCIABILITY, AND COFFEEHOUSES

As trading networks expanded, merchants in Europe, Asia, Africa, and the Americas distributed many new commodities. By far the most popular were a group of stimulants—coffee, cocoa, sugar, tobacco, and tea—all of which (except for sugar) were addictive and also produced a sense of well-being. Previously, many of these products had been grown in isolated parts of the world: the coffee bean in Yemen, tobacco and cocoa in the New World, and sugar in Bengal. Yet, by the seventeenth century, in nearly every corner of the world, the well-to-do began to congregate in coffeehouses, consuming these new products and engaging in sociable activities.

Coffeehouses everywhere served as locations for social exchange, political discussions, and business activities. Yet they also varied from cultural area to cultural area, reflecting the values of the societies in which they arose.

The coffeehouse first appeared in Islamic lands late in the fifteenth century. As coffee consumption caught on among the wealthy and leisured classes in the Arabian Peninsula and the Ottoman Empire, local growers protected their advantage by monopolizing its cultivation and sale and refusing to allow any seeds or cuttings from the coffee tree to be taken abroad.

Despite some religious opposition, coffee spread into Egypt and throughout the Ottoman Empire in the sixteenth century. Ottoman bureaucrats, merchants, and artists assembled in coffeehouses to trade stories, read, listen to poetry, and play chess and backgammon. Indeed, so deeply connected were coffeehouses with literary and artistic pursuits that people referred to them as schools of knowledge.

From the Ottoman territories, the culture of coffee drinking spread to western Europe. The first coffeehouse in London opened in 1652, and within sixty years the city claimed no fewer than 500 such establishments. In fact, the Fleet Street area of London had so many that the English essayist Charles Lamb commented, "[T]he man must have a rare recipe for melancholy who can be dull in Fleet Street." Although coffeehouses attracted people from all levels of society, they especially appealed to the new mercantile and professional classes as locations where stimulating beverages like coffee, cocoa, and tea promoted lively conversations. Here, too, opponents claimed that excessive coffee drinking destabilized the thinking processes and even caused conversions to Islam. But against such opposition, the pleasures of coffee, tea, and cocoa prevailed. These bitter beverages in turn required liberal doses of the sweetener sugar. A smoke of tobacco topped off the experience. In this environment of pleasure, patrons of the coffeehouses indulged their addictions, engaged in gossip, conducted business, and talked politics.

Coffee. Coffee drinkers at an Ottoman banquet (*left*) and in an English coffeehouse (*right*).

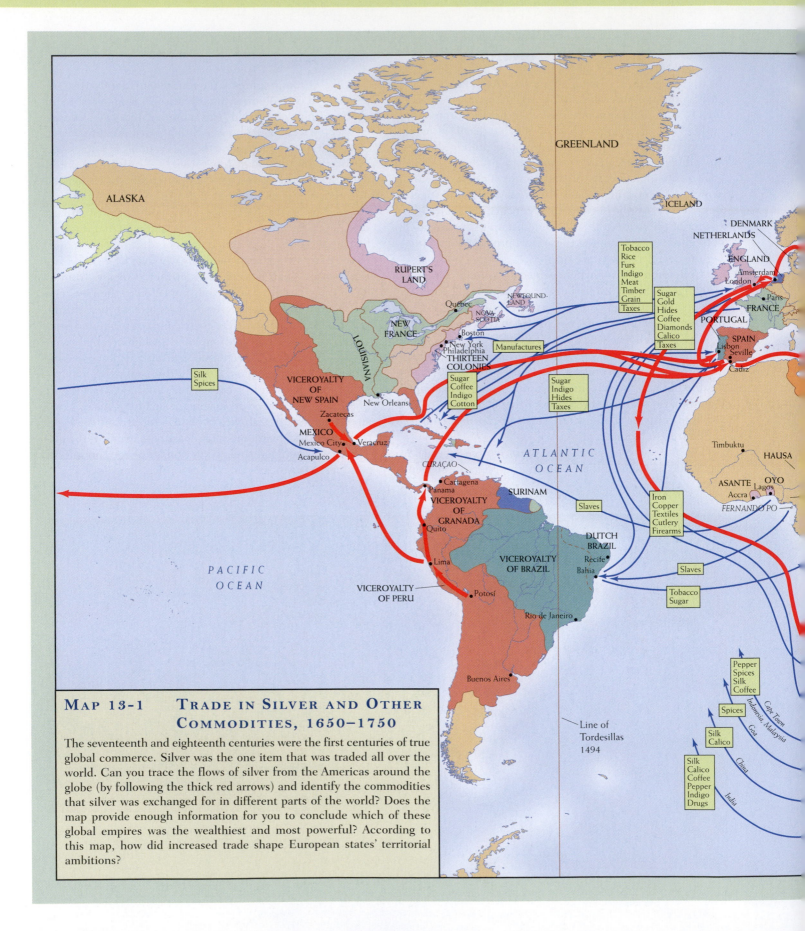

ALASKA

GREENLAND

ICELAND

DENMARK
NETHERLANDS

RUPERT'S
LAND

ENGLAND
Amsterdam
London

NEWFOUND-
LAND

FRANCE

Québec

Paris

NEW
FRANCE

NOVA
SCOTIA

PORTUGAL

SPAIN

Boston

Lisbon
Seville

New York
Philadelphia

Manufactures

THIRTEEN
COLONIES

Cadiz

LOUISIANA

Tobacco
Rice
Furs
Indigo
Meat
Timber
Grain
Taxes

Sugar
Gold
Hides
Coffee
Diamonds
Calico
Taxes

Silk
Spices

Sugar
Coffee
Indigo
Cotton

Sugar
Indigo
Hides
Taxes

VICEROYALTY
OF NEW SPAIN

Timbuktu

HAUSA

Zacatecas

New Orleans

ASANTE

OYO

MEXICO

Mexico City Veracruz

Acapulco

*ATLANTIC
OCEAN*

Accra   Lagos

FERNANDO PO

CURAÇAO

Cartagena

SURINAM

Iron
Copper
Textiles
Cutlery
Firearms

Panama

VICEROYALTY
OF
GRANADA

Slaves

*PACIFIC
OCEAN*

Quito

DUTCH
BRAZIL

VICEROYALTY
OF BRAZIL

Recife

Bahia

Slaves

Lima

VICEROYALTY
OF PERU

Potosí

Tobacco
Sugar

Pepper
Spices
Silk
Coffee

Rio de Janeiro

Indonesia, Malaysia

Cape Town

Buenos Aires

Spices

Goa

Silk
Calico

Line of
Tordesillas
1494

China

Silk
Calico
Coffee
Pepper
Indigo
Drugs

India

Map 13-1   Trade in Silver and Other Commodities, 1650–1750

The seventeenth and eighteenth centuries were the first centuries of true global commerce. Silver was the one item that was traded all over the world. Can you trace the flows of silver from the Americas around the globe (by following the thick red arrows) and identify the commodities that silver was exchanged for in different parts of the world? Does the map provide enough information for you to conclude which of these global empires was the wealthiest and most powerful? According to this map, how did increased trade shape European states' territorial ambitions?

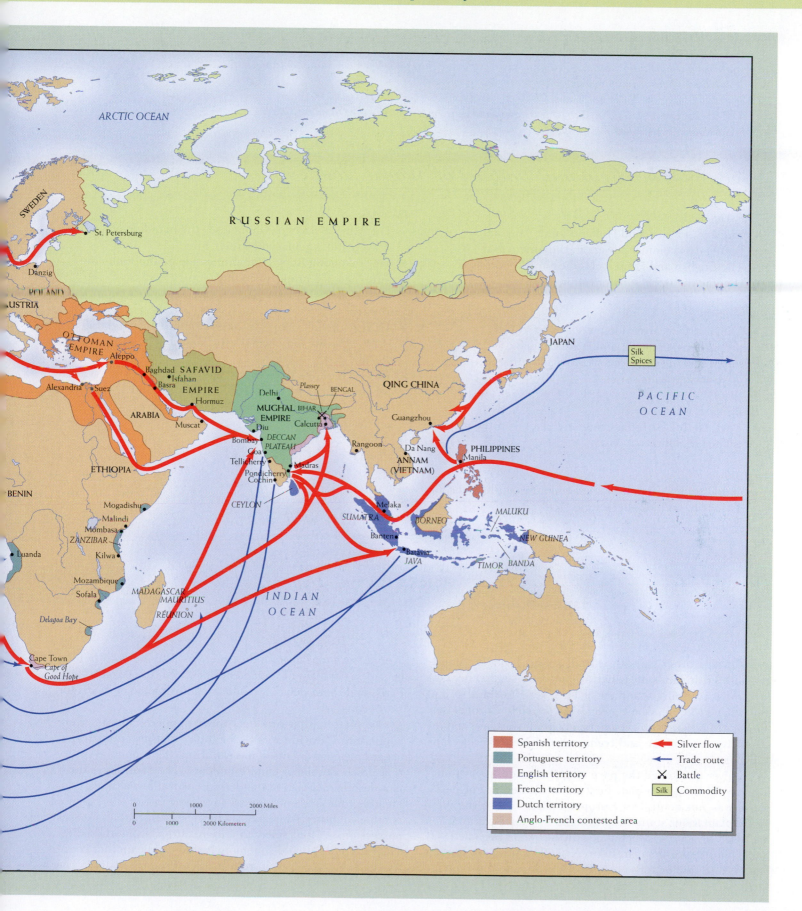

ARCTIC OCEAN

RUSSIAN EMPIRE

SWEDEN
St. Petersburg
Danzig
POLAND
AUSTRIA
OTTOMAN EMPIRE
Aleppo
Alexandria
Suez
Baghdad
Isfahan
Basra
SAFAVID EMPIRE
Hormuz
ARABIA
Muscat
ETHIOPIA
BENIN
Mogadishu
Malindi
Mombasa
ZANZIBAR
Luanda
Kilwa
Mozambique
Sofala
MADAGASCAR
MAURITIUS
RÉUNION
Delagoa Bay
Cape Town
Cape of Good Hope

Delhi
MUGHAL EMPIRE
Diu
Bombay
DECCAN PLATEAU
Goa
Tellicherry
Pondicherry
Cochin
CEYLON
Plassey
BENGAL
BIHAR
Calcutta
Madras
Rangoon

QING CHINA
Guangzhou
JAPAN

Da Nang
ANNAM (VIETNAM)
PHILIPPINES
Manila

Melaka
SUMATRA
BORNEO
MALUKU
NEW GUINEA
Banten
Batavia
JAVA
TIMOR
BANDA

INDIAN OCEAN

PACIFIC OCEAN

Silk Spices

Spanish territory	Silver flow
Portuguese territory	Trade route
English territory	Battle
French territory	Silk — Commodity
Dutch territory	
Anglo-French contested area	

0   1000   2000 Miles
0   1000   2000 Kilometers

MAIN THEMES

→ *Increased global trade brings the regions of the world more closely together, enriching some, destabilizing others, and provoking bitter rivalries.*

→ *Silver and sugar are the major commodities of world trade.*

→ *Western European states and Tsarist Russia expand their empires while the Ottoman, Safavid, Mughal, and Ming dynasties are shaken.*

FOCUS ON *The Regional Impact of World Trade*

The Americas

◆ England, France, and Holland join Spain and Portugal as colonial powers in the Americas.

◆ The English and French colonies in the Caribbean become the world's major exporters of sugar.

Africa

◆ The Atlantic slave trade increases to record proportions, creating gender imbalances, impoverishing some regions, and elevating the power of slave-supplying states.

Southeast Asia

◆ The Dutch East India Company takes over the major islands of Southeast Asia.

Islam

◆ World trade destabilizes the economies of the Safavid, Ottoman, and Mughal empires.

East Asia

◆ The Ming dynasty in China loses the mandate of heaven and is replaced by the Ching.

◆ The Tokugawa Shogunate unifies Japan and limits the influence of Europeans in the country.

Europe

◆ Tsarist Russia expands toward the Baltic Sea and the Pacific Ocean and becomes the largest state in the world.

◆ Europe recovers from thirty years of political and religious warfare (1618–1648), with Holland, England, and France emerging as economic powerhouses.

---

they devised other ways to extract wealth, for the Americas had fertile lands on which to cultivate sugarcane, cotton, tobacco, indigo, and rice. The New World also had fur-bearing wildlife, whose pelts were prized in Europe. Better still from the colonizers' perspective, it was easy and inexpensive to produce and transport the New World crops and skins.

If silver quickened the pace of global trade, sugar transformed the European diet. First domesticated in Polynesia, sugar was not central to European diets before the New World plantations started exporting it. Previously, Europeans had used honey for sweetener, but they soon became insatiable consumers of sugar. Between 1690 and 1790, Europe imported 12 million tons of sugar—approximately one ton for

every African enslaved in the Americas. Public tooth-pulling became a popular entertainment (for spectators!) in cities like Paris, and tooth decay became a leading cause of death for Europeans.

No matter what products they supplied, colonies were supposed to provide wealth for their "mother countries"— according to exponents of mercantilism, the economic theory that drove European empire-builders. The term **mercantilism** described a system that saw the world's wealth as fixed, meaning that any one country's wealth came at the expense of other countries. Mercantilism further assumed that overseas possessions existed solely to enrich European motherlands. Thus, colonies should ship more "value" to the mother country than they received in return. (See Primary Source: The

THE PRINCIPLES OF MERCANTILISM

In 1757, a British commercial expert by the name of Malachy Postlewayt published a commercial dictionary, The Universal Dictionary of Trade and Commerce. *Under the entry "trade," he set forth "some maxims relating to trade that should seem to be confirmed in the course of this work." The first five convey the economic philosophy of mercantilism and the importance that countries attached to the acquisition of precious metals.*

I. That the lasting prosperity of the landed interest depends upon foreign commerce.

II. That the increase of the wealth, splendour, and power of Great Britain and Ireland depends upon exporting more in value of our native produce and manufactures than we import of commodities from other nations and bringing thereby money into the kingdom by means of freight by shipping.

III. That domestic and foreign trade, as they are the means of increasing national treasure, of breeding seamen, and of augmenting our mercantile and royal navies they necessarily become the means of our permanent prosperity and of the safety and preservation of our happy constitution.

IV. That the constant security of the public credit and the payment of interest and principal of the public creditors depend upon the prosperous state of our trade and navigation.

V. That gold and silver is the measure of trade, and that silver is a commodity and may be exported, especially in foreign coin as well as any other commodity.

➔ *According to this reading, whom does mercantilism serve?*
➔ *What are the key tenets of mercantilism?*
➔ *Why is silver more important than gold in trade?*

SOURCE: Malachy Postlewayt, *The Universal Dictionary of Trade and Commerce,* vol. 2, p. 792.

Principles of Mercantilism.) In addition to creating trade surpluses, colonies were supposed to be closed to competitors, lest foreign traders drain precious resources from an empire's exclusive domain. As the mother country's monopoly over its colonies' trade generated wealth for royal treasuries, European states grew rich enough to wage almost unceasing wars against one another. Ultimately, mercantilists believed, as did the English philosopher Thomas Hobbes (1588–1679), that "wealth is power and power is wealth."

The mercantilist system required an alliance between the state and its merchants. Mercantilists understood economics and politics as interdependent, with the merchant needing the monarch to protect his interests and the monarch relying on the merchant's trade to enrich the state's treasury. **Chartered companies**, such as the (English) Virginia Company and the Dutch East India Company, were the most visible examples of the collaboration between the state and the merchant classes. European monarchs awarded these firms monopoly trading rights over vast areas.

NEW COLONIES IN THE AMERICAS

➔ *How did European mercantilism and colonialism transform the Americas?*

Entanglement and conflict were unavoidable once newcomers joined Spain and Portugal in the rush to reap riches from American colonies and to take a greater share of global commerce. As rulers in England, France, and Holland granted monopolies to merchant companies, they began to dominate the settlement and trade of new colonies in the Americas (see Map 13-2). Although the search for precious metals or water routes to Asia had initially spurred many of these enterprises, the new colonizers learned that only by exploiting other resources could their claims in the

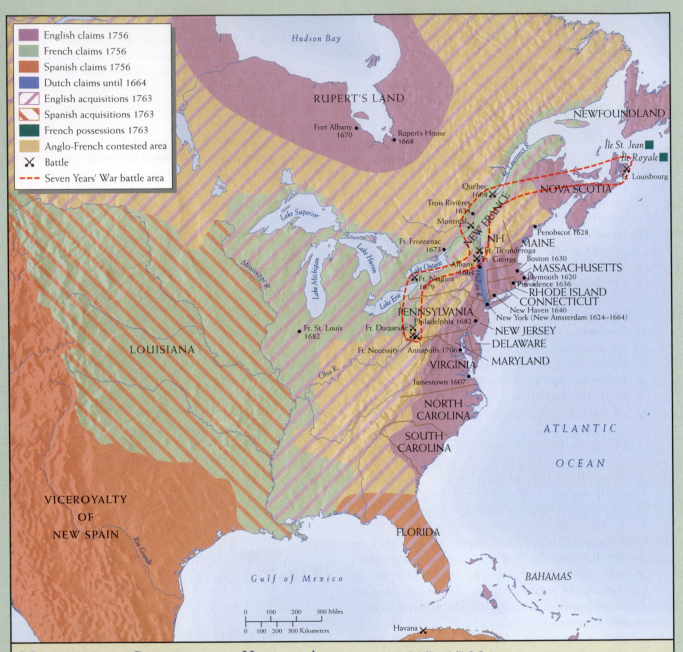

Legend:
- English claims 1756
- French claims 1756
- Spanish claims 1756
- Dutch claims until 1664
- English acquisitions 1763
- Spanish acquisitions 1763
- French possessions 1763
- Anglo-French contested area
- ✕ Battle
- - - - Seven Years' War battle area

MAP 13-2 COLONIES IN NORTH AMERICA, 1607–1763

France, England, and Spain laid claim to much of North America at this time. Where was each of these colonial powers strongest before the outbreak of the Seven Years' War in 1756? (See p. 521 for a discussion of the Seven Years' War.) Which empire gained the most North American territory, and who lost the most at the end of the war in 1763? How do you think Native American peoples reacted to the territorial arrangements agreed to by Spain, France, and England at the Peace of Paris, which ended the war?

Americas generate profits. Also, differences among New World societies required rethinking the character of colonial regimes.

HOLLAND'S TRADING COLONIES

The Dutch first settled in North America at the mouth of the Hudson River, which was named for an Englishman (Henry Hudson) whom the Dutch East India Company had hired to find a "northwest passage" to Asia via North America's Atlantic coast. By 1624, thirty Dutch families were living on an island at the Hudson's mouth (Manhattan); many soon moved upriver to trade with the Iroquois and other Indians.

But trading with Indians was not the original inspiration for the Dutch to enter the Americas. Rather, profits from shipping had lured them to cross oceans. Defying mercantilist precepts, Dutch vessels transported other nations' cargo to any corner of the world. As Dutch merchants profited from handling other colonizers' slaves, spices, textiles, and silver, they also coveted the riches flowing from Spanish and Portuguese possessions. Especially tempting were some of the Spanish island possessions in the Caribbean. In 1621, Amsterdam merchants founded the Dutch West India Company to regulate commerce, promote settlement, and maintain the flow of slaves to the Caribbean. Within fifteen years the Dutch claimed islands in the West Indies (see Map 13-3) and important sugar zones in Brazil. These colonies never yielded satisfactory profits, however, and by 1674 the Dutch West India Company was bankrupt.

Despite their largely unsuccessful efforts to establish colonies in the Americas, Dutch businessmen profited from financing foreign merchants and transporting other nations' cargoes. They were, in fact, often called the world's "universal carriers." Nor were they completely excluded from possessing colonies, for ultimately the Dutch took over lucrative sugar-producing islands in the East Indies and then established a small colony in South Africa (Cape Town). The latter served as a refreshment station for ships sailing between the Atlantic and Indian Oceans.

FRANCE'S FUR-TRADING EMPIRE

The French also began their colonizing in North America with a search for a water route to the Pacific that turned into a fur-trading enterprise. Jacques Cartier (1491–1557) led the initial explorations. Sailing up the St. Lawrence River, Cartier and subsequent French explorers, notably Samuel de Champlain (1567–1635), found huge bodies of fresh water—the Great Lakes—in the midst of the massive continent. Following this discovery Champlain founded the colony of New France, based in Québec. From there, French traders and missionaries penetrated deep into the interior of North Amer-

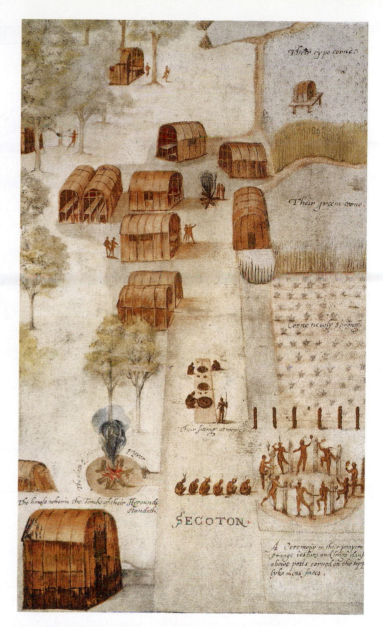

Woodlands Indians. This late-sixteenth-century drawing by John White, a pioneer settler on Roanoke Island off the coast of North Carolina, depicts the Indian village of Secoton in eastern Virginia. In contrast to the great empires that the Spanish conquered in the valley of Mexico and in the Andes, the Indians whom English, French, and Dutch colonizers encountered in the woodlands of eastern North America generally lived in villages that were politically autonomous entities.

ica, eager to trade with Indian natives and to convert them to Catholicism.

Crucial to this trade was the beaver, an animal for which Indian peoples previously had little use. But Europeans coveted its barbed underfur and offered numerous goods in return. Thus, in response to the Europeans' interest, one native hunter proclaimed, "The beaver does everything perfectly

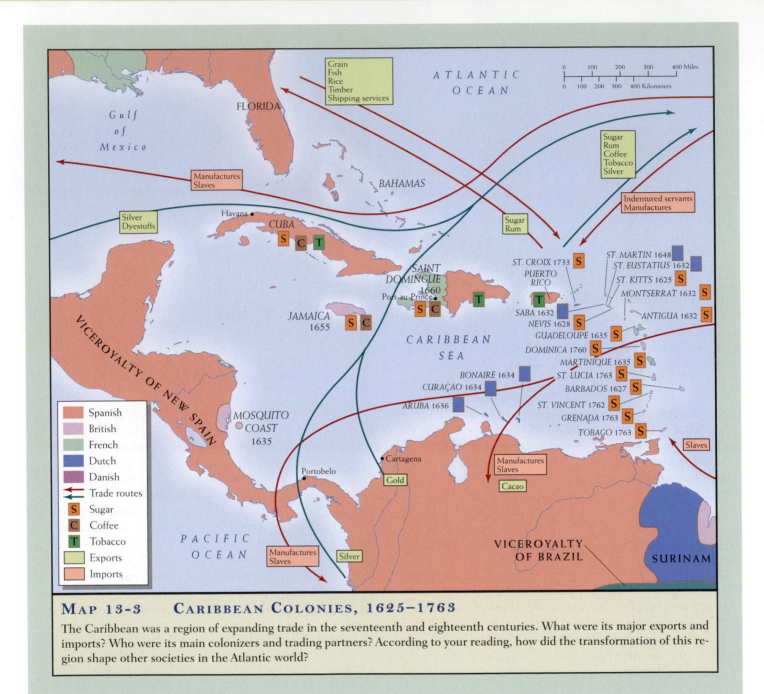

MAP 13-3   CARIBBEAN COLONIES, 1625–1763

The Caribbean was a region of expanding trade in the seventeenth and eighteenth centuries. What were its major exports and imports? Who were its main colonizers and trading partners? According to your reading, how did the transformation of this region shape other societies in the Atlantic world?

well; it makes kettles, hatchets, swords, knives, bread; in short it makes everything." As long as there were beavers to be trapped, trade between the French and their Indian partners flourished.

The distinctive aspect of the fur trade was the Europeans' utter dependence on Indian know-how. After all, trapping required familiarity with the beaver's habits and habitats, which Europeans lacked. This reliance forced the French to adapt

to Indian ways, which is evident in their pattern of exchange. Although the French wanted to export furs purely as a commercial venture, they were willing to permit exchanges with their Indian partners to go beyond material concerns. Responding to Indian desires to use trade as an instrument to cement familial bonds, the French gave gifts, participated in Indian diplomatic rituals, and even married into Indian families. As a result, *métis* (French-Indian offspring) played an

The Fur Trade. For Europeans in northern North America, no commodity was as important as beaver skins. For the French especially, the fur trade determined the character of their colonial regime in North America. For Indians, it offered access to European goods, but overhunting depleted resources and provoked intertribal conflicts.

important role in New France as interpreters, traders, and guides. Thus, the French colonization of the Americas—owing to their reliance on Indians as trading partners, military allies, and mates—rested more on cooperation than conquest, especially compared to the empires built by their European rivals.

ENGLAND'S LANDED EMPIRE

Part of the rationale for the French alliance with the Indians was strategic: they shared a deep mistrust of the English, who were also pressing into North America. Initially, the English sought colonies that would yield precious metals. But their early settlements along the Atlantic coast lacked such resources. Nor did these temperate lands boast beavers with the thick furs that French traders "mined" in the north. However, the English territories had land suitable for growing a variety of crops. And as the population grew, these settlements encroached more and more on Indian lands. Therefore, relations between English colonists and Indians were far less cordial than those between the French and their native trading partners.

The English colonies all possessed a hunger for land that came at the expense of Indian inhabitants. Around Massachusetts Bay, Protestant refugees (Puritans) founded a colony whose population surged after 1630. As the population grew, so did the demand for fresh farmlands. The result: a souring of relations between natives and newcomers, which led to

ferocious wars. These conflicts left devastating casualties among both Puritans and Indians, but over the course of the seventeenth century they led to the dispossession of Indians from much of southern New England.

A similar cycle of hostile Indian-English relations unfolded around Chesapeake Bay to the south. In Virginia, the impulse for colonization was more commercial and less religious than the Puritans' of Massachusetts, but the pattern of intercultural relations was similar. After settlers founded Jamestown in 1607, the first disastrous winters wiped out many of the gentlemen adventurers who had aimed to make money but held little interest in hard work. Like the Puritans, the Chesapeake colonists would not have survived their "starving times" had local Indians not brought them food and other assistance. Within a few years the colony was thriving, especially once the settlers found a suitable staple for export: tobacco, a weed that Indians cultivated. Before long, a tobacco boom transformed the colony into a commercial powerhouse.

As the lure of prosperity drew thousands of English men and women to Virginia, pressures on Indian lands intensified. As in Massachusetts, the hunger for plantations resulted in wars that ejected Indians from their homelands. Although the French intermixed with their trading partners and the Spanish married into Indian societies, the English migrants (who included a larger number of women) avoided such alliances with natives. Instead of developing trading networks, the English based their New World empire on land ownership—and did not hesitate to push deeper into Indian territory.

Tobacco. The cultivation of tobacco saved the Virginia colony from ruin and brought prosperity to increasing numbers of planters. The spread of tobacco plantations also pushed Indians off their lands and led planters to turn to Africa for a labor force.

THE PLANTATION COMPLEX IN THE CARIBBEAN

As late as 1670, the most populous English colony was not on the North American mainland, but on the Caribbean island of Barbados. Because sugar was so desirable, from the mid-seventeenth century onward the English- and French-controlled islands of the Caribbean replicated the Portuguese sugarcane plantations of Brazil. All was not sweet here, however. Because no colonial power held a monopoly, competition to control the region—and sugar production—was fierce. The resulting turbulence did not simply reflect imperial rivalry; it also reflected labor arrangements in the colonies. Because the native populations had been wiped out in Columbus's wake (see Chapter 12), owners of Caribbean estates looked to Africa to obtain workers for their plantations.

Sugar was a killing crop. So deadly was the hot, humid environment in which sugarcane flourished (as fertile for disease as for sugarcane) that many sugar barons spent little time on their plantations. Management fell to overseers, who worked their slaves to death. Despite having immunities to yellow fever and malaria from their homeland's similar environment, Africans could not withstand the regimen. Inadequate food, atrocious living conditions, and filthy sanitation added to their miseries. Moreover, plantation managers treated their slaves as nonhumans: for example, on the first day all new slaves suffered branding with the planter's seal. One English gentleman commented that slaves were like cows, "as near as beasts may be, setting their souls aside."

More than disease and inadequate rations, the work itself decimated the enslaved. Average life expectancy was three years. Six days a week slaves rose before dawn, labored until noon, ate a short lunch, and then worked until dusk. At harvest time, sixteen-hour days saw hundreds of men, women, and children doubled over to cut the sugarcane and transport it to refineries, sometimes seven days per week. Under this brutal schedule, slaves occasionally dropped dead from exhaustion.

Amid disease and toil, the enslaved resisted as they could. The most dramatic expression of resistance was violent revolt. In the early sixteenth century, in fact, slave revolts were so frequent in Panama that the crown banned all slave trade to the region. In the early seventeenth century, in parts of coastal Mexico, the viceroy negotiated an armistice with slaves to pacify the region. A more common form of resistance was flight. Seeking refuge from overseers, thousands of slaves took to the hills—for example, to the remote highlands of Caribbean islands or to Brazil's vast interior. Those who remained on the plantations resisted via foot dragging, pilfering, and sabotage.

Slaves Cutting Cane. Sugar was the preeminent agricultural export from the New World for centuries. Owners of sugarcane plantations relied almost exclusively on African slaves to produce the sweetener. Labor in the fields was especially harsh, as slaves worked in the blistering sun from dawn until dusk. This image shows how women and men toiled side by side.

Caribbean settlements and slaveholdings were not restricted to any single European power. But it was the latecomers—the Dutch, the English, and especially the French—who concentrated on the Antilles. The English took Jamaica from the Spanish and made it the premier site of Caribbean sugar by the 1740s. When the French seized half of Santo Domingo in the 1660s (renaming it Saint Domingue, which is present-day Haiti), they created one of the wealthiest societies based on slavery of all time. This French colony's exports eclipsed those of all the Spanish and English Antilles combined. The capital, Port-au-Prince, was one of the richest cities in the Atlantic world. The colony's merchants and planters built immense mansions worthy of the highest European nobles. Thus the Atlantic system benefited elite Europeans, who amassed new fortunes by exploiting the colonies' natural resources and the African slaves' labor.

THE SLAVE TRADE AND AFRICA

> → *How did the slave trade affect African societies?*

Although the slave trade began in the mid-fifteenth century, only in the seventeenth and eighteenth centuries did the numbers of human exports from Africa begin to soar (see Map 13-4). By 1800, two slaves had crossed the Atlantic for every European. Those numbers were essential to the prosperity of Europe's American colonies. At the same time, the departure of so many inhabitants depopulated and destabilized many parts of Africa.

CAPTURING AND SHIPPING SLAVES

Before the Europeans' arrival, Africa had an already existing system of slave commerce, mainly flowing across the Sahara to North Africa and Egypt and eastward to the Red Sea and the Swahili coast of East Africa. From the Red Sea and Swahili coast destinations, Muslim and Hindu merchants shipped slaves to ports around the Indian Ocean. However, the number of these slaves could not match the volume destined for the Americas once plantation agriculture began to spread. Indeed, twelve and a half million Africans survived forcible enslavement and shipment to Atlantic ports from 1525 (the date of the first direct voyage from Africa to the Americas) until 1867 (when the last voyage took place).

Merchants in Europe and the New World prospered as the slave trade soared, but their fortunes depended on trading and political networks in Africa. In fact, European slavers took little interest in the happenings in the African interior. They were not involved in capturing slaves; this was a business left to their African partners, whose networks linked moneylenders and traders on the coast with allies in the interior. In the West African Bight (bay) of Biafra, for instance, English merchants relied on traditional African practices of pawnship—the use of human "pawns" to secure European commodities in advance of the delivery of slaves. According to custom, a secret male society called Ekpe enforced payments of promised slave deliveries. If a trader failed to deliver on his promise, his pawns (often members of his own kin group) were sold instead. By the mid-eighteenth century, Ekpe had powerful networks stretching deep into African hinterlands and supplying the slave trade in the port of Old Calabar.

Now the slave ports along the African coast became gruesome entrepôts. Indeed, high death rates occurred on the

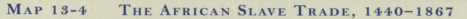

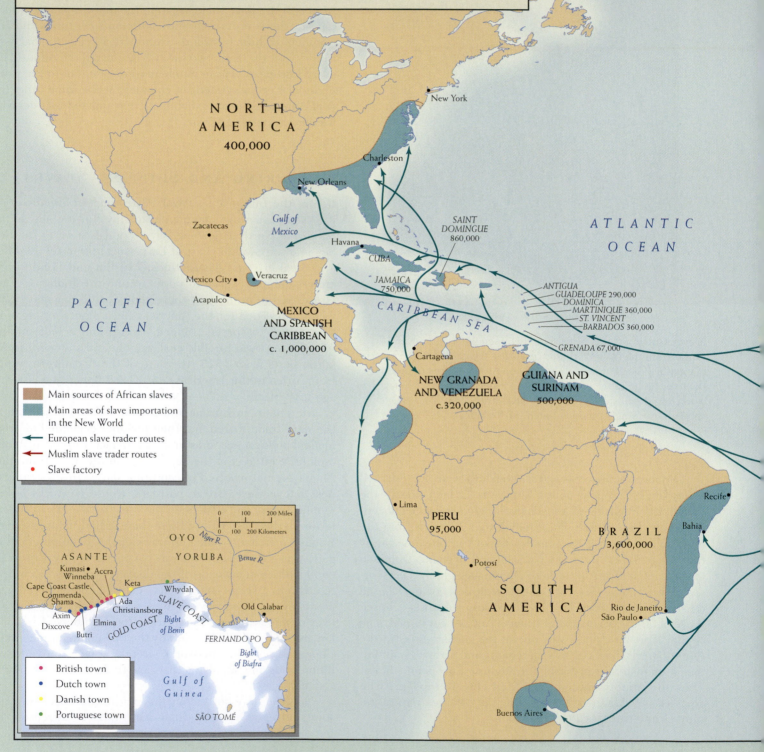

MAP 13-4 THE AFRICAN SLAVE TRADE, 1440–1867

The Atlantic slave trade flourished in the seventeenth, eighteenth, and nineteenth centuries, linking many parts of Africa with the Americas. What were the main areas in Africa from which the slaves were taken? What were the main areas that they were taken to in the Americas? What was the relationship between sugar cultivation in the Americas and the demand for African slave labor? How and where did the slave trade reshape African societies?

NORTH AMERICA 400,000

New York

Charleston

New Orleans

Gulf of Mexico

Zacatecas

Havana

CUBA

SAINT DOMINGUE 860,000

ATLANTIC OCEAN

Mexico City • Veracruz

Acapulco

JAMAICA 750,000

ANTIGUA
GUADELOUPE 290,000
DOMINICA
MARTINIQUE 360,000
ST. VINCENT
BARBADOS 360,000

MEXICO AND SPANISH CARIBBEAN c. 1,000,000

CARIBBEAN SEA

GRENADA 67,000

PACIFIC OCEAN

Cartagena

NEW GRANADA AND VENEZUELA c.320,000

GUIANA AND SURINAM 500,000

Lima

PERU 95,000

Potosí

Recife

BRAZIL 3,600,000

Bahia

SOUTH AMERICA

Rio de Janeiro
São Paulo

Buenos Aires

Legend:
- Main sources of African slaves
- Main areas of slave importation in the New World
- ← European slave trader routes
- ← Muslim slave trader routes
- Slave factory

Inset map:
OYO
YORUBA
Niger R.
Benue R.
ASANTE
Kumasi • Accra
Winneba
Cape Coast Castle
Commenda
Shama
Axim
Dixcove
Butri
Elmina
Keta
Ada
Christiansborg
Whydah
SLAVE COAST
Old Calabar
GOLD COAST
Bight of Benin
FERNANDO PO
Bight of Biafra
Gulf of Guinea
SÃO TOMÉ

0   100   200 Miles
0   100   200 Kilometers

- British town
- Dutch town
- Danish town
- Portuguese town

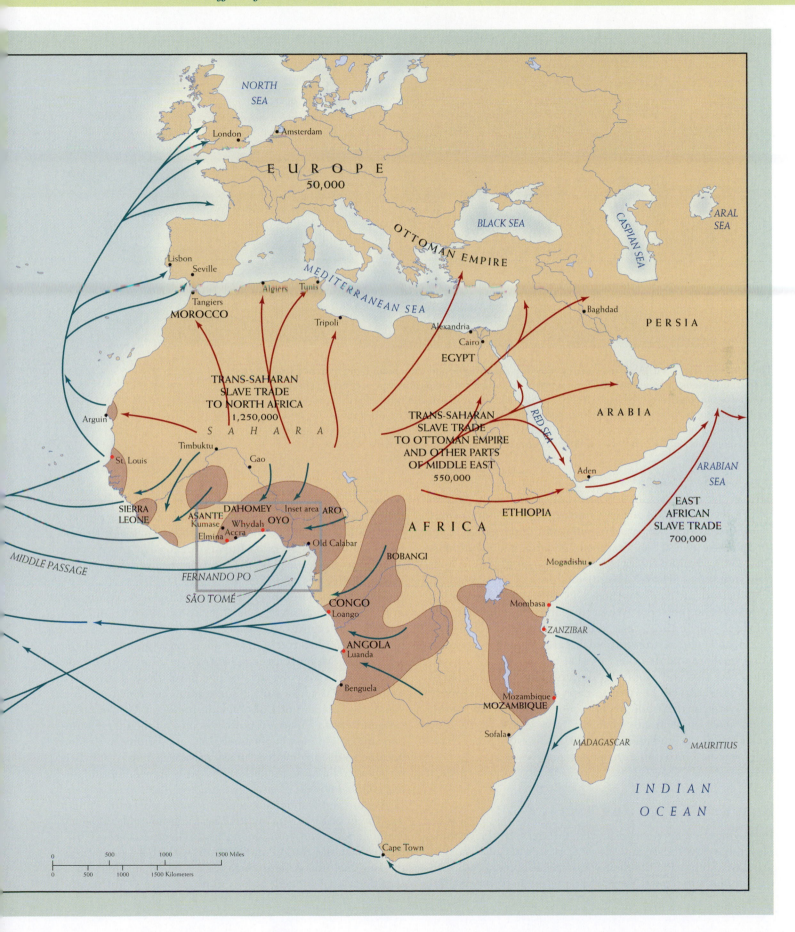

The Slave Trade. (*Left*) Africans were captured in the interior and then bound and marched to the coast. Note that there is only one woman among the men (and a couple of children), reflecting the gender imbalance among those captured. (*Right*) After reaching the coast, the captured Africans would be crammed into the holds of slave vessels, where they suffered grievously from overcrowding and unsanitary conditions. Long voyages were especially deadly. If the winds failed or ships had to travel longer distances than usual, many of the captives would die en route to the slave markets across the ocean.

African side of the shipping; many slaves who perished did so before losing sight of Africa. Stuck in vast holding camps where disease and hunger were rampant, the slaves were then forced aboard vessels in cramped and wretched conditions. These ships waited for weeks to fill their holds while their human cargoes wasted away below deck. Crew members tossed dead Africans overboard as they loaded on other Africans from the shore. When the cargo was complete, the ships set sail. In their wake, crews continued to dump bodies. Most died of gastrointestinal diseases leading to dehydration. Smallpox and dysentery were also scourges. Either way, death was slow and agonizing. Because high mortality led to lost profits, slavers learned to carry better food and more fresh water as the trade became more sophisticated. Still, when slave ships finally reached New World ports, they reeked of disease and excrement. (See Primary Source: Olaudah Equiano on the Atlantic Crossing.)

SLAVERY'S GENDER IMBALANCE

In moving so many Africans to the Americas, the slave trade played havoc with sex ratios in both places because most of the slaves shipped to the Americas were adult men. Although the numbers indicated Europeans' preferences for male la-

borers, they also reflected African slavers' desire to keep female slaves, primarily for household work. The gender imbalance made it difficult for slaves to reproduce in the Americas. So planters and slavers had to return to Africa to procure more captives—especially for the Caribbean islands, where slaves' death rates were so high.

Male slaves outnumbered females in the New World, but in the slave-supplying regions of Africa women outnumbered men. Female captives were especially prized in Africa because of their traditional role in the production of grains, leathers, and cotton. Moreover, the slave trade reinforced the traditional practice of polygyny—allowing relatively scarce men to take several wives. But in some states, notably the slave-supplying kingdom of Dahomey on the West African coast, women were able to assert power because of their large numbers and heightened importance. In fact, Dahomean women became so deeply involved in succession disputes that their intrigues could make the difference between winning and losing political power.

Within the Dahomean court the most powerful woman was the queen mother, the *kpojito*. Each new ruler selected his queen mother from among his predecessors' wives. Believing that she could communicate with the supernatural, the king and his courtiers consulted her before making important decisions. Indeed, queen mothers were so influential that in reality the king and the *kpojito* were joint rulers. Ultimately, though, the fact that powerful women rose to power in a few societies did not diminish the destabilizing effects of the Atlantic slave trade or the chaos that slave raiding and slave trading had on the relations among African states.

AFRICA'S NEW SLAVE-SUPPLYING POLITIES

Africans did not passively let captives fall into the arms of European slave buyers; instead, local political leaders and merchants were active suppliers. This activity promoted the growth of centralized polities, particularly in West African rain forest areas. The trade also shifted control of wealth away from households owning large herds or lands to those who profited from the capture and exchange of slaves—urban merchants and warrior elites.

THE KONGO KINGDOM In some parts of Africa, the booming slave trade wreaked havoc as local leaders feuded over control of the traffic. In the Kongo kingdom, civil wars raged for over a century after 1665, and captured warriors were sold as slaves. As members of the royal family clashed, entire provinces saw their populations vanish. Most important to the conduct of war and the control of trade were firearms and gunpowder, which made the capturing of slaves highly efficient. Moreover, kidnapping became so prevalent that cultivators worked their fields bearing weapons, leaving their children behind in guarded stockades.

Some leaders of the Kongo kingdom fought back. Consider Queen Nzinga (1583–1663), a masterful diplomat and a shrewd military planner. Having converted to Christianity, she managed to keep the Portuguese slavers at bay during her long reign. Even after Portuguese forces defeated her troops in open battle, she conducted effective guerrilla warfare into her sixties.

Consider also the Christian visionary Dona Beatriz Kimpa Vita. Born in the Kongo in 1684 and baptized as a Christian, at age twenty she claimed to have received visions from St. Anthony of Padua. She believed that she died every Friday and was transported to heaven to converse with God, returning to earth on Monday to broadcast God's commands to believers. Her message aimed to end the Kongo civil wars and re-create a unified kingdom. Although she gained a large following, she failed to win the support of leading political figures. In 1706 she was captured and burned at the stake.

OYO, ASANTE, AND OTHER GROUPS As some African merchants and warlords sold other Africans, their commercial success enabled them to consolidate political power and grow wealthy. Their wealth financed additional weapons, with which they subdued neighbors and extended political control. Among the most durable new polities was the Asante state, which arose in the West African tropical rain forest in 1701 and expanded through 1750. This state benefited from its access to gold, which it used to acquire firearms (from European traders) to raid nearby communities for servile workers. From its capital city at Kumasi, the state eventually encompassed almost all of present-day Ghana. Main roads spread out from the capital like spokes of a wheel, each approximately twenty days' travel from the center. Through the

The Port of Loango. Partly as a result of the profits of the slave trade, African rulers and merchants were able to create large and prosperous port cities such as Loango, pictured here, which was on the west coast of south-central Africa.

OLAUDAH EQUIANO ON THE ATLANTIC CROSSING

The most compelling description of the horrifying conditions that captives endured on the African coast as they awaited the arrival of slaving ships and the perils of the Atlantic crossing came from the pen of a former slave, Olaudah Equiano (c. 1745–1797). After purchasing his freedom and becoming a skilled writer, Equiano published The Interesting Narrative of the Life of Olaudah Equiano, or Gustavus Vassa, the African. Written by Himself *(1789). An instantaneous best seller, within ten years the book saw nine English editions and appeared in American, Dutch, German, Russian, and French editions. Although some critics have questioned the authenticity of Equiano's birth and early life in Africa, the scholarly consensus remains that he was indeed born in Igboland (in the eastern part of present-day Nigeria) and made the voyage across the Atlantic after his capture at age nine.*

The first object which saluted my eyes when I arrived on the coast was the sea, and a slave ship, which was then riding at anchor, and waiting for its cargo. These filled me with astonishment, which was soon converted into terror when I was carried on board. I was immediately handled and tossed up to see if I were sound by some of the crew; and I was now persuaded that I had gotten into a world of bad spirits, and that they were going to kill me. Their complexions too differing so much from ours, their long hair, and the language they spoke, (which was very different from any I had ever heard) united to confirm me in this belief. Indeed such were the horrors of my views and fears at the moment, that, if ten thousand worlds had been my own, I would have freely parted with them all to have ex-changed my condition with that of the meanest slave in my own country. When I looked round the ship too and saw a large furnace or copper boiling, and a multitude of black people of every description chained together, every one of their countenances expressing dejection and sorrow, I no longer doubted of my fate; and, quite overpowered with horror and anguish, I fell motionless on the deck and fainted. When I recovered a little I found some black people about me, who I believed were some of those who brought me on board, and had been receiving their pay; they talked to me in order to cheer me, but all in vain. I asked them if we were not to be eaten by those white men with horrible looks, red faces, and loose hair. They told me I was not . . .

Asante trading networks African traders bought, bartered, and sold slaves, who wound up in the hands of European merchants waiting in ports with vessels carrying manufactures and weaponry.

Also active in the slave trade—and enriched by it—was the Oyo Empire. This territory, which straddled the main trade routes, linked tropical rain forests with interior markets of the northern savannah areas. The empire's strength rested on its impressive army brandishing weapons secured from trade with Europeans. Deploying cavalry units in the savannah and infantry units in the rain forest, the Oyo's military campaigns became annual events, only suspended so that warriors could return home for their agricultural duties. Every dry season, Oyo armies marched on their neighbors to capture entire villages.

Slavery and the emergence of new political organizations enriched and empowered some Africans, but they cost Africa dearly. For the princes, warriors, and merchants who organized the slave trade, their business (like that of Amerindian fur suppliers) enabled them to obtain European goods—especially alcohol, tobacco, textiles, and guns. The Atlantic system also tilted wealth away from rural dwellers and village elders and increasingly toward port cities. Across the landmass, the slave trade thinned the population. True, Africa was spared a demographic catastrophe equal to the devastation of American Indians. The introduction of American food crops—notably maize and cassava, producing many more calories per acre than the old staples of millet and sorghum—blunted the trade's depopulating aspects. Yet some areas suffered grievously from three centuries of heavy involvement in the slave trade. The Atlantic trade enhanced the warrior class, who carried out raids for captives; the dislocations, internal power struggles, and economic hardships that followed precipitated the rise and fall of West African kingdoms.

In a little time after, amongst the poor chained men, I found some of my own nation, which in a small degree gave ease to my mind. I inquired of these what was to be done with us; they gave me to understand we were to be carried to these white people's country to work for them. I then was a little revived, and thought, if it were no worse than working, my situation was not so desperate: but still I feared I should be put to death, the white people looked and acted, as I thought, in so savage a manner; for I had never seen among any people such instances of brutal cruelty; and this not only shewn towards us blacks, but also to some of the whites themselves. . . .

At last, when the ship we were in had got in all her cargo, they made ready with many fearful noises, and we were all put under deck, so that we could not see how they managed the vessel. But this disappointment was the least of my sorrow. The stench of the hold while we were on the coast was so intolerably loathsome, that it was dangerous to remain there for any time, and some of us had been permitted to stay on the deck for the fresh air; but now that the whole ship's cargo were confined together, it became absolutely pestilential. The closeness of the place, and the heat of the climate, added to the number in the ship, which was so crowded that each had scarcely room to turn himself, almost suffocated us. This produced copious perspirations, so that the air soon became unfit for respiration, from a variety of loathsome smells, and brought on a sickness among the slaves, of which many died, thus falling victims to the improvident avarice, as I may call it, of their purchasers. This wretched situation was again aggravated by the galling of the chains, now become insupportable; and the filth of the necessary tubs [latrines], into which the children often fell, and were almost suffocated. The shrieks of the women, and the groans of the dying, rendered the whole a scene of horror almost inconceivable.

→ *The slave trade involved capturing Africans from various parts of the interior of the continent. Which lines in the reading give evidence of this?*

→ *Equiano's book came out in 1789 in the midst of a campaign to abolish the slave trade. Considering the formality of his language, what type of audience do you suppose he was seeking to reach?*

→ *Why would this book describing the horrors of the slave trade have appeared only in the late 1700s, even though such brutal conditions had been existing for more than two centuries?*

SOURCE: Werner Sollors, ed., *The Interesting Narrative of the Life of Olaudah Equiano, or Gustavus Vassa, the African, Written by Himself,* A Norton Critical Edition (New York: Norton, 2001), pp. 38–41.

ASIA IN THE SEVENTEENTH AND EIGHTEENTH CENTURIES

→ *How did global trade affect the Asian dynasties?*

Global trading networks blossomed as vigorously in Asia as they did in the Americas. In Asia, however, the Europeans were less dominant. Although they could penetrate Asian markets with American silver, they could not conquer Asian empires or colonize vast portions of the region. Nor were they able to enslave Asian peoples as they had Africans. The Mughal Empire continued to grow, and the Qing dynasty, which had wrested control from the Ming, significantly expanded China's borders. China remained the richest state in the world, but in some places the balance of power was tilting in Europe's direction. Not only did the Ottomans' borders contract, but by the late eighteenth century Europeans had established economic and military dominance in parts of India and much of Southeast Asia.

THE DUTCH IN SOUTHEAST ASIA

In Southeast Asia the Dutch already enjoyed a dominant position by the seventeenth century. Although the Portuguese had seized the vibrant port city of Melaka in 1511 and the Spaniards had taken Manila in 1571, neither was able to monopolize the lucrative spice trade. To challenge them, the Dutch government persuaded its merchants to charter the Dutch East India Company (abbreviated as VOC) in 1602.

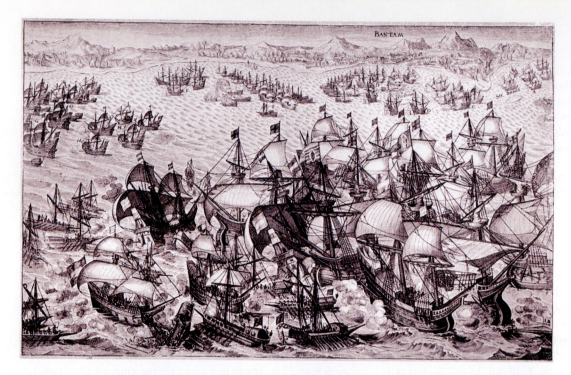

Attack on Bantam. This engraving depicts a Dutch attack on Bantam in the late seventeenth century as part of the VOC's effort to expand its empire in Southeast Asia.

Benefiting from Amsterdam's position as the most efficient money market with the lowest interest rates in the world, the VOC raised ten times the capital of its English counterpart—the royal chartered English East India Company. The advantages of chartered companies were evident in the VOC's scale of operation: at its peak the company had 257 ships and employed 12,000 persons. Throughout two centuries it sent ships manned by a total of one million men to Asia.

The VOC's main impact was in Southeast Asia, where spices, coffee, tea, and teak wood were key exports (see again Map 13-1). The company's objective was to secure a trade monopoly wherever it could, fix prices, and replace the native population with Dutch planters. In 1619, under the leadership of Jan Pieterszoon Coen (who once said that trade could not be conducted without war nor war without trade), the Dutch swept into the Javanese port of Jakarta (renamed Batavia by the Dutch). In defiance of local rulers and English rivals, the Dutch burned all the houses, drove out the population, and constructed a fortress from which to control the Southeast Asian trade. Two years later, Coen's forces took over a cluster of nutmeg-producing islands known as Banda. The traditional chiefs and almost the entire population were killed outright, left to starve, or taken into slavery. Dutch planters and their slaves replaced the decimated local population and sent their produce to the VOC. The motive for such rapacious action was the huge profit to be made by buying nutmeg at a low price in the Bandanese Islands and selling it at many times that price in Europe.

With their monopoly of nutmeg secured, the Dutch went after the market in cloves. Their strategy was to control production in one region and then destroy the rest, which entailed, once again, wars against producers and traders in other areas. Portuguese Melaka soon fell to the Dutch and became a VOC outpost. Although this aggressive expansion met widespread resistance from the local population and other merchants involved in the region's trade, by 1670 the Dutch controlled all of the lucrative spice trade from the Maluku islands.

Next, the VOC set its sights on pepper. In this gambit, it gained control of Bantam (present-day Banten), the largest pepper-exporting port. However, the Dutch had to share this commerce with Chinese and English competitors. Moreover, since there was no demand for European products in Asia, the Dutch had to participate more in inter-Asian trade as a way to reduce their need to make payments in precious metals. So they purchased, for example, calicoes (plain white cotton cloths) in India or copper in Japan for resale in Melaka and Java. They also diversified into trading silk, cotton, tea, and coffee, in addition to spices.

As a result of the Dutch enterprise, European outposts such as Dutch Batavia and Spanish Manila soon eclipsed old cosmopolitan cities such as Bantam. Indeed, as Europeans competed for supremacy in the borderlands of Southeast Asia, they made local societies serve their own ambitions and began replacing traditional networks with trade routes that primarily served European interests.

TRANSFORMATIONS IN ISLAM

Compared with Southeast Asia, the Islamic empires did not feel such direct effects of European intrusion. They did, however, face internal difficulties. While the Ottoman and

Mughal empires remained resilient, the Safavid Empire fell into chaos.

THE SAFAVID EMPIRE   From its inception, the Safavid Empire had always required a powerful, religiously inspired ruler to enforce Shiite religious orthodoxy and to hold together the realm's tribal, pastoral, mercantile, and agricultural factions. The founding figure and his strongest successor had succeeded at this challenge. But when such a figure was not present, the state foundered. By 1722, after a series of weak rulers, it was under assault from within and without.

Internal turmoil was partly the result of a change in trade routes away from Persia and partly the result of tribal incursions against the central government. Such incursions were always a threat to political stability, but especially so when weak rulers sat on the throne. Meanwhile, neighboring Afghan clansmen invaded Safavid territory, overran the inept and divided armies, and besieged the capital at Isfahan (see Map 13-1). As the city's inhabitants perished from hunger and disease, some desperate survivors ate the corpses of the deceased. After the shah abdicated, the invaders executed thousands of officials and members of the royal household. The empire limped along until 1773, when a revolt toppled the last ruler from the throne.

THE OTTOMAN EMPIRE   Having attained a high point under Suleiman (see Chapter 11), the Ottoman Empire, too, entered a period of decline. After Suleiman's reign, Ottoman armies and navies tried unsuccessfully to expand the empire's borders—losing, for example, on the western flank to the European Habsburgs. As military campaigns and a growing population strained the realm's limited resources, Ottoman intellectuals worried that the empire's glory was ebbing.

Even as the empire's strength waned, by the seventeenth century its sultans faced a commercially more connected world. Once New World silver entered Ottoman networks of commerce and money lending, its presence eventually destabilized the empire. Although early Ottoman rulers had avoided trade with the outside world, the lure of silver broke through state regulations. Now Ottoman merchants established black markets for commodities that eager European buyers paid for in silver—especially wheat, copper, and wool. Because these exports were illegal, their sale did not generate tax revenues to support the state's civilian and military administration. So Ottoman rulers had to rely on loans of silver from the merchants. Such financial dependence meant that rulers could ill afford to impose official rules on those who bankrolled them.

More silver and budget deficits were a recipe for inflation. Indeed, prices doubled and then tripled between 1550 and 1650. Runaway inflation caused hard-hit peasants in Anatolia, suffering from high food prices, shortages, and increasing taxes (used to pay off dynastic debts), to join together in uprisings that threatened the state's stability. By the time of Sultan Ibrahim's reign (1640–1648), the cycle of spending, taxing, borrowing, and inflation was so severe that his own officials murdered him. Moreover, disorder at the center of the empire was accompanied by difficulties in the provinces, where breakaway regimes appeared.

THE MAMLUKS IN OTTOMAN EGYPT   The most threatening of the breakaway pressures occurred in Egypt beginning in the seventeenth century. In 1517, Egypt had become the Ottoman Empire's greatest conquest. As the wealthiest Ottoman territory, it was an important source of revenue, and its people shouldered heavy tax burdens.

The group that asserted Egypt's political and commercial autonomy from Istanbul were military men, known as **Mamluks** (Arabic for "owned" or "possessed"), who had ruled Egypt as an independent regime until the Ottoman conquest of the country (see Chapter 10). Although the Ottoman army had routed Mamluk forces on the battlefield in 1517, Ottoman governors in Egypt allowed the Mamluks to reform themselves. By the seventeenth century, these military men were nearly as powerful as their ancestors had been in the fifteenth century when they ruled Egypt independently. Turning the Ottoman administrator of Egypt into a mere figurehead, this new provincial elite kept much of the area's fiscal resources for themselves at the expense not only of the imperial coffers but also of the local peasantry. Mamluk households also enhanced their power by aligning with Egyptian merchants and catering to the Egyptian *ulama*.

THE OTTOMANS' KOPRULU REFORMS   The Ottoman system also had elements of resilience—especially at the center, where decaying leadership provoked demands for reform from administrative elites. Late in the seventeenth century, the Koprulu family controlled the office of grand vizier and spearheaded changes to revitalize the empire. Mehmed Koprulu, the first to assume office, had been born into an obscure Albanian family. Taken as a slave in the *devshirme* (see Chapter 11), he slowly ascended the bureaucratic ladder and became grand vizier at age eighty. Pragmatic and incorruptible, Mehmed not only rooted out his corrupt peers but also balanced the budget and reversed the Ottoman armies' misfortunes. His death in 1661 did not halt the reforms, for he had groomed his son, Fazil Ahmed Koprulu, to continue them. The young grand vizier continued to trim the administration and strengthen the armies for another fifteen years.

Known as the Koprulu reforms, the changes in administration gave the state a new burst of energy and enabled the military to reacquire some of its lost possessions. Revenues again increased, and inflation decreased. Fired by revived expansionist ambitions, Istanbul decided to renew its assault on Christianity (see Chapter 11)—beginning with rekindled plans to seize Vienna under the leadership of Fazil Ahmed's

Siege of Vienna. This seventeenth-century painting depicts the Ottoman siege of Vienna, which began on July 14, 1683, and ended on September 12. The city might have fallen if the Polish king, John III, had not answered the pope's plea to defend Christendom and sent an army to assist German and Austrian troops in defeating the Ottomans.

brother-in-law, Kara Mustafa Pasha. Although the Ottomans gathered an enormous force outside the Habsburg capital in 1683, both sides suffered heavy losses and the Ottoman forces ultimately retreated. They planned to renew the assault months later, but the sultan, fearing disgrace, had Kara Mustafa strangled. Thereafter, the Ottomans halted their military advances. Worse still, under the treaty that ended the Austro-Ottoman war, the Ottomans lost major European territorial possessions, including Hungary.

Whereas in the sixteenth century rulers of the Ottoman Empire had wanted to create a self-contained and self-sufficient imperial economy, silver undermined this vision as it had elsewhere in the global economy. Indeed, the influx of silver opened Ottoman-controlled lands to trade with the rest of the world, producing intellectual ferment, breakaway regimes, widespread inflation, and social discontent.

THE MUGHAL EMPIRE In contrast to the Ottomans' setbacks, the Mughal Empire reached its height in the 1600s. The period saw Mughal rulers extend their domain over almost all of India and enjoy increased domestic and international trade. But they eventually had problems governing dispersed and resistant provinces, where many villages retained traditional religions and cultures.

Before the Mughals, India had never had a single political authority. Akbar and his successors had conquered territory in the north (see Chapter 12, Map 12-5), so now the Mughals turned to the south and gained control over most of that region by 1689. As the new provinces provided an additional source of resources, local lords, and warriors, the Mughal bureaucracy grew better at extracting services and taxes.

Imperial stability and prosperity did not depend entirely on the Indian Ocean trading system. Indeed, although the Mughals profited from seaborne trade, they never undertook overseas expansion. The main source of their wealth was land rents, which increased via incentives to bring new land into cultivation. Here peasants planted, in part, New World crops like maize and tobacco. But the imperial economy also benefited from Europeans' increased demand for Indian goods and services—such as a sixfold rise in the English East India Company's textile purchases within twenty years. Dutch trade with India saw similar trends. As precious metals flowed in from Japan and the New World to finance this booming trade, the imperial mint struck increasing numbers of silver coins, which fueled a cycle of greater trade and the use of **specie** (money in coin) for exchange.

LOCAL AUTONOMY IN MUGHAL INDIA Mughals were victims of their own success. More than a century of imperial expansion, commercial prosperity, and agricultural development placed substantial resources in the hands of

Indian Cotton. European traders were drawn to India by its famed cotton textiles. This image from c. 1800 shows a woman separating the cotton from the seeds; it captures the preindustrial technology of cotton production in India.

local and regional authorities. As a result, local warrior elites became more autonomous. By the late seventeenth century, many regional leaders were well positioned to resist Mughal authority.

As in the Ottoman Empire, then, distant provinces began to challenge central rulers. Under Aurangzeb (r. 1658–1707), as the Mughals pushed their frontier deep into southern India, they encountered fierce opposition from the Marathas in the northwestern Deccan plateau (see Map 13-1). To finance this expansion, Aurangzeb raised taxes on the peasants. Then resentment spread, and even the elite grew restive at the drain on imperial finances. Seeking support from the orthodox *ulama*, the monarch abandoned the toleration of heterodoxy and of non-Muslims that his predecessors had allowed. Ultimately, only the strong hand of Aurangzeb kept order in the empire.

When Aurangzeb died in 1707, a war of succession broke out. The revenue system eroded as local tax collectors pocketed more of the returns. Prosperous local elites rallied military forces of their own, annexing neighboring lands and chipping away at imperial authority. All this turmoil set the stage for successful peasant revolts.

Now the Indian peasants (like their counterparts in Ming China, Safavid Persia, and the Ottoman Empire) capitalized on weakening central authority to assert their independence. Many rose in rebellions; others took up banditry. Consider the revolt of the Jat peasant caste in northern India in the late seventeenth century: refusing to pay taxes, the Jat people killed a Mughal official and then seized lands and plundered the region. A half-century later, peasant cultivators of the Punjab turned their own closely knit community into a military power that stymied the Mughal forces. Peasants were also critical in the rise of the Marathas of western India, whose charismatic leader harnessed hatred of imperial oppression to fiercely resist Mughal control.

At this point the Mughal emperors had to accept diminished power over a loose unity of provincial "successor states." Most of these areas accepted Mughal control in name only, administering semiautonomous regimes through access

Aurangzeb. The last powerful Mughal emperor, Aurangzeb continued the conquest of the Indian subcontinent. Pictured in his old age, he is shown here with his courtiers.

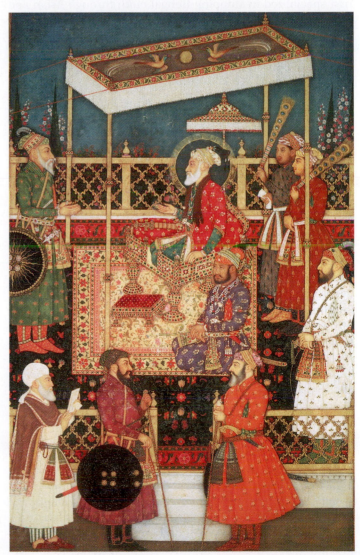

to local resources. Yet India still flourished, and landed elites brought new territories into agrarian production. Cotton, for instance, supported a thriving textile industry as peasant households focused on weaving and cloth production. Much of their production was destined for export as the region deepened its integration into world trading systems.

PRIVATE COMMERCIAL ENTERPRISE   The Mughals themselves paid scant attention to commercial matters, but local rulers welcomed Europeans into Indian ports. As more European ships arrived, these authorities struck deals with merchants from Portugal and, increasingly, from England and Holland. Some Indian merchants formed trading companies of their own to control the sale of regional produce to competing Europeans; others established intricate trading networks that reached as far north as Russia.

One of these companies built a trading and banking empire that demonstrated how local prosperity could undercut imperial power. This was the house of Jagat Seths, which at first specialized in shipping Bengal cloth through Asian and European merchants. Increasingly, however, most of their business in the provinces of Bengal and Bihar was tax-farming, whereby they collected taxes for the imperial coffers. (See Map 13-1.) The Jagat Seths maintained their own retinue of agents to gather levies from farmers while pocketing substantial profits for themselves. In this way, they and other mercantile houses grew richer and gained greater political influence over financially strapped emperors. Thus, even as global commercial entanglements enriched some in India, the effects undercut the Mughal dynasty.

FROM MING TO QING IN CHINA

Like India, China prospered in the seventeenth and eighteenth centuries; but here, too, sizeable wealth undermined central control and contributed to the fall of a long-lasting dynasty. As in Mughal India, local power holders in China increasingly defied the Ming government. Moreover, because Ming sovereigns discouraged overseas commerce and forbade travel abroad, they did not reap the rewards of long-distance exchange. Rather, such profits went to traders and adventurers who evaded imperial edicts. Together, the persistence of local autonomy and the accelerating economic and social changes brought unprecedented challenges until finally, in 1644, the Ming dynasty collapsed.

ADMINISTRATIVE PROBLEMS   How did a dynasty that in the early seventeenth century governed the world's most economically advanced society (and perhaps a third of the world's population) fall from power? As in the Ottoman Empire, responsibility often lay with the rulers. Consider the disastrous reign of Zhu Yijun, the Wanli Emperor (r. 1573–1620). This precocious youth ascended to the throne at age nine and, like his predecessors, grew up within the confines of the Forbidden City (see Chapter 11). The emperor was secluded despite being surrounded by a staff of 20,000 eunuchs and 3,000 women. The "Son of Heaven" rarely ventured outside the palace compound, and when he moved within it a large retinue accompanied him, led by eunuchs clearing his path with whips. His day was filled with state functions, for which he had to change clothes to suit each occasion—including formal headgear with curtain-like beads that forced him to move solemnly and deliberately.

Ming emperors like Wanli quickly discovered that despite the elaborate arrangements and ritual performances affirming their position as the Son of Heaven, they had scant control over the vast bureaucracy. An emperor frustrated with his officials could do little more than punish them or refuse to cooperate. Unable to change this system, Wanli avoided any involvement with managing the realm; he even refused to meet with officials or preside over state rituals. A mountain of reports and petitions piled up in his study unattended, while some of his bureaucrats exploited his neglect to accumulate wealth for themselves. During his long reign, Wanli's inaction as a ruler was in clear contrast to the ideal image of a wise and caring emperor.

ECONOMIC PROBLEMS   The timing of administrative breakdown in the Ming government was unfortunate, because expanding opportunities for trade led many individuals to circumvent official rules. From the mid-sixteenth century, bands of supposedly Japanese pirates ravaged the Chinese coast. Indeed, the Ming government had difficulties regulating trade with Japan. Japanese missions, often armed and several hundred people strong, looted Chinese coastal villages. Yet, while Ming officials labeled all pirates as Japanese, many of the marauders were in fact Chinese.

Operating out of the empire's coastal towns, as well as from ports in Japan and Southeast Asia, these maritime adventurers deeply disturbed the Ming authorities. In tough times, the roving gangs terrorized sea-lanes and harbors. In better times, some functioned like mercantile groups: their leaders mingled with elites, foreign trade representatives, and imperial officials. What made these predators so resilient—and their business so lucrative—was their ability to move among the mosaic of East Asian cultures.

Just like in the Islamic empires, the influx of silver from the New World and Japan, while at first stimulating the Chinese economy, led to severe economic (and, eventually, political) dislocations. As noted in Chapter 12, Europeans used New World silver to pay for their purchases of Chinese goods. As a result, by the early seventeenth century silver imports exceeded domestic **bullion** production (uncoined gold or silver) by some twentyfold. Increasing **monetization** of the economy, which entailed silver becoming the primary medium of exchange, bolstered market activity and state revenues at the same time.

Silver. This seventeenth-century helmet from the Ming (1368–1633) or the Qing dynasties (1644–1911) features steel, gold, silver, and textiles, all of which were vital to the Chinese economy during this century. Silver was especially important, for its large influx from Japan and the Americas led to severe economic problems, political unrest, and the overthrow of Ming dynasts.

Yet the primacy of silver pressured peasants, who now needed that metal to pay their taxes and purchase goods. (See Primary Source: Huang Liuhong on Eliminating Authorized Silversmiths.) When silver supplies were abundant, the peasants faced inflationary prices. When supplies were scant, the peasants could not meet their obligations to state officials and merchants. The frustrated masses thus often seethed with resentment, which quickly turned to rebellion.

Market fluctuations abroad also affected the Chinese economy, introducing new sources of instability. After 1610, Dutch and English assaults on Spanish ships heading to Asia cut down on silver flows into China. Then, in 1639, Japanese authorities clamped down on foreign traders, a move that curbed the outflow of Japanese specie to China. All these blows to the Asian trading system destabilized China's money supply and weakened its economy.

THE COLLAPSE OF MING AUTHORITY By the seventeenth century, the Ming's administrative and economic difficulties were affecting their subjects' daily lives. This was particularly evident when the regime failed to cope with devastation caused by natural disasters, as in the northwestern province of Shaanxi. As the price of grain soared there, the poor and the hungry fanned out to find food by whatever means they could muster. To deal with the crisis, the government imposed heavier taxes and cut the military budget. Bands of dispossessed Chinese peasants and mutinous soldiers then vented their anger at local tax collectors and officials.

Now the cycle of rebellion and weakened central authority that played out in so many other places took its predictable toll. Outlaw armies grew large under charismatic leaders. Numerous mobile armies—the so-called roving bandits—took shape. The most famous rebel leader, the "dashing prince" Li Zicheng, arrived at the outskirts of Beijing in 1644. Only a few companies of soldiers and a few thousand eunuchs were there to defend the capital's twenty-one miles of walls, so Li Zicheng seized Beijing easily. Two days later, the emperor hanged himself. On the following day, the triumphant "dashing prince" rode into the capital and claimed the throne.

News of the fall of the Ming capital sent shock waves around the empire. One hundred and seventy miles to the northeast, where China meets Manchuria, the army's commander received the news within a matter of days. His task in the area was to defend the Ming against their menacing neighbor, a group that had begun to identify itself as Manchu. Immediately the commander's position became precarious. Caught between an advancing rebel army on the one side and the Manchus on the other, he made a fateful decision: he appealed for the Manchus' cooperation to fight the "dashing prince," promising his new allies that "gold and treasure" awaited them in the capital. Thus, without shedding a drop of blood, the Manchus joined the Ming forces. After years of coveting the Ming Empire, the Manchus were finally on their way to Beijing (see Map 13-5).

THE QING DYNASTY ASSERTS CONTROL Despite their small numbers, the Manchus overcame early resistance to their rule and oversaw an impressive expansion of their realm. The **Manchus**—the name was first used in 1635—were descendants of the Jurchens (see Chapter 10). They emerged as a force early in the seventeenth century, when their leader claimed the title of khan after securing the allegiance of various Mongol groups in northeastern Asia, paving the way for their eventual conquest of China.

When the Manchus defeated Li Zicheng and seized power in Beijing, they numbered around 1 million. Assuming control of a domain that included perhaps 250 million people, they were keenly aware of their minority status. Taking power was one thing; keeping it was another. But keep it they did. In fact, during the eighteenth century, the Manchu **Qing** ("pure") **dynasty** (1644–1911) incorporated new territories, experienced substantial population growth, and sustained significant economic growth. All this occurred without the kind of economic and political turmoil that rocked the societies of the Atlantic world.

The key to China's relatively stable economic and geographic expansion lay in its rulers' shrewd and flexible policies. The early Manchu emperors were able and diligent administrators. They also knew that to govern a diverse population

HUANG LIUHONG ON ELIMINATING AUTHORIZED SILVERSMITHS

The influx of silver into China had profound effects on its economy and government. For instance, silver became the medium for assessing taxes. In his magistrate's manual from around 1694, Huang Liuhong (Huang Liu-hung) indicated the problems that arose from involving authorized silversmiths in the payment process. The situation demonstrates how silver had become an integral part of the lives of the Chinese people.

The purpose of using an authorized silversmith in the collection of tax money is twofold. First, the quality of the silver delivered by the taxpayers must be up to standard. The authorized silversmith is expected to reject any substandard silver. Second, when the silver is delivered to the provincial treasury, it should be melted and cast into ingots to avoid theft while in transit. But, to get his commission, the authorized silversmith has to pay a fee and arrange for a guarantor. In addition, he has to pay bribes to the clerks of the revenue section and to absorb the operating expenses of his shop—rent, food, coal, wages for his employees, and so on. If he does not impose a surcharge on the taxpayers, how can he maintain his business?

There are many ways for an authorized silversmith to defraud the taxpayers. First, he can declare that the quality of the silver is not up to standard and a larger amount is required. Second, he can insist that all small pieces of silver have to be melted and cast into ingots; hence there will be wastage in the process of melting. Third, he may demand that all ingots, no matter how small they are, be stamped with his seal, and of course charge a stamping fee. Fourth, he may require a fee for each melting as a legitimate charge for the service. Fifth, he can procrastinate until the taxpayer becomes impatient and is willing to double the melting fee. Last, if the taxpayer seems naive or simple minded, the smith can purposely upset the melting container and put the blame on the taxpayer. All these tricks are prevalent, and little can be done to thwart them.

When the silver ingots are delivered to the provincial treasury, few of them are up to standard. The authorized silversmith often blames the taxpayers for bringing in silver of inferior quality although it would be easy for him to reject them at the time of melting. Powerful official families and audacious licentiates often put poor quality silver in sealed envelopes, which the authorized silversmith is not empowered to examine. Therefore, the use of an authorized silversmith contributes very little to the business of tax collection; it only increases the burden of small taxpayers. . . .

→ *What are the six ways that an authorized silversmith can defraud taxpayers?*

→ *Why does the author suggest that the use of authorized silversmiths increases the burden of small taxpayers?*

→ *What reasons would the Chinese state have for maintaining such a "flawed" system?*

SOURCE: Huang Liu-hung, "Elimination of Authorized Silversmiths" from *A Complete Book Concerning Happiness and Benevolence: A Manual for Local Magistrates in Seventeenth Century China*, translated and edited by Djang Chu, pp. 190–91. Copyright © 1984 the Arizona Board of Regents. Reprinted by permission of the University of Arizona Press.

---

they had to adapt to local ways. To promote continuity with previous practices, they respected Confucian codes and ethics and kept the classic texts as the basis of the prestigious civil service examinations (see Chapter 9). Social hierarchies of age, gender, and kin—indeed, the entire image of the family as the bedrock of social organization—endured. In some areas, like Taiwan, the Manchus added new territories to existing provinces. Elsewhere, they gave newly acquired territories, like Mongolia, Tibet, and Xinjiang, their own form of local administration. Imperial envoys in these regions administered through staffs of locals and relied on native institutions. Until

the late nineteenth century, the Qing dynasty showed little interest in integrating those regions into "China proper."

At the same time, Qing rulers were determined to convey a clear sense of their own majesty and legitimacy. Rulers relentlessly promoted patriarchal values. Widows who remained "chaste" enjoyed public praise, and women in general were urged to lead a "virtuous" life serving male kin and family. To the majority Han population, the Manchu emperor represented himself as the worthy upholder of familial values and classical Chinese civilization; to the Tibetan Buddhists, the Manchu state offered imperial patronage. So, too, with

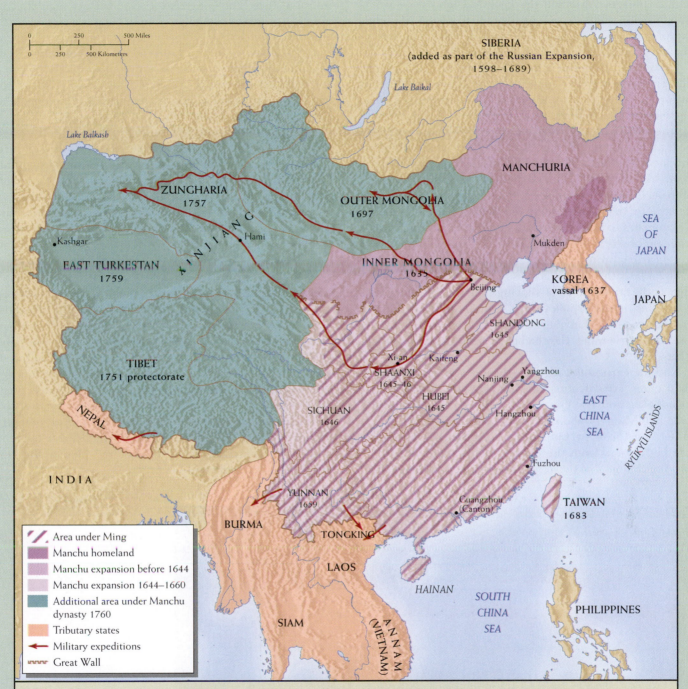

Map 13-5   From Ming to Qing China, 1644–1760

Qing China under the Manchus expanded its territory significantly during this period. Find the Manchu homeland and then the area of Manchu expansion after 1644, when the Manchus established the Qing dynasty. Where did the Qing dynasty expand? Based on the map, why do you think the Qing dynasty expanded so aggressively during this period? What does the location of Manchuria tell you about the historical origins of the Qing?

Islamic subjects. Although the Islamic Uighurs, as well as other Muslim subjects, might have disliked the Manchus' easygoing religious attitude, they accepted the emperor's favors and generally endorsed his claim to rule.

However, insinuating themselves into an existing order and appeasing subject peoples did not satisfy the Manchu yearning to leave their imprint. They also introduced measures that emphasized their authority, their distinctiveness, and the submission of their mostly Han Chinese subjects. For example, Qing officials composed or translated important documents into Manchu and banned intermarriage between Manchu and Han (although this was difficult to enforce). Other edicts imposed Manchu ways. For example, the day after the Manchus entered Beijing, a decree required all Han males to follow the Manchu practice of shaving their foreheads and braiding their hair at the back in a queue. Although strong protests led to temporary shelving of the policy, a year later the Manchus reissued the order and gave their subjects the stark choice of shaving their hair or losing their heads. This time, the policy stood firm. In a similar vein, the Qing decreed that Han males adopt Manchu garb: instead of loose Ming-style robes, they had to wear high collars and tight jackets.

Nothing earned the regime's disapproval more than the urban elites' conspicuous consumption and indulgence in sensual pleasure. The Qing court regarded the "decadence" of the late Ming, symbolized by its famous actresses, as one of the Ming's principal failings. In 1723 the Qing banned female performers from the court, after which the practice spread to commercial theaters, with young boys taking female roles on stage. The Qing also tried to further regulate commercial theater by excluding women from the audience. The popularity of female impersonators on stage, however, brought a new cachet to homosexual relationships. A gulf began to open between the government's aspirations and its ability to police society. For example, the urban public continued to flock to performances by female impersonators in defiance of the Qing's bans.

Manchu impositions fell mostly on the peasantry, for the Qing financed their administrative structure through taxes on peasant households. In response the peasants sought new lands to cultivate in border areas, often planting New World crops that grew well in difficult soils. This move introduced an important change in Chinese diets: while rice remained the staple diet of the wealthy, peasants increasingly subsisted on corn and sweet potatoes.

EXPANSION AND TRADE UNDER THE QING Despite public disregard for certain imperial edicts, the Qing dynasty enjoyed a heyday during the eighteenth century. It forged tributary relations with Korea, Vietnam, Burma, and Nepal, and its territorial expansion reached far into central Asia, Tibet, and Mongolia. In particular, the Manchus confronted the Junghars of western Mongolia, who controlled much of central Asia in the mid-seventeenth century and whose predecessors had once captured an early Ming emperor. Wary of a potential alliance between the Junghars and an emerging Russia on its northern frontiers, the Qing dynasty launched successive campaigns and dealt a decisive blow to the Junghars by the mid-eighteenth century.

Qing Theater with Female Impersonators. The Qing court banned women from performing in theaters, which led to the practice of using young boys in female roles.

→ *How did global trade affect the Asian dynasties?*

Canton. Not only were foreigners not allowed to trade with the Chinese outside of Canton, but they were also required to have Chinese guild members act as guarantors of their good behavior and payment of fees.

While officials redoubled their reliance on an agrarian base, trade and commerce flourished. Chinese merchants continued to ply the waters stretching from Southeast Asia to Japan, exchanging textiles, ceramics, and medicine for spices and rice. Although the Qing state vacillated about permitting maritime trade with foreigners in its early years, it sought to regulate external commerce more formally as it consolidated its rule. In 1720, in Canton, a group of merchants formed a monopolistic guild to trade with Europeans seeking coveted Chinese goods and peddling their own wares. Although the guild disbanded in the face of opposition from other merchants, it revived after the Qing restricted European trade to Canton. The **Canton system**, officially established by imperial decree in 1759, required European traders to have guild merchants act as guarantors for their good behavior and payment of fees.

China, in sum, negotiated a century of upheaval without dismantling established ways in politics and economics. The peasantry continued to practice popular faiths, cultivate crops, and stay close to fields and villages. Trade with the outside world was marginal to overall commercial life; like the Ming, the Qing cared more about the agrarian than the commercial health of the empire, believing the former to be the foundation of prosperity and tranquility. As long as China's peasantry could keep the dynasty's coffers full, the government was content to squeeze the merchants when it needed funds. Some historians view this practice as a failure to adapt to a changing world order, as it ultimately left China vulnerable to outsiders—especially Europeans. But this view puts the historical cart before the horse. By the mid-eighteenth century, Europe still needed China more than the other way around. For the majority of Chinese, no superior model of

belief, politics, or economics was conceivable. Indeed, although the Qing had taken over a crumbling empire in 1644, a century later China was enjoying a new level of prosperity.

TOKUGAWA JAPAN

Integration with the Asian trading system exposed Japan to new external pressures, even as the islands grappled with internal turmoil. But the Japanese dealt with these pressures more successfully than the mainland Asian empires (Ottoman, Safavid, Mughal, and Ming), which saw political fragmentation and even the overthrow of ruling dynasties. In Japan, a single ruling family emerged. This dynastic state, the **Tokugawa shogunate**, accomplished something that most of the world's other regimes did not: it regulated foreign intrusion. While Japan played a modest role in the expanding global trade, it remained free of outside exploitation.

UNIFICATION OF JAPAN During the sixteenth century, Japan had suffered from political instability as banditry and civil strife disrupted the countryside. Regional ruling families, called *daimyos,* had commanded private armies of warriors known as samurai. The daimyos sometimes brought order to their domains, but no one family could establish preeminence over others. Although Japan had an emperor, his authority did not extend beyond the court in Kyoto.

Ultimately, several military leaders attempted to unify Japan. One general, who became the supreme minister, arranged marriages among the children of local authorities to solidify political bonds. Also, to coax cooperation from the daimyos, he ordered that their wives and children be kept as semihostages in the residences they were required to maintain in Edo. After the general died, one of the daimyos, Tokugawa Ieyasu, took power for himself. This was a decisive moment. In 1603, Ieyasu assumed the title of shogun (military ruler). He also solved the problem of succession, declaring that rulership would be hereditary and that his family would be the ruling household. This hereditary Tokugawa shogunate lasted until 1867.

Now administrative authority shifted from Kyoto to the site of Ieyasu's domain headquarters: the castle town called Edo (later renamed Tokyo; see Map 13-6). The Tokugawa built Edo out of a small earthen fortification clinging to a coastal bluff. Behind Edo lay a village in a swampy plain. In a monumental work of engineering, the rulers ordered the swamp drained, the forest cleared, many of the hills leveled, canals dredged, bridges built, the seashore extended by landfill, and a new stone castle completed. By the time Ieyasu died, Edo had a population of 150,000.

The Tokugawa shoguns ensured a flow of resources from the working population to the rulers and from the provinces to the capital. Villages paid taxes to the daimyos, who transferred resources to the seat of shogunate authority. No longer

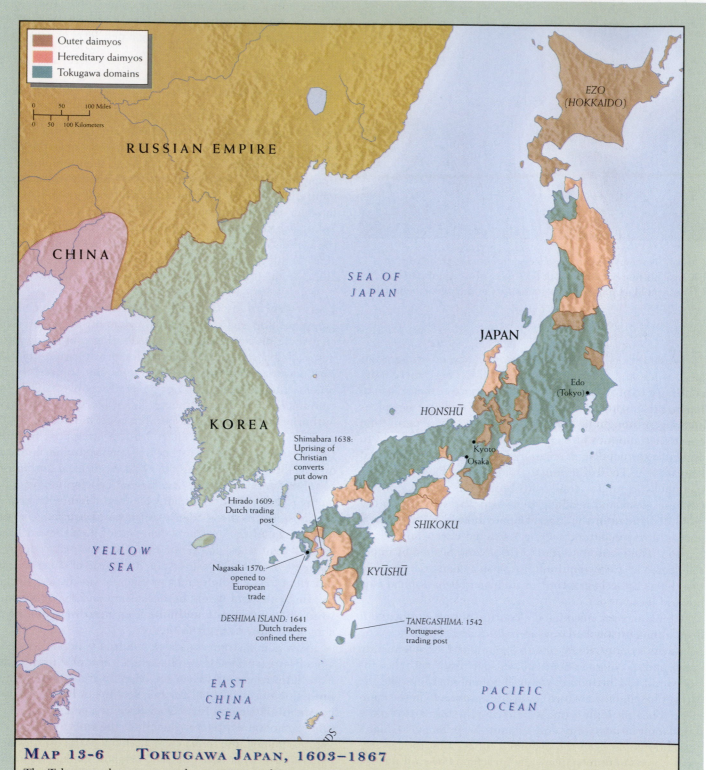

Outer daimyos
Hereditary daimyos
Tokugawa domains

0   50   100 Miles
0   50   100 Kilometers

RUSSIAN EMPIRE

CHINA

EZO
(HOKKAIDO)

SEA OF
JAPAN

JAPAN

Edo
(Tokyo)

HONSHŪ

KOREA

Shimabara 1638:
Uprising of
Christian
converts
put down

Kyoto
Osaka

Hirado 1609:
Dutch trading
post

SHIKOKU

YELLOW
SEA

Nagasaki 1570:
opened to
European
trade

KYŪSHŪ

DESHIMA ISLAND: 1641
Dutch traders
confined there

TANEGASHIMA: 1542
Portuguese
trading post

EAST
CHINA
SEA

PACIFIC
OCEAN

MAP 13-6   TOKUGAWA JAPAN, 1603–1867

The Tokugawa shoguns created a strong central state in Japan at this time. According to this map, how extensive was their control? What foreign states were interested in trade with Japan? How did Tokugawa leaders attempt to control relations with foreign states and other entities?

Edo in the Rain. This facsimile of an *ukiyo-e* ("floating world") print by Hiroshige (1797–1858) depicts one of several bridges in the bustling city of Edo (later Tokyo), with Mount Fuji in the background.

engaged in constant warfare, the samurai became administrators. Peace brought prosperity. Agriculture thrived. Improved farming techniques and land reclamation projects enabled the country's population to grow from 10 million in 1550 to 16 million in 1600 and 30 million in 1700.

FOREIGN AFFAIRS AND FOREIGNERS Internal peace and prosperity did not insulate Japan from external challenges. When Japanese rulers tackled foreign affairs, their most pressing concern was the intrusion of Christian missionaries and European traders. Initially, Japanese officials welcomed these foreigners out of an eagerness to acquire muskets, gunpowder, and other new technology. But once the ranks of Christian converts swelled, Japanese authorities realized that Christians were intolerant of other faiths, believed Christ to be superior to any authority, and fought among themselves. Trying to stem the tide, the shoguns prohibited conversion to Christianity and attempted to ban its practice. After a rebellion in which converted peasants rose up in protest against high rents and taxes, the government suppressed Christianity and drove European missionaries from the country.

Even more troublesome was the lure of trade with Europeans. The Tokugawa knew that trading at various Japanese ports would pull the commercial regions in various directions, away from the capital. When it became clear that European traders preferred the ports of Kyūshū (the southernmost island), the shogunate restricted Europeans to trade only in ports under Edo's direct rule in Honshū. Then, Japanese authorities expelled all European competitors. Only the Protestant (and nonmissionizing) Dutch won permission to remain in Japan, confined to an island near Nagasaki. The Dutch were allowed to unload just one ship each year, under strict supervision by Japanese authorities.

These measures did not close Tokugawa Japan to the outside world, however. Trade with China and Korea flourished, and the shogun received missions from Korea and the Ryūkyū islands. Edo also gathered information about the outside world from the resident Dutch and Chinese (who included monks, physicians, and painters). A few Japanese were permitted to learn Dutch and to study European technology, shipbuilding, and medicine (see Chapter 14). By limiting such encounters, the authorities ensured that foreigners would not threaten Japan's security.

Ruling over three islands, Tokugawa Japan was surrounded by "vassals" that were neither part of the realm nor entirely independent. Most important were the Ryūkyūs in the south and the island of Ezo to the north, which the Japanese maintained as buffers. Such areas helped define a distinct Japanese identity for all peoples living "on the inside." When, beginning in 1697, the Russians approached Japan to open relations, the Japanese instead sought to deal with them through the northern buffer zone. As the Russians tried harder to open Japan to trade, the Japanese annexed and began to colonize Ezo (what would eventually be called Hokkaidō), the country's fourth main island and a strong barrier to foreign penetration. In regulating outside contacts, Japanese rulers suppressed potential sources of upheaval and

Portuguese Arriving in Japan. In the 1540s, the Portuguese arrival on the islands of Japan sparked a fascination with the strange costumes and the great ships of these "southern barbarians" (so called because they had approached Japan from the south). Silk-screen paintings depicted Portuguese prowess in exaggerated form, such as in the impossible height of the fore and aft of the vessel pictured here.

consolidated a dynasty that lasted well into the nineteenth century.

The rulers of Japan invented an approach to relations with the outside world on Japanese terms. They permitted trade and diplomatic relations with the Dutch, Chinese, and Koreans, but in a controlled fashion, and they generally did not permit such relations with the Russians or Christian missionaries. In this, the Japanese were aided by their island status, which had also protected them from the Mongols.

TRANSFORMATIONS IN EUROPE

> → *Why did Europe's economic and political centers shift northward?*

Between 1600 and 1750, religious conflict, commercial expansion, and the consolidation of dynastic power transformed Europe. Commercial centers shifted northward, and Spain and Portugal lost ground to England and France. Even farther to the north, the state of Muscovy expanded dramatically to become the sprawling Russian Empire.

EXPANSION AND DYNASTIC CHANGE IN RUSSIA

During this period the Russian Empire expanded to become the world's largest-ever state. It gained positions on the Baltic Sea and the Pacific Ocean, and it established political borders with both the Qing Empire and Japan. These momentous shifts involved the elimination of steppe nomads as an inde-

pendent force. Culturally, Europeans as well as Russians debated whether Russia belonged more to Europe or to Asia. The answer was both.

MUSCOVY BECOMES THE RUSSIAN EMPIRE The principality of Moscow, or Muscovy, like Japan and China, used territorial expansion and commercial networks to consolidate a powerful state. This was the Russian Empire, the name given to Muscovy by Tsar Peter the Great around 1700. Originally a mixture of Slavs, Finnish tribes, Turkic speakers, and many others, **Muscovy** expanded to become a huge empire that spanned parts of Europe, much of northern Asia, numerous North Pacific islands, and even—for a time—a corner of North America (Alaska).

Like Japan, Russia emerged out of turmoil. Three factors inspired the regime to seize territory: security concerns; the ambitions of private individuals; and religious conviction. Security concerns were foremost, as expansion was inseparable from security. Because the steppe, which stretches deep into Asia, remained a highway for nomadic peoples (especially descendants of the powerful Mongols), Muscovy sought to dominate the areas south and east of Moscow. By marrying the niece of the last Byzantine emperor, the Muscovite grand prince Ivan III (r. 1462–1505) added a religious dimension to his expansionist claims: he could assert that Moscow was the center of the Byzantine faith and heir to the conquered city of Constantinople. Later expansion secured Muscovy's eastern borders by reaching into Siberia. Beginning in the 1590s, Russian authorities built forts and trading posts along Siberian rivers at the same time that privateers, enticed by the fur trade, pushed even farther east. By 1639 the state's borders had reached the Pacific. Thus in just over a century, Muscovy had claimed an empire straddling Eurasia and incorporating peoples of many languages and religions (see Map 13-7).

Much of this expansion occurred despite dynastic chaos that followed the death of Ivan IV in 1584. Ultimately a group

MAP 13-7 RUSSIAN EXPANSION, 1462–1795

The state of Muscovy incorporated vast territories through overland expansion as it grew and became the Russian Empire. It did so in part because of its geographical position and its strategic needs. Using the map key, identify how many different expansions the Russian Empire underwent between 1462 and 1795 and in what directions generally. With what countries and cultures did the Russian Empire come into contact? What drove such dramatic expansion?

of prominent families reestablished central authority and threw their weight behind a new family of rulers. These were the Romanovs, court barons who set about reviving the Kremlin's fortunes. (The Kremlin was a medieval walled fortress where the Muscovite grand princes—later, tsars—resided.) Like the Ottoman and Qing dynasts, Romanov tsars and their aristocratic supporters would retain power into the twentieth century.

ABSOLUTIST GOVERNMENT AND SERFDOM In the seventeenth and eighteenth centuries, the Romanovs created an absolutist system of government. Only the tsar and his ret-

inue had the right to make war, tax, judge, and coin money. The Romanovs also made the nobles serve as state officials. Now Russia became a despotic state that had no political assemblies for nobles or other groups, other than mere consultative bodies like the imperial senate. Indeed, away from Moscow, local aristocrats enjoyed nearly unlimited authority in exchange for loyalty and tribute to the tsar.

During this period, Russia's peasantry bore the burden of maintaining the wealth of the small nobility and the monarchy. Most peasant families gathered into communes, isolated rural worlds where people helped one another deal with the harsh climate, severe landlords, and occasional poor harvests.

Communes functioned like extended kin networks in that members reciprocated favors and chores. The typical peasant hut was a single chamber heated by a wood-burning stove with no chimney. Livestock and humans often shared the same quarters. In 1649, peasants were legally bound as serfs to the nobles and the tsar, meaning they had to perform obligatory services and deliver part of their produce to their lords. In fact, the lords essentially controlled all aspects of their serfs' lives.

IMPERIAL EXPANSION AND MIGRATION Three factors were key to Russia's becoming an empire: (1) the conquest of Siberia, which brought vast territory and riches in furs; (2) incorporation of the fertile southern steppes, known as Ukraine; and (3) victory in a prolonged war with Sweden. Peter the Great (r. 1682–1725) accomplished the victory in Sweden, after which he founded a new capital at St. Petersburg. Yet even as he triumphed over Sweden he sought to imitate a Swedish-style bureaucracy in Russia. Thereafter Russia developed a formidable military-fiscal state bureaucracy, but the aristocracy, not the civil service, remained predominant.

Under Peter's successors, including the hard-nosed Catherine the Great, Russia added even more territory. Catherine placed her former lover on the Polish throne and subsequently, together with the Austrians and Prussians, carved up the medieval state of Poland. Her victories against the Ottomans allowed Russia to annex Ukraine, the grain-growing "breadbasket" of eastern Europe. By the late eighteenth century, Russia's grasp extended from the Baltic Sea

Catherine the Great. Catherine the Great styled herself an enlightened despot of the baroque epoch, furthering the Russian Empire's adaptation of European high culture.

through the heart of Europe, Ukraine, and the Crimea on the Black Sea and into the ancient lands of Armenia and Georgia in the Caucasus Mountains.

The Russian Empire was a harsh but colossal space that induced the movement of peoples within it. Many people migrated eastward, into Siberia. Some were fleeing serfdom; others were being deported for having rejected changes in the state's official Eastern Orthodox religious services. Battling astoundingly harsh temperatures (falling to –40 degrees Centigrade/Fahrenheit) and frigid Arctic winds, these individuals traveled on horseback and trudged on foot to resettle in the east. But the difficulties of clearing forested lands or planting crops in boggy Siberian soils, combined with extraordinarily harsh winters, meant that many settlers died or tried to return. Isolation was a problem, too. There was no established land route back to Moscow until the 1770s, when exiles completed the Great Siberian Post Road through the swamps and peat bogs of western Siberia. The writer Anton Chekhov later called it "the longest and ugliest road in the whole world."

Whereas initially over 90 percent of Siberia's inhabitants were natives, by 1750 the number of immigrants almost matched the native population and soon surpassed it. Although many of the immigrants were runaway serfs, others who were religious or political outcasts would later make Siberia infamous as a land for prisoners instead of a destination of freedom. "The road to Siberia is wide," went the saying, "the way back, narrow."

Nenets Hunters. Hunters of the Nenets tribe in far North Asia's treeless tundra, showing off their warm animal-skin clothing and self-fashioned weapons, as depicted in a 1620 engraving by Theodore de Bry, one of the first Europeans to come into contact with them.

ECONOMIC AND POLITICAL FLUCTUATIONS IN WESTERN EUROPE

During this period European economies became more commercialized, especially after recovering from the Thirty Years' War. As in Asia, developments in distant parts of the world shaped the region's economic upturns and downturns. Com-

The Thirty Years' War. The mercenary armies of the Thirty Years' War were renowned for pillaging and tormenting the civilians of central Europe. Here, the townsfolk exact revenge on some of these soldiers, hanging, as the engraving's caption claims, "damned and infamous thieves, like bad fruit, from this tree."

pounding these pressures was the continuation of dynastic rivalries and religious conflicts.

THE THIRTY YEARS' WAR For a century after Martin Luther broke with the Catholic Church (see Chapter 12), religious warfare raged in Europe. So did contests over territory, power, and trade. The **Thirty Years' War** (1618–1648) was all three of these—a war between Protestant princes and the Catholic emperor for religious predominance in central Europe; a struggle for regional control among Catholic powers (the Spanish and Austrian Habsburgs and the French); and a bid for independence (from Spain) by the Dutch, who wanted to trade and worship as they liked.

The brutal conflict began as a struggle between Protestants and Catholics within the Habsburg Empire, but it soon became a war for preeminence in Europe. It took the lives of civilians as well as soldiers. Just when it seemed as if Protestantism would vanish from central Europe, the Swedish king made a timely intervention, reenergizing the Protestant cause. In the course of a war fought heavily by ill-paid and poorly fed mercenaries, both sides committed many atrocities against civilians. Most famously, in 1631, Catholic forces besieged and then destroyed the beautiful German town of Magdeburg, killing three-quarters of the civilian inhabitants. In total, fighting, disease, and famine wiped out a third of the German states' urban population and two-fifths of their rural population. The war also depopulated Sweden and Poland. Ultimately the Treaty of Westphalia (1648) stated, in essence, that as there was a rough balance of power between Protestant and Catholic states, they would simply have to put

up with each other. The Dutch won their independence, but the war's enormous costs provoked severe discontent in Spain, France, and England. Central Europe was so devastated that it did not recover in economic or demographic terms for more than a century.

The Thirty Years' War transformed war making. Whereas most medieval struggles had been sieges between nobles leading small armies, centralized states fielding standing armies now waged decisive, grand-scale campaigns. The war also changed the ranks of soldiers: as the conflict ground on, local enlisted men defending their king, country, and faith gave way to hired mercenaries or criminals doing forced service. Even officers, who previously obtained their stripes by purchase or royal decree, now had to earn them. Gunpowder, cannons, and handguns became standardized. By the eighteenth century, Europe's wars featured huge standing armies boasting a professional officer corps, deadly artillery, and long supply lines bringing food and ammunition to the front. The costs—material and human—of war began to soar.

WESTERN EUROPEAN ECONOMIES In spite of the toll that warfare took on economic activity, the European states enjoyed significant commercial expansion. Northern Europe gained more than did the south, however. Spain, for example, started losing ground to its rivals as the costs of defending its empire soared and merchants from northern Europe cut in on its trading networks. The weighty costs of its involvement in the Thirty Years' War dealt the Spanish economy a final, disastrous blow. Other previously robust economies also

Amsterdam Stock Exchange. Buying and selling shares in the new joint-stock companies was daily business at the stock exchange in seventeenth-century Amsterdam. This image depicts gentlemanly negotiations between prosperous merchants and investors, but panics could also occur, as during the South Sea Bubble.

suffered under the pressures of greater economic connection and competition. Venice, for example, which before the era of transoceanic shipping had been Europe's chief gateway to Asia, saw its economy decline.

As European commercial dynamism shifted northward, the Dutch led the way with innovative commercial practices and a new mercantile elite. They specialized in shipping and in financing regional and long-distance trade. Their famous *fluitschips* carried heavy, bulky cargoes (like Baltic wood) with relatively small crews. Now shipping costs throughout the Atlantic world dropped as Dutch ships transported their own and other countries' goods. Amsterdam's merchants founded an exchange bank, established a rudimentary stock exchange, and pioneered systems of underwriting and insuring cargoes. As Europe's other mercantile centers followed suit, the Dutch share of commercial activity eventually shrank. But their pioneering ways set an early example for trading and financing practices that further integrated the Atlantic economies.

England and France also became commercial powerhouses, establishing aggressive policies to promote national business and drive out competitors. Consider the English Navigation Act of 1651. By stipulating that only English ships could carry goods between the mother country and its colonies, it protected English shippers and merchants—especially from the Dutch. The English subsequently launched several effective trade wars against Holland. The French, too, followed

aggressive mercantilist policies and ultimately joined forces with England to invade Holland.

Economic development was not limited to port towns: the countryside, too, enjoyed breakthroughs in production. Most important was expansion in the production of food. In northwestern Europe investments in water drainage, larger livestock herds, and improved cultivation practices generated much greater yields. Also, a four-field crop rotation involving wheat, clover, barley, and turnips kept nutrients in the soil and provided year-round fodder for livestock. As a result (and as we have seen many times throughout history), increased output supported a growing urban population. By contrast, in Spain and Italy, agricultural change and population growth came more slowly.

Production rose most where the organization of rural property changed. Consider again the transformation that occurred in England. Here, in a movement known as **enclosure**, landowners took control of lands that traditionally had been common property serving local needs. Claiming exclusive rights to these lands, the landowners planted new crops or pastured sheep with the aim of selling the products in distant markets—especially cities. The largest landowners put their farms in the hands of tenants, who hired wage laborers to till, plant, and harvest. Thus, in England, peasant agriculture gave way to farms run by wealthy families who exploited the marketplace to buy what they needed (includ-

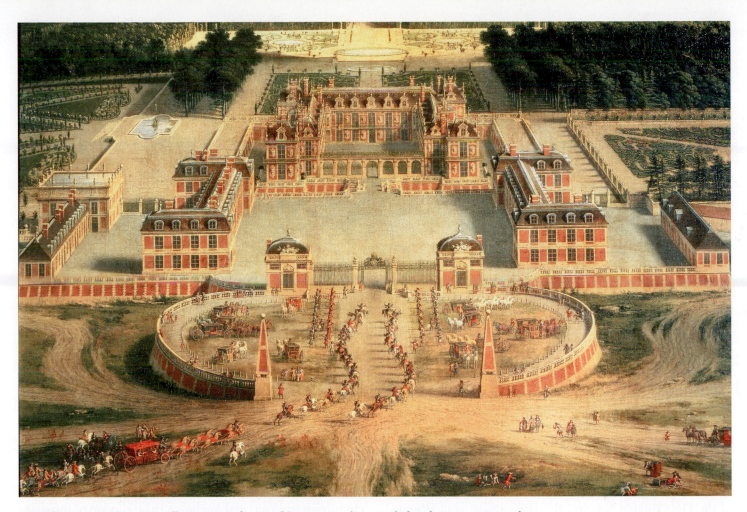

Versailles. Louis XIV's Versailles, just southwest of Paris, was a hunting lodge that was converted at colossal cost in the 1670s–1680s into a grand royal chateau with expansive grounds. Much envied and imitated across Europe, the palace became the epicenter of a luxurious court life that included entertainments such as plays and musical offerings, state receptions, royal hunts, boating, and gambling. Thousands of nobles at Versailles vied with each other for closer proximity to the king in the performance of court rituals.

ing labor) and to sell what they produced. In this regard, England led the way in a Europe-wide process of commercializing the countryside.

DYNASTIC MONARCHIES: FRANCE AND ENGLAND European monarchs had varying success with centralizing state power. In France, Louis XIII (r. 1610–1643) and especially his chief minister, Cardinal Richelieu, concentrated power in the hands of the king. Under his successor, the Bourbon family established a monarchy in which succession passed to the oldest male in the male line. After 1614, kings refused to convene the Estates-General, a medieval advisory body. Composed of representatives of three groups—the clergy (the First Estate, those who pray), the nobility (the Second Estate, those who fight), and the unprivileged remainder of the population (the Third Estate,

those who work)—the Estates-General was an obstacle to the king's full empowerment. Instead of sharing power, the king and his counselors wanted him to rule free of external checks, to create in the words of the age an **absolute monarchy.** The ruler was not to be a tyrant, but his authority was to be complete and thorough, and his state free of bloody disorders. The king's rule would be lawful; but he, not his jurists, would dictate the last legal word. If the king made a mistake, only God could call him to account. Thus the Europeans believed in the "divine right of kings," a political belief not greatly different from imperial China where the emperor was thought to rule with the mandate of heaven.

In absolutist France, privileges and state offices flowed from the king's grace. All patronage networks ultimately linked to the king. The great palace Louis XIV built at Versailles

Queen Elizabeth of England. This portrait (c. 1600) depicts an idealized Queen Elizabeth near the end of her long reign. The queen is pictured riding in a procession in the midst of an admiring crowd composed of the most important nobles of the realm.

teemed with nobles from all over France seeking favor, dressing according to the king's expensive fashion code, and attending the latest tragedies, comedies, and concerts. Just as the Japanese shogun monitored the daimyos by keeping their families in Edo, Louis XIV kept a watchful eye on the French nobility at Versailles.

The French dynastic monarchy provided a model of absolute rule for other European dynasts, like the Habsburgs of the Holy Roman Empire, the Hohenzollerns of Prussia, and the Romanovs of Muscovy. The king and his ministers controlled all public power, while other social groups, from the nobility to the peasantry, had no formal body to represent their interests. Nonetheless, French absolutist government was not as absolute as the king would have wished. Pockets of stalwart Protestants practiced their religion secretly in the plateau villages of central France. Peasant disturbances continued. Criticism of court life, wars, and religious policies filled anonymous pamphlets, jurists' notebooks, and courtiers' private journals. Members of the nobility also grumbled about their political misfortunes, but since the king would not call the Estates-General, they had no formal way to express their concerns.

England might also have evolved into an absolutist regime, but there were important differences between England and France. Queen Elizabeth (r. 1558–1603) and her successors used many policies similar to those of the French monarchy, such as control of patronage (to grant privileges) and elaborate court festivities. Also, refusing to share her power with a man, the "Virgin Queen" never married and exerted sole control over the church, military, and aristocracy. However, not only did the English system of succession allow women to rule as queens in their own right, but the English

Parliament remained an important force. Whereas the French kings did not need the consent of the Estates-General to enact taxes, the English monarchs had to convene Parliament to raise money.

Under Elizabeth's successors, fierce quarrels broke out over taxation, religion, and royal efforts to rule without parliamentary consent. Tensions ran high between Puritans (who preferred a simpler form of worship and more egalitarian church government) and Anglicans (who supported the state-sponsored, hierarchically organized Church of England headed by the king). Social and economic grievances led to civil war in the 1640s and an ultimate victory for the parliamentary army (largely Puritan)—and the beheading of King Charles I. Twelve years of government as a commonwealth without a king followed. During that time the middle and lower classes enjoyed political and religious power, but the commonwealth became a military dictatorship.

In 1660 the monarchy was restored, but without resolving issues of religious tolerance and the king's relation to Parliament. Charles II and his successor, James II, aroused opposition by their autocracy and secret efforts to bring England back into the Catholic fold. The conflict between an aspiring absolutist throne and Parliament's insistence on shared sovereignty and Protestant succession culminated in the Glorious Revolution of 1688–1689. In a bloodless upheaval, James II fled to France and Parliament offered the crown to William of Orange and his wife, Mary (a Protestant). The outcome of the conflict established the principle that English monarchs must rule in conjunction with Parliament. Although the Church of England was reaffirmed as the official state church, Presbyterians and Jews were allowed to practice their religions. Catholic worship, still officially forbidden, was tolerated as long as the Catholics kept quiet. By 1700, then, England's nobility and merchant classes had a guaranteed say in public affairs and assurance that state activity would privilege the propertied classes as well as the ruler.

Events in France and England stimulated much political writing. In England, Thomas Hobbes published *Leviathan* (1651), a defense of the state's absolute power over all competing forces. John Locke published *Two Treatises of Civil Government* (1689), which argued not only for the natural rights to liberty and property but also for the rights of peoples to form a government and then to disband and reform it when it did not live up to its contract. French theorists also proposed new ways of conducting politics and making law. As writers discussed the costs of unchecked state power, they differed over the extent to which elites could check the king. As the eighteenth century unfolded, the question of where sovereignty lay grew more pressing.

MERCANTILIST WARS The rise of new powers in Europe, especially France and England, intensified rivalries for control of the Atlantic system. As conflicts over colonies and sea-lanes replaced earlier religious and territorial struggles, commercial struggles became worldwide wars. Across the globe, European empires constantly skirmished over control of trade and territory. English and Dutch trading companies took aim at Portuguese outposts in Asia and the Americas, and then at each other. Ports in India suffered repeated assaults and counterassaults. In response, European powers built huge navies to protect their colonies and trade routes and to attack their rivals.

Smuggling became rampant. English and French traders, sometimes backed by political authorities, violated the sovereign claims of rival colonies. Curaçao, for instance, became an entrepôt for traders from England and the Low Countries selling illegal goods in South America (see Map 13-1). French and English traders set up shop in southern Brazil to smuggle goods in return for Andean silver. All around the Gulf of Mexico and the Caribbean, merchants sneaked their goods into enemies' colonies.

After 1715, mercantilist wars occurred mainly outside Europe, as empires feuded over colonial possessions. These conflicts were especially bitter in border areas, particularly in the Caribbean and North America. Each round of warfare ratcheted up the scale and cost of fighting.

The **Seven Years' War** (known as the French and Indian War in the United States) marked the culmination of this rivalry among European empires around the globe. Fought from 1756 to 1763, it saw Native Americans, African slaves, Bengali princes, Filipino militiamen, and European footsoldiers dragged into a contest over imperial possessions and control of the seas. Some fleets, like the French at the Battle of Quiberon Bay, were dispatched to the bottom of the ocean. Some fortresses, like Spain's Havana, and Quebec

City fell to invaders. The battles in Europe were relatively indecisive (despite being large), except in the hinterlands. After all, what sparked the war was a skirmish of British colonial troops (featuring a lieutenant colonel named George Washington) allied with Seneca warriors against French soldiers in the Ohio Valley (see Map 13-2 for North American references). In India, the war had a decisive outcome, for here the East India Company trader Robert Clive rallied 850 European officers and 2,100 Indian recruits to defeat the French (there were but 40 French artillerymen) and their 50,000 Maratha allies at Plassey. The British seized the upper hand—over everyone—in India. Not only did the British drive off the French from the rich Bengali interior, but they also crippled Indian rulers' resistance against European intruders (see Map 12-5 for India references).

The Seven Years' War changed the balance of power around the world. Britain emerged as the foremost colonial empire. Its rivals, especially France and Spain, took a pounding; France lost its North American colonies, and Spain lost Florida (though it gained the Louisiana Territory west of the Mississippi in a secret deal with France). In India, as well, the French were losers and had to acknowledge British supremacy in the wealthy provinces of Bihar and Bengal. But overwhelmingly, the biggest losers were indigenous peoples everywhere. With the rise of one empire over all others, it was harder for Native Americans to play the Europeans off against each other. Maratha princes faced the same problem. Clearly, as worlds became more entangled, the gaps between winners and losers grew more pronounced.

CONCLUSION

In the 1750s, the world's regions were more economically connected than they had been a century and a half earlier. The process of integrating the resources of previous worlds apart that had begun with Christopher Columbus's voyages intensified during this period. Traders shipped a wider variety of commodities—from Baltic wood to Indian cotton, from New World silver and sugar to Chinese silks and porcelain—over longer distances. People increasingly wore clothes manufactured elsewhere, consumed beverages made from products cultivated in far-off locations, and used imported guns to settle local conflicts.

Everywhere, this integration and the consumer opportunities that it made possible came at a heavy price. Nowhere was it more costly than in the Americas, where colonization and exploitation led to the expulsion of Indians from their lands and the decimation of their numbers. The cost was also very high for the millions of Africans forced across the Atlantic to work New World plantations and for the millions more who did not survive the journey.

Along with sugar, silver was the product from the Americas that most transformed global trading networks and that showed how greater entanglements could both enrich and destabilize. Although Spanish colonizers mined New World silver and shipped it to western Europe and Asia, it was Spain's main competitors in Europe that gained the upper hand in the seventeenth and eighteenth centuries. Nearly one-third of the silver from the New World ended up in China as payment for products like porcelains and silks that consumers still regarded as the world's finest manufactures. But if China's economy remained vibrant, silver did play a part in the fall of one dynasty and the rise of another. For the Ottoman, Mughal, and Safavid empires, the influx of silver created rampant inflation and undermined their previous economic autonomy.

Certain societies coped with increased commercial exchange more successfully than others. The Safavid and Ming dynasties could not withstand the pressures; both collapsed. The Spanish, Ottoman, and Mughal dynasties managed to survive but faced increasing pressure from aggressive rivals. For newcomers to the integrating world, the opportunity to trade helped support new dynasties. Japan, Russia, and England emerged on the world stage. But even in these newer regimes, commerce and competition did not erase conflict. To the contrary, while the world was more together economically than ever before, greater prosperity for some hardly translated into peace for most.

Review and research materials are available at StudySpace: ⑤ WWNORTON.COM/STUDYSPACE

KEY TERMS

absolute monarchy (p. 519)	monetization (p. 506)
bullion (p. 506)	Muscovy (p. 514)
Canton system (p. 511)	Qing dynasty (p. 507)
chartered companies (p. 489)	Seven Years' War (p. 521)
enclosure (p. 518)	specie (p. 504)
Mamluks (p. 503)	Thirty Years' War (p. 517)
Manchus (p. 507)	Tokugawa shogunate
mercantilism (p. 488)	(p. 511)

Chronology

	1600	1650
THE AMERICAS	◆ 1607 *English establish Jamestown colony* ◆ 1608 *French establish colony of New France* ◆ 1624 *Dutch settle New Amsterdam*	
SOUTH ASIA		1658–1707 *Aurangzeb expands Mughal Empire* ◆- - - - - -
RUSSIA	1613 *Romanov dynasty established in Russia* ◆- - - - - - - - - - - - - - - - - - - -	◆ 1639 *Russian state's frontier reaches Pacific* 1682–1725 *Peter the Great rules Russia* ◆- - - -
EAST ASIA	1603 *Tokugawa Shogunate founded in Japan* ◆- -	◆ 1637 *Japanese expel European missionaries* ◆ 1641 *Dutch seize Melaka from Portuguese* 1644 *Ming dynasty falls to the Qing (rule from 1644 to 1912)* - - -
EUROPE	◆ 1600 *English East India Company established* ◆ 1602 *Dutch East India Company established* ◆- - - - - - - - - - - - - - - - - - - ◆ 1618–1648 *Thirty Years' War* ◆ 1621 *Dutch West India Company founded* 1643–1715 *Reign of France's Louis XIV* ◆- - - - -	
AFRICA	◆- 1600–1800 *Massive expansion of the Atlantic slave trade*	1690s–1713 *Oyo Empire expands to coast of Africa* ◆-
SOUTHWEST ASIA	1656–1676 *Koprulu reforms revitalize Ottoman Empire* ◆- - - - - - - - - - - - ◆	

STUDY QUESTIONS

1. Define mercantilism, and analyze how mercantilist practices affected all regions of the Atlantic world between 1600 and 1750.
2. Describe the plantation complex in the Caribbean. Why was it so valued by Europeans relative to other regions of the Americas?
3. Analyze how the Atlantic slave trade reshaped sub-Saharan African societies. Which regions and groups benefited from Africa's growing entanglements in global commerce?
4. Analyze how global trade affected the Ottoman and Mughal empires during this era. How did each regime respond to these growing entanglements?
5. List and describe major factors that caused the end of the Ming dynasty and the rise of the Qing dynasty in China. How did global trade affect this outcome? How did Qing rulers react to global commerce?
6. Analyze to what extent the Tokugawa shogunate succeeded in creating a strong central government in Japan. How did it avoid the problems associated with expanding trade that many other dynasties faced at this time?
7. Compare and contrast the expansionist policies of the Russian state with those pursued by the British and French regimes during this period. How were they similar and how were they different?
8. Analyze how increased global trade shaped the history of Europe during this period. Why did England tend to be the largest beneficiary of these trends in terms of regional dynastic rivalries? What other social and political groups were strongly affected by Europe's increased global entanglements?
9. Compare and contrast the impact of global commerce on European and Asian dynasties. Did any dynasty hold an advantage over others in controlling commercial networks and using them to enrich their societies?

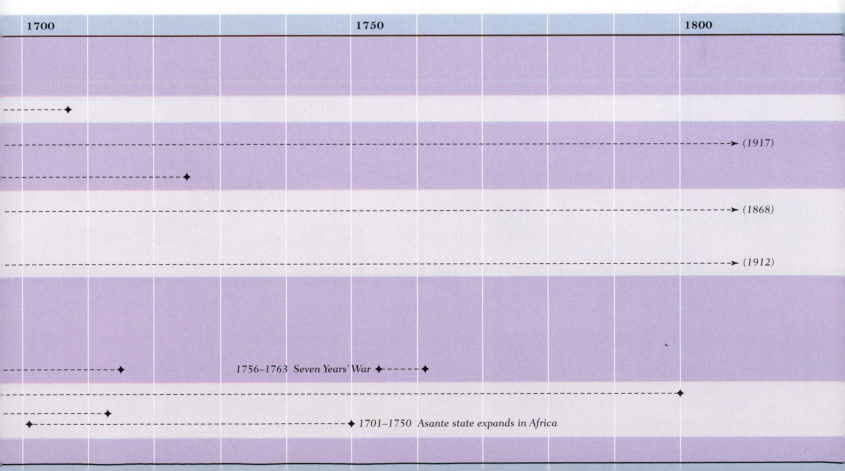

1700   1750   1800

(1917)

(1868)

(1912)

1756–1763 Seven Years' War

1701–1750 Asante state expands in Africa

Chapter

14

CULTURES OF SPLENDOR AND POWER, 1500–1780

In 1664, a sixteen-year-old girl from the provinces of New Spain asked her parents for permission to attend the university in the capital. Although she had mastered Greek logic, taught Latin, and become a proficient mathematician, she had two strikes against her: she was a woman, and her thinking ran against the grain of the Catholic Church. So keen was she to pursue her studies that she proposed to disguise herself as a man. But her parents denied her requests, and instead of attending the university she entered a convent in Mexico City, where she would spend the rest of her life. Fortunately, the convent turned out to be a sanctuary for her. There she studied science and mathematics and composed remarkable poetry. Sor (Sister) Juana Inés de la Cruz was her name, and she was the bard of a new world where people mixed in faraway places, where new wealth created new customs, and where new ideas began to take hold. One of her poems, called "You Men," began: "Silly, you men—so very adept / at wrongly faulting womankind, not seeing you're alone to blame / for faults you plant in woman's mind." Her poetry is an example of how new discoveries and new knowledge challenged old ways. But her life story also reminds us of the fierce resistance to new ways. Sor Juana's poetry enraged church authorities, who forced her to recant her words and who burned her books. Only the intervention of the viceroy's wife prevented officials from torching the nun's complete works before she died of a plague in 1695.

Sor Juana's story attests to the conflicts between new ideas and old orders that occurred once the entanglements of commerce and the consolidation of empires fostered knowledge of foreign ways. On the one hand, global commerce created riches that supported arts, architecture, and scientific ventures. On the other, experimentations in new ways caused discomfort among defenders of the old order and provoked backlashes against purveyors of innovation.

This chapter explores how global commerce enriched and reshaped cultures in the centuries after the Americas ceased to be worlds apart from Afro-Eurasia. Profiting from trade in New World commodities, many rulers and merchants displayed their power by commissioning fabulous works of art and majestic palaces and sprawling plazas. These cultural splendors were meant to impress, which they surely did. These efforts also demonstrated the growing connections between distant societies, reflecting how exotic, borrowed influences could blend with domestic traditions. Book production and consumption soared with some publications finding their way around the world. The spread of books and ideas and increasing cultural contact led to experiments in religious toleration and helped foster cultural diversity. Yet even as Europeans, who were the greatest beneficiaries of New World riches, claimed to advance new universal truths, cultural productions around the globe still showed the resilience of local traditions.

TRADE AND CULTURE

> → *How did world trade begin to change world cultures?*

It is not surprising that in 1500 the world's most dynamic cultures were in Asia, in areas profiting from the Indian Ocean and China Sea trades. It was in China and the Islamic world that the spice and luxury trades first flourished; here, too, rulers had successfully established political stability and centralized control of taxation, law making, and military force. This often involved recruiting people from diverse backgrounds and promoting new kinds of secular (nonreligious) education. Although older ways did not die out, both trade and empire building contributed to the spread of knowledge about distant people and foreign cultures.

Of course, some rulers and polities were more eager for change than others. Moreover, certain societies—in the Americas and the South Pacific, for example—found that contact, conquest, and commerce undermined indigenous cultural life. Although Europeans and native peoples often exchanged ideas and practices, these transfers were not equal. Native Americans, for example, adapted to European missionizing by creating mixed forms of religious worship—but only because they were under pressure to do so. And as the Europeans swallowed up new territories, it was *their* culture that spread and diversified. Indeed, the Europeans absorbed much from Native Americans and African slaves

Focus Questions

Ⓢ WWNORTON.COM/STUDYSPACE

→ *How did world trade begin to change world cultures?*

→ *How did the Islamic empires mix cultures?*

→ *How and why did Chinese and Japanese governments attempt to control culture and knowledge?*

→ *What were the major tenets of Enlightenment thought?*

→ *How did involvement in the slave trade reshape African cultures?*

→ *How did cultural developments in the Americas reflect global entanglements?*

→ *What role did "race" play in how Europeans viewed others, especially those from Oceania?*

MAIN THEMES

→ *Growing global commerce enriches and shapes cultures worldwide.*
→ *The major regions demonstrate pride in their traditions and celebrate political, economic, and cultural achievements.*
→ *Europeans and peoples of European descent in the Americas argue that their races and cultures are superior to all others.*

FOCUS ON *The Flourishing of Regional Cultures*

The Islamic World

◆ The Ottomans' unique cultural synthesis accommodates not only mystical Sufis and ultraorthodox ulama but also military men, administrators, and clerics.
◆ The Safavid state proclaims the triumph of Shiism and Persian influences in the sumptuous new capital, Isfahan.
◆ Mughal courtly culture values art and learning and welcomes non-Muslim contributions.

East Asia

◆ China's cultural flourishing, coming from within, is evident in the broad circulation of traditional ideas, publishing, and mapmaking.
◆ Japan's imperial court at Kyoto develops an elite culture of theater, stylized painting, tea ceremonies, and flower arranging.

Europe

◆ Cultural flourishing known as the Enlightenment yields a faith in reason and a belief in humans' ability to fathom the laws of nature and human behavior.
◆ European thinkers articulate a belief in unending human progress.
◆ Europeans expand into Australia and the South Pacific.

Africa

◆ Slave-trading states such as Asante, Oyo, and Benin celebrate royal power and wealth through art.

The Americas

◆ Even as Euro-Americans participate in the Enlightenment, their culture reflects Native American and African influences.

but offered them little share of sovereignty or wealth in return.

For many groups, the global cultural flourishing of this period owed much to the benefits of burgeoning world trade, which allowed some rulers to consolidate wealth, administration, and military power. These rulers were eager to patronize the arts as a way to legitimize their power and reflect their cultural sophistication. In Europe, monarchs known as **enlightened absolutists** restricted the clergy and nobility and hired loyal bureaucrats who championed the knowledge of the new age. British monarchs, though they were not absolutists (because they shared power with Parliament), followed suit. Mughal emperors, Safavid shahs, and Ottoman sultans glorified their regimes by bringing artists

and artisans from all over the world to give an Islamic flavor to their major cities and buildings. Rulers in China and Japan also looked to artists to extol their achievements. And in Africa, the wealth garnered from slave trading underwrote cultural productions of extraordinary merit.

Despite the unifying aspects of world trade, each society retained core aspects of its individuality. Ruling classes disseminated values based on cherished classical texts and long-established moral and religious principles. They mapped their geographies and wrote their histories according to their traditional visions of the universe. Even as global trade drew their attention outward and in some cases introduced foreign influences, societies celebrated their achievements in politics, economics, and culture with pride in their own heritages.

CULTURE IN THE ISLAMIC WORLD

→ *How did the Islamic empires mix cultures?*

For centuries, Muslim elites had generously funded cultural development. As the Ottoman, Safavid, and Mughal empires gained greater expanses of territory, they acquired new resources to fund more such pursuits. Rulers supported new schools and building projects, and the elite produced books, artworks, and luxury goods. Cultural life was connected to the politics of empire building, as emperors and elites sought greater prestige by patronizing intellectuals and artists.

Forged under contrasting imperial auspices, Islamic cultural and intellectual life now reflected three distinct worlds. In place of an earlier Islamic cosmopolitanism, unique cultural patterns prevailed within each empire. Although the Ottomans, the Safavids, and the Mughals shared a common faith, each developed a relatively autonomous form of Muslim culture.

THE OTTOMAN CULTURAL SYNTHESIS

By the sixteenth century, the Ottoman Empire was enjoying a remarkably rich culture that reflected a variety of mixing influences. Its blend of ethnic, religious, and linguistic elements exceeded those of previous Islamic empires. The Ottomans' cultural synthesis accommodated both Sufis (mystics who stressed contemplation and ecstasy through poetry, music, and dance) and ultraorthodox *ulama* (Islamic jurists who stressed tradition and religious law). It also balanced the interests of military men and administrators with those of clerics. Finally, it allowed autonomy to the minority faiths of Christianity and Judaism.

RELIGION AND LAW The Ottoman world achieved cultural unity, above all, by an outstanding intellectual achievement—its system of administrative law. As the empire absorbed diverse cultures and territories, the sultans realized that the *sharia* (Islamic holy law) would not suffice because it was silent on many secular matters. Moreover, the Ottoman state needed comprehensive laws to bridge differences among the many social and legal systems under its rule. Mehmed II, conqueror of Constantinople, began the reform. By recruiting young boys, rather than noblemen, for training as bureaucrats or military men and making them accountable directly to the sultan, he fashioned a professional bureaucracy with unswerving loyalty to the ruler. Mehmed's successor, Suleiman the Magnificent and the Lawgiver, continued this

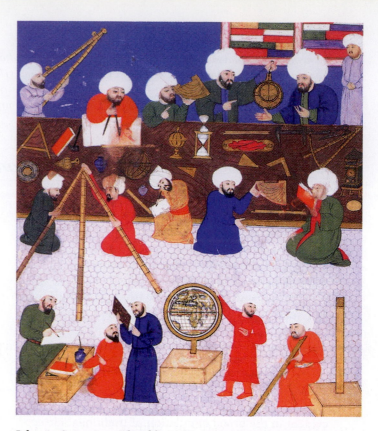

Islamic Scientists. This fifteenth-century Persian miniature shows Islamic scholars working with sophisticated navigational and astronomical instruments and reflects the importance that the educated classes in the Islamic world attached to observing and recording the regularities in the natural world. Indeed, many of Europe's advances in sailing drew upon knowledge from the Muslim world.

work by compiling a comprehensive legal code. The code addressed subjects' rights and duties, proper clothing, and how Muslims were to relate to non-Muslims. The code also reconciled many differences between administrative and religious law.

EDUCATION A sophisticated educational system was crucial for the empire's religious and intellectual integration and for its cultural achievements. Here, too, the Ottomans tolerated difference. They encouraged three educational systems that produced three streams of talent—civil and military bureaucrats, *ulama*, and Sufi masters. The administrative elite attended hierarchically organized schools that culminated in the palace schools at Topkapi (see Chapter 11). Graduates from these institutions staffed the civil and military bureaucracy all across the empire. In the religious sphere, an equally elaborate system took students from elementary schools (where they learned reading, writing, and numbers) on to higher schools, or *madrasas* (where they learned law, religious sciences, the Quran, and the regular sciences). These graduates became *ulama* who served as judges, experts in religious law, or teachers. Yet another set of schools, *tekkes*, taught the devotional strategies and religious knowledge for students to enter Sufi orders.

Each set of schools created lasting linkages between the ruling elite and the orthodox religious elite. The *tekkes*, especially, promoted social and religious solidarity and helped integrate Muslim peoples living under Ottoman rule. The value that the Ottomans placed on education and scholarship was evident in the saying that "an hour of learning was worth more than a year of prayer." It was also evident in the important advances that those schooled in Ottoman institutions made in astronomy and physics, as well as in history, geography, and politics.

SCIENCE AND THE ARTS Under the patronage of a reformist-minded grand vizier, Ottoman intellectuals also took an interest in works of European science. Some of these appeared in Turkish translation for the first time in the eighteenth century. The Ottomans' most impressive effort to spread European knowledge occurred when a Hungarian convert to Islam, Ibrahim Muteferrika, set up a printing press in Istanbul in 1729. Muteferrika published works on science, history, and geography. One included sections on geometry; the works of Copernicus, Galileo, and Descartes; and a plea to the Ottoman elite to learn from Europe. When his patron was killed, however, the *ulama* promptly closed off this promising avenue of contact with western learning.

The Ottomans combined inherited traditions with new elements in art as well. For example, portraiture became popular after the Italian painter Gentile Bellini visited Istanbul and composed a portrait of Mehmed II. In other areas, though, the Ottomans kept their own styles. Consider the magnificent architectural monuments of the sixteenth through eighteenth centuries, including mosques, gardens, tombs, forts, and palaces: these showed scant western influence. Nor were the Ottomans interested in western literature or music. For the most part, they believed that God had given the Islamic world a monopoly on truth and enlightenment and that their military successes proved his favor.

The Ottomans' capacity to celebrate their well-being and prosperity was most elegantly displayed during the so-called Tulip Period, which occurred in the first half of the eighteenth century. The elite had long admired the tulip's bold colors and graceful blooms, and for centuries the flower served as the sultans' symbol. In fact, both Mehmed the Conqueror and Suleiman the Magnificent grew tulips in the most secluded and prestigious courtyards at Topkapi Palace in Istanbul. And many Ottoman warriors heading into battle wore undergarments embroidered with tulips to ensure victory. By the early eighteenth century, estate owners had begun to specialize in growing the bulb; tulip designs appeared on tiles, fabrics, and public buildings, and authorities sponsored elaborate tulip festivals.

Fascination with the tulip represented a widespread delight in worldly things, which Grand Vizier Damat Ibrahim (r. 1718–1730) encouraged. As well as restoring order to the empire, Ibrahim loosened the *ulama*'s controls over social activities and sanctioned the elite's consumption of luxury goods. Commoners, too, now celebrated life's pleasures—in coffeehouses and taverns. Indeed, Ottoman demand for luxury goods grew so extensive (seeking lemons, soap, pepper, metal tools, coffee, and wine) that a well-traveled diplomat looked askance at the supposed wealth of Europe. He wrote, "In most of the provinces [of Europe], poverty is widespread, as a punishment for being infidels."

Ottoman Court Women. This eighteenth-century watercolor found in Topkapi Palace in Istanbul shows various musical instruments being played by court women, who were often called upon to provide entertainment.

The Ottomans and the Tulip. From the earliest times, the Ottomans admired the beauty of the tulip. (*Left*) Sultan Mehmed II smelling a tulip, symbol of the Ottoman sultans. (*Right*) The Ottomans used tulip motifs to decorate tiles in homes and mosques and pottery wares, as on the plate shown here.

Anyone who travels in these areas must confess that goodness and abundance are reserved for the Ottoman realms." Thus, despite challenges from western Europe and foreboding that their best days were behind them, the Ottomans took some foreign elements into their culture while preserving inherited ways.

SAFAVID CULTURE

The Safavid Empire in Persia (modern-day Iran) was not as long-lived as the Ottoman Empire, but it was significant for giving Shiism a home base and a location for displaying Shiite culture. There had been Shiite governments before, such as the Fatimid state in Egypt (see Chapter 9). But once the Mamluks overthrew the Fatimids in the thirteenth century, Shiism became overwhelmingly a religion of opposition to established rulers.

THE SHIITE EMPHASIS The Safavids faced a critical dilemma when they seized power. They had owed their rise to the support of Turkish-speaking tribesmen who followed a populist form of Islam. But in order to hold on to power, the Safavid shahs needed to cultivate powerful and conservative elements of Iranian society: Persian-speaking landowners and orthodox *ulama*. Thus they turned away from the more popular Turkish-speaking Islamic brotherhoods with their mystical and Sufi qualities and, instead, built a mixed political and religious system that extolled a Shiite vision of law and society and drew on older Persian imperial traditions. The brilliant culture that emerged during the Safavid period provided a unique blend of Shiism and Persia's distinctive historical identity. It found its highest expression in the city of Isfahan,

capital of the Safavid state from its creation in 1598 until the empire's end in 1722.

Just as the Ottomans' great achievement was in blending Sufism and clerical orthodoxy, so the Safavids' triumph was in creating a mixed political and religious system based on Shiism and loyalty to the royal family. Also like the Ottomans, the Safavids used established institutions like the *madrasas*, brotherhood lodges, and the *ulama* to promote Shiite orthodoxy and a Shiite-dominated culture. Even after the Safavids lost power in the eighteenth century, Shiism remained the fundamental religion of the Iranian people.

The most effective architect of a cultural life based on Shiite religious principles and Persian royal absolutism was shah Abbas I (r. 1587–1629). The location that he chose to display the wealth and royal power of his state, its Persian and Shiite heritages, and its artistic sensibility was the new capital city of Isfahan. For this purpose the shah hired skilled artists and architects to design a city that would dwarf even Delhi and Istanbul, the other showplaces of the Islamic world. The architectural goal was to create an earthly representation of heavenly paradise.

ARCHITECTURE AND OTHER CULTURAL PRODUCTIONS The Safavid shahs were unique among Afro-Eurasian rulers of this era, for they sought to project both absolute authority and accessibility. For example, their dwellings were unlike those of other rulers—such as Topkapi palace in Istanbul, the Citadel in Cairo, and the Red Forts of the Mughals. Those were enclosed and fortified buildings, designed to enhance rulers' power by concealing them from their subjects. In contrast, the buildings of Isfahan were open to the outside, demonstrating the Safavid rulers' desire to connect with their people.

Isfahan's centerpiece was the great plaza next to the royal palace and the royal mosque at the heart of the capital. The plaza, surrounded by elaborate public and religious buildings, measured 83,000 square meters—only slightly less than Tiananmen Square in Beijing, and seven times bigger than the plaza of San Marco in Venice. A seventeenth-century English visitor was suitably impressed, noting that the plaza was 1,000 paces from north to south and 200 from east to west and far larger than the largest urban squares in London and Paris. He added that it "is without doubt as spacious, as pleasant, and aromatic a market as any in the universe."

Other aspects of intellectual life also reflected the elites' aspirations, wealth, and commitment to Shiite principles. Safavid artists perfected the illustrated book, the outstanding example being *The King's Book of Kings*, which contained 250 miniature illustrations. Here, artists demonstrated their mastery of three-dimensional representation and their ability to harmonize different colors. In areas other than painting, proficient weavers produced highly ornate and beautiful silks and carpets for trade throughout the world; artisans painted tiles in vibrant colors and created mosaics that adorned mosques and other buildings. Moreover, the Safavids developed an elaborate calligraphy that was the envy of artists throughout the Islamic world. (See Primary Source: Islamic Views of the World.) In all these ways—but especially in shah Abbas's pride and joy, the city of Isfahan—the Safavids gave a Persian and Shiite emphasis to their stunning cultural flourishing.

POWER AND CULTURE UNDER THE MUGHALS

Like the Safavids and the Ottomans, the Mughals fostered a courtly high culture. Because they ruled over a large non-Muslim population, the culture that they developed in South Asia was broad and open. So highly did it value art and learning that it welcomed non-Muslims into its circle. Thus, while Islamic traditions dominated the empire's political and judicial systems, Hindus shared with Muslims the flourishing of learning, music, painting, and architecture. In this arena, aesthetic refinement and philosophical sophistication could bridge religious differences.

RELIGION The promise of an open Islamic high culture found its greatest fulfillment under the Mughal emperor Akbar (r. 1556–1605). This skillful military leader was also a popular ruler who allowed common people as well as nobles from all ethnic groups to converse with him at court. His quest for universal truths outside the strict *sharia* led him to develop a religion of his own, which incorporated many aspects of Hindu belief and ritual practice (see Chapter 12). His trusted advisor Abulfazl encouraged these multifaceted

pursuits and composed a tribute to the ruler and his predecessors, the *Akbarnamah* (the Book of Akbar). It describes Akbar as receiving kingship as a gift from God because he was a true philosopher and had been born a perfect person in the Sufi sense. The akbarnamah remains one of the major sources of early Mughal history.

ARCHITECTURE AND THE ARTS In architecture, too, the Mughals produced masterpieces that blended styles. This was already evident as builders combined Persian, Indian, and Ottoman elements in tombs and mosques built by Akbar's predecessors. But Akbar enhanced this mixture in the elaborate city he built at Fatehpur Sikri, beginning in 1571. The buildings included residences for nobles (whose loyalty Akbar wanted), gardens, a drinking and gambling zone, and even an experimental school devoted to studying language acquisition in children. Building the huge complex took a decade, much less time than it took for construction of Louis XIV's comparable royal residence—a century later—at Versailles.

Akbar Leading Religious Discussion. This miniature painting from 1604 shows Akbar receiving Muslim theologians and Jesuits. The Jesuits (in the black robes on the left) hold a page relating, in Persian, the birth of Christ. A lively debate will follow the Jesuits' claims on behalf of Christianity.

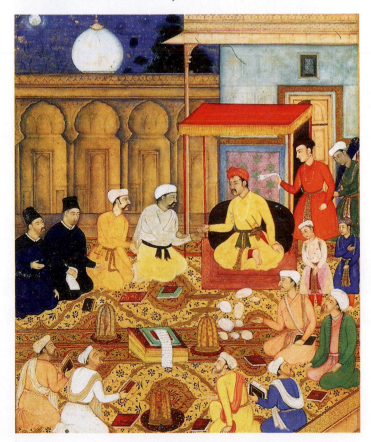

ISLAMIC VIEWS OF THE WORLD

Although maps give the impression of objectivity and geographic precision, they actually reveal the mapmakers' views of the world (via the way they arrange the world, names of locations, areas placed in the center or at the peripheries, and accompanying text). In most cultures, official maps located their own major administrative and religious sites at the center of the universe and reflected local elites' ideas about how the world was organized.

The two maps shown here are from the Islamic world. The map of al-Idrisi, dating from the twelfth century, was a standard one of the period. Showing the world as Afro-Eurasian peoples knew it at that time, the map features only three landmasses: Africa, Asia, and Europe. The second map, made in Iran around 1700, was unabashedly Islamic: it offers a grid that measures the distances from any location in the Islamic world to the holy city of Mecca.

→ *What does each map reveal about the worldview of these Islamic societies?*

→ *What purposes do you think each map was used for?*

SOURCES: (left) Giraudon/Art Resource, NY; (right) Private Collection, courtesy of the owner and D. A. King, contributor; phot. by Christie's of London.

Al-Idrisi map, twelfth century

Iranian map, seventeenth century

Akbar's descendant Shah Jahan was also a lavish patron of architecture and the arts. In 1630, Shah Jahan ordered the building in Agra of a magnificent white marble tomb for his beloved wife, Mumtaz Mahal. Like many other women in the Mughal court, she had been an important political counselor. Designed by an Indian architect of Persian origin, this structure, the **Taj Mahal**, took 20 years and 20,000 workers to build. The 42-acre complex included a main gateway, a garden, minarets, and a mosque. The translucent marble mausoleum lay squarely in the middle of the structure, enclosed by four identical facades and crowned by a majestic central dome rising to 240 feet. The stone inlays of different types and hues, organized in geometrical and floral patterns, and featuring Quranic verses inscribed in Arabic

The Taj Mahal. A symbol of Mughal splendor, the Taj Mahal was a mausoleum that was built of white marble. Often described as poetry in stone, it was constructed under Shah Jahan as an homage to his deceased wife, Mumtaz Mahal (*right*).

calligraphy gave the surface an appearance of delicacy and lightness. Blending Persian and Islamic design with Indian materials and motifs, this poetry in stone represented the most splendid example of Mughal high culture and the combining of cultural traditions. Like Shah Abbas's great plaza, the Taj Mahal gave a sense of refined grandeur to this empire's power and splendor. (See Global Connections & Disconnections: Royal Architecture in the Age of Splendor and Power.)

FOREIGN INFLUENCES VERSUS ISLAMIC CULTURE Under later emperors, Mughal culture remained vibrant although not quite so brilliant. François Bernier, a seventeenth-century French traveler, wrote admiringly of the broad philosophical interests of Danishmand Khan, whom the emperor Aurangzeb had appointed as governor of Delhi. According to Bernier, Khan avidly read the works of the French philosophers Gassendi and Descartes and studied Sanskrit treatises to understand different philosophical traditions. But Aurangzeb, a pious Muslim, favored Islamic arts and sciences. He dismissed many of the court's painters and musicians, and in 1669 ordered that all recently built non-Islamic places of worship be torn down. In his court, intellectuals debated whether metaphysics, astronomy, medicine, mathematics, and ethics were of use in the practice of Islam. Women, at least at court, apparently were allowed to pursue the arts, for two of Aurangzeb's daughters were accomplished poets.

Well into the eighteenth century, the Mughal nobility exuded confidence and lived in unrivaled luxury. The presence of foreign scholars and artists enhanced the courtly culture, and the elite eagerly consumed exotic goods from China and Europe. Foreign trade also brought in more silver, advancing the money economy and supporting the nobles' sumptuous lifestyles. In addition, the Mughals assimilated European military technology: they hired Europeans as gunners and military engineers in their armies, employed them to forge guns, and bought guns and cannons from them. However, Mughal appreciation for other European knowledge and technology was limited. Thus, when a representative of the English East India Company presented an edition of Mercator's *Maps of the World* to the emperor in 1617, the emperor returned it a fortnight later with the remark that no one could read or understand it. The Mughals, like the Ottomans, remained supremely confident of their own cultural world.

The Islamic world drew on intellectual currents that spanned the Eurasian–North African landmass, for its centers were in Istanbul, Cairo, Isfahan, and Delhi. From Islam's founding, Muslims had looked to India and China, not to Europe, for inspiration. True, the Crusades had proved that Europeans could be worthy military rivals (see Chapter 10), and the increasing wealth and power of Christian kingdoms enriched by New World colonies made those cultures more imposing. Yet even as Muslims brought a few new European elements into their cultural mix, most still regarded Europeans as rude barbarians. More impressive in the eyes of elites in Persia, India, and the Ottoman Empire were the cultural splendors to be found to the east, not the west.

ROYAL ARCHITECTURE IN THE AGE OF
SPLENDOR AND POWER

By the seventeenth century, all the great imperial monarchies of Afro-Eurasia had elaborate architectural structures that projected their states' power and values. All were ornate and splendid, were expensive to construct, and involved the best craftsmen and artists available. In the case of the Ottoman, Safavid, and Mughal royal structures, emperors brought in skilled craftsmen from outside their empires, thereby indirectly borrowing from other cultures. Yet, each structure reflected unique elements of its own culture as well as the vision of the rulers who paid for its construction.

The **Forbidden City of Beijing** was the earliest of these impressive sites of royal power. (See illustration on p. 437.) Beijing became the capital of a unified Chinese empire under the Mongols in the thirteenth century, although it had enjoyed prominence in earlier times. Chinggis Khan destroyed the old city, but his successor, Kubilai Khan, restored it as his imperial capital. Following the classical ideal of early Chinese capitals, he rebuilt it along north-south and east-west axes, surrounded it with high walls, and housed the emperor and his court deep within—in the Imperial City and the Forbidden City. These represented the center of the Chinese state. Here, government took place; only those who had business with the state won permission to enter, and they had to bow and scrape ("kowtow") to indicate utmost respect for the

Isfahan. On the great plaza at Isfahan, markets and government offices operated in close proximity to the public Shah Abbas Mosque, shown here, and the shah's private mosque. This structure represented Shah Abbas's desire to unite control of trade, government, and religion under one leader.

emperor's power. The ruler remained within the confines of the imperial quarters (although later Qing emperors traveled somewhat), relying on envoys and chief ministers for information about the kingdom and the world beyond its borders.

The center of Safavid power in the seventeenth century was the **great plaza at Isfahan**, the inspiration of Shah Abbas (r. 1587–1629). This structure reflected his desire to bring trade, government, and religion together under the authority of the supreme political leader. An enormous public mosque, the Shah Abbas Mosque, dominated one end of the plaza, which measured 1,667 feet by 517 feet. At the other end were trading stalls and markets. Along one side sat government offices; the other side offered the exquisite Mosque of Shaykh Lutfollah for the shah's personal use. Many of Shah Abbas's most proficient craftsmen came from India and were familiar with the architecture of the Mughal Empire.

The French monarch Louis XIV built the **Palace of Versailles** in the 1670s–1680s at the site of a royal hunting lodge outside Paris, the French capital. (See illustration on p. 519.) This elaborate structure has many similarities with the Isfahan plaza, although the French builders had no knowledge of Isfahan. Here, too, the royal palace opens onto an expansive courtyard. The buildings adjoining the central palace housed important nobles and clergy, whom the French monarchs wanted to keep an eye on.

The **Topkapi Palace** in Istanbul, capital of the Ottoman Empire, began to take shape in 1458 under Mehmed II and underwent steady expansion over the years. (See illustration on p. 422.) Topkapi projected royal authority in much the same way as the Forbidden City emphasized Chinese emperors' power: governing officials worked enclosed within massive walls, and monarchs rarely went outside their inner domain. By isolating their rulers from the rest of society, Ottomans and Chinese alike made their monarchs' power seem even more awesome.

Another advocate of royal architecture was the Mughal emperor Shah Jahan (r. 1628–1658). He is best known for his peacock throne; for the Taj Mahal, which he built as a magnificent tomb for his wife, Mumtaz Mahal (see illustration on p. 533); and for his building program for the state's capital at Delhi.

Shah Jahan's Peacock Throne. Embedded with precious stones, Shah Jahan's peacock throne was meant to present the shah as the supreme ruler.

CULTURE AND POLITICS IN EAST ASIA

> → *How and why did Chinese and Japanese governments attempt to control culture and knowledge?*

Like the Ottomans, Safavids, and Mughals, the Chinese did not need to prove the richness of their scholarly and artistic traditions. China had long been a renowned center of learning, with its emperors and elites supporting artists, poets, musicians, scientists, and teachers. But in late Ming and early Qing China, cultural flourishing owed less to imperial patronage than to a booming internal market. Indeed, a growing population and extensive commercial networks propelled the circulation of ideas as well as goods. As a result, China's cultural sphere expanded and diversified well before similar changes occurred elsewhere.

In Japan, too, prosperity promoted cultural dynamism. Because of its giant neighbor across the sea, the Japanese people had always been aware of outside influences. Like the Chinese government, the Tokugawa shogunate tried to promote Confucian notions of a social hierarchy organized on the basis of social position, age, gender, and kin. It also tried to shield the country from highly egalitarian ideas that would threaten the strict social hierarchy. But the forces that undermined governmental control of knowledge in China proved even stronger in Japan. Here, a decentralized political system enabled different cultural influences to spread, including European ideas and practices. By the eighteenth century, in struggling to define its own identity through these contending currents, the cultural scene in Japan was more lively, open, and varied than its counterpart in China.

CHINA: THE CHALLENGE OF EXPANSION AND DIVERSITY

While China had become increasingly connected with the outside world in the sixteenth and seventeenth centuries, the sources for its cultural flourishing during the period came primarily from within. Although new opportunities for cultural exchange with foreigners left their mark, it was internal social changes that propelled the circulation of books and ideas.

PUBLISHING AND THE TRANSMISSION OF IDEAS
Broader circulation of ideas had more to do with the decentralization of book production than with technological innovations. After all, woodblock and moveable type printing had been present in China for centuries. Although initially the state had spurred book production by printing Confucian texts, before long the economy's increasing commercialization

weakened government controls over what got printed. Even as officials clamped down on unorthodox texts, there was no centralized system of censorship, and unauthorized opinions circulated freely.

By the late Ming era, a burgeoning publishing sector catered to the diverse social, cultural, and religious needs of educated elites and urban populations. European visitors admired the vast collections of printed materials housed in Chinese libraries, describing them as "magnificently built" and "finely adorn'd." In fact, the late Ming was an age of collections of other sorts as well. Members of the increasingly affluent elite acquired objects for display (such as paintings, ceramics, and calligraphy) as a sign of their status and refinement. Connoisseurship of all the arts reached unprecedented levels. Consumers could build collections by purchasing artworks from multiple sources—from roadside peddlers to monks to gentlemen dealers, whose proclaimed love of art masked the commercial orientation of their passions.

Perhaps more important, books and other luxury goods were now more affordable. For example, a low-quality commentary on the Confucian classics published in 1615 cost only half a tael of silver (a measurement based on the silver's weight). Even a low-level private tutor could earn more than forty taels a year, making it possible to gradually develop a small personal library. Increasingly, publishers offered a mix of wares: guidebooks for patrons of the arts, travelers, or merchants; handbooks for performing rituals, choosing dates for ceremonies, or writing proper letters; almanacs and encyclopedias; morality books; medical manuals.

Especially popular were study aids for the civil service examination. In fact, after the late fifteenth century, when examinees had to submit a highly structured eight-part essay, model essays flooded the market. In 1595, Beijing reeled with scandal over news that the second-place graduate had reproduced verbatim several model essays published by commercial printers. Just over twenty years later, the top graduate plagiarized a winning essay submitted years earlier. Ironically, then, the increased circulation of knowledge led critics to bemoan a decline in real learning; instead of mastering the classics, they charged, examination candidates were simply memorizing the work of others.

Examination hopefuls were not the only beneficiaries of the book trade, for elite women also joined China's literary culture. As readers, writers, and editors, these women now began to penetrate what used to be an exclusively male domain. Anthologies of women's poetry were especially popular, not only in the market but when issued in limited circulation to celebrate the refinement of the writer's family. Men of letters soon recognized the market potential of women's writings; some also saw women's less regularized style (usually acquired through family channels rather than state-sponsored schools) as a means to challenge stifling stylistic conformity. On rare occasions, women even served as publishers themselves.

Chinese Civil Service Exam. Lining the sides of this Chinese examination compound were cells in which candidates sat for the examination. Other than three long boards—the highest served as a shelf, the middle one as a desk, and the lowest as a seat—the cell had neither furniture nor a door. Indeed, the cells were little more than spaces partitioned on three sides by brick walls and covered by a roof; the floors were packed dirt. Generations of candidates spent three days and two nights in succession in these cells as they strove to enter officialdom.

Although elite women enjoyed success in the world of culture, the period brought increasing restrictions on their lives. Remarriage of widows and premarital sex might have met with disapproval in earlier times, but now they were utterly unthinkable for women from "good" families. Ironically, the thriving publishing sector indirectly promoted the stricter morality by printing plays and novels that echoed the government's conservative attitudes. Meanwhile, the practice of footbinding (which elite women first adopted around the late Tang-Song period) continued to spread among common people, as small, delicate feet came to signify femininity and respectability. (For more on footbinding, see Chapter 18.)

POPULAR CULTURE AND RELIGION Important as the book trade was, it had only an indirect impact on most men and women in late Ming China. Those who could not read well or at all absorbed cultural values through oral communication, ritual performance, and daily practices. The Ming government tried to control these channels, too. It appointed village elders as guardians of local society, and it instituted "village compacts" to ensure shared responsibility for proper conduct and observation of the laws.

Still, the everyday life of rural and small-town dwellers went on outside these official networks. Apart from toiling in the field, villagers participated in various religious and cultural practices, such as honoring local guardian spirits, patronizing Buddhist and Daoist temples, or watching performances by touring theater groups. Furthermore, villagers often took group pilgrimages to religious sites and attended markets in nearby towns, which drew them in with restaurants, brothels, and other types of entertainment. At the marketplaces the visitors would gather news and gossip in the teahouses or listen to the tales of itinerant storytellers and traveling monks. The open-ended nature of such cultural activities meant that village audiences had opportunities to reinterpret official norms to serve their own purposes and to contest the government's rules. For example, the common people could take officially approved morality tales celebrating the deeds of just and impartial officials and use them to challenge the real-life behavior of government bureaucrats.

Another manifestation of late-Ming cultural flourishing was the fervor associated with popular religions that mingled various cultural traditions. Here, at the grassroots level, there was little distinction among Buddhist, Daoist, and local cults. After all, the Chinese believed in cosmic unity; and although they venerated spiritual forces, they did not consider any of them to be a Supreme Being who favored one sect over another. They believed it was the emperor, rather than any religious group, who held the Mandate of Heaven. To the Chinese, the enforcement of orthodox values was more a matter of political than of religious control. Unless sects posed an obvious threat, the emperor had no reason to regulate their spiritual practices. This situation promoted religious tolerance and avoided the sectarian warfare that plagued post-Reformation Europe.

TECHNOLOGY AND CARTOGRAPHY Belief in cosmic unity did not prevent the Chinese from devising technologies to master nature's operations in this world. For example, the magnetic compass, gunpowder, and the printing press were all Chinese inventions. Moreover, Chinese technicians had mastered iron casting and produced mechanical clocks centuries before Europeans did. Chinese astronomers also compiled accurate records of eclipses, comets, novae, and meteors. In part, the emperor's needs drove their interest in astronomy and calendrical science. After all, it was his job as the Son of Heaven, and thus mediator between heaven and earth, to determine the best dates for planting, holding

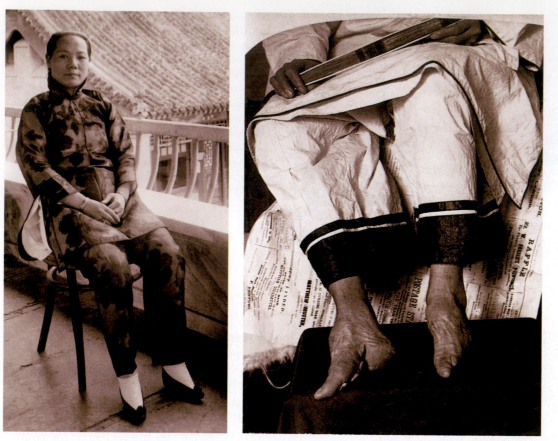

Footbinding. Two images of bound feet: (*left*) as an emblem of feminine respectability when wrapped and concealed, as on this well-to-do Chinese woman; (*right*) as an object of curiosity and condemnation when exposed for the world to see.

festivities, scheduling mourning periods, and convening judicial court sessions. The Chinese believed that the empire's stability depended on correct calculation of these dates.

European missionaries and traders arriving in China were awed by Chinese technological expertise, eloquence, and artistic refinement. Nonetheless, convinced that their sciences were superior, Christian missionaries tried to promote their own knowledge in areas such as astronomy and **cartography** (mapmaking). Possessing sophisticated sciences of their own, the Chinese were selective in appropriating these novel European practices. To be sure, members of the Jesuit order served in the imperial astronomy bureau and, in the early eighteenth century, undertook monumental surveys for the Qing emperor. However, the Europeans' overall cultural impact in China during this period was limited.

In the realm of cartography, the Chinese demonstrated most clearly their understanding of the world. Their maps encompassed elements of history, literature, and art—not just technical detail. It was not that "scientific" techniques were lacking; a map made as early as 1136 reveals that Chinese cartographers could readily draw to scale. Yet, valuing written text over visual and other forms of representation, Chinese elites did not always treat geometric and mathematical precision as the main objective of cartography. Reflecting the elites' worldview, most maps placed the realm of the Chinese emperor, as the ruler of "All under Heaven," at the center, surrounded by foreign countries. Thus the physical scale of China and distances to other lands were distorted. Still, some of the maps cover a vast expanse: one includes an area stretching from Japan to the Atlantic, encompassing Europe and Africa. (See Primary Source: Chinese Views of the World.)

Europeans did not know what to make of the Chinese resistance to their science. In 1583, the Jesuit missionary Matteo Ricci brought European maps to China, hoping to impress the elite with European learning. Challenging their belief that the world was flat, his maps demonstrated that the earth was spherical—and that China was just one country among many others. Yet Chinese critics complained that Ricci treated the Ming Empire as "a small unimportant country." As a concession, he placed China closer to the center of the maps and provided additional textual information. Still, his maps had a negligible impact, as neither the earth's shape nor precise scale was particularly important to most Chinese geographers.

Before the nineteenth century, the Chinese had fairly incomplete knowledge about foreign lands despite a long history of contact. The empire saw itself as superior to all others (a common feature of many cultures). Chinese writers, for example, often identified groups of other people through distinctive and, to them, odd physical features. A Ming geographical publication portrayed the Portuguese as "seven feet tall, having eyes like a cat, a mouth like an oriole, an ash-

Primary Source

CHINESE VIEWS OF THE WORLD

The Chinese developed cartographical skills early in their history. A third-century map, no longer extant, was designed to enable the emperors to "comprehend the four corners of the world without ever having to leave their imperial quarters." The Huayi tu (Map of Chinese and Foreign Lands) from 1136 depicted the whole world on stone stele, including 500 place names and textual information on foreign lands. Chinese maps typically devoted more attention to textual explanations with moral and political messages than to locating places accurately. One such map, the Chinese wheel map from the 1760s, is full of textual explanations.

➔ *Why do you think Chinese maps included messages that focused on moral and political themes?*

➔ *How are these maps similar to and different from the Islamic maps shown on p. 532?*

SOURCES: (left) The Needham Research Institute; (right) The British Library, London.

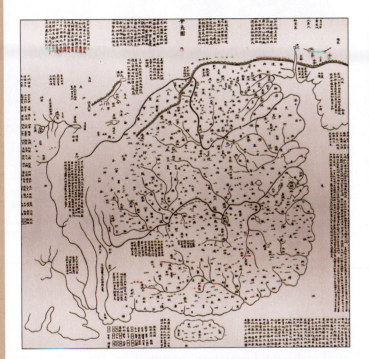

The *Huayi tu* map, 1136

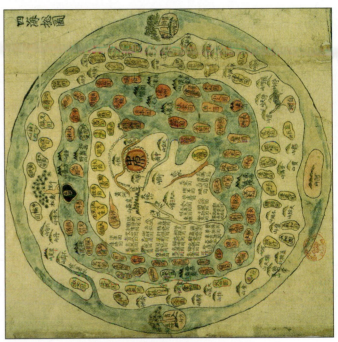

Chinese wheel map, 1760s

white face, thick and curly beards like black gauze, and almost red hair." Chinese elites glorified their "white" complexions against the peasants' dark skin; against the black, wavy-haired "devils" of Southeast Asia; and against the Europeans' "ash-white" pallor. Qing authors in the eighteenth century confused France with the Portugal known during Ming times, and they characterized England and Sweden as dependencies of Holland. During this period of cultural flourishing, in short, most Chinese did not feel compelled to revise their view of the world.

CULTURAL IDENTITY AND TOKUGAWA JAPAN

Chinese cultural influence had long crossed the Sea of Japan, but under the Tokugawa shogunate there was also interest in European culture. This interest grew via the Dutch presence in Japan and via limited contacts with Russians. At the same time, there was a surge in the study of Japanese traditions and culture. Thus, Tokugawa Japan engaged in a three-cornered conversation among time-honored Chinese ways (transmitted via Korea), European teachings, and distinctly Japanese traditions.

NATIVE ARTS AND POPULAR CULTURE   Until the sixteenth and seventeenth centuries, the main patrons of Japanese culture were the imperial court in Kyoto, the hereditary shogunate, religious institutions, and a small upper class. These groups developed an elite culture of theater and stylized painting. Samurai (former warriors turned bureaucrats) and daimyo (regional lords) favored a masked theater, called Nō, and an elegant ritual for making tea and engaging in contemplation. In their gardens, the lords built teahouses with stages for Nō drama. These gave rise to hereditary schools of actors, tea masters, and flower arrangers. The elites also hired commoner-painters to decorate tea utensils and other fine articles and to paint the brilliant interiors and standing screens in grand stone castles. Some upper-class men did their own painting, which conveyed philosophical thoughts. Calligraphy was proof of refinement.

Alongside the elite culture arose a rougher urban one that artisans and merchants patronized. Urban dwellers could purchase, for example, works of fiction and colorful prints (often risqué) made from carved wood blocks, and they could enjoy the company of female entertainers known as geisha. These women were skilled (*gei*) in playing the three-stringed instrument (*shamisen*), storytelling, and performing; some were also prostitutes. Geisha worked in the cities' pleasure quarters, which were famous for their geisha houses, public baths, brothels, and theaters. Kabuki—a type of theater that combined song, dance, and skillful staging to dramatize conflicts between duty and passion—became wildly popular. This art form featured dazzling acting, brilliant makeup, and sumptuous costumes. In 1629 the shogunate, concerned for public order, banned female actors; thereafter men played women's roles. These male actors sometimes maintained their impersonations offstage, inspiring fashion trends for urban women.

Much popular entertainment chronicled the world of the common people rather than politics or high society. The urbanites' pleasure-oriented culture was known as "the floating world" (*ukiyo*), and the woodblock prints depicting it as *ukiyo-e* (*e* meaning "picture"). Here, the social order was temporarily turned upside down. Those who were usually considered inferior—actors, musicians, courtesans, and others seen as possessing low morals—became idols. Even some upper-class samurai partook of this "lower" culture. But to enter the pleasure quarters they had to leave behind their swords, a mark of rank, since commoners were not allowed to carry such weapons.

Literacy in Japan now surged, especially among men. The most popular novels sold 10,000 to 12,000 copies. In the late eighteenth century, Edo had some sixty booksellers and hundreds of book lenders. In fact, the presence of so many lenders allowed books to spread to a wider public that

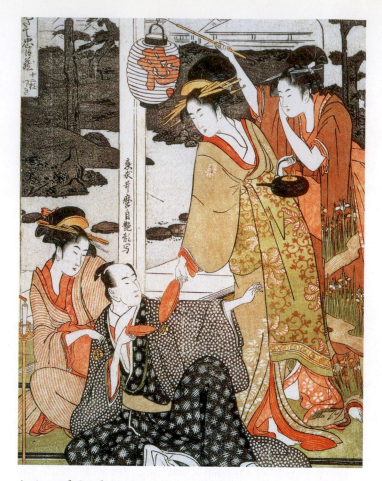

Artist and Geisha at Tea. The erotic, luxuriant atmosphere of Japan's urban pleasure quarters was captured in a new art form, the *ukiyo-e*, or "pictures from a floating world." In this image set in Tokyo's celebrated Yoshiwara district, several geisha flutter about a male artist.

previously could not afford to buy them. By the late eighteenth century, as more books circulated and some of them criticized the government, officials tried to censor certain publications.

THE INFLUENCE OF CHINA   In the realm of higher culture, China loomed large in the Tokugawa world. Japanese scholars wrote imperial histories of Japan in the Chinese style, and Chinese law codes and other books attracted a significant readership. Some Japanese traveled south to Nagasaki to meet Zen Buddhist masters and Chinese residents there. A few Chinese monks even won permission to found monasteries outside Nagasaki and to give lectures and construct temples in Kyoto and Edo.

Although Buddhist temples grew in number, they did not displace the native Japanese practice of venerating ancestors and worshipping gods in nature. Later called Shintō ("the way of the gods"), this practice boasted a network of shrines throughout the country. Shintō developed from time-honored beliefs in spirits, or *kami*, who were associated with places (mountains, rivers, waterfalls, rocks, the moon) and activities (harvest, fertility). Seeking healing or other assistance, adherents appealed to these spirits in nature and daily life through incantations and offerings. Some women under Shintō served as *mikos*, a kind of shamaness with special divinatory powers.

Shintō rituals competed with a powerful strain of neo-Confucianism that issued moral and behavioral guidelines. For example, in 1762 "Greater Learning for Females" appeared—an influential text that made Confucian teachings understandable for nonscholars. In particular, it outlined social roles that stressed hierarchy based on age and gender as a way to ensure order. At the same time, merit became important in determining one's place in the social hierarchy. Doing the right thing (propriety) and being virtuous were key.

By the early eighteenth century, neo-Confucian teachings of filial piety and loyalty to superiors had become the official state creed. This philosophy legitimated the social hierarchy and the absolutism of political authorities, but it also instructed the shogun and the upper class to provide "benevolent administration" for the people's benefit. That meant taking into account petitioners' complaints and requests, whether for improved irrigation and roads or for punishment of unfair officials.

Reacting to a creed adapted from non-native traditions, and desiring to honor their own country's greatness, some thinkers promoted intellectual traditions from Japan's past. These efforts stressed "native learning," Japanese texts, and Japanese uniqueness. In so doing, they formalized a Japanese religious and cultural tradition, and they denounced Confucianism and Buddhism as foreign contaminants. A few thinkers also looked to the uninterrupted imperial line in Kyoto (which did not govern) for validation of Japan's intellectual lineage and cultural superiority. Some who called for restored rule by the emperor faced arrest by the shogun's military men, but others went on to develop Japanese poetry. This art form, which expressed a yearning for a glorious lost age, became popular with both upper and lower classes.

EUROPEAN INFLUENCES Not only did Chinese intellectual influences compete with revived native learning, but by the late seventeenth century Japan was also tapping other sources of knowledge. At this time Portuguese was the common language in East Asia, and even the Dutch used it in communicating with the Japanese. By 1670, however, a guild of Japanese interpreters in Nagasaki who could speak and read Dutch accompanied Dutch merchants on trips to Edo. As European knowledge spread to high circles in Edo, in 1720 the shogunate lifted its ban on foreign books. Thereafter European ideas, called "Dutch learning," circulated more openly. Scientific, geographical, and medical texts appeared in Japanese translations and in some cases displaced Chinese texts. A Japanese-Dutch dictionary appeared in 1745, and the first official school of Dutch learning followed. Students of Dutch or European teachings remained a limited segment of Japanese society, but the demand for translations intensified.

One strong proponent of the European orientation was Honda Toshiaki (1744–1821), who visited the northern frontier in Ezo, studied European texts, and set down his thoughts in unpublished manuscripts. Toshiaki believed that Japan should learn about European advances in science—especially geography and astronomy, which aided ocean trade. He also praised European economic progress while extolling Japan's neighbor to the north, the Russian Empire. For Toshiaki, Japan's greatness depended on its ability to keep pace with advances outside Japan. But he did not reject Confucianism or Japan's system of social ranks based on Confucianism, and he showed Confucian contempt for unethical businessmen. His celebrations of European prowess mainly conveyed his pragmatism about adaptation and his aspirations for Japan's future.

Kabuki Theater. Kabuki originated among dance troupes in the environs of temples and shrines in Kyoto in the late sixteenth and early seventeenth centuries. As kabuki spread to the urban centers of Japan, the theater designs enabled the actors to enter and exit from many directions and to step out into the audience, lending the skillful, raucous shows great intimacy.

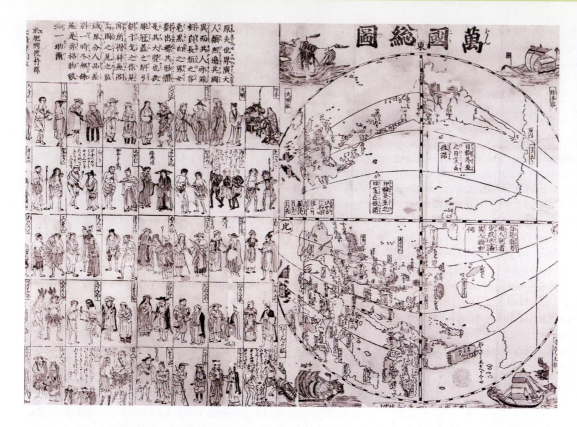

Japanese Map of the World. Japanese maps underwent a shift in connection with encounters with the Dutch. Here, in a map dated 1671, much information is incorporated about distant lands, both cartographically on the globe and pictorially, to the left, in two-person images representing various peoples of the world in their purported typical costumes.

Japan's internal debates about what to borrow from the Europeans and the Chinese illustrate the changes that the world had undergone in recent centuries. A few hundred years earlier, products and ideas generally did not travel beyond coastal regions and had only a limited effect (especially inland) on local cultural practices. By the eighteenth century, though, expanded networks of exchange and new prosperity made the integration of foreign ideas feasible and, sometimes, desirable. The Japanese were especially eager to transform useful new ideas and practices. They did not consider the embracing of outside influences as a mark of inferiority or subordination, particularly when they could put those influences to good use. This was not the case for the great Asian land-based empires, which were eager lenders but hesitant borrowers.

THE ENLIGHTENMENT IN EUROPE

> → *What were the major tenets of Enlightenment thought?*

An extraordinary cultural flowering also blossomed in Europe during the seventeenth and eighteenth centuries. Often the **Enlightenment** is defined purely in intellectual terms as the spreading of faith in reason and in universal rights and laws, but this era encompassed broader developments, such as the expansion of literacy, the spread of critical thinking, and the decline of religious persecution. Part of what gave Enlightenment thinkers such influence in Europe and beyond was that they wanted not just to convey new ideas to the elite but also to spread them widely. They hoped to change their contemporaries' worldviews and to transform political and social institutions.

Crucial for the success of this endeavor were widening patronage networks. Previously such networks had involved religious and monarchical supporters of arts and sciences, but they now extended to the lower aristocracy and bureaucratic and commercial elites as well. Equally important were cafés and intellectual salons, public theaters, exchanges of correspondence, and newspaper and book publishing. The male and female thinkers of this period disagreed about many things, but they shared a desire to "spread light" and to speak their minds about how to improve their societies, something that often made them troublesome to religious and political authorities.

Abandoning Christian belief in God's mysterious tampering with natural forces and human events, Enlightenment thinkers wanted to know the world in new ways. They sought universal and objective knowledge that would not reflect any particular religion, political view, class, or gender. Recognizing no territorial boundaries, these scholars struggled to formulate natural laws that would, they presumed, apply everywhere and to all peoples. Most of these thinkers were unaware of the extent to which European, upper-class male perspectives colored their "objective" knowledge.

ORIGINS OF THE ENLIGHTENMENT

While the sixteenth century brought new prosperity, the seventeenth century produced civil and religious wars, dynastic conflicts, and famine. These crises devastated central Europe. They bankrupted the Spanish, caused chaos in France, led to the execution of the English king, and saw the Dutch break free from Spanish control. They also contributed to the spread of Protestantism in Europe. At the same time, the crises made some intellectuals wish to turn their backs on religious strife, and to develop useful ways for understanding and improving *this* world. By 1750, too, in some western countries, a larger share of the population was eager to join in these discussions. As literate, middle-class men and women gained confidence in being able to reason for themselves, to understand the world without calling on traditional authorities, and to publicly criticize what they found distasteful or wrong, contemporaries recognized that they were living in an increasingly "enlightened" age.

It helps to pause and consider the development of this confidence, and of Enlightenment knowledge as a whole. First, the Reformation and Counter-Reformation (see Chapter 12) were significant in increasing literacy and diffusing the new science and its premises. Second, greater contacts between Europeans and the wider world after the fourteenth century were key. After all, Europeans had become eager consumers of other peoples' cultural goods. From Native American trapping methods to African slaves' crop cultivation techniques, from Chinese porcelain to New World tobacco and chocolate, contact with others influenced Europe in the seventeenth and eighteenth centuries. Yet the more they learned, the more European intellectuals became critical of other cultures—and more confident that their own culture was unique, superior, and the standard against which to judge all others. (See Primary Source: European Views of the World.)

THE NEW SCIENCE

The search for new, testable knowledge began centuries before the Enlightenment, in the efforts of Nicolaus Copernicus (1473–1542) and Galileo Galilei (1564–1642) to understand the behavior of the heavens. These men were both astronomers and mathematicians. Making their own mathematical calculations and observations of the stars and planets, these scholars came to conclusions that contradicted age-old assumptions. By no means was trusting one's own work rather than the accepted authorities easy, or without risk: when Galileo confirmed Copernicus's claims that the earth revolved around the sun, he was put on trial for heresy.

In the seventeenth century, a small but influential group of scholars committed themselves, similarly, to experimentation, calculation, and observation. They adopted a method

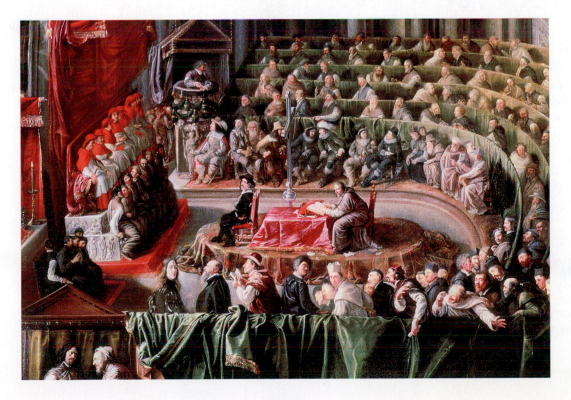

Galileo. The Catholic Church was initially worried that the new science would undermine Christian faith. In 1633, the Italian scientist Galileo was put on trial for espousing heretical beliefs and was condemned to house arrest.

EUROPEAN VIEWS OF THE WORLD

As Europeans became world travelers and traders, they needed accurate information on places and distances so they could get home as well as return to the sites they had visited. Europe's first printed map of the New World, the Waldseemüller map (produced in 1507), portrayed the Americas as a long and narrow strip of land. Asia and Africa dwarf its unexplored landmass. By the mid-seventeenth century, European maps were seemingly more objective, yet they still grouped the rest of the world around the European countries. Moreover, the effort to make world maps that served navigational purposes led to distortions (like the stretching of polar zones in the 1569 Mercator projection) that made Europe seem disproportionately large and central.

→ *What are the most striking differences between the two maps?*
→ *How are these European maps similar to and different from the Islamic and Chinese ones shown on pp. 532 and 539?*

SOURCES: (top) Courtesy Wychwood Editions; (bottom) Rare Books Division, The News York Public Library, Astor, Lenox and Tilden Foundations.

Waldseemüller map, 1507

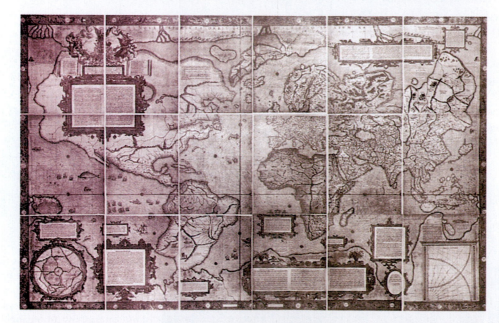

Mercator projection, 1569

for "scientific" inquiry laid out by the philosopher Sir Francis Bacon (1561–1626), who claimed that real science entailed the formulation of hypotheses that could be tested in carefully controlled experiments. Bacon believed that traditional authorities could never be trusted; only by conducting experiments could humans begin to comprehend the workings of nature. Bacon was chiefly wary of classical and medieval authorities, but his principle also applied to traditional knowledge that European scientists were encountering in the rest of the world. Confident of their calculations performed according to the new **scientific method**, scientists like Isaac Newton (1642–1727) defined what they believed were universal laws that applied to all matter and motion; they criticized older conceptions of nature (from Aristotelian ideas to folkloric and foreign ones) as absurd and obsolete. Thus, in his *Principia Mathematica* Newton set forth the laws of motion—including the famous law of gravitation, which simultaneously explained falling bodies on earth and planetary motion.

It is no longer fashionable to call these changes a scientific revolution, for European thinking did not change overnight. Only gradually did thinkers come to see the natural world as operating according to inviolable laws that experimenters could figure out. But by the late seventeenth century many rulers had developed a new interest in science's discoveries, and they established royal academies of science to encourage local endeavors. This patronage, of course, had a political function. By incorporating the British Royal Society in 1662, for example, Charles II hoped to show not only that the crown backed scientific progress but also that England's great minds backed the crown. Similar reasoning lay behind the founding of the French Royal Academy of Sciences and behind support for artistic monuments. In France, Louis XIV's fabulously expensive palace complex at Versailles demonstrated not only his refined taste but also his supreme power. The nobility, he meant to say, needed to look to him for both cultural and political guidance.

Gradually, the new science expanded beyond the court to gain popularity among elite circles. Marquise de Chatelet-Lomont built a scientific laboratory in her home and translated Newton's *Principia* into French. Well-to-do landowners formed societies to discuss the latest methods of animal breeding. Military schools increasingly stressed engineering methods and produced graduates with sophisticated technical skills. By about 1750, even artisans and journalists were applying Newtonian mechanics to their practical problems and inventions. In Italy, numerous female natural philosophers emerged, and the genre of scientific literature for "ladies" took hold. In 1763, the mathematician Diamante Medaglia Faini delivered an oration recommending that all women increase their knowledge of science. A consensus emerged among proponents of the new science that useful knowledge came from collecting data and organizing them into universally valid systems, rather than from studying revered classical texts.

Marquise de Chatelet-Lomont. The Marquise de Chatelet-Lomont (1706–1749) was one of the few in her day to understand Newtonian physics. Her French translation of Newton's *Principia Mathematica* included extensive explanations of the science that informed Newton's thinking. Her lover and admirer Voltaire wrote of her, "She was a great man whose only fault was in being a woman."

By no means, however, did the scientific worldview dominate European thinking. Most people still understood their relationships with God, nature, and fellow humans via Christian doctrines and local customs. Although literacy was increasing, it was far from universal; schools remained church-governed or elite, male institutions. All governments employed censors and punished radical thinkers, peasants still suffered under arbitrary systems of taxation, and judicial regimes were as harsh as during medieval times. Science and rationality certainly did not pervade all spheres of European life by 1700. If that had been so, there would have been no need for the movement we now call the Enlightenment.

ENLIGHTENMENT THINKERS

Enlightenment thinkers believed in the power of human reason and the perfectibility of humankind; they rejected the medieval belief in man's sinful nature and helplessness in the face of earthly evils. Such thinkers included the French writers Voltaire (1694–1778) and Denis Diderot (1713–1784) and the Scottish economist Adam Smith (1723–1790). But these writers also called attention to the evils and flaws of human society: Voltaire criticized the torture of criminals, Diderot denounced the despotic tendencies of the French kings Louis XIV and Louis XV, and Smith exposed the inefficiency of mercantilism.

In general, Enlightenment thinkers trusted nature and individual human reason and distrusted institutions and traditions. "Man is born good," wrote Jean-Jacques Rousseau (1712–1778); "it is society that corrupts him." He also wrote about government as the expression of the general will and how the people could withdraw their support if the government violated the "social contract." Moreover, Voltaire warned against excessive optimism in a world full of stupidity, greed, and injustice. Like Rousseau and Voltaire, other Enlightenment thinkers saw the need for great improvements in human society. They mainly criticized contemporary European conditions, and they often suffered imprisonment or exile for writing about what they considered to be superstitious beliefs and corrupt political structures.

The Enlightenment touched all of Europe, but the extent of its reach varied. In France and Britain, enlightened learning spread widely; in Spain, Poland, and Scandinavia, enlightened circles were small and had little influence on rulers or the general population. Enlightened thought flourished in commercial centers like Amsterdam and Edinburgh and in colonial ports like Philadelphia and Boston. As education and literacy levels rose in these cities, book sales and newspaper circulation surged. By 1770, approximately 3,500 different books and pamphlets were appearing each year in France alone, compared to 1,000 fifty years earlier. By 1776, about 12 million copies of newspapers were circulating in Britain.

POPULAR CULTURE In the emerging marketplace for new books and new ideas, some of the most popular works were not from high intellectuals. They came from the pens of more sensationalist essayists. Pamphlets charging widespread corruption, fraudulent stock speculation, and insider trading circulated widely. Sex, too, sold well. Works like *Venus in the Cloister or the Nun in a Nightgown* racked up as many sales as the now-classic works of the Enlightenment. Bawdy and irreligious, these vulgar best sellers exploited consumer demand—but they also seized the opportunity to mock authority figures, such as nuns and priests. Some even dared to go after the royal family, portraying Louis XV as fond of getting spanked or Marie Antoinette as having sex with her court confessor. In these cases, pornography—some of it even philosophical—spilled into the literary marketplace for political satire. Such works displayed the seamier side of the Enlightenment, but they also revealed a willingness (on the part of high and low intellectuals alike) to explore modes of thought that defied established beliefs and institutions.

The reading public itself helped generate new cultural institutions and practices. In Britain and Germany, book clubs and coffeehouses sprang up to cater to sober men of business and learning; here, aristocrats and well-to-do commoners could read news sheets or discuss stock prices, political affairs, and technological novelties. The same sort of noncourtly socializing occurred in Parisian salons, where aristocratic women presided. Speaking their minds more openly in these

Salon of Madame Geoffrin. Much of the important work—and wit—of the Enlightenment was the product of private gatherings known as salons. Often hosted, like the one depicted here, by aristocratic women, these salons also welcomed down-at-the-heels writers and artists, offering everyone, at least in theory, the opportunity to discuss the sciences, the arts, politics, and the idiocies of their fellow humans on an equal basis.

private settings than at court or at public assemblies, women here freely exchanged ideas with men. The most successful salons were the ones that spread witty gossip, but would-be philosophers and writers attended in hopes of finding jobs as secretaries or obtaining commissions for their projects. Moreover, libraries now opened their doors to the public.

It is important to note, however, that most funding for intellectuals still came from aristocrats, royal families, and the church. For example, in the German states, Enlightenment thinkers were chiefly university professors, bureaucrats, and pastors. Art collecting boomed—primarily because it gave aristocrats a way to display their good taste, wealth, and distance from the common people.

Challenges to Authority and Tradition

Even though they took the aristocracy's money, many Enlightenment thinkers tried overturn the status distinctions that characterized European society. They emphasized merit rather than birth as the basis for status. The English philosopher John Locke (1632–1704) claimed that man was born with a mind that was a clean slate (*tabula rasa*) and acquired all his ideas through experience. Locke stressed that cultural differences were not the result of unequal natural abilities, but of unequal opportunities to develop one's abilities. Similarly, in *The Wealth of Nations*, Adam Smith remarked that there was little difference (other than education) between a philosopher and a street porter: both were born, he claimed, with the ability to reason, and both were (or should be) free to rise in society according to their talents. Yet, Locke and Smith still believed that a mixed set of social and political institutions was necessary to regulate relationships among ever-imperfect humans. Moreover, they did not believe that women could act as independent, rational individuals in the same way that all men, presumably, could. Although educated women like Mary Wollstonecraft and Olympe de Gouges took up the pen to protest these inequities (see Chapter 15 for further discussion), the Enlightenment did little to change the subordinate status of women in European society.

Seeking Universal Laws

Inspired by the new science, many thinkers sought to discover the "laws" of human behavior, an endeavor linked with criticism of existing governments. Explaining the laws of economic relations was chiefly the work of Adam Smith, whose book *The Wealth of Nations* described universal economic laws. It became one of the most influential and long-lived of enlightened works. Smith claimed that unregulated markets in a laissez-faire economy best suited mankind because they allowed man's "trucking and bartering" nature to express itself fully. (**Laissez-faire** expresses the concept that the economy works best when it is left alone—that is, when the state does not regulate or interfere with the workings of the market.) In Smith's view, the "invisible hand" of the market, rather than govern-

ment regulations, would lead to prosperity and social peace. Smith was conscious of growing economic gaps between "civilized and thriving" nations and "savage" ones; the latter were so miserably poor that, Smith claimed, they were reduced to infanticide, starvation, and euthanasia. Yet, he believed that until these nations learned to play by what he called nature's laws, they could not expect a happy fate. Smith was just one of many writers who felt that non-Europeans had no other choice but to follow the Enlightenment's "universal" laws.

One of the most controversial areas for applying universal laws was religion. Although few Enlightenment thinkers were atheists (people who do not believe in any god), most of them called for religious toleration. They insisted that the use of reason, not force, was the best way to create a community of believers and morally good people. Their critiques of church authorities and practices were highly controversial. Governments often reacted by censoring books or exiling writers, but the arguments managed to persuade some rulers. Thus, in the late eighteenth century, governments from Denmark to Austria passed acts offering religious minorities some freedom of worship. However, toleration did not mean full civil rights—especially for Catholics in England or Jews anywhere in Europe. Toleration simply meant a loosening of religious uniformity, and the population as a whole often resented even this.

Seeking Universal Knowledge

The Enlightenment produced numerous works that attempted to encompass universal knowledge. Most important was the French *Encyclopedia*, which ultimately comprised twenty-eight volumes containing essays by nearly 200 intellectuals. It was extremely popular among the elite despite its political, religious, and intellectual radicalism. Its purpose was "to collect all the knowledge scattered over the face of the earth" and to make it useful to men and women in the present and future. Indeed, the *Encyclopedia* offered a wealth of information about the rest of the world, including more than 2,300 articles on Islam. Here, quite typically, the authors praised Arab culture for preserving and extending Greek and Roman science—and in doing so, preparing the way for scientific advances in Europe. But at the same time the authors portrayed Islam with the same ill will that they applied to other organized religions, condemning Muhammad for promoting a bloodthirsty religion and Muslim culture in general for not rejecting superstition.

Enlightenment thinkers valued commerce and rationality, so they placed all regions that supposedly lacked these ingredients at the bottom of the world's cultures. While praising some cultures like the Chinese for having achieved much in these areas, Enlightenment thinkers were confident that Europe was advancing over the rest of the world in its acquisition of goods and universal knowledge.

Absolutist governments did not entirely reject enlightened ideas. After all, they recognized the virtues of universality (as

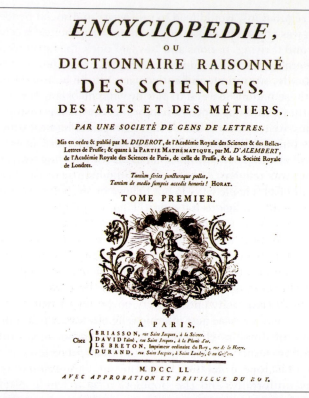

The *Encyclopedia*. Originally published in 1751, the *Encyclopedia* was the most comprehensive work of learning of the French Enlightenment. The title page (*left*) features an image of light and reason being dispersed throughout the land. The title itself identifies the work as a dictionary, based on reason, that deals not just with the sciences but also with the arts and occupations. It identifies two of the leading men of letters (*gens de lettres*), Denis Diderot and Jean le Rond d'Alembert, as the primary authors of the work. Contributors to the *Encyclopedia* included craftsmen as well as intellectuals. The detailed illustrations of a pin factory and the processes and machinery employed in pin making shown below are from a plate in the fourth volume of the *Encyclopedia* and demonstrate its emphasis on practical information.

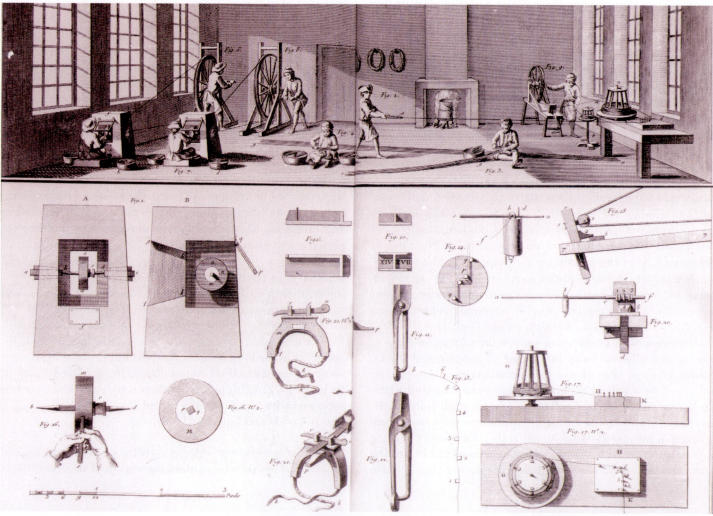

in a universally applicable system of taxation) and precision (as in a well-drilled army). Also, social mobility allowed more skilled bureaucrats to rise through the ranks, while commerce provided the state with new riches. The idea of collecting knowledge, too, appealed to states that wanted greater control over their subjects. Consider Louis XIV, who was persuaded to establish a census (though he never carried it out) so that he could "know with certitude in what consists his grandeur, his wealth, and his strength." Some enlightened princes—in Prussia and Austria, for example—even made impressive legal reforms and supported innovations in the arts and agriculture. Indeed, the Enlightenment spread the idea of liberty far and wide, even to women, lower-class men, and enslaved peoples whom European elites felt might not deserve it. In fact, many other eighteenth-century male thinkers, like their absolutist rulers, were uncomfortable with the idea of offering liberty and equality (not to mention sovereignty) to *all* the people.

AFRICAN CULTURAL FLOURISHING

> → *How did involvement in the slave trade reshape African cultures?*

Power and splendor were nothing new in parts of Africa. Although much of the rest of the world did not know it, kingdoms throughout Africa had strong artisanal and artistic traditions dating back centuries. But now, as in Europe, wealth from the slave trade enabled the African upper classes to fund new cultural achievements. Africa was like East Asia, however, in that it maintained local forms of cultural production, such as woodcarving, weaving, and metalworking.

Cultural traditions in Africa varied from kingdom to kingdom, but there were patterns among them. For example, all West African elites encouraged local artisans to produce carvings, statues, masks, and other objects that would glorify the power and achievements of rulers. (Royal patrons in Europe, Asia, and the Islamic world did the same with architecture and painting). There was also a widespread belief that rulers and their families had the blessing of the gods. Arts and crafts not only celebrated royal power but also captured the energy of a universe that people believed was suffused with spiritual beings. Starting in the 1500s and continuing into the 1700s when the slave trade reached its peak, African rulers had even more reason—and means—to support cultural pursuits. After all, as destructive as the slave trade was for African peoples, it made the slave-trading states wealthy and powerful.

THE ASANTE, OYO, AND BENIN CULTURAL TRADITIONS

Not surprisingly, the kingdom of Asante, which grew rich through the slave trade, led the way in cultural attainments. Its access to gold enabled its artisans to celebrate its royal tradition through the crafting of magnificent seats or stools coated with gold as symbols of authority. The most ornate royal stool was reserved for the head of the Asante federation, who ruled his far-flung empire from the capital city of Kumasi and ventured out from his secluded palace only on ceremonial and feast days. At those times he wore sumptuous silk garments featuring many dazzling colors and geometric patterns, all joined together in interwoven strips. Known as Kente cloth, this fabric could be worn only by the ruler. He also held aloft maces, spears, staffs, and other symbols of power fashioned from the kingdom's abundant gold supplies. These articles displayed his connection to the gods.

Equally resplendent were rulers of the Oyo Empire and Benin, located in the territory that now constitutes Nigeria. Elegant, refined metalwork in the form of West African bronzes reflects these rulers' awesome power and their peoples' highest esteem. The bronze heads of Ife, capital city of the Yoruba Oyo Empire, are among the world's most sophisticated pieces of art. According to one commentator, "little that Italy or Greece or Egypt ever produced could be finer, and the appeal of their beauty is immediate and universal." The Ife heads mark the high point of Yoruba craft and artistic tradition that dates back to the first millennium CE. Artisans fashioned the best known of these works in the thirteenth century (before the slave trade era), but the tradition continued and became more elaborate in the seventeenth and eighteenth centuries.

Equally stunning were bronzes from Benin. Although historical records have portrayed Benin as one of Africa's most brutal slave-trading regimes, it also produced art of the highest order. Whether Benin's reputation for brutality was deserved or simply part of Europeans' later desire to label African rulers as "savage" in order to justify their conquest of the landmass, it cannot detract from the splendor of its artisans' creations.

Brass Oba Head. The brass head of an Oba, or king, of Benin. The kingdom's brass and bronze work was among the finest in all of Africa.

HYBRID CULTURES IN THE AMERICAS

> → *How did cultural developments in the Americas reflect global entanglements?*

In the Americas, mingling between European colonizers and native peoples (as well as African slaves) produced hybrid cultures. But the mixing of cultures grew increasingly unbalanced as Europeans imposed authority over more of the Americas. For Native Americans, the pressure to adapt their cultures to those of the colonists began from the start. Over time, Indians faced mounting pressure as Europeans insisted that their conquests were not simply military endeavors but also spiritual errands. In addition to guns and germs, all of Europe's colonizers brought Bibles, prayer books, and crucifixes. With these, they set out to Christianize and "civilize" Indian and African populations in the Americas. Yet missionary efforts produced uneven and often unpredictable outcomes. Even as Indians and African slaves adopted Christian beliefs and practices, they often retained older religious practices too.

European colonists likewise borrowed from the peoples they subjugated and enslaved. This was especially true in the sixteenth and seventeenth centuries, when the colonists' survival in the New World often depended on adapting. Before long, however, many American settlements had become stable and prosperous, to the extent that colonists preferred not to admit their past dependence on others. New sorts of hierarchies emerged, and elites in Latin America and North America increasingly followed the tastes and fashions of European aristocrats. Yet, even as they imitated Old World ways, these colonials forged identities that separated them from Europe.

SPIRITUAL ENCOUNTERS

Settlers in the New World had the military and economic power to impose their culture—especially their religion—on indigenous peoples. Although the Jesuits had little impact in China and the Islamic world, Christian missionaries in the Americas had armies and officials to back up their insistence that Native Americans and African slaves abandon their own deities and spirits for Christ.

FORCING CONVERSIONS   European missionaries, especially Catholics, used numerous techniques to bring Indians within the Christian fold. Smashing idols, razing temples, and whipping backsliders all belonged to the missionaries' arsenal. Catholic orders (principally Dominicans, Jesuits, and Franciscans) also learned what they could about Indian be-

Indians Becoming Christians. This image is from a colonial chronicle, illustrated and narrated by indigenous scribes who had converted to Christianity. The picture of Indians before the conquest entering a house of prayer is intended to represent the Indians as proto-Christians.

liefs and rituals—and then exploited that knowledge to make conversions to Christianity. For example, many missionaries found it useful to demonize local gods, subvert indigenous spiritual leaders, and transform Indian iconography into Christian symbols. But at the same time, the missionaries preserved much linguistic and ethnographic information about Native American communities. In sixteenth-century Mexico, the Dominican friar Bernardino de Sahagún compiled an immense ethnography of Mexican ways and beliefs. In seventeenth-century Canada, French Jesuits prepared dictionaries and grammars of the Iroquoian and Algonquian languages and translated Christian hymns into Amerindian tongues.

Neither gentle persuasion nor violent coercion produced the results that missionaries desired. When conversions did occur, the Christian practices that resulted were usually hybrid forms in which indigenous deities and rituals merged with Christian ones. Among Andean mountain people, for example, priestesses of local cults took the Christian name Maria to mask their secret worship of traditional deities. In other cases, indigenous communities turned their backs on Christianity and accused missionaries of bringing disease and death. Those who did convert saw Christian spiritual power as an addition to, not a replacement for, their own religions.

MIXING CULTURES More distressing to missionaries than the blending of beliefs or outright defiance were the Indians' successes in converting captured colonists. Many Indian groups had a tradition of adopting their captives as a way to replace lost kin. It deeply troubled the missionaries that quite a few captured colonists adjusted to their situation, accepted their adoptions, and refused to return to colonial society when given the chance. Moreover, some other Europeans voluntarily chose to live among the Indians. Comparing the records of cultural conversion, one eighteenth-century colonist suggested that "thousands of Europeans are Indians," yet "we have no examples of even one of those Aborigines having from choice become European." (Aborigines are original, native inhabitants of a region, as opposed to invaders, colonizers, or later peoples of mixed ancestry.) While this calculation may be exaggerated, it reflects the fact that Europeans who adopted Indian culture, like Christianized Indians, lived in a mixed cultural world. In fact, their familiarity with both Indian and European ways made them ideal intermediaries for diplomatic arrangements and economic exchanges.

Beyond the attractions of Indian cultures, Europeans mixed with Indians because there were many more men than women among the colonists. Almost all the early European traders, missionaries, and settlers were men (although the British North American settlements saw more women arrive relatively early on). In response to the scarcity of women and as a way to help Amerindians accept the newcomers' culture, the Portuguese crown authorized intermarriage between Portuguese men and local women. These relations often amounted to little more than rape, but longer-lasting relationships developed in places where Indians kept their independence—as among French fur traders and Indian women in Canada, the Great Lakes region, and the Mississippi Valley. Whether by coercion or consent, sexual relations between European men and Indian women resulted in offspring of mixed ancestry. In fact, the mestizos of Spanish colonies and the métis of French outposts soon outnumbered settlers of wholly European descent.

The increasing numbers of African slaves in the Americas complicated the mix of New World cultures even further. Unlike marriages between fur traders and Indian women, in which the women held considerable power because of their connections to Indian trading partners, sexual intercourse between European men and enslaved African women was almost always forced. Children born from such unions swelled the ranks of mixed-ancestry people in the colonial population. Europeans attempted to Christianize slaves, though many slave owners doubted the wisdom of converting persons they regarded as mere property. Protestants had more difficulty than Catholics in accepting that Africans could be both slaves and Christians, and their missionary efforts were less aggressive than the Catholics'.

Sent forth with the pope's blessing, Catholic priests targeted slave populations in the American colonies of Portugal, Spain, and France. Applying many of the same techniques that missionaries used with Indian "heathens," these priests produced similarly mixed results. Often converts blended Islamic or traditional African religions with Catholicism. Converted slaves wove remembered practices and beliefs from their homeland into their American Christianity, transforming both along the way. In northeastern Brazil, for example, slaves combined the Yoruba faiths of their ancestors with

Racial Mixing. (*Left*) This image shows racial mixing in colonial Mexico—the father is Spanish, the mother Indian, and the child a mestizo. This is a well-to-do family, illustrating how Europeans married into the native aristocracy. (*Right*) Here too we see a racially mixed family. The father is Spanish, the mother black or African, and the child a mulatto. Observe, however, the less aristocratic and markedly less peaceful nature of this family.

Catholic beliefs, and they frequently attributed powers of African deities to Christian saints. Sometimes Christian and African faiths were practiced side by side. In Saint Domingue, slaves and free blacks practiced *vodun* ("spirit" in the Dahomey tongue); in Cuba, *santería* ("cult of saints" in Spanish), a faith of similar origins.

Just as slaveholders feared, Christianity—especially in its hybrid forms—could inspire resistance, even revolt, among slaves. Indeed, a major runaway slave leader in mid-eighteenth-century Surinam was a Christian. Those held in bondage in the English colonies drew inspiration from Christian hymns that promised deliverance, and they embraced as their own the Old Testament story of Moses leading the Israelites out of Egypt. By the late eighteenth century, freed slaves like the Methodist Olaudah Equiano (see Chapter 13) were saying in their own voices that slavery was unjust and incompatible with Christian brotherhood.

THE MAKING OF COLONIAL CULTURES

The colonization of the Americas brought Europeans, Africans, and Indians into sustained contact, though the nature of the colonies and the character of the contact varied considerably. Where their dominance was most certain, European colonists imposed their ways on subjugated populations and imported what they took to be the chief attributes of the countries and cultures they had left behind. Yet Europeans were not immune to cultural influences from the groups they dispossessed and enslaved, and over time the colonists developed a sense of their own distinctive "American" identities. The cultures and identities of Indians and African slaves also underwent significant transformations, though often what Europeans imposed was only partially and selectively adapted.

THE CREOLE IDENTITY In Spanish America, ethnic and cultural mixing produced a powerful new class, the **creoles**—persons of European descent who were born in the Americas. By the late eighteenth century, creoles increasingly resented the control that **peninsulars**—men and women born in Spain or Portugal but living in the Americas—had over colonial society. Creoles especially chafed under the exclusive privileges given to peninsular rulers, like those that forbade creoles from trading with other colonial ports. Also, they disliked the fact that royal ministers gave most official posts to peninsulars. While the Spanish and Portuguese rulers did occasionally soften their discrimination for fear of angering the creoles, their reforms usually aggravated tensions with peninsulars.

The growing creole identity gained strength from new ideas spreading in the colonies, especially those circulating under the umbrella of the Enlightenment. The French writer Abbé

Raynal's *History of the Settlements and Trade of the Europeans in the East and West Indies* (1770), for example, was a favorite text among colonial reading circles in Buenos Aires and Rio de Janeiro. As a history of colonization in the New World, it was unkind to Iberian (Spanish and Portuguese) emperors and conquerors—and often helped creoles justify their dissatisfaction. Other French works were also popular, especially those of Rousseau. So were some English texts, like Adam Smith's *The Wealth of Nations*. Smith's reformist spirit contributed to creole impressions that mercantilist Iberian authorities lagged behind them in political and economic matters.

In many cities of the Spanish and Portuguese empires, reading clubs and salons hosted energetic discussions of fresh ideas. In one university in Peru, Catholic scholars taught their students that Spanish labor drafts and taxes on Andean natives not only violated divine justice but also offended the natural rights of free men. The Spanish crown, recognizing the role of printing presses in spreading troublesome ideas, strictly controlled the number and location of printers in the colonies. In Brazil, royal authorities banned them altogether. Nonetheless books, pamphlets, and simple gossip allowed new notions of science, history, and politics to circulate among literate creoles.

ANGLICIZATION In one important sense, wealthy colonists in British America were similar to the creole elites in Spanish and Portuguese America: they, too, copied European ways. For example, they constructed "big houses" (in Virginia) modeled on the country estates of English gentlemen, imported opulent furnishings and fashions from the finest British stores, and exercised more control over colonial assemblies. Imitating the English also involved tightening patriarchal authority. In seventeenth-century Virginia, men had vastly outnumbered women, which gave women some power (widows in particular gained greater control over property and more choices when they remarried). During the eighteenth century, however, sex ratios became more equal, and women's property rights diminished as English customs took precedence. Overall, patriarchal authority was evident in family portraits, where husband-patriarchs sat or stood in front of their wives and children.

Intellectually, too, British Americans were linked to Europe. Importing enormous numbers of books and journals, these Americans played a significant role in the Enlightenment as producers and consumers of political pamphlets, scientific treatises, and social critiques. Indeed, drawing on the words of numerous Enlightenment thinkers, American intellectuals created the most famous of enlightened documents: the Declaration of Independence. It announced that all men were endowed with equal rights and were created to pursue worldly happiness. In this way Anglicized Americans showed themselves, like the creole elites of Latin America, to be products of both European and New World encounters.

IMPERIALISM IN OCEANIA

> → *What role did "race" play in how Europeans viewed others, especially those from Oceania?*

Not only in Europe and the Americas but also in the South Pacific, an "enlightened" form of cultural expansionism took shape in the eighteenth century. Though in centuries past Hindu, Buddhist, Islamic, and Chinese missionaries and traders had traveled to Malaysia and nearby islands, they had not ventured beyond Timor (see Map 14-1). Europeans began to do so in the years after 1770, turning their sights on **Oceania** (Australia, New Zealand, and the islands of the southwest Pacific). Using their new wealth to fund voyages with scientific and political objectives, Europeans invaded these remaining unexplored areas. The results were mixed: while some islands maintained their autonomy, the biggest prize, Australia, underwent thorough Anglicization.

Until Europeans colonized it in the late eighteenth century, Australia was, like the Americas before Columbus, truly a world apart. Separated by water and sheer distance from other regions, Australia's main features were harsh natural conditions and a sparse population. At the time of the European colo-nization, the island was home to around 300,000 people, mostly hunter-gatherers. While seafarers from Java, Timor, and particularly the port of Makassar may have ventured into the area in the past, there was little evidence that either Chinese or Muslim merchants had ever strayed that far south.

Europeans had visited Oceania before the eighteenth century. Spices had drawn the Portuguese and Dutch into the South Pacific (see Chapter 13), and the Spanish had plied Pacific waters while traveling between Manila and Acapulco, but they had stopped only in Guam and the Mariana Islands. In the 1670s and 1680s they attempted to conquer these islands, and despite considerable resistance they succeeded by 1700. The Dutch visited Easter Island in 1722, and the French arrived in Tahiti in 1767. Both the Portuguese and the Dutch had seen the northern and western coasts of Australia, but they had found only sand, flies, and Aborigines. Not until the late eighteenth century did Europeans see Australia's more hospitable eastern coast or find grounds for serious interest in colonization. Now the intrusion into Oceania presented Europeans with a previously unknown region that could serve as a laboratory for studying other peoples and geographical settings.

THE SCIENTIFIC VOYAGES OF CAPTAIN COOK

In Oceania and across the South Pacific, Europeans experimented with a scientific form of imperialism. The story of the region's most famous explorer, Captain James Cook (1728–1779), shows how closely related science and imperialist ventures could be, and how unequal cultural exchange could be. Cook's voyages and his encounter with the South Sea Islanders opened up the Pacific, and particularly Australia, to European colonizers.

Captain Cook has become a legendary figure in European cultural history, portrayed as one of the saintly scientists of enlightened progress. His first voyage had two objectives. The Royal Society charged him with the scholarly task of observing the movement of the planet Venus from the Southern Hemisphere, and the British government assigned him the secret mission of finding and claiming "the southern continent" for Britain. Cook set sail in 1768, and his voyage was so fruitful that he subsequently undertook two more scientific-imperial adventures. The extremely popular accounts of his discoveries, and the engravings that accompanied them, opened up the exotic worlds of Tahiti, New Zealand, Australia, and Hawaii to European scrutiny. They also prepared the way for a new, more intensive sort of cultural colonization.

SCIENTIFIC AND CULTURAL ASPECTS   Cook was chosen to head the first expedition because of his scientific interests and skills. Although he had little schooling, he had

Chronometer. In the 1760s, the English clockmaker John Harrison perfected the chronometer, a timepiece mariners could use to reckon longitude while at sea. Although the Royal Scientific Society initially refused to believe that Harrison had solved this long-standing problem, Harrison's instrument made navigation so much safer and more predictable that it became standard equipment on European ships.

MAP 14-1 SOUTHEAST ASIA

Captain Cook's voyages throughout the Pacific Ocean symbolized a new era in European exploration of other societies. According to this map, how many voyages did Cook take? Where did Cook explore, and what peoples did he encounter? According to your reading, how did Cook's endeavors symbolize "scientific" imperialism?

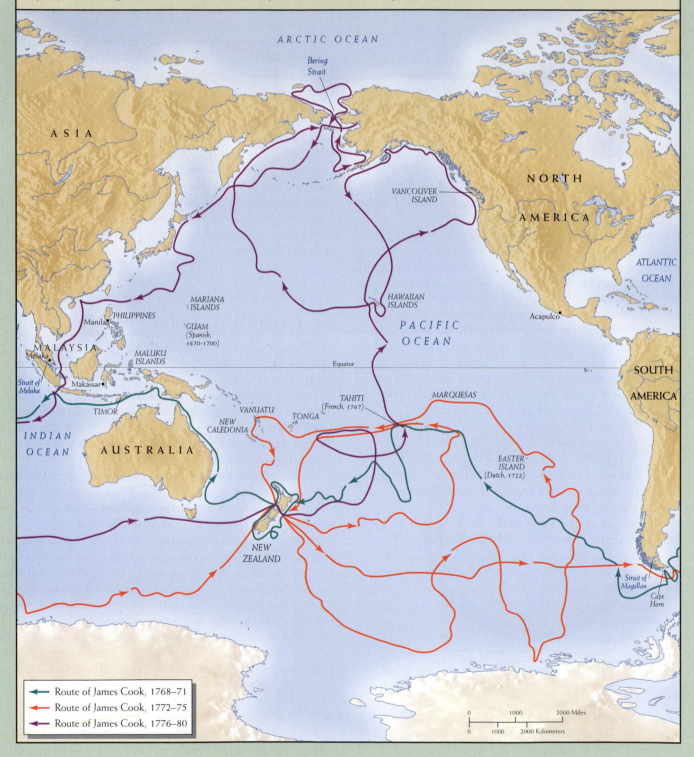

← Route of James Cook, 1768–71
← Route of James Cook, 1772–75
← Route of James Cook, 1776–80

The Voyages of Captain James Cook. During his celebrated voyages to the South Pacific, Cook (*left*) kept meticulous maps and diaries. Although he had little formal education, he became one of the great exemplars of enlightened learning through experience and experiment. (*Right*) Kangaroos were unknown in the West until Cook and his colleagues encountered (and ate) them on their first visit to Australia. This engraving of the animal (which unlike most animals, plants, and geographical features actually kept the name the Aborigines had given it) from Cook's 1773 travelogue, *A Voyage Round the World in the Years 1768–1771,* lovingly depicts the kangaroo's environs and even emotions.

gone to sea early and, through long experience in navigating the uncharted North American waters of Newfoundland, had developed excellent surveying skills. Besides Cook, the Royal Society sent along one of its members who was a botanist; a doctor and student of the renowned Swedish naturalist Carolus Linnaeus (1707–1778); and numerous artists and other scientists. The crew also carried sophisticated instruments and had instructions to keep detailed diaries. This was to be a grand data-collecting journey.

Cook's voyages surpassed even the Royal Society's hopes. The scientists made approximately 3,000 drawings of Pacific plants, birds, landscapes, and peoples never seen in Europe. The men described the region's flora and fauna according to Swedish naturalist Carolus Linnaeus's recently developed system for classifying all natural phenomena, and they gave English names to geographical features.

More than science was at stake, however, for Australia was intended to supply Britain with raw materials. But as in the Americas, extracting those materials required a labor force, and the Aborigines of Australia, like the Indians of the Americas, perished in great numbers from imported diseases. Those who survived generally fled to escape control by British masters. Thus, to secure a labor force, plans arose for grand-scale conquest and resettlement by British colonists. On his third voyage, Cook took along an astonishing array of animals

and plants with which to turn the South Pacific into a European-style garden. His lieutenant later brought apples, quinces, strawberries, and rosemary to Australia; the seventy sheep imported in 1788 laid the foundations for the region's wool-growing economy. In fact, the domestication of Australia arose from the Europeans' certainty about their superior know-how and a desire to make the entire landmass serve British interests.

In 1788, a British military expedition took official possession of the eastern half of Australia. The intent was, in part, to establish a prison colony far from home. This plan belonged as well to the realm of "enlightened" dreams: that of ridding "civilized" society of all evils by resettling lawbreakers among the "uncivilized." The intent was also to exploit Australia for its timber and flax and to use it as a strategic base against Dutch and French expansion. In the next decades, immigration—free and forced—increased the Anglo-Australian population from an original 1,000 to about 1.2 million by 1860. Importing their customs and their capital, British settlers turned Australia into a frontier version of home, just as they had done in British America. Yet, such large-scale immigration had disastrous consequences for the surviving Aborigines. Like the Native Americans, the original inhabitants of Australia were decimated by diseases and increasingly forced westward by European settlement.

Omai. Omai, the South Sea Islander brought to England by Captain Cook, was the object of much curiosity in London in the 1780s.

STUDYING FOREIGNERS In one important way, Cook continued practices of the past. Earlier travelers had developed an efficient way to study foreign peoples and their languages: by taking some of them to Europe, through kidnapping if necessary. On Columbus's first voyage to the New World, he had captured six Amerindians and taken them back to Spain—to show them off as exotic people, and to enable them to learn Spanish so they could serve as intermediaries between the two cultures. Other explorers did the same, seizing local people, taking them to Europe, and putting them on display.

This was not the way that Europeans learned about peoples whom they considered to be civilized—for example, the Chinese and the Arabs. For such "civilized" peoples, texts stood in for living bodies. But exhibiting live individuals continued to be a crude means for studying those whom the Europeans considered uncivilized. Cook himself captured and transported to England a highly skilled Polynesian naviga-

tor, Omai. Omai quickly became the talk of London society and symbolized for some people the innocence and beauty that were vanishing as Europe developed complicated machines and stock exchanges. Cook's return of Omai to his home on his third voyage was a sensation of equal proportions, seen as a colossally generous act by the revered British explorer.

CLASSIFICATION AND "RACE"

Cook's description of the South Sea Islanders underscores the place that "race" had come to occupy in Europeans' views of themselves and others. Previously, the word *race* referred to a swift current in a stream or a test of speed, and sometimes it meant a lineage (mainly that of a royal or noble family). By the late seventeenth century, a few writers were expanding the definition to designate a European ethnic lineage, identifying, for example, the indomitable spirit and freedom-loving ethos of the Anglo-Saxon race.

The Frenchman François Bernier, who had traveled in Asia, may have been the first European to attempt to classify the peoples of the world. He used a variety of criteria, including those that were to become standard from the late eighteenth century down to the present, such as skin color, facial features, and hair texture. Bernier published this work in his *New Division of the Earth by the Different Groups or Races Who Inhabit It* (1684). In addition to the Swedish naturalist Carolus Linnaeus, the French scholar Georges Louis LeClerc, the comte de Buffon (1707–1788), and the German anatomist Johann Friedrich Blumenbach (1752–1840) were the first to use racial principles to classify humankind.

CATEGORIZING HUMAN GROUPS In his *Systema Naturae* (1735), Europe's most accomplished naturalist, Carolus Linnaeus, sought to classify all the world's plants and animals by giving each a binomial, or two-worded, name. In subsequent editions of his *Systema* Linnaeus perfected his system, identifying five subspecies of the mammal he called *Homo sapiens*, or "wise man." Linnaeus gave each of the continents a subspecies: there was *Homo europaeus*, *Homo americanus*, *Homo afer*, and *Homo asiaticus*. He added a fifth category, *Homo monstrosus*, for "wild" men and "monstrous" types.

Linnaeus's classifications were based on a combination of physical characteristics that included skin color and social qualities. He characterized Europeans as light-skinned and governed by laws; Asians as "sooty" and governed by opinion; indigenous American peoples as copper-skinned and governed by custom; and Africans (whom he consigned to the lowest rung of the human ladder) as ruled by personal whim. Later eighteenth-century natural historians dismissed Linnaeus's fifth category, which contained mythical monstrous races and people with mental and physical disabilities, but the habit of ranking "races" and lumping together physical and cultural characteristics persisted.

THE EUROPEAN BIAS   In inventorying the world's peoples and assigning each group a place on the ladder of human achievement, Europeans applied their reverence for classical sculpture. Those who most resembled Greek nudes were considered the most beautiful, as well as the most civilized and suited for world power. In his *Natural History* (1750), the comte de Buffon insisted that classical sculptures had established the proper proportion for the human form. Having divided humans into distinct "races," he determined that white peoples were the most admirable, and Africans the most contemptible.

In these emerging racial hierarchies, South Sea Islanders fell somewhere between Caucasians and Ethiopians. To some, their isolation from European and Asian cultures and their residence in a tropical "paradise" made them seem like direct descendants of Adam and Eve—a virtuous, uncorrupted people who fit the description of the "noble savage" coined by Jean-Jacques Rousseau. But in succeeding decades Europeans would come to emphasize not the nobility but the savagery of the South Sea Islanders. Declining appreciation for their innocence and simplicity may have begun with the final act in the Cook legend: his killing by the Hawaiians in 1779. The news scandalized Cook's homeland; the king himself, it is said, shed tears. Thereafter Europeans began to write about a "darker side" of South Pacific cultures.

CONCLUSION

New wealth produced by commerce and state building created the conditions for a global cultural renaissance in the sixteenth, seventeenth, and eighteenth centuries. It began in the Chinese and Islamic empires and then stretched into Europe, Africa, and previous worlds apart in the Americas and Oceania. Experiments in religious toleration encouraged cultural exchange; book production and consumption soared; grand new monuments took shape; luxury goods became available for wider enjoyment.

A striking aspect of this cultural renaissance was its unevenness. While elites and sometimes the middle classes benefited, the poor did not. They remained illiterate, undernourished, and often subjected to brutal treatment by rulers and landowners. Elite women in Europe and China increasingly joined literate society, but they gained no new rights. Urban areas also profited more from the new wealth than rural ones, so people seeking refinement flocked to the cities. Some former cultural centers, like the Italian peninsula, lost their luster as new, more commercially and culturally dynamic centers took their place.

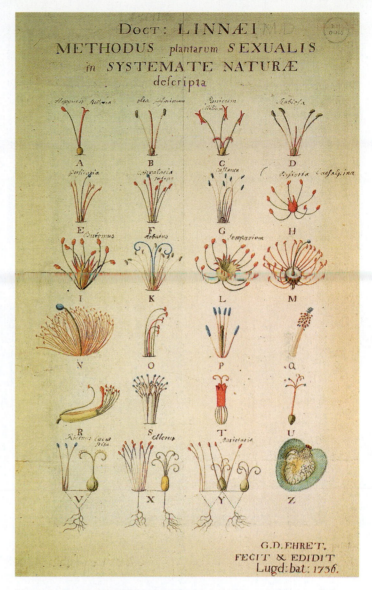

Linnaeus and Classification. Linnaeus's famous system of plant and animal classifications, which depended on sexual forms (such as the stamen and pistil in plants), was in wide use by the end of the eighteenth century.

Among states, too, cultural inequalities were glaring. Although the Islamic and Chinese worlds confidently retained their own systems of knowing, believing, and representing, the Americas and Oceania increasingly faced European cultural pressures. Here, while hybrid practices became widespread by the late eighteenth century, European beliefs and habits took over as the standards for judging degrees of "civilization." African cultures largely escaped this influence, though their homelands felt the impact of European expansionism because of the slave trade.

From a commercial standpoint, the world was more integrated than ever before. But the exposure and cultural borrowing that global trade promoted largely reconfirmed established ways. The Chinese, for instance, still believed in the superiority of their traditional knowledge and customs. Muslim rulers, confident of the primacy of Islam, allowed others to form subordinate cultural communities within their realm and adopted the Europeans' knowledge only when it served their own imperial purposes.

Only the Europeans were constructing knowledge that they believed was both universal and objective, enabling mortals to master the world of nature and all its inhabitants. This view would prove consequential, as well as controversial, in the centuries to come.

Review and research materials are available at StudySpace: Ⓢ WWNORTON.COM/STUDYSPACE

KEY TERMS

cartography (p. 538)
creoles (p. 552)
enlightened absolutists (p. 527)
Enlightenment (p. 542)
Forbidden City of Beijing (p. 534)
great plaza at Isfahan (p. 535)
laissez-faire (p. 547)
Oceania (p. 553)
Palace of Versailles (p. 535)
peninsulars (p. 552)
scientific method (p. 545)
Taj Mahal (p. 532)
Topkapi Palace (p. 535)

Chronology

		1600		1650	
THE ISLAMIC WORLD		◆----------◆ 1587–1602 *Abulfazl's Akbarnamah in Mughal India*			
		◆----------------------◆ 1598–1629 *Building of palace and plaza in Isfahan, I*			
		1630–1650 *Building of Taj Mahal in Agra, India* ◆----------------◆			
EUROPE		1632 *Galileo Galilei's Dialogue on the Two Chief Systems of the World* ◆			
				1661 *Building of Versailles begins outside Paris* ◆	
				1662 *Incorporation of British Royal Society* ◆	
AMERICAS		1600s *Hybrid cultures emerge in Americas*			
		◆---			
AFRICA		◆ 1600s *Oyo and Asante kingdoms produce vibrant artistic work*			
EAST ASIA		◆ 1583 *Jesuit missionary Matteo Ricci brings European cartography to China*			
		1600s *Growing circulation of books and ideas in China*			
		◆--			
		◆ 1600s *Kabuki theater appears in Japan*			

STUDY QUESTIONS

1. Explain the processes that brought forth cultural syntheses in the three Islamic dynasties during this era. To what extent did European culture influence each empire?

2. Describe Chinese and Japanese cultural achievements during this period. How did foreign influences affect each dynasty?

3. Define the term *Enlightenment* as it pertained to Europe. How did Enlightenment ideas shape European attitudes toward other cultures?

4. Explain the various factors that contributed to the growth of hybrid cultures in the Americas during this era. How similar and different were these new societies across the Americas?

5. Analyze the impact of Enlightenment ideas in the Americas. Did the spread of this philosophy bring communities across the Atlantic together, or did it drive them apart?

6. Compare and contrast European exploration of Oceania in the eighteenth century to European exploration of the Americas in the sixteenth century (see Chapter 12). How did European exploration of Oceania transform European attitudes toward non-European groups around the world?

7. Explain how global trade changed world cultures at this time.

8. Analyze to what extent dynastic rulers around the world were able to control cultural developments during this period. How did new cultural productions potentially undermine local governments?

1700	1750	1800

♦ 1720s *Tulip Period in Ottoman Empire*

♦ 1687 *Isaac Newton's Principia Mathematica*   ♦ 1735 *Carolus Linnaeus's Systema Naturae*

♦ 1690 *John Locke's Essay Concerning Human Understanding*   ♦------------------♦ 1751–1772 *Denis Diderot's Encyclopedia*

1768–1779 *Voyages of Captain James Cook* ♦--------♦

1776 *Adam Smith's The Wealth of Nations* ♦

------------------→ ♦ 1700s *Enlightenment philosophy introduces elite thought in American colonies*

♦ 1728 *Movement for "native learning" begins in Japan*

REORDERING THE WORLD, 1750–1850

In 1798, the French commander Napoleon Bonaparte invaded Egypt. At the time, Europeans regarded this territory as the cradle of a once-great culture, a land bridge to the Red Sea and trade with Asia, and an outpost of the Ottoman Empire. Occupying the country would allow Napoleon to introduce some of the principles of the French Revolution and to seize control of trade routes to Asia. Napoleon also hoped that by defeating the Ottomans, who controlled Egypt, he would augment his and France's historic greatness. But events did not go as Napoleon planned, for his troops faced a resentful Egyptian population.

Although Napoleon soon returned to France and his dream of a French Egypt was short-lived, his invasion challenged Ottoman rule and threatened the balance of power in Europe. Indeed, Napoleon's actions in Africa, the Americas, and Europe, combined with the principles of the French Revolution, laid the foundations for a new era—one based on the radically new idea of freedom, which was expected to manifest itself in personal relationships, economic arrangements, and political action. In Europe and the Americas, though not elsewhere, the era also witnessed the emergence of the nation-state. This new form of political organization derived legitimacy from its inhabitants,

561

often referred to as citizens, who in theory, if not always in practice, shared a common culture, ethnicity, and language.

This broad reordering had its roots in the Atlantic world, where political upheavals destroyed the American colonial domains of Spain, Portugal, Britain, and France and brought new nations to the stage. But even as western European countries lost their New World colonies, they gained economic and military power, which further challenged Asian and African governments. In response, reform-minded leaders in Egypt and the Ottoman Empire tried to modernize. The impulse for the changes that had their epicenter in the Americas and western Europe was a belief that new, less restricted institutions would bring benefits to all. The watchwords of the age were free inquiry, free markets, free labor, and governments freely chosen by free individuals. Meanwhile, in China, the ruling Manchus faced European pressure to permit expanded trade. Clearly, the worldwide balance of power was changing.

REVOLUTIONARY TRANSFORMATIONS AND NEW LANGUAGES OF FREEDOM

> → *How did Enlightenment ideas transform the world?*

In the eighteenth century, the circulation of goods, people, and ideas created pressures for reform around the Atlantic world. As economies expanded, many people felt that the restrictive mercantilist system prevented them from sharing in the new wealth and power. Similarly, an increasingly literate public called for their states to adopt just practices, including the abolition of torture and the accountability of rulers. Although elites resisted the demands for more freedom to trade and more influence in government, power holders could not stamp out these demands before they became—in several places—full-scale revolutions.

Reformers wanted to establish **popular sovereignty** (power residing in the people themselves) and argued that unregulated economies would produce faster economic growth. In fact, they argued that three important aspects of such economies would yield more just and more efficient societies, ultimately benefiting everyone everywhere in the world. These three aspects were **free trade**, that is, domestic and international trade unencumbered by tariff barriers, quotas, and fees; **free markets**, which would be unregulated; and **free labor,** which meant wage-paying rather than slave labor.

The struggle to create new political and economic relationships gave people the chance to think differently. Two new ideas were especially appealing: **nationalism** (the idea that members of a shared community called a "nation" should have sovereignty within the borders of their state) and **democracy** (the idea that these people, through membership in a nation, should choose their own representatives and be governed by them). The first expression of this new thinking occurred in thirteen of Britain's North American colonies and in France. In both places, the "nation" and the "people" toppled their former rulers.

As democratic and nationalist ideas emerged in the American and French revolutions, questions arose as to how far freedom should be extended. Should women, Native Americans, and slaves be given the rights of citizens? Should people without property be given the vote? Should freedom be extended to non-Europeans? For the most part, European and Euro-American elites answered no. The same elites who wanted a freer world often exploited slaves, denied women equal treatment, restricted colonial economies, and tried to forcibly open Asia's and Africa's markets to European trade

Focus Questions

Ⓖ WWNORTON.COM/STUDYSPACE

→ *How did Enlightenment ideas transform the world?*

→ *What major changes in government and society grew out of the Atlantic revolutions?*

→ *How did abolition of the slave trade affect African society?*

→ *How did the industrial revolution reorder society?*

→ *How did the Atlantic revolutions affect Afro-Eurasian societies?*

MAIN THEMES

➔ *A new era based on radically new ideas of freedom and the nation-state emerges in Europe and the Americas.*
➔ *The watchwords of the age are free inquiry, free markets, free labor, and governments freely chosen by free individuals.*
➔ *The worldwide balance of power changes.*

FOCUS ON *The Global Effects of the "New Ideas"*

The Atlantic World

✦ North American colonists revolt against British rule and establish a nonmonarchical, republican form of government.
✦ Inspired by the American Revolution, the French citizenry abolishes feudalism; proclaims a new era of liberty, equality, and fraternity; and executes opponents of their revolution, notably the king and queen of France.
✦ Napoleon's French empire extends many principles of the French Revolution throughout Europe.
✦ Drawing on the ideals of the French Revolution, Haitian slaves throw off French rule, abolish slavery, and create an independent state.
✦ Napoleon's invasion of Iberia frees Portuguese and Spanish America from colonial rule.

✦ The British lead a successful campaign to abolish the Atlantic slave trade and promote new sources of trade with Africa.
✦ An industrial revolution spreads outward from Britain to the rest of the world.
✦ The Russian monarchy strengthens its power through modest reforms and suppression of rebellion.

Africa, India, and Asia

✦ In Egypt a military adventurer, Muhammad Ali, modernizes the country and threatens the political integrity of the Ottoman Empire.
✦ The British East India Company increasingly dominates the Indian subcontinent.
✦ The Qing Empire persists despite major European encroachments on its sovereignty.

---

and investment. In Africa, another corner of the Atlantic world, idealistic upheavals did not lead to free and sovereign peoples, but to greater enslavement.

 POLITICAL REORDERINGS

➔ *What major changes in government and society grew out of the Atlantic revolutions?*

Late in the eighteenth century, revolutionary ideas spread across the Atlantic world (see Map 15-1) following the trail of Enlightenment ideas about freedom and reason. As more newspapers, pamphlets, and books circulated in European countries and American colonies, readers began to discuss their societies' problems and to believe they had the right to participate in governance. Gradually, on both sides of the Atlantic, politics drew in a wider group beyond kings, court advisers, and landowning elites. Increasingly, those who supported political revolutions claimed to be acting for the good of "the people."

The slogans of independence, freedom, liberty, and equality seemed to promise an end to oppression, hardship, and inequities. In the North American colonies and in France, revolutions ultimately brought down monarchies and blossomed in republics. The examples of the United States and France soon encouraged others in the Caribbean and Central and South America to reject the rule of monarchs. In all these revolutionary environments, new institutions—such as written constitutions and permanent parliaments—claimed to represent the people. The claims of popular sovereignty also became rooted in the idea of the nation (people of a common language, common culture, and common history), giving rise to the notion of the **nation-state**.

RUSSIA

BRITISH NORTH AMERICA

Hudson Bay

OREGON
(Claimed by Spain,
Russia and Britain)

LOUISIANA

Quebec

Boston
New York
Philadelphia
Washington, D.C.

UNITED STATES
✳ 1776
(independence recognized
by Great Britain 1783)

Charleston

Santa Fe

MEXICO
✳ 1821

FLORIDA

Gulf of Mexico

ATLANTIC

OCEAN

Mexico City

CUBA

PUERTO RICO

BELIZE

JAMAICA

GUADELOUPE (Fr.)

REPUBLIC OF HAITI
✳ 1804

MARTINIQUE (Fr.)

UNITED PROVINCES
OF CENTRAL AMERICA
✳ 1823

Cartagena

Caracas

TRINIDAD (Br.)

PACIFIC

OCEAN

REPUBLIC OF
COLOMBIA
✳ 1819

GUIANA

Quito

PERU
✳ 1821

Lima

BRAZIL
✳ 1822

BOLIVIA
✳ 1825

PARAGUAY
✳ 1811

Rio de Janeiro

CHILE
✳ 1818

PROVINCES
OF LA PLATA
✳ 1816

URUGUAY
✳ 1828

Buenos Aires

Montevideo

British possessions
Spanish possessions
French possessions
Portuguese possessions
Dutch possessions
Ottoman possessions
Russian Empire
✳ 1776 Date of political independence
from European (or Ottoman)
colonial rule

0   1000   2000 Miles

0   1000   2000 Kilometers

MAP 15-1   REVOLUTIONS OF NATIONAL INDEPENDENCE IN THE ATLANTIC WORLD, 1776–1829

Influenced by Enlightenment thinkers and the French Revolution, colonies gained independence from European powers (and in the case of Greece, from the Ottoman Empire) in the late eighteenth and early nineteenth centuries. Which European powers granted independence to their colonial possessions in the Americas during this period? What were the first two colonial territories to become independent in the Americas? Given that the second American republic arose from a violent slave revolt, why do you suppose the United States was reluctant to recognize its political independence? According to your reading, why did colonies in Spanish and Portuguese America obtain political independence decades after the United States won its independence?

THE NORTH AMERICAN WAR OF INDEPENDENCE, 1776–1783

By the mid-eighteenth century, Britain's colonies in North America swelled with people and prosperity. Bustling port cities like Charleston, Philadelphia, New York, and Boston saw inflows of African slaves, European migrants, and manufactured goods, while agricultural staples flowed out. A "genteel" class of merchants and landowning planters dominated colonial affairs.

But with settlers arriving from Europe and slaves from Africa, land was a constant source of dispute. Planters struggled with independent farmers (yeomen). Sons and daughters of farmers, often unable to inherit or acquire land near their parents, moved westward, where they came into conflict with Indian peoples. To defend their lands, many Indians allied with Britain's rival, France. After losing the Seven Years' War (see Chapter 13), however, France ceded its Canadian colony to Britain. This left many Indians no choice but to turn to Britain to help them resist the aggressive advances of land-hungry colonists. British officials did make some concessions to Indian interests, most visibly by issuing the Proclamation of 1763, which drew a line at the crest of the Appalachians beyond which Indian lands were to be protected from colonial settlement. Still, Britain did not have the troops to police the line, so while the proclamation antagonized some colonists, it did not really secure Indian lands.

ASSERTING INDEPENDENCE FROM BRITAIN Even as tensions simmered and sometimes boiled over into bloodshed on the western frontier of British North America, the situation of the British in North America still looked very strong in the mid-1760s. At that point, Britain stood supreme in the Atlantic world, with its greatest foes defeated and its empire expanding. Political revolution seemed unimaginable. And yet, a decade later, that is what occurred.

The spark came from King George III, who insisted that colonists help pay for Britain's war with France and for the benefits of being subjects of the British Empire. It seemed only reasonable to King George and his ministers, faced with staggering war debts, that colonists contribute to the crown that protected them. Accordingly, the king's officials imposed taxes on a variety of commodities and tried to end the lucrative smuggling by which colonists had been evading the restrictions that mercantilism was supposed to impose on colonial trade. To the king's surprise and dismay, colonists raised vigorous objections to the new measures and protested having to pay taxes when they lacked political representation in the British Parliament. (See Primary Source: The Other Revolution of 1776.)

In 1775, resistance in the form of petitions and boycotts turned into open warfare between a colonial militia and British troops in Massachusetts. Once blood was spilled, more radical voices came to the fore. Previously, leaders of the resistance to taxation without representation had claimed to revere the British Empire while fearing its corruptions. Now calls for severing the ties to Britain became more prominent. Thomas Paine, a recent immigrant from England, captured the new mood in a pamphlet he published in 1776, arguing that it was "common sense" for people to govern themselves. Later that year, the Continental Congress (in which representatives from thirteen colonies gathered) adapted part of Payne's popular pamphlet for the Declaration of Independence.

Drawing on Enlightenment themes (see Chapter 14), the declaration written by Thomas Jefferson stated the people's "natural rights" to govern themselves. It also drew inspiration from the writings of the British philosopher John Locke, notably the idea that governments should be based on a **social contract** in which the law binds both ruler and people. Locke had even written that the people had the right to rebel against their government if it broke the contract and infringed on their rights.

With the Declaration of Independence, the rebels announced their right to rid themselves of the English king and form their own government. But neither the Declaration of Independence nor Locke's writings explained how these colonists (now calling themselves Americans) should organize a nonmonarchical government—or how thirteen weakly connected colonies (now calling themselves states) might prevail against the world's most powerful empire. Nonetheless,

The Boston Massacre. Paul Revere's idealized view of the Boston Massacre of March 5, 1770. In the years after the Seven Years' War, Bostonians grew increasingly disenchanted with British efforts to enforce imperial regulations. When British troops fired on and killed several members of an angry mob in what came to be called the "Boston Massacre," the resulting frenzy stirred revolutionary sentiments among the populace.

THE OTHER REVOLUTION OF 1776

The year 1776 is mainly known as the year American colonists declared their independence from the British Empire. But it also marked the publication of Adam Smith's An Inquiry into the Nature and Causes of the Wealth of Nations, *the most important book in the history of economic thought. Smith, a Scottish philosopher, felt that constraints on trade (by governments or private monopolies) prevented people from achieving their full potential and thereby impoverished nations. Although he was not opposed to colonies per se, in this selection Smith warns British authorities that mercantilist controls on their colonies are not only unjust but counterproductive. Thus, "free trade" is tied to the fate of Europe's colonies.*

The exclusive trade of the mother countries tends to diminish, or, at least, to keep down below what they would otherwise rise to, both the enjoyments and industry of all those nations in general, and of the American colonies in particular. . . . By rendering the colony produce dearer in all other countries, it lessens its consumption, and thereby cramps the industry of the colonies, and both the enjoyments and the industry of all other countries, which both enjoy less when they pay more for what they enjoy, and produce less when they get less for what they produce.

By rendering the produce of all other countries dearer in the colonies, it cramps, in the same manner, the industry of all other countries, and both the enjoyments and the industry of the colonies. It is a clog which, for the supposed benefit of some particular countries, embarrasses the pleasures, and encumbers the industry of all other countries; but of the colonies more than of any other.

It not only excludes, as much as possible, all other countries from one particular market; but it confines, as much as possible, the colonies to one particular market: and the difference is very great between being excluded from one particular market, when all others are open, and being confined to one particular market, when all others are shut up. The surplus produce of the colonies, however, is the original source of all that increase of enjoyments and industry which Europe derives from the discovery and colonization of America; and the exclusive trade of the mother countries tends to render this source much less abundant than it otherwise would be.

→ *In terms of the American colonies, who is "the mother country"?*

→ *According to Smith, how does exclusive trade between the mother country and the colonists diminish the colonies' development?*

SOURCE: Adam Smith, *An Inquiry into the Nature and Causes of the Wealth of Nations*, Book 4, edited by Edwin Cannan (Chicago: University of Chicago Press, 1776/1977), pp. 105–106.

the colonies soon became embroiled in a revolution that would turn the world upside down.

During their War of Independence, Americans designed new political arrangements. First, individual states elected delegates to constitutional conventions, where they drafted written constitutions to govern the workings of each state. Second, by eliminating royal authority, the state constitutions gave extensive powers to legislative bodies, whose members "the people" would elect. But who constituted the people? That is, who had voting rights? Not women. Not slaves. Not Indians. Not even adult white men who owned no property.

Despite the limited extent of voting rights, the notion that all men were created equal overturned former social hierarchies. Thus common men no longer automatically deferred to gentlemen of higher rank. Many women claimed that their contributions to the revolution's cause (by managing farms and shops in their husbands' absence) earned them greater equality in marriage, including property rights. In letters to her husband, John Adams, who was a representative in the Continental Congress and a champion of American independence, Abigail Adams stopped referring to the family farm as "yours" and instead called it "ours." Most revolutionary of all, many slaves sided against the Revolution, for it was the British who offered them freedom—most directly in exchange for military service.

Alas, their hopes for freedom were thwarted when Britain conceded the loss of its rebellious American colonies. That improbable outcome owed to a war in which British armies won most of the major battles but could not finish off the

Abigail Adams. Abigail Adams was the wife of John Adams, a leader in the movement for American independence and later the second president of the United States. Abigail's letters to her husband testified to the ways in which revolutionary enthusiasm for liberty and equality began to reach into women's minds. In the spring of 1776, Abigail wrote to implore that the men in the Continental Congress "remember the ladies, and be more generous and favorable to them than your ancestors. . . . If particular care and attention is not paid to the Ladies we are determined to foment a Rebellion, and will not hold ourselves bound by any Laws in which we have no voice, or Representation."

Continental Army under the command of General George Washington. Washington hung on and held his troops together long enough to convince the French that the American cause was not hopeless and that supporting it might be a way to settle a score against the British. This they did, and with the Treaty of Paris (1783) the United States gained its independence.

BUILDING A REPUBLICAN GOVERNMENT With independence, the former colonists had to build a new government. They generally agreed that theirs was not to be a monarchy. But what it *was* to be remained through the 1780s a source of much debate, involving heated words and sometimes heated action.

Amid the political revolution against monarchy, the prospect of a social revolution of women, slaves, and artisans generated a reaction against what American elites called the "excesses of democracy." Their fears increased after farmers in Massachusetts, led by Daniel Shays, interrupted court proceedings in which the state tried to foreclose on their properties for nonpayment of taxes. The farmers who joined in Shays's rebellion in 1786 also denounced illegitimate taxation—this time, by their state's government. Acting in the interests of the fledgling government, Massachusetts militiamen defeated the rebel army. But to save the young nation from falling into "anarchy," propertied men convened the Constitutional Convention in Philadelphia a year later.

This gathering aimed to forge a document that would create a more powerful national government and a more unified nation. After fierce debate, the convention drafted a charter for a **republican government** in which power and rulership would rest with representatives of the people—not a king. When it went before the states for approval, the Constitution was controversial. Its critics, known as Anti-Federalists, feared the growth of a potentially tyrannical national government and insisted on including a Bill of Rights to protect individual liberties from abusive government intrusions. Ultimately the Constitution won ratification, and the Bill of Rights was soon amended to it.

Ratification of the Constitution and the addition of the Bill of Rights did not end arguments about the scope and power of the national government of the United States, although they did quiet the most heated controversies. In an uneasy truce, political leaders agreed not to let the debate over whether to abolish slavery escalate into a cause for disunion. As the frontier pushed westward, however, the question of which new states would or would not allow slavery sparked debates again. Initially the existence of ample land postponed a confrontation. In 1800, Thomas Jefferson's election as the third president of the United States marked the triumph of a model of sending pioneers out to new lands in order to reduce conflict on old lands. In the same year, however, a Virginia slave named Gabriel Prosser raised an army of slaves to seize the state capital at Richmond and won support from white artisans and laborers for a more inclusive republic. His dream of an egalitarian revolution fell victim to white terror and black betrayal, though: twenty-seven slaves, including Prosser, went to the gallows. With them, for the moment, died the dream of a multiracial republic in which all men were truly created equal.

But the issue of slavery did not go away. Indeed, with ideas of the dignity and rights of free labor gaining popularity in the northern states, the truce by which political leaders tried to keep debates over slavery from escalating into a cause for disunion became even more uneasy.

In a larger Atlantic world context, the American Revolution ushered in a new age based on ideas of freedom. The successful defiance of Europe's most powerful empire and the establishment of a nonmonarchical, republican form of government sent shock waves through the Americas and Europe and even into distant corners of Asia and Africa.

THE FRENCH REVOLUTION, 1789–1799

Partly inspired by the American Revolution, French men and women soon began to call for liberty too—and the result profoundly shook Europe's dynasties and social hierarchies. Its impact, though, reached well beyond Europe, for the French Revolution, even more than the American, inspired rebels and terrified rulers around the globe.

The "Tennis Court Oath." Locked out of the chambers of the Estates-General, the deputies of the Third Estate reconvened at a nearby indoor tennis court in June 1789; there they swore an oath not to disband until the king recognized the sovereignty of a national assembly.

ORIGINS AND OUTBREAK For decades, enlightened thinkers had attacked France's old regime—the court, the aristocracy, and the church—at the risk of imprisonment or exile. But by the mid-eighteenth century, discontent had spread beyond the educated few. In the countryside, peasants grumbled about having to pay taxes and tithes to the church, whereas nobles and clergy paid almost no taxes. Also, despite improved health and nutrition, peasants still suffered occasional deprivation. A combination of these pressures, as well as a fiscal crisis, unleashed the French Revolution of 1789.

Ironically, the king himself opened the door to revolution. Eager to weaken his rival, England, Louis XVI spent huge sums in support of the American rebels—and thereby overloaded the state's debt. It was not the size of the debt but the French king's inability to raise funds that put him in a bind. To restore his credit, Louis needed to raise taxes on the privileged classes, but to do so he was forced to convene the Estates-General, a medieval advisory body that had not met for over a century. Like the American colonists, French nobles argued that taxation gave them the right of representation. When the king reluctantly agreed to summon the Estates-General in 1788, he still thought he would prevail. After all, the delegates of the clergy (the First Estate) and the aristocracy (the Second Estate) could overrule the delegates representing everyone else (the Third Estate), because each estate voted as one body. This meant that it was possible to outvote the Third Estate.

However, when the delegates assembled, the Third Estate refused to be outvoted. It insisted that those who worked and paid taxes *were* the nation, and it demanded that all delegates sit together in one chamber and vote as individuals. The privileged few, critics claimed, were parasites. As arguments raged, peasants began to attack castles in another indication that "the people" were throwing off old inequalities. Soon delegates of the Third Estate declared themselves to be the "National Assembly," the body that should determine France's future.

On July 14, 1789, a Parisian crowd attacked a medieval armory in search of weapons. Not only did this armory—the Bastille—hold gunpowder, but it was also an infamous prison for political prisoners. The crowd stormed the prison and murdered the commanding officer, then cut off his head and paraded it through the streets of Paris. On this day (Bastille Day), the king made the fateful decision not to call out the army, and the capital city belonged to the crowd. As news spread to the countryside, peasants torched manor houses and destroyed municipal archives containing records of the hated feudal dues. Barely three weeks later, the French National Assembly abolished the feudal privileges of the nobility and the clergy. It also declared a new era of liberty, equality, and fraternity.

REVOLUTIONARY TRANSFORMATIONS The "Declaration of the Rights of Man and Citizen" followed a few weeks later. It echoed the Americans' Declaration of Independence, but in more radical terms. It guaranteed all citizens of the French nation inviolable liberties and gave all men equality under the law. It also proclaimed that "the principle of all sovereignty rests essentially in the nation." Thus, the French Revolution connected more closely the concept of a people with a nation. Both the rhetorical and the real war against feudal privileges ushered in the end of dynastic and aristocratic rule in Europe.

Relations in social hierarchies changed too, as women felt that the new principles of citizenship should include women's

Women March on Versailles. On October 5, 1789, a group of market women, many of them fishwives (traditionally regarded as leaders of the poor), marched on the Paris city hall to demand bread. Quickly, their numbers grew, and they redirected their march to Versailles, some twelve miles away and the symbol of the entire political order. In response to the women, the king finally appeared on the balcony and agreed to sign the revolutionary decree and return with the women to Paris.

rights. In 1791, a group of women demanded the right to bear arms to defend the revolution, but they stopped short of claiming equal rights for both sexes. In their view, women would become citizens by being good revolutionary wives and mothers, not because of any natural rights. In the same year, Olympe de Gouges composed the "Declaration of the Rights of Woman and Citizen," proposing rights to divorce, hold property in marriage, be educated, and have public careers. The all-male assembly did not take up these issues, believing that a "fraternity" of free *men* composed the nation. (For a statement claiming similar rights for women in Britain, see Primary Source: Mary Wollstonecraft on the Rights of Women.)

As the revolution gained momentum, more nobles and clergy fled the country. In late 1790, all clergy had to take an oath of loyalty to the new state—an action that enraged Catholics. Meanwhile, the revolutionary ranks began to splinter, as men and women argued over the revolution's proper goals. Soon a new National Convention was elected by universal manhood suffrage, meaning that all adult males could vote—the first such election in Europe. In 1792, the first French Republic was proclaimed. But radicalization continued, and by early 1793 Louis XVI had lost his head to the guillotine, and France was at war with many of its neighbors.

THE TERROR   After the king's execution, radicals known as Jacobins, who wanted to extend the revolution beyond France's borders, launched the Reign of Terror to purge the nation of its internal enemies. Jacobin leaders, including the lawyer Maximilien Robespierre, oversaw the execution of as many as 40,000 so-called enemies of the people—mostly peasants and laborers.

To spread revolution to other parts of Europe, the radicals instituted the first national draft. By 1794 France's army numbered some 800,000 soldiers, making it the world's largest. Most French officers now came from the middle classes, some even from the lower class. Foot soldiers identified with the French fatherland and demonstrated their solidarity by singing songs like "The Marseillaise."

The revolutionaries understood that to change society they would have to eliminate all symbols of the old regime. So they changed street names to honor revolutionary heroes, destroyed monuments to the royal family, adopted a new flag, eliminated titles, and insisted that everyone be addressed as "Citizen." They were so exhilarated by the new world they were creating that they changed time itself. Now they reckoned time not from the birth of Christ but from the moment the French Republic was proclaimed. Thus September 22, 1792, became day 1 of year 1 of the new age. The radicals also unsuccessfully attempted to replace the Catholic faith, which they accused of corruption and inequality, with a religion of reason.

By mid-1794, enthusiasm for Robespierre's measures had lost popular support, and Robespierre himself went to the guillotine on 9 Thermidor (July 28, 1794). His execution marked the end of the Terror. Several years later, following more political turmoil, a coup d'état brought to power a thirty-year-old general from the recently annexed Mediterranean island of Corsica.

The general, **Napoleon Bonaparte** (1769–1821), put security and order ahead of social reform. True, his regime retained many of the revolutionary changes, especially those associated with more efficient state government, but retreating from the Jacobins' anti-Catholicism, he allowed religion to be freely practiced again in France. Determined not only to reform France but also to prevail over its enemies, he retreated from republican principles. Napoleon first was a member of a three-man consulate; then he became first consul; finally, he proclaimed himself emperor. But he took the title Emperor of the French, not Emperor of France, and prepared a constitution subject to a vote of approval. He also

Primary Source

MARY WOLLSTONECRAFT ON THE RIGHTS OF WOMEN

As revolutionaries stressed the rights of "man" across the Atlantic world, Mary Wollstonecraft (1759–1797), an English writer, teacher, editor, and proponent of spreading education, resented her male colleagues' celebration of their newfound liberties. In A Vindication of the Rights of Woman *(1792), one of the founding works of modern feminism, she argued that the superiority of men was as arbitrary as the divine right of kings. For this, male progressives denounced her. The author is a "hyena in petticoats," noted one critic. In fact, she was arguing that women had the same rights to be reasonable creatures as men and that education should be available equally to both sexes.*

I love man as my fellow; but his sceptre, real or usurped, extends not to me, unless the reason of an individual demands my homage; and even then the submission is to reason, and not to man. In fact, the conduct of an accountable being must be regulated by the operations of its own reason; or on what foundation rests the throne of God?

It appears to me necessary to dwell on these obvious truths, because females have been insulated, as it were; and while they have been stripped of the virtues that should clothe humanity, they have been decked with artificial graces that enable them to exercise a short-lived tyranny. Love, in their bosoms, taking the place of every nobler passion, their sole ambition is to be fair, to raise emotion instead of inspiring respect; and this ignoble desire, like the servility in absolute monarchies, destroys all strength of character. Liberty is the mother of virtue, and if women be, by their very constitution, slaves, and not allowed to breathe the sharp invigorating air of freedom, they must ever languish like exotics, and be reckoned beautiful flaws in nature. Let it also be remembered, that they are the only flaw.

As to the argument respecting the subjection in which the sex has ever been held, it retorts on man. The many have always been enthralled by the few; and monsters, who scarcely have shown any discernment of human excellence, have tyrannized over thousands of their fellow-creatures. Why have men of superior endowments submitted to such degradation? For, is it not universally acknowledged that kings, viewed collectively, have ever been inferior, in abilities and virtue, to the same number of men taken from the common mass of mankind—yet have they not, and are they not still treated with a degree of reverence that is an insult to reason? China is not the only country where a living man has been made a God. *Men* have submitted to superior strength to enjoy with impunity the pleasure of the moment; *women* have only done the same, and therefore till it is proved that the courtier, who servilely resigns the birthright of a man, is not a moral agent, it cannot be demonstrated that woman is essentially inferior to man because she has always been subjugated.

→ *Wollstonecraft compares men to kings and women to slaves. What are her criticisms of kings, and why does she call them "monsters"?*

→ *In what ways are Wollstonecraft's ideas an outgrowth of Enlightenment thinking?*

→ *Do you find Wollstonecraft's arguments compelling? Explain why or why not.*

SOURCE: Mary Wollstonecraft, *A Vindication of the Rights of Woman*, edited by Miriam Brody (New York: Penguin Books, 1792/1993), pp. 122–23.

centralized government administration and created a system of rational tax collection. Most important, he created a civil legal code—the "Code Napoleon"—that applied throughout all of France (and the French colonies, including the Louisiana Territory). By designing a law code applicable to the nation as a whole, Napoleon created a model that would be widely imitated by emerging nation-states in Europe and the Americas in the century to come.

NAPOLEON'S EMPIRE, 1799–1815

Determined to extend the reach of French influence, Napoleon had his armies trumpet the principles of liberty, equality, and fraternity wherever they went. Many local populations actually embraced the French, regarding them as liberators from the old order. Although Napoleon thought the entire world would take up his cause, this was not always the case, as he learned in Egypt. After defeating Mamluk troops there in 1798, Napoleon soon faced a rebellious local Egyptian population.

In Portugal, Spain, and Russia, French troops also faced fierce popular resistance. Portuguese and Spanish soldiers and peasants formed bands of resisters called guerrillas, and British troops joined them to fight the French in the Peninsular War (1808–1813). In Germany and Italy, as local inhabitants grew tired of hearing that the French occupiers' ways were superior, many looked to their past for inspiration to oppose the French. Now they discovered something they had barely recognized before: *national* traditions and borders.

Battle of the Pyramids. The French army invaded Egypt with grand ambitions and high hopes. Napoleon brought a large cadre of scholars along with his 36,000-man army, intending to win Egyptians to the cause of the French Revolution and to establish a French imperial presence on the banks of the Nile. This idealized portrait of the famous Battle of the Pyramids, fought on July 21, 1798, shows Napoleon and his forces crushing the Mamluk military forces.

In fact, one of the ironies of Napoleon's attempt to bring all of Europe under French rule was that instead of creating a unified continent, it laid the foundations for nationalist strife.

In Europe, Napoleon extended his empire from the Iberian Peninsula to the Austrian and Prussian borders (see Map 15-2). By 1812, when he invaded Russia, however, his forces were too overstretched and undersupplied to survive the harsh winter. Until this point, divisions among his enemies had aided Napoleon's progress. But after his failed attack on Russia, all the major European powers united against him. Forced to retreat, Napoleon and his army were vanquished in Paris. Subsequently Napoleon escaped exile to lead his troops one last time; but at the Battle of Waterloo in Belgium in 1815, armies from Prussia, Austria, Russia, and Britain crushed his troops as they made their last stand.

In 1815, delegates from the victorious states met at the Congress of Vienna. They agreed to respect one another's borders and to cooperate in preventing future revolutions and war. They restored thrones to monarchs deposed by the French under Napoleon, and they returned France itself to the care of a new Bourbon king. Great Britain and Russia—one a constitutional monarchy (ruled by a prime minister and legislative body, with oversight by a king), the other an autocracy (in which the ruler did not share power with anyone)—cooperated to prevent any future attempts to dominate the continent.

The impact of the French Revolution and Napoleon's conquests, however, was far-reaching. In numerous German states, the changes introduced under French revolutionary occupation remained in place. Napoleon's occupation of the Italian peninsula also sparked underground movements for liberty and for Italian unification, much to the chagrin of Austrian and French monarchs. These upheavals even affected Spain and Portugal's links to their colonies in the Americas. The stage was now set for a century-long struggle between those who wanted to restore society as it was before the French Revolution and those who wanted to guarantee a more liberal order based on individual rights, limited government, and free trade.

REVOLUTIONS IN THE CARIBBEAN AND IBERIAN AMERICA

From North America and France, revolutionary enthusiasm spread through the Caribbean and into Spanish and Portuguese America. But unlike the colonists' war of independence that produced the United States, political upheaval in the rest of the Americas began first of all from subordinated people of color (see Map 15-3).

Even before the French Revolution, Andean Indians rebelled against Spanish colonial authority. In a spectacular uprising in the 1780s, they demanded freedom from forced labor and compulsory consumption of Spanish wares. After an army

MAP 15-2   NAPOLEON'S EMPIRE, 1812

Early in the first decade of the nineteenth century, Napoleon controlled almost all of Europe. What major states were under French control? What countries were allied to France? Compare this map with the European part of Map 15-1, and explain how Napoleon redrew the map of Europe. What major country was not under French control? How was Napoleon able to control and build alliances with so many states and kingdoms?

of 40,000 to 60,000 Andean Indians besieged the ancient capital of Cuzco and nearly vanquished Spanish armies, it took Spanish forces many years to eliminate the insurgents.

After this uprising, Iberian American elites who feared their Indian or slave majorities renewed their loyalty to the Spanish or Portuguese crown. They hesitated to imitate the independence-seeking Anglo-American colonists, lest they unleash a social revolution. Ultimately, however, the French Revolution and Napoleonic wars shattered the ties between

Spain and Portugal and their American colonies. Nonetheless, elites limited local power by interpreting "liberty" to apply just to property-owning classes.

REVOLUTION IN SAINT DOMINGUE (HAITI) It was only in the French colony of Saint Domingue (modern-day Haiti) that slaves carried out a successful revolt. The French Revolution had sent shock waves through this highly prized French colony. There, it led to loss of the colony and

MAP 15-3 LATIN AMERICAN NATION BUILDING

Creating strong, unified nation-states proved difficult in Latin America. The map highlights this experience in Mexico, the United Provinces of Central America, and the Republic of Colombia. In each case, the governments' territorial and nation-building ambitions failed to some degree. During what period did a majority of the colonies in Latin America gain independence? Which European countries lost the most in Latin America during this period? Why did all these colonies gain their independence during this time?

emancipation for its slaves, along with considerable bloodshed. At the time the island's black slave population numbered 500,000, compared with 40,000 white French settlers and about 30,000 free "people of color" (individuals of mixed black and white ancestry, as well as freed black slaves). Almost two-thirds of the slaves were relatively recent arrivals, brought to the colony to toil on its renowned sugar plantations. The slave population was an angry majority.

After the events of 1789 in France, white settlers in Saint Domingue sought self-government, while slaves borrowed the revolutionary language to denounce their masters. As civil war erupted, Dominican slaves fought French forces that had arrived to restore order. (See Global Connections & Disconnections: Inspirations for Slave Rebellion on Haiti.) Finally, in 1793, the National Convention in France abolished slavery. The argument that revolutionary principles (liberty, fraternity, equality) should apply to the French colonies as well as to the nation won out over claims that abolition would mean economic disaster.

Once liberated, the former slaves took control of the island, but their struggles were not over. First they had to fight British and Spanish forces on the island. Then Napoleon took power in France, restored slavery, and sent an army to suppress forces led by Toussaint L'Ouverture, a former slave. But before long a combination of guerrilla fighters and yellow fever crippled the French army, which

INSPIRATIONS FOR SLAVE REBELLION ON HAITI

As the ideals of the French Revolution spread through Europe and overseas, they had a tumultuous effect on the island of Saint Domingue (renamed Haiti after it acquired independence). By the 1780s Saint Domingue was France's richest colony, whose wealth came from sugar plantations that used a vast, highly coerced slave population. About 40,000 whites ruthlessly exploited 500,000 enslaved Africans. The slaves' lives were short and brutal, lasting on average only fifteen years; hence the wealthy planter class had to replenish their labor supplies from Africa at frequent intervals.

White planters on the island had the reputation of great wealth. But they knew their privileges were vulnerable, so they were eager to amass quick fortunes so that they could sell out and return to France. These men and women were vastly outnumbered by the enslaved, who were seething with resentment, at a time when abolitionist sentiments were gaining ground in Europe and even circulating among slaves in the Americas.

Yet, the planters greeted the onset of the French Revolution in 1789 with enthusiasm. They saw an opportunity to assert their independence from France and to engage in wider trading contacts with North America and the rest of the world. They ignored the fact that the ideals of the French Revolution—especially its slogan of liberty, equality, and fraternity—could inspire the island's free blacks, free mulattoes, and slaves. Indeed, no sooner had the white planters thrown in their lot with the Third Estate in France than a slave rebellion broke out in Saint Domingue. From its beginnings in 1791, it led, after great loss of life to African slaves and French soldiers, to the proclamation of an independent state in Haiti in 1804, ruled by African Americans. Haiti became the Americas' second independent republican government.

The revolution had many sources of inspiration. It was both French and African. According to a later West Indian scholar, a group of black Jacobins, determined to carry the ideals of the French Revolution to their logical end point—the abolition of slavery—made up the revolutionary cadre. Their undisputed leader was Toussaint L'Ouverture, a freed black who had learned about French abolitionist writings. But given that most of the slaves had arrived from Africa very recently, African cultural and political ideals also fueled slave resistance.

At a secret meeting in 1791, the persons who were to lead the initial stage of the revolution gathered to affirm their commitment to one another at a voodoo ritual, presided over by a tall, black priestess "with strange eyes and bristly hair." Voodoo was a mixture of African and New World religious beliefs that existed among slave communities in many parts of the Americas (see Chapter 14). One

Toussaint L'Ouverture. In the 1790s, Toussaint L'Ouverture led the slaves of the French colony of Saint Domingue in the world's largest and most successful slave insurrection. Toussaint embraced the principles of the French Revolution and demanded that universal rights be applied to people of African descent.

description of the ceremony relates that after performing a ritual dance accompanied by an African song, the priestess sacrificed a pig and served its blood to each participant. Then, "at a signal from the priestess, everyone threw themselves on their knees and swore blindly to obey the orders of Boukman, who had been proclaimed supreme chief of the rebellion." Boukman, a voodoo chief himself, initiated the revolution against the planters, though Toussaint L'Ouverture later assumed leadership of the revolt.

Inspired by both voodoo and the French Revolution, the rebellion in Saint Domingue caused the deaths or maiming of hundreds of thousands of African slaves and French soldiers. Thereafter, as white planters yielded to a black political elite, the old sugar economy collapsed. Slave shipments no longer arrived, and sugar was no longer exported.

ultimately surrendered and left. Toussaint L'Ouverture died in a French jail, having been captured while negotiating a settlement. Nonetheless, in 1804 General Jean-Jacques Dessalines declared "Haiti" independent.

The revolt had serious environmental consequences. Not only did sugarcane fields become scorched battlefields, but freed slaves rushed to stake out independent plots on the old plantations and in wooded areas. In both places, the new peasant class energetically cleared the land. The small country soon became deforested, and intensive cultivation caused erosion and soil depletion. Haiti fell into a vicious cycle of environmental degradation and poverty.

Moreover, independence did not bring international recognition from fellow revolutionaries. France's commitment to empire ultimately overrode its commitment to the ideals of republican citizenship. Indeed, Toussaint and the slaves of Saint Domingue had been more loyal to the ideals of liberty than the French themselves were. Even Thomas Jefferson, author of the Declaration of Independence and U.S. president at the time, refused to recognize Haiti. Like other American slave owners, he worried that the example of a successful slave uprising might inspire similar revolts in the United States.

BRAZIL AND CONSTITUTIONAL MONARCHY Brazil was a prized Portuguese colony whose path to independence saw little political turmoil and no social revolution. In 1807, French troops stormed Lisbon, the capital of Portugal, but not before the royals and their associates fled to Rio de Janeiro, then the capital of Brazil. There they made reforms in administration, agriculture, and manufacturing, and they established schools, hospitals, and a library. In fact, the royals' migration prevented the need for colonial claims for autonomy, because with their presence Brazil was now the center of the Portuguese empire. Furthermore, the royal family willingly shared power with the local planter aristocracy, so the economy prospered and slavery expanded.

In 1821, the exiled Portuguese king returned to Lisbon, instructing his son Pedro to preserve the family lineage in Rio de Janeiro. Soon, however, Brazilian elites rejected Portugal altogether. Fearing that colonists might topple the dynasty in Rio de Janeiro and spark regional disputes, in 1822 Pedro declared Brazil an independent empire. Shortly thereafter he established a constitutional monarchy, which would last until the late nineteenth century.

Now Brazilian business elites and bureaucrats cooperated to minimize conflicts, lest a slave revolt erupt. They crushed regional uprisings, like the fledgling Republic of the Equator, and a campaign seeking a decentralized federation of southern provinces free from the Rio de Janeiro rulers. Even the largest urban slave revolt in the Americas, led by African Muslims in the state of Bahia, was quashed in a matter of days. By the 1840s, Brazil had achieved a political stability unmatched in the Americas. Its socially controlled transition from colony to nation was unique in Latin America.

Revolution in Saint Domingue. In 1791, slaves and people of color rose up against white planters. This engraving was based on a German report on the uprising and depicts white fears of slave rebellion as much as the actual events themselves.

As the Brazilian state and its ruling elite expanded the agrarian frontier, here, too, occurred the same kind of terrible environmental degradation that had taken place in Haiti. Landowners oversaw the clearing of ancient hardwood forests so that slaves and squatters could plant coffee trees. The clearing process had begun with sugarcane in the coastal regions, but it accelerated with coffee plantings in the hilly regions of São Paulo. In fact, coffee was a worse threat to Brazil's forests than any other invader in the previous 300 years. Consider that coffee trees thrive on soils that are neither soggy nor overly dry. Therefore planters razed the "virgin" forest, which contained a balanced variety of trees and undergrowth, and Brazil's once-fertile soil suffered rapid depletion by the single-crop industry. Within one generation the clear-cutting led to infertile soils and extensive erosion, which drove planters further into the frontier to destroy even more old forest and plant more coffee groves. The environmental impact was monumental: between 1788 and 1888, when slavery was abolished, Brazil produced about 10 million tons of coffee at the expense of 300 million tons of ancient forest biomass (the accumulated biological material from living organisms).

MEXICO'S INDEPENDENCE When Napoleon occupied Spain, he sparked a crisis in the Spanish empire. Because the ruling Spanish Bourbons fell captive to Napoleon in 1807 and then spent many years under comfortable house

Miguel Hidalgo y Costilla. At the center of this mural by Juan O'Gorman is the revolutionary Mexican priest Miguel Hidalgo y Costilla, who led the first uprising against Spanish rulers. This painting suggests the rebellion was a multiclass and multiethnic movement.

arrest, colonial elites in Buenos Aires (Argentina), Caracas (Venezuela), and Mexico City (Mexico) enjoyed self-rule without an emperor. Once the Bourbons returned to power in 1814 after Napoleon was crushed, creoles (American-born Spaniards) resented it when Spain reinstated peninsulars (colonial officials born in Spain). Inspired by Enlightenment thinkers and chafing at the efforts to restore Iberian authority, the creoles wanted to keep their elite privileges and get rid of the peninsulars.

In Mexico, the royal army prevailed as long as there was any hope that the emperor in Madrid could maintain political authority. But from 1810 to 1813 two rural priests, Father Miguel Hidalgo and Father José María Morelos, galvanized an insurrection of peasants, Indians, and artisans. They sought an end to abuses by the elite, denounced bad government, and called for redistribution of wealth, return of land to the Indians, and respect for the Virgin of Guadalupe (who later became Mexico's patron saint). The rebellion nearly choked off Mexico City, the colony's capital, which horrified peninsulars and creoles alike. In response, they overcame their own disputes to plead with Spanish armies to rescue them from the rebels. Years later, the royal armies eventually crushed the uprising.

Despite the military victory, Spain's hold on its colony weakened. After all, during the years of conflict the colonists had enjoyed some autonomy and had begun electing representatives to local assemblies. Moreover, like the creoles of South America, those of Mexico were identifying themselves more as Mexicans and less as Spanish Americans. So when the Spanish king appeared unable to govern effectively abroad and even within Spain, the colonists considered home rule. A critical factor was the army, which remained faithful to the crown. However, when anarchy seemed to spread through Spain in 1820, Mexican generals (with support of the creoles) proclaimed Mexican independence in 1821. In many ways, as with Brazil, independence from Spain was a way to curb further turmoil within Mexico. But unlike in Brazil, Mexican secession did not lead to stability.

OTHER SOUTH AMERICAN REVOLUTIONS   The loosening of Spain's grip on its colonies was more prolonged and militarized than Britain's separation from its American colonies. Indeed, the struggle for independence from Spain transformed the nature of political leadership in South America. Venezuela's **Simón Bolívar** (1783–1830), the son of a merchant-planter family who was educated on Enlightenment texts, dreamed of a land governed by reason. He revered Napoleonic France as a model state built on military heroism and constitutional proclamations. So did the Argentine leader General José de San Martín (1778–1850). Men like Bolívar, San Martín, and their many generals waged extended wars of independence against Spanish armies and their allies between 1810 and 1824. In some areas, like present-day Uruguay and Venezuela, the wars left entire provinces depopulated.

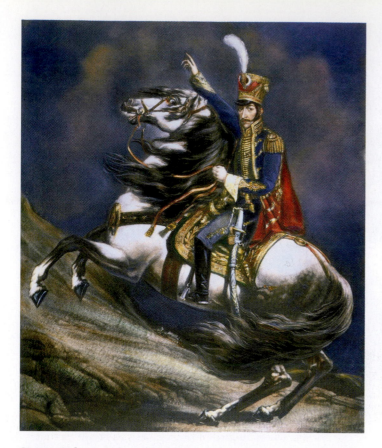

Simón Bolívar. Bolívar fought Spanish armies from Venezuela to Bolivia, securing the independence of five countries. He wanted to transform the former colonies into modern republics and used many of the icons of revolution from the rest of the Atlantic world—among his favorite models were George Washington and Napoleon Bonaparte. This image portrays Bolívar in a quintessential Napoleonic pose on horseback.

What started in South America as a political revolution against Spanish colonial authority escalated into a social struggle among Indians, mestizos, slaves, and whites. The militarized populace threatened the planters and merchants; rural folk battled against aristocratic creoles; Andean Indians fled the mines and occupied great estates. Provinces fought their neighbors. Popular armies, having defeated Spanish forces by the 1820s, fought civil wars over the new postcolonial order.

New states and collective identities of nationhood now emerged. However, a narrow elite led these political communities, and their guiding principles were contradictory. Simón Bolívar, for instance, urged his followers to become "American," to overcome their local identities. He wanted the liberated countries to form a Latin American confederation, urging Peru and Bolivia to join Venezuela, Ecuador, and Colombia in the "Gran Colombia." But local identities prevailed, giving way to unstable national republics. Bolívar died surrounded by enemies; San Martín died in exile. The real heirs to independence were local military chieftains, who often forged alliances with landowners. Thus the legacy of the Spanish American revolutions was contradictory: the triumph of wealthy elites under a banner of liberty, yet often at the expense of poorer, ethnic, and mixed populations.

CHANGE AND TRADE IN AFRICA

→ *How did abolition of the slave trade affect African society?*

Africa also was swept up in revolutionary tides, as increased domestic and world trade—including the selling of African slaves—shifted the terms of state building across the continent. Around Lake Victoria, in the highlands of present-day Rwanda and Burundi, and in southern Africa, the early nineteenth century saw new, more powerful kingdoms emerge. Other regimes shattered from internal rivalries. The main catalyst for Africa's political shake-up was the rapid growth and then the demise of the Atlantic slave trade.

ABOLITION OF THE SLAVE TRADE

Even as it enriched and empowered some Africans and many Europeans, the slave trade became a subject of fierce debate in the late eighteenth century. Some European and American revolutionaries argued that slave labor was inherently less productive than free wage labor and ought to be abolished. At the same time, another group favoring abolition of the slave trade insisted that traffic in slaves was immoral. In London they created committees, often led by Quakers, to lobby Parliament for an end to the slave trade. Quakers in Philadelphia did likewise. Pamphlets, reports, and personal narratives denounced the traffic in people. (See Primary Source: Frederick Douglass Asks, "What to the Slave Is the Fourth of July?")

In response to abolitionist efforts, North Atlantic powers moved to prohibit the slave trade. Denmark acted first in 1803, Great Britain followed in 1807, and the United States joined the campaign in 1808. Over time, the British persuaded the French and other European governments to do likewise. To enforce the ban, Britain posted a naval squadron off the coast of West Africa to prevent any slave trade above the equator and compelled Brazil's emperor to end slave imports. After 1850, Atlantic slave-shipping dropped sharply.

But until the 1860s, slavers continued to buy and ship captives illegally. British squadrons that stopped these smugglers took the freed captives to the British base at Sierra Leone and resettled them there. Liberia, too, became a refuge for freed captives and for former slaves returning from the Americas.

Primary Source

FREDERICK DOUGLASS ASKS, "WHAT TO THE SLAVE IS THE FOURTH OF JULY?"

Frederick Douglass spent the first twenty years of his life as a slave. After running away in 1838, he toured the northern United States delivering speeches that attacked the institution of slavery. The publication of his autobiography in 1845 cemented his standing as a leading abolitionist. In the excerpt below, taken from an address delivered on July 5, 1852, Douglass contrasts the freedom and natural rights extolled in the Declaration of Independence and celebrated on the Fourth of July with the dehumanizing condition—and lack of freedom—of African American slaves.

Fellow-Citizens—pardon me, and allow me to ask, why am I called upon to speak here to-day? What have I, or those I represent, to do with your national independence? Are the great principles of political freedom and of natural justice, embodied in that Declaration of Independence, extended to us? and am I, therefore, called upon to bring our humble offering to the national altar, and to confess the benefits, and express devout gratitude for the blessings, resulting from your independence to us? . . .

But, such is not the state of the case. I say it with a sad sense of the disparity between us. I am not included within the pale of this glorious anniversary! Your high independence only reveals the immeasurable distance between us. The blessings in which you this day rejoice, are not enjoyed in common. The rich inheritance of justice, liberty, prosperity, and independence, bequeathed by your fathers, is shared by you, not by me. The sunlight that brought life and healing to you, has brought stripes and death to me. This Fourth of July is *yours*, not *mine*. *You* may rejoice, *I* must mourn. . . .

. . . Must I undertake to prove that the slave is a man? That point is conceded already. Nobody doubts it. The slaveholders themselves acknowledge it in the enactment of laws for their government. They acknowledge it when they punish disobedience on the part of the slave. There

are seventy-two crimes in the state of Virginia, which, if committed by a black man (no matter how ignorant he be) subject him to the punishment of death; while only two of these same crimes will subject a white man to the like punishment. What is this but the acknowledgment that the slave is a moral, intellectual, and responsible being. The manhood of the slave is conceded. It is admitted in the fact that southern statute books are covered with enactments forbidding, under severe fines and penalties, the teaching of the slave to read or write. When you can point to any such laws, in reference to the beasts of the field, then I may consent to argue the manhood of the slave. When the dogs in your streets, when the fowls of the air, when the cattle on your hills, when the fish of the sea, and the reptiles that crawl, shall be unable to distinguish the slave from a brute, then will I argue with you that the slave is a man!

❖ *What examples does Douglass give of the disparity between slaves and free white Americans?*

❖ *How does Douglass suggest that slaves are human beings?*

❖ *What is the significance of the last sentence of the speech?*

SOURCE: David W. Blight (ed.), *Narrative of the Life of Frederick Douglass: An American Slave, Written by Himself* (Boston: Bedford Books, 1993), pp. 141–45.

NEW TRADE WITH AFRICA

Even as the Atlantic slave trade died down, Europeans promoted commerce with Africa. Now they wanted Africans to export raw materials and to purchase European manufactures. This "legitimate" trade aimed to raise the Africans' standards of living by substituting trade in produce for trade in slaves. West Africans responded by exporting palm kernels and peanuts. The real bonanza was in vegetable oils to lubri-

cate machinery and make candles and in palm oil to produce soap. European merchants argued that by becoming vibrant export societies, Africans would earn the wealth to profitably import European wares.

LEGITIMATE COMMERCE Arising in the age of legitimate commerce, Africa's palm and peanut plantations were less devastating to the environment than their predecessors in the West Indies had been. There, planters had felled

Chasing Slave Dhows. From being the major proponents of the Atlantic slave trade the British became its chief opponents, using their naval forces to suppress those European and African slave traders who attempted to subvert the injunction against slave trading. Here a British vessel chases an East African slaving dhow trying to run slaves from the island of Zanzibar.

forests to establish sugar estates (see Chapter 12). In West Africa, where palm products became crucial exports, the palm tree had always grown wild. Although intensive cultivation caused some deforestation, the results were not as extreme as in the Caribbean.

Legitimate commerce gave rise to a new generation of successful West African merchants. There were many rags-to-riches stories, like that of King Jaja of Opobo (1821–1891). Kidnapped and sold into slavery as a youngster, he started out paddling canoes carrying palm oil to coastal ports. Ultimately becoming the head of a coastal canoe house, as a merchant-prince and chief he founded the port of Opobo and could summon a flotilla of war canoes on command. Another freed slave, a Yoruba, William Lewis, made his way back to Africa and settled in Sierra Leone in 1828. Starting with a few utensils and a small plot of land, he became a successful merchant who sent his son Samuel to England for his education. Samuel eventually became an important political leader in Sierra Leone.

EFFECTS IN AFRICA   Just as the slave trade shaped African political communities, its demise brought sharp adjustments. For some, it was a welcome end to the constant drainage of people. For others, it was a disaster because it cut off income necessary to buy European arms and luxury goods. Many West African regimes, like the Yoruba kingdom, collapsed once chieftains could no longer use the slave trade to finance their retinues and armies.

The rise of free labor in the Atlantic world and the dwindling foreign slave trade had another effect: they strengthened slavery in Africa itself. In some areas by the mid-nineteenth century, slaves accounted for more than half the population. No longer did they comfortably serve in domestic employment; instead, they toiled on palm oil plantations or, in East Africa, on clove plantations. They also served in the military forces, bore palm oil and ivory to markets as porters, or paddled cargo-carrying canoes along rivers leading to the coast. In 1850, northern Nigeria's ruling class had more slaves than independent Brazil, and almost as many as the United States. No longer the world's supplier of slaves, Africa itself had become the world's largest slaveholding region.

ECONOMIC REORDERING

> → *How did the industrial revolution reorder society?*

Behind the political and social upheavals, profound changes were occurring in the world economy. Until the middle of the eighteenth century, global trade touched only the edges of societies, most of which produced for their own subsistence. Surpluses of special goods, from porcelains to silks, entered trade arteries but did not change the cultures that produced them. An exception was the Americas, where especially in the slave societies of the Caribbean, Brazil, and the southern United States, plantations produced goods for export. Yet, this commercial specialization anticipated developments to come, in which communities would be transformed to produce for other societies and less and less for themselves. This gradual, halting, but ineluctable process would gather speed in the eighteenth century and bring the world together in ways that were unimaginable during the age of older European empires.

AN INDUSTRIOUS REVOLUTION

Many of these developments took place first in northwestern Europe and British North America. Here, as elsewhere in the world, households had always produced mainly for themselves and made available for marketplaces only meager surpluses of goods and services. But dramatic changes occurred when family members, including wives and children, decided to work harder and longer in order to produce more for the market and purchase more in the market. For the first time, farmers were able to produce enough food to feed large and growing nonagrarian populations. In these locations, peasant farming gave way to specialized production for the market. In what scholars recently have come to call an **industrious revolution,** households in the countryside and the cities devoted less time to leisure activities; by working more and using income earned through hard work, they were able to live at higher standards than they had before.

This industrious revolution began in the second half of the seventeenth century, gained speed in the eighteenth century, and laid the foundations for the industrial revolution of the late eighteenth and early nineteenth centuries. The willingness on the part of families to work more and an eagerness to eat more diverse foods, to wear better clothes, and to consume products that had once been available as luxuries only to the wealthy classes led in turn to a large expansion in trade—both regionally and globally. By the eighteenth century, separate trading spheres described in earlier chapters were merging increasingly into integrated circuits. As we have observed, sugar and silver were the pioneering products. But by the eighteenth century, other staples joined the long-distance trading business; these staples, moreover, were linked to each other. Tea, for instance, was truly a beverage of world trade. Its leaves came from China, the sugar to cut its bitterness from the Caribbean, the slaves to harvest the sweetener from Africa, and the ceramics from which to drink a proper cup from the English Midlands.

The significance of growing cross-cultural trade and specialization, and the shift away from a few precious cargoes to basic staples, can be seen in the story of a single commodity: soap. By the 1840s, the American entrepreneur William Colgate was importing palm oil from West Africa, coconut oil from Malabar and Ceylon, and poppy seed oil from South Asia, all to make aromatic bars of soap. A London barber called Andrew Pears added glycerine to his product to give it a clean transparent look, and his grandson-in-law, Thomas Barratt, launched an aggressive marketing campaign—in 1886 buying a painting from the *Illustrated London News* called "Bubbles" to enhance the image of his family's soap. Colgate and his Atlantic rivals in the toiletry trade like Pears advertised their products as necessities for the prim and proper home. Pears promised African and Indian buyers that his product would actually whiten their skin.

Global trading trickled its way down from elites to ordinary folk. Even ordinary people could purchase imported goods with their earnings. Thus, the poor began to enjoy—some would say the addictions of—coffee, tea, and sugar, and eventually even felt the need to use soap. European artisans and farmers purchased tools, furnishings, and home decorations. Slaves and colonial laborers also used their meager earn-

New Farming Technologies. Although new technologies only gradually transformed agriculture, the spread of more intensive cultivation led to increased yields.

ings to buy imported cotton cloth made in Europe from the raw cotton they themselves had picked several seasons earlier.

The expansion of global trade had important social and political consequences. In many dynastic societies, merchants had long stood high in the social hierarchy, but few extended their business beyond provincial confines. As new goods flowed from ever more distant corners of the globe, immense fortunes grew. To support their enterprise, traders needed new services, in insurance, bookkeeping, and the recording of legal documents. Trade helped nurture the emergence of new classes of professionals—accountants and lawyers. The new cities of the commercial revolution hubs like Bristol, Bombay, and Buenos Aires provided the homes and flourishing neighborhoods for a class of men and women known as the **bourgeoisie.**

As Europe moved to the center of a new economic order, one class in particular moved to the top: the trader-financiers. Like the merchandiser, the financier did not have to emerge from the high and mighty of Eurasia's dynasties. Consider Mayer Amschel Rothschild (1744–1812): born the son of a money changer in the Jewish ghetto of Frankfurt, Rothschild progressed from coin dealing to money changing, then from trading textiles to lending funds to kings and governments. By the time of his death he owned the world's biggest banking operation and his five sons were running powerful branches in London, Paris, Vienna, Naples, and Frankfurt.

By extending credit, families like the Rothschilds also enabled traders to ship goods across long distances without having to worry about immediate payment. All these financial changes implied world integration through the flow of goods as well as the flow of money. In the 1820s, sizeable funds amassed in London flowed to Egypt, Mexico, and New York to support trade, public investment, and, of course, speculation.

THE INDUSTRIAL REVOLUTION

Trade and finance repositioned western Europe's relationship with the rest of the world. So did the emergence of manufacturing—a big leap, as in agriculture, in the output, in this case of industrial commodities. The heart of this process was a gradual accumulation and diffusion of technical knowledge. Lots of little inventions, their applications, and their diffusion across the Atlantic world gradually built up a stock of technical knowledge and practice. Historians have traditionally called these changes the **industrial revolution,** a term first used by the British economic historian Arnold Toynbee in the late nineteenth century. Although the term suggests radical and rapid economic change, the reality was much more gradual and less dramatic than originally believed. Yet, the term still has great validity, for the major economic changes that occurred in Britain, northwestern Europe, and North America catapulted these countries ahead of the rest of the world in industrial and agricultural output and standards of living.

Nowhere was this industrial revolution more evident than in Britain. Britain had a few advantages, like large supplies of coal and iron—key materials used in manufactured products. It also had a political and social environment that allowed merchants and industrialists to invest heavily while also expanding their internal and international markets. Among their investments was the application of steam power to textile production—which enabled Britain's manufacturers to produce cheaper goods in larger quantities. Finally, Britain had access to New World lands as sources of financial investment, raw materials, and markets for manufactured goods. These factors' convergence in Britain promoted self-sustaining economic growth.

An example of the new alliance of the inventor and the investor that fueled the industrial revolution was the advent of the steam engine. Such engines burned coal to boil water, and the resulting steam drove mechanized devices. There were several tinkerers working on the device. But the most famous was James Watt (1736–1819) of Scotland, who managed to separate steam condensers from piston cylinders so that pistons could stay hot and run constantly, and who also joined forces with the industrialist Matthew Boulton, who marketed the steam engine and set up a laboratory where Watt could refine his device. The steam engine catalyzed a revolution in transportation. Steam-powered engines also improved sugar refining, pottery making, and other industrial processes, generating more products at lower cost than when workers had made them by hand.

Technical changes made possible the consolidation of textile manufacturing within a single factory. With new machinery, a single textile operator handled many looms and spindles at once and produced bolts of cloth with stunning efficiency. Gone were the hand tools, the family traditions, and the loosely organized and dispersed systems of households putting out cloth for local merchants to carry to markets. The material was also stronger, finer, and more uniform. All the while, the price of cotton cloth almost halved between 1780 and 1850. As England became the world's largest cloth producer, it imported cotton from Brazil, Egypt, India, and the United States.

Most raw cotton for the British cloth industry had come from colonial India until 1793, when the American inventor Eli Whitney (1765–1825) patented a "cotton gin" that separated cotton seeds from fiber. After that, cotton farming spread so quickly in the southern United States that by the 1850s it was producing more than 80 percent of the world's cotton supply. In turn, every black slave in the Americas and many Indians in British India were consumers of cheap, British-produced cotton shirts.

It is important to note that the industrial revolution did not imply the creation of large-scale industries. The large factory was rare in manufacturing. Indeed, the largest employers at the time were the slave plantations of the Americas that produced the staples for industrial consumption. Small-scale production remained the norm, mass production the exception. Lyonese silks relied on the Jacquard loom, refined between 1800 and 1820, which allowed weavers to reassert their traditional control over the production of fashionable fabrics while increasing productivity. The new looms cut labor costs by eliminating some tasks, but they required skilled, precision handling. Here, as in many places, innovations in-

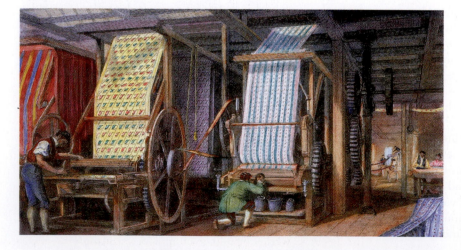

A Cotton Textile Mill in the 1830s. The region of Lancashire became one of the major industrial hubs for textile production in the world. By the 1830s, mills had made the shift from artisanal work to highly mechanical mass production. Among the great breakthroughs was the discovery that cloth could be printed with designs, such as paisley or calico (as in this image), and marketed to middle-class consumers.

→ *How did the industrial revolution reorder society?*

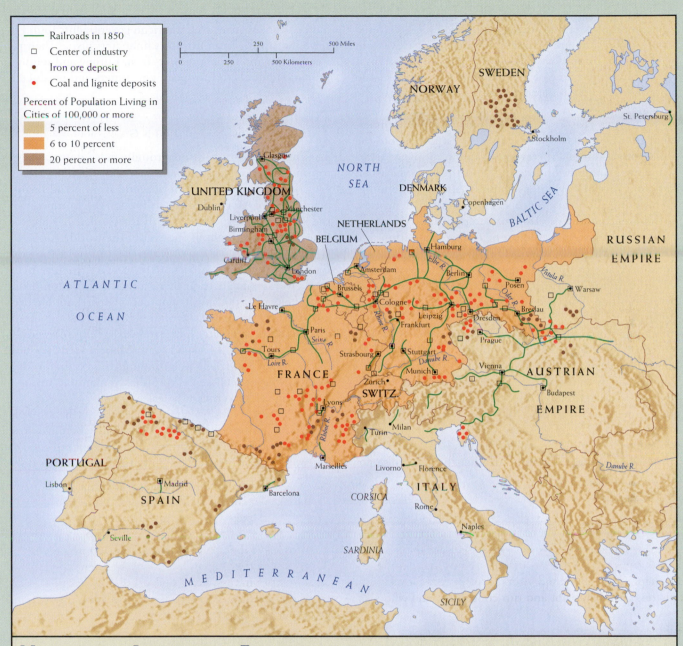

MAP 15-4 INDUSTRIAL EUROPE AROUND 1850

By 1850 much of western Europe was industrial and urban, with major cities linked to one another through a network of railroads. According to this map, what natural resources contributed to the growth of the industrial revolution? What effects did it have on urban population densities? Explain how the presence of an extensive railroad system helped to accelerate industrialization. According to your reading, why were the effects of the industrial revolution more rapidly apparent in Great Britain and in north-central Europe?

creased the efficiency and quality of production and saved labor, but they did not lead to large-scale production. The silks of Lyon, cutlery of Solingen, calicoes of Alsace, and cottons of Pawtucket, Rhode Island, were all products of small firms in heavily industrialized belts.

Wherever the industrial revolution took hold, it allowed societies to outdistance rivals in manufacturing and elevated them to a new place in the emerging global economic order (see Map 15-4). But why did this revolution cluster mainly in the Atlantic world? This is an important question, because the unequal distribution of global wealth, the gap between the haves and have-nots, really took off in this era of revolutions. In much of Asia and Africa, technical change altered modes of production and business practices, but it was not followed by a continuous cascade of changes. The great mystery was China, the home of astronomical water clocks and gunpowder. Why did China not become the epicenter of the industrial revolution?

There are two reasons. China did not foster experimental science of the kind that allowed Watt to stumble onto the possibility of steam, or Procter and Gamble to invent floating soap. Experimentation, testing, and the links between thinkers and investors were a distinctly Atlantic phenomenon. The Qing, like the Mughal and Ottoman dynasties, swept the great minds into the bureaucracy and reinforced the old agrarian system based on peasant exploitation and tribute. Second, Chinese rulers did not support overseas expansion and trade that helped create the commercial revolution in the Atlantic world. The agrarian dynasties of China and India neither showered favors on local merchants nor effectively shut out interlopers. This made them vulnerable to cheap manufactured imports from European traders backed by their governments extolling the virtues of free trade.

The effects were profound. Historically, Europe had a trade imbalance with partners to the east—furs from Russia, and spices and silks from Asia. It made up for this with silver from the Americas. But the new economic order meant that by the nineteenth century, western Europe not only had manufactures like soap to export to Asia, it also had capital. One of Europe's biggest debtors was none other than the sultan of

the Ottoman Empire, whose tax system could not keep up with spending necessary to keep the realm together. More and more, Asian, African, and American governments found themselves borrowing from Europe's financiers just as their people were buying industrial products from Europe and selling their primary products to European consumers and producers.

WORKING AND LIVING

The industrious revolution brought more demanding work routines—not only in the manufacturing economies of western Europe and North America but also on the farms and plantations of Asia and Africa. Although the European side of the story is better known, cultivators toiled harder and for longer hours throughout the rest of the world.

URBAN LIFE AND WORK ROUTINES Increasingly, Europe's workers made their livings in cities. London, Europe's largest city in 1700, saw its population nearly double over the next century to almost 1 million. By the 1820s, population growth was even greater in the industrial hubs of Leeds, Glasgow, Birmingham, Liverpool, and Manchester. By contrast, in the Low Countries (Belgium and the Netherlands) and France, where small-scale, rural-based manufacturing flourished, the shift to cities was less extreme.

For most urban dwellers, cities were not healthy places. Water that powered the mills, along with chemicals used in dyeing, went directly back into waterways that provided drinking water. Overcrowded tenements shared just a few out-

A Model Textile Mill. In the nineteenth century, the English industrialist and reformer Robert Owen tried to create humane factories. Worried about the terrible conditions in most textile mills, Owen created clean and orderly working environments in his mills and had the work rules posted on the walls. Like most of his contemporaries, Owen employed children, as can be seen in this image.

houses. Most European cities as late as 1850 had no running water, no garbage pickup, no underground sewer system. The result was widespread disease. (In fact, no European city at this time had as clean a water supply as the largest towns of the ancient Roman Empire once had.)

As families found jobs in factories, their wages bolstered family revenues. Children, wives, and husbands increasingly worked outside the home for cash, though some still made handicrafts inside the home as well. Urban employers experimented with paying according to the tasks performed or the number of goods produced per day. To earn subsistence wages, men, women, and children frequently stayed on the job for twelve or more hours at a time.

Changes in work affected the understanding of time. Whereas most farmers' workloads had followed seasonal rhythms, after 1800 industrial settings imposed a rigid concept of work discipline. To keep the machinery operating, factory and mill owners installed huge clocks and used bells or horns to signify the workday's beginning and end. Employers also measured output per hour and compared workers' performance. Josiah Wedgwood, a maker of teacups and other porcelain, installed a Boulton & Watt steam engine in his manufacturing plant and made his workers use it efficiently. He rang a bell at 5:45 in the morning so employees could start work as day broke. At 8:30 the bell rang for breakfast, 9:00 to call them back, and 12:00 for a half-hour lunch; it last tolled when darkness put an end to the workday. Sometimes, though, factory clocks were turned back in the morning and forward at night, falsely extending the exhausted laborers' workday.

Despite higher production, industrialization imposed numbing work routines and paltry wages. Worse, however, was having no work at all. As families abandoned their farmland and depended on wages, being idle meant having no income. Periodic downturns in the economy put wage workers at risk, and many responded by organizing protests. In 1834, the British Parliament centralized the administration of all poor relief and deprived able-bodied workers of any relief unless they joined a workhouse, where working conditions resembled those of a prison.

SOCIAL PROTEST AND EMIGRATION While entrepreneurs accumulated private wealth, the effects of the industrial revolution on working-class families raised widespread concern. In the 1810s in England, groups of jobless craftsmen, called Luddites, smashed the machines that had left them unemployed. In 1849, the English novelist Charlotte Brontê published a novel, *Shirley,* depicting the misfortunes caused by the power loom. Charles Dickens described a mythic Coketown to evoke pity for the working class in his 1854 classic, *Hard Times.* Both Elizabeth Gaskell, in England, and Émile Zola, in France, described the hardships of women whose malnourished children were pressed into the workforce too early. Gaskell and Zola also highlighted the hunger, loneliness, and illness that prostitutes and widows endured. These social advocates sought protective legislation for workers, including curbing child labor, limiting the workday, and, in some countries, legalizing prostitution for the sake of monitoring the prostitutes' health.

Some people, however, could not wait for legislative reform. Thus, the period saw unprecedented emigration, as unemployed workers or peasants abandoned their homes to seek their fortunes in America, Canada, and Australia. During the Irish Potato Famine of 1845–1849, at least one million Irish citizens left their country (and a further million or so died) when fungi attacked their subsistence crop. Desperate to escape starvation, they booked cheap passage to North America on ships so notorious for disease and malnutrition that they earned the name "Coffin Ships." Those who did survive faced discrimination in their new land, for many Americans feared the immigrants would drive down wages or create social unrest.

PERSISTENCE AND CHANGE IN AFRO-EURASIA

➔ *How did the Atlantic revolutions affect Afro-Eurasian societies?*

Western Europe's military might, its technological achievements, and its economic strength represented a threat to the remaining Afro-Eurasian empires. Across the continent, western European merchants and industrialists sought closer economic and (in some cases) political ties. They did so in the name of gaining "free" access to Asian markets and products. In response, Russian and Ottoman rulers modernized their military organizations and hoped to achieve similar economic strides while distancing themselves from the democratic principles of the French Revolution. The remote Chinese empire was largely unaffected by the upheavals in Europe and America—until the first Opium War of the early 1840s forced the Chinese to acknowledge their military weaknesses. Thus, changes in the Atlantic world unleashed new pressures around the globe, though with varying degrees of intensity.

REVAMPING THE RUSSIAN MONARCHY

Some eastern European dynasties responded to the pressures by strengthening their traditional rulers, through modest reforms and the suppression of domestic opposition. This was how Russian rulers reacted. Tsar Alexander I (r. 1801–1825) was fortunate that Napoleon committed several blunders and

Decembrists in St. Petersburg. Russians energetically participated in the coalition that defeated Napoleon, but the ideas of the French Revolution greatly appealed to the educated upper classes, including aristocrats of the officer corps. In December 1825, at the death of Tsar Alexander I, some regimental officers staged an uprising of about 3,000 men, demanding a constitution and the end of serfdom. But Nicholas I, the new tsar, called in loyal troops and brutally dispersed the "Decembrists," executing or exiling their leaders.

lost his formidable army in the Russian snows. Yet the French Revolution and its massive, patriotic armies struck at the heart of Russian political institutions, which rested upon a huge peasant population laboring as serfs.

The tsars could no longer easily justify their absolutism by claiming that enlightened despotism was the most advanced form of government, since a new model, rooted in popular sovereignty and the concept of the nation, had arisen. One response was to highlight the heroic resistance of the Russian people that had led to victory over the French. Tsar Alexander glorified patriots who had either fought in the war or grown up hearing about it, but he was not interested in allowing any new political order.

In December 1825, when Alexander died unexpectedly and childless, there was a question over succession. Some Russian officers launched a patriotic revolt, hoping to convince Alexander's brother Constantine to take the throne (and to guarantee a constitution) in place of a more conservative brother, Nicholas. The Decembrists, as they were called, came primarily from elite families and were familiar with western European life and institutions. A few Decembrists called for a constitutional monarchy to replace Russia's despotism; others favored a tsar-less republic and the abolition of serfdom. But the officers' conspiracy failed to win over conservatives or the peasantry, who still believed in the tsar's divine right to rule. Constantine supported Nicholas's claim to power, so Nicholas (r. 1825–1855) became tsar and brutally suppressed the insurrectionists. For the time being, the influence of the French Revolution was quashed.

Still, Alexander's successors faced a world in which powerful European states had constitutions and national armies of citizens, not subjects. In trying to maintain absolute rule, Russian tsars portrayed the monarch's family as the ideal historical embodiment of the nation with direct ties to the peo-

ple. Nicholas himself prevented rebellion by expanding the secret police, enforcing censorship, conducting impressive military exercises, and maintaining serfdom. After suppressing a revolt in the empire's Polish provinces, he sought a closer alliance with conservative monarchies in Austria and Prussia. And in the 1830s he introduced a conservative ideology that stressed religious faith, hierarchy, and obedience. Even some officials and members of society who supported the monarchy wondered whether this would be enough to enable Russia to remain a competitive great power.

REFORMING EGYPT AND THE OTTOMAN EMPIRE

Unlike in Russia, where Napoleon's army had reached Moscow, the Ottoman capital in Istanbul never faced a threat by French troops. Still, Napoleon's invasion of Egypt shook the Ottoman Empire and led European merchants to press Ottoman rulers for more commercial concessions. Even before this trauma, imperial authorities faced the challenge posed by increased trade with Europe—and the greater presence of European merchants and missionaries. In addition, many non-Muslim religious communities in the sultan's empire wanted the European powers to advance their interests. In the wake of Napoleon, who had promised to remake Egyptian society, reformist energies swept from Egypt to the center of the Ottoman domain. (See Primary Source: An Egyptian Intellectual's Reaction to the French Occupation of Egypt.)

REFORMS IN EGYPT In Egypt, far-reaching changes came with **Muhammad Ali**, a skillful modernizing ruler. After the French withdrawal in 1801, Muhammad Ali (r. 1805–1848) won a chaotic struggle for supreme power in Egypt and

AN EGYPTIAN INTELLECTUAL'S REACTION TO THE FRENCH OCCUPATION OF EGYPT

In the 1798 invasion of Egypt, Napoleon Bonaparte attempted to win rank-and-file Egyptian support against the country's Mamluks, who were the most powerful group in Egypt at the time though the country was still under the authority of the Ottoman sultan. Bonaparte portrayed himself as a liberator and invoked the ideals of the French Revolution, as he had done with great success all over Europe. His Egyptian campaign did not succeed, however, and local opposition was bitter. The chronicler Abd al-Rahman al-Jabarti has left one of the most perceptive accounts of these years.

On Monday news arrived that the French had reached Damanhur and Rosetta [in the Nile Delta]. . . . They printed a large proclamation in Arabic, calling on the people to obey them. . . . In this proclamation were inducements, warnings, all manner of wiliness and stipulations. Some copies were sent from the provinces to Cairo and its text is:

In the name of God, the Merciful, the Compassionate. There is no God but God. He has no son nor has He an associate in His Dominion.

On behalf of the French Republic which is based upon the foundation of liberty and equality, General Bonaparte, Commander-in-Chief of the French armies makes known to all the Egyptian people that for a long time the Sanjaqs [its Mamluk rulers] who lorded it over Egypt have treated the French community basely and contemptuously and have persecuted its merchants with all manner of extortion and violence. Therefore the hour of punishment has now come.

Unfortunately, this group of Mamluks . . . have acted corruptly for ages in the fairest land that is to be found upon the face of the globe. However, the Lord of the Universe, the Almighty, has decreed the end of their power.

O ye Egyptians . . . I have not come to you except for the purpose of restoring your rights from the hands of the oppressors and that I more than the Mamluks serve God. . . .

And tell them also that all people are equal in the eyes of God and the only circumstances which distinguish one from the other are reason, virtue, and knowledge. . . . Formerly, in the lands of Egypt there were great cities, and wide canals and extensive commerce and nothing ruined all this but the avarice and the tyranny of the Mamluks.

[Jabarti then challenged the arguments in the French proclamation and portrayed the French as godless invaders, inspired by false ideals.] They follow this rule: great and small, high and low, male and female are all equal. Sometimes they break this rule according to their whims and inclinations or reasoning. Their women do not veil themselves and have no modesty. . . . Whenever a Frenchman has to perform an act of nature he does so where he happens to be, even in full view of people, and he goes away as he is, without washing his private parts after defecation. . . .

His saying "[all people] are equal in the eyes of God" the Almighty is a lie and stupidity. How can this be when God has made some superior to others as is testified by the dwellers in the Heavens and on Earth? . . .

So those people are opposed to both Christians and Muslims, and do not hold fast to any religion. You see that they are materialists, who deny all God's attributes. . . . May God hurry misfortune and punishment upon them, may He strike their tongues with dumbness, may He scatter their hosts, and disperse them.

→ *When the proclamation speaks of "the fairest land that is to be found upon the face of the globe," what land is it referring to?*
→ *Why do you think Napoleon's appeals to the ideals of the French Revolution failed with Egyptians?*
→ *Why does al-Jabarti claim that the invaders are godless even though the proclamation clearly suggests otherwise?*

SOURCE: Abd al-Rahman al-Jabarti, *Napoleon in Egypt: al-Jabarti's Chronicle of the French Occupation, 1798,* translated by Shmuel Moreh (Princeton, NJ: Markus Wiener Publishing, 1993), pp. 24–29.

Muhammad Ali. The Middle Eastern ruler who most successfully assimilated the educational, technological, and economic advances of nineteenth-century Europe was Muhammad Ali, ruler of Egypt from 1805 until 1848.

aligned himself with influential Egyptian families. Yet he looked to revolutionary France for a model of modern state-building. As with Napoleon (and with Simón Bolívar in Latin America), the key to his hold on power was the army. With the help of French advisors, the modernized Egyptian army became the most powerful fighting force in the Middle East.

Muhammad Ali also made reforms in education and agriculture. He established a school of engineering and opened the first modern medical school in Cairo under the supervision of a French military doctor. And his efforts in the countryside made Egypt one of the world's leading cotton exporters. A summer crop, cotton required steady watering when the Nile's irrigation waters were in short supply. So Muhammad Ali's Public Works Department, advised by European engineers, deepened the irrigation canals and constructed a series of dams across the Nile. These efforts transformed Egypt, making it the most powerful state in the eastern Mediterranean and alarming the Ottoman state (which still controlled Egypt) and the great powers in Europe.

Muhammad Ali's modernizing reforms, however, disrupted the habits of the peasantry. After all, incorporation into the industrial world economy involved harder work (as English wage workers had discovered), often with little addi-

tional pay. Because irrigation improvements permitted year-round cultivation, Egyptian peasants now had to plant and harvest three crops instead of one or two. Moreover, the state controlled the prices of cultivated products, so peasants saw little profit from their extra efforts. Young men also faced conscription into the state's enlarged army, while whole families had to toil, unpaid, on public works projects. In addition, a state-sponsored program of industrialization aimed to put Egypt on a par with Europe: before long, textile and munitions factories employed 200,000 workers. But Egypt had few skilled laborers or cheap sources of energy, so by the time of Muhammad Ali's death in 1849 few of the factories survived.

External forces also limited Muhammad Ali's ambitious plans. At first, his new army enjoyed spectacular success. At the bidding of the Ottoman sultan, the Egyptian military fought well against Greek nationalists (who ultimately won independence in 1829) and carried out conquests in Sudan. But Muhammad Ali overplayed his hand when he sent forces into Syria in the 1830s and later when he threatened Anatolia, the heart of the Ottoman state. Fearing that an Egyptian ruler might attempt to overthrow the Ottoman sultan and threaten the balance of power in the eastern Mediterranean region, the European powers compelled Egypt to withdraw from Anatolia and reduce its army. In the name of free trade, European merchants pressed for free access to Egyptian markets, just as they did in Latin America and Africa.

OTTOMAN REFORMS Under political and economic pressures like those facing Muhammad Ali in Egypt, Ottoman rulers also made reforms. Indeed, military defeats and humiliating treaties with Europe were painful reminders of the sultans' vulnerability. Stunned by Napoleon's defeat of the Mamluks in Egypt and disenchanted with privileged janissaries who resisted reform efforts, in 1805 Sultan Selim III tried to create a new source of military strength: the New Order infantry, trained by western European officers. But before he could bring this force up to fighting strength, the janissaries stormed the palace and killed New Order officers. They overturned the New Order army and deposed Selim in 1807. Over the next few decades, janissary military men and clerical scholars (*ulama*) cobbled together an alliance that continuously thwarted reformers.

Why did reform falter in the Ottoman state before it could be implemented? After all, in France and Spain, the old regimes were also inefficient and burdened with debts and military losses. But reform was possible only if the forces of restraint—especially in the military—were weak and the reformers strong. In the Ottoman Empire, the janissary class had grown powerful, providing the main resistance to change. Ottoman authority depended on clerical support, and the Muslim clergy also resisted change. Blocked at the top, Ottoman rulers were hesitant to appeal for popular support in a struggle against anti-reformers. Such an appeal, in the new age of popular sovereignty and national feeling, would be dangerous for an unelected dynast in a multiethnic and multireligious realm.

Mahmud II (r. 1808–1839), who acknowledged Europe's rising power, broke the political deadlock. He shrewdly manipulated his conservative opponents. Convincing some clerics that the janissaries neglected traditions of discipline and piety, and promising that a new corps would pray fervently, the sultan won the *ulama*'s support and in 1826 established a European-style army corps. When the janissaries plotted their inevitable mutiny, Mahmud rallied clerics, students, and subjects. The schemers retreated to their barracks, only to be shelled by the sultan's artillery and then destroyed in flames. Thousands of other janissaries were rounded up and executed.

The sultan could now pursue reform within an autocratic framework. Like Muhammad Ali in Egypt, Mahmud brought in European officers to advise his forces. Here, too, military reform spilled over into nonmilitary areas. The Ottoman modernizers created a medical college, then a school of military sciences. To understand Europe better and to create a first-rate diplomatic corps, the Ottomans schooled their officials in European languages and had European classics translated into Turkish. As Mahmud's successors extended reforms into civilian life, this era—known as the Tanzimat, or Reorganization period—saw legislation that guaranteed equality for all Ottoman subjects, regardless of religion.

The reforms, however, stopped well short of revolutionary change. For one thing, reform relied too much on the personal whim of rulers. Also, the bureaucratic and religious infrastructure remained committed to old ways. Moreover, any effort to reform the rural sector met resistance by the landed interests. Finally, the merchant classes profited from business with a debt-ridden sultan. By preventing the empire's fiscal collapse through financial support to the state, bankers lessened the pressure for reform and removed the spark that had fired the revolutions in Europe. Together, these factors impeded reform in the Ottoman Empire.

Yet, by failing to make greater reforms, the empire lost economic and military ground to its European neighbors. For centuries, European traders had needed Islam's goods and services more than the other way around. By the nineteenth century, however, the ties of trade and financial dependency bound the Ottomans to Europe on terms that the Europeans controlled.

COLONIAL REORDERING IN INDIA

Europe's most important colonial possession in Asia between 1750 and 1850 was British India. Unlike in North America, the changes that the British fostered in Asia did not lead to political independence. Instead, India was increasingly dominated by the **East India Company**, which the crown had chartered in 1600. The company's control over India's imports and exports in the eighteenth and nineteenth centuries, however, contradicted British claims about their allegiance to a world economic system based on "free trade."

THE EAST INDIA COMPANY'S MONOPOLY   Initially the British, through the East India Company, tried to control India's commerce by establishing trading posts along the

Indian Resistance to Company Rule. Tipu Sultan, the Mysore ruler, put up a determined resistance against the British. This painting by Robert Home shows Cornwallis, the East India Company's governor, receiving Tipu's two sons as hostages after defeating him in the 1792 war. The boys remained in British custody for two years. Tipu returned to fighting the British and was killed in the war of 1799.

coast but without taking complete political control. After conquering the state of Bengal in 1757, the company began to fill its coffers and its officials began to amass personal fortunes. Even the British governor of Bengal pocketed a portion of the tax revenues. Such unbridled abuse of power caused the Bengal army, along with forces of the Mughal emperor and of the ruler of Awadh, to revolt. Although the rebels were unsuccessful, British officials left the emperor and most provincial leaders in place—as nominal rulers. Nonetheless, the British secured the right for the East India Company to collect tax revenues in Bengal, Bihar, and Orissa and to trade free of duties throughout Mughal territory. In return, the emperor would receive a hefty annual pension. The company went on to annex other territories, bringing much of South Asia under its rule by the early 1800s (see Map 15-5).

To carry out its responsibilities, the East India Company needed to establish a civil administration. Rather than place Britons in these positions, the company enlisted Hindu kings and Muslim princes; they retained royal privileges while losing their autonomy. The emperor himself was now permanently under the thumb of the company's administrators. Yet the company did not depend entirely on local leaders, for it also maintained a large standing army and a centralized bureaucracy. Together, the military force, the bureaucracy, and an array of local leaders enabled the company state to guarantee security and the smooth collection of revenues.

To rule with minimal interference, however, required knowing the conquered society. This led to Orientalist scholarship: English scholar-officials wrote the first modern histories of South Asia, translated Sanskrit and Persian texts, identified philosophical writings, and compiled Hindu and Muslim law books. Through their efforts, the company state presented itself as a force for revitalizing authentic Hinduism and recovering India's literary and cultural treasures. Although the Orientalist scholars admired Sanskrit language and literature, they still supported English colonial rule and did not necessarily agree with local beliefs.

EFFECTS IN INDIA   Maintaining a sizeable military and civilian bureaucracy also required taxation. Indeed, taxes on land were the East India Company's largest source of revenue. From 1793 onward, land policies required large and small landowners alike to pay taxes to the company. As a result, large estate owners gained more power and joined with the company in determining who could own property. Whenever smaller proprietors defaulted on their taxes, the company put their properties up for auction, with the firm's own employees and large estate owners often obtaining title.

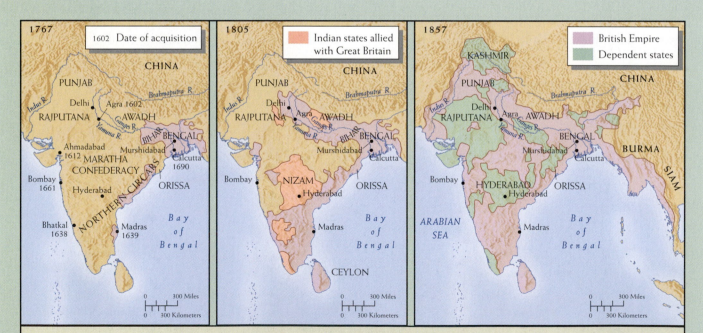

MAP 15-5   THE BRITISH IN INDIA, 1767–1857

Starting from locations in eastern and northeastern India, the British East India Company extended its authority over much of South Asia prior to the outbreak of the Indian Rebellion of 1857. What type of location did the British first acquire in India? How did the company expand into the interior of India and administer these possessions? Why did it choose a strategy of direct and indirect rule over different areas within the larger region?

Company rule and booming trade altered India's urban geography as well. By the early nineteenth century, colonial cities like Calcutta, Madras, and Bombay became the new centers at the expense of older Mughal cities like Agra, Delhi, Murshidabad, and Hyderabad. As the colonial cities attracted British merchants and Indian clerks, artisans, and laborers, their populations surged. Calcutta's reached 350,000 in 1820; Bombay's jumped to 200,000 by 1825. In these cities, Europeans lived close to the company's fort and trading stations, while migrants from the countryside clustered in crowded quarters called "black towns."

Back in Britain, the debts of rural Indians and the conditions of black towns generated little concern. Instead, calls for reform focused on the East India Company's monopoly: its sole access to Indian wealth, and its protection of company shareholders and investors. In 1813 the British Parliament, responding to merchants' and traders' demands to participate in the Indian economy, abolished the company's monopoly over trade with India.

India now had to serve the interests of an industrializing Britain, so it became an importer of British textiles and an exporter of raw cotton—a reversal of its traditional pattern of trade. In the past, India had been an important textile manufacturer, exporting fine cotton goods throughout the Indian Ocean and to Europe. But its elites could not resist the appeal of cheap British textiles. As a result, India's own process of industrialization slowed down. In addition, the import of British manufactures caused unfavorable trade balances that changed India from a net importer of gold and silver to an exporter of these precious metals.

Packing Cotton Bales. This 1864 engraving of the packing of cotton bales registers the shift in cotton trade between India and Britain: from being an exporter of cotton manufactures up to the eighteenth century, India became a source of raw cotton in the nineteenth century.

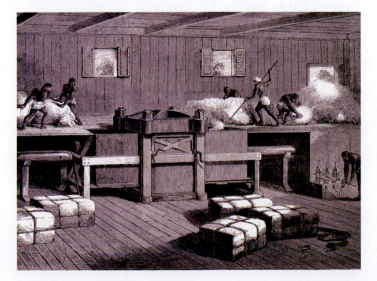

PROMOTING CULTURAL CHANGE The British did more than alter the Indian economy; they also advocated far-reaching changes in Indian culture so that its people would value British goods and culture. In 1817, James Mill, a philosopher and an employee of the East India Company, condemned what he saw as backward social practices and cultural traditions. He and his son, John Stuart Mill, argued that only dictatorial rule could bring good government and economic progress to India, whose people they considered unfit for self-rule or liberalism. (See Primary Source: James Mill on Indian Tradition.)

Evangelicals and liberal reformers also tried to change Hindu and Muslim social practices, through legislation and European-style education. For example, they sought to stop the practice of *sati*, by which women burned to death on the funeral pyres of their dead husbands. Now the mood swung away from the Orientalists' respect for India's classical languages, philosophies, cultures, and texts. In 1835, when the British poet, historian, and Liberal politician Lord Macaulay was making recommendations on educational policies, he urged that English replace Persian as the language of administration and that European education replace Oriental learning. The result, reformers hoped, would be a class that was Indian in blood and color but English in tastes and culture.

This was a new colonial order, but it was not stable. Most wealthy landowners resented the loss of their land and authority. Peasants, thrown to the mercy of the market, moneylenders, and landlords, were in turmoil. The non-Hindu forest dwellers and roaming cultivators, faced with the hated combination of a colonial state and moneylenders, revolted. Dispossessed artisans stirred up towns and cities. And merchants and industrialists chafed under the British-dominated economy. However, the British continued to extend their colonial state with its commitment to free trade, combining reform with autocracy. Even though India was part of a more interconnected world and thereby supported Europe's industrialization, it was doing so as a colony. As freedom expanded in Europe, exploitation expanded in India.

PERSISTENCE OF THE QING EMPIRE

The Qing dynasty, which had taken power in 1644, was still enjoying prosperity and territorial expansion as the nineteenth century dawned. The Chinese were largely unaware of revolutionary events occurring in North America, France, and Britain. Their sense of imperial splendor continued to rest on the political structure and social order inherited from the Ming (see Chapter 11). Although some Chinese felt that the Manchu Qing were foreign occupiers, the Qing rulers carefully adapted Chinese institutions and philosophies. Thus, Chinese elites at court did not challenge the dynasty's authority (as delegates to the Estates-General in France did).

JAMES MILL ON INDIAN TRADITION

James Mill was a Scottish political economist and philosopher who believed that according to the principles of utilitarianism, law and government were essential for maximizing a people's usefulness and happiness. Thus his History of British India *(1818) criticized India's Hindu and Muslim cultures and attributed their so-called backwardness to the absence of a systematic form of law. Mill's critique was also an attack on earlier British Orientalists, whose close engagement with Indian culture and Indian texts led them to oppose interfering in traditional practices. A year after the book's publication, the East India Company appointed him as an official.*

The condition of the women is one of the most remarkable circumstances in the manners of nations. Among rude people, the women are generally degraded; among civilized people they are exalted.

———

Nothing can exceed the habitual contempt which the Hindus entertain for their women. Hardly are they ever mentioned in their laws, or other books, but as wretches of the most base and vicious inclinations, on whose natures no virtuous or useful qualities can be engrafted. "Their husbands," says the sacred code, "should be diligently careful in guarding them: though they well know the disposition with which the lord of creation formed them; Manu allotted to such women a love of their bed, of their seat, and of ornament, impure appetites, wrath, weak flexibility, desire of mischief, and bad conduct."

———

They are held, accordingly, in extreme degradation. They are not accounted worthy to partake of religious rites but in conjunction with their husbands. They are entirely excluded from the sacred books. . . .

———

They [the Hindus] are remarkably prone to flattery; the most prevailing mode of address from the weak to the strong, while men are still ignorant and unreflecting. The Hindus are full of dissimulation and falsehood, the universal concomitants of oppression. The vices of falsehood, indeed, they carry to a height almost unexampled among other races of men. Judicial perjury is more than common; it is almost universal.

———

This religion has produced a practice, which has strongly engaged the curiosity of Europeans; a superstitious care of the life of the inferior animals. A Hindu lives in perpetual terror of killing even an insect; and hardly any crime can equal that of being unintentionally the cause of death to any animal of the more sacred species. This feeble circumstance, however, is counteracted by so many gloomy and malignant principles, that their religion, instead of humanizing the character, must have had no inconsiderable effect in fostering that disposition to revenge, that insensibility to the sufferings of others, and often that active cruelty, which lurks under the smiling exterior of the Hindu.

———

Few nations are surpassed by the Hindus, in the total want of physical purity, in their streets, houses, and persons. Mr. Forster, whose long residence in India, and knowledge of the country, render him an excellent witness, says of the narrow streets of Benares: "In addition to the pernicious effect which must proceed from a confined atmosphere, there is, in the hot season, an intolerable stench arising from the many pieces of stagnated water dispersed in different quarters of the town. The filth also which is indiscriminately thrown into the streets, and there left exposed, (for the Hindus possess but a small portion of general cleanliness) add to the compound of ill smells so offensive to the European inhabitants of this city."

———

The attachment with which the Hindus, in common with all ignorant nations, bear to astrology, is a part of their manners exerting a strong influence upon the train of their actions. "The Hindus of the present age," says a partial observer, "do not undertake any affair of consequence without consulting their astrologers, who are always Brahmans." The belief of witchcraft and sorcery continues universally prevalent.

→ *What did James Mill hold to be the chief indicator of a civilization's accomplishment?*
→ *In what ways do Mill's views on India reflect a deep disagreement with British Orientalists?*

SOURCE: James Mill, *The History of British India* (New Delhi: Atlantic Publishers & Distributors, 1990), pp. 279, 281–82, 286–87, 288, 289, 297, 299.

EXPANSION OF THE EMPIRE The Qing had a talent for extending the empire's boundaries and settling frontier lands. Before 1750, they conquered Taiwan (the stronghold of remaining Ming forces), pushed westward into central Asia, and annexed Tibet. Qing troops then eliminated the threat of the powerful Junghars in western Mongolia and halted Russian efforts to take southern Siberia in the 1750s. To secure these territorial gains, the Qing encouraged settlement of frontier lands like Xinjiang. New crops from the Americas aided this process—especially corn and sweet potatoes, which grow well in less fertile soils.

Through rising agricultural productivity and population growth, rural life became commercialized and state revenues surged. Furthermore, despite the Chinese ideal for women to stay home while men worked the land, in reality most rural women had toiled at fieldwork for centuries—and now their labor became even more important. In the eighteenth century, rural markets participated in more interregional trade in grain, cotton, tea, and silk. As rural industries proliferated, peasant households became the backbone of early manufactures (as in Europe), especially in textiles.

Like their European counterparts, Chinese peasants were on the move. But migration occurred in Qing China for different reasons. The state-sponsored westward movement into Xinjiang, for example, aimed to secure a recently pacified frontier region through military colonization, after which

Rice Paddies. Farmers working in neatly planted rice paddy fields in late imperial China. The process was labor intensive, but it reduced wastage.

civilians would follow. So peasants received promises of land, tools, seed, and the loan of silver and a horse—all with the dual objectives of producing enough food grain to supply the troops and relieving pressure on the poor and arid northwestern part of the country. These efforts brought so much land under cultivation by 1840 that the region's ecological and social landscape completely changed.

Other migrants were on the move by their own initiative. The ever-growing competition for land even drove them into areas where the Qing regime had tried to restrict migration (because of excessive administrative costs), such as Manchuria and Taiwan. As the migrants introduced their own agricultural techniques, they reshaped the environment through land reclamation and irrigation projects and sparked large population increases.

PROBLEMS OF THE EMPIRE Despite their success in expanding the empire, the Qing faced nagging problems. As a ruling minority, they took a conservative approach to innovation. And only late in the eighteenth century did they deal with rapid population growth. On the one hand, the tripling of China's population since 1300 demonstrated the realm's prosperity; on the other, a population of over 300 million severely strained resources—especially soil for growing crops and wood for fuel.

Even as rulers recognized the problems, they had limited ability to tackle them. The taxes they levied were light (compared to the ones European monarchs levied).

Bureaucrats were understaffed. And as local authorities introduced many new taxes, the common people regarded them as corrupt. In the late eighteenth and early nineteenth centuries, uprisings inspired by mystical beliefs in folk Buddhism, and at times by the idea of restoring the Ming, engulfed northern China.

In spite of the difficulties that beset the Qing, European rulers and upper classes remained eager consumers of Chinese silks, teas, carved jade, tableware, jewelry, paper for covering walls, and ceramics. The Chinese, for their part, had little interest in most European manufactures. In 1793, Emperor Qianlong wrote in response to a request for trade by Britain's king that "as your ambassador can see for himself, we possess all things," adding, "I have no use for your country's manufactures."

By the mid-nineteenth century, however, extraordinary changes had made western European powers stronger than ever before, and the Qing could no longer dismiss their demands. The first clear evidence of an altered balance of power was not the rise of Napoleon, but a British-Chinese war over a narcotic. Indeed, the **Opium War** exposed China's vulnerability in a new era of European ascendancy.

THE OPIUM WAR AND THE "OPENING" OF CHINA Europeans had been selling staples and intoxicants in China for a long time. For example, tobacco, a New World crop, had become widely popular in China by the seventeenth century. Initially, few people would have predicted that tobacco smoking would lead to the widespread use of opium, previously used as a medicine or an aphrodisiac. But before long people in Southeast Asia, Taiwan, and China were smoking crude opium mixed with tobacco. By the late eighteenth century, opium smokers with their long-stemmed pipes were conspicuous at every level of Chinese society.

Although the Qing banned opium imports in 1729, the Chinese continued to smoke the drug and import it illegally. Sensing its economic potential, the East India Company created an opium monopoly in India in 1773. The reason was a rapid growth in the company's purchase of tea. Because the Chinese showed little taste for British goods, the British had been financing their tea imports with exports of silver to China. But by the late eighteenth century, the company's tea purchases had become too large to finance with silver. Fortunately for the company, the Chinese were eager for Indian cotton and opium, and then mostly just opium. Thus the British exported essentially no silver after 1804. Given the drug's importance, the company expanded its cultivation by offering loans to Indian peasants: they agreed to grow opium and sell it to the company's agents at a predetermined price.

The illegal opium traffic could not have flourished without the involvement of corrupt Chinese bureaucrats and a network of local brokers and distributors. Although another official ban in 1799 slowed the flow of opium into China for a while, the volume increased eightfold by 1839. The dramatic increase reflected an influx of private British merchants after the British government revoked the East India Company's monopoly over trade with China.

Opium's impact on the empire's balance of trade was devastating. In a reversal from earlier trends, silver began to flow out of instead of into China. Once silver shortages occurred, the peasants' tax burden grew heavier because they had to pay in silver (see Chapter 13). Consequently, long-simmering unrest in the countryside gained momentum. At the Qing court, some officials wanted to legalize the opium trade so as to eliminate corruption and boost revenues. (After all, as long as opium was an illegal substance, the government could not tax its traffic). Others wanted stiffer prohibitions. In 1838 the emperor sent a special commissioner to Canton, the main center of the trade, to eradicate the influx of opium. In a letter to Queen Victoria of Britain, the commissioner, Lin Zexu, claimed that China exported tea and silk for no other reason than "to share the benefit with the people of the whole world." He asked, therefore, why the British inflicted harm on the Chinese people through opium imports.

Lin demanded that foreigners hand over their opium stocks to the Chinese government (for destruction) and stop the trade. When British merchants in Canton resisted, Lin ordered the arrest of the president of the British Chamber of Commerce. After this man refused to comply, 350 foreigners were blockaded inside their own quarters. Lin ultimately convinced the foreign community to surrender 20,283 chests of opium with an estimated value of $9 million—an enormous sum in those days. But merchants had overstocked in anticipation of the trade's legalization, and the British government representative in Canton promised to compensate them for their losses. For Lin, the surrendering of the opium (which the Chinese flushed out to sea) was proof that the foreigners accepted submission. The Chinese victory, however, was short-lived. War soon broke out.

Opium. (*Left*) A common sight in late Qing China were establishments catering specifically to opium smoking. Taken from a volume condemning the practice, this picture shows opium smokers idling their day away. (*Right*) Having established a monopoly in the 1770s over opium cultivation in India, the British greatly expanded their manufacture and export of opium to China to balance their rapidly growing import of Chinese tea and silk. This picture from the 1880s shows an opium warehouse in India where the commodity was stored before being transported to China.

→ *How did the Atlantic revolutions affect Afro-Eurasian societies?*

MAP 15-6   THE QING EMPIRE AND THE OPIUM WAR
How many treaty ports were there after the opium war? What was their significance? How did the opium war change relations between China and the western powers?

Though determined, the Chinese were no match for Britain's modern military technology. After a British fleet—including four steam-powered battleships—entered Chinese waters in June 1840, the warships bombarded coastal regions near Canton and sailed upriver for a short way (see Map 15-6). On land, Qing soldiers used spears, clubs, and a few imported matchlock muskets against the modern artillery of British troops, many of whom were Indians supplied with percussion cap rifles. Along the Yangzi River, outgunned Qing forces fought fiercely, as soldiers killed their own wives and children before committing suicide themselves.

FORCING MORE TRADE The British triumphed as the Qing ruling elite wanted to avoid further conflicts with the militarily superior British. With the 1842 Treaty of Nanjing, the British acquired the island of Hong Kong and the right to trade in five treaty ports, and they forced the Chinese to repay their costs for the war—and the value of the opium Lin had destroyed. British traders now won the right to trade directly with the Chinese and to live in the treaty ports.

Subsequent treaties guaranteed that the British and other foreign nationals would be tried in their own courts for crimes, rather than in Chinese courts, and would be exempt from Chinese law. Moreover, the British insisted that any privileges granted through treaties with other parties would also apply to them. Other Western nations followed the British example

Trade in Canton. In this painting, we can see the hongs, the buildings that made up the factories, or establishments, where foreign merchants conducted their business in Canton. From the mid-eighteenth century to 1842, Canton was the only Chinese port open to European trade.

in demanding the same right, and the arrangement thus guaranteed all Europeans and North Americans a privileged position in China.

Still, China did not become a formal colony. To the contrary, in the mid-nineteenth century Europeans and North Americans were trading only on its outskirts. Most Chinese did not encounter the Europeans. Daily life for most people went on as it had before the Opium War. Only the political leaders and urban dwellers were beginning to feel the foreign presence and wondering what steps China might take to acquire European technologies, goods, and learning.

 CONCLUSION

During the period 1750–1850, changes in politics, commerce, industry, and technology reverberated throughout the Atlantic world and, to varying degrees, elsewhere around the globe. By 1850, the world was more integrated economically, with Europe increasingly at the center.

In the Americas, colonial ties broke apart. In France, the people toppled the monarchy. Dissidents threatened the same in Russia. Such upheavals introduced a new public vocabulary—the language of the nation—and made the idea of revolution empowering. In the Americas and parts of Europe, nation-states took shape around redefined hierarchies of class, gender, and color. Britain and France emerged from the political crises of the late eighteenth century to expand their borders. Their drive forced older empires such as Russia and the Ottoman state to make reforms.

As commerce and industrialization transformed economic and political power, European governments compelled others (including Egypt, India, and China) to expand their trade with European merchants. Ultimately, such countries had to participate in a European-centered economy as exporters of raw materials and importers of European manufactures.

Chronology

	1750	1775
THE AMERICAS		◆--------------◆ 1776–1783 *American Revolution* 1791–1804 *Haitian Rebellion* ◆---------- 1793 *Eli Whitney invents the cotton gin* ◆
EUROPE		◆ 1769 *James Watt invents steam engine* 1789–1799 *French Revolution* ◆--------------
RUSSIA AND OTTOMAN EMPIRE		
AFRICA		
SOUTH ASIA		◆ 1765 *British establish company rule in India*
EAST ASIA	←——— 1736–1796 *Chinese expansion under Qianlong emperor*	

By the 1850s, many of the world's peoples became more industrious, producing less for themselves and more for distant markets. Through changes in manufacturing, some areas of the world also made more goods than ever before. With its emphasis on free trade, Europe began to force open new markets—even to the point of colonizing them. Gold and silver now flowed out of China and India to pay for European-dominated products like opium and textiles.

However, global reordering did not mean that Europe's rulers had uncontested control over other people, or that the institutions and cultures of Asia and Africa ceased to be dynamic. Some countries became dependent on Europe commercially; others became colonies. China escaped colonial rule but was forced into unfavorable trade relations with the Europeans. In sum, dramatic changes combined to unsettle systems of rulership and to alter the economic and military balance between western Europe and the rest of the world.

Review and research materials are available at StudySpace: ⓢ WWNORTON.COM/STUDYSPACE

KEY TERMS

Simón Bolívar (p. 577)
Napoleon Bonaparte (p. 570)
bourgeoisie (p. 581)
democracy (p. 562)
East India Company (p. 589)
free labor (p. 562)
free markets (p. 562)
free trade (p. 562)
industrial revolution (p. 582)

industrious revolution (p. 581)
Muhammad Ali (p. 586)
nationalism (p. 562)
nation-state (p. 563)
Opium War (p. 593)
popular sovereignty (p. 562)
republican government (p. 568)
social contract (p. 566)

STUDY QUESTIONS

1. Describe the political and social revolutions that occurred in the Atlantic world between 1750 and 1850. What ideas inspired these changes? How far did revolutionaries extend these changes?

2. Compare and contrast the way Latin American peoples achieved independence to the similar process in the United States. How similar were their goals? How well did they achieve these goals?

3. Explain Napoleon's role in spreading the ideas of political and social revolution. How did his armies spread the concept of nationalism? How did Napoleon's military pursuits affect political and social ferment in the Americas?

4. Explain how the Atlantic world's political and social revolution led to the end of the Atlantic slave trade. What economic, social, and political consequences did this development have on sub-Saharan Africa?

5. Explain the relationship between industrialization and the "industrious revolution." Where did the industrial revolution begin? What other parts of the Atlantic world did it spread to during this time?

6. Explore how industrialization altered the societies that began to industrialize during this time. What impact did this process have on the environment? How were gender roles and familial relationships altered?

7. Analyze how the two intertwined Atlantic revolutions (political and industrial) altered the global balance of power. How did the Russian, Mughal, Ottoman, and Qing dynasties respond to this change?

8. To what extent did Great Britain emerge as the leading global power between 1750 and 1850? How did the British state shape political and economic developments around the world during this time?

1800	1825	1850

◆ 1807 Robert Fulton launches first commercial steamship

◆ 1810–1824 Revolutions in South America

◆ 1804–1815 Napoleon's empire

◆ 1830 First railway launched in England

◆ 1808–1839 Reign of Mahmud II, Ottoman Empire

1825 Decembrist Revolt in Russia ◆

1829 Greek independence ◆

◆ 1798–1801 French invasion of Egypt

1803–1867 Abolition of Atlantic slave trade

1805–1848 Reign of Muhammad Ali, Egypt

◆ 1813 Abolition of company trade monopoly in India

1839–1842 Opium War, China ◆

Chapter 9 New Empires and Common Cultures, 600–1000 CE

Ahmed, Leila, *Women and Gender in Islam* (1992). A superb overview of the relations between men and women throughout the history of Islam.

Aneirin, *Y Gododdin: Britain's Oldest Heroic Poem*, ed. and trans. A. O. H. Jarman (1988). A sixth-century Welsh text that describes the battle of the last Britons against the invading Anglo-Saxons.

Arberry, Arthur J., introduction to *The Koran Interpreted: A Translation*, trans. Arthur J. Arberry (1986). One of the most eloquent appreciations of this classical work of religion.

Augustine, *The City of God*, trans. H. Bettenson (1976). An excellent translation of Augustine's monumental work of history, philosophy, and religion.

Berkey, Jonathan P., *The Formation of Islam: Religion and Society in the Near East, 600–1800* (2005). A recent overview of the history of Islam before the modern era. It is particularly sensitive to the influence of external elements on the history of the Muslim peoples.

Bol, Peter, *This Culture of Ours: Intellectual Transitions in T'ang and Sung China* (1994). A study tracing the transformation of the shared culture of the Chinese learned elite from the seventh to the twelfth centuries.

Brown, Peter, *The Rise of Western Christendom: Triumph and Diversity, AD 200–1000*, 2nd ed. (2003). A description of the changes in Christianity in northern Europe and the emergence of the new cultures and political structures that coincided with this development.

Bulliet, Richard W., *Conversion to Islam in the Medieval Period: An Essay in Quantitative History* (1979). A study of the rate at which the populations overrun by Arab conquerors in the seventh century CE embraced the religion of their rulers.

Cook, Michael, *The Koran: A Very Short Introduction* (2000). A useful overview of Islam's holy book.

————, *Muhammad* (1983). A brief but careful life of the Prophet that takes full account of the prolific and often controversial preexisting scholarship.

Creswell, K. A. C., *A Short Account of Early Muslim Architecture, Revised and supplemented by James W. Allan* (1992). The definitive treatment of the subject, brought up to date.

Cross, S. H., and O. P. Sherbowitz-Westor, trans., *The Russian Primary Chronicle* (1953). A vivid record of the Viking settlement of Kiev, of the conversion of Kiev, and of the princes of Kiev in the tenth and eleventh centuries.

Donner, Fred M., *The Early Islamic Conquests* (1981). The best account of the Arab conquests in the Persian and Byzantine empires in the seventh century.

Duncan, John, *The Origins of the Chosŏn Dynasty* (2000). A historical account of the early Korean dynasties from 900 to 1400.

Fage, J. D., *Ghana: A Historical Introduction* (1966). A brief but authoritative history of Ghana from earliest times to the present.

Fisher, Humphrey J., *Slavery in the History of Muslim Black Africa* (2001). A general history of the relations between North Africa and black Africa, focusing on one of the most important aspects of contact—the slave trade.

Graham-Campbell, James, *Cultural Atlas of the Viking World* (1994). A positioning of the Vikings against their wider background in both western and eastern Europe.

Hawting, G. R., *The First Dynasty of Islam: The Umayyad Caliphate, A.D. 661–750* (2000). The essential scholarly treatment of Islam's first dynasty.

Herrmann, Georgina, *Iranian Revival* (1977). The structure and horizons of the Sasanian Empire as revealed in its monuments.

Hillgarth, J. N. (ed.), *Christianity and Paganism, 350–750: The Conversion of Western Europe*, rev. ed. (1986). A collection of contemporary sources.

Hodges, Richard, and David Whitehouse, *Mohammed, Charlemagne, and the Origins of Europe* (1983). A spirited comparison of Islam and the rise of Europe.

Hodgson, Marshall G. S., *The Venture of Islam: Conscience and History in a World Civilization* (1977), 3 vols. A magnificent history of the Islamic peoples. Its first volume, *The Classical Age of Islam,* is basic reading for anyone interested in the history of the Muslim world.

Holdsworth, May, *Women of the Tang Dynasty* (1999). An account of women's lives during the Tang dynasty.

Hourani, Albert, *History of the Arab Peoples* (2002). The best overview of Arab history.

Jones, Gwynn, *The Norse Atlantic Saga* (1986). The Viking discovery of America.

Kennedy, Hugh, *The Prophet and the Age of the Caliphate: The Islamic Near East from the Sixth to the Eleventh Century* (2004). A very good recent synthesis of the rise and spread of Islam.

Lee, Peter, et al. (eds.), *Sources of Korean Tradition,* vol. 1 (1996). A unique view of Korean history through the eyes and words of the participants or witnesses themselves, as provided in translations of official documents, letters, and policies.

Levtzion, Nehemia, *Ancient Ghana and Mali* (1980). The best introduction to the kingdoms of West Africa.

Levtzion, Nehemia, and Jay Spaulding, *Medieval West Africa: Views from Arab Scholars and Merchants* (2003). An indispensable source book on early West African history.

Lewis, Bernard, *The Middle East: Two Thousand Years of History from the Rise of Christianity to the Present Day* (1995). A stimulating introduction to an area that has seen the emergence of three of the great world religions.

——— (trans.), *Islam from the Prophet Muhammad to the Capture of Constantinople* (1974). Vol. 2: Religion and Society. A fine collection of original sources that portray various aspects of classical Islamic society.

Lewis, David Levering, *God's Crucible: Islam and the Making of Europe, 570–1215* (2008). An exciting and well-written overview of the high period of Islamic power and cultural attainments.

Middleton, John, *The Swahili: The Social Landscape of a Mercantile Community* (2000). An exciting synthesis of the Swahili culture of East Africa.

Miyazaki, Ichisada, *China's Examination Hell* (1981). A study of China's examination system.

Nurse, Derek, and Thomas Spear, *The Swahili: Reconstructing the History and Language of an African Society, 800–1500* (1984). A work that explores the history of the Muslim peoples who lived along the coast of East Africa.

Peters, F. E., *Muhammad and the Origins of Islam* (1994). A work that explores the early history of Islam and highlights the critical role that Muhammad played in promoting a new religion and a powerful Arab identity.

Schirokauer, Conrad, et al., *A Brief History of Japanese Civilization,* 2nd ed. (2005). A balanced account; chapters focus on developments in art, religion, literature, and thought as well as on Japan's economic, political, and social history in medieval times.

Smith, Julia, *Europe after Rome: A New Cultural History, 500–1000* (2005). A vivid analysis of society and culture in so-called Dark Age Europe.

Totman, Conrad, *History of Japan* (2004). A recent and readable summary of Japanese history from ancient to modern times.

Twitchett, Denis, *The Birth of the Chinese Meritocracy: Bureaucrats and Examinations in T'ang China* (1976). A description of the role of the written civil examinations that began during the Tang dynasty.

———, *Financial Administration under the T'ang Dynasty* (1970). A pioneering account—based on rare Dunhuang documents that survived from medieval times in Buddhist grottoes in central Asia—of the political and economic system undergirding the Chinese imperial state.

Whittow, Mark, *The Making of Byzantium, 600–1025* (1996). A study on the survival and revival of the eastern Roman empire as a major power in eastern Europe and Southwest Asia.

Wood, Ian, *The Missionary Life: Saints and the Evangelization of Europe, 400–1050* (2001). The horizons of Christians on the frontiers of Europe.

Chapter 10 Becoming "The World," 1000–1300 CE

Allsen, Thomas, *Commodity and Exchange in the Mongol Empire: A Cultural History of Islamic Textiles* (1997). A study that uses golden brocade, the textile most treasured by Mongol rulers, as a lens through which to analyze the vast commercial networks facilitated by the Mongol conquests and control.

———, *Culture and Conquest in Mongol Eurasia* (2001). A work that emphasizes the cultural and scientific exchanges that took place across Afro-Eurasia as a result of the Mongol conquest.

Bartlett, Robert, *The Making of Europe: Conquest, Colonization and Cultural Change, 950–1350* (1993). The modes of cultural, political, and demographic expansion of feudal Europe along its frontiers, especially in eastern Europe.

Bay, Edna G., *Wives of the Leopards: Gender, Politics, and Culture in the Kingdom of Dahomey* (1998). A work that stresses the role of women in an important West African society and dips into the early history of this area.

Beach, D. N., *Shona and Zimbabwe, 900–1850: An Outline of Shona History* (1980). A good place to start for exploring the history of Great Zimbabwe.

Brooks, George E., *Landlords and Strangers: Ecology, Society, and Trade in Western Africa, 1000–1630* (1993). A survey assembled from primary sources of early West African history that stresses transregional connections.

Buzurg ibn Shahriyar of Ramhormuz, *The Book of the Wonders of India: Mainland, Sea and Islands,* ed. and trans. G. S. P. Freeman-Greenville (1981). A collection of stories told by sailors, both true and fantastic; they help us imagine the lives of sailors of the era.

Chappell, Sally A. Kitt, *Cahokia: Mirror of the Cosmos* (2002). A thorough and vivid account of the "mound people"; it explores not just what we know of Cahokia but how we know it.

Christian, David, *A Short History of Russia, Central Asia, and Mongolia,* vol. 1, *Inner Eurasia from Prehistory to the Mongol Empire*

(1998). Essential reading for students interested in interconnections across the Afro-Eurasian landmass.

Curtin, Philip, *Cross-Cultural Trade in World History* (1984). A groundbreaking book on intercultural trade with a primary focus on Africa, especially the cross-Saharan trade and Swahili coastal trade.

Dawson, Christopher, *Mission to Asia* (1980). Accounts of China and the Mongol Empire brought back by Catholic missionaries and diplomats after 1240 CE.

Foltz, Richard C., *Religions of the Silk Road: Overland Trade and Cultural Exchange from Antiquity to the Fifteenth Century* (1999). A study of the populations and the cities of the Silk Road as transmitters of culture across long distances.

Franklin, Simon, and Jonathan Shepherd, *The Emergence of Rus: 750–1200* (1996). The formation of medieval Russia between the Baltic and Black seas.

Gibb, Hamilton A. R., *Saladin: Studies in Islamic History*, ed. Yusuf Ibish (1974). A sympathetic portrait of one of Islam's leading political and military figures.

Goitein, S. D., *Letters of Medieval Jewish Traders* (1973). The classic study of medieval Jewish trading communities based on the commercial papers deposited in the Cairo Geniza (a synagogue storeroom) during the tenth and eleventh centuries; it explores not only commercial activities but also the personal lives of the traders around the Indian Ocean basin.

———, *A Mediterranean Society: An Abridgment in One Volume*, rev. and ed. Jacob Lassner (1999). A portrait of the Jewish merchant community with ties across the Afro-Eurasian landmass, based largely on the documents from the Cairo Geniza (of which Goitein was the primary researcher and interpreter).

———, "New Light on the Beginnings of the Karim Merchant," *Journal of Social and Economic History of the Orient* 1 (1958). Goitein's description of Egyptian trade.

Harris, Joseph E., *The African Presence in Asia: Consequences of the East African Slave Trade* (1971). One of the few books that looks broadly at the impact of Africans and African slavery on the societies of Asia.

Hartwell, Robert, "Demographic, Political, and Social Transformations of China, 750–1550," *Harvard Journal of Asiatic Studies* 42 (1982): 365–442. A pioneering study of the demographic changes that overtook China during the Tang and Song dynasties, which are described in light of political reform movements and social changes in this crucial era.

Historical Relations across the Indian Ocean: Report and Papers of the Meeting of Experts Organized by UNESCO at Port Louis, Mauritius, from 15 to 19 July, 1974 (1980). Excellent essays on the connections of Africa with Asia across the Indian Ocean.

Hitti, Philip, *An Arab-Syrian Gentleman and Warrior in the Period of the Crusades: Memoirs of Usāmah ibn-Munqidh* (1929). The Crusaders seen through Muslim eyes.

Hodgson, Natasha, *Women, Crusading, and the Holy Land in Historical Narrative* (2007). A book dealing with the Crusades and focusing on the place of women in them.

Holt, P. M., *The Age of the Crusades: The Near East from the Eleventh Century to 1517* (1984). The Crusades period as seen from the eastern Mediterranean and through the lens of a leading British scholar of the area.

Hymes, Robert, and Conrad Schirokauer (eds.), *Ordering the World: Approaches to State and Society in Sung Dynasty China* (1993). A collection of essays that traces the intellectual, social, and political movements that shaped the Song state and its elites.

Ibn Battuta, *The Travels of Ibn Battuta*, trans. H. A. R. Gibb (2002). A readable translation of the classic book, originally published in 1929.

Ibn Fadlan, Ahmad, *Ibn Fadlan's Journey to Russia: A Tenth Century Traveler from Baghdad to the Volga River*, trans. with commentary by Richard Frye (2005). A coherent summary of the observations of an envoy who traveled from Baghdad to Russia.

Irwin, Robert, *The Middle East in the Middle Ages: The Early Mamluk Sultanate, 1250–1582* (1986). Egypt under Mamluk rule.

Jeppie, Shamil, and Diagne, Souleymane Bachir, editors, *The Meanings of Timbuktu* (2008). New materials on the ancient Muslim city of Timbuktu by scholars who have been preserving its manuscripts and writing about its historical importance.

Lancaster, Lewis, Kikun Suh, and Chai-shin Yu (eds.), *Buddhism in Koryo: A Royal Religion* (1996). A description of Buddhism at its height in the Koryo period, when the religion made significant contributions to the development of Korean culture.

Levtzion, Nehemia, and Randall L. Pouwels (eds.), *The History of Islam in Africa* (2000). A useful general survey of the place of Islam in African history.

Lewis, Bernard (trans.), *Islam: From the Prophet Muhammad to the Capture of Constantinople* (1974). Vol. 2: *Religion and Society*. A fine collection of original sources that portray various aspects of classical Islamic society.

Lopez, Robert S., *The Commercial Revolution of the Middle Ages, 950–1350* (1976). An account focusing on the development around the Mediterranean of commercial practices such as the use of currency, accounting, and credit.

Maalouf, Amin, *The Crusades through Muslim Eyes*, trans. Jon Rothschild (1984). The European Crusaders as seen by the Muslim world.

Marcus, Harold G., *A History of Ethiopia* (2002). An authoritative overview of the history of this great culture.

Mass, Jeffrey, *Yoritomo and the Founding of the First Bakufu: The Origins of Dual Government in Japan* (1999). A revisionist account of how the Kamakura military leader Minamoto Yoritomo established the "dual polity" of court and warrior government in Japan.

McDermott, Joseph, *A Social History of the Chinese Book: Books and Literati Culture in Late Imperial China* (2006). The history of the book in China since the Song dynasty, with comparisons to the book's role in other civilizations, particularly the European.

McIntosh, Roderik, *The Peoples of the Middle Niger: The Island of Gold* (1988). A historical survey of an area often omitted from other textbooks.

Moore, Jerry D., *Cultural Landscapes in the Ancient Andes: Archaeologies of Place* (2005). The most recent and up-to-date analysis of findings based on recent archaeological evidence, emphasizing the importance of local cultures and diversity in the Andes.

Niane, D. T. (ed.), *Africa from the Twelfth to the Sixteenth Century*, vol. 4 of *General History of Africa* (1984). The general UNESCO history of Africa's volume on four centuries of African history. This work features the scholarship of Africans.

Oliver, Roland (ed.), *From c. 1050 to c. 1600*, vol. 3 of *The Cambridge History of Africa*, ed. J. D. Fage and Roland Oliver (1977). Another general survey of African history. This volume draws heavily on the work of British scholars.

Peters, Edward, *The First Crusade* (1971). The Crusaders as seen through their own eyes.

Petry, Carl F. (ed.), *Islamic Egypt, 640–1517*, vol. 1 of *The Cambridge History of Egypt*, ed. M. W. Daly (1998). A solid overview of the history of Islamic Egypt up to the Ottoman conquest.

Polo, Marco, *The Travels of Marco Polo*, ed. Manuel Komroff (1926). A solid translation of Marco Polo's famous account.

Popovic, Alexandre, *The Revolt of African Slaves in Iraq in the 3rd/9th Century*, trans. Leon King (1999). The account of a massive revolt against their slave masters by African slaves taken to labor in Iraq's mines and fields.

Scott, Robert, *Gothic Enterprise: A Guide to Understanding the Medieval Cathedral* (2003). The meaning and social function of religious building in medieval cities in northern Europe.

Shaffer, Lynda Norene, *Maritime Southeast Asia to 1500* (1996). A history of the peoples of the southeast fringe of the Eastern Hemisphere, up to the time that they became connected to the global commercial networks of the world.

Shimada, Izumi, "Evolution of Andean Diversity: Regional Formations (500 BCE–CE 600)," in Frank Salomon and Stuart Schwartz (eds.), *South America*, vol. 3 of *The Cambridge History of the Native Peoples of the Americas* (1999), part 1, pp. 350–517. A splendid overview that contrasts the varieties of lowland and highland cultures.

Steinberg, David Joel, et al., *In Search of Southeast Asia: A Modern History* (1987). An account of the emergence of the modern Southeast Asian polities of Cambodia, Burma, Thailand, and Indonesia.

Tyerman, Christopher, *God's War: A New History of the Crusades* (2006). The balance of religious and nonreligious motivations in the Crusades.

Waley, Daniel, *The Italian City-Republics*, 3rd ed. (1988). The structures and culture of the new cities of medieval Italy.

Watson, Andrew, *Agricultural Innovation in the Early Islamic World: The Diffusion of Crops and Farming Techniques, 700–1100* (1983). An impressive study of the spread of new crops throughout the Muslim world.

Chapter 11 Crises and Recovery in Afro-Eurasia, 1300–1500

Bois, Guy, *The Crisis of Feudalism: Economy and Society in Eastern Normandy, c. 1300–1550* (1984). A good case study of a French region that illustrates the turmoil in fourteenth-century Europe.

Brook, Timothy, *Praying for Power: Buddhism and the Formation of Gentry Society in Late Ming China* (1994). An analysis of the role of a significant religious force in the political and social developments of the Ming.

Dardess, John, *A Ming Society: T'ai-ho County, Kiangsi, Fourteenth to Seventeenth Centuries* (1996). A work that covers the different changes and developments of a single locality in China through the centuries.

Dols, Michael W., *The Black Death in the Middle East* (1977). One of the few scholarly works to examine the Black Death outside Europe.

Dreyer, Edward, *Early Ming China: A Political History, 1355–1435* (1982). A useful account of the early years of the Ming dynasty.

Finkel, Caroline, *Osman's Dream: The Story of the Ottoman Empire, 1300–1923* (2005). The most authoritative overview of Ottoman history.

Hale, John, *The Civilization of Europe in the Renaissance* (1994). A beautifully crafted account of the politics, economics, and culture of the Renaissance period in western Europe.

Hodgson, Marshall, *The Venture of Islam: Conscience and History in a World Civilization*, vol. 3 (1974). A good volume on the workings of the Ottoman state.

Itzkowitz, Norman, *Ottoman Empire and Islamic Tradition* (1972). Another good book on the Ottoman state.

Jackson, Peter, *The Delhi Sultanate* (1999). A meticulous, highly specialized, political and military history.

Jackson, Peter, and Lawrence Lockhart (eds.), *The Cambridge History of Iran*, vol. 6 (1986). A volume that deals with the Timurid and Safavid periods in Iran.

Jones, E. L., *The European Miracle* (1981). A provocative work on the economic and social recovery from the Black Death.

Kafadar, Cemal, *Between Two Worlds: The Construction of the Ottoman State* (1995). A thorough reconsideration of the origins of one of the world's great land empires.

Karamustafa, Ahmed, *God's Unruly Friends: Dervish Groups in the Islamic Later Middle Period, 1200–1550* (1994). A book that describes the unorthodox Islamic activities that were occurring in the Islamic world prior to and alongside the establishment of the Ottoman and Safavid empires.

Levathes, Louise, *When China Ruled the Seas: The Treasure Fleet of the Dragon Throne, 1405–33* (1994). A book that provides a lively account of the Zheng He expeditions.

Lowry, Heath W., *The Nature of the Early Ottoman State* (2003). New perspectives on the rise of the Ottomans to prominence.

McNeill, William, *Plagues and Peoples* (1976). A pathbreaking work with a highly useful chapter on the spread of the Black Death throughout the Afro-Eurasian landmass.

Morgan, David, *Medieval Persia, 1040–1797* (1988). Contains an informative discussion of the Safavid state.

Peirce, Leslie, *The Imperial Harem: Women and Sovereignty in the Ottoman Empire* (1993). A work that describes the powerful place that imperial women had in political affairs.

Pirenne, Henri, *Economic and Social History of Medieval Europe* (1937). A classic study of the economic and social recovery from the Black Death.

Reid, James J., *Tribalism and Society in Islamic Iran, 1500–1629* (1983). A useful account of how the Mongols and other nomadic steppe peoples influenced Iran in the era when the Safavids were establishing their authority.

Singman, Jeffrey L. (ed.), *Daily Life in Medieval Europe* (1999). An introductory description of the social and material world experienced by Europeans of different walks of life.

Tuchman, Barbara W., *A Distant Mirror: The Calamitous Fourteenth Century* (1978). A book that shows, in a vigorous way, how war, famine, and pestilence devastated Europeans in the fourteenth century.

Wittek, Paul, *The Rise of the Ottoman Empire* (1958). A work that contains vital insights on the emergence of the Ottoman state amid the political chaos in Anatolia.

Chapter 12 Contact, Commerce, and Colonization, 1450–1600

Axtell, James, *Beyond 1492: Encounters in Colonial North America* (1992). A wonderfully informed speculation about Indian reactions to Europeans.

Brady, Thomas A., et al. (eds.), *Handbook of European History 1400–1600: Late Middle Ages, Renaissance, and Reformation, Structures and Assertions* (1996). A good synthetic survey of recent literature and historiographical debates.

Brook, Timothy, *Vermeer's Hat: The Seventeenth Century and the Dawn of the Global World* (2008). An interesting look at the connections forged across the globe through the works of a well-known European artist.

Cass, Victoria, *Dangerous Women: Warriors, Grannies, and Geishas of the Ming* (1999). An original study of Chinese female archetypes in memoirs, miscellanies, short stories, and novels.

Chaudhuri, K. N., *Trade and Civilisation in the Indian Ocean: An Economic History from the Rise of Islam to 1750* (1985). An excellent, comprehensive work that deals with the Indian Ocean economy and the appearance of European merchants there from the sixteenth century onward.

Clendinnen, Inga, *Aztecs: An Interpretation* (1991). Brilliantly reconstructs the culture of Tenochtitlán in the years before its conquest.

Crosby, Alfred W., *The Columbian Exchange: Biological and Cultural Consequences of 1492* (1972). A provocative discussion of the ecological consequences that followed the European "discovery" of the Americas.

———, *Ecological Imperialism: The Biological Expansion of Europe, 900–1900* (1986). Another important work on the ecological consequences of European expansion.

Curtin, Philip, *Cross-Cultural Trade in World History* (1984). A work stressing the role of trade and commerce in establishing cross-cultural contacts.

Febvre, Lucien, *The Problem of Unbelief in the Sixteenth Century: The Religion of Rabelais* (1982). A tour de force of intellectual history by the man who moved the study of the Reformation away from great men to the broader question of religious revival and mentalities.

Flynn, Dennis, and Arturo Giráldez (eds.), *Metals and Monies in an Emerging Global Economy* (1997). Contains several articles relating to silver and the Asian trade.

Frank, Andre Gunder, *ReOrient: Global Economy in the Asian Age* (1998). A reassessment of the role of Asia in the economic development of the world from around 1400 onward.

Gruzinski, Serge, *The Conquest of Mexico* (1993). An important work on the conquest of Mexico.

Habib, Irfan, *The Agrarian System of Mughal India* (1963). One of the best studies on the subject.

Hall, Richard Seymour, *Empires of the Monsoon: A History of the Indian Ocean and Its Invaders* (1996). A very engaging journalistic account with fabulous details.

Hodgson, Marshall, *The Venture of Islam*, vols. 2 and 3 (1974). A magisterial work that includes the Indian subcontinent in its careful study of the political and cultural history of the whole Islamic world.

Hulme, Peter, *Colonial Encounters: Europe and the Native Caribbean, 1492–1797* (1986). Presents an interesting interpretation of the encounters of Europeans and Native Americans.

Lach, Donald F., *Asia in the Making of Europe*, 5 books in 3 vols. (1965–). Perhaps the single most comprehensive and innovative guide to the European voyages of discovery.

Lockhart, James, and Stuart Schwartz, *Early Latin America* (1983). One of the finest studies of European expansion in the late fifteenth century.

Melville, Elinor G. K., *A Plague of Sheep: Environmental Consequences of the Conquest of Mexico* (1994). A history of the transformation of a valley in Mexico from the Aztec period to the era of Spanish rule.

Mignolo, Walter D., *The Darker Side of the Renaissance: Literacy, Territoriality, and Colonization* (1995). Uses literary theory and literary images to present provocative interpretations of the encounter of Europeans and Native Americans.

Pagden, Anthony, *European Encounters with the New World* (1993). A complex look at the deep and lasting imprint of the New World on its conquerors.

Parker, Geoffrey, *The Military Revolution: Military Innovation and the Rise of the West, 1500–1800* (1996). Traces the changes in technology and tactics in the early modern period and discusses the political significance of this "revolution."

Pelikan, Jaroslav, *Reformation of Church and Dogma (1300–1700)* (1988). An important overview of major religious controversies.

Phillips, William D., and Carla Rahn Phillips, *The World of Christopher Columbus* (1992). One of the finest studies of European expansion in the late fifteenth century.

Russell-Wood, A. J. R., *The Portuguese Empire, 1415–1808* (1992). An important survey of early Portuguese exploration.

Von Glahn, Richard, *Fountain of Fortune: Money and Monetary Policy in China, 1000–1700* (1996). Includes an excellent analysis of the history of silver in Ming China.

Chapter 13 Worlds Entangled, 1600–1750

Alam, Muzaffar, *The Crisis of Empire in Mughal North India* (1993). Represents the best of the new scholarly interpretations on the subject.

Bay, Edna, *Wives of the Leopard: Gender, Politics, and Culture in the Kingdom of Dahomey* (1998). A useful treatment of gender issues in Dahomey.

Blackburn, Robin, *The Making of New World Slavery: From the Baroque to the Modern, 1492–1800* (1997). A good place to begin when studying African slavery and the Atlantic slave trade, it compares the early expansion of the plantation systems across the Atlantic and throughout the Americas.

Crossley, Pamela, *A Translucent Mirror: History and Identity in Qing Imperial Ideology* (1999). The author deals with the formation of identities such as "Manchu" and "Chinese" during the Qing period.

Dennis, Matthew, *Cultivating a Landscape of Peace: Iroquois-European Encounters in Seventeenth-Century America* (1993). An excellent discussion of the relations of the Iroquois and the European colonists.

Flynn, Dennis O., and Arturo Giraldez (eds.), *Metals and Money in an Emerging World Economy* (1997). A collection of articles about the place of silver in the world economy.

Forsyth, James, *A History of the Peoples of Siberia: Russia's North Asian Colony 1581–1990* (1992). A narrative overview of a violent history reminiscent of the western expansion of the United States.

Glahn, Richard von, *Fountains of Fortune: Money and Monetary Policy in China, 1000–1700* (1996). A discussion of the place of silver in the Chinese economy.

Halperin, Charles J., *Russia and the Golden Horde: The Mongol Impact on Medieval Russian History* (1985). A book on the rise of Muscovy, forebear of the Russian Empire, from within the Mongol realm.

Hattox, Ralph S., *Coffee and Coffeehouses: The Origins of a Social Beverage in the Medieval Near East* (1985). This work shows how widespread and popular coffee consumption and coffeehouses were around the world.

Huang, Ray, *1587, A Year of No Significance: The Ming Dynasty in Decline* (1981). An insightful analysis of the problems confronting the late Ming.

Lensen, George, *The Russian Push Toward Japan: Russo-Japanese Relations 1697–1875* (1959). A discussion of why and how Japan established its first border with another state and how Russia pursued its ambitions in the Pacific.

Lockhart, James, *The Nahuas After the Conquest* (1992). A landmark study of the social reorganization of Mesoamerican societies under Spanish rule.

Lovejoy, Paul, *Transformations in Slavery: A History of Slavery in Africa* (1983). An excellent discussion of African slavery.

Nakane, Chie, and Shinzaburo Oishi (eds.), *Tokugawa Japan: The Social and Economic Antecedents of Modern Japan* (1990). First-rate essays on Japanese village society, urban life, literacy, and culture.

Pamuk, Sevket, *A Monetary History of the Ottoman Empire* (2000). A discussion of the place of silver in the Ottoman Empire.

Parker, Geoffrey (ed.), *The Thirty Years' War* (1997). The standard account of the conflict and its outcomes.

Perdue, Peter C., *China Marches West: The Qing Conquest of Central Asia* (2005). This volume chronicles the expansion of the Qing Empire to its northwest, drawing comparisons to other colonial empires and their legacies.

Platonov, S. F., *Ivan the Terrible* (1986). Covers the controversies over Russia's infamous tsar.

Rawski, Evelyn, *The Last Emperors: A Social History of Qing Imperial Institutions* (1998). This volume explores the mechanisms and processes through which the Qing court negotiated its Manchu identity.

Reid, Anthony, *Charting the Shape of Early Modern Southeast Asia* (1999). A collection of articles by a leading historian of Southeast Asia.

Richter, Daniel, *The Ordeal of the Longhouse: The Peoples of the Iroquois League in the Era of European Colonization* (1992). A superb analysis of the Iroquois and their relations with Dutch, English, and French colonists.

Spence, Jonathan, and John Wills (eds.), *From Ming to Ch'ing: Conquest, Region, and Continuity in Seventeenth-Century China* (1979). Covers the various aspects of a tumultuous period of dynastic transition.

Taylor, Alan, *American Colonies: The Settling of North America* (2001). Brings together British, French, and Spanish colonial histories and shows how the fortunes of each were entangled with one another and with those of diverse Native American peoples.

Thornton, John, *Africa and Africans in the Making of the Atlantic World, 1400–1800* (1998). A wonderful discussion of how African slaves played a large role in the formation of the Atlantic world.

Thornton, John K., *The Kongolese Saint Anthony: Dona Beatriz Kimpa Vita and the Antonian Movement, 1684–1706* (1998). An excellent monograph on religious movements in the Kongo.

Toby, Ronald P., *State and Diplomacy in Early Modern Japan: Asia in the Development of the Tokugawa Bakufu* (1984). The author shows that the Japanese, far from being isolated from the outside world, engaged in vigorous and successful diplomacy.

Vilar, Pierre, *A History of Gold and Money* (1991). An excellent study of the development of the early silver and gold economies.

Chapter 14 Cultures of Splendor and Power, 1500–1780

Axtell, James, *The Invasion of America: The Contest of Cultures in Colonial North America* (1985). Discusses the strategies of Christian missionaries in converting the Indians, as well as the success of Indians in converting Europeans.

Babaie, Sussan, *Isfahan and Its Palaces: Statecraft, Shi'ism and the Architecture of Conviviality in Early Modern Iran* (2008). An overview of the city of Isfahan, as the capital of the Safavid state.

Berlin, Ira, *Many Thousands Gone: The First Two Centuries of Slavery in North America* (1998). Surveys the development of African-American culture in colonial North America.

Brook, Timothy, *The Confusions of Pleasure: Commerce and Culture in Ming China* (1999). An insightful survey of Ming society.

Clunas, Craig, *Superfluous Things: Material Culture and Social Status in Early Modern China* (1991). A good account of the late Ming elite's growing passion for material things.

Collcutt, Martin, Marius Jansen, and Isao Kumakura, *A Cultural Atlas of Japan* (1988). A sweeping look at the many different forms of Japanese cultural expression over the centuries, including the flourishing urban culture of Edo.

Darnton, Robert, *The Business of the Enlightenment: A Publishing History of the Encyclopédie, 1775–1800* (1979). The classic study of Europe's first great compendium of knowledge.

Dash, Mike, *Tulipomania: The Story of the World's Most Coveted Flower and the Extraordinary Passions It Aroused* (1999). A global perspective on and lively account of the spread of the tulip around the world as a flower signifying both beauty and status.

Elman, Benjamin A., *On Their Own Terms: Science in China, 1550–1900* (2005). A study of the development of "native" Chinese science and how the process interacted with the introduction of western science to China over the course of three and a half centuries.

Eze, Emmanuel Chukwudi (ed.), *Race and the Enlightenment: A Reader* (1997). Readings examining the idea of race in the context of the Enlightenment.

Fleischer, Cornell, *Bureaucrat and Intellectual in the Ottoman Empire: The Historian Mustafa Ali (1540–1600)* (1986). Offers good insight into the world of culture and intellectual vitality in the Ottoman Empire.

Grafton, Anthony, April Shelford, and Nancy Siraisi, *New Worlds, Ancient Texts: The Power of Tradition and the Shock of Discovery* (1995). A concise discussion of the impact of the New World on European thought.

Gutierrez, Ramon, *When Jesus Came, the Corn Mothers Went Away: Marriage, Sexuality, and Power in New Mexico, 1500–1846* (1991). A provocative dissection of the spiritual dimensions of European colonialism in the Americas.

Harley, J. B., and David Woodward (eds.), *The History of Cartography*. Vol. 2, Book 2: *Cartography in the Traditional East and Southeast Asian Societies* (1994). An authoritative treatment of the subject.

Horton, Robin, *Patterns of Thought in Africa and the West: Essays on Magic, Religion, and Science* (1993). Reflections on African patterns of thought and attitudes toward nature, which can help us understand African-American religious beliefs and resistance movements.

Keene, Donald, *The Japanese Discovery of Europe: Honda Toshiaki and Other Discoverers, 1720–1798* (1952). A study of the ways Japan managed to incorporate knowledge from the outside world with the development of national traditions.

Ko, Dorothy, *Teachers of the Inner Chambers: Women and Culture in Seventeenth-Century China* (1994). Explores the lives of elite women in late Ming and early Qing China.

Lewis, Bernard, *Race and Color in Islam* (1979). Examines the Islamic attitude toward race and color.

Morgan, Philip D., *Slave Counterpoint: Black Culture in the Eighteenth-Century Chesapeake and Lowcountry* (1998). Describes the development of African-American culture in colonial North America.

Munck, Thomas, *The Enlightenment: A Comparative Social History, 1721–1794* (2000). A wonderful survey, with unusual examples from the periphery, especially from Scandinavia and the Habsburg Empire.

Necipoglu, Gulru, *Architecture, Ceremonial, and Power: The Topkapi Palace in the Fifteenth and Sixteenth Centuries* (1991). A magnificently illustrated book that shows the enormous artistic talent that the Ottoman rulers poured into their imperial structure.

Publishing and the Print Culture in Late Imperial China (Special Issue). *Late Imperial China*, Vol. 17:1 (June 1996). Contains a collection of important articles with a foreword by the French cultural historian Roger Chartier.

Qaisar, Ahsan Jan, *The Indian Response to European Technology, AD 1498–1707* (1998). A meticulous, scholarly work on this little-studied subject.

Rizvi, Athar Abbas, *The Wonder That Was India*. Vol. 2: *A Survey of the History and Culture of the Indian Sub-continent from the Coming of the Muslims to the British Conquest, 1200–1700* (1987). A deeply learned work in intellectual history.

Smith, Bernard, *European Vision and the South Pacific* (1985). An excellent cultural history of Cook's voyages.

Smith, Richard J., *Chinese Maps: Images of "All under Heaven"* (1996). Provides a good introduction to the history of cartography in China.

Welch, Anthony, *Shah Abbas and the Arts of Isfahan* (1973). Describes the astonishing architectural and artistic renaissance of the city of Isfahan under the Safavid ruler Shah Abbas.

Whitfield, Peter, *The Image of the World: Twenty Centuries of World Maps* (1994). A good introduction to the history of cartography in different parts of the world.

Zilfi, Madeline C., *The Politics of Piety: The Ottoman Ulema in the Post-Classical Age (1600–1800)* (1988). Explores the cultural flourishing that took place within the Islamic world in this period.

Chapter 15 Reordering the World, 1750–1850

Allen, Robert C., *The British Industrial Revolution in Global Perspective* (2009). The most recent and authoritative study of the industrial revolution in Britain and its implications around the world.

Anderson, Fred, *Crucible of War: The Seven Years' War and the Fate of Empire in British North America, 1754–1766* (2000). The best synthesis of the "great war for empire" that set the stage for the American Revolution.

Bayly, C. A., *Indian Society and the Making of the British Empire* (1998). A useful work on the early history of the British conquest of India.

Blackburn, Robin, *The Overthrow of Colonial Slavery, 1776–1848* (1988). Places the abolition of the Atlantic slave trade and colonial slavery in a large historical context.

Cambridge History of Egypt: Modern Egypt from 1517 to the End of the Twentieth Century, Vol. 2 (1998). Volume 2 contains authoritative essays on all aspects of modern Egyptian history, including the impact of the French invasion and the rule of Muhammad Ali.

Chaudhuri, K. N., *The Trading World of Asia and the East India Company, 1660–1760* (1978). An authoritative economic history of the East India Company's operations.

Crafts, N. F. R., *British Economic Growth during the Industrial Revolution* (1985). A pioneering study that emphasizes a long-term, more gradual process of adaptation to new institutional and social circumstances.

de Vries, Jan, *Industrious Revolution: Consumer Behavior and the Household Economy, 1650 to the Present* (2008). A book on the lead-up to the industrial revolution, written by the leading economic historian who coined the term industrious revolution.

Doyle, William, *The Oxford History of the French Revolution* (1990). A highly detailed discussion of the course of events.

Drescher, Seymour, *Abolition: A History of Slavery and Anti-Slavery* (2009). A recent and authoritative overview of slavery and its opponents.

Elvin, Mark, *The Retreat of the Elephants: An Environmental History of China* (2004). A study of the different ways in which China's natural environment was shaped.

Fick, Carolyn E., *The Making of Haiti: The Saint Domingue Revolution from Below* (1990). Provides a detailed account of the factors that led to the great slave rebellion on the island of Haiti at the end of the eighteenth century.

Findley, Carter, *Bureaucratic Reform in the Ottoman Empire: The Sublime Porte, 1789–1922* (1980). A useful guide to Ottoman reform efforts in the nineteenth century.

Hevia, James, *Cherishing Men from Afar: Qing Guest Ritual and the Macartney Embassy of 1793* (1995). Offers a definitive interpretation of the nature of Sino-British conflict in the Qing period.

Hobsbawm, Eric, *Nations and Nationalism since 1780* (1990). An important overview of the rise of the nation-state and nationalism around the world.

Howe, Daniel Walker, *What Hath God Wrought: The Transformation of America, 1815–1848* (2007). A Pulitzer Prize–winning interpretation of how new technologies and new ideas reshaped the economy, society, culture, and politics of the United States in the first half of the nineteenth century.

Hunt, Lynn, *Politics, Culture and Class in the French Revolution* (1984). Examines the influence of sociocultural shifts as causes and consequences of the French Revolution, emphasizing the symbols and practice of politics invented during the revolution.

Inikori, Joseph, *Africans and the Industrial Revolution in England* (2002). Author demonstrates the important role that Africa and Africans played in facilitating the industrial revolution.

Isset, Christopher Mills, *State, Peasant, and Merchant in Qing Manchuria, 1644–1862* (2007). A study of the relationships between the sociopolitical structures and peasant lives in a key region during the Qing.

Jones, E. L., *Growth Recurring* (1988). Discusses the controversy over why the industrial revolution took place in Europe, stressing the unique ecological setting that encouraged long-term investment.

Kinsbruner, Jay, *Independence in Spanish America* (1994). A fine study of the Latin American revolutions that argues that the struggle was as much a civil war as a fight for national independence.

Mokyr, Joel, *Enlightened Economy: An Economic History of Britain, 1700–1850* (2009). Perspectives on the evolution of the British economy in the era that produced the industrial revolution.

———, *The Lever of Riches* (1990). An important study of the causes of the industrial revolution that emphasizes the role of small technological and organizational breakthroughs.

Naquin, Susan, and Evelyn Rawski, *Chinese Society in the Eighteenth Century* (1987). A survey of mid-Qing society.

Neal, Larry, *The Rise of Financial Capitalism* (1990). An important study of the making of financial markets.

Nikitenko, Aleksandr, *Up from Serfdom: My Childhood and Youth in Russia, 1804–1824* (2001). One of the very few recorded life stories of a Russian serf.

Pomeranz, Kenneth, *The Great Divergence: Europe, China, and the Making of the Modern World Economy* (2000). Offers explanations of why Europe and not some other place in the world, like parts of China or India, forged ahead economically in the nineteenth century.

Rudé, George, *Europe in the Eighteenth Century* (1972). Emphasizes the rise of a new class, the bourgeoisie, against the old aristocracy, as a cause of the French Revolution.

Wakeman, Frederic, Jr., "The Canton Trade and the Opium War," in John K. Fairbank (ed.), *The Cambridge History of China*, Vol. 10 (1978), pp. 163–212. The standard account of the episode.

Wong, R. Bin, *China Transformed: Historical Change and the Limits of European Experience* (2000). Draws attention to the relative autonomy of merchant capitalists in relation to dynastic states in Europe compared to China.

Wood, Gordon S., *Empire of Liberty: A History of the Early Republic, 1789–1815* (2009). An excellent synthesis of the history of the United States in the tumultuous years between the ratification of the Constitution and the War of 1812.

Wortman, Richard, *Scenarios of Power: Myth and Ceremony in Russian Monarchy*, 2 vols. (1995–2000). Examines how dynastic Russia confronted the challenges of the revolutionary epoch.

Abd al-Rahman III Islamic ruler in Spain who held a countercaliphate and reigned from 912 to 961 CE.

aborigines Original, native inhabitants of a region, as opposed to invaders, colonizers, or later peoples of mixed ancestry.

absolute monarchy Form of government where one body, usually the monarch, controls the right to tax, judge, make war, and coin money. The term *enlightened absolutists* was often used to refer to state monarchies in seventeenth- and eighteenth-century Europe.

acid rain Precipitation containing large amounts of sulfur, mainly from coal-fired plants.

adaptation Ability to alter behavior and to innovate, finding new ways of doing things.

African National Congress (ANC) Multiracial organization founded in 1912 in an effort to end racial discrimination in South Africa.

Afrikaners Descendants of the original Dutch settlers of South Africa; formerly referred to as Boers.

Agones Athletic contests in ancient Greece.

Ahmosis Egyptian ruler in the southern part of the country who ruled from 1550 to 1525 BCE; Ahmosis used Hyksos weaponry—horse chariots in particular—to defeat the Hyksos themselves.

Ahura Mazda Supreme God of the Persians believed to have created the world and all that is good and to have appointed earthly kings.

AIDS (Acquired Immunodeficiency Syndrome) Virus that compromises the ability of the infected person's immune system to ward off disease. First detected in 1981, AIDS was initially stigmatized as a "gay cancer," but as it spread to heterosexuals, public awareness about it increased. In its first two decades, AIDS killed 12 million people.

Akbarnamah Mughal intellectual Abulfazl's *Book of Akbar*, which attempted to reconcile the traditional Sufi interest in the inner life within the worldly context of a great empire.

Alaric II Visigothic king who issued a simplified code of innovative imperial law.

Alexander the Great (356–323 BCE) Leader who used novel tactics and new kinds of armed forces to conquer the Persian Empire, which extended from Egypt and the Mediterranean Sea to the interior of what is now Afghanistan and as far as the Indus River valley. Alexander's conquests broke down barriers between the Mediterranean world and Southwest Asia and transferred massive amounts of wealth and power to the Mediterranean, transforming it into a more unified world of economic and cultural exchange.

Alexandria Port city in Egypt named after Alexander the Great. Alexandria was a model city in the Hellenistic world. It was built up by a multiethnic population from around the Mediterranean world.

Al-Khwarizmi Scientist and mathematician who lived from 780 to 850 CE and is known for having modified Indian digits into Arabic numerals.

Allied powers Name given to the alliance between Britain, France, Russia, and Italy, who fought against Germany and Austria-Hungary (the Central powers) in World War I. In World War II the name was used for the alliance between Britain, France, and America, who fought against the Axis powers (Germany, Italy, and Japan).

allomothering System by which mothers relied on other women, including their own mothers, daughters, sisters, and friends, to help in the nurturing and protecting of children.

alluvium Area of land created by river deposits.

American Railway Union Workers' union that initiated the Pullman Strike of 1894, which led to violence and ended in the leaders' arrest.

Amnesty International Non-governmental organization formed to defend "prisoners of conscience"—those detained for their beliefs, race, sex, ethnic origin, language, or religion.

Amorites Name that Mesopotamian urbanites called the transhumant herders from the Arabian desert. Around 2300 BCE, the Amorites, along with the Elamites, were at the center of newly formed dynasties in southern Mesopotamia.

Amun Once insignificant Egyptian god elevated to higher status by Amenemhet (1991–1962 BCE). *Amun* means "hidden" in Ancient Egyptian; the name was meant to convey the god's omnipresence.

Analects Texts that included the teachings and cultural ideals of Confucius.

anarchism Belief that society should be a free association of its members, not subject to government, laws, or police.

Anatolia Now mainly the area known as modern Turkey; in the sixth millennium BCE, people from Anatolia, Greece, and the Levant took to boats and populated the Aegean. Their small villages endured almost unchanged for two millennia.

Angkor Wat Magnificent Khmer Vaishnavite temple that crowned the royal palace in Angkor. It had statues representing the Hindu pantheon of gods.

Anglo-Boer War (1899–1902) Anticolonial struggle in South Africa between the British and the Afrikaners over the gold-rich Transvaal. In response to the Afrikaners' guerrilla tactics and in order to contain the local population, the British instituted the first concentration camps. Ultimately, Britain won the conflict.

animal domestication Gradual process that occurred simultaneously with or just before the domestication of plants, depending on the region.

annals Historical records. Notable annals are the cuneiform inscriptions that record successful Assyrian military campaigns.

Anti-Federalists Critics of the U.S. Constitution who sought to defend the people against the power of the federal government and insisted on a bill of rights to protect individual liberties from government intrusion.

Apartheid Racial segregation policy of the Afrikaner-dominated South African government. Legislated in 1948 by the Afrikaner National Party, it had existed in South Africa for many years.

Arab-Israeli War of 1948–1949 Conflict between Israeli and Arab armies that arose in the wake of a U.N. vote to partition Palestine into Arab and Jewish territories. The war shattered the legitimacy of Arab ruling elites.

Aramaic Dialect of a Semitic language spoken in Southwest Asia; it became the lingua franca of the Persian Empire.

Aristotle (384–322 BCE) Philosopher who studied under Plato but came to different conclusions about nature and politics. Aristotle believed in collecting observations about nature and discerning patterns to ascertain how things worked.

Aryans Nomadic charioteers who spoke Indo-European languages and entered South Asia in 1500 BCE. The early Aryan settlers were herders.

Asante state State located in present-day Ghana, founded by the Asantes at the end of the seventeenth century. It grew in power in the next century because of its access to gold and its involvement in the slave trade.

ascetic One who rejects material possessions and physical pleasures.

Asiatic Society Cultural organization founded by British Orientalists who supported native culture but still believed in colonial rule.

Aśoka Emperor of the Mauryan dynasty from 268 to 231 BCE; he was a great conqueror and unifier of India. He is said to have embraced Buddhism toward the end of his life.

Assur One of two cities on the upper reaches of the Tigris River that were the heart of Assyria proper (the other was Nineveh).

Aśvaghosa First known Sanskrit writer. He may have lived from 80 to 150 CE and may have composed a biography of the Buddha.

Ataturk, Mustafa Kemal (1881–1938) Ottoman army officer and military hero who helped forge the modern Turkish nation-state. He and his followers deposed the sultan, declared Turkey a republic, and constructed a European-like secular state, eliminating Islam's hold over civil and political affairs.

Atlantic system New system of trade and expansion that linked Europe, Africa, and the Americas. It emerged in the wake of European voyages across the Atlantic Ocean.

Atma Vedic term signifying the eternal self, represented by the trinity of deities.

Atman In the Upanishads, an eternal being who exists everywhere. The atman never perishes but is reborn or transmigrates into another life.

Attila Sole ruler of all Hunnish tribes from 433 to 453 CE. Harsh and much feared, he formed the first empire to oppose Rome in northern Europe.

Augustus Title meaning "Revered One," assumed in 27 BCE by the Roman ruler Octavian (63–14 BCE). This was one of many titles he assumed; others included *imperator*, *princeps*, and *Caesar*.

Australopithecines Hominid species that appeared 3 million years ago and, unlike other animals, walked on two legs. Their brain capacity was a little less than one-third of a modern human's or about the size of the brain capacity of today's African apes. Although not humans, they carried the genetic and biological material out of which modern humans would later emerge.

Austro-Hungarian Empire Dual monarchy established by the Habsburg family in 1867; it collapsed at the end of World War I.

authoritarianism Centralized and dictatorial form of government, proclaimed by its adherents to be superior to parliamentary democracy and especially effective at mobilizing the masses. This idea was widely accepted in parts of the world during the 1930s.

Avesta Compilation of holy works transmitted orally by priests for millennia and eventually recorded in the sixth century BCE.

Axis powers The three aggressor states in World War II: Germany, Japan, and Italy.

Aztec Empire Mesoamerican empire that originated with a league of three Mexica cities in 1430 and gradually expanded through the Central Valley of Mexico, uniting numerous small, independent states under a single monarch who ruled with the help of counselors, military leaders, and priests. By the late fifteenth century, the Aztec realm may have embraced 25 million people. In 1521, they were defeated by the conquistador Hernán Cortés.

baby boom Post–World War II upswing in U.S. birth rates; it reversed a century of decline.

bactrian camel Two-humped animal domesticated in central Asia around 2500 BCE. The bactrian camel was heartier than the one-humped dromedary and became the animal of choice for the harsh and varied climates typical of Silk Road trade.

Baghdad Capital of the Islamic Empire under the Abbasid dynasty, founded in 762 CE (in modern-day Iraq). In the medieval period, it was a center of administration, scholarship, and cultural growth for what came to be known as the Golden Age of Islamic science.

Baghdad Pact (1955) Middle Eastern military alliance between countries friendly with America who were also willing to align themselves with the western countries against the Soviet Union.

Balam Na Stone temple and place of pilgrimage for the Mayan people of Mexico's Yucatan peninsula.

Balfour Declaration Letter (November 2, 1917) by Lord Arthur J. Balfour, British foreign secretary, that promised a homeland for the Jews in Palestine.

Bamboo Annals Shang stories and foundation myths that were written on bamboo strips and later collected.

Bantu Language first spoken by people who lived in the southeastern area of modern Nigeria around 1000 CE.

Bantu migrations Waves of rapid population movement from West Africa into eastern and southern Africa during the first millennium CE that brought advanced agricultural practices to these regions and absorbed most of the preexisting hunting-and-gathering populations.

barbarian Derogatory term used to describe pastoral nomads, painting them as enemies of civilization; the term *barbarian* used to have a more neutral meaning than it does today.

barbarian invasions Violent migration of people in the late fourth and fifth centuries into Roman territory. These migrants had long been used as non-Roman soldiers.

basilicas Early church buildings, based on old royal audience halls.

Battle of Adwa (1896) Battle in which the Ethiopians defeated Italian colonial forces; it inspired many of Africa's later national leaders.

Battle of Wounded Knee (1890) Bloody massacre of Sioux Ghost Dancers by U.S. armed forces.

Bay of Pigs (1961) Unsuccessful invasion of Cuba by Cuban exiles supported by the U.S. government. The invaders intended to incite an insurrection in Cuba and overthrow the communist regime of Fidel Castro.

Bedouins Nomadic pastoralists in the deserts of the Middle East.

Beer Hall Putsch (1923) Nazi intrusion into a meeting of Bavarian leaders in a Munich beer hall; the Nazis were attempting to force support for their cause; Adolf Hitler was imprisoned for a year after the incident.

Beghards (1500s) Eccentric European group whose members claimed to be in a state of grace that allowed them to do as they pleased— from adultery, free love, and nudity to murder; also called Brethren of Free Speech.

bell beaker Ancient drinking vessel, an artifact from Europe, so named because its shape resembles an inverted bell.

Berenice of Egypt Egyptian "queen" who helped rule over the Kingdom of the Nile from 320 to 280 BCE.

Beringia Prehistoric thousand-mile-long land bridge that linked Siberia and North America (which had not been populated by hominids). About 18,000 years ago, *Homo sapiens* edged into this landmass.

Berlin Airlift (1948) Supply of vital necessities to West Berlin by air transport primarily under U.S. auspices. It was initiated in response to a land and water blockade of the city instituted by the Soviet Union in the hope that the Allies would be forced to abandon West Berlin.

Berlin Wall Wall built by the communists in Berlin in 1961 to prevent citizens of East Germany from fleeing to West Germany; torn down in 1989.

Bhakti Religious practice that grew out of Hinduism and emphasizes personal devotion to gods.

Bhakti Hinduism Popular form of Hinduism that emerged in the seventh century. The religion stresses devotion (*bhakti*) to God and uses vernacular languages (not Sanskrit) spoken by the common people.

big men Leaders of the extended household communities that formed village settlements in African rain forests.

big whites French plantation owners in Saint Domingue (present-day Haiti) who created one of the wealthiest slave societies.

Bilad al-Sudan Arabic for "the land of the blacks"; it consisted of the land lying south of the Sahara.

bilharzia Debilitating water-borne illness. It was widespread in Egypt, where it infected peasants who worked in the irrigation canals.

Bill of Rights First ten amendments to the U.S. Constitution; ratified in 1791.

bipedalism Walking on two legs, thereby freeing hands and arms to carry objects such as weapons and tools; one of several traits that distinguished hominids.

Black Death Great epidemic of the bubonic plague that ravaged Europe, East Asia, and North Africa in the fourteenth century, killing large numbers, including perhaps as many as one-third of the European population.

Black Jacobins Nickname for the rebels in Saint Domingue, including Toussaint L'Ouverture, a former slave who led the slaves of this French colony in the world's largest and most successful slave insurrection.

Black Panthers Radical African American group in the 1960s and 1970s; they advocated black separatism and pan-Africanism.

black shirts Fascist troops of Mussolini's regime; the squads received money from Italian landowners to attack socialist leaders.

Black Tuesday (October 29, 1929) Historic day when the U.S. stock market crashed, plunging the United States and international trading systems into crisis and leading the world into the "Great Depression."

Blitzkrieg "Lightning war"; type of warfare in which the Germans, during World War II, used coordinated aerial bombing campaigns along with tanks and infantrymen in motorized vehicles.

Bodhisattvas In Mahayan Buddhism, enlightened demigods who were ready to reach *nirvana* but delayed so that they might help others attain it.

Bolívar, Simón (1783–1830) Venezuelan leader who urged his followers to become "American," to overcome their local identities. He wanted the liberated countries to form a Latin American confederation, urging Peru and Bolivia to join Venezuela, Ecuador, and Colombia in the "Gran Colombia."

Bolsheviks Former members of the Russian Social Democratic Party who advocated the destruction of capitalist political and economic institutions and started the Russian Revolution. In 1918 the Bolsheviks changed their name to the Russian Communist Party.

Book of the Dead Ancient Egyptian funerary text that contains drawings and paintings as well as spells describing how to prepare the jewelry and amulets that were buried with a person in preparation for the afterlife.

bourgeoisie The middle class. In Europe, they sought to be recognized not by birth or title, but by capital and property.

Boxer Protocol Written agreement between the victors of the Boxer Uprising and the Qing Empire in 1901 that placed western troops in Beijing and required the regime to pay exorbitant damages for foreign life and property.

Boxer Uprising (1899–1900) Chinese peasant movement that opposed foreign influence, especially that of Christian missionaries; it was put down after the Boxers were defeated by an army composed mostly of Japanese, Russians, British, French, and Americans.

Brahma One of three major deities that form a trinity in Vedic religion. Brahma signifies birth. *See also* Vishnu *and* Siva.

Brahmans Vedic priests who performed rituals and communicated with the gods. Brahmans provided guidance on how to live in balance with the forces of nature as represented by the various deities. The codification of Vedic principles into codes of law took place at the hands of the Brahmans. They memorized Vedic works and compiled commentaries on them. They also developed their own set of rules and rituals, which developed into a full-scale theology. Originally memorized and passed on orally, these may have been written down sometime after the beginning of the Common Era. Brahmanism was reborn as Hinduism sometime during the first half of the first millennium CE.

British Commonwealth of Nations Union formed in 1926 that conferred "dominion status" on Britain's white settler colonies in Canada, Australia, and New Zealand.

British East India Company *See* East India Company.

bronze Alloy of copper and tin brought into Europe from Anatolia; used to make hard-edged weapons.

brown shirts Troops of German men who advanced the Nazi cause by holding street marches, mass rallies, and confrontations and by beating Jews and anyone who opposed the Nazis.

bubonic plague Acute infectious disease caused by a bacterium that is transmitted to humans by fleas from infected rats. It ravaged Europe and parts of Asia in the fourteenth century. Sometimes referred to as the "Black Death."

Buddha (Siddhartha Gautama; 563–483 BCE) Indian ascetic who founded Buddhism.

Buddhism Major South Asian religion that aims to end human suffering through the renunciation of desire. Buddhists believe that removing the illusion of a separate identity would lead to a state of contentment (nirvana). These beliefs challenged the traditional Brahmanic teachings of the time and provided the peoples of South Asia with an alternative to established traditions.

bullion Uncoined gold or silver.

Cahokia Commercial center for regional and long-distance trade in North America. Its hinterlands produced staples for urban consumers. In return, its crafts were exported inland by porters and to North American markets in canoes. *See also* Mound people.

Calaveras Allegorical skeleton drawings by the Mexican printmaker and artist José Guadalupe Posada. The works drew on popular themes of betrayal, death, and festivity.

caliphate Institution that arose as the successor to Muhammad's leadership and became both the political and religious head of the Islamic community. Although the caliphs exercised political authority over the Muslim community and were the head of the religious community, the *ummah*, they did not inherit Muhammad's prophetic powers and were not authorities in religious doctrine.

Candomblé Yoruba-based religion in northern Brazil; it interwove African practices and beliefs with Christianity.

canton system System officially established by imperial decree in 1759 that required European traders to have Chinese guild merchants act as guarantors for their good behavior and payment of fees.

caravan cities Set of networks at long-distance trade locations where groups of merchants could assemble during their journeys. Several of these developed into full-fledged cities, especially in the deserts of Arabia.

caravans Companies of men who transported and traded goods along overland routes in North Africa and central Asia; large caravans consisted of 600–1,000 camels and as many as 400 men.

caravansarais Inns along major trade routes that accommodated large numbers of traders, their animals, and their wares.

caravel Sailing vessel suited for nosing in and out of estuaries and navigating in waters with unpredictable currents and winds.

carrack Ship used on open bodies of water, such as the Mediterranean.

Carthage City in what is modern-day Tunisia; emblematic of the trading aspirations and activities of merchants in the Mediterranean. Pottery and other archaeological remains demonstrate that trading contacts with Carthage were as far-flung as Italy, Greece, France, Iberia, and West Africa.

cartography Mapmaking.

caste system Hierarchical system of organizing people and distributing labor.

Caste War of Yucatan (1847–1901) Conflict between Mayan Indians and the Mexican state over Indian autonomy and legal equality, which resulted in the Mexican takeover of the Yucatan peninsula.

Castro, Fidel (1926–) Cuban communist leader whose forces overthrew Batista's corrupt regime in early January 1959. Castro became increasingly radical as he consolidated power, announcing a massive redistribution of land and the nationalization of foreign oil refineries; he declared himself a socialist and aligned himself with the Soviet Union in the wake of the 1961 CIA-backed Bay of Pigs invasion.

Çatal Hüyük Site in Anatolia discovered in 1958. It was a dense honeycomb of settlements filled with rooms whose walls were covered with paintings of wild bulls, hunters, and pregnant women. Çatal Hüyük symbolizes an early transition into urban dwelling and dates to the eighth millennium BCE.

Cathedra Bishop's seat, or throne, in a church.

Catholic Church Unifying institution for Christians in western Europe after the collapse of the Roman Empire. Rome became the spiritual capital of western Europe and the bishops of Rome emerged as popes, the supreme head of the church, who possessed great moral authority.

Cato the Elder (234–149 BCE) Roman statesman, often seen as emblematic of the transition from a Greek to a Roman world. Cato the Elder wrote a manual for the new economy of slave plantation agriculture, invested in shipping and trading, learned Greek rhetoric, and added the genre of history to Latin literature.

Caudillos South American local military chieftains.

cave drawings Images on cave walls. The subjects are most often large game, although a few are images of humans. Other elements are impressions made by hands dipped in paint and pressed on a wall or abstract symbols and shapes.

Celali revolts (1595–1610) Peasant and artisan uprisings against the Ottoman state.

Central powers Defined in World War I as Germany and Austria-Hungary.

Chan Chan City founded between 850 and 900 CE by the Moche people in what is now modern-day Peru. It had a core population of 30,000 inhabitants.

Chan Santa Cruz Separate Mayan community formed as part of a crusade for spiritual salvation and the complete cultural separation of the Mayan Indians; means "little holy cross."

Chandra Gupta II King who reigned in South Asia from 320 to 335 CE. He shared his name with Chandragupta, the founder of the Mauryan Empire.

Chandravamsha One of two main lineages (the lunar one) of Vedic society, each with its own creation myth, ancestors, language, and rituals. Each lineage included many clans. *See* Suryavamsha.

chapatis Flat, unleavened Indian bread.

chariots Horse-driven carriages brought by the pastoral nomadic warriors from the steppes that became the favored mode of transportation for an urban aristocratic warrior class and for other men of power in agriculture-based societies. Control of chariot forces was the foundation of the new balance of power across Afro-Eurasia during the second millennium BCE.

charismatic Person who uses personal strengths or virtues, often laced with a divine aura, to command followers.

Charlemagne Emperor of the West and heir to Rome from 764 to 814 CE.

chartered companies Firms that were awarded monopoly trading rights over vast areas by European monarchs (e.g., Virginia Company, Dutch East India Company).

Chartism (1834–1848) Mass democratic movement to pass the Peoples' Charter in Britain, granting male suffrage, secret ballot, equal electoral districts, and annual parliaments, and absolving the requirement of property ownership for members of the parliament.

chattel slavery Form of slavery that sold people as property, the rise of which coincided with the expansion of city-states. Chattel slavery was eschewed by the Spartans, who also rejected the innovation of coin money.

Chavín A people who lived in what is now northern Peru from 1400 to 200 BCE. They were united more by culture and faith than by a unified political system.

Chernobyl (1986) Site in the Soviet Union (in Ukraine) of the meltdown of a nuclear reactor.

Chiang Kai-shek (1887–1975) Leader of the Guomindang following Sun Yat-sen's death who mobilized the Chinese masses through the New Life movement. In 1949 he lost the Chinese Revolution to the communists and moved his regime to Taiwan.

Chimu Empire South America's first empire; it developed during the first century of the second millennium in the Moche Valley on the Pacific coast.

chinampas Floating gardens used by Aztecs in the 1300s and 1400s to grow crops.

China's Sorrow Name for the Yellow River, which, when it changed course or flooded, could cause mass death and waves of migration.

chinoiserie Chinese silks, teas, tableware, jewelry, and paper; popular among Europeans in the seventeenth and eighteenth centuries.

Christendom Entire portion of the world in which Christianity prevailed.

Christianity Religion that originated at the height of the Roman Empire and in a direct confrontation with Roman imperial authority: the trial of Yeshua ben Yosef (Joshua son of Joseph; we know him today by the Greek form of his name, Jesus). Jesus was condemned for sedition and crucified. His followers believed that he was resurrected and that his teachings were not that of a man, but a god who had walked among human beings. At first, the Roman Empire refused to recognize Christianity and persecuted its followers, but in the fourth century CE Christianity was officially recognized as the Roman state religion.

Church of England Established form of Christianity in England dating from the sixteenth century.

city Highly populated concentration of economic, religious, and political power. The first cities appeared in river basins, which could produce a surplus of agriculture. The abundance of food freed most city inhabitants from the need to produce their own food, which allowed them to work in specialized professions.

city-state Political organization based on the authority of a single, large city that controls outlying territories.

Civil Rights Act (1964) U.S. legislation that banned segregation in public facilities, outlawed racial discrimination in employment, and marked an important step in correcting legal inequality.

civil rights movement Powerful movement for equal rights and the end of racial segregation in the United States that began in the 1950s with court victories against school segregation and nonviolent boycotts.

civil service examinations The world's first written civil service examination system, instituted by the Tang dynasty to recruit officials and bureaucrats. Open to most males, the exams tested a candidate's literary skills and knowledge of the Confucian classics. They helped to unite the Chinese state by making knowledge of a specific language and Confucian classics the only route to power.

Civil War, American (1861–1865) Conflict between the northern and southern states of

America; this struggle led to the abolition of slavery in the United States.

clan A social group comprising many households, claiming descent from a common ancestor.

clandestine presses Small printing operations that published banned texts in the early modern era, especially in Switzerland and the Netherlands.

Clovis people Early humans in America who used basic chipped blades and pointed spears in pursuing prey. They extended the hunting traditions they had learned in Afro-Eurasia, such as establishing campsites and moving with their herds. They were known as "Clovis people" because the arrowhead point that they used was first found by archaeologists at a site near Clovis, New Mexico.

codex Early form of book, with separate pages bound together; it replaced the scroll as the main medium for written texts. The codex emerged around 300 CE.

cognitive skills Skills such as thought, memory, problem-solving, and—ultimately—language. Hominids were able to use these skills and their hands to create new adaptations, like tools, which helped them obtain food and avoid predators.

Cohong Chinese merchant guild that traded with Europeans under the Qing dynasty.

coins Form of money that replaced goods, which previously had been bartered for services and other products. Originally used mainly to hire mercenary soldiers, coins became the commonplace method of payment linking buyers and producers throughout the Mediterranean.

cold war (1945–1990) Ideological conflict in which the Soviet Union and eastern Europe opposed the United States and western Europe.

colonies Regions under the political control of another country.

Colons French settler population in Algeria.

colosseum Huge amphitheater completed by Titus and dedicated in 80 CE. Originally begun by Flavian, the structure is named after a colossal statue of Nero that formerly stood beside it.

Columbian exchange Movements between Afro-Eurasia and the Americas of previously unknown plants, animals, people, diseases, and products that followed in the wake of Columbus's voyages.

commanderies Provinces. Shi Huangdi (First August Emperor) divided China into commanderies (*jun*) to enable the Qin dynasty to rule the massive state effectively. The thirty-six commanderies were then subdivided into counties (*xian*).

Communist Manifesto Pamphlet published by Karl Marx and Friedrich Engels in 1848 at a time when political revolutions were sweeping Europe. It called on the workers of all nations to unite in overthrowing capitalism.

Compromise of 1867 Agreement between the Habsburgs and the peoples living in Hungarian parts of the empire that the Habsburg state would be officially known as the Austro-Hungarian Empire.

concession areas Territories, usually ports, where Chinese emperors allowed European merchants to trade and European people to settle.

Confucian ideals The ideals of honoring tradition, emphasizing the responsibility of the emperor, and respect for the lessons of history, promoted by Confucius, which the Han dynasty made the official doctrine of the empire by 50 BCE.

Confucianism Ethics, beliefs, and practices stipulated by the Chinese philosopher Kong Qiu, or Confucius, which served as a guide for Chinese society up to modern times.

Confucius (551–479 BCE) Influential teacher, thinker, and leader in China who developed a set of principles for ethical living. He believed that coercive laws and punishment would not be needed to maintain order in society if men following his ethics ruled. He taught his philosophy to anyone who was intelligent and willing to work, which allowed men to gain entry into the ruling through education.

cong tube Ritual object crafted by the Liangzhu. A cong tube was made of jade and was used in divination practices.

Congo Independent State Large colonial state in Africa created by Leopold II, king of Belgium, during the 1880s, and ruled by him alone. After rumors of mass slaughter and enslavement, the Belgian parliament took the land and formed a Belgian colony.

Congress of Vienna (1814–1815) International conference to reorganize Europe after the downfall of Napoleon. European monarchies agreed to respect each other's borders and to cooperate in guarding against future revolutions and war.

conquistadors Spanish military leaders who led the conquest of the New World in the sixteenth century.

Constantine Roman emperor who converted to Christianity in 312 CE. In 313, he issued a proclamation that gave Christians new freedoms in the empire. He also founded Constantinople (at first called "New Rome").

Constantinople Capital city, formerly known as Byzantium, which was founded as the New Rome by Constantine the Great.

Constitutional Convention (1787) Meeting to formulate the Constitution of the United States of America.

Contra rebels Opponents of the Sandinistas in Nicaragua; they were armed and financed by the United States and other anticommunist countries (1980).

Conversion of Constantine A significant political and religious turning point in the Roman Empire. Before the decisive battle for Rome in 312 CE, Constantine supposedly had a dream in which he was told to place a sign with the opening letters of Christ's name on his soldiers' shields. Constantine won the ensuing battle; he soon issued a proclamation giving privileges to Christian bishops. The edict spread Christianity through the institutions and across the byways of the Roman Empire.

Conversos Jewish and Muslim converts to Christianity in the Iberian Peninsula and the New World.

Coptic Form of Christianity practiced in Egypt. It was doctrinally different from Christianity elsewhere, and Coptic Christians had their own views of Christology, or the nature of Christ.

Corn Laws Laws that imposed tariffs on grain imported to Great Britain, intended to protect British farming interests. The Corn Laws were abolished in 1846 as part of a British movement in favor of free trade.

cosmology Branch of metaphysics devoted to understanding the order of the universe.

Council of Nicaea Church council convened in 325 CE by Constantine and presided over by him as well. At this council, a Christian creed was articulated and made into a formula that expressed the philosophical and technical elements of Christian belief.

Counter-Reformation Movement to counter the spread of the Reformation; initiated by the Catholic Church at the Council of Trent in 1545. The Catholic Church enacted reforms to attack clerical corruption and it placed a greater emphasis on individual spirituality. During this time, the Jesuits were founded to help revive the Catholic Church.

coup d'état Overthrow of established state by a group of conspirators, usually from the military.

creed Formal statement of faith or expression of a belief system. A Christian creed or "credo" was formulated by the Council of Nicaea in 325 CE.

creoles Persons of full-blooded European descent who were born in the Spanish American colonies.

Crimean War (1853–1856) War waged by Russia against Great Britain and France. Spurred by Russia's encroachment on Ottoman territories, the conflict revealed Russia's military weakness when Russian forces fell to British and French troops.

crossbow Innovative weapon used at the end of the Warring States period that allowed archers to shoot their enemies with accuracy, even from a distance.

Crusades Wave of attacks launched in the late eleventh century by western Europeans. The First Crusade began in 1095, when Pope Urban II appealed to the warrior nobility of France to free Jerusalem from Muslim rule. Four subsequent Crusades were fought over the next two centuries.

Cuban Missile Crisis (1962) Diplomatic standoff between the United States and the Soviet Union that was provoked by the Soviet Union's attempt to base nuclear missiles in Cuba; it brought the world close to a nuclear war.

cult Religious movement, often based on the worship of a particular god or goddess.

cultigen Organism that has diverged from its ancestors through domestication or cultivation.

cuneiform Wedge-shaped form of writing. As people combined rebus symbols with other visual marks that contained meaning, they became able to record and transmit messages over long distances by using abstract symbols or signs to denote concepts; such signs later came to represent syllables, which could be joined into words. By impressing these signs into wet clay with the cut end of a reed, scribes engaged in cuneiform.

Cyrus the Great Founder of the Persian Empire. This sixth-century ruler (559–529 BCE) conquered the Medes and unified the Iranian kingdoms.

Daimyo Ruling lords who commanded private armies in pre-Meiji Japan.

dan Fodio, Usman (1754–1817) Fulani Muslim cleric whose visions led him to challenge the Hausa ruling classes, whom he believed were insufficiently faithful to Islamic beliefs and practices. His ideas gained support among those who had suffered under the Hausa landlords. In 1804, his supporters and allies overthrew the Hausa in what is today northern Nigeria.

Daoism School of thought developed at the end of the Warring States period that focused on the importance of following the Dao, or the natural way of the cosmos. Daoism emphasized the need to accept the world as it was rather than trying to change it through politics or the government. Unlike Confucianism, Daoism scorned rigid rituals and social hierarchies.

Dar al-Islam Arabic for "the House of Islam"; it describes a sense of common identity.

Darius I (521–486 BCE) Leader who put the emerging unified Persian Empire onto solid footing after Cyrus's death.

Darwin, Charles (1809–1882) British scientist who became convinced that the species of organic life had evolved under the uniform pressure of natural laws, not by means of a special, one-time creation as described in the Bible.

D-Day (June 6, 1944) Day of the Allied invasion of Normandy under General Dwight Eisenhower to liberate western Europe from German occupation.

Dear Boy Nickname of an early human remain discovered in 1931 by a team of archaeologists named the Leakeys. They discovered an almost totally intact skull. Other objects discovered with Dear Boy demonstrated that by the time of Dear Boy, early humans had begun to fashion tools and to use them for butchering animals and possibly for hunting and killing smaller animals.

Decembrists Russian army officers who were influenced by events in revolutionary France and formed secret societies that espoused liberal governance. They were put down by Nicholas I in December 1825.

Declaration of Independence U.S. document stating the theory of government on which America was founded.

Declaration of the Rights of Man and Citizen (1789) French charter of liberties formulated by the National Assembly that marked the end of dynastic and aristocratic rule. The seventeen articles later became the preamble to the new constitution, which the assembly finished in 1791.

decolonization End of empire and emergence of new independent nation-states in Asia and Africa as a result of the defeat of Japan in World War II and weakened European influence after the war.

Delhi Sultanate (1206–1526) Turkish regime of Northern India. The regime strengthened the cultural diversity and tolerance that were a hallmark of the Indian social order, which allowed it to bring about political integration without enforcing cultural homogeneity.

democracy The idea that people, through membership in a nation, should choose their own representatives and be governed by them.

Democritus Thinker in ancient Greece who lived from 470 to 360 BCE; he deduced the existence of the atom and postulated that there was such a thing as an indivisible particle.

demotic writing The second of two basic forms of ancient Egyptian writing. Demotic was a cursive script written with ink on papyrus, on pottery, or on other absorbent objects. It was the most common and practical form of writing in Egypt and was used for administrative record keeping and in private or pseudo-private forms like letters and works of literature. *See also* Hieroglyphs.

developing world Term applied to countries collectively called the Third World during the cold war and seeking to develop viable nation-states and prosperous economies.

Devshirme System of taking non-Muslim children in place of taxes in order to educate them in Ottoman Muslim ways and prepare them for service in the sultan's bureaucracy.

Dhamma Moral code espoused by Aśoka in the Kalinga edict, which was meant to apply to all—Buddhists, Brahmans, and Greeks alike.

Dhimmis Followers of religions, other than Islam, that were permitted by Ottoman law: Armenian Christians, Greek Orthodox Christians, and Jews.

dhows Ships used by Arab seafarers; the dhow's large sails were rigged to maximize the capture of wind.

Dien Bien Phu (1954) Defining battle in the war between French colonialists and the Viet Minh that secured North Vietnam for Ho Chi Minh and his army and left the south to form its own government to be supported by France and the United States.

Din-I-Ilahi "House of worship" in which the Mughal emperor Akbar engaged in religious debate with Hindu, Muslim, Jain, Parsi, and Christian theologians.

Diogenes Greek philosopher who lived from 412 to 323 BCE and who espoused a doctrine of self-sufficiency and freedom from social laws and customs. He rejected cultural norms as out of tune with nature and therefore false.

Directory Temporary military committee that took over the affairs of the state of France in 1795 from the radicals and held control until the coup of Napoleon Bonaparte.

divination The interpretation of rituals used to communicate the wishes of gods or royal ancestors to foretell future events. Divination was used to legitimize royal authority and demand tribute.

Djoser Ancient Egyptian king who reigned from 2630 to 2611 BCE. He was the second king of the Third Dynasty and celebrated the Sed festival in his tomb complex at Saqqara.

domestication Bringing a wild animal or plant under human control.

Dominion in the British Commonwealth Canadian promise to keep up the country's fealty to the British crown, even after its independence in 1867. Later applied to Australia and New Zealand.

Dong Zhongshu Emperor Wu's chief minister, who advocated a more powerful view of Confucius by promoting texts that focused on Confucius as a man who possessed aspects of divinity.

double-outrigger canoes Vessels used by early Austronesians to cross the Taiwan Straits and colonize islands in the Pacific. These sturdy canoes could cover over 120 miles per day.

Duma Russian parliament.

Dutch learning Broad term for European teachings that were strictly regulated by the shoguns inside Japan.

dynastic cycle Political narrative in which influential families vied for supremacy. Upon gaining power, they legitimated their authority by claiming to be the heirs of previous grand dynasts and by preserving or revitalizing the ancestors' virtuous governing ways. This continuity conferred divine support.

dynasty Hereditary ruling family that passed control from one generation to the next.

Earth Summit (1992) Meeting in Rio de Janeiro between many of the world's governments in an effort to address international environmental problems.

East India Company (1600–1858) British charter company created to outperform Portuguese and Spanish traders in the Far East; in the eighteenth century the company became, in effect, the ruler of a large part of India.

Eastern Front Battlefront between Berlin and Moscow during World War I and World War II.

Edict of Nantes (1598) Edict issued by Henry IV to end the French Wars of Religion. The edict declared France a Catholic country but tolerated some Protestant worship.

Egyptian Middle Kingdom Period of Egyptian history lasting from about 2040 to 1640 BCE, characterized by a consolidation of power and building activity in Upper Egypt.

Eiffel Tower Steel monument completed in 1889 for the Paris Exposition. It was twice the height of any other building at the time.

eight-legged essay Highly structured essay form with eight parts, required on Chinese civil service examinations.

Ekklesia Church or early gathering committed to leaders chosen by God and fellow believers.

Ekpe Powerful slave trade institution that organized the supply and purchase of slaves inland from the Gulf of Guinea in West Africa.

Elamites A people with their capital in the upland valley of modern Fars who became a cohesive polity that incorporated transhumant people of the Zagros Mountains. A group of Elamites who migrated south and west into Mesopotamia helped conquer the Third Dynasty of Ur in 2400 BCE.

empire Group of states or different ethnic groups under a single sovereign power.

Enabling Act (1933) Emergency act passed by the Reichstag (German parliament) that helped transform Hitler from Germany's chancellor, or prime minister, into a dictator following the suspicious burning of the Reichstag building and a suspension of civil liberties.

enclosure A movement in which landowners took control of lands that traditionally had been common property serving local needs.

Encomenderos Commanders of the labor services of the colonized peoples in Spanish America.

Encomiendas Grants from European Spanish governors to control the labor services of colonized people.

Endeavor Ship of Captain James Cook, whose celebrated voyages to the South Pacific in the late eighteenth century supplied Europe with information about the plants, birds, landscapes, and people of this uncharted territory.

Engels, Friedrich (1820–1895) German social and political philosopher who collaborated with Karl Marx on many publications, including *The Communist Manifesto*.

English Navigation Act of 1651 Act stipulating that only English ships could carry goods between the mother country and its colonies.

English Peasants' Revolt (1381) Uprising of serfs and free farm workers that began as a protest against a tax levied to raise money for a war on France. The revolt was suppressed but led to the gradual emergence of a free peasantry as labor shortages made it impossible to keep peasants bound to the soil.

enlightened absolutists Seventeenth- and eighteenth-century monarchs who claimed to rule rationally and in the best interests of their subjects and who hired loyal bureaucrats to implement the knowledge of the new age.

Enlightenment Intellectual movement in eighteenth-century Europe stressing natural laws and reason as the basis of authority.

entrepôts Trading stations at the borders between communities, which made exchange possible among many different partners. Long-distance traders could also replenish their supplies at these stations.

Epicurus Greek philosopher who espoused emphasis on the self. He lived from 341 to 279 BCE and founded a school in Athens called The Garden. He stressed the importance of sensation, teaching that pleasurable sensations were good and painful sensations bad. Members of his school sought to find peace and relaxation by avoiding unpleasantness or suffering.

Estates-General French quasi-parliamentary body called in 1789 to deal with the financial problems that afflicted France. It had not met since 1614.

Etruscans A dominant people on the Italian peninsula until the fourth century BCE. The Etruscan states were part of the foundation of the Roman Empire.

eunuchs Loyal and well-paid men who were surgically castrated as youths and remained in service to the caliph or emperor. Both Abbasid and Tang rulers relied for protection on a cadre of eunuchs.

Eurasia The combined area of Europe and Asia.

European Union (EU) International body organized after World War II as an attempt at reconciliation between Germany and the rest of Europe. It initially aimed to forge closer industrial cooperation. Eventually, through various treaties, many European states relinquished some of their sovereignty, and the cooperation became a full-fledged union with a single currency, the euro, and with a somewhat less powerful common European parliament.

evolution Process by which the different species of the world—its plants and animals—made changes in response to their environment that enabled them to survive and increase in numbers.

Exclusion Act of 1882 U.S. congressional act prohibiting nearly all immigration from China to the United States; fueled by animosity toward Chinese workers in the American West.

Ezo Present-day Hokkaido, Japan's fourth main island.

Fascism Mass political movement founded by Benito Mussolini that emphasized nationalism, militarism, and the omnipotence of the state.

Fascists Radical right-wing group of disaffected veterans that formed around Mussolini in 1919 and a few years later came to power in Rome.

Fatehpur Sikri Mughal emperor Akbar's temporary capital near Agra.

Fatimids Shiite dynasty that ruled parts of the Islamic Empire beginning in the tenth century CE. They were based in Egypt and founded the city of Cairo.

February Revolution (1917) The first of two uprisings of the Russian Revolution, which led to the end of the Romanov dynasty.

Federal Deposit Insurance Corporation (FDIC) Organization created in 1933 to guarantee all bank deposits up to $5,000 as part of the New Deal in the United States.

Federal Republic of Germany (1949–1990) Country formed of the areas occupied by the Allies after World War II. Also known as West Germany, this country experienced rapid demilitarization, democratization, and integration into the world economy.

Federal Reserve Act (1913) U.S. legislation that created a series of boards to monitor the supply and demand of the nation's money.

Federalists Supporters of the ratification of the U.S. Constitution, which was written to replace the Articles of Confederation.

feminist movements Movements that called for equal treatment for men and women—equal pay and equal opportunities for obtaining jobs and advancement. Feminism arose mainly in Europe and in North America in the 1960s and then became global in the 1970s.

Ferangi Arabic word meaning "Frank" that was used to describe Crusaders.

Fertile Crescent Site of the world's first agricultural revolution; an area in Southwest Asia, bounded by the Mediterranean Sea in the west and the Zagros Mountains in the east.

feudalism System instituted in medieval Europe after the collapse of the Carolingian Empire (814 CE) whereby each peasant was under the authority of a lord.

fiefdoms Medieval economic and political units.

First World Term invented during the cold war to refer to western Europe and North America (also known as the "free world" or the West); Japan later joined this group. Following the principles of liberal modernism, First World states sought to organize the world on the basis of capitalism and democracy.

Five Pillars of Islam The five tenets, or main aspects, of Islamic practice: testification or bearing witness that there is no God other than God (Allah, in Arabic) and that Muhammad is the messenger of God; praying five times a day; fasting from sunup to sundown every day during Ramadan (a month on the Islamic calendar); giving alms; and making a pilgrimage to Mecca.

Five-Year Plan Soviet effort launched under Stalin in 1928 to replace the market with a state-owned and state-managed economy, to promote rapid economic development over a five-year period of time and thereby "catch and overtake" the leading capitalist countries. The First Five-Year Plan was followed by the Second Five-Year Plan (1933–1937), and so on, until the collapse of the Soviet Union in 1991.

Flagellants European social group that came into existence during the bubonic plague in the fourteenth century; they believed that the plague was the wrath of God.

floating population Poor migrant workers in China who supplied labor under Emperor Wu.

Fluitschips Dutch shipping vessels that could carry heavy bulky cargo with relatively small crews.

flying cash Letters of exchange—early predecessors of paper cash instead of coins—first developed by guilds in the northwestern Shanxi. By the thirteenth century, paper money had eclipsed coins.

Fondûqs Complexes in caravan cities that included hostels, storage houses, offices, and temples.

Forbidden City Palace city of the Ming and Qing dynasties.

Force Publique Colonial army used to maintain order in the Belgian Congo; during the early stages of King Leopold's rule, it was responsible for bullying local communities.

Fourierism Form of utopian socialism based on the ideas of Charles Fourier (1772–1837). Fourier envisioned communes where work was made enjoyable and systems of production and distribution were run without merchants. His ideas appealed to middle-class readers, especially women, as a higher form of Christian communalism.

free labor Wage-paying rather than slave labor.

free markets Unregulated markets.

Free Officers Movement Secret organization of Egyptian junior military officers who came to power in a coup d'état in 1952, forced King Faruq to abdicate, and consolidated their own control through dissolving the parliament, banning opposing parties, and rewriting the constitution.

free trade Domestic and international trade unencumbered by tariff barriers, quotas, and fees.

Front de Libération Nationale (FLN) Algerian anticolonial, nationalist party that waged an eight-year war against French troops, beginning in 1854, that forced nearly all of the 1,000,000 colonists to leave.

Fulani Muslim group in West Africa that carried out religious revolts at the end of the eighteenth and the beginning of the nineteenth centuries in an effort to return to the pure Islam of the past.

fur trade Trading of animal pelts (especially beaver skins) by Indians for European goods in North America.

Gandhi, Mohandhas Karamchand (Mahatma) (1869–1948) Indian leader who led a nonviolent struggle for India's independence from Britain.

garrison towns Stations for soldiers originally established in strategic locations to protect territorial acquisition. Eventually, they became towns. Alexander the Great's garrison towns evolved into cities that served as centers from which Hellenistic culture was spread to his easternmost territories.

garrisons Military bases inside cities; often used for political purposes, such as protecting rulers and putting down domestic revolts or enforcing colonial rule.

gauchos Argentine, Brazilian, and Uruguayan cowboys who wanted a decentralized federation, with autonomy for their provinces and respect for their way of life.

Gdansk shipyard Site of mass strikes in Poland that led in 1980 to the formation of the first independent trade union, Solidarity, in the communist bloc.

gendered relations A relatively recent development that implies roles emerged only with the appearance of modern humans and perhaps Neanderthals. When humans began to think imaginatively and in complex symbolic ways and give voice to their insights, perhaps around 150,000 years ago, gender categories began to crystallize.

genealogy History of the descent of a person or family from a distant ancestor.

Geneva Peace Conference (1954) International conference to restore peace in Korea and Indochina. The chief participants were the United States, the Soviet Union, Great Britain, France, the People's Republic of China, North Korea, South Korea, Vietnam, the Viet Minh party, Laos, and Cambodia. The conference resulted in the division of North and South Vietnam.

Genoa One of two Italian cities (the other was Venice) that linked Europe, Africa, and Asia as nodes of commerce in 1300 CE. Genoese ships linked the Mediterranean to the coast of Flanders through consistent routes along the Atlantic coasts of Spain, Portugal, and France.

German Democratic Republic Nation founded from the Soviet zone of occupation of Germany after World War II; also known as East Germany.

German Social Democratic Party Founded in 1875, the most powerful Socialist party in Europe before 1917.

Ghana The most celebrated medieval political kingdom in West Africa.

Ghost Dance American Indian ritual performed in the nineteenth century in the hope of restoring the world to precolonial conditions.

Gilgamesh Heroic narrative written in the Babylonian dialect of Semitic Akkadian. This story and others like it were meant to circulate and unify the kingdom.

Girondins Liberal revolutionary group that supported the creation of a constitutional monarchy during the early stages of the French Revolution.

global warming Release into the air of human-made carbons that contribute to rising temperatures worldwide.

globalization Development of integrated worldwide cultural and economic structures.

Gold Coast Name that European mariners and merchants gave to that part of West Africa from which gold was exported. This area was conquered by the British in the nineteenth century and became a British colony; upon independence, it became Ghana.

Goths One of the groups of "barbarian" migrants into Roman territory in the fourth century.

government schools Schools founded by the Han dynasty to provide an adequate number of officials to fill positions in the administrative bureaucracy. The Imperial University had 30,000 members by the second century BCE.

Gracchus brothers Two tribunes, the brothers Tiberius and Gaius Gracchus, who in 133 and 123–21 BCE attempted to institute land reforms that would guarantee all of Rome's poor citizens a basic amount of land that would qualify them for army service. Both men were assassinated.

Grand Canal Created in 486 BCE, a thousand-mile-long connector between the Yellow and Yangzi rivers, linking the north and south, respectively.

grand unity Guiding political idea embraced by Qin rulers and ministers, with an eye toward joining the states of the Central Plain into one empire and centralizing administration.

"Greased cartridge" controversy Controversy spawned by the rumor that cow and pig fat had been used to grease the shotguns of the sepoys in the British army in India. Believing that this was a British attempt to defile their religion and speed their conversion to Christianity, the sepoys mutinied against the British officers.

Great Depression Worldwide depression following the U.S. stock market crash on October 29, 1929.

great divide The division between economically developed nations and less developed nations.

Great East Asia Co-Prosperity Sphere Term used by the Japanese during the 1930s and 1940s to refer to Hong Kong, Singapore, Malaya, Burma, and other states that they seized during their run for expansion.

Great Flood One of many traditional Mesopotamian stories that were transmitted orally from one generation to another before being recorded. The Sumerian King List refers to this crucial event in Sumerian memory and identity. The Great Flood was assigned responsibility for Uruk's demise to the gods.

Great Game Competition over areas such as Turkistan, Persia (present-day Iran), and Afghanistan. The British (in India) and the Russians believed that controlling these areas was crucial to preventing their enemies' expansion.

Great League of Peace and Power Iroquois Indian alliance that united previously warring communities.

Great Leap Forward (1958–1961) Plan devised by Mao Zedong to achieve rapid agricultural and industrial growth in China. The plan failed miserably and more than 20 million people died.

Great Proletarian Cultural Revolution (1966–1976) Mass mobilization of urban Chinese youth inaugurated by Mao Zedong in an attempt to reinvigorate the Chinese revolution and to prevent the development of a bureaucratized Soviet style of communism; with this movement, Mao turned against his longtime associates in the communist party.

Great Trek Afrikaner migration to the interiors of Africa after the British abolished slavery in the empire in 1833.

Great War (August 1914–November 1918) A total war involving the armies of Britain, France, and Russia (the Allies) against those of Germany, Austria-Hungary, and the Ottoman Empire (the Central Powers). Italy joined the Allies in 1915, and the United States joined them in 1917, helping tip the balance in favor of the Allies, who also drew upon the populations and material of their colonial possessions. Also known as World War I.

Greek Orthodoxy Enduring form of Christianity that used the framework of the "Roman" state inherited from Constantine and Justinian to protect itself from Roman Catholicism and Muslim forces. The Greek Orthodox capital was Constantinople and its spiritual empire included the Russian peoples, Baltic Slavs, and peoples living in southwest Asia.

Greenbacks Members of the American political party of the late nineteenth century that worked to advance the interest of farmers by promoting cheap money.

griots Counselors and other officials to the royal family in African kingships. They were also responsible for the preservation and transmission of oral histories and repositories of knowledge.

Group Areas Act (1950) Act that divided South Africa into separate racial and tribal areas and required Africans to live in their own separate communities, including the "homelands."

guerrillas Portuguese and Spanish peasant bands who resisted the revolutionary and expansionist efforts of Napoleon; after the French word *guerre*.

guest workers Migrants looking for temporary employment abroad.

Gulag Administrative name for the vast system of forced labor camps under the Soviet regime; it originated in a small monastery near the Arctic Circle and spread throughout the Soviet Union and to other Soviet-style socialist countries. Penal labor was required of both ordinary criminals (rapists, murderers, thieves) and those accused of political crimes (counterrevolution, anti-Soviet agitation).

Gulf War (1991) Armed conflict between Iraq and a coalition of thirty-two nations, including the United States, Britain, Egypt, France, and Saudi Arabia. It was started by Iraq's invasion of Kuwait, which it had long claimed, on August 2, 1990.

gunpowder Explosive powder. By 1040, the first gunpowder recipes were being written down. Over the next 200 years, Song entrepreneurs invented several incendiary devices and techniques for controlling explosions.

gunpowder empires Muslim empires of the Ottomans, Safavids, and Mughals that used cannonry and gunpowder to advance their military causes.

Guomindang Nationalist party of China, founded just before World War I by Sun Yat-sen and later led by Chiang Kai-shek.

Habsburg Empire Ruling house of Austria, which once ruled both Spain and central Europe but came to settle in lands along the Danube River; it played a prominent role in European affairs for many centuries. In 1867, the Habsburg Empire was reorganized into the Austro-Hungarian Dual Monarchy, and in 1918 it collapsed.

Hadith Sayings attributed to the Prophet Muhammad and his early converts. Used to guide the behavior of Muslim peoples.

Hagia Sophia Enormous and impressive church sponsored by Justinian and built starting in 532 CE. At the time, it was the largest church in the world.

Hajj Pilgrimage to Mecca; an obligation for Muslims.

Hammurapi's Code Legal code created by Hammurapi, the most famous of the Mesopotamian rulers, who reigned from 1792 to 1750 BCE. Hammurapi sought to create social order by centralizing state authority and creating a grand legal structure that embodied paternal justice. The code was quite stratified, dividing society into three classes: free men, dependent men, and slaves, each with distinct rights and responsibilities.

Han agrarian ideal Guiding principle for the free peasantry that made up the base of Han society. In this system, peasants were honored for their labors, while merchants were subjected to a range of controls, including regulations on luxury consumption, and were belittled for not engaging in physical labor.

Han Chinese Inhabitants of China proper who considered others to be outsiders. They felt that they were the only authentic Chinese.

Han Fei Chinese state minister who lived from 280 to 223 BCE; he was a proponent and follower of Xunzi.

Han military Like its Roman counterpart, a ruthless military machine that expanded the empire and created stable conditions that permitted the safe transit of goods by caravans. Emperor Wu heavily influenced the transformation of the military forces and reinstituted a policy that made military service compulsory.

Hangzhou City and former provincial seaport that became the political center of the Chinese people in their ongoing struggles with northern steppe nomads. It was also one of China's gateways to the rest of the world by way of the South China Sea.

Hannibal Great Roman general from Carthage whose campaigns in the third century BCE swept from Spain toward the Italian peninsula. He crossed the Pyrenees and the Alps mountain ranges with war elephants. He was unable, however, to defeat the Romans in 217 BCE.

Harappa One of two cities that, by 2500 BCE, began to take the place of villages throughout the Indus River valley (the other was Mohenjo Daro). Each covered an area of about 250 acres and probably housed 35,000 residents.

harem Secluded women's quarters in Muslim households.

Harlem Renaissance Cultural movement in the 1920s that was based in Harlem, a part of New York City with a large African American population. The movement gave voice to black novelists, poets, painters, and musicians, many of whom used their art to protest racism; also referred to as the "New Negro movement."

harnesses Tools made from wood, bone, bronze, and iron for steering and controlling chariot horses. Harnesses discovered by archaeologists reveal the evolution of headgear from simple mouth bits to full bridles with headpiece, mouthpiece, and reins.

Hatshepsut Leader known as ancient Egypt's most powerful woman ruler. Hatshepsut served as regent for her young son, Thutmosis III, whose reign began in 1479 BCE. She remained co-regent until her death.

Haussmannization Redevelopment and beautification of urban centers; named after the city planner who "modernized" mid-nineteenth-century Paris.

Hegira "Emigration" of Muhammad and his followers out of a hostile Mecca to Yathrib, a city that was later called Medina. The year in which this journey took place, 622 CE, is also year 1 of the Islamic calendar.

Heian period Period from 794 to 1185, during which began the pattern of regents ruling Japan in the name of the sacred emperor.

Hellenism Process by which the individuality of the cultures of the earlier Greek city-states gave way to a uniform culture that stressed the common identity of all who embraced Greek ways. This culture emphasized the common denominators of language, style, and politics to which anyone, anywhere in the Afro-Eurasian world, could have access.

hieroglyphs One of two basic forms of Egyptian writing that were used in conjunction throughout antiquity. Hieroglyphs are pictorial symbols; the term derives from a Greek word meaning "sacred carving"—they were employed exclusively in temple, royal, and divine contexts. *See also* Demotic writing.

Hijra Tradition of Islam, whereby one withdraws from one's community to create another, more holy, one. The practice is based on the Prophet Muhammad's withdrawal from the city of Mecca to Medina in 622 CE.

Hinayana (Lesser Vehicle) Buddhism Form of Buddhism that accepted the divinity of Buddha himself but not of demigods, or bodhisattvas.

Hinduism A refashioning of the ancient Brahmanic Vedic religion, bringing it in accord with rural life and agrarian values. It emerged as the dominant faith in Indian society in the third century CE. Believers became vegetarians and adopted rituals of self-sacrifice. Three major deities— Brahma, Vishnu, and Siva—formed a trinity representing the three phases of the universe (birth, existence, and destruction, respectively) and the three expressions of the eternal self, or *atma*.

Hindu revivalism Movement to reconfigure traditional Hinduism to be less diverse and more amenable to producing a narrowed version of Indian tradition.

Hiroshima Japanese port devastated by an atomic bomb on August 6, 1945.

Hitler, Adolf (1889–1945) German dictator and leader of the Nazi Party who seized power in Germany after its economic collapse in the Great Depression. Hitler and his Nazi regime started World War II in Europe and systematically murdered Jews and other non-Aryan groups in the name of racial purity.

Hittites One of the five great territorial states. The Hittites campaigned throughout Anatolia, then went east to northern Syria, though they eventually faced weaknesses in their own homeland. Their heyday was marked by the reign of the king Supiliulimua (1380 to 1345 BCE), who preserved the Hittites' influence on the balance of power in the region between Mesopotamia and the Nile.

Holocaust Deliberate racial extermination of the Jews by the Nazis that claimed around 6 million European Jews.

Holy Roman Empire Enormous realm that encompassed much of Europe and aspired to be the Christian successor state to the Roman Empire. In the time of the Habsburg dynasts, the empire was a loose confederation of principalities that obeyed an emperor elected by elite lower-level sovereigns. Despite its size, the empire never effectively centralized power; it was split into Austrian and Spanish factions when Charles V abdicated to his sons in 1556.

Holy Russia Name applied to Muscovy and then to the Russian Empire by Slavic Eastern Orthodox clerics who were appalled by the Muslim conquest in 1453 of Constantinople (the capital of Byzantium and of Eastern Christianity) and who were hopeful that Russia would become the new protector of the faith.

home charges Fees India was forced to pay to Britain as its colonial master; these fees included interest on railroad loans, salaries to colonial officers, and the maintenance of imperial troops outside India.

hominids Humanlike beings who walked erect and preceded modern humans.

Homo A word used by scientists to differentiate between pre-human and "true human" species.

Homo caudatus "Tailed man," believed by some European Enlightenment thinkers to be an early species of humankind.

Homo erectus Species that emerged about 1.5 million years ago and had a large brain and walked truly upright. *Homo erectus* means "Standing man."

Homo habilis Scientific term for "Skillful man." Toolmaking ability truly made *Homo habilis* the forerunners, though very distant, of modern humans.

Homo sapiens The first humans; they emerged in a small region of Africa about 200,000 years ago and migrated out of Africa about 100,000 years ago. They had bigger brains and greater dexterity than previous hominid species, whom they eventually eclipsed.

homogeneity Uniformity of the languages, customs, and religion of a particular people or place. It can also be demonstrated by a consistent calendar, set of laws, administrative practices, and rituals.

horses Animals used by full-scale nomadic communities to dominate the steppe lands in western Afro-Eurasia by the second millennium BCE. Horse-riding nomads moved their large herds across immense tracts of land within zones defined by rivers, mountains, and other natural geographical features. In the arid zones of central Eurasia, the nomadic economies made horses a crucial component of survival.

Huguenots French Protestants who endured severe persecution in the sixteenth and seventeenth centuries.

humanism The Renaissance aspiration to know more about the human experience beyond what the Christian scriptures offered by reaching back into ancient Greek and Roman texts.

Hundred Days' Reform (1898) Abortive modernizing reform program of the Qing government of China.

hunting and gathering Lifestyle in which food is acquired through hunting animals, fishing, and foraging for wild berries, nuts, fruit, and grains, rather than planting crops, vines, or trees. As late as 1500, as much as 15 percent of the world's population still lived by this method.

Hyksos A western Semitic-speaking people whose name means "Rulers of Foreign Lands"; they overthrew the unstable Thirteenth Dynasty in Egypt around 1640 BCE. The Hyksos had mastered the art of horse chariots, and with those chariots and their superior bronze axes and composite bows (made of wood, horn, and sinew), they were able to defeat the pharaoh's foot soldiers.

Ibn Sina Philosopher and physician who lived from 980 to 1037 CE. He was also schooled in the Quran, geometry, literature, and Indian and Euclidian mathematics.

ideology Dominant set of ideas of a widespread culture or movement.

Il Duce Term designating the fascist Italian leader Benito Mussolini.

Iliad Epic Greek poem about the Trojan War, composed several centuries after the events it describes. It was based on oral tales passed down for generations.

Il-khanate Mongol-founded dynasty in thirteenth-century Persia.

Imam Muslim religious leader and politico-religious descendant of Ali; believed by some to have a special relationship with Allah.

imperialism Acquisition of new territories by a state and the incorporation of these territories into a political system as subordinate colonies.

Imperium Latin word used to express Romans' power and command over their subjects. It is the basis of the English words *empire* and *imperialism*.

Inca Empire Empire of Quecha-speaking rulers in the Andean valley of Cuzco that encompassed a population of 4 to 6 million. The Incas lacked a clear inheritance system, causing an internal split that Pizarro's forces exploited in 1533.

Indian Institutes of Technology (IIT) Institutions originally designed as engineering schools to expand knowledge and to modernize India, which produced a whole generation of pioneering computer engineers, many of whom moved to the United States.

Indian National Congress Formed in 1885, a political party deeply committed to constitutional methods, industrialization, and cultural nationalism.

Indian National Muslim League Founded in 1906, an organization dedicated to advancing the political interests of Muslims in India.

Indo-Greek Fusion of Indian and Greek culture in the area under the control of the Bactrians, in the northwestern region of India, around 200 BCE.

Indu What we would today call India. Called "Indu" by Xuanzang, a Chinese Buddhist pilgrim who visited the area in the 630s and 640s CE.

indulgences Church-sponsored fund-raising mechanism that gave certification that one's sins had been forgiven in return for money.

industrial revolution Gradual accumulation and diffusion of old and new technical knowledge that led to major economic changes in Britain, northwestern Europe, and North America, catapulting these countries ahead of the rest of the world in manufacturing and agricultural output and standards of living.

industrious revolution Dramatic economic change in which households that had traditionally produced for themselves decided to work harder and longer hours in order to produce more for the market, which enabled them to increase their income and standard of living. Areas that underwent the industrious revolution shifted from peasant farming to specialized production for the market.

innovation Creation of a new method that allowed humans to make better adaptations to their environment such as the making of new tools.

Inquisition Tribunal of the Roman Catholic Church that enforced religious orthodoxy during the Protestant Reformation.

internal and external alchemy In Daoist ritual, use of trance and meditation or chemicals and drugs, respectively, to cause transformations in the self.

International Monetary Fund (IMF) Agency founded in 1944 to help restore financial order in Europe and the rest of the world, to revive international trade, and to support the financial concerns of Third World governments.

invisible hand As described in Adam Smith's *The Wealth of Nations*, the idea that the operations of a free market produce economic efficiency and economic benefits for all.

iron Malleable metal found in combined forms almost everywhere in the world; it became the most important and widely used metal in world history after the Bronze Age.

Iron Curtain Term popularized by Winston Churchill after World War II to refer to a rift, or an iron curtain, that divided western Europe, under American influence, from eastern Europe, under the domination of the Soviet Union.

irrigation Technological advance whereby water delivery systems and water sluices in floodplains or riverine areas were channeled or redirected and used to nourish soil.

Islam A religion that dates to 610 CE, when Muhammad believed God came to him in a vision. Islam ("submission"—in this case, to the will of God) requires its followers to act righteously, to submit themselves to the one and only true God, and to care for the less fortunate. Muhammad's most insistent message was the oneness of God, a belief that has remained central to the Islamic faith ever since.

Jacobins Radical French political group that came into existence during the French Revolution and executed the French king and sought to remake French culture.

Jacquerie (1358) French peasant revolt in defiance of feudal restrictions.

jade The most important precious substance in East Asia. Jade was associated with goodness, purity, luck, and virtue, and was carved into such items as ceremonial knives, blade handles, religious objects, and elaborate jewelry.

Jagat Seths Enormous trading and banking empire in eastern India.

Jainism Along with Buddhism, one of the two systems of thought developed in the seventh century BCE that set themselves up against Brahmanism. Its founder, Vardhamana Mahavira, taught that the universe obeys its own everlasting rules that no god or other supernatural being could affect. The purpose of life was to purify one's soul in order to attain a state of permanent bliss, which could be accomplished through self-denial and the avoidance of harming other creatures.

Janissaries Corps of infantry soldiers recruited as children from the Christian provinces of the Ottoman Empire and brought up with intense loyalty to the Ottoman state and its sultan. The Ottoman sultan used these forces to clip local autonomy and to serve as his personal bodyguards.

Jati Social groups as defined by Hinduism's caste system.

Jesuits Religious order founded by Ignatius Loyola to counter the inroads of the Protestant Reformation; the Jesuits, or the Society of Jesus, were active in politics, education, and missionary work.

Jihad Literally, "striving" or "struggle." This word also connotes military efforts or "striving in the way of God." It also came to mean spiritual struggles against temptation or inner demons, especially in Sufi, or mystical, usage.

Jih-pen Chinese for "Japan."

Jim Crow laws Laws that codified racial segregation and inequality in the southern part of the United States after the Civil War.

Jizya Special tax that non-Muslims were forced to pay to their Islamic rulers in return for which they were given security and property and granted cultural autonomy.

jong Large ocean-going vessels, built by Southeast Asians, which plied the regional trade routes from the fifteenth century to the early sixteenth century.

Judah The southern kingdom of David, which had been an Assyrian vassal until 612 BCE, when it became a vassal of Assyria's successor, Babylon, against whom the people of Judah rebelled, resulting in the destruction of Jerusalem in the sixth century BCE.

Julius Caesar Formidable Roman general who lived from 100 to 44 BCE. He was also a man of letters, a great orator, and a ruthless military man who boasted that his campaigns had led to the deaths of over a million people.

junks Trusty seafaring vessels used in the South China Seas after 1000 CE. These helped make shipping by sea less dangerous.

Justinian Roman or Byzantine emperor who ascended to the throne in 527 CE. In addition to his many building projects and military expeditions, he issued a new law code.

Kabuki Theater performance that combined song, dance, and skillful staging to dramatize conflicts between duty and passion in Tokogawa, Japan.

Kamikaze Japanese for "divine winds" or typhoons; such a storm saved Japan from a Mongol attack.

Kanun Highly detailed system of Ottoman administrative law that jurists developed to deal with matters not treated in the religious law of Islam.

Karim Loose confederation of shippers banding together to protect convoys.

karma Literally "fate" or "action," in Confucian thought; this is a universal principle of cause and effect.

Kassites Nomads who entered Mesopotamia from the eastern Zagros Mountains and the Iranian plateau as early as 2000 BCE. They gradually integrated into Babylonian society by officiating at temples. By 1745 BCE, they had asserted order over the region, and they controlled southern Mesopotamia for the next 350 years, creating one of the territorial states.

Keynesian Revolution Post-Depression economic ideas developed by the British economist John Maynard Keynes, wherein the state took a greater role in managing the economy, stimulating it by increasing the money supply and creating jobs.

KGB Soviet political police and spy agency, formed as the Cheka not long after the Bolshevik coup in October 1917. Grew to more than 750,000 operatives with military rank by the 1980s.

Khan Ruler who was acclaimed at an assembly of elites and supposedly descended from Chinngis Khan on the male line; those not descended from Chinggis continually faced challenges to their legitimacy.

Khanate Major political unit of the vast Mongol empire. There were four Khanates, including the Yuan Empire in China, forged by Chinggis Khan's grandson Kubilai.

Kharijites Radical sect from the early days of Islam. The Kharijites seceded from the "party of Ali" (who themselves came to be known as the Shiites) because of disagreements over succession to the role of the caliph. They were known for their strict militant piety.

Khmers A people who created the most powerful empire in Southwest Asia between the tenth and thirteenth centuries in what is modern-day Cambodia.

Khomeini, Ayatollah Ruhollah (1902–1989) Iranian religious leader who used his traditional Islamic education and his training in Muslim ethics to accuse the shah's government of gross violations of Islamic norms. He also identified the shah's ally, America, as the great Satan. The shah fled the country in 1979; in his wake, Khomeini established a theocratic state ruled by a council of Islamic clerics.

Khufu A pyramid, among those put up in the Fourth Dynasty in ancient Egypt (2575–2465 BCE), which is the largest stone structure in the world. It is in an area called Giza, just outside modern-day Cairo.

Khusro I Anoshirwan Sasanian emperor who reigned from 530 to 579 CE. He was a model ruler and was seen as the personification of justice.

Kiev City that became one of the greatest cities of Europe after the eleventh century. It was built to be a small-scale Constantinople on the Dnieper.

Kikuyu Kenya's largest ethnic group; organizers of a revolt against the British in the 1950s.

King, Martin Luther, Jr. (1929–1968) Civil rights leader who borrowed his most effective weapon—the commitment to nonviolent protest and the appeal to conscience—from Gandhi.

Kingdom of Awadh One of the most prized lands for annexation and the fertile, opulent, and traditional vestige of Mughal rule in India.

Kingdom of Jerusalem What Crusaders set out to liberate when they launched their attack.

Kizilbash Mystical, Turkish-speaking tribesmen who facilitated the Safavid rise to power.

Knossos Area in Crete where, during the second millennium BCE, a primary palace town existed.

Koine Greek Common form of Greek that became the international spoken and written language in the Hellenistic world. This was a simpler everyday form of the ancient Greek language.

Koprulu reforms Reforms named after two grand viziers who revitalized the Ottoman Empire in the seventeenth century through administrative and budget trimming as well as by rebuilding the military.

Korean War (1950–1953) Cold war conflict between Soviet-backed North Korea and U.S.- and UN-backed South Korea. The two sides seesawed back and forth over the same boundaries until 1953, when an armistice divided the country at roughly the same spot as at the start of the war. Nothing had been gained. Losses, however, included 33,000 Americans, at least 250,000 Chinese, and up to 3 million Koreans.

Koryo dynasty Leading dynasty of the northern-based Koryo kingdom in Korea. It is from this dynasty that the name "Korea" derives.

Kremlin Once synonymous with the Soviet government; refers to Moscow's walled city center.

Kshatriyas Originally the warrior caste in Vedic society, the dominant clan members and ruling caste who controlled the land.

Ku Klux Klan Racist organization that first emerged in the U.S. South after the Civil War and then gained national strength as a radically traditionalist movement during the 1920s.

Kubilai Khan (1215–1294) Mongol leader who seized southern China after 1260 and founded the Yuan dynasty.

kulak Originally a pejorative word used to designate better-off peasants, the term used in the late 1920s and early 1930s to refer to any peasant, rich or poor, perceived as an opponent of the Soviet regime. Russian for "fist."

Kumarajiva Renowned Buddhist scholar and missionary who lived from 344 to 413 CE. He was brought to China by Chinese regional forces from Kucha, modern-day Xinjiang.

Kushans Northern nomadic group that migrated into South Asia in 50 CE. They unified the tribes of the region and set up the Kushan dynasty. The Kushans' empire embraced a large and diverse territory and played a critical role in the formation of the Silk Road.

Labour Party Founded in Britain in 1900, the party that represented workers and was based on socialist principles.

laissez-faire The concept that the economy works best when it is left alone—that is, when the state does not regulate or interfere with the workings of the market.

"Land under the Yoke of Ashur" Lands not in Assyria proper, but under its authority; they had to pay the Assyrian Empire exorbitant amounts of tribute.

language System of communication reflecting cognitive abilities. Natural language is generally defined as words arranged in particular sequences to convey meaning and is unique to modern humans.

language families Related tongues with a common ancestral origin; language families contain languages that diverged from one another but share grammatical features and root vocabularies. More than a hundred language families exist.

Laozi Also known as Master Lao; perhaps a contemporary of Confucius and the person after whom Daoism is named. His thought was elaborated upon by generations of thinkers.

Latifundia Broad estates that produced goods for big urban markets, including wheat, grapes, olives, cattle, and sheep.

Laws of Manu Part of the handiwork of Brahman priests; a representative code of law that incorporated social sanctions and practices and provided guidance for living within the caste system.

League of Nations Organization founded after World War I to solve international disputes through arbitration; it was dissolved in 1946 and its assets were transferred to the United Nations.

Legalism Also called Statism, a system of thought about how to live an ordered life. It was developed by Master Xun, or Xunzi (310–237 BCE). It is based on the principle that people, being inherently inclined toward evil, require authoritarian control to regulate their behavior.

Lenin, Nikolai (1870–1924) Leader of the Bolshevik Revolution in Russia and the first leader of the Soviet Union.

Liangzhu Culture spanning centuries from the fourth to the third millennium BCE that represented the last new Stone Age culture in the Yangzi River delta. One of the Ten Thousand States, it was highly stratified and is known for its jade objects.

liberalism Political and social theory that advocates representative government, free trade, and freedom of speech and religion.

limited-liability joint-stock company Company that mobilized capital from a large number of investors, called shareholders, who were not to be held personally liable for financial losses incurred by the company.

Linear A and B Two linear scripts first discovered on Crete in 1900. On the island of Crete and on the mainland areas of Greece, documents of the palace-centered societies were written on clay tablets in these two scripts. Linear A script, apparently written in Minoan, has not yet been deciphered. Linear B was first deciphered in the early 1950s.

"Little Europes" Urban landscapes between 1100 and 1200 CE composed of castles, churches, and towns in what are today Poland, the Czech Republic, Hungary, and the Baltic States.

Liu Bang Chinese emperor from 206 to 195 BCE; after declaring himself the prince of his home area of Han, in 202 BCE, Liu declared himself the first Han emperor.

llamas Animals similar in utility and function to camels in Afro-Eurasia. Llamas could carry heavy loads for long distances.

Long March (1934–1935) Trek of over 10,000 kilometers by Mao Zedong and his communist followers to establish a new base of operations in northwestern China.

Longshan peoples Peoples who lived in small agricultural and riverine villages in East Asia at the end of the third millennium BCE. They set the stage for the Shang in terms of a centralized state, urban life, and a cohesive culture.

lord Privileged landowner who exercised authority over the people who lived on his land.

lost generation The 17 million former members of the Red Guard and other Chinese youth who were denied education from the late 1960s to the mid-1970s as part of the Chinese government's attempt to prevent political disruptions.

Louisiana Purchase (1803) American purchase of French territory from Napoleon, including much of the present-day United States between the Mississippi River and the Rocky Mountains.

Lucy Relatively intact skeleton of a young adult female australopithecine unearthed in the valley of the Awash River in 1974 by an archaeological team working at a site in present-day Hadar, Ethiopia. The researchers nicknamed the skeleton Lucy. She stood just over three feet tall and walked upright at least some of the time. Her skull contained a brain within the ape size range. Also, her jaw and teeth were humanlike. Lucy's skeleton was relatively complete and was the oldest hominid skeleton ever discovered.

Luftwaffe German air force.

Maastricht Treaty (1991) Treaty that formed the European Union, a fully integrated trading and financial bloc with its own bureaucracy and elected representatives.

Ma'at Term used in ancient Egypt to refer to stability or order, the achievement of which was the primary task of Egypt's ruling kings, the pharaohs.

Maccabees Leaders of a riot in Jerusalem in 166 BCE; the riot was a response to a Roman edict outlawing the practice of Judaism.

Madhyamika (Middle Way) Buddhism Chinese branch of Mahayana Buddhism established by Kumarajiva (344–413 CE) that used irony and paradox to show that reason was limited.

madrassas Higher schools of Muslim education that taught law, the Quran, religious sciences, and the regular sciences.

Mahayana (Greater Vehicle) Buddhism School of Buddhist theology that believed that the Buddha was a deity, unlike previous groups that had considered him a wise human being.

Mahdi The "chosen one" in Islam whose appearance was supposed to foretell the end of the world and the final day of reckoning for all people.

maize Grains, the crops that the settled agrarian communities across the Americas cultivated, along with legumes (beans) and tubers (potatoes).

Maji-Maji Revolt (early 1900s) Swahili insurrection against German colonialists; inspired by the belief that those who were anointed with specially blessed water (*maji*) would be immune to bullets. It resulted in 200,000–300,000 African deaths.

Mamluks (Arabic for "owned" or "possessed") Military men who ruled Egypt as an independent regime from 1250 until the Ottoman conquest in 1517.

Manaus Opera House Opera house built in the interior of Brazil in a lucrative rubber-growing area at the turn of the twentieth century.

Manchukuo Japanese puppet state in Manchuria in the 1930s.

Manchus Descendants of the Jurchens who helped the Ming army recapture Beijing in 1644 after its seizure by the outlaw Li Zicheng. The Manchus numbered around 1 million but controlled a domain that included perhaps 250 million people. Their rule lasted more than 250 years and became known as the Qing dynasty.

mandate of heaven Ideology established by Zhou dynasts to communicate the moral transfer of power. Originally a pact between the Zhou people and their supreme god, it evolved in the first century BCE into Chinese political doctrine.

Mande A people who lived in the area between the bend in the Senegal River and the bend in the Niger River east to west and from the Senegal River and Bandama River north to south. Also known as the Mandinka. Their civilization emerged around 1100.

Mandela, Nelson (1918–) Leader of the African National Congress (ANC) who was imprisoned for more than two decades by the apartheid regime in South Africa for his political beliefs; worldwide protests led to his release in 1990. In 1994 Mandela won the presidency in South Africa's first free mass elections.

Manifest Destiny Belief that it was God's will for the American people to expand their territory and political processes across the North American continent.

Mao Zedong (1893–1976) Chinese communist leader who rose to power during the Long March (1934). In 1949, he defeated the Nationalists and established a communist regime in China. Although many of Mao's efforts to transform China, such as the industrialization program of 1958 (known as the Great Leap Forward) and the Cultural Revolution of 1966, failed and brought great suffering to the people, he did instill a new spirit of independence in China and a sense of purpose after many decades of political and economic failure.

maroon community Sanctuary for runaway slaves in the Americas.

Marshall Plan Economic aid package given by the United States to Europe after World War II in hopes of a rapid period of reconstruction and economic gain, thereby securing the countries that received the aid from a communist takeover.

martyrs People executed by the Roman authorities for persisting in their Christian beliefs and refusing to submit to pagan ritual or belief.

Marx, Karl (1818–1883) German philosopher and economist who created Marxism and believed that a revolution of the working classes would overthrow the capitalist order and create a classless society.

Marxism Form of scientific socialism created by Karl Marx and Friedrich Engels that was rooted in a materialist theory of history: what mattered in history were the production of material goods and the ways in which society was organized into classes of producers and exploiters.

mass consumption Increased purchasing power in the early-twentieth-century prosperous and mainly middle-class societies, stemming from mass production.

mass culture Distinctive form of popular culture that arose in the wake of World War I. It reflected the tastes of the working and the middle classes, who now had more time and money to spend on entertainment, and relied on new technologies, especially film and radio, which could reach an entire nation's population and consolidate their sense of being a single state.

mass production System in which factories were set up to produce huge quantities of identical products, reflecting the early-twentieth-century world's demands for greater volume, faster speed, reduced cost, and standardized output.

Mastaba Word meaning "bench" in Arabic; it refers to a huge flat structure identical to earlier royal tombs of ancient Egypt.

Mau-Mau Revolt (1952–1957) Uprising orchestrated by a Kenyan guerrilla movement; this conflict forced the British to grant independence to the black majority in Kenya.

Mauryan Empire Dynasty extended by the Mauryans from 321 to 184 BCE, from the Indus Valley to the northwest areas of South Asia, in a region previously controlled by Persia. It was the first large-scale empire in South Asia and was to become the model for future Indian empires.

Mawali Non-Arab "clients" to Arab tribes in the early Islamic Empire. Because tribal patronage was so much a part of the Arabian cultural system, non-Arabs who converted to Islam affiliated themselves with a tribe and became clients of that tribe.

Maxim gun European weaponry that was capable of firing many bullets per second; it was used against Africans in the conquest of the continent.

Mayans Civilization that ruled over large stretches of Mesoamerica; it was composed of a series of kingdoms, each built around ritual centers rather than cities. The Mayans engaged neighboring peoples in warfare and trade and expanded borders through tributary relationships. They were not defined by a great ruler or one capital city, but by their shared religious beliefs.

McCarthyism Campaign by Republican senator Joseph McCarthy in the late 1940s and early 1950s to uncover closet communists, particularly in the State Department and in Hollywood.

Meat Inspection Act (1906) Legislation that provided for government supervision of meat-packing operations; it was part of a broader "Progressive" reform movement dedicated to correcting the negative consequences of urbanization and industrialization in the United States.

Mecca Arabian city in which Muhammad was born. Mecca was a trading center and pilgrimage destination in the pre-Islamic and Islamic periods. Exiled in 622 CE because of resistance to his message, Muhammad returned to Mecca in 630 CE and claimed the city for Islam.

Medes Rivals of the Assyrians and the Persians. The Medes inhabited the area from the Zagros Mountains to the modern city of Tehran; known as expert horsemen and archers, they were eventually defeated by the Persians.

megaliths Literally, "great stone"; the word *megalith* is used when describing structures such as Stonehenge. These massive structures are the result of cooperative planning and work.

Megarons Large buildings found in Troy (level II) that are the predecessors of the classic Greek temple.

Meiji Empire Empire created under the leadership of Mutsuhito, emperor of Japan from 1868 until 1912. During the Meiji period Japan became a world industrial and naval power.

Meiji Restoration Reign of the Meiji emperor, which was characterized by a new nationalist identity, economic advances, and political transformation.

Mencius Disciple of Confucius who lived from 372 to 289 BCE.

mercantilism Economic theory that drove European empire builders. In this economic system, the world had a fixed amount of wealth, which meant one country's wealth came at the expense of another's. Mercantilism assumed that colonies existed for the sole purpose of enriching the country that controlled the colony.

Mercosur Free-trade pact between the governments of Argentina, Brazil, Paraguay, and Uruguay.

meritocracy Rule by persons of talent.

Meroe Ancient kingdom in what is today Sudan. It flourished for nearly a thousand years, from the fifth century BCE to the fifth century CE.

mestizos Mixed-blood offspring of Spanish settlers and native Indians.

métis Mixed-blood offspring of French settlers and native Indians.

Mexican Revolution (1910) Conflict fueled by the unequal distribution of land and by disgruntled workers; it erupted when political elites split over the succession of General Porfirio Díaz after decades of his rule. The fight lasted over ten years and cost one million lives, but it resulted in a widespread reform and a new constitution.

Mfecane movement African political revolts in the first half of the nineteenth century that were caused by the expansionist methods of King Shaka of the Zulu people.

microsocieties Small-scale communities that had little interaction with others. These communities were the norm for peoples living in the Americas and islanders in the Pacific and Aegean from 2000 to 1200 BCE.

migration Long-distance travel for the purpose of resettlement. In the case of early man, the need to move was usually a response to an environmental shift, such as climate change during the Ice Age.

millenarian Convinced of the imminent coming of a just and ideal society.

millenarian movement Broad, popular upheaval calling for the restoration of a bygone moral age, often led by charismatic spiritual prophets.

Millets Minority religious communities of the Ottoman Empire.

minaret Slender tower within a mosque from which Muslims are called to prayer.

Minbar Pulpit inside a mosque from which Muslim religious speakers broadcast their message to the faithful.

Minoans A people who built a large number of elaborate, independent palace centers on Crete, at Knossos, and elsewhere around 2000 BCE. Named after the legendary King Minos, said to have ruled Crete at the time, they sailed throughout the Mediterranean and by 1600 BCE had planted colonies on many Aegean islands, which in turn became trading and mining centers.

mission civilisatrice Term French colonizers used to refer to France's form of "rationalized" colonial rule, which attempted to bring "civilization" to the "uncivilized."

mitochondrial DNA Form of DNA found outside the nucleus of cells, where it serves as cells' microscopic power packs. Examining mitochondrial DNA enables researchers to measure the genetic variation among living objects, including human beings.

Moche A people who extended their power and increased their wealth at the height of the Chimu Empire over several valleys in what is now modern-day Peru.

Model T First automobile, manufactured by the Ford Motor Company of Henry Ford, to be priced reasonably enough to be sold to the masses.

Modernists A generation of exuberant young artists, writers, and scientists in the late nineteenth century who broke with older conventions and sought new ways of seeing and describing the world.

Mohism School of thought in ancient China, named after Mo Di, or Mozi, who lived from 479 to 438 BCE. It emphasized one's obligation to society as a whole, not just to one's immediate family or social circle.

monarchy Political system in which one individual holds supreme power and passes that power on to his or her next of kin.

monasticism Christian way of life that originated in Egypt and was practiced as early as 300 CE in the Mediterranean. The word itself contains the meaning of a person "living alone" without marriage or family.

monetization An economic shift from a barter-based economy to one dependent on coin.

Mongols Combination of nomadic forest and prairie peoples who lived by hunting and livestock herding and were expert horsemen. Beginning in 1206, the Mongols launched a series of conquests that brought far-flung parts of the world together under their rule. By incorporating conquered peoples and adapting some of their customs, the Mongols created a unified empire that stretched from the Pacific Ocean to the shores of the eastern Mediterranean and the southern steppes of Eurasia.

Moors Term employed by Europeans in the medieval period to refer to Muslim occupants of North Africa, the western Sahara, and the Iberian Peninsula.

mosque Place of worship for the people of Islam.

"Mound people" Name for the people of Cahokia, since its landscape was dominated by earthen monuments in the shapes of mounds. The mounds were carefully maintained and were the loci from which Cahokians paid respect to spiritual forces. *See also* Cahokia.

Mu Chinese ruler (956–918 BCE) who put forth a formal bureaucratic system of governance, appointing officials, supervisors and military captains to whom he was not related. He also instituted a formal legal code.

muckrakers Journalists who aimed to expose political and commercial corruption in late-nineteenth- and early-twentieth-century America.

Muftis Experts on Muslim religious law.

Mughal Empire One of Islam's greatest regimes. Established in 1526, it was a vigorous, centralized state whose political authority encompassed most of modern-day India. During the sixteenth century, it had a population of between 100 and 150 million.

Muhammad (570–632 CE) Prophet and founder of the Islamic faith. Born in Mecca in Saudi Arabia and orphaned when young, Muhammad lived under the protection of his uncle. His career as a prophet began around

610 CE, with his first experience of spiritual revelation.

Muhammad Ali Ruler of Egypt between 1805 and 1848. He initiated a set of modernizing reforms that sought to make Egypt competitive with the great powers.

mullahs Religious leaders in Iran who in the 1970s led a movement opposing Shah Reza Pahlavi and denounced American materialism and secularism.

multinational corporations Corporations based in many different countries that have global investment, trading, and distribution goals.

Muscovy The principality of Moscow. Originally a mixture of Slavs, Finnish tribes, Turkic speakers, and many others, Muscovy used territorial expansion and commercial networks to consolidate a powerful state and expanded to become the Russian Empire, a huge realm that spanned parts of Europe, much of northern Asia, numerous North Pacific islands, and even—for a time—a corner of North America (Alaska).

Muslim Brotherhood Egyptian organization founded in 1938 by Hassan al-Banna. It attacked liberal democracy as a cover for middle-class, business, and landowning interests and fought for a return to a purified Islam.

Muslim League National Muslim party of India.

Mussolini, Benito (1883–1945) Italian dictator and founder of the fascist movement in Italy. During World War II, he allied Italy with Germany and Japan.

Muwahhidin Term meaning "unitarians"; these were followers of the Wahhabi movement that emerged in the Arabian Peninsula in the eighteenth century.

Mycenaeans Mainland competitors of the Minoans; they took over Crete around 1400 BCE. Migrating to Greece from central Europe, they brought their Indo-European language, horse chariots, and metalworking skills, which they used to dominate until 1200 BCE.

Nagasaki Second Japanese city to be hit by an atomic bomb near the end of World War II.

Napoleon Bonaparte (1769–1821) General who rose to power in a post-Revolutionary coup d'état, eventually proclaiming himself emperor of France. He placed security and order ahead of social reform and created a civil legal code. Napoleon expanded his empire through military action, but after his disastrous Russian campaign, the united European powers defeated Napoleon and forced him into exile. He escaped and reassumed command of his army but was later defeated at the Battle of Waterloo.

Napoleonic Code Legal code drafted by Napoleon in 1804; it distilled different legal traditions to create one uniform law. The code confirmed the abolition of feudal privileges of all kinds and set the conditions for exercising property rights.

National Assembly of France Governing body of France that succeeded the Estates-General in 1789 during the French Revolution. It was composed of, and defined by, the delegates of the Third Estate.

National Association for the Advancement of Colored People (NAACP) Founded in 1910, the U.S. civil rights organization dedicated to ending inequality and segregation for black Americans.

National Recovery Administration (NRA) New Deal agency created in 1933 to prepare codes of fair administration and to plan for public works. It was later declared unconstitutional.

nationalism The idea that members of a shared community called a "nation" should have sovereignty within the borders of their state.

nation-state Form of political organization that derived legitimacy from its inhabitants, often referred to as citizens, who in theory, if not always in practice, shared a common language, common culture, and common history.

native learning Japanese movement to promote nativist intellectual traditions and the celebration of Japanese texts.

native paramountcy British form of "rationalized" colonial rule, which attempted to bring "civilization" to the "uncivilized" by proclaiming that when the interests of European settlers in Africa clashed with those of the African population, the latter should take precedence.

natural rights Belief that emerged in eighteenth-century western Europe and North America that rights fundamental to human nature were discernible to reason and should be affirmed in human-made law.

natural selection Charles Darwin's theory that populations grew faster than the food supply, creating a "struggle for existence" among species. In later work he showed how the passing on of individual traits was also determined by what he called sexual selection—according to which the "best" mates are chosen for their strength, beauty, or talents. The outcome: the "fittest" survived to reproduce, while the less adaptable did not.

Nazis (National Socialist German Workers Party) German organization dedicated to winning workers over from socialism to nationalism; the first Nazi Party platform combined nationalism with anticapitalism and anti-Semitism.

Neanderthals Members of an early wave of hominids from Africa who settled in western Afro-Eurasia, in an area reaching from present-day Uzbekistan and Iraq to Spain, approximately 150,000 years ago.

needle compass Crucial instrument made available to navigators after 1000 CE that helped guide sailors on the high seas. It was a Chinese invention.

negritos Hunter-gatherer inhabitants of the East Asian coastal islands who migrated there around 28,000 BCE but by 2000 BCE had been replaced by new migrants.

Negritude Statement of the virtues of the black identity and the validation of African culture and the African past, even in a westernizing world. This idea was shaped by African and African American intellectuals like Senegal's first president, Léopold Sédar Senghor.

Nehemiah Jewish eunuch of the Persian court who was given permission to rebuild the fortification walls around the city of Jerusalem from 440 to 437 BCE.

Neo-Assyrian Empire Afro-Eurasian empire that dominated around 950 BCE. The Neo-Assyrians extended their control over resources and people beyond their own borders, and their empire lasted for three centuries.

Nestorian Christians Denomination of Christians whose beliefs about Christ differed from those of the official Byzantine church. Named after Nestorius, former bishop of Constantinople, they emphasized the human aspects of Jesus.

New Deal President Franklin Delano Roosevelt's package of government reforms that were enacted during the 1930s to provide jobs for the unemployed, social welfare programs for the poor, and security to the financial markets.

New Economic Policy Enacted decrees of the Bolsheviks between 1921 and 1927 that grudgingly sanctioned private trade and private property.

New Negro movement *See* Harlem Renaissance.

New World Term applied to the Americas that reflected the Europeans' view that anything previously unknown to them was "new," even if it had existed and supported societies long before European explorers arrived on its shores.

Nirvana Literally, nonexistence; nirvana is the state of complete liberation from the concerns of worldly life, as in Buddhist thought.

Nō drama Masked theater favored by Japanese bureaucrats and regional lords during the Tokugawa period.

Noble Eightfold Path Buddhist concept of a way of life by which people may rid themselves of individual desire to achieve nirvana. The path consists of wisdom, ethical behavior, and mental discipline.

Nok culture Spectacular culture that arose in what is today Nigeria, in the sixth century BCE. Iron smelting occurred there around 600 BCE. Thus the Nok people made the transition from stone to iron materials.

nomads People who move across vast distances without settling permanently in a particular place. Often pastoralists, nomads and transhumant herders introduced new forms of chariot-based warfare that transformed the Afro-Eurasian world.

non-governmental organizations (NGOs) Term used to refer to private organizations like the Red Cross that play a large role in international affairs.

nonviolent resistance (*Satyagraha*) Moral and political philosophy of resistance developed by Indian National Congress leader Mohandas Gandhi. Gandhi believed that if Indians pursued self-reliance and self-control in a nonviolent way, the British would eventually have to leave.

North American Free Trade Agreement (NAFTA) Treaty negotiated in the early 1990s to promote free trade between Canada, the United States, and Mexico.

North Atlantic Treaty Organization (NATO) International organization set up in 1949 to provide for the defense of western European countries and the United States from the perceived Soviet threat.

Northern Wei dynasty Regime founded in 386 CE by the Tuoba, a people originally from Inner Mongolia, that lasted one and a half centuries. The rulers of this dynasty adopted many practices of the earlier Chinese Han regime. At the same time, they struggled to consolidate authority over their own nomadic people. Ultimately, several decades of intense internal conflict led to the dynasty's downfall.

northwest passage Long-sought marine passageway between the Atlantic and Pacific oceans.

Oceania Collective name for the lands of Australia and New Zealand and the islands of the southwest Pacific Ocean.

Odyssey Composed in the eighth century BCE, an epic tale of the journey of Odysseus, who traveled the Mediterranean back to his home in Ithaca after the siege of Troy.

Oikos The word for "small family unit" in ancient Greece, similar to the *familia* in Rome. Its structure, with men as heads of household over women and children, embodied the fundamental power structure in Greek city-states.

oligarchy Clique of privileged rulers.

Olmecs A people who emerged around 1500 BCE and lived in Mesoamerica. The name means those who "lived in the land of the rubber." Olmec society was composed of decentralized villages. Its members spoke the same language and worshipped the same gods.

Open Door Policy Policy proposed by American Secretary of State John Hay that would give all foreign nations equal access to trade with China. As European imperial powers carved out spheres of trade in late-nineteenth-century China, American leaders worried that the United States would be excluded from trade with China. To prevent this, Hay proposed the Open Door Policy.

Opium War (1839–1842) War fought between the British and Qing China over British trade in opium; resulted in the granting to the British the right to trade in five different ports and the ceding of Hong Kong to the British.

oracle bones Animal bones used by Shang diviners. Diviners applied intense heat to the shoulder bones of cattle or to turtle shells, which caused them to crack. The diviners would then interpret the cracks as signs from the ancestors regarding royal plans and actions.

Organization of Petroleum Exporting Countries (OPEC) International association established in 1960 to coordinate price and supply policies of oil-producing states.

orientalism Genre of literature and painting that portrayed the nonwestern peoples of North Africa and Asia as exotic, sensuous, and economically backward with respect to Europeans.

orientalists Western scholars who specialized in the study of the East.

Orrorin tugenensis Predecessor to hominids that first appeared 6 million years ago.

Ottoman Empire Rulers of Anatolia, the Arab world, and much of southern and eastern Europe in the early sixteenth century. They transformed themselves from nomadic warrior bands who roamed the borderlands between Islamic and Christian worlds in Anatolia into sovereigns of a vast, bureaucratic empire. The Ottomans embraced a Sunni view of Islam. They adapted traditional Byzantine governmental practices but tried new ways of integrating the diverse peoples of their empire.

Pacific War (1879–1883) War between Chile and the alliance of Bolivia and Peru.

Pagani Pejorative word used by Christians to designate pagans.

palace Official residence of the ruler, his family, and his entourage. The palace was both a social institution and a set of buildings. It first appeared around 2500 BCE, about a millennium later than the Mesopotamian temple, and quickly joined the temple as a defining landmark of city life. Eventually, it became a source of power rivaling the temple, and palace and temple life often blurred, as did the boundary between the sacred and the secular.

Palmyra Roman trading depot in modern-day Syria; part of a network of trading cities that connected various regions of Afro-Eurasia.

pan movements Groups that sought to link people across state boundaries in new communities based on ethnicity or, in some cases, religion (e.g., pan-Germanism, pan-Islamism, pan-Slavism).

Pansophia Ideal republic of inquisitive Christians united in the search for knowledge of nature as a means of loving God.

papacy The institution of the pope; the Catholic spiritual leader in Rome.

papal Of, relating to, or issued by a pope.

Parthians Horse-riding people who pushed southward around the middle of the second century BCE and wiped out the Greek kingdoms in Iran. They then extended their power all the way to the Mediterranean, where they ran up against the Roman Empire in Anatolia and Mesopotamia.

pastoral nomadic communities Groups of people that moved their domesticated animals from place to place to meet the animals' demanding grazing requirements. Around 3500 BCE, western Afro-Eurasia witnessed the growth and spread of pastoral nomadic communities.

pastoralism Herding and breeding of sheep and goats or other animals as a primary means of subsistence.

Paterfamilias Latin for "Father of the family," which itself was the foundation of the Roman social order.

Patria Latin, meaning "fatherland."

patrons In the Roman system of patronage, men and women of wealth and high social status who protected dependents or "clients" of a lower class.

Pax Mongolica Term that refers to the political and especially the commercial stability that the vast Mongol Empire provided for the travelers and merchants of Eurasia during the thirteenth and fourteenth centuries.

Pax Romana Latin for "Roman Peace"; refers to the period between 25 BCE and 235 CE during which conditions in the Roman Empire were settled and peaceful.

Pax Sinica Period of peace (149–87 BCE) during which agriculture, commerce, and industry flourished in East Asia under the rule of the Han.

Peace Preservation Act (1925) Act instituted in Japan that specified up to ten years' hard labor for any member of an organization advocating a basic change in the political system or the abolition of private property.

Pearl Harbor American naval base in Hawaii on which the Japanese launched a surprise attack on December 7, 1941, bringing the United States into World War II.

Peloponnesian War War fought between 431 and 404 BCE between two of Greece's most powerful city-states, Athens and Sparta.

Peninsular War (1808–1814) Conflict in which the Portuguese and Spanish populations, supported by the British, resisted the French invasion under Napoleon of the Iberian Peninsula.

Peninsulars Spaniards who, although born in Spain, resided in the Spanish colonial territories. They regarded themselves as superior to Spaniards born in the colonies (Creoles).

Peoples' Charter Document calling for universal suffrage for adult males, the secret ballot, electoral districts, and annual parliamentary elections. It was signed by over 3 million British between 1839 and 1842.

periplus Book that reflected sailing knowledge; in such books captains would record landing spots and ports. The word *periplus* literally means "sailing around."

Persepolis Darius I's capital city in the highlands of Fars; a ceremonial center and expression of imperial identity as well as an important administrative hub.

Peterloo Massacre (1819) The killing of 11 and wounding of 460 following a peaceful demonstration for political reform by workers in Manchester, England.

Petra City in modern-day Jordan that was the Nabataean capital. It profited greatly by supplying provisions and water to travelers and traders. Many of its houses and shrines were cut into the rocky mountains. *Petra* means "rock."

phalanx Military formation used by Philip II of Macedonia, whereby heavily armored infantry were closely arrayed in battle formation.

Philip II of Macedonia Father of Alexander the Great, under whose rule Macedonia developed into a large ethnic and territorial state. After unifying Macedonia, Philip went on to conquer neighboring states.

philosophia Literally "love of wisdom"; this system of thought originally included speculation on the nature of the cosmos, the environment, and human existence. It eventually came to include thought about the nature of humans and life in society.

Phoenicians Known as the Canaanites in the Bible, an ethnic group in the Levant under Assyrian rule in the seventh century BCE; they provided ships and sailors for battles in the Mediterranean. The word *Phoenician* refers to the purple dye they manufactured and widely traded, along with other commercial goods and services, throughout the Mediterranean. While part of wider Mesopotamian culture, their major contribution was the alphabet, first introduced in the second millennium BCE, which made far-reaching communication possible.

phonemes Primary and distinctive sounds that are characteristic of human language.

piety Strong sense of religious duty and devoutness, often inspiring extraordinary actions.

plant domestication Process of growing plants, harvesting their seeds, and saving some of the seeds for planting in subsequent growing cycles, resulting in a steady food supply. This process occurred as far back as 5000 BCE, when plants began to naturally retain their seeds. Plant domestication was practiced first in the southern Levant and spread from there into the rest of Southwest Asia.

Plato (427–347 BCE) Disciple of the great philosopher Socrates; his works are the only record we have of Socrates' teaching. He was also the author of formative philosophical works on ethics and politics.

plebs In Rome, term that referred to the "common people." Their interests were protected by officials called tribunes.

Pochteca Archaic term for merchants of the Mexicos.

polities Politically organized communities or states.

polyglot communities Societies composed of diverse linguistic and ethnic groups.

popular culture Affordable and accessible forms of art and entertainment available to people at all levels of society.

popular sovereignty The idea that the power of the state resides in the people.

populists Members of a political movement that supported U.S. farmers in late-nineteenth-century America. The term is often used generically to refer to political groups who appeal to the majority of the population.

potassium-argon dating Major dating technique based on the changing chemical structure of objects over time, since over time potassium decays into argon. This method makes possible the dating of objects up to a million years old.

potato famine (1840s) Severe famine in Ireland that led to the rise of radical political movements and the migration of large numbers of Irish to the United States.

potter's wheel Fast wheel that enabled people to mass-produce vessels in many different shapes. This advance, invented at the city of Uruk, enabled potters to make significant technical breakthroughs.

pottery Vessels made of mud and later clay that were used for storing and transporting food. The development of pottery was a major breakthrough.

Prague Spring (1968) Program of liberalization under a new communist party in Czechoslovakia that strove to create a democratic and pluralist socialism.

predestinarian Belief of many sixteenth- and seventeenth-century Protestant groups that God had foreordained the lives of individuals, including their bad and good deeds.

primitivism Western art movement of the late-nineteenth and early-twentieth centuries that drew upon the so-called primitive art forms of Africa, Oceania, and pre-Columbian America.

progressive reformers Members of the U.S. reform movement in the early twentieth century that aimed to eliminate political corruption, improve working conditions, and regulate the power of large industrial and financial enterprises.

proletarians Industrial wage workers.

prophets Charismatic freelance religious men of power who found themselves in opposition to the formal power of the kings, bureaucrats, and priests.

Prophet's Town Indian village that was burned down by American forces in the early nineteenth century.

Protestant Reformation Religious movement initiated by sixteenth-century monk Martin Luther, who openly criticized the corruption in the Catholic Church and voiced his belief that Christians could speak directly to God. His doctrines gained wide support, and those who followed this new view of the Christianity rejected the authority of the papacy and the Catholic clergy, broke away from the Catholic Church, and called themselves "Protestants."

Protestantism Division of Christianity that emerged in western Europe from the Protestant Reformation.

Proto-Indo-European The parent of all the languages in the Indo-European family, which includes, among many others, English, German, Norwegian, Portuguese, French, Russian, Persian, Hindi, and Bengali.

Pullman Strike (1894) American Railway Union strike in response to wage cuts and firings.

puppet states Governments with little power in the international arena that follow the dictates of their more powerful neighbors or patrons.

Puritans Seventeenth-century reform group of the Church of England; also known as dissenters or nonconformists.

Qadiriyya Sufi order that facilitated the spread of Islam into West Africa.

Qadis Judges in the Ottoman Empire.

qanats Underground water channels, vital for irrigation, which were used in Persia. Little evaporation occurred when water was being moved through qanats.

Qing dynasty (1644–1911) Minority Manchu rule over China that incorporated new territories, experienced substantial population growth, and sustained significant economic growth.

Questions of King Milanda (Milindapunha) Name of a second-century BCE text espousing the teachings of Buddhism as set forth by Menander, a Yavana king. It featured a discussion between the king and a sophisticated Buddhist sage named Nagasena.

Quetzalcoatl Ancient deity and legendary ruler of Native American peoples living in Mexico.

Quran The scripture of the Islamic faith. Originally a verbal recitation, the Quran was eventually compiled into a book in the order in which we have it today. According to traditional Islamic interpretation, the Quran was revealed to Muhammad by the angel Gabriel over a period of twenty-three years.

radicals Widely used term in nineteenth-century Europe that referred to those individuals and political organizations that favored the total reconfiguration of Europe's old state system.

radiocarbon isotope C^{14} Isotope contained by all living things, which plants acquire directly from the atmosphere and animals acquire indirectly when they consume plants or other animals. When living things die, the C^{14} isotope they contain begins to decay into a stable nonradioactive element, C^{12}. The rate of decay is regular and measurable, making it possible to ascertain the date of fossils that leave organic remains for ages of up to 40,000 years.

raj British crown's administration of India following the end of the East India Company's rule after the Rebellion of 1857.

raja "King" in the Kshatriya period in South Asia; could also refer to the head of a family, but indicated the person who had control of land and resources in South Asian city-states.

Ramadan Ninth month of the Muslim year, during which all Muslims must fast during daylight hours.

Rape of Nanjing Attack against the Chinese in which the Japanese slaughtered at least 100,000 civilians and raped thousands of women between December 1937 and February 1938.

Rashtriya Swayamsevak Sangh **(RSS)** (1925) Campaign to organize Hindus as a militant, modern community in India; translated in English as "National Volunteer Organization."

Rebellion of 1857 Indian uprising against the East India Company to bring religious purification, an egalitarian society, and local and communal solidarity without the interference of British rule.

rebus Probably originating in Uruk, a representation that transfers meaning from the name of a thing to the sound of that name. For example, a picture of a bee can represent the sound "b." Such pictures opened the door to writing: a technology of symbols that uses marks to represent specific discrete sounds.

Reconquista Spanish reconquest of territories lost to the Islamic Empire, beginning with Toledo in 1061.

Red Guards Chinese students who were the shock troopers in the early phases of Mao's Cultural Revolution in 1966–1968.

Red Lanterns Female supporters of the Chinese Boxers who rebelled against foreign intrusions in China at the turn of the twentieth century. Most were teenage girls and unmarried women and dressed in red garments.

Red Turban movement Diverse religious movement in China during the fourteenth century that spread the belief that the world was drawing to an end as Mongol rule was collapsing.

Reds Bolsheviks.

Reich German empire composed of Denmark, Austria, and parts of western France.

Reichstag The German parliament.

Reign of Terror Campaign at the height of the French Revolution in the early 1790s that used violence, including systematic execution of opponents of the revolution, to purge France of its enemies and to extend the revolution beyond its borders; radicals executed as many as 40,000 persons who were judged enemies of the state.

Renaissance Term meaning "rebirth" that historians use to characterize the expanded cultural production of European nations between 1430 and 1550. Emphasized a break from the church-centered medieval world and a new concept of humankind as the center of the world.

republican government Government in which power and rulership rest with representatives of the people—not a king.

Res publica Literally "public thing"; this referred to the Roman republic, in which policy and rules of behavior were determined by the Senate and by popular assemblies of the citizens.

Restoration period (1815–1848) European movement after the defeat of Napoleon to restore Europe to its pre-French revolutionary status and to quash radical movements.

Rift Valley Area of northeastern Africa where some of the most important early human archaeological discoveries of fossils were found, especially one of an intact skull that is 1.8 million years old.

river basin Area drained by a river, including all its tributaries. River basins were rich in fertile soil, water for irrigation, and plant and animal life, which made them attractive for human habitation. Cultivators were able to produce surplus agriculture to support the first cities.

riverine Term denoting an area whose inhabitants depended on irrigation for their well-being and whose populations are settled near great rivers. Egypt was, in a sense, the most riverine of all these cultures, in that it had no hinterland of plains as did Mesopotamia and the Indus valley. Away from the banks of the Nile, there is only largely uninhabitable desert.

Roman army Military force of the Roman Empire. The Romans devised a military draft that could draw from a huge population. In their encounter with Hannibal, they lost up to 80,000 men in three separate encounters and still won the war.

Roman Catholicism Branch of Christianity established by 1000 CE in western Europe and led by the Roman papacy. In contrast to ancient Greek Orthodoxy, Western Catholics believed that their church was destined to expand everywhere, and they set about converting the pagan tribes of northern Europe. Western Catholics contemptuously called the East Romans "Greeks" and condemned them for their "Byzantine" cunning.

Roman law Roman legal system, under which disputes were brought to the public courts and decisions were made by judges and sometimes by large juries. Rome's legal system featured written law and institutions for settling legal disputes.

roving bandits Large bands of dispossessed and marginalized peasants who vented their anger at tax collectors in the waning years of the Ming dynasty.

Royal Road A 1,600-mile road from Sardis in Anatolia to Susa in Iran; used by messengers, traders, the army, and those taking tribute to the king.

Russification Programs to assimilate people of over 146 dialects into the Russian Empire.

S.S. (*Schutzstaffel*) Hitler's security police force.

Sack of Constantinople Rampage in 1204 by the Frankish armies on the capital city of Constantinople.

sacred kingships Institutions that marked the centralized politics of West Africa. The inhabitants of these kingships believed that their kings were descendants of the gods.

Sahel region Area of sub-Saharan Africa with wetter and more temperate locations, especially in the upland massifs and their foothills, villages, and towns.

St. Bartholomew's Day Massacre (1572) Roman Catholic massacre of French Protestants in Paris.

St. Patrick Former slave brought to Ireland from Briton who later became a missionary, or the "Apostle of Ireland." He died in 470 CE.

Salt March (1930) A 240-mile trek to the sea in India, led by Mohandas Gandhi, to gather salt for free, thus breaking the British colonial monopoly on salt.

Samurai Japanese warriors who made up the private armies of Japanese daimyos.

Sandinista coalition Left-leaning Nicaraguan coalition of the 1970s and 1980s.

Santería African-based religion, blended with Christian influences, that was first practiced by slaves in Cuba.

Sargon the Great King of Akkad, a city-state near modern Baghdad. Reigning from 2334 to 2279 BCE, Sargon helped bring the competitive era of city-states to an end and sponsored monumental works of architecture, art, and literature.

Sasanian Empire Empire that succeeded the Parthians in the mid-220s CE in Inner Eurasia. The Sasanian Empire controlled the trade crossroads of Afro-Eurasia and possessed a strong armored cavalry, which made them a powerful rival to Rome. The Sasanians were also tolerant of Judaism and Christianity, which allowed Christians to flourish.

Sati Hindu practice whereby a woman was burned to death on the pyre of her dead husband.

satrap Governor of a province in the Persian Empire. Each satrap was a relative or intimate associate of the king.

Satyagraha See nonviolent resistance.

scientific method Method of inquiry based on experimentation in nature. Many of its principles were first laid out by the philosopher Sir Francis Bacon (1561–1626), who claimed that real science entailed the formulation of hypotheses that could be tested in carefully controlled experiments.

Scramble for Africa European rush to colonize parts of Africa at the end of the nineteenth century.

scribes Those who wield writing tools; from the very beginning they were at the top of the social ladder, under the major power brokers.

Scythian ethos Warrior ethos that embodied the extremes of aggressive mounted-horse culture, c. 1000 BCE. In part the Scythian ethos was the result of the constant struggle between settlers, hunter-gatherers, and nomads on the northern frontier of Europe.

Sea Peoples Migrants from north of the Mediterranean who invaded the cities of Egypt and the Levant in the second millennium BCE. Once settled along the coast of the Levant, they became known as the Philistines and considerably disrupted the settlements of the Canaanites.

SEATO (Southeast Asia Treaty Organization) Military alliance of pro-American, anticommunist states in Southeast Asia in 1954.

Second World Term invented during the cold war to refer to the communist countries, as opposed to the West (or First World) and the former colonies (or Third World).

second-generation societies Societies that expanded old ideas and methods by incorporating new aspects of culture and grafting them onto, or using them in combination with, established norms.

Seleucus Nikator Successor of Alexander the Great who lived from 358 to 281 BCE. He controlled Mesopotamia, Syria, Persia, and parts of the Punjab.

Self-Strengthening movement In the latter half of the nineteenth century, a movement of reformist Chinese bureaucrats that attempted to adopt western elements of learning and technological skill while retaining their core Chinese culture.

Semu Term meaning "outsiders" or non-Chinese people—Mongols, Tanguts, Khitan, Jurchen, Muslims, Tibetans, Persians, Turks, Nestorians, Jews, and Armenians—who became a new ruling elite over a Han majority population in the late thirteenth century.

sepoys Hindu and Muslim recruits of the East India Company's military force.

serfs Peasants who farmed the land and paid fees to be protected and governed by lords under a system of rule called feudalism.

settled agriculture Application of human labor and tools to a fixed plot of land for more than one growing cycle. It entails the changeover from a hunting and gathering lifestyle to one based on agriculture, which requires staying in one place until the soil has been exhausted.

Seven Years' War (1756–1763) Worldwide war that ended when Prussia defeated Austria, establishing itself as a European power, and when Britain gained control of India and many of France's colonies through the Treaty of Paris.

sexual revolution Increased freedom in sexual behavior, resulting in part from the advances in contraception, notably the introduction of oral contraception in 1960, which allowed men and women to limit childbearing and to have sex with less fear of pregnancy.

shah Traditional title of Persian rulers.

shamans Certain humans whose powers supposedly enabled them to commune with the supernatural and to transform themselves wholly or partly into beasts.

Shamisen Three-stringed instrument, often played by Japanese geisha.

Shandingdong Man A *Homo sapiens* whose fossil remains and relics can be dated to about 18,000 years ago. His physical characteristics were closer to those of modern humans, and he had a similar brain size.

Shang state Dynasty in northeastern China that ruled from 1600 to 1045 BCE. Though not as well defined by borders as the territorial states in the southwest of Asia, it did have a ruling lineage. Four fundamental elements of the Shang state were a metal industry based on copper, pottery making, standardized architectural forms and walled towns, and divination using animal bones.

Shanghai School Late-nineteenth-century style of painting characterized by an emphasis on spontaneous brushwork, feeling, and the incorporation of western influences into classical Chinese pieces.

sharecropping System of farming in which tenant farmers rented land and gave over a share of their crops to the land's owners. Sometimes seen as a cheap way for the state to conduct agricultural affairs, sharecropping often resulted in the impoverishment and marginalization of the underclass.

Sharia Literally, "the way"; now used to indicate the philosophy and rulings of Islamic law.

Sharpeville Massacre (1960) Massacre of sixty-nine black Africans when police fired upon a rally against the recently passed laws requiring nonwhite South Africans to carry identity papers.

Shawnees Native American tribe that inhabited the Ohio valley during the eighteenth century.

Shays's Rebellion (1786) Uprising of armed farmers that broke out when the Massachusetts state government refused to offer them economic relief.

Shiism One of the two main branches of Islam, practiced in the Safavid Empire. Although always a minority sect in the Islamic world, Shiism contains several subsects, each of which has slightly different interpretations of theology and politics.

Shiites Group of supporters of Ali, Muhammad's cousin and son-in-law, who wanted him to be the first caliph and believed that members of the Prophet's family deserved to rule. The leaders of the Shiite community are known as "Imam," which means "leaders."

Shinto Japan's official religion; it promoted the state and the emperor's divinity. The term means "the way of the gods."

shoguns Japanese military commanders. From 1192 to 1333, the Kamakura shoguns served as military "protectors" of the ruler in the city of Heian.

Shotoku Prince in the early Japanese Yamoto state (574–622 CE) who is credited with having introduced Buddhism to Japan.

shudras Literally "small ones"; workers and slaves from outside the Vedic lineage.

Siddhartha Gautama Another name for the Buddha; the most prominent opponent of the Brahman way of life; he lived from 563 to 483 BCE.

Sikhism Islamic-inspired religion that calls on its followers to renounce the caste system and to treat all believers as equal before God.

Silicon Valley Valley between the California cities of San Francisco and San Jose, known for its innovative computer and high-technology industries.

silk Luxury textile that became a vastly popular export from China (via the Silk Road) to the cities of the Roman world.

Silk Road Trade route linking China with central Asia and the Mediterranean; it extended over 5,000 miles, land and sea included, and was so named because of the quantities of silk that were traded along it. The Silk Road was a major factor in the development of civilizations in China, Egypt, Persia, India, and even Europe.

Silla One of three independent Korean states that may have emerged as early as the third century BCE. These states lasted until 668 CE, when Silla took control over the entire peninsula.

Silver Islands Term used by European merchants in the sixteenth century to refer to Japan, because of its substantial trade in silver with China.

Sino-Japanese War (1894–1895) Conflict over the control of Korea in which China was forced to cede the province of Taiwan to Japan.

Sipahi Urdu for "soldier."

Siva The third of three Vedic deities, signifying destruction. *See also* Brahma *and* Vishnu.

slave plantations System whereby labor was used for the cultivation of crops wholly for the sake of producing surplus that was then used for profit; slave plantations were a crucial part of the growth of the Mediterranean economy.

small seal script Unified script that was used to the exclusion of other scripts under the Qin, with the aim of centralizing administration; its use led to a less complicated style of clerical writing than had been in use under the Han.

social contract The idea, drawn from the writings of British philosopher John Locke, that the law should bind both ruler and people.

Social Darwinism Belief that Charles Darwin's theory of evolution was applicable to humans and justified the right of the ruling classes or countries to dominate the weak.

social hierarchies Distinctions between the privileged and the less privileged.

Social Security Act (1935) New Deal act that instituted old-age pensions and insurance for the unemployed.

socialism Political ideology that calls for a classless society with collective ownership of all property.

Socrates (469–399 BCE) Philosopher in Athens who encouraged people to reflect on ethics and morality. He stressed the importance of honor and integrity as opposed to wealth and power. Plato was his student.

Sogdians A people who lived in central Asia's commercial centers and maintained the stability and accessibility of the Silk Road. They were crucial to the interconnectedness of the Afro-Eurasian landmass.

Solidarity The communist bloc's first independent trade union, it was established in Poland at the Gdansk shipyard.

Song dynasty Chinese dynasty that took over the mandate of heaven for three centuries starting in 976 CE. It ruled an era of many economic and political successes, but it eventually lost northern China to nomadic tribes.

Song porcelain Type of porcelain perfected during the Song period that was light, durable, and quite beautiful.

South African War (1899–1902) Conflict between the British and Dutch colonists of South Africa which resulted in bringing two Afrikaner republics under the control of the British. Often called the Boer War.

Soviet bloc International alliance that included the east European countries of the Warsaw Pact as well as the Soviet Union but also came to include Cuba.

Spanish-American War (1898) War between the United States and Spain in Cuba, Puerto Rico, and the Philippines. It ended with a treaty in which the United States took over the Philippines, Guam, and Puerto Rico; Cuba won partial independence.

speciation The formation of different species.

specie Money in coin.

species Group of animals or plants possessing one or more distinctive characteristics.

spiritual ferment Process that occurred after 300 CE in which religion touched more areas of society and culture than before and touched them in different, more demanding ways.

Spring and Autumn period Period between the eighth and fifth centuries BCE, during which China was ruled by the feudal system. Considered an anarchic and turbulent time, there were 148 different tributary states in this period.

Stalin, Joseph (1879–1953) Leader of the communist party and the Soviet Union; sought to create "socialism in one country."

steel A metal more malleable and stronger than iron that became essential for industries like shipbuilding and railways.

stoicism Widespread philosophical movement initiated by Zeno (334–262 BCE). Zeno and his followers sought to understand the role of people in relation to the cosmos. For the Stoics, everything was grounded in nature. Being in love with nature and living a good life required being in control of one's passions and thus indifferent to pleasure or pain.

Strait of Malacca Seagoing gateway to Southeast and East Asia.

Strategic Defense Initiative ("Star Wars") Master plan, championed by U.S. president Ronald Reagan in the 1980s, that envisions the deployment of satellites and space missiles to protect the United States from incoming nuclear bombs.

stupa Dome monument marking the burial site of relics of the Buddha.

Suez Canal Channel built in 1869 across the Isthmus of Suez to connect the Mediterranean Sea with the Red Sea and to lower the costs of international trade.

Sufi brotherhoods Mystics within Islam who were responsible for the expansion of Islam into many regions of the world.

Sufism Emotional and mystical form of Islam that appealed to the common people.

sultan Islamic political leader. In the Ottoman Empire, the sultan combined a warrior ethos with an unwavering devotion to Islam.

Sumerian King List Text that recounts the making of political dynasties. Recorded around 2000 BCE, it organizes the reigns of kings by dynasty, one city at a time.

Sumerian pantheon The Sumerian gods, each of whom had a home in a particular floodplain city. In the Sumerian belief system, both gods and the natural forces they controlled had to be revered.

Sumerian temples Homes of the gods and symbols of Sumerian imperial identity. Sumerian temples also represented the gods' ability to hoard wealth at sites where people exchanged goods and services. In addition, temples distinguished the urban from the rural world.

Sun Yat-sen (1866–1925) Chinese revolutionary and founder of the Nationalist Party in China.

Sunnis Orthodox Muslims. The majority sect of Islam, Sunnis originally supported the succession of Abu Bakr over Ali and supported the rule of consensus rather than family lineage for the succession to the Islamic caliphate. *See also* Shiism.

superior man In the Confucian view, a person of perfected moral character, fit to be a leader.

superpowers Label applied to the United States and the Soviet Union after World War II because of their size, their possession of the atomic bomb, and the fact that each embodied a model of civilization (capitalism or communism) applicable to the whole world.

supranational organizations International organizations such as NGOs, the World Bank, and the IMF.

survival of the fittest Charles Darwin's belief that as animal populations grew and resources became scarce, a struggle for existence arose, the outcome of which was that only the "fittest" survived.

Suryavamsha The second lineage of two (the solar) in Vedic society. *See* Chandravamsha.

Swadeshi movement Voluntary organizations in India that championed the creation of indigenous manufacturing enterprises and schools of nationalist thought, in order to gain autonomy from Britain.

Syndicalism Organization of workplace associations that included unskilled labor.

tabula rasa Term used by John Locke to describe the human mind before it begins to acquire ideas from experience; French for "clean slate."

Taiping Heavenly Kingdom (Heavenly Kingdom of Great Peace) Religious sect established by the Chinese prophet Hong Xiuquan in the mid-nineteenth century. Hong Xiuquan believed that he was Jesus's younger brother. The group struggled to rid the world of evil and "restore" the heavenly kingdom, imagined as a just and egalitarian order.

Taiping Rebellion Rebellion by followers of Hong Xiuquan and the Taiping Heavenly Kingdom against the Qing government over the economic and social turmoil caused by the Opium War. Despite raising an army of 100,000 rebels, the rebellion was crushed.

Taj Mahal Royal palace of the Mughal Empire, built by Shah Jahan in the seventeenth century in homage to his wife, Mumtaz.

Tale of Genji Japanese work written by Lady Murasaki that gives vivid accounts of Heian court life; Japan's first novel (early eleventh century).

talking cures Psychological practice developed by Sigmund Freud whereby the symptoms of neurotic and traumatized patients would decrease after regular periods of thoughtful discussion.

Talmud Huge volumes of oral commentary on Jewish law eventually compiled in two versions, the Palestinian and the Babylonian, in the fifth and sixth centuries BCE.

Talmud of Jerusalem Codified written volumes of the traditions of Judaism; produced by the rabbis of Galilee around 400 CE.

Tang dynasty (608–907 CE) Regime that promoted a cosmopolitan culture, turning China into the hub of East Asia cultural integration, while expanding the borders of their empire. In order to govern such a diverse empire, the Tang established a political culture and civil service based on Confucian teachings. Candidates for the civil service were required to take examinations, the first of their kind in the world.

Tanzimat Reorganization period of the Ottoman Empire in the mid-nineteenth century; modernizing reforms affected the military, trade, foreign relations, and civilian life.

tappers Rubber workers in Brazil, mostly either Indian or mixed-blood people.

Tarascans Mesoamerican society of the 1400s; rivals to and sometimes subjects of the Aztecs.

Tatish Ruler of Chan Santa Cruz during the Mexican Caste War. The term means "father."

Tecumseh (1768–1813) Shawnee who circulated Tenskwatawa's message of Indian renaissance among Indian villages from the Great Lakes to the Gulf Coast. He preached the need for Indian unity, insisting that Indians resist any American attempts to get them to sell more land. In response, thousands of followers renounced their ties to colonial ways and prepared to combat the expansion of the United States.

Tekkes Schools that taught devotional strategies and the religious knowledge for students to enter Sufi orders and become masters of the brotherhood.

temple Building where believers worshiped their gods and goddesses and where some peoples believed the deities had earthly residence.

Tenskwatawa (1768–1834) Shawnee prophet who urged disciples to abstain from alcohol and return to traditional customs, reducing dependence on European trade goods and severing connections to Christian missionaries. His message spread to other tribes, raising the specter of a pan-Indian confederacy.

Teotihuacán City-state in a large, mountainous valley in present-day Mexico; the first major community to emerge after the Olmecs.

territorial state Political form that emerged in the riverine cities of Mesopotamia, which was overwhelmed by the displacement of nomadic peoples. These states were kingdoms organized around charismatic rulers who headed large households; each had a defined physical border.

Third Estate The French people minus the clergy and the aristocracy; this term was popularized in the late eighteenth century and used to exalt the power of the bourgeoisie during the French Revolution.

Third Reich The German state from 1933 to 1945 under Adolf Hitler.

Third World Nations of the world, mostly in Asia, Latin America, and Africa, that were not highly industrialized like First World nations or tied to the Soviet Bloc (the Second World).

Thirty Years' War (1618–1648) Conflict begun between Protestants and Catholics in Germany that escalated into a general European war fought against the unity and power of the Holy Roman Empire.

Tiananmen Square Largest public square in the world and site of the pro-democracy movement in 1989 that resulted in the killing of as many as a thousand protesters by the Chinese army.

Tiers monde Term meaning "Third World," coined by French intellectuals to describe countries seeking a "third way" between Soviet communism and western capitalism.

Tiglath Pileser III Assyrian ruler from 745 to 728 BCE. This leader instituted reforms that changed the administrative and social structure of the empire to make it more efficient and introduced a standing army.

Tiwanaku Another name for Tihuanaco, the first great Andean polity, on the shores of Lake Titicaca.

Tlaxcalans Mesoamerican society of the 1400s; these people were enemies of the powerful Aztec Empire.

Tokugawa shogunate Hereditary military administration founded in 1603 that ruled Japan while keeping the emperor as a figurehead; it was toppled in 1868 by reformers who felt that Japan should adopt, not reject, Western influences.

Toltecs A Mesoamerican people who, by 1000 CE, had filled the political vacuum created by the decline of the city of Teotihuacán.

tomb culture Warlike group from northeast Asia who arrived by sea in the middle of the third century CE and imposed their military and social power on southern Japan. These conquerors are known today as the "Tomb culture" because of their elevated necropolises near present-day Osaka.

Topkapi Palace Political headquarters of the Ottoman Empire, located in Istanbul.

total war All-out war involving civilian populations as well as military forces, often used in reference to World War II.

transhumant migrants Nomads who entered settled territories in the second millennium BCE and moved their herds seasonally when resources became scarce.

Trans-Siberian Railroad Railroad built over very difficult terrain between 1891 and 1903 and subsequently expanded; it created an overland bridge for troops, peasant settlers, and commodities to move between Europe and the Pacific.

Treaty of Brest-Litovsk (1918) Separate peace between imperial Germany and the new Bolshevik regime in Russia. The treaty acknowledged the German victory on the Eastern Front and withdrew Russia from the war.

Treaty of Nanjing (1842) Treaty between China and Britain following the Opium War; it called for indemnities, the opening of new ports, and the cession of Hong Kong to the British.

Treaty of Tordesillas (1494) Treaty in which the pope decreed that the non-European world would be divided into spheres of trade and missionary responsibility between Spain and Portugal.

trickle trade Method by which a good is passed from one village to another, as in the case of obsidian among farming villages; the practice began around 7000 BCE. Also called "down the line trade."

Tripartite Pact (1940) Pact that stated that Germany, Italy, and Japan would act together in all future military ventures.

Triple Entente Alliance developed before World War I that eventually included Britain, France, and Russia.

Troy Important site founded around 3000 BCE in Anatolia, to the far west. Troy is legendary as the site of the war that was launched by the Greeks (the Achaeans) and that was recounted by Homer in the *Iliad*.

Truman Doctrine (1947) Declaration promising U.S. economic and military intervention, whenever and wherever needed, for the sake of preventing communist expansion.

Truth and Reconciliation Commission Quasi-judicial body established after the overthrow of the apartheid system in South Africa and the election of Nelson Mandela as the country's first black president in 1994. The commission was to gather evidence about crimes committed during the apartheid years. Those who showed remorse for their actions could appeal for clemency. The South African leaders believed that an airing of the grievances from this period would promote racial harmony and reconciliation.

truth commissions Elected officials' inquiries into human rights abuses by previous regimes. In Argentina, El Salvador, Guatemala, and South Africa, these commissions were vital for creating a new aura of legitimacy for democracies and for promising to uphold the rights of individuals.

tsar/czar Russian word derived from the Latin *Caesar* to refer to the Russian ruler of Kiev, and eventually to all rulers in Russia.

Tula Toltec capital city; a commercial hub and political and ceremonial center.

Uitlanders British populations living in Afrikaner republics; they were denied voting rights and subject to other forms of discrimination in the late nineteenth century. The term means "outsiders."

Ulama Arabic word that means "learned ones" or "scholars"; used for those who devoted themselves to knowledge of Islamic sciences.

Umayyads Family who founded the first dynasty in Islam. They established family rule and dynastic succession to the role of caliph. The first Umayyad caliph established Damascus as his capital and was named Mu'awiya ibn Abi Sufyan.

Umma Arabic word for "community"; used to refer to the "Islamic polity" or "Islamic community."

Universal Declaration of Human Rights (1948) U.N. declaration that laid out the rights to which all human beings are entitled.

universitas Term used from the end of the twelfth century to denote scholars who came together, first in Paris. The term is borrowed from the merchant communities, where it denoted the equivalent of the modern "union."

Untouchables Caste in the Indian system whose jobs, usually in the more unsanitary aspects of urban life, rendered them "ritually and spiritually" impure.

Upanishads Vedic wisdom literature collected in the first half of the first millennium BCE. It took the form of dialogues between disciples and a sage.

urban-rural divide Division between those living in cities and those living in rural areas. One of history's most durable worldwide distinctions, the urban-rural divide eventually encompassed the globe. Where cities arose, communities adopted lifestyles based on the mass production of goods and on specialized labor. Those living in the countryside remained close to nature, cultivating the land or tending livestock. They diversified their labor and exchanged their grains and animal products for necessities available in urban centers.

utopian socialism The most visionary of all Restoration-era movements. Utopian socialists like Charles Fourier dreamed of transforming states, workplaces, and human relations and proposed plans to do so.

Vaishyas Householders or lesser clan members in Vedic society who worked the land and tended livestock.

Vardhamana Mahavira Advocate of Jainism who lived from 540 to 468 BCE; he emphasized interpretation of the Upanishads to govern and guide daily life.

Varna Caste system established by the Vedas in 600 BCE.

vassal states Subordinate states that had to pay tribute in luxury goods, raw materials, and manpower as part of a broad confederation of polities under the kings' protection.

Vedas Rhymes, hymns, and explanatory texts composed by Aryan priests; the Vedas became their most holy scripture and part of their religious rituals. They were initially passed down orally, in Sanskrit. Brahmans, priests of Vedic culture, incorporated the texts into ritual and society. The Vedas are considered the final authority of Hinduism.

Vedic people People who came from the steppes of Inner Asia around 1500 BCE and entered the fertile lowlands of the Indus River basin, gradually moving as far south as the Deccan plateau. They called themselves Aryan, which means "respected ones," and spoke Sanskrit, an Indo-European language.

veiling Practice of modest dress required of respectable women in the Assyrian Empire, introduced by Assyrian authorities in the thirteenth century BCE.

Venus figures Representations of the goddess of fertility drawn on the Chauvet Cave in southeastern France. Discovered in 1994, they are probably about 35,000 years old.

Versailles Conference (1919) Peace conference between the victors of World War I; resulted in the Treaty of Versailles, which forced Germany to pay reparations and to give up its colonies to the victors.

Viet Cong Vietnamese communist group committed to overthrowing the government of South Vietnam and reunifying North and South Vietnam.

Viet Minh Group founded in 1941 by Ho Chi Minh to oppose the Japanese occupation of Indochina; it later fought the French colonial forces for independence. Also known as the Vietnamese Independent League.

Vietnam War (1965–1975) Conflict that resulted from concern over the spread of communism in Southeast Asia. The United States intervened on the side of South Vietnam in its struggle against peasant-supported Viet Cong guerrilla forces, who wanted to reunite Vietnam under a communist regime. Faced with antiwar opposition at home and ferocious resistance from the Vietnamese, American troops withdrew in 1973; the puppet South Vietnamese government collapsed two years later.

Vikings A people from Scandinavia who replaced the Franks as the dominant warrior class in northern Europe in the ninth century. They used their superior ships to loot other seagoing peoples and sailed up the rivers of central Russia to establish a trade route that connected Scandinavia and the Baltic with Constantinople and Baghdad. The Vikings established settlements in Iceland and Greenland and, briefly, North America.

Vishnu The second of three Vedic deities, signifying existence. *See also* Brahma *and* Siva.

viziers Bureaucrats of the Ottoman Empire.

Vodun Mixed religion of African and Christian customs practiced by slaves and free blacks in the colony of Saint Domingue.

Voting Rights Act (1965) Law that granted universal suffrage in the United States.

Wafd Nationalist party that came into existence during a rebellion in Egypt in 1919 and held power sporadically after Egypt was granted limited independence from Britain in 1922.

Wahhabism Early-eighteenth-century reform movement organized by Muhammad Ibn abd al-Wahhab, who preached the absolute oneness of Allah and a return to the pure Islam of Muhammad.

Wang Mang Han minister who usurped the throne in 9 CE because he believed that the Han had lost the mandate of heaven. He ruled until 23 CE.

war ethos Strong social commitment to a continuous state of war. The Roman army constantly drafted men and engaged in annual spring military campaigns. Soldiers were taught to embrace a sense of honor that did not allow them to accept defeat and commended those who repeatedly threw themselves into battle.

War of 1812 Conflict between Britain and the United States arising from U.S. grievances over oppressive British maritime practices in the Napoleonic Wars.

War on Poverty President Lyndon Johnson's push for an increased range of social programs and increased spending on social security, health, education, and assistance for the disabled.

Warring States period Period extending from the fifth century BCE to 221 BCE, when the regional warring states were unified by the Qin dynasty.

Warsaw Pact (1955–1991) Military alliance between the Soviet Union and other communist states that was established in response to the creation of the NATO alliance.

Weimar Republic (1919–1933) Constitutional Republic of Germany that was subverted by Hitler soon after he became chancellor.

Western Front Military front that stretched from the English Channel through Belgium and France to the Alps during World War I.

White and Blue Niles The two main branches of the Nile, rising out of central Africa and Ethiopia. They come together at the present-day capital city of Sudan, Khartoum.

White Lotus Rebellion Series of uprisings in northern China (1790–1800s) inspired by mystical beliefs in folk Buddhism and, at times, the idea of restoring the Ming dynasty.

White Wolf Mysterious militia leader, depicted in popular myth as a Chinese Robin Hood whose mission was to rid the country of the injustices of Yuan Shikai's government in the early years of the Chinese Republic (1910s).

Whites "Counterrevolutionaries" of the Bolshevik Revolution (1918–1921) who fought the Bolsheviks (the "Reds"); included former supporters of the tsar, Social Democrats, and large independent peasant armies.

witnessing Dying for one's faith, or becoming a martyr.

Wokou Supposedly Japanese pirates, many of whom were actually Chinese subjects of the Ming dynasty.

Works Progress Administration (WPA) New Deal program instituted in 1935 that put nearly 3 million people to work building roads, bridges, airports, and post offices.

World Bank International agency established in 1944 to provide economic assistance to war-torn and poor countries. Its formal title is the International Bank for Reconstruction and Development.

World War II (1939–1945) Worldwide war that began in September 1939 in Europe, and even earlier in Asia, and pitted Britain, the United States, and the Soviet Union (the Allies) against Nazi Germany, Japan, and Italy (the Axis).

Wu or Wudi Chinese leader known as the "Martial Emperor" because of his many military campaigns during the Han dynasty. He reigned from 141 to 87 BCE.

Wu Zhao Chinese empress who lived from 626 to 706 CE. She began as a concubine in the court of Li Shimin and became the mother of his son's child. She eventually gained power equal to that of the emperor, and named herself regent when she finagled a place for one of her own sons after their father's death.

Xiongnu The most powerful and intrusive of the nomadic peoples; originally pastoralists from the eastern part of the Asian steppe in what is modern-day Mongolia. They appeared along the frontier with China in the late Zhou dynasty and by the third century BCE had become the most powerful of all the pastoral communities in that area.

Xunzi Confucian moralist whose ideas were influential to Qin rulers. He lived from 310 to 237 BCE and believed that rational statecraft was more reliable than fickle human nature and that strict laws and severe punishments could create stability in society.

Yalta Accords Results of the meeting between President Roosevelt, Prime Minister Churchill, and Premier Stalin that occurred in the Crimea in 1945 to plan for the postwar order.

Yavana kings Sanskrit name for Greek rulers, derived from the Greek name for the area of western Asia Minor called Ionia, a term that then extended to anyone who spoke Greek or came from the Mediterranean.

yellow press Newspapers that sought a mass circulation by featuring sensationalist reporting.

Yellow Turbans One of several local Chinese religious movements that emerged across the empire, especially under Wang Mang's officials, who considered him a usurper. The Yellow Turbans, so called because of the yellow scarves they wore around their heads, were Daoist millenarians.

Yin City that became the capital of the Shang in 1350 BCE, ushering in a golden age.

Young Egypt Antiliberal, fascist group that gained a large following in Egypt during the 1930s.

Young Italy Nationalist organization made up of young students and intellectuals, devoted to the unification and renewal of the Italian state.

Yuan dynasty Dynasty established by the Mongols after the defeat of the Song. The Yuan dynasty was strong from 1280 to 1368; its capital was at Dadu, or modern-day Beijing.

Yuan Mongols Mongol rulers of China who were overthrown by the Ming dynasty in 1368.

Yuezhi A Turkic nomadic people who roamed on pastoral lands to the west of the Xiongnu territory of central Mongolia. They had friendly relationships with the farming societies in China, but the Yuezhi detested the Xiongnu and had frequent armed clashes with them.

Zaibatsu Large-scale, family-owned corporations in Japan consisting of factories, import-export businesses, and banks that dominated the Japanese economy until 1945.

Zamindars Archaic tax system of the Mughal Empire where decentralized lords collected tribute for the emperor.

Zapatistas Group of indigenous rebels that rose up against the Mexican government in 1994 and drew inspiration from an earlier Mexican rebel, Emiliano Zapata.

Zheng King during the Qin era who defeated what was left of the Warring States between 230 and 221 BCE. He assumed the mandate of heaven from the Zhou and declared himself First August Emperor, to distinguish himself from other kings.

Zheng He (1371–1433) Ming naval leader who established tributary relations with Southeast Asia, Indian Ocean ports, the Persian Gulf, and the east coast of Africa.

Zhong Shang Administrative central complex of the Shang.

Zhongguo Term originating in the ancient period and subsequently used to emphasize the central cultural and geographical location of China in the world; means "Middle Kingdom."

ziggurat By the end of the third millennium BCE, the elevated platform base of a Sumerian temple had transformed into a stepped platform called a *ziggurat*.

Zionism Political movement advocating the reestablishment of a Jewish homeland in Palestine.

Zoroaster Sometimes known as Zarathustra, thought to have been a teacher around 1000 BCE in eastern Iran and credited with having solidified the region's religious beliefs into a unified system that moved away from animistic nomadic beliefs. The main source for his teachings is a compilation called the Avesta.

Zoroastrianism Religion based on the teachings of Zoroaster that became the dominant religion of the Persian Empire.

Zulus African tribe that, under Shaka, created a ruthless warrior state in southern Africa in the early 1800s.

Photo Credits

p. 519: Chateau de Versailles, France/Bridgeman Art Library; p. 520: Private Collection/The Bridgeman Art Library.

CHAPTER 14

Pages 524–25: Scala/Art Resource, NY; p. 528: Topkapi Palace Museum, Istanbul; p. 529: Réunion des Musées Nationaux/Art Resource, NY; p. 530 (left): Topkapi Palace Museum, Istanbul; (right): Victoria & Albert Museum/Art Resource, NY; p. 531: Reproduced by the kind permission of the trustees of the Chester Beatty Library and Gallery of Oriental Art, Dublin; p. 532 (left): Giraudon/Art Resource; (right): Private Collection, courtesy of the owner and D. A. King; photo by Christie's of London; p. 533 (left): Scala/Art Resource, NY; (right): Granger Collection; p. 534: Werner Forman/Art Resource, NY; p. 535: British Library/akg-images; p. 537: from *World Civilizations* Addison Wesley Longman, 2001; p. 538

(left): Underwood & Underwood/Corbis; (right): Underwood & Underwood/Corbis; p. 539 (left): The Needham Research Institute; (right): The British Library, London; p. 540: The British Library/The Bridgeman Art Library; p. 541: Reunion de Musees Nationaux/Art Resource, NY; p. 542: The Fotomas Index; p. 543: Bridgeman Art Library; p. 544 (top): Wikipedia; (bottom): Rare Books Division, The New York Public Library, Astor, Lenox and Tilden Foundations; p. 545: Bridgeman Art Library; p. 546: Musee des Beaux-Arts, Rouen/Superstock; p. 548 (top) Private Collection/The Bridgeman Art Library; (bottom): Private Collection/The Bridgeman Art Library; p. 549: Image copyright © The Metropolitan Museum of Art/Art Resource, NY; p. 550: Bridgeman Art Library; p. 551 (both): Museo de America, Madrid; p. 553: National Maritime Museum, London; p. 555 (left): HIP/Art Resource, NY; (right): Granger Collection; p. 556: The Art Archive/Castle Howard/Eileen Tweedy; p. 557: Natural History Museum, London/ The Bridgeman Art Library.

CHAPTER 15

Pages 560–61: Stefano Bianchetti/Corbis; p. 566: Library of Congress; p. 568: Granger Collection; p. 569: Hulton Archive/Getty Images; p. 570: Musee de la Ville de Paris, Musee Carnavalet/Giraudon/Art Resource, NY; p. 572: Lauros-Giraudon/The Bridgeman Art Library; p. 575: North Wind Picture Archives; p. 576: Granger Collection; p. 577: The Art Archive/Museo Nacional de Historia, Castillo de Chapultepec, Mexico City/Dagli Orti; p. 578: Granger Collection; p. 580: Private Collection/The Bridgeman Art Library; p. 581–82: Granger Collection; p. 584: Granger Collection; p. 586: Novotsi/The Bridgeman Art Library; p. 588: Corbis; p. 589: Courtesy of the director, National Army Museum, London; p. 591: Granger Collection; p. 592: The Art Archive; p. 594 (left): The British Library, London/The Bridgeman Art Library; (right): North Wind Picture Archives; p. 596: Roy Miles Fine Paintings/The Bridgeman Art Library.

WORLD · POLITICAL

NATIONAL BOUNDARIES

While man's impact is quite evident, and even striking, on many remotely sensed scenes, sometimes, as in the case with most political boundaries, it is invisible. State, provincial, and national boundaries can follow natural features, such as mountain ridges, rivers, or coastlines. Artificial constructs that possess no physical reality—for example, lines of latitude and longitude—can also determine political borders. The world political map (right) represents man's imaginary lines as they slice and divide Earth.

The National Geographic Society recognizes 192 independent states in the world as represented here. Of those nations, 185 are members of the United Nations.

Winkel Tripel Projection